South of France

timeout.com/southoffrance

The South of France

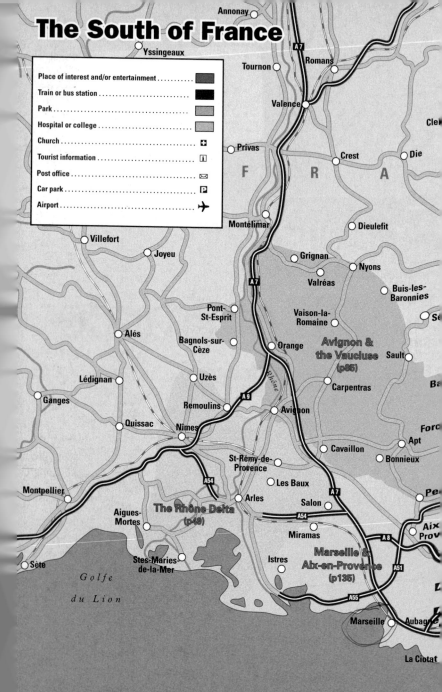

Place of interest and/or entertainment	
Train or bus station	
Park	
Hospital or college	
Church	✠
Tourist information	ℹ
Post office	✉
Car park	🅿
Airport	✈

Annonay

Yssingeaux

Tournon

Romans

Valence

Privas

Crest

Die

Cle

F R A

Montélimar

Dieulefit

Villefort

Grignan

Nyons

Joyeu

Valréas

Buis-les-
Baronnies

Pont-
St-Esprit

Vaison-la-
Romaine

Sé

Alès

Bagnols-sur-
Cèze

Orange

**Avignon &
the Vaucluse**
(p85)

Sault

Lédignan

Uzès

Carpentras

Ba

Ganges

Remoulins

A9

Avignon

Quissac

Nîmes

Cavaillon

Apt

Montpellier

St-Rémy-de-
Provence

Bonnieux

Forc

Les Baux

A54

Arles

Salon

A7

Pe

Aigues-
Mortes

The Rhône Delta
(p49)

Miramas

A54

A8

Aix
Prov

Sète

Istres

**Marseille &
Aix-en-Provence**
(p135)

A51

Stes-Maries-
de-la-Mer

*Golfe
du Lion*

A55

Marseille

Aubagn

La Ciotat

M E D I T E R R A N E A N   S E A

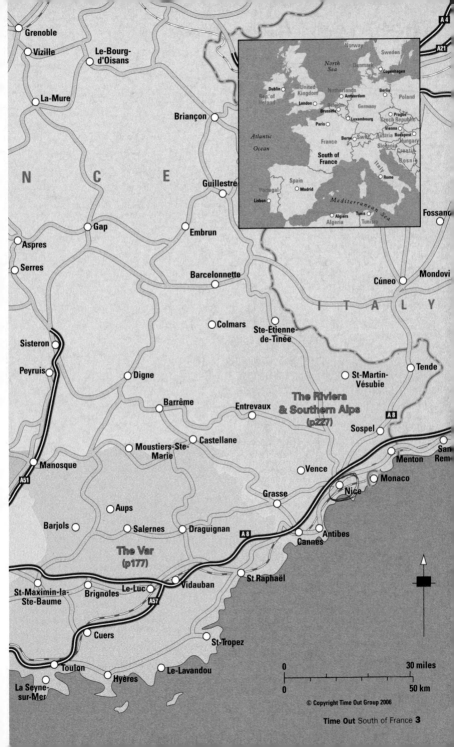

Grenoble

Vizille

Le-Bourg-
d'Oisans

La-Mure

Briançon

Guillestre

Gap

Aspres

Embrun

Serres

Barcelonnette

Fossano

Cúneo   Mondovi

Colmars

Ste-Etienne-
de-Tinée

I T A L Y

Sisteron

Peyruis

Digne

Barrême

Entrevaux

St-Martin-
Vésubie

Tende

**The Riviera
& Southern Alps
(p227)**

Sospel

Castellane

Moustiers-Ste-
Marie

Manosque

Vence

Menton

San
Rem

Grasse

Monaco

Nice

Aups

Barjols

Salernes

Draguignan

Antibes

**The Var
(p177)**

Cannes

St Raphaël

St-Maximin-la-
Ste-Baume

Brignoles

Le-Luc

Vidauban

Cuers

St-Tropez

Toulon

Hyères

Le-Lavandou

La Seyne-
sur-Mer

| 0 | | | 30 miles |
| 0 | | | 50 km |

© Copyright Time Out Group 2006

Published by Time Out Guides Ltd, a wholly owned subsidiary of Time Out Group Ltd.
Time Out and the Time Out logo are trademarks of Time Out Group Ltd.

© **Time Out Group Ltd 2006**
Previous editions 2004, 2002, 2000

10 9 8 7 6 5 4 3 2 1

This edition first published in Great Britain in 2006 by Ebury Publishing
Ebury Publishing is a division of The Random House Group Ltd,
20 Vauxhall Bridge Road, London SW1V 2SA

Random House Australia Pty Limited 20 Alfred Street, Milsons Point, Sydney, New South Wales 2061, Australia
Random House New Zealand Limited 18 Poland Road, Glenfield, Auckland 10, New Zealand
Random House South Africa (Pty) Limited Isle of Houghton, Corner Boundary
Road & Carse O'Gowrie, Houghton 2198, South Africa

Random House UK Limited Reg. No. 954009

Distributed in USA by Publishers Group West
1700 Fourth Street, Berkeley, California 94710

Distributed in Canada by Penguin Canada Ltd
10 Alcorn Avenue, Toronto, Ontario, Canada M4V 3B2

For further distribution details, see www.timeout.com

ISBN
To 31 December 2006: 1904978010
From 1 January 2007: 9781904978015

A CIP catalogue record for this book is available from the British Library.

Colour reprographics by Icon, Crowne House, 56-58 Southwark Street, London SE1 1UN.

Printed and bound in Germany by Appl

Papers used by Ebury Publishing are natural, recyclable products made from wood grown in sustainable forests.

Time Out Guides Limited
Universal House
251 Tottenham Court Road
London W1T 7AB
Tel + 44 (0)20 7813 3000
Fax + 44 (0)20 7813 6001
Email guides@timeout.com
www.timeout.com

Editorial

Editor Sam Le Quesne
Deputy Editor Simon Coppock
Listings Editors Anna Samson, The Content Works
Proofreader Tamsin Shelton
Indexer Anna Norman

Editorial/Managing Director Peter Fiennes
Series Editor Ruth Jarvis
Deputy Series Editor Lesley McCave
Business Manager Gareth Garner
Guides Co-ordinator Holly Pick
Accountant Kemi Olufuwa

Design

Art Director Scott Moore
Art Editor Tracey Ridgewell
Senior Designer Josephine Spencer
Digital Imaging Dan Conway
Ad Make-up Jenni Prichard

Picture Desk

Picture Editor Jael Marschner
Deputy Picture Editor Tracey Kerrigan
Picture Researcher Helen McFarland

Advertising

Sales Director Mark Phillips
International Sales Manager Ross Canadé
International Sales Executive Simon Davies
Advertising Sales (South of France) Carlos Pineda
Advertising Assistant Lucy Butler

Marketing

Marketing Director Mandy Martinez
Marketing & Publicity Manager, US Rosella Albanese

Production

Production Director Mark Lamond
Production Controller Marie Howell

Time Out Group

Chairman Tony Elliott
Managing Director Mike Hardwick
Group Financial Director Richard Waterlow
Group Commercial Director Lesley Gill
Group General Manager Nichola Coulthard
Group Circulation Director Jim Heinemann
Group Art Director John Oakey
Online Managing Director David Pepper
Group Production Director Steve Proctor
Group IT Director Simon Chappell

Contributors

Introductions Sam Le Quesne. **History** Simon Coppock, Natasha Edwards (*Crossing the holy sea* Rik Mulder; *The other D-Day* Fiona Johnson). **The South of France Today** Ian Sparks (*Auto pilot* Isabel Pitman). **Provençal Food** Rosa Jackson. **Provençal Wine** Richard James (*Tasting notes* Rupert Wright; *A fruitful enterprise* Jamie Ivey). **The Creative South** Sam Le Quesne, Natasha Edwards (*Algeria on the page* Sarah Adams). **The Festive South** Anna Samson. **Nîmes & the Pont du Gard** Stephen Mudge. **St-Rémy & Les Alpilles** Lisa Plumridge. **Arles** Stephen Mudge. **The Camargue** Stephen Mudge. **Avignon** Stephen Mudge (*Inn the family way* Isabel Pitman). **Orange & Châteauneuf-du-Pape** Stephen Mudge. **Carpentras & Mont Ventoux** Isabel Pitman. **The Drôme Provençale** Isabel Pitman. **The Luberon** Lisa Plumridge. **Marseille** Sam Le Quesne (*Rap and raï* Sarah Adams). **Cassis, the Calanques & La Ciotat** Sam Le Quesne. **Aix-en-Provence** Sam Le Quesne (*Portrait of the artist* Anna Samson). **Toulon & Western Côte** Lisa Plumridge. **Hyères to Les Maures** Rik Mulder. **St-Tropez** Tristan Rutherford. **St-Raphaël & the Estérel** Lisa Plumridge. **Brignoles & the Ste-Baume** Rik Mulder. **Draguignan & the Central Var** Lisa Plumridge. **The Gorges du Verdon** Rik Mulder (*Ministry of hilly walks* Sarah Fraser). **Cannes** Sarah Fraser (*Too hot to handle?* Rik Mulder). **Antibes to Cagnes** Rosa Jackson (*Plane sailing* Tristan Rutherford). **Nice** Rosa Jackson. **The Corniches** Tristan Rutherford. **Monaco & Monte-Carlo** Peterjon Cresswell. **Roquebrune to Menton** Rosa Jackson. **Grasse & the Gorges du Loup** Sarah Fraser. **Vence & St-Paul** Tristan Rutherford. **Into the Alps** Sarah Fraser. **Directory** Alexia Loundras.

Maps JS Graphics, Kerpenru, 56330 Camors, France (john@jsgraphics.co.uk). Street plans are based on material supplied by Thomas Cook Publishers.

Photography by Karl Blackwell, except: page 12 Getty Images; pages 14, 17 akg-images; page 21 AFP/Getty Images; page 34 Barry J Holmes; pages 38, 175 JC Carbonne; page 47 Laurent Masson; page 98 Scott Wishart; page 99 Rob Greig; page 221 OT Moustiers; page 222 OTSI Castellane; page 252 Nice Convention & Visitors Bureau. The following image was provided by the featured establishment/artist: page 192.

The Editor would like to thank Mélody Raynaud and all contributors to previous editions of *Time Out South of France*, whose work forms the basis for parts of this book.

Contents

Introduction

Provence and the Riviera have been visited, often adopted, by so many painters, writers and photographers over the years that the South of France has acquired the image of a shimmering promised land. This is where café terraces are shaded by plane trees and the warm air is filled with the scent of lavender; it's where loveable village folk throw open their blue-painted shutters each morning and greet life with sunny dispositions and salt-of-the-earth wisdom.

Or is it? From the windows of a coach, perhaps. But there is so much more to this region than the spectacle of its *villages perchés* or its fields of sunflowers. The Riviera has long since ceased to be an aristocratic theme park of cocktails and casino chips. The South of the 21st century is a thoroughly modern place.

Marseille, the oldest port in France, is now home to some of the country's most cutting-edge art and music. Near neighbour Aix-en-Provence, while it may lack the gritty cachet of Marseille, is the chosen site for the construction of the South's most adventurous contemporary dance centre, while also being the playground of rowdy throngs of students. Further west, Avignon hosts one of Europe's most significant cultural festivals.

But for all its modernity, the South of France is steeped in history and natural beauty. Classicists can marvel at the amphitheatres of Nîmes and Arles, while the rugged coastline of the Calanques or the hiking trails of the Gorges du Verdon make you feel like the only person left on earth.

Go, then, for the culture, the nature, the wine, the food: the main thing is, just go.

ABOUT TIME OUT CITY GUIDES

This is the fourth edition of *Time Out South of France*, one of an expanding series of Time Out guides produced by the people behind the successful listings magazines in London, New York and Chicago. Our guides are all written by resident experts who have striven to provide all the most up-to-date information you'll need to explore the city or read up on its background, whether you're a local or a first-time visitor.

THE LIE OF THE LAND

The South of France is as much about an image and a lifestyle as technical boundaries. The main area we cover coincides with the southern portion of the modern French administrative region of Provence-Alpes-Côte d'Azur, taking in the *départements* of Bouches-du-Rhône, Vaucluse, Var, Alpes-Maritimes and the south of the Alpes de Haute-Provence. But we also extend our coverage further west into the Gard *département* to Nîmes and Uzès, which fell within Roman Provincia, to Aigues-Mortes as the western boundary of the Camargue, and north to the southern reaches of the Drôme *département*, an area that is often dubbed 'the Drôme Provençale', where the vegetation of olives and herbs already augurs the South.

Our regional sections are arranged in a roughly west-east order. All the areas covered, from big cities to rural backwaters, start with the background history and sightseeing information, followed by where to eat, where to stay and visitor information, including the addresses of the relevant tourist offices. Listings for restaurants, bars and hotels are more detailed in larger conurbations. We give essential road and public transport information at the end of chapters, but sometimes suggested routes between villages are detailed in the main text. Bear in mind that public transport in inland rural areas is often extremely limited.

ESSENTIAL INFORMATION

For all the practical information you might need for visiting the area – including visa and customs information, details of local transport, a listing of emergency numbers, information on local weather and a selection of useful websites – turn to the Directory at the back of this guide. It begins on page 313.

THE LOWDOWN ON THE LISTINGS

We have tried to make this book as easy to use as possible. Addresses, phone numbers, bus information, opening times and admission prices are all included in the listings. However, businesses can change their arrangements at any time. Before you go out of your way, we'd strongly advise you to phone ahead to check opening times and other particulars. While every effort and care has been made to ensure the accuracy of the information contained in this guide, the publishers cannot accept responsibility for any errors it may contain.

PRICES AND PAYMENT

We have noted where venues such as shops, hotels, restaurants and theatres accept the following credit cards: American Express (AmEx), Diners Club (DC), MasterCard (MC) and Visa (V). The most widely accepted credit card is Visa. Note that credit cards are often not accepted for less than €15.

The prices we've supplied should be treated as guidelines, not gospel. If you encounter prices that vary wildly from those we've quoted, ask whether there's a good reason. If not, go elsewhere. For hotels we have listed the price for a double room as the best indication for the price bracket within which a hotel falls (although these hotels may well equally have single rooms or, indeed, triples, quadruples or suites). The range for a double takes in different categories of room and/or variations between low- and high-season prices. French hotel prices generally do not include breakfast, although those for *chambres d'hôtes*, the French equivalent of B&B, generally do. For restaurants, we give the price range for set menus (referred to in French as *formule*, *menu* or *prix-fixe*); note that the lowest-priced *menu* is often available only on weekday lunches. Where no *menus* are served, we give an average for a three-course meal without drinks, for one person.

Advertisers

TELEPHONE NUMBERS

All French phone numbers have ten digits. Numbers for the area covered in this guide (except Monaco, code 00 377) start with 04. From outside France, dial the country code (33) and leave off the zero at the beginning of the number. Numbers prefixed by 06 are mobile phones, 08.36 numbers are premium rate and 08.00 are freephone numbers (sometimes available from outside France at standard international rates).

POSTCODES

All addresses in France have a five-figure postcode, starting with the two figures that indicate the *département* (eg. 06000 Nice, 06400 Cannes). For questions of space and readability, we have not put postcodes in each address but, should you need to write to someone in a particular town or village, we have included them in the address of tourist information offices.

MAPS

Each of the regional sections of the guide (*see p8* **The lie of the land**) starts with a map of the region and a summary of its major features and attractions. We have also included detailed maps of the larger cities. A map of the entire region can be found at the front of the guide.

LET US KNOW WHAT YOU THINK

We hope you enjoy *Time Out South of France*, and we'd like to know what you think of it. We welcome tips for places that you consider we should include in future editions and take note of your criticism of our choices. You can email us at guides@timeout.com.

There is an online version of this book, along with guides to over 45 other international cities, at **www.timeout.com**.

In Context

Features

Fighting against **cholera**. *See p17.*

History

Greek, Latin, Provençal, Arabic, English, even French, spoken here.

Penguins in Provence? Perhaps so. Alongside the familiar bison, horses and handprints, the ancient cave paintings in Grotte Cosquer in the Calanques depict penguins – but then the paintings do date back beyond the last Ice Age, putting the first date of human habitation in the South of France somewhere around 27,000 BC. Later Neolithic communities settled in the fertile lands near present-day Nice and Monaco, or sheltered in caves in the Verdon gorges.

Around 1200 BC the Gauls – a Celtic people – began to migrate from the Rhine Valley into France and Italy. The southernmost front of this advance developed into the Ligurian culture, which stretched from Spain into Italy. Skilled metalworkers and stone carvers, the Ligurians lived in oppidums (fortified villages), such as that at Entremont, near Aix.

Western civilisation first came to Provence in the form of the Greeks from the Ionian city of Phocaea, who founded the colony of Massalia (Marseille) in about 600 BC. By the fifth century BC, Massalia was so powerful it was minting its own money and had begun to plant colonies along the coast at Nikaïa (Nice), Olbia (Hyères), Taureontum (Les Lecques) and Agde, as well as inland at Arles. The Greeks planted vines and olives, and the pan-Mediterranean trade in wine, olive oil and other goods soon filtered through to neighbouring Celtic areas.

NOUVEAUX ROMANS

Marseille took the Roman side during the Carthaginian Wars, a smart move that stood it in good stead when Rome went annexing beyond the Alps towards the end of the second century BC. Called in by Marseille to help the city repulse a Celtic attack, the Romans stayed on, destroying the Oppidum of Entremont and founding the city of Aquae Sextiae (Aix-en-Provence) in 122 BC. In recognition of its support, Marseille was allowed to remain an independent state within Roman territory.

The main reason, however, for expansion into the South of France was the need to secure the land route to Spain. From around 120 BC,

Roman consul Gnaeus Domitius Ahenobarbus created the Via Domitia (Domitian Way) with staging posts at Nîmes, Beaucaire, Cavaillon and Apt. By 118 BC Rome controlled the whole coast westwards to the Pyrenees and a large swathe of the hinterland. The Romans subdued by colonisation: vast numbers of settlers were attracted by the promise of free land. The Celtic town at Vaison-la-Romaine became a semi-autonomous federated city; Narbonne, further west, became the capital of Gallia Narbonensis, also known, more simply, as 'Provincia'. After 115 BC the Celtic tribe of the Cimbri and the Germanic Teutons mounted a series of raids on Provence, culminating in a humiliating defeat for the Romans at Orange in 105 BC.

Under the Pax Romana, Gallia Narbonensis became a model province. Provence became an important supplier of grain, olive oil and ships to the ever-hungry empire. In return, it was treated more as an extension of the motherland than a colonial outpost. The aqueducts, baths, amphitheatres and temples that serviced fine cities, such as Aix, Arles, Nîmes, Orange and Glanum (St-Rémy), often surpassed those of similar-sized Italian cities. Further east the Romans constructed the major port of Fréjus (probable birthplace of the historian Tacitus), Cemenelum (Nice) and a ring of fortified settlements in what is now the eastern Var. Even after Julius Caesar had subdued the rest of Gaul in the Gallic Wars (58-51 BC), this remained the most Roman of the empire's transalpine possessions.

Marseille was eclipsed after it supported Pompey against Caesar in the Civil Wars. Besieged in 49 BC, its possessions were transferred to Arles, Narbonne and the nascent Fréjus – though it continued to be a centre of scholarship. The imperial connection with Provence was reinforced under Antoninus Pius (emperor AD 138-161), whose family came from Nîmes; in the fourth century, under Constantine, Arles became a favoured imperial residence.

CHRISTIANITY AND THE COUNTS

The Christian community came into the open in the early fifth century with the foundation of the St-Honorat monastery on the Iles de Lérins and the Abbaye de St-Victor in Marseille. The latter was the centre of a monastic diaspora that gave the South a generous sprinkling of abbeys from Le Barben to Castellane, ensuring the land was worked even in times of crisis – although the monks could be as tyrannical in exploiting the peasantry as any feudal landlord.

When the Roman Empire finally fell apart in 476, the bishoprics maintained some semblance of order in the face of invasions by Visigoths and Ostrogoths. It was the Franks who eventually gained the upper hand, after a period of anarchy during which Roman embellishments fell into ruin and fields returned to swampland. The new rulers looked north rather than south, and the Mediterranean trade that had sustained cities like Arles or Marseille gradually dried up.

The three-way partition of the Carolingian Empire between the sons of Louis I in the Treaty of Verdun in 843 made the Rhône a frontier and provided the basis for the later division between Provence and Languedoc. In 931 the kingdom of Provence – one of many fragments of Charlemagne's former empire – was allied with Burgundy. Over the next couple of centuries, imperial rule gave way to out-and-out feudalism, as local lords used brute force and taxes to subdue the territory around their castle strongholds. The Saracens terrorised the coast and launched raids on the surrounding countryside from their base at La Garde-Freinet in the Massif des Maures, until they were driven out by William I, Count of Arles, in 974, confirming the power of the kingdom of Arles, which became part of the Holy Roman Empire.

'Out of the apparent anarchy, a distinctive local culture emerged.'

From the end of the 11th century more efficient agriculture, the revival of trade and the rise of the guilds provided the money for the construction of new religious foundations, such as the impressive abbey of St-Gilles in the Camargue, with its richly carved façade, and the restoration and embellishment of Cathédrale St-Trophime in Arles. A sober, pared-back style of Romanesque also evolved in the 12th century at the great Cistercian foundations of Silvacane, Senanque and Thoronet. Northern French Gothic (which had its beginnings at St-Denis in the 12th century) was slow to percolate through to the South, where Romanesque continued to hold sway, but a few fine Gothic edifices were built, notably the Palais des Papes in Avignon, the Cathédrale St-Siffrein in Carpentras and the magnificent Basilique St-Maximin-la-Ste-Baume.

Some time in the 11th century, a small local dynasty had felt confident enough to award itself the title of Counts of Provence. When the line died out in 1113 the title passed to the House of Barcelona, which became the nominal ruler of the area. However, the larger cities soon asserted their independence, setting up governments known as Consulates. In the country, local bosses such as the Lords of Les Baux and Count of Forcalquier put up fierce resistance to those claiming higher authority.

Crossing the holy sea

Did Mary Magdalene, repentant sinner and first witness of Christ's resurrection, end her days in the South of France? The Provençal like to think so and, thanks to the rampaging success of Dan Brown's *The Da Vinci Code* (not to mention the earlier bestseller *The Holy Blood and the Holy Grail*), a great many others have taken an interest too. According to a legend that became popular in Provence around the tenth century, hostile Jews tossed Mary Magdalene, along with Lazarus, Martha, Maximin and a few others (including Joseph of Arimathea, who later headed to Britain with the Holy Grail), into a small boat without sails, oars or helm. Miraculously, the castaways drifted across the Mediterranean to the southern coast of Gaul and landed either in Stes-Maries-de-la-Mer (*see p81*) or in Marseille. A wonderful 16th-century painting in the Musée du Vieux Marseille (*see p144*), thought to be the work of Antoine Ronzen or one of his apprentices, shows Mary Magdalene preaching to a crowd of local dignitaries next to what is now the Vieux Port of Marseille, her boat docked nearby. The crunchy biscuits called navettes provençales take their canoe shape from this legend, and 'La Cantinella de la Santa Maria Magdalena', a 23-stanza song describing the life and death of Christ's

female follower, was sung every Easter in Marseille's churches from the 11th to the 18th centuries.

After landing, the story goes, the exiled Palestinians separated to preach the Gospel throughout Provence. Lazarus converted the Marseillais, while Martha went west to beat the Tarasque (the mythical beast of Tarascon, *see p68*) and Maximin became the first bishop of the plain now called St-Maximin-la-Ste-Baume. But Mary Magdalene retired to a wet, north-facing cave in the Ste-Baume hills and spent the next 30-odd years sitting on the only dry rock available, atoning for her promiscuous youth and eating roots – though in some versions angels descend seven times a day to feed her nectar from heaven. After her death, St Maximin buried her at the site where the Basilique Ste-Marie-Madeleine (*see p209*) would be erected 12 centuries later.

Mary's remains were supposedly moved to Vézelay, in Burgundy, around the eighth century, though they were inexplicably dug up intact in St-Maximin-la-Ste-Baume in 1280, when work began on the basilica. The ensuing dispute between Vézelay and St-Maximin was bitter, as large groups of pilgrims – and a lot of money – had begun pouring into both sites. Today Vézelay still claims (though rather less vocally) to have the saint's relics in its crypt, while the Ste-Baume cave displays what may be her skull. In truth, historical evidence supporting either theory is extremely slim, and in any case the evangelisation of Provence did not begin in earnest before the third century. Greek Catholics believe that Mary Magdalene sailed to Ephesus, an Ionic colony on what is now the Turkish coast, and died there; her remains may or may not have been moved to Constantinople and subsequently to Rome. But in Provence the redeemed prostitute, fittingly appointed patron saint of the Toulon-Fréjus diocese, remains well loved by pilgrims, tourist offices and conspiracy theorists alike.

Every year, thousands of pilgrims visit Stes-Maries-de-la-Mer (04.90.97.82.55, www.saintesmaries.com) and St-Maximin-la-Ste-Baume (04.94.59.84.59), while those who want to investigate the legend more fully enlist the help of **Magdalene Tours** (www.magdalenetours.com). For just £1,750 guides will whisk you from Marseille to Mary's cave, pointing out all the clues along the way.

Barcelona's sway over Mediterranean France was helped along by language. Provençal, the eastern dialect of Occitan or *langue d'Oc*, was a close cousin of Catalan. Out of the apparent anarchy and the frequent shifts in the balance of power among the warring seigneuries, a distinctive local culture emerged, which reached its fullest expression in the poetry and ballads of the troubadours, itinerant love poets.

FROM ANJOU TO AVIGNON

Provence was spared the destruction visited on south-western France during the Albigensian Crusade against the Cathars. But the crusade altered the balance of power in the South: the Counts of Toulouse were crushed, and Languedoc passed to the French Crown in 1271, except for the Comtat Venaissin (including Avignon, Carpentras, Cavaillon and Fontaine-de-Vaucluse), which Philippe III of France gave to the Papacy in 1274.

The Counts of Provence emerged as sole rulers of the land between the Rhône and the Alps. The last Count of Provence, Raymond-Bérenger V, was also one of the shrewdest and most cultured. He gave his territories an efficient administration and dealt with the increasingly muscular power of France in a masterful piece of dynastic planning, marrying all four daughters to kings or future kings: the eldest, Marguerite, to Louis IX of France, Eleanor to Henry III of England, Sanchia to Richard of Cornwall and, in 1246, Beatrice to Charles d'Anjou, brother of Louis IX, thus bringing Provence under Angevin rule.

The Anjou princes ruled for two and a half centuries, bringing a new degree of stability. They made Aix their administrative capital, although, until they were chased out of Sicily in 1282, they preferred to reside in Palermo or Naples; Louis II of Anjou founded the University of Aix in 1409. Good King René (1434-80) likewise concentrated first on Italy, until he lost Naples to Aragon in 1442, thereafter dividing his time between Angers and Provence, where he established his court at Aix and built a lavishly furnished château at Tarascon. His reign was longer and more stable than most, and the poet-king encouraged a minor artistic revival from his court. The administrative reforms introduced by the last Count of Provence were continued with the establishment of the *états généraux*, a regional assembly that had the power to raise taxes and take over the reins of government in times of crisis. The last of the local warlords, the Baux family, retreated to Orange, setting off the dynastic daisy chain that would lead to the latter becoming a corner of Protestant Holland in the 16th century.

In 1306 French-born pope Clement V made good use of papal bolthole the Comtat Venaissin, transferring his whole court first to Carpentras and then to Avignon, and ushering in the Papacy's 70-year 'Babylonian captivity'. When the Jews were expelled from France, first in 1306 by Philippe le Bel and again in 1394 under Charles VI, they found refuge in the papal enclave, where fine synagogues survive at Carpentras and Cavaillon. The Black Death hit Provence in 1348, entering through the port of Marseille and decimating the population.

The Avignon Papacy spurred an economic, intellectual and cultural renaissance in the region, from new industries like glass-making, paper manufacture and melon-growing to the rise of an artistic school, now known as the Provençal Primitives. Enguerrand Quarton and Nicolas Froment, King René's court painter, were the leading figures of the school, which developed a Flemish-influenced style of crystalline painterly detail that also used strong shadows and simplified forms to echo the strong southern light. To the east, in the territory of Nice (grabbed by the House of Savoy in 1388) – and especially its mountainous hinterland – Niçois painter Louis Bréa and Piedmontese imports Giovanni Canavesio and Jean Baleison would found a distinctive school between the mid-15th and mid-16th centuries.

UNION AND WARS OF RELIGION

Charles du Maine, René's nephew, survived his uncle by only a year. Dying without an heir in 1481, he bequeathed Anjou, Maine and Provence (excluding Savoy, Monaco and the Comtat Venaissin) to portly King Louis XI of France. Not only Provence but Roussillon, Burgundy, Lorraine and parts of northern Italy came under the sway of this fat controller.

After trying strong-arm tactics for the first three years, France decided to allow Provence at least the illusion of independence, with the Act of Union (1486) granting the region substantial autonomy within the French state. A *parlement* was established at Aix in 1501, but there were still several pockets of autonomy – notably Marseille, which stoutly defended its republican traditions. Francis I subdued the city with the fort on the Ile d'If and used the Marseille shipyards in the Italian wars, waged against his arch-enemy the Holy Roman Emperor Charles V; Charles V replied by besieging the city in 1523. Francis added similar fortifications on the Ile de Porquerolles and at St-Paul-de-Vence, where they survive pretty much intact.

On the ground the dominant issue became that of religious difference. Protestantism had achieved a firm foothold in Provence and eastern Languedoc, especially among the rural poor. Even before Luther, the Waldensian or Vaudois sect – whose tweaking of Catholic doctrine was more than enough for them to be branded heretical – had put down roots in the Luberon, where feudal landlords encouraged them to repopulate the land after the Black Death. The movement was brutally put down in April 1545, when Vaudois villages were pillaged and burned and their populations massacred. This was only the opening salvo of the Wars of Religion, which really kicked in when French Calvinism – or Huguenotism – spread throughout France in the 1550s. There were Protestant enclaves in Orange, Haute-Provence and the Luberon, but the main seedbed of the new faith lay west of the Rhône: in Nîmes three-quarters of the population became Huguenot. The 1560s saw atrocities on both sides. Most of the Huguenots of Orange were massacred in 1563. In reprisal, the Baron des Adrets, converted from Catholicism only the year before, went on the rampage (he specialised in throwing Catholic prisoners from the top of the nearest castle); two years later he reconverted and retired to the family estate.

> ### 'When Marseille dared to set up a rebel council, Louis XIV turned the town's cannons on itself.'

In 1593 the first Bourbon monarch, the Protestant Henri de Navarre (Henry IV), converted to Catholicism and assumed power. He issued the Edict of Nantes in 1598 to reconcile the warring factions: the Edict guaranteed civil and religious liberties to Protestants. In the South its main effect was to reconfirm the Rhône split, this time as a religious rather than political frontier.

Under Louis XIII and his minister Cardinal Richelieu, the Catholic Counter-Reformation reached its apogée. Flamboyant baroque churches were built at l'Isle-sur-la-Sorgue, Martigues and in Italian-ruled Nice; sculptor and architect Pierre Puget built his masterpiece Vieille Charité in Marseille. The Royals made a few trips south. In 1638 Queen Anne of Austria, still childless after 22 years of marriage to Louis XIII, made a pilgrimage to Cotignac to pray for a son; she subsequently visited Apt in 1660 in gratitude for the birth of Louis XIV.

In 1685 Louis XIV, encouraged by his fervently Catholic mistress Madame de Maintenon, revoked the Edict of Nantes, leading to massacres of Protestants in Nîmes and Arles; Protestant churches were demolished and schools closed. The main effect, though, was to deprive Nîmes and Uzès of their industrious Huguenot manufacturers, who emigrated in their thousands. A few did convert, though, and stayed on to make silk and the blue linen 'de Nîmes' that English merchants called 'denim'.

TYRANNY AND THE BOURGEOISIE

By the 17th century the history of the South had become bound up with that of France. Of use to Paris mainly as a source of fruit, olive oil, wine, textiles and taxes, and as a builder of ships for royal wars, the Midi was drained of funds and, at the same time, kept firmly in line by the increasingly centralised state and absolutist rule of the Sun King (*l'état c'est moi*) Louis XIV. When restless Marseille dared to set up a rebel council in 1658, Louis XIV turned the town's cannons on itself and built an additional fort designed above all to keep an eye on the unruly citizens. The port of Toulon was expanded and turned into the main base of the Mediterranean fleet, which was busy waging war against the Spanish. Louis XIV's military architect Vauban added his characteristic star-shaped defences to both Toulon and Antibes.

Marseille took a further body blow in 1720, when a visiting Syrian ship caused one of the last big outbreaks of plague in the West, killing 50,000 people in the city alone. A plague wall was built that stretched as far as the Luberon, but the disease spread all the same.

The 18th century was also a time of growing prosperity. A wealthy bourgeoisie developed in the main industrial centres – textiles at Nîmes, salt at Aigues-Mortes and Hyères, furniture at Beaucaire (site of the most important fair in the South), faïence in Marseille and Moustiers, perfumery and tanning in Grasse. In the 'parliamentary' city of Aix (capital of the *états généraux* administrative area of Provence), a caste of politicians with plenty of time on their hands built themselves sumptuous townhouses and lavish country bastides.

REVOLUTION, EMPIRE AND REPUBLIC

Resentment of Paris and its taxes continued to simmer, fuelled by bad harvests and rising unemployment. When the Revolution broke out in 1789, Provence was swift to join. Among its primary movers was the Comte de Mirabeau, elected as *député* of Aix when the Third Estate was finally convened later that year. The dockers of Marseille were particularly active, taking the forts of St-Jean and St-Nicolas in an echo of the storming of the Bastille. The republic's battle-hymn 'La Marseillaise' was in fact written by Alsatian Rouget de l'Isle, and was only associated with Marseille after having been adopted by its Jacobin national guard (*les Féderés*) on the march to Paris in 1792.

The Revolution was anti-clerical as well as anti-royal. Religious foundations and churches became state property and religious festivals were replaced by the cult of the Supreme Being. There were some lucky escapes: Toulon cathedral survived as an arms depot; St-Maximin-la-Ste-Baume was saved by an organ rendition of 'La Marseillaise' by Napoleon's brother Lucien. The papal enclave of the Comtat Venaissin was reincorporated into France in 1791 and in 1792 Revolutionary forces took Nice (subsequently handed back to Italy in 1814). Anarchy soon broke out all over France, with counter-revolutionary uprisings brutally put down by Robespierre's Terror of 1793, notably in Marseille and Toulon. The British took advantage of the confusion to occupy Toulon in 1793; they were sent packing by artillery commanded by a rising military star, 24-year-old Napoleon Bonaparte. In 1799, after a military coup, Napoleon became First Consul; in 1804 he declared himself Emperor.

Perhaps the main legacy of the Revolution was a further weakening of regional autonomy with the abolition of the *états généraux* and the carving up of France in 1790 into centrally administered *départements*. Under his rule, Napoleon gave France the *lycée* educational system and the Napoleonic Code of civil law.

Though he had undergone his military training in Antibes and Toulon, Bonaparte had little affection for Provence – a feeling that was entirely mutual. Defeated in 1814, Napoleon was exiled to Elba. His return to France and flight north to Paris through the Alps are commemorated by the Route Napoléon, but his reinstatement was brief. After Waterloo, the monarchy was restored under Louis XVII.

The radical spirit endured, despite heavy losses sustained during the 1832 cholera epidemic, which left a lasting mark on the region. Defiance was nurtured in the shipyards of Toulon and Marseille, and most of the South threw its weight behind the 1848 Revolution, which saw the monarchy again overthrown and Louis-Napoleon Bonaparte, the nephew of Napoleon I, elected first President and later, in 1852, Emperor Napoleon III. The glittery Second Empire was a period of colonial and industrial expansion. The opening of the Suez Canal in 1869 and the spread of colonial France quadrupled Marseille's port traffic, and long boulevards, a new cathedral, the Bourse Maritime and Palais Longchamp were all built. Toulon expanded beyond its walls and gained a glamorous opera house. Steamships poured out of the shipyards of La Ciotat and La Seyne-sur-Mer, and the coastal railway, an impressive

The city's most famous immigrant:
La Marseillaise. *See p16.*

feat of engineeering with its tunnels and viaducts, had reached Nice by 1865 and Monaco by 1868.

The last of the major territorial reshuffles took place in 1860, when Napoleon III received Nice and its mountainous hinterland from the House of Savoy in return for his diplomatic neutrality during the unification of Italy. Monaco was now a one-town state, having lost Roquebrune and Menton in 1848 when the inhabitants revolted against the Grimaldis' exorbitant taxes. Ironically, it was his principality's isolation and threatened bankruptcy that spurred Charles III to reinvent Monaco as the gambling capital of Europe.

PROVENCE RESURGENT?

In parallel with the arrival of the industrial revolution, tourism arrived in the South, initially in the form of winter stop-offs in Hyères or Nice for aristos. In 1822 the promenade des Anglais, then a picturesque footpath, was laid out by the English colony in Nice. In 1834 Lord Brougham wintered in Cannes. Russians and English, including Queen Victoria, began flocking to the Riviera.

Yet the 19th century also witnessed the rediscovery of Provence's ancient heritage: by the end of the century the Arènes had been cleared in Arles, Viollet-le-Duc had restored the ramparts of Avignon and excavation had started at Vaison-la-Romaine.

While the centralised administrative and education system meant Provence was more a part of France than ever, and the Provençal language had largely died out except in remote rural communities, there was an ever-present current of Catholic fundamentalism that created different reactionary minorities. Some, led by Frédéric Mistral, pursued the revival of the Provençal language and traditions; others supported Action Française, the proto-Fascist movement founded by Southerner Charles Maurras in Paris in 1899. Mistral, author of epic Provençal poem Mirèio (Mireille), was one of seven young poets who founded the Félibrige movement in Avignon in 1854; he was to win the Nobel Prize for Literature in 1904.

The early 20th century was the era of the great waterfront hotels, built in response to a surge in tourism: between 1890 and 1910 the number of foreigners visiting Nice each year grew almost sixfold to more than 150,000. Amused by these eccentric milords, the French bourgeoisie continued to winter in the country; only in the 1920s did French artists, designers and socialites begin to descend on Le Midi in any great number: American railroad magnate Frank Jay Gould opened up the summer season in Juan-les-Pins and built the Palais de la Méditerranée in Nice. The artistic avant-garde came too, and modernist architects put up radical new villas.

World War I was a distant, rain-soaked northern affair, although it took its toll among provençal conscripts and Fréjus found itself a curious role as acclimatisation zone for colonial troops. In the 1930s France saw its first socialist government, under Leon Blum's Front Populaire, enthusiastically supported in the south – and the arrival of paid holidays for all.

World War II marked the South. After Paris fell in June 1940 and nominal rule of France was transferred to Maréchal Pétain in Vichy, the South became part of the zone libre or free France (except Menton, which was occupied by the Italian army) – not that this prevented the creation of a number of internment camps for aliens, notably at Les Milles, just outside Aix. Marseille served as an important escape route. Then, from autumn 1942, the South was occupied by German troops. Hardest hit were the strategic naval ports of Marseille and Toulon, ravaged by both Allied bombing and retreating Germans in 1944. Groups of maquis, the Resistance, hid out in the hills. The Alpes-Maritimes were occupied by Italian troops until the fall of Italy in September 1943, when they were replaced by Germans. The liberation of Provence by Allied forces based in North Africa came on 15 August, in an attack centred on the Var (see p19 **The other D-Day**).

Post-war reconstruction was responsible for some of the architectural horrors that dog the South; lax or corrupt planning departments did the rest, suffocating the Côte d'Azur in concrete in a misguided attempt to deal with mass tourism and the urban housing shortage of the major towns. Environmental damage is also a growing concern. Heavy industry did its share, especially west of Marseille where the salt marsh of the Etang de Berre became a huge oil dump; wild fires – destroying a fifth of the Massif des Maures in 2003 and causing the evacuation of 2,000 people from the Bouches-du-Rhône in 2004 – remain a concern each summer and the culling of wolves to protect sheep flocks is an increasingly vexed question.

Since the 1980s – when Mitterrand granted the regions limited autonomy – the centralising impetus of the previous centuries has begun to be reversed. The regional assembly is largely about economic power, especially in the South of France, which – with its large number of expat second-homers and immigrants, from outside and within France – has a less fierce sense of regional identity than the Pays Basque and Brittany. Nonetheless, Provençal lessons are now available in schools and dual-language street signs have appeared.

The other D-Day

On Sunday 15 August 2004 a 60-year-old injustice was laid to rest, when French president Jacques Chirac finally presented the Legion of Honour to 21 World War II veterans who had fought heroically in the French army – no matter that they were African.

On 15 August 1944 the beaches of Cavalaire, St-Raphaël and Le Lavandou had become the stage upon which unfolded a dramatic and intense battle to restore battered French national pride. Operation Dragoon, a 250,000-strong wave of Allied manpower, hit the provençal shores between Toulon and Cannes on 15 August. The forces significantly included the 1st French Army under General de Lattre de Tassigny. This was the military representation of Charles de Gaulle's alternative French government, a body recognised – but only with firmly gritted teeth – by the British and American establishment. There was a deep and entirely mutual repulsion felt between Roosevelt and de Gaulle: 'Prima donna!' sneered Roosevelt; 'Corpse!' muttered our Frenchman.

As American forces, who had been airdropped inland at Le Muy, barrelled up the Rhône Valley in the direction of Lyon and Grenoble, General de Lattre's forces landed on the coast at Pramousquier and Cap Nègre to take care of the strategic ports of Toulon and Marseille, and 20,000 GIs from the 36th Texan Division landed on the Plage du Dramont. After just over a week of intense fighting and despite suffering high casualties, the Allies managed to capture Marseille on 23 August, Cannes on 25 August – ecstatically echoing the liberation of Paris on the same day – and Toulon on 27 August.

To the British, the Provence landings seem an afterthought to the Normandy triumph of June 1944. For the French, events in Provence are intimately tied up with the euphoria of the liberation of Paris and a wider sense of the French recapturing their country. However, many of these 'French' soldiers actually came from the colonies of Algeria, Morocco, Senegal and Cameroon, a fact gracelessly forgotten by the Toulonnois in 1995, when they voted for Le Pen's Front National at local election time. De Lattre's army apparently bred related concerns in de Gaulle, who ordered that it should be 'whitened' by the introduction of exiled Resistance fighters. It is, then, a delicious irony that the French aircraft carrier on which these hitherto disregarded veterans were honoured, in front of more than a dozen African leaders, should have been the *Charles de Gaulle*. 'The sons of your nations joined their names to the military legend of France and forever mingled their blood with ours,' intoned Chirac in his address.

Memorials to the dead of that campaign now pepper the coast, but they are easily missed amid the crush of a Côte d'Azur summer. For quiet reflection, there are national cemeteries at Boularis, Rayol-Canadel and Luynes. The main commemorative museum is the **Musée-Mémorial du Débarquement** (*see p182*) in Toulon; you can also visit the **Musée de la Libération** (*see p217*) at Le Muy and the US war cemetery outside Draguignan. A more general history of the occupation and *maquis* resistance can be found at the **Musée d'Histoire 1939-1945** (*see p127*) in Fontaine-de-Vaucluse.

The economy of the South remains highly skewed, with great disparities between rich and poor, the highest property prices outside Paris, above-national-average unemployment, and a population that soars in summer and plummets in winter. High-tech industry poles in Aix and Sophia-Antipolis, biotechnology in Nîmes and the petrochemicals of the Etang de Berre are counterparts to the largely agricultural interior (an important producer of fruit and veg). Marseille, France's second city, is perhaps symbolic of the new South, trying to secure a reputation for its dynamic service industries rather than a declining agrifood industry and 'Popeye' Doyle-style drug dealings.

While international conventions and congresses bolster the economies of Nice and Cannes, much of the South remains heavily dependent on tourism. The arrival of the TGV in 2001 brought the South closer than ever to Paris, and formal discussion of an extension to Nice began in February 2005. This would not only cut journey times from the capital to four hours, but also open up the tantalising possibility of onward links to Barcelona and Genoa. The influx of especially British tourists (increasingly, second-homers) on the budget airlines remains a source of revenue and a cause of muttering in the local cafés (*see also chapter* **South of France Today**).

Key events

c25,000 BC Cave paintings in Calanques.
5000 BC-2500 BC Rock engravings made in Vallée des Merveilles.
c600 BC Phocaean Greeks found Massalia (modern-day Marseille).
122 BC Romans defeat Oppidum of Entremont and found Aquae Sextiae (Aix-en-Provence).
120 BC Romans build Via Domitia, with staging posts at Apt, Beaucaire and Nîmes.
105 BC Romans defeated by Celts at Orange.
49 BC Caesar besieges Marseille.
6 BC Trophée des Alpes built at La Turbie.
cAD 40-60 Construction of Pont du Gard.
476 Fall of Roman Empire.
843 Treaty of Verdun – the former Carolingian Empire divided between Louis I's three sons.
974 William I drives Saracens from their last stronghold, La Garde-Freinet in the Maures.
1113 Provence passes to the House of Barcelona; Languedoc to Toulouse.
1160 Construction of Abbaye de Thoronet.
1195 Marriage of Alphonse, Count of Provence, to Gersande, Countess of Forcalquier, unites the two Comtés.
1240 Louis IX founds Aigues-Mortes.
1246 Beatrice of Provence marries Charles d'Anjou, brother of French king Louis IX.
1274 Comtat Venaissin given to Papacy.
1295 Charles II founds Basilique of St Mary Magdalene at Ste-Maximin-la-Ste-Baume.
1297 The Grimaldis come to power in Monaco.
1306 Philippe le Bel expels Jews from France.
1306-1417 Avignon Papacy.
1348 Black Death decimates the population.
1372 Raymond de Turenne becomes guardian of the last princess of Les Baux.
1409 Louis II of Anjou founds University of Aix.
1471 Good King René moves court to Aix.
1481 Provence bequeathed to Louis XI.
1486 Act of Union between France and Provence.
1501 Parlement de Provence held at Aix.
1503 Nostradamus born in St-Rémy.
1523 Holy Roman Emperor Charles V besieges Marseille.
1538 Francis I signs peace treaty with Charles V in Château de Villeneuve-Loubet.
1540s-90s Wars of Religion.
1545 Massacre of Mérindol.
1563 Huguenots massacred in Orange.
1567 Catholics massacred in Nîmes.
1598 Henry IV issues the Edict of Nantes.
1608 Henry IV buys Antibes from the Grimaldis.
1637 Battle of St-Tropez: royal troops force Spanish galleys into retreat.

1649 Cours Mirabeau laid out in Aix.
1671 La Vieille Charité begun in Marseille.
1680 Darse Neuve naval docks at Toulon.
1685 Louis XIV revokes the Edict of Nantes.
1690s Louis XIV's military architect Vauban builds forts in Marseille, Toulon and Entrevaux.
1720 Plague spreads from Marseille.
1789 French Revolution begins.
1791 Avignon and the Comtat Venaissin incorporated into France.
1792 Nice taken by Revolutionary forces.
1793 Napoleon captures Royalist Toulon.
1799 Coup d'état by Napoleon.
1804 Bonaparte proclaimed Emperor.
1815 1 March: Napoleon lands at Golfe Juan.
1822 Bauxite discovered at Baux-de-Provence; promenade des Anglais laid out in Nice.
1834 Lord Brougham settles in Cannes.
1848 Revolution; Louis-Philippe overthrown.
1853 Joliette port opens in Marseille.
1854 Félibrige movement founded.
1860 Nice, Roquebrune and Menton become part of France.
1863 Casino de Monte-Carlo opens.
1869 First Chorégies d'Orange opera festival.
1888 Van Gogh settles in Arles.
1892 Queen Victoria stays in Hyères.
1906 Matisse, Braque and Derain spend the summer at L'Estaque.
1936 Front Populaire introduces paid summer holidays.
1940 Fall of France in World War II; the South becomes the *zone libre*.
1942 South occupied by German troops.
1944 15 August: Liberation of Provence.
1946 First Cannes film festival.
1947 Roya and Bevera valleys become part of France; first Avignon theatre festival.
1951 Matisse's Chapelle du Rosaire opens.
1956 Severe frost kills off most of olive crop; Bardot makes a star of St-Tropez.
1960s Ecole de Nice art movement flourishes.
1962 Algerian independence: thousands of pieds noirs settle in the South of France.
1969 Creation of Sophia-Antipolis.
1971 Isola 2000 ski resort opens.
1982 Death of Princess Grace of Monaco.
2001 TGV Méditérranée high-speed train links Paris to Marseille and to Nîmes.
2002 Presidential election: Jacques Chirac re-elected after Front National candidate Jean-Marie Le Pen gets through to second round.
2003 Summer fires destroy 20% of Maures.
2005 Prince Rainier III of Monaco dies and is succeeded by his son, Albert II.

Leader of the far-right Front National party, **Jean-Marie Le Pen**. *See p24.*

The South of France Today

It's getting hot and steamy down on the coast, and not everyone's managing to keep their cool.

From the palm-fringed beaches of Nice to snow-capped Alpine peaks, from lavish villas and luxury yachts to graffiti-covered tower blocks and from the sterile sophistication of Sophia-Antipolis to the goat farms of Caussols, the South of France is – and always has been – a melting pot of contrasts and contradictions. The Côte d'Azur, a single 128-kilometre (80-mile) stretch of coastline, accommodates the rich and the poor, the glitzy and the shabby, the ancient and the ultra-modern side-by-side on one of the most expensive, sought-after and overpopulated strips of land on earth.

For many visitors, the South is a summer playground where, for the right money, they can be pampered in some of Europe's finest hotels, sunbathe for a tenner an hour on an exclusive private beach and fork out a small fortune for a tiny cup of coffee so they can watch the surgically enhanced beauties, ageing lotharios in white loafers and jewel-encrusted old women with small dogs file past on Cannes' famous Croisette.

It is a region where, in April and May, you can ski in the morning at Isola 2000 or Auron, then swim in the Mediterranean in the afternoon. You can hike through the Gorges du Loup and not see another living soul all day, or fight your way through the crowds for a café table at St-Tropez's bustling port.

Where other places may strive to appear cosmopolitan, the Côte d'Azur, in particular, has had the honour thrust upon it. It is the region of France where the indigenous locals – if you can find one – are most greatly outnumbered by outsiders. Over the past ten years, the French themselves, especially Parisians, have been flooding in in increasing numbers to escape overcrowded and expensive city life, only to find that their arrival – along with, among others, tens of thousands of Britons, Germans, Dutch, Italians and, more recently, an influx of wealthy Russians, is making it as overcrowded and expensive as the city they left behind.

The British are among the Riviera's most long-established immigrants. The area became popular with Victorians after their queen spent

Auto pilot

Dangerous French driving is an art form. Its virtuosos are called *chauffards* – note the frightening proximity to the word *chauffeur* and gauge the safety distance. The Southern take on the genre is famously lethal: tanked on *pastis* and Mediterranean sun, provençal drivers treat the road like a not-so-virtual round of Gran Turismo. The safety belt is just superfluous car-couture. Marseille holds the road-rage title, its official manual being Luc Besson's high-speed auto-action flick *Taxi*, tellingly the highest French grosser in 1998.

To watch, take a spin down the A7 motorway. It's a sophisticated act: flying fag-butts, wagging fists and disco brake lights. Suddenly, blackened windows swerve out from nowhere, slaloming in and out of caravans, and come up the rear to smooch your bumper. Many British holidaymakers have feared for their lives braving the descent to Provence by car, tempting them to make U-turns back north. But this year is different.

French road deaths have dropped by eight per cent over the last three years, taking 'only' 5,232 victims in 2004. Weary of its reputation as training ground for Europe's worst drivers, the French government finally put its foot on the brakes by placing a campaign to fight against *insécurité routière* at the centre of Chirac's second presidency. And he's taking it seriously, so seriously, in fact, that he's prepared to stoop so low as to suggest that the nation takes a page out of the British Highway Code of courtesy and low accident rates. Cue a furious, turbo-speed backlash.

The new laws promise to boost fines and multiply speed cameras. Even the wine and spirits giant Pernod Ricard has recognised that strong measures of alcohol are behind the problem, and has given away key rings and breathalysers at student parties as part of its charter to reduce drink-driving. The driving test has got tougher too, wangling its own TV slot on the France 2 terrestial television channel. Low viewing figures were only to be expected. Pass rates have plummeted; only a mildly reassuring triumph, given that two-thirds of offenders don't have the pink *permis* anyway. As an indicator of candidates' violent calibre, driving examiners now announce results by post to avoid being bludgeoned by the disappointed.

Since 2001 the fight has even threatened the dreamy plane-tree avenues, symbol of the South, with the politically correct chop. Their alignment is said to slice the sunlight into a hazardous strobe, blinding drivers' vision and causing accidents. So far, these unlikely 'corridors of hell' remain standing, avoiding a provençal chainsaw massacre.

But many see the government as the slowcoaches in the fight against road violence. Jean-Pierre Giraud, a sculptor from the Hérault area who lost his son in a car accident, took the crisis into his own hands and launched *Opération Silhouette* in 2000. His colony of black, human cutouts haunts the Southern road network, a bolt of blood-red lightening splicing each through the head. Every figure marks the spot of a fatal accident. You can't miss them, and their effect is chilling enough to make you bolt off the road in terror.

Towns and villages have joined in the shock tactics, brandishing huge warning signs on the way out, announcing the death toll of the road ahead. So what's the traffic report for years to come? Dangerous French drivers RIP?

a winter in Grasse to escape the British weather. Since then, the British have settled in enclaves along the whole coast from St-Tropez to Menton, with, it seems, a particular affection for Antibes, scathingly referred to by locals as 'Angle-tibes'. Valbonne, with its grocery shop selling English tea, Marmite and baked beans, and its own pub and English-language bookshop, is another favourite with the British.

But the Côte d'Azur is far more than a luxury holiday destination or retreat for rich expats. It is a busy, working region riddled with all the inherent problems of maintaining and developing its infrastructure, looking after its elderly and creating jobs to sustain its population.

Chelsea FC boss Roman Abramovich and Microsoft tycoon Paul Allen are among the billionaires who moor their super-yachts at Antibes's Port Vauban. A four-bedroom house with swimming pool on the nearby Cap d'Antibes costs well in excess of a million quid. But drive just ten minutes inland to the dilapidated social housing projects of Vallauris, and the stark division of wealth provoked by low wages, the high cost of living and mounting unemployment is brutally evident.

Ten per cent of the French workforce is unemployed, but on the Côte d'Azur, almost 40 per cent of North African Arabs are out of work and living on state handouts. Gangs of youths

In the wake of the initial national improvements, drivers are already beginning to take their foot off the brake, cruising on smugness back towards old speeds. Recent surveys show that in spite of the clamp down, the number of road injuries in the Bouche-du-Rhône area has actually risen. For the full horror show, the Ligue Contre la Violence Routière, the pressure group for road safety, flash the number of road deaths per hour on its website www.violenceroutiere.org (75 when we went to print).

Moreover, the road network is designed like a sprawling entertainment park. Decorated roundabouts mushroom by the day – islets of kitsch, they booby-trap your journey as you swerve in shock at their ugliness. Service stations outshine Disney World Paris. Radio Info, the motorway radio station, keeps feet dangerously tapping at the pedal to its groovy tunes, hence the rhythmic lane waltzing. It's so much fun, you'll simply never want to leave your car.

More worrying still, the government's campaign has started to get confused. Debate rages over how many speed cameras to introduce, and rumours have spread that some were sold to a company that forgot to pay the electricity bill. Meanwhile, murderers zoom past the blind eyes at 180kph (110 mph).

Things may be a bit slower right now, but it's still terrifying out there, hot with hormones and tarmac. The summer holiday warpath south continues, all mad jerks and motorbikes, with free-range kiddies crawling over the seats. So make the most of the lull while it lasts.

drift into Vallauris's historic village centre to scowl at the tourists browsing the disused pottery workshops that were once the town's thriving industry.

But nowadays there is no real manufacturing on the Côte d'Azur. Even Grasse, once – yet still boasting to be – the perfume capital of the world, is more of a museum than a scent factory. In the summer months, tourist buses are parked six deep for multilingual tours of the old Fragonard and Molinard distilleries, while, with generous EU farming subsidies available, many flower farmers now find it more profitable to let their jasmine, rose and lavender fields lie fallow than actually grow real crops.

Apart from the increasing numbers of Eastern European prostitutes that haunt the promenade des Anglais in Nice and the backstreets of Cannes and Antibes, the coast's boom industry is now tourism, and this is proving to be both a blessing and a curse for the region. Café-owners, restaurateurs and hoteliers can make three-quarters of their annual income in just one quarter of the year, but the influx of wealthy foreigners hoovering up holiday homes only to leave them lying empty for 11 months of the year, or second home-owners spurred on by the raft of television programmes about renovating foreign properties has sent house prices soaring by up to 20 per cent a year.

Local councils have been quick to identify tourism as their biggest potential money-spinner, with towns like Grasse, Valbonne and Vence embarking on the lavish cobbling and closing to traffic of quaint streets and squares to attract more tourists seeking the 'real Provence'. Seasonal businesses like smart restaurants, souvenir shops and provençal art galleries are moving in, pushing up rents and forcing out the local butcher, baker and crumbling corner café. Developers are renovating antiquated village flats and houses, pushing up rents and property prices and forcing the mostly Arab immigrant families out of town centres into suburban tower blocks.

But it is not just dispossessed North African immigrants who could never hope to own their own homes. Many first-time buyers whose families have lived on this coast for generations are now finding it almost impossible to get on to the property ladder. With houses and apartments costing up to £2,000 per square metre, the same as smart districts of Paris, young people are being forced to rent, creating a demand that is sending those prices spiralling beyond the reach of many.

The well-paid young executives of Sophia Antipolis, the Riviera's own miniature silicon valley and home to high-tech giants like Cisco Systems and Hewlett Packard, may still be able to afford a home, but the high prices are causing a now serious shortage of lower-paid, but socially crucial key workers like nurses, teachers or firemen. As with London, Paris and New York, many of these indispensable public servants in large towns like Nice, Cannes and Antibes are forced to live long distances from their place of work, with all the stresses on family life that that brings. A recent initiative by Nice's mayor to offer lower rents and travel perks to key workers has so far proved mostly ineffective, and many have begun a new trend of reverse immigration and simply quit the Côte d'Azur for the cheaper regions of France.

This gradual exodus is creating a subtle polarisation of communities in the South that is becoming more noticeable with every passing year. With middle-class French families drifting away from the region, they are leaving behind wealthier French and foreigners, and a disproportionately large, jobless underclass living in council accommodation and existing on state handouts. This yawning gulf in lifestyles and living standards is mirrored by the political climate of the South, which is also the region of France where there is the most striking division of the vote between the extreme right- and extreme left-wing parties, with relatively less space occupied in the middle for more moderate views. The National Front party, thriving on the votes of the white *pieds noirs* French who resettled along the coast when Charles de Gaulle granted Algeria independence, sees the South as its natural home. Although its heartland may be in towns west of the Côte d'Azur like Vitrolles, Toulon and Orange, Jean-Marie Le Pen's party still managed to reap around a quarter of the vote in Grasse, St-Raphaël and Fréjus in the last presidential election.

'The whiff of an apartheid wafts over the region, with those Arabs who are in work often occupying the most menial positions.'

This whiff of an unmentionable apartheid wafts over the region, from the ubiquitous fly-posters supporting the National Front to the politically embarrassing and highly visible reality that those Arabs who are in work often occupy the most menial positions, or the incontrovertible government statistic that two out of three white adults over the age of 50 in Vallauris voted for the party that wants all non-French residents repatriated.

The centre-right national government has been accused of pandering to the South's large numbers of National Front voters with recent legislation banning the wearing of ostentatious religious symbols in schools. Although the rules ban everything from skullcaps to crucifixes, North African Muslims said the law was really aimed at outlawing the traditional Islamic headscarves worn by many schoolgirls, and its implementation at the end of 2004 triggered angry demonstrations by Arabs in the region.

But state investment in the South's infrastructure means hospitals are slick and well funded and state schools are so highly regarded that the children of a British expat,

a Russian billionaire and a jobless North African can all be found sitting side by side in the local primary school. Perhaps in decades to come this academic democracy – aided by the gradual passing away of the *pieds noirs* – will iron out the coast's racial divisions by itself.

The future prosperity of the Côte d'Azur would also receive a significant boost from another of the proposed 'grands projets' designed to inject new life into the region. The 322kph (200mph) TGV trains whisk passengers the 800 kilometres (500 miles) from Paris to Marseilles in just under three hours, but it then takes the same amount of time again for the trains to crawl along the remaining 250 kilometres (150 miles) of picturesque coastal line between Marseille and the Italian border just outside Menton. Consecutive mayors of Nice have been petitioning the Paris government for years to extend the high-speed track to bring their city within a feasible three hours 45 minutes of the capital, thus opening it up to businesses that have so far considered it too isolated. In mid 2005 a series of options of where to route the new line was drawn up by the Transport Ministry in the hope that construction of the multi-billion-pound project could be under way within five years.

Up in the remote mountain wilderness of Alpes-Maritimes villages like Caussols and Coursegoules, where wolves and wild boar still roam, it can be hard to imagine that one is less than an hour's drive from the Ferraris, the casinos, super-yachts, luxury villas, council estates and sprawling developments of new houses that are linking up the already tightly packed seaside resorts and turning the entire coastline into a strip of urban development, creeping ever further back from the coast and with barely a green space in between.

Some tourists come seeking the real Provence, of a cobbled village street with beret-wearing locals playing *boules* and sipping *pastis*. But this is a place where foreigners have not yet trod, and the moment they do find it, another village morphs into a provençal theme park with an out-of-town coach park, a gift shop and multi-language restaurant menus. Others are lured to the region by a mythical kudos, by a kind of old-world technicolour glamour, by visions of strolling into Monaco's casino in a dinner jacket or roaring down the Corniches in a cabriolet with the mountains on one side and the sea on the other.

Both worlds still exist, and it is these idyllic extremes that still define the South, preserve its magical allure and keep the tourists flooding in. But when the lights go down, the reality, like a cabaret singer without her make-up, is perhaps not quite as glamorous as it first appeared.

A feast of beasts: the one and only **bouillabaisse**.

Provençal Food

Let Provence march on your stomach.

It's Saturday morning at the cours Saleya market in Nice and recipes are whizzing around like volleyballs on a patch of sandy beach, with the occasional decisive spike as a *grand-mère* spits out the last word in a heated culinary debate. 'Cut these into thick slices and bake them with onion, olive oil and herbes de Provence,' advises one market gardener with a pierced nose, straw hat and piles of trumpet-shaped squash. 'It's simple but sublime.' Shoppers exchange their recipes for petits farcis (stuffed vegetables), while the tomato specialist beams from behind his display of yellow, green, orange, red and striped varieties. The more experienced cooks are buying kilos of delicate purple figs for jam-making (they know the season only lasts a few weeks), while novices get advice on how to deep-fry golden courgette flowers. No wonder so few people here own more than a couple of cookbooks.

In markets across Provence, similar scenes are taking place – and yet with a difference. Just a few kilometres away in Cagnes-sur-Mer, fresh fish is more bountiful than in Nice. Menton has its own tropical microclimate, some of the world's best lemons and, hardly surprising given its proximity to the border, an Italian-influenced cooking style. Cannes, though better known for its glitz, quietly houses the finest collection of small fruit and vegetable

producers on the Côte d'Azur in its Forville market, while on the Vieux Port in Marseille you can watch little wooden fishing boats deliver the live catch. St-Tropez, with its daily fish market, serves as a magnet not just for luxury yachts but also for serious foodies. Inland, fish gives way to beef, lamb and, in the Camargue, slow-cooked bull's meat (taureau). In the Rhône Valley the food often takes a back seat to some of the world's most sensual wines. Elsewhere, copious quantities of chilled rosé make a perfect match for the summer fare, while bold provençal reds, particularly the celebrated Bandol, take over in winter.

Despite this apparent abundance, Provence has not always basked in such a wealth of produce. As in Tuscany, provençal cooking uses great ingenuity to turn rustic ingredients into something extraordinary: sardines farcies, a delectable dish of sardine fillets topped with swiss chard and breadcrumbs, are a perfect example. Hard winters, when the populace is whipped by the Mistral or the Tramontagne, call for rib-sticking dishes, such as long-simmered daube (beef stew). Stuffed vegetables were invented to use up leftover daube, while pan bagnat is salade niçoise stuffed into a bun, all the better for taking into the fields. Though the original versions of these dishes were always delicious, they were rarely refined

DIY cuisine

Few visitors to Provence pass up the chance of lazing away a few hours over some quality nosh, having never lifted a finger except to beckon over le garçon. Yet a growing number of holiday-makers are choosing to spend precious leisure time slaving in a variety of French kitchens. Whether they are located in homely farmhouses or grandiose châteaux, the region's Ecoles de Cuisine (cooking schools) are run along similar lines: raw ingredients are gathered at the local market, prepared using any number of provençal techniques, then eaten with smug satisfaction by the budding chefs, buoyed up with insights gained into local produce and cooking techniques. Classes range from half a day to a full week, all include food and wine, some include accommodation and excursions – but expect to pay as much, or more, to cook it yourself as to dine at a good restaurant. The following courses are taught in English, unless stated otherwise.

The Atelier Culinaire Provençal at **Château de Clapier** (Mirabeau, 04.42.93.11.80, www.acp-aix.com; 1-day course from €65, 1wk course from €750) is on a wine estate in the Luberon. Chef Daniel Peyraud guides the group through Aix market, letting seasonal produce inspire his menus. His style is a light, modern take on regional produce: think roast red mullet with a lemon-caper sauce and raspberry sorbet. Both one-day and week-long classes include a wine tasting at the estate.

The Ecole de Cuisine at Côtes de Provence wine-producer **Château de Berne** (Lorgues, 04.94.60.48.88, www.chateauberne.com; 1-day course €100, 3-day course from €916) is run by chef Jean-Louis Vosgien in a house overlooking a pool and vineyards. The surroundings are gorgeous and the facilities excellent, but the feel is that of a luxury resort and perhaps less relaxed than other schools.

The atmosphere is more domestic when you learn with **Ghislaine Daniel** (06.20.66.06.80, http://site.voila.fr/lacuisinedeghislaine; 4 classes €100, in French only). She teaches simple provençal cooking in her home in Aix-en-Provence. Students cook, clean up and eat their creations together – and you're encouraged to have seconds. To give the experience extra authenticity, Ghislaine and her husband sit at each end of the table preventing the mostly foreign students from speaking languages other than French.

The Ecole de Cuisine at **Mas de Cornud** (04.90.92.39.32, www.mascornud.com; half-day course from €130, 1wk course from €2,000) takes place in a stone farmhouse B&B near St-Rémy. Chef Nito Carpitas, a consummate hostess, draws dual inspiration from her Egyptian background and provençal cuisine. These intensive courses are ideal for experienced cooks wanting to hone their skills – Carpitas regularly brushes up her own skills at professional cooking schools.

In Arles, **Cuisine et Tradition School of Provençale Cuisine** (04.90.49.69.20, www.cuisineprovencale.com; 5-day course from €895) is led by French chef Erick Vedel and his wife Madeleine. Hands-on classes are held in their ancient stone kitchen, but also include visits to the market and local artisans, like a goat's-cheese maker and a beekeeper. Erick's recipes for provençal mussels and Etruscan duck are delicious.

In a 16th-century stone farmhouse in the Drôme Provençale, **Ecole Culinaire Tuillières** (Pont de Barret, 04.75.90.43.91; 1wk course from €1,300) is both cooking school and rustic guesthouse. Classes, with Austrian chef Hermann Jenny and his wife Susan, are thorough, entertaining and cater to all levels, as budding cooks learn to prepare dishes such as chicken terrine, lamb stew and the authentically provençal tarte aux pignons.

Kathie Alex's **Cooking with Friends in France** (04.93.60.10.56, www.cookingwith friends.com; 1wk course from €2,450) combines the acquisition of new cooking techniques with 'cultural experience' in the former house of pioneering American chef Julia Child near Grasse. At **Haute Provence** (www.georgeannebrennan.com; 1wk course approx €2,750), US cookbook author Georgeanne Brennan gives courses in a restored farmhouse outside Aups.

There are also shorter options. You can take the lunch or dinner classes, taught by a professional chef at Avignon hotel **La Mirande** (04.90.85.93.93; half-day course from €100), or head to **Les Petits Farcis** (06.81.67.41.22, www.petitsfarcis.com; 1-day course €200-€290), where Rosa Jackson offers market visits followed by a hands-on cooking class, four-course lunch and optional afternoon walking tour. Classes take place in her renovated flat in Vieux Nice, just behind the cours Saleya market.

(and that's where the current generation of chefs comes in). The stars of provençal cooking – Alain Llorca at Moulin de Mougins; Jacques Chibois at Bastide Saint-Antoine in Grasse; Franck Cerutti of the Louis XV in Monaco; Christian Etienne at his eponymous restaurant in Avignon; the legendary Jacques Maximin, with his convivial Table d'Amis in Vence; Daniel Hébet, at his outstanding new bistro Le Jardin du Quai in l'Isle sur la Sorgue; Joël Robuchon, who oversees the restaurant in Monaco's splashily renovated Hôtel Métropole – bring finesse to peasant cooking, using their technical prowess to let magical ingredients speak for themselves.

'It would be dishonest to pretend that simply being in Provence provides a guarantee of good food.'

It would be dishonest to pretend, however, that simply being in Provence provides a guarantee of good food. Marvellous ingredients are there for the taking, yet relatively few chefs bother seeking them out. With so many potential victims coming through their doors in high season, they easily fall prey to cynicism – particularly near the seafront (with some notable exceptions) and during major events, such as the Festival d'Avignon. If you hope to get to the heart of provençal cooking, it pays to do some research – and perhaps rent a gîte with a kitchen so you can try out the word-of-mouth recipes for yourself.

MEAT AND POULTRY
Beef, a provençal favourite, might be grilled with herbs, simmered in a daube (an aromatic stew made with wine, herbs and orange zest) or sautéed with morels. In the Camargue look out for dark, tender bull's meat (taureau), simply grilled or stewed in a hearty boeuf à la gardiane. Sheep raised in Les Alpilles, the Crau plain and Haute Provence (most famously Sisteron) produce tender lamb, perhaps roast with rosemary, summer savory or whole heads of garlic; daube à l'avignonnaise features lamb rather than beef. Game includes rabbit, hare and wild boar from the *garrigues* (brush hillsides) and woodland, which find their way into rich stews and saucissons. Rabbit is stewed with white wine, herbs and tomatoes. Chicken was for so long thought uninteresting that few recipes exist for it in the provençal repertoire; canard aux olives is a classic way to prepare duck. Thrift is at the heart of provençal cooking and the less noble parts of the animals are also used, as in the pieds et paquets of Marseille

(stuffed tripe and sheep's feet stewed in wine) or the type of porchetta found in Nice (whole pig stuffed with every possible part of the beast). Charcuteries along the coast sell delicious Italian-style sausages.

FISH
Coastal Provence has developed a splendid battery of fish and shellfish dishes. Over-fishing of the Mediterranean means that a lot of the fish actually comes from the Atlantic or Italy, but there is still a pricey local catch, seen in the Marseille and St-Tropez fish markets or delivered direct to seashore restaurants (some have their own fishing boats). The celebrated bouillabaisse is found all along the coast, though Marseille is its acknowledged home; a group of restaurateurs even signed a charter to defend the authentic recipe. Bouillabaisse is traditionally served in two courses: first the saffron-tinted soup, accompanied by toasted baguette, fiery rouille and a sprinkling of gruyère, then the fish. Purists insist on 12 varieties of fish and shellfish, but the three essentials are rascasse (scorpion fish), grondin (red gurnard) and congre (conger eel). Mussels are generally included too, though langouste or lobster is often considered a false luxury touch.

Less well-known but equally delicious is bourride, a creamy garlic-spiked fish soup made from one or more of John Dory, sea bass and monkfish bound with aïoli. If you're lucky, you may find poutargue, the pressed, salted grey mullet roe that is a speciality of Martigues. Mussels are raised in the bay of Toulon and are popular on the Var coast, eaten à la marinière (with white wine, onions and shallots), à la provençale (with white wine, tomatoes, onion and garlic) or gratinéed. You might also come across Mediterranean oysters, saltier than the Atlantic variety. Other fish preparations include loup au fenouil (sea bass baked with fennel) and red mullet with tapenade. Brandade de morue, salt cod soaked in milk and puréed with olive oil, is a speciality of Nîmes. Some of the best meals consist of just-out-of-the-sea fish, chosen at table, then charcoal-grilled. Expect to pay by weight (allow roughly 400g-500g or 14oz-18oz per person).

FRUIT AND VEGETABLES
The quality and variety of the vegetables and fruit are superb, whether they come from fields and orchards along the Durance and Var rivers or from tiny coastal gardens. This part of France is thus a paradise for vegetarians, even though specifically vegetarian menus are rare. As well as ratatouille, other favourites include artichauts à la barigoule, tomates provençales (slow-baked tomatoes with breadcrumbs and

garlic on top) and courgette-flower fritters. There are all manner of stuffed vegetables and baked tians (gratins named after the dish in which they are cooked). And what could be simpler or more delicious than grilled red peppers, served cold and drizzled with olive oil?

In spring, the region produces some of the best asparagus in France, followed by a summer abundance of aubergines, peppers, courgettes (look out for yellow and round varieties) and tomatoes. Artichokes are usually of the violet, almost chokeless, variety. Humbler chickpeas, broad beans and fennel also feature in traditional recipes, as do blettes – pieces of swiss chard, braised and served with cream as a vegetable or in the curious sweet-savoury tourte that is a speciality of Nice. Epeautre (spelt), grown on Mont Ventoux, has made a bit of a comeback, and excellent rice is still grown in the Camargue. Autumn brings squash, wild mushrooms and pumpkins, and winter is the time for truffles in the Drôme, Luberon and the Var. Mesclun, a distinctly provençal salad of mixed leaves and herbs, is available year-round.

Delicious orange-fleshed melon of Cavaillon has been grown here since being introduced by the Avignon Papacy in the 14th century. Other fruit cultivated in the region includes early strawberries from Carpentras, cherries, apricots and table grapes, citrus fruits from Menton and a sumptuous glut of figs in late summer.

CHEESE

Dairying is limited, but you'll find plenty of farmhouse goat's cheeses at markets. Look out for unctuous banon, made in the area around Forcalquier with goat's milk, wrapped in a chestnut leaf and aged to a pungent runniness; picodon, a small, young, tangy goat's cheese from north Provence; pelardon, similar to picodon, but aged and very firm; and brousse de Rove, a ricotta-like soft, mild, fresh cheese made from goat's or ewe's milk and used to fill ravioli or eaten drizzled with olive oil or honey.

MARKETS

Even in the most touristy village or glamorous resort, markets remain a vital force and stands selling scented candles and lavender sachets remain squarely outnumbered by stalls laden with goat's cheeses, herbs, aubergines and tomatoes. You'll also find stalls specialising in saucissons secs, olives and tapenades, jams and honey. In larger towns, there are daily markets; in smaller towns and villages they're often held once or twice a week, usually in the morning. Many vendors stock up at nearby wholesale markets in the early hours, while others sell their own lovingly tended wares (to spot the producers, look for those with dirt under their fingernails). A growing trend is for farmers' markets, sometimes in the evening, where you buy direct from the producer.

THE RESTAURANTS

At the grandest establishments, with their famous chefs, you'll eat sublime food and pay sublimely ridiculous prices. Locals tend to patronise these places only on special occasions or for lunch, when many renowned kitchens offer relatively affordable menus. Instead, they are more likely to seek out good value, accepting less silverware and perhaps a single waiter or waitress, for cooking that's spot on.

The traditional emphasis on vegetables, olive oil and fish in the provençal diet already perfectly matches the health concerns of today, but the Southern restaurant scene has not stood still. If many restaurants delight in trad Provence, with print tablecloths and the comforting reassurance of age-old daubes and tians, other eateries are renewing Southern cuisine with the creative use of seasonal, regional produce or by adding cosmopolitan touches drawn from elsewhere. Outside influences are not new: the Italian kitchen had a strong impact in Nice – for a long time part of the kingdom of Genoa – and Italianate gnocchi and ravioli (the latter often filled with daube) are common alongside all sorts of other local snacks. Marseille cuisine goes well beyond bouillabaisse; the city boasts superb ethnic restaurants, reflecting the kaleidoscopic variety of people who've settled there. The city has large Italian, Spanish, North African, Greek and Armenian communities, and these cuisines have made their mark on many chefs.

When possible, think carefully before choosing your restaurant – €30 per person can buy you a feast in a bistro headed by a passionate chef, but these are not exactly thick on the ground in the tourist centres. Be especially cautious in high season, when restaurants often hire unqualified staff. A worthwhile alternative is *tables d'hôtes*, offered in many bed and breakfasts, where the hosts prepare a simple country-style meal; if they are doing this, the chances are they want to share their love of the local food.

Restaurants are generally relaxed in France. Although you shouldn't come to the table in a bathing costume unless you're right on the beach, ties are rarely required and T-shirts and shorts are usually fine. However, the French are often well dressed (think smart-casual), especially in the evening. Seaside showbiz destinations can be distinctly glitzy (gold jewellery and tans, real or fake, required), while haute cuisine establishments, even in a village, can be as dressy as Paris – if not more so.

Decoding the menu

Agneau lamb. **aiglefin** haddock. **ail** garlic. **aïoli** garlic mayonnaise. **airelle** cranberry. **alouettes sans têtes** literally 'headless skylarks', actually small stuffed beef parcels. **amande** almond; – **de mer** small clam. **ananas** pineapple. **anchoïade** anchovy and olive sauce, served with raw vegetables. **anchois** anchovy. **andouillette** sausage made from pig's offal. **anguille** eel. **artichauts à la barigoule** small purple artichokes braised in white wine. **anis** aniseed. **asperge** asparagus. **aubergine** aubergine (UK); eggplant (US). **Bar** sea bass. **barbue** brill. **baudroie** coastal monkfish. **bavarois** moulded cream dessert. **bavette** beef flank steak. **béarnaise** sauce of butter and egg yolk, flavoured with tarragon. **beignet** fritter or doughnut; – **de fleur de courgette** courgette flower fritters. **betterave** beetroot. **biche** venison. **biftek** steak. **biologique** organic. **bisque** shellfish soup. **blanc** white; – **de poulet** chicken breast. **blanquette** 'white' stew, usually veal, made with eggs and cream. **blette** swiss chard. **boudin noir** black pudding (blood sausage); – **blanc** white pudding. **boeuf** beef; – **à la gardiane** (Camargue) bull's beef stewed with carrots and celery; – **gros sel** boiled beef with vegetables. **bourride** thick, garlicky fish soup. **brandade de morue** (Nîmes) purée of salt cod, milk, garlic and olive oil (often also with potato). **brébis** ewe's milk cheese. **brochet** pike. **brouillade** scrambled egg; – **aux truffes** scrambled egg with truffles. **brousse** soft, mild, white cheese. **bulot** whelk. **Cabillaud** fresh cod. **caille** quail. **caillette** pork terrine with herbs and spinach or chard cooked in caul. **calmar** squid. **calisson d'Aix** (Aix-en-Provence) diamond-shaped sweet of almonds, sugar and preserved fruit. **canard** duck. **cannelle** cinnamon. **cardon** cardoon (edible thistle). **câpre** caper. **carrelet** plaice. **cassis** blackcurrants; also blackcurrant liqueur. **cassoulet** stew of haricot beans, sausage and preserved duck. **catégau d'anguilles** (Camargue) eels cooked with red wine and garlic. **céleri** celery; –**rave** celeriac. **cèpe** cep. **cerise** cherry. **cervelle** brains. **champignon** mushroom. **charlotte** moulded cream dessert with biscuit edge. **châtaigne** chestnut. **chateaubriand** thick fillet steak. **cheval** horse. **à cheval** with an egg on top. **chêvre** goat's cheese. **chevreuil** young

roe deer. **chichis** deep-fried dough sticks. **chou** cabbage. **choucroute** sauerkraut, usually served garnie with cured ham and sausages. **chou-fleur** cauliflower. **ciboulette** chive. **citron** lemon; – **vert** lime. **citronelle** lemongrass. **civet** game stew. **clafoutis** baked batter dessert filled with fruit, usually cherries. **cochon de lait** suckling pig. **colin** hake. **confit de canard** preserved duck. **congre** conger eel. **contre-filet** sirloin steak. **coquille** shell; – **Saint-Jacques** scallop. **côte** chop; – **de boeuf** beef rib. **crème chantilly** whipped cream. **crème fraîche** thick, slightly soured cream. **cresson** watercress. **crevette** prawn (UK), shrimp (US). **croquant** crunchy; –**e de Nîmes** hard nut biscuit. **croque-monsieur** toasted cheese and ham sandwich. **en croûte** in a pastry case. **cru** raw. **crudités** assorted raw vegetables. **crustacé** shellfish. **Daube** meat (beef or lamb) braised slowly in red wine with *lardons* (qv), onions, garlic and herbs. **daurade** sea bream. **désossé** boned. **dinde** turkey. **Echalote** shallot. **écrevisse** freshwater crayfish. **endive** chicory (UK), Belgian endive (US). **entrecôte** beef rib steak. **entremêts** milk-based dessert. **épeautre** spelt. **épices** spices. **épinards** spinach. **escabèche** sautéed, marinated fish, served cold. **escargot** snail. **espadon** swordfish. **estocafinado** (Nice) salt cod, stewed with garlic and tomato. **estouffade** beef, braised with carrots, onions, garlic and orange zest. **Faisan** pheasant. **farci** stuffed. **farcis niçois** (Nice) vegetables stuffed with meat or mushrooms and herbs. **fenouil** fennel. **faux-filet** sirloin steak. **feuilleté** 'leaves' of (puff) pastry. **fève** broad bean (UK), fava bean (US). **filet mignon** tenderloin. **flageolet** small, green, kidney bean. **flambé(e)** flamed in alcohol. **flétan** halibut. **foie** liver; – **gras** fattened goose or duck liver. **forestière** with mushrooms. **fougasse** flat bread made with olive oil, flavoured with *lardons* (qv) or olives; also sweet versions of the same. **au four** baked. **fraise** strawberry. **framboise** raspberry. **frisée** curly endive. **fromage** cheese; – **blanc** smooth cream cheese. **fruit** fruit; –**s de mer** shellfish; –**s rouge** red summer berries. **Galette** flat, flaky-pastry cake, potato pancake or buckwheat savoury crêpe.

galinette tub gurnard. **gardiane de boeuf** (Camargue) beef stew. **garni(e)** garnished. **gésiers** gizzards. **gibier** game. **gigot d'agneau** leg of lamb. **gingembre** ginger. **girolle** chanterelle. **glace** ice-cream. **glacé(e)** frozen or iced. **gras** fat. **gratin dauphinois** sliced potatoes, baked with cream and garlic. **grillé(e)** grilled. **grondin** red gurnard.
Langouste spiny lobster. **langoustine** Dublin Bay prawn/scampi. **langue** tongue. **lapin** rabbit; **– à la provençale** rabbit in white wine with tomato and herbs. **lard** bacon. **lardon** small cube of bacon. **laurier** bay leaf. **légume** vegetable. **lentilles** lentils. **lieu** pollock. **lièvre** hare. **limande** lemon sole. **lotte** monkfish. **loup** sea bass.
Mâche lamb's lettuce. **magret** duck breast. **maquereau** mackerel. **marcassin** wild boar. **mariné** marinated. **marmite** small cooking pot. **marquise** mousse-like cake. **marron** chestnut. **merguez** spicy lamb/beef sausage. **merlan** whiting. **merlu** hake. **mesclun** salad of tiny leaves and herbs. **miel** honey. **mirabelle** tiny yellow plum. **moelle** bone marrow; **os à la – marrow bone. **morille** morel. **moules** mussels. **morue** dried, salted cod. **mulet** grey mullet. **mûre** blackberry. **muscade** nutmeg. **myrtille** bilberry.
Navarin lamb and vegetable stew. **navet** turnip. **navette** boat-shaped biscuit flavoured with orange flower water. **noisette** hazelnut; small round portion of meat. **noix** walnut; **– de coco** coconut. **nouilles** noodles.
Oeuf egg; **– en cocotte** baked egg; **– en meurette** egg poached in red wine; **– à la neige** poached whipped egg white floating in vanilla custard. **oie** goose. **oignon** onion. **onglet** cut of beef, similar to *bavette* (qv). **oseille** sorrel. **oursin** sea urchin.
Pageot pandora, similar to sea bream. **pain** bread; **– perdu** French toast. **palombe** wood pigeon. **palourde** type of clam. **pamplemousse** grapefruit. **pan bagnat** (Nice) bread roll filled with tuna, tomatoes, onions and egg in olive oil. **panais** parsnip. **en papillote** cooked in a packet. **pastèque** water melon. **pâte** pastry. **pâtes** pasta. **paupiette** slice of meat or fish, stuffed and rolled. **pavé** thick steak. **pêche** peach. **perdrix** partridge. **persil** parsley. **petits farcis** (Nice) vegetables stuffed with meat or mushrooms and herbs. **petits pois** peas. **petit salé** salt pork. **pied** trotter. **pieds et paquets** (Marseille) stew of

stuffed tripe and sheep's feet. **pignon** pine kernel. **piment** hot pepper or chilli. **pintade** guinea fowl. **pissaladière** pizza-like onion and anchovy tart. **pistou** pesto-like basil and garlic sauce served with vegetable soup. **pleurotte** oyster mushroom. **poire** pear. **poireau** leek. **pois chiche** chickpea. **poisson** fish. **poivre** pepper. **poivron** red or green (bell) pepper. **pomme** apple; **– de terre** potato. **porc** pork. **porchetta** rolled and stuffed meat, usually pork. **potage** soup. **potiron** pumpkin. **poulet** chicken. **poulpe** octopus. **poutargue** (Martigues) preserved grey mullet roe. **pressé** squeezed. **prune** plum. **pruneau** prune. **Quenelle** light, poached fish dumpling. **quetsche** damson. **queue de boeuf** oxtail. **Rabasse** truffle. **raie** skate. **raisin** grape; **– sec** raisin. **rascasse** scorpion fish. **ratatouille** provençal stew of onion, aubergine, courgette, tomato and peppers. **réglisse** liquorice. **reine-claude** greengage plum. **ris de veau** veal sweetbreads. **riz** rice. **rognon** kidney. **romarin** rosemary. **roquette** rocket. **rouget** red mullet. **rouille** spicy red pepper, garlic and olive oil sauce. **Sablé** shortbread biscuit. **St-Pierre** John Dory. **salade niçoise** (Nice) salad of tuna, lettuce, green beans, egg and anchovies. **salé** salted. **sandre** pike-perch. **sanglier** wild boar. **sarde** bream-like Mediterranean fish. **saucisse** sausage. **saucisson sec** small, dried sausage. **saumon** salmon. **seiche** squid. **socca** (Nice) thin pancake made with chickpea flour. **souris d'agneau** lamb knuckle. **stockfisch** dried cod. **supion** small squid. **Tapenade** provençal olive and caper paste. **tartare** raw, minced steak; also tuna or salmon. **tarte Tatin** caramelised apple tart, cooked upside-down and served warm. **taureau** (Camargue) bull's meat. **tête de veau** calf's-head jelly. **thon** tuna. **thym** thyme. **tian** vegetable gratin baked in an earthenware dish. **topinambour** Jerusalem artichoke. **tourte** covered pie or tart, usually savoury; **– de blettes** (Nice) swiss chard pie with pine nuts and raisins. **travers de porc** pork spare ribs. **tripoux** dish of sheep's tripe and feet. **tropézienne** (St-Tropez) sponge cake filled with custard cream. **truffe** truffle. **truite** trout. **Vacherin** dessert of meringue, cream, fruit and ice-cream; a soft, cow's-milk cheese. **veau** veal. **velouté** stock-based white sauce; creamy soup. **viande** meat. **violet** sea potato.

PARIS ON A PLATTER

Moulin des Costes. *See p36.*

Provençal Wine

O for a beaker full of the warm South!

Teetotallers, head for the hills, purge yourselves with crystal draughts of Evian, tickle your taste buds with Badoit's mineral mousse. Beer lovers, get on a train to Belgium; cider fans, Normandy awaits you. But for those with even the most fleeting interest in wine, look no further. South-east France is home to a bewildering array of wine appellations: from minuscule Palette just east of Aix and Nice's bijou Bellet (*see p272* **Nice's corking neighbour**) to the huge sweeping Côtes de Provence and Coteaux d'Aix; up-and-coming Costières de Nîmes, Côtes du Ventoux, Cairanne and Rasteau to established royalty like Châteauneuf-du-Pape, Gigondas and Bandol. And if the Provence Côte d'Azur region currently seems less dynamic than the Languedoc-Roussillon, there's still plenty of good wine to be found amid the plonk. The relatively hot and dry climate favours red grape varieties, although certain appellations, such as Cassis, are rated for their whites.

There's a long tradition of making dry rosés in the Mediterranean. Ideal for summer drinking, they have the fullness of a red to go with local food yet retain the refreshing edge of a chilled white. Provence is quintessentially the land of rosé (it makes up 70 per cent of some appellations). The best – and alas the dearest – are from Bandol and Les Baux, made from free-run juice drained or 'bled' off (hence the French term saignée) shortly after crushing, having macerated on the skins of the (red) grapes for a few hours. The juice is then fermented fairly cool to preserve fresh aromas and fruit – thus it is made like a white wine. Only the heartiest, more expensive styles will improve in bottle, so make sure you buy the youngest possible.

TOUR 1: LES BAUX-DE-PROVENCE

This youthful sub-region, which was given a separate AOC (*appellation d'origine contrôlée*) only in 1995, centres on the historic hilltop village of Les Baux-de-Provence in Les Alpilles. The appellation encompasses just 12 growers spread over 330 hectares (815 acres), thus

Tasting notes

No longer just a purveyor of plonk produced in industrial quantities, the Midi is fast becoming France's New World wine region. These days, the area is producing some excellent quality wines to match the best of the rest of France, Australia and America, and at altogether better prices. Much has happened to transform the Midi's vast output – Provence and the Languedoc combine to make the largest vineyard in the world – from its emphasis on quantity to one of quality. It is now more than 20 years since the pioneers and flying wine-makers brought their energy and techniques to bear in the area. Today it is an exciting place to visit due to the tremendous variety of wine that is being produced locally, from claret copies, to dark syrah, fresh sauvignon blanc, chardonnay (of course), vermentino (called *rolle* in France), lemony picpouls and mourvèdre from the coast, sangiovese (the grape of chianti) and pinot noir. Believe it or not, there's even a gewürztraminer, and carignan is currently experiencing something of a renaissance.

So what should you drink in the South of France? Obviously, there are few drinks more refreshing on a hot summer's day than a glass of rosé. But you should ensure that the wine you are drinking is the freshest possible. That means you want to be drinking last year's crop, not one made five years ago. Rosé does not age well. In fact it goes off. So if it's 2006, you want to be drinking wine with 2005 on the label. Much the same applies for the whites, although you could probably risk going a year earlier. The red wine from the South of France will probably improve with a couple of years in the bottle, but not a whole lot more. If you pick a red wine that is more than five years old, you run the risk of being disappointed.

Not every wine you will be offered will be first-rate. There is still an enormous amount of second-rate wine being produced, particularly by the co-operatives. You can buy wine now for less than the equivalent amount of petrol, but generally it won't taste much better.

Rupert Wright is the author of Notes from the Languedoc, *published by Ebury Press, £7.99.*

making it ideal for a compact tour to discover rich individual reds, full dry rosés and beautiful wild countryside. Here syrah and cabernet sauvignon – ironically perceived as an Australian blend – harmoniously collide with grenache and mourvèdre. The best reds do age well and may justify the high prices Les Baux commands, but some should be more convincing at this level. The AOC white wines are currently classified as Coteaux d'Aix-en-Provence but the growers are lobbying for Les Baux status, which could be seen as a cynical attempt to boost the prices of generally average whites. However, they want to base it on the marsanne and roussanne varieties (not

permitted for appellation whites at the moment) and sémillon. Tasting the complex, barrel-fermented *vins de pays* made from these grapes confirms their potential, and they are an admirable improvement on grenache blanc, rolle and clairette.

The majority of estates in Les Baux are farmed organically and one, **Château Romanin** (St-Rémy-de-Provence, 04.90.92.45.87), near the airfield, is run on biodynamic principles (with homeopathic methodology, taking account of astronomical and atmospheric conditions). Owners Colette and Jean-Pierre Peyraud have successfully followed this philosophy since they bought the property in 1990. Back towards

St-Rémy is the **Domaine Hauvette** (Quartier de la Haute Galine, St-Rémy, 04.90.92.03.90), which makes a rich oaky white and highly rated reds. Heading east again, off the D99 before the turning for Eygalières, is the **Domaine de Terres Blanches** (St-Remy, 04.90.95.91.66).

A few kilometres south along the D24, you'll come across **Domaine de la Vallongue** (Quartier de la Vallongue, Eygalières, 04.90.95.91.70), which makes a fab rosé and traditional reds. South of here and east of Le Destet you'll spot the vineyards of **Domaine de Lauzières** (Mouriès, 04.90.47.62.88), but there's no cellar – Jean-André Charial of the luxurious Oustau de Baumanière hotel (www.oustaudebaumaniere.com) makes his wines from this estate's grapes. **Mas de Gourgonnier** (Mouriès, 04.90.47.50.45) is situated on the other side of Le Destet.

Moving back towards Les Baux via Maussane on the D5, **Mas de la Dame** (04.90.54.32.24, www.masdeladame.com) is where Anne Poniatowski and Caroline Missoffe make their award-winning wines, including the elegant Cuvée La Stèle red and creamy Coin Caché white. Not far from the ancient Bauxite city along the D27 is **Mas Ste-Berthe** (Les Baux, 04.90.54.39.01), whose lovely 1995 red shows the wines' ageing potential. Heading west, the Auge Valley is home to **Olivier Penel** (Fontvieille, 04.90.54.62.95, www.olivier dauge.com) and his 'new wave'-leaning but good reds. Further along this road towards

Fontvieille, stop off at **Château d'Estoublon** (rte de Maussane, Fontvieille, 04.90.54.64.00, www.estoublon.com) before travelling north again via St-Etienne-du-Grès to **Château Dalmeran** (St-Etienne-du-Grès, 04.90.49.04.04). Hopefully, you'll be able to buy a bottle of its superb 1997 red.

TOUR 2: BANDOL

'Le Rond-Point des mourvèdres' stands at exit 11 off the A50, La Cadière-Le Castellet to the north of Bandol. A roundabout dedicated to the mourvèdre grape variety lets you know who's boss around here. Majestic mourvèdre shapes not only the heart of the region but the hearts and minds of the growers too. This beefy, late-ripening red grape needs plenty of sunshine and intimate handling to control its yield and tannins, thus producing structured, complex yet rounded wines suited to barrel ageing.

Elsewhere in the South, winemakers use only a small proportion of mourvèdre as they struggle to coax a fine performance out of it. Here, at least 50 per cent is required in the red wines to qualify as AOC Bandol. And the best rosés, which are serious, full bodied and dry, also contain quite a lot of mourvèdre along with cinsault and/or grenache. Bandol's reputation stems from its reds yet it produces two-thirds rosé (plus five per cent often overpriced white); at the leading estates, however, the focus is firmly on reds.

AOC Bandol, totalling 1,400 hectares (3,460 acres) – less than half the area of Châteauneuf-du-Pape – also takes in Sanary, Le Castellet, La Cadière d'Azur and parts of St-Cyr-sur-Mer, Le Beausset, Evenos and Ollioules, in a sweeping amphitheatre around Bandol itself. The rosés go well with local food such as anchovies, sea urchin, mullet and also ethnic cuisine; red Bandol is a good match for pigeon or duck.

Heading south briefly on the D82 from the rond-point towards Le Plan du Castellet, you'll find **Domaine Tempier** (1082 chemin des Fanges, 04.94.98.70.21, www.domainetempier.com), owned by the Peyraud family. Back in the early days, Lucien pushed for mourvèdre to become the main variety (re)planted and hence the backbone of the appellation. Its rosé develops nicely in bottle and two reds are excellent: La Migoua – a single vineyard comprising mourvèdre, syrah, cinsault and grenache – and La Tourtine, made up of 80 per cent mourvèdre, and therefore very sturdy and concentrated.

Follow the D559b south out of Le Plan, then take the lane on the right under the motorway. **Moulin des Costes** (La Cadière d'Azur, 04.94.98.58.98, www.bunan.com), resting on steep terraces laden with flat stones, is one of four estates that collectively create Domaines Bunan (also including Château la Rouvière and Mas de la Rouvière). Château la Rouvière red, the pinnacle of the range, is enriched with over 90 per cent mourvèdre and a little syrah. Its full-bodied Blanc de Blancs is made from clairette pointue and the lovely intense rosé half mourvèdre, with gutsy 14 per cent alcohol.

The vineyards of celebrated **Château de Pibarnon** (Chemin de la Croix des Signaux, La Cadière, 04.94.90.12.73, www.pibarnon.com) border the Bunans but the only way there is to wind back on the D559b south to the right and up the hill again. Laid-back aristos Eric de Saint Victor and his father Henri, the Comte, cultivate the highest slopes of Bandol at 300 metres (985 feet). Here the soil is particularly chalky, which they believe tames mourvèdre. As Eric put it: 'It's very macho, on this soil we manage to make something quite fine.'

TOUR 3: COTES DE PROVENCE – MASSIF DES MAURES

Getting to grips with the Côtes de Provence as a whole isn't easy. A region on this scale – the appellation extends across the Var over 19,000 hectares (46,950 acres) from within the Bouches-du-Rhône to the edge of Alpes-Maritimes – naturally bears very diverse terrain, producers and personalities. The result is wines ranging from rough, harmless but cheap, through very

drinkable to serious and pricey, all officially wearing the same AOC badge. So it's worth concentrating on a specific area, and selecting the best within it.

The coastal strip between Hyères and St-Tropez bordering the Massif des Maures offers scenic touring and some high-quality estates. La Londe-les-Maures provides a good place to start and a *terroir* particularly successful for white wines – not the norm in rosé country. Take a left at the main lights in the town, heading north over the N98, and follow the signs for **Château Ste-Marguerite** (Le Haut Pansard, 04.94.00.44.44, www.chateausainte marguerite.com). This peaceful spot surrounded by handsome vines is owned by Jean-Pierre Fayard, whose Cru Classé (an ancient, unofficial classification) wines include a fine white made from low-yielding rolle, sémillon and ugni blanc, and smoky-textured red from syrah and cabernet sauvignon.

Rejoin the D559 in La Londe, then turn right just out of town. Follow this twisty lane until you reach a mini-roundabout where another right takes you to **Clos Mireille** (rte de Brégançon, 04.94.01.53.53, www.domaines-ott.com), signposted Domaines Ott, which owns this and other properties in Côtes de Provence and Bandol. Clos Mireille, also a Cru Classé, is unusual in that it currently only produces white wines: the floral citrussy Blanc de Blancs and richer oak-aged L'Insolent.

Turn right back on to the country lane and follow the signs for Brégançon; a quarter of an hour or so later you'll come across the aristocratic **Château de Brégançon** itself (639 route de Léoube, Bormes-les-Mimosas, 04.94.64.80.73, www.chateaudebregancon.fr), appropriately another Cru Classé. Recommended tastings include its Prestige rosé and limited edition Cuvée Hermann Sabran red, with one-third cabernet sauvignon lending a Bordeaux-like finesse and power.

A further 30-40 minutes (depending on traffic) towards St-Tropez on the winding D559 coastal road will eventually bring you to Gassin, home of one of the grandest Cru Classé estates, **Château Minuty** (rte de Ramatuelle, 04.94.56.12.09) with its smart gardens and cute Napoléon III chapel. To find it, either turn right on to the D89 and climb almost to the village but go left just before the top, descend a little and take a right into the side entrance; or circle around and approach from the Ramatuelle road via the main gate. Its Cuvée Réserve rosé and red are pretty special. You could finish the tour by visiting **Château Barbeyrolles** (04.94.56.33.58, www.barbeyrolles.com) next door, where you can also taste wines from the owners' other property, Château la Tour de l'Evêque.

In Context

A fruitful enterprise

You are bent double in the baking sun, a searing pain is shooting up your spinal cord, great clots of hair are matted to your head and your vision is blurred from grape juice dripping into your eyes. This is the *vendange à main*, the centuries-old hand harvest of the grapes that will make this year's crop of wines. Inevitably, too, there will be a couple of decrepit locals in the adjacent row of vines, snipping grapes at twice your rate and gleefully debating how *les Anglais* ever ruled the world.

After a couple more hours your fingers begin to swell and redden and you can barely clasp the secateurs. There's a squadron of dive-bombing flies circling overhead and tributaries of blood run from grazes on your knees. But just as you are considering commando-rolling away to safety, it's finally time for lunch.

After bread, cheese and a vat of red wine, the pain recedes to a dull throb, and by mid-afternoon you've even convinced yourself that the whole experience is actually quite enjoyable. There's a certain knack to swiftly untangling the grapes from the vines, and you find that suddenly, with a quick jerk and a snip, you are managing to deftly deposit the bunches in the bucket behind you. The flies are less irksome now you've borrowed a baseball cap from one of your fellow *vendangers*, and as the late evening sun melts between the vines, the sight of a fully laden tractor trundling away towards the *cave* makes you swell with pride. Even so, at the end of the day, as you relax in a warm bath (turned pink by the grape juice oozing from your hair) and contemplate a life of osteopathy, you wonder why in this age of machines anyone still bothers to hand harvest.

The answer is all in the taste. Wine made from hand-harvested grapes is typically a purer product. *Vignerons* who use machines may have to book the harvesting equipment months in advance and, as a result, the *vendange* begins when the machines arrive, not when the grapes are ready. And because of the nature of mechanical harvesting the grapes can be bruised as they are picked and piled on top of each other, allowing juice to seep through their skins and fermentation to begin in the field as opposed to the controlled conditions of the *cave*. Chemicals such as sulphur then need to be added to the wine to preserve it, resulting (for the over indulgent consumer, at least) in a raging hangover.

Sadly, fewer and fewer vineyards in the South of France can afford the labour costs associated with hand harvesting. It's most common in the superior wine-producing areas such as Bandol, to the east of Marseille, where the appellation rules and the price commanded by each bottle have reinforced the tradition. But even in other areas, provided you have a thick skin and no history of back complaints, you can still get involved in a hand harvest.

The *vendange* at an average-sized vineyard will typically last for two weeks. Harvesting begins in late August by the coast and starts progressively later as you head inland, finishing in most areas by the beginning of October. The easiest way to participate is to rise with the sun and head out into the countryside. Look for lines of beaten-up cars parked on the grass verges by the side of the road and scan the rows of vines for the tractors, which transport the harvested grapes back to the *cave*. If you find one of these tractors, you'll usually find the *vigneron* and you can volunteer your services. You are likely to be fed at lunchtime and, if it's the last day of the harvest, you might even be invited to the *fête de la vendange*, a feast held at the vineyard to thank the workers for all their efforts.

If you are taking part in the *vendange* to help subsidise your travel around France, be warned: rates of pay are low. Don't expect much more than €5 per hour, and if you are only prepared to help out for the day (rather than the full two weeks of the harvest) you are unlikely to be paid at all.

For those wanting to organise their *vendange* in advance, trips are available through UK-based agencies such as **Responsible Travel** (www.responsible travel.com). Another option, if you are a student with some agricultural experience, is a work placement, which can be set up through Paris-based agency **Sesame** (9 square Gabriel Fauré, 40.54.07.08, www.agriplanete.com). Alternatively, if you are planning to be down south anyway, visit the **Conseil Interprofessionnel des Vins de Provence** (Maison de Vin, F83460, Les Arcs Sur Argens, 04.94.99.50.10, www.vinsdeprovence.fr) and ask to be put in touch with *vignerons* who hand harvest their wine.

The Creative South

Where generations of bright young things have lived, loved, died and gone mad – all in the name of art.

So many artists, writers and musicians have sucked their inspiration from its sun-baked landscape that the South of France has long been famed as a cradle of creativity. And from the bling of the Riviera to the street poetry of Marseille, the beat goes on.

ART
The South of France's phenomenal modern art legacy is a difficult act to live up to and has tended to spawn a morass of sub-Picasso potters and neo-Impressionist daubers. Yet a number of important older-generation artists who marked the 1960s and '70s are still active here today, including Support-Surface founder **Claude Viallat** in Nîmes, sculptor **Bernard Pagès** and Fluxus artist **Ben**. There's also a

dynamic, conceptually based, emerging young art scene, centred in particular on Marseille.

Among the young artists who are making their mark in France and internationally is **Gilles Barbier**, whose installations composed of multiple wax clones of himself in different vaguely sinister situations suggest questions of identity, science and belonging, fiction and reality. **Natacha Lesueur**'s elaborately set-up glossy photos deal with issues of femininity, fetishism and food. Extravagant cocktail headdresses, chignons with cucumber curls and caviar dreadlocks comment on food, ceremony, glamour and fashion, while mouths replaced by vegetable teeth tread a neat line between attraction and repugnance. **Francesco Finizio** creates tragi-comic situations using video, soundworks and installation to treat issues related to consumer society.

The perpetual issue of the revival (or not) of painting is present too. Nice-based **Pascal Pinaud** works with the motifs and structures of abstraction. One series uses car paint and titles such as *Volkswagen* and *Porsche*, others use acrylic gel and even knitting or aluminium. The stripy, lacquer paintings and installations of **Cédric Tesseire** (like Lesueur part of La Station collective in Nice in the late-1990s) similarly play with and break the rules of pop art and minimalism. **Anne Pesce**'s paintings derive from photographs and voyages to Greenland and the Antarctic, as well as the view of the sea from where she lives in Vence.

A number of public institutions and artist-run spaces play an important role on the contemporary art scene. As well as the **Frac** (Fonds Régional d'Art Contemporain), based in Marseille but organising events all over the region, and the two modern art museums **MAC** in Marseille and **MAMAC** in Nice, **La Friche La Belle de Mai** and the **Villa Arson** in Nice act as artistic hothouses. The commercial gallery scene is smaller, but led by **Galerie Roger Pailhas** in Marseille and **Galerie Catherine Issert** in Vence.

Occupying some 45,000 square metres (484, 375 sqaure feet) of an old tobacco factory, and place of exchange for over 300 artists, dancers, performers, musicians, graphic and web designers, puppeteers and street acts, **La Friche La Belle de Mai** is wilfully pluridisciplinary and experimental – a melting pot of art, music, theatre, performance and dance, as well as an umbrella for several artist-run organisations. According to director Philippe Foulquié, 'La Friche's mission is to make the artist the centre of a system of socialisation founded on the dual necessity of creating works and interaction with the public.'

Within the Friche, associations like Astérides and the Triangle organise artists' residencies and temporary exhibitions, nourished by exchanges with similar outfits, such as Triangle Arts at the Gasworks in London, the Tramway in Glasgow or the Hangar in Barcelona. Astérides, run by a group of artists including Gilles Barbier, invites mainly young artists for studio residencies of up to six months, but has also included well-established names like Tony Cragg or international up-and-comers such as Tatiana Trouvé, Hugues Reip and Virginie Barré. Triangle similarly organises exhibitions, residencies and the Action-Man-Oeuvres pluridisciplinary performances.

In Nice, the **Villa Arson**, which comes under the aegis of the Ministry of Culture, has a more institutional edge, but its combination of art school, residencies and international exhibitions and cultural programmes also makes it an important forum for debate.

LITERATURE

In recent years, the contemporary voices of French literature have had a youthful and distinctly North African accent (*see p41* **Algeria on the page**), exciting the interest of a fresh reading public, especially in the South where the influence of France's Algerian and Moroccan communities is arguably at its strongest. But the region's distinguished literary past continues to draw many readers.

In 1895 writer and filmmaker **Marcel Pagnol** was born in Aubagne (where his *maison natale* is now a museum dedicated to his life's work) and his creative vision is inseparable from the landscape of his youth. For many, the highlight of his fruitful career is the enchanting autobiography *Souvenirs d'enfance*, whose first volume, *La Gloire de mon père*, was made into a successful French film. *Jean de Florette* and *Manon des Sources*, 1980s film adaptations of Pagnol's *L'Eau des collines*, must have been responsible for thousands of first-time visits to Provence since the 1990s, but it is the Marseille trilogy for which he is most fondly remembered in France. This triptych of films (*Marius*, 1931; *Fanny*, 1932; *César*, 1936) has been called by *American Film Magazine* 'one of the most cherished love stories of the century'. Early 20th-century novelist **Jean Giono**'s cholera-riven page-turner *Le Hussard sur le toit* (*The Horseman on the Roof*) has also been made into a big-budget French film. A celebrated son of Manosque, where literary competitions and themed walks are regular reminders of his legacy, Giono is best known for his pantheistic trilogy *Colline, Un de Baumugnes* and *Regain*, but his eco-fable 'The Man who Planted Trees' – a shepherd patiently fighting deforestation, acorn by acorn – may have the most contemporary resonance.

Further west, celebrated 19th-century novelist **Alphonse Daudet** began his lifelong love affair with the region in Nîmes. He came to popular attention in 1860 with a delightful collection of short stories, *Lettres de mon Moulin*. The *moulin* in question is a windmill in Fontvieille, which remains a landmark to this day. The darker side of Daudet's life – he contracted syphilis in the 1880s – is explored in his short memoir *In the Land of Pain*, published in English in 2002, which records with excoriating honesty and acerbic humour his failed cures and many sufferings.

Literary visitors to the region from abroad have also, of course, been legion. Novelist **DH Lawrence**, perhaps most notable of the Brits, died in Vence back in 1930, but the tradition continues: in 2005 New Englander **Gustaf Sobin**, made famous by his third novel *The Fly-Truffler*, died in his adopted Provence after living here for four decades.

ARCHITECTURE AND DESIGN

From his agency in Bandol, with the sound of cicadas screeching outside the window, Rudy Ricciotti is a rare architect outside the Paris power-base to have made it on the international scene. A *grande gueule* (big mouth) not afraid to speak out against the establishment or architectural mediocrity, Ricciotti has become known, on the one hand, for his radical, often sculptural and minimalist modern buildings and, on the other, for his subtle adaptation of historic buildings for new cultural use.

The latter include the **Abbaye de Montmajour** near Arles and the **Collection Lambert** in Avignon. Ricciotti sees no contradiction between the two: 'There is no difference between working with a historic building or designing a contemporary one: in both cases we are talking about the urban. There is no break between history and modernity.' After the **Centre Chorégraphique National** currently under construction in Aix-en-Provence – 'a spidery, complex and fleeting structure in concrete and glass' – the conversion of the semi-derelict Grands Moulins de Paris into a new university faculty in Paris and the Nikolaisaal concert hall in Potsdam, Germany, Ricciotti has just been named as the winner of the competition for the new Musée National des Civilisations de l'Europe et de la Méditerranée in Marseille. He also works for private clients in the South, where he has almost single-handedly revived the tradition of the avant-garde seaside villa. Minimalist constructions, such as the Villa Le Goff in Marseille and the Villa Lyprendi in Toulon, are both radical interventions and camouflaged into the natural landscape – literally, in the case of Villa Le Goff, whose glass façade, opening on to a long, narrow swimming pool, is hung with a curtain of camouflage netting that provides a dialogue between interior and exterior.

On the design front, **Fred Sathal**, who recently returned to live in her birthplace Marseille, is one of a select group of young designers invited to show at the haute couture *défilés*, and in 2003 featured in a solo show at the Musée de la Mode in Marseille. Her clothes are typically colourful, favouring wafty, multi-layered, asymmetric cuts and mixing different fabrics and textures from sequins to felt.

Marseille-based design group **Cooked in Marseille** uses silicone to create the funky Expres'soft espresso cup, the brilliantly simple silicone Oeugy ring egg cup and silicone lightbulb shades, or colourful neo-1960s pouffes and mouldable seats in pvc or foam.

DANCE AND THEATRE

The Ballet National de Marseille (BNM) was in crisis at the beginning of 2004, when artistic director **Marie-Claude Pietragalla** was forced to resign following a strike by 80 per cent of the personnel of the company and its dance school. The strikers complained that Pietragalla, an acclaimed dancer in her own right, spent too much of the budget on her own productions at the expense of prestigious touring engagements. In her defence, Pietragalla claimed she had been left with zero repertoire when celebrated choreographer Roland Petit retired in 1990, taking his creations with him. She had renewed the classical ballet programme, invited guest choreographers such as William Forsythe and Jeri Kylian, toured in China and Thailand and pulled in more than 303,000 spectators. Following in the footsteps of Petit, who had created the ballet company in 1972 and whose name was as intrinsically linked with it as Diaghilev's with the Ballets Russes, was never going to be easy and whoever takes on the job next still has a tough act to follow.

Since he arrived in Monaco in 1993, **Jean-Christophe Maillot**, previously at the Centre National Chorégraphique de Tours, has rejuvenated the Ballets de Monte-Carlo and brought it to the forefront of the dance scene with his slimmed-down updatings of the classics. **Angelin Preljocaj**, previously at the CNCDC in Châteauvallon and now in Aix-en-Provence, similarly creates a bridge between contemporary dance and ballet. As well as creating a repertoire for his own company, he has choreographed pieces including Le Parc for the Opéra National de Paris.

More strictly contemporary, **Georges Appaix** and his La Liseuse company (again based at La Friche La Belle de Mai) often starts from a poem or philosophical essay. He works closely with jazz and popular Mediterranean music.

In theatre, Marseille's Théâtre de la Criée continues to play a major role, along with more alternative outfits and experimental circus pioneers **Archaos**. There is also new blood at the Théâtre de Nîmes where **Macha Makeieff** and **Jérôme Deschamps** have recently been appointed artistic directors. Deschamps and Makeieff, famous for the over-the-top Deschiens clan who made it from the stage to a prime spot on the Canal+ TV station, create theatre that is at once radical and accessible. They are likely to spend the next few years hopping between Paris and the South, using Nîmes as a platform for new work and a meeting point for other directors and southern companies. Their latest piece, *Les Etourdis* (which translates roughly as 'the scatterbrains'), premièred at Nîmes in December 2003, takes a typically Makeieff and Deschamps perspective of socially downtrodden and confused non-conformists, innocents in the modern world.

Algeria on the page

'It's not just about rap, pit bulls, violence and hoodlums,' is how Faïza Guène described the housing projects of Courtillières, north-east of Paris, where she grew up. By the age of 19 Guène had become one of France's surprise success stories with her coming-of-age novel *Kiffe-Kiffe Demain*. Published in 2004 and described by *American Elle* as 'a teenage Bridget Jones of the Paris suburbs' (Zadie Smith might be a more relevant parallel), her title is a pun that means both 'same shit, different day' and plays on the Arabic-influenced French slang *kiffer*, to really like somebody.

As a *beurette*, or young French woman born to Algerian parents, Guène represents a new generation of Maghreb writers publishing in France. (The term *beur* itself is generally acknowledged to be *verlan* – or backslang – for *arabe*, though the latest permutation is *rebeu*.) Engagingly comic and outspoken about the lot of women in France's immigrant communities, Guène has turned down offers to work for the French Interior Ministry, scoffing 'How can discrimination be positive anyway?' In the wake of *La Haine*, male-dominated rap and the laddish gynmastics of *le parkour* (free running), and with a short film already under her belt, she offers instead a sassy new and alternative take on France's urban problems.

If Guène's generation was born in France, her literary forebears were mostly forced to flee the politics and censorship of *al-Maghrib* ('where the sun sets') for *le metropole*. Arguably the best known of these is the Moroccan Tahar Ben Jelloun, the first Maghreb writer to win Le Prix Goncourt (in 1987), for *La Nuit Sacrée*. He is an author who describes himself both as a guest and a mischievous host writing in the French language. Then, as if finally waking up to the phenomenal talents of francophone writers, the same prize was awarded in 1992 to the Martiniquais Patrick Chamoiseau for *Texaco*, and the following year to the Lebanese author Amin Maalouf. *This Blinding Absence of Light*, published in Linda Coverdale's English translation in 2004, and based on Ben Jelloun's interviews with the few survivors (or 'living cadavers') of one of King Hassan II's concentration camps, won author and translator the world's richest international literary prize (in euros, anyway), the Impac Dublin Award. Other recent works include *Racism Explained To My Daughter* and *Islam Explained for Children*.

One of the survivors of Hassan's imprisonment was the brother of fellow Moroccan writer Mahi Binebine, whose *Welcome to Paradise*, about a disparate group of African immigrants trying to steal their way across to Europe in an ill-fated boat, was shortlisted for the 2004 Independent Foreign Fiction prize. Binebine has recently returned to Marrakech after years of exile in Paris, despite his understated quip that life back home 'isn't very practical'.

Currently an academic based in the US, Assia Djebar (the pseudonym for Fatima Zohra Imalayen) is a contemporary of Ben Jelloun and often tipped for the Nobel Prize. She was the first Algerian woman to win a place at Sartre's alma mater, the Ecole Normale Supérieure. A poet and filmmaker too, she stopped writing novels for a decade following Algerian independence, while reconsidering her role as an intellectual expressing herself in French. Her later novels deliberately reflect the influence of her studies in classical Arabic, hinting at the distinctive sounds and rhythms of her native language.

Maïssa Bey, on the other hand, has remained in her native western Algeria throughout its ongoing political turmoil. Her first novel (*In the Beginning was the Sea*) appeared in 1996, with Bey going on to write about the 1993 earthquake (*Whatever You Do, Don't Turn Round*), as well as tackling the subject of repudiated women. Rather like the young Guène in her Paris suburb, Bey insists on the need for taking a different stance: 'As a writer, as someone who lives in Algeria, who wants to see this country on its feet, I'd like to show that there is a different kind of Algeria from that of the massacres, an Algeria that creates and wants to live.'

The Festive South

If you're looking for fun, the South of France has it in spades – or in chestnuts, garlic and lemons at least.

Festivals are a way of life throughout the South of France, providing full-on entertainment for locals and visitors alike. Many festivals, especially those dedicated to performing arts, take place in the summer – international acts are as fond as tourists of holidays that combine plenty of suntanning opportunities with a spot of culture thrown in.

One of this year's highlights is the 60th anniversary of the prestigious **Festival d'Avignon**, which will offer a fantastic line-up of international theatre, dance and music. For jazz lovers, there's the world-famous **Jazz à Juan**, and the less-known **Nice Jazz Festival** (held in a Roman amphitheatre) and **Jazz Festival de Ramatuelle**. The **Cannes Film Festival** is, of course, unmissable for film buffs, and those passionate about photography will enjoy the **Rencontres d'Arles**.

In addition to these high-culture events, there are numerous village celebrations that see locals proudly dressing up in provençal or medieval costumes to parade the streets, singing and dancing to traditional bands accompanied by flamboyant floats. Indeed, the desire to pay tribute to century-old customs is characteristic of provincial French life across the country. The variety of eccentric and obscure activities on offer is immense, even running to **Napoléon à Golfe-Juan**, a re-enactment of the conquering Corsican's arrival from Elba, involving a 400-strong army, cavalry included.

It doesn't stop there. For sport enthusiasts, there's the **Tennis Master Series Monte-Carlo**, the **Grand Prix de Monaco** and the **Rallye Automobile Monte-Carlo**, while if wine-tasting is more up your street, there are festivals offering *dégustations* in wine cellars. Festive indeed, the South caters to every taste and all manner of pastimes.

INFORMATION

All of the local and regional tourist offices are able to supply information on specific events and concerts, as well as a comprehensive free booklet *Terre de Festivals*, which covers summer arts festivals in the Provence-Alpes-Côtes d'Azur region. Information is also available online at www.cr-paca.fr and www.festivals.laregie-paca.com. Tickets can often be bought at tourist offices, branches of Fnac (www.fnac.fr) or through agencies such as France Billet (08.92.69.26.94, www.france billet.com) and Globaltickets (01.42.81.88.98, www.globaltickets.com).

Spring

Transhumance

Throughout rural Provence, including St-Rémy-de-Provence, La Garde-Freinet, St-Etienne-de-Tinée & Riez. **Date** May-June.

Late spring sees the traditional movement of flocks from winter to summer pastures. Hundreds of sheep, accompanied by dogs, carts and donkeys, are driven through the villages to the sound of flutes and tambourines. In St-Rémy-de-Provence on the Monday of Pentecost, flocks parade two or three times around the town centre. Check local tourist offices for details.

The Rhône Delta

Feria Pascale

Arènes, Arles (04.90.96.03.70/www.arenes-arles.com). **Date** Easter Sat-Easter Mon. **Tickets** €12-€86.

Arles's famous Roman arena is the venue for three days of Spanish-style bullfighting taking place over the Easter weekend.

Fête des Gardians

Arènes, Arles, & around town (information Office de Tourisme, 04.90.18.41.20). **Date** 1 May.

The mounted 'Queen of Arles' is crowned, prior to a procession of traditional bands and, in the arena, displays of horsemanship.

Feria de Pentecôte

Arènes, Nîmes (04.66.02.80.80/www.arenesdenimes.com). **Date** late May-early June. **Tickets** €15-€92.

Corridas during the main féria in Nîmes (held in the amphitheatre) are accompanied by an orchestra, and there are parties throughout the city. Smaller férias take place in September and February.

Pèlerinage de Mai

Stes-Maries-de-la-Mer (information 04.90.97.82.55/www.saintesmaries.com). **Date** 24-25 May.

Gypsies from across Europe come to honour the patron saint of gypsies, Black Sarah, who (according to legend) met Mary Magdalene, Mary Jacob and Mary Salome on their arrival by boat from Palestine. On Sarah's saint day (24 May), her relics are taken to the sea from the church, in a procession of gypsies, locals in traditional costumes and mounted *gardians*, and are blessed by a priest. The next day is devoted to Mary Salome and Mary Jacob, whose relics are also carried in procession to the sea to receive benediction.

Avignon & the Vaucluse

Ascension Day

Cavaillon (information Office de Tourisme, 04.90.71.32.01). **Date** late May.

Locals dress up in provençal costumes for this traditional *corso* (parade), which features decorated carnival floats and traditional bands. Similar processions are organised in Apt and Pertuis.

Fête de la Vigne et du Vin

Avignon, Châteauneuf-du-Pape, Gigondas & other villages (information 04.90.84.01.67/www.fetedela vigneetduvin.com). **Date** late May.

On the Friday and Saturday of Ascension weekend, the *département* of Vaucluse celebrates its three wines – the Côtes du Rhône, Côtes du Luberon and Côtes du Ventoux – in a wine village set up in front of the Palais des Papes. On the Saturday many wine cellars and vintners across the region offer tastings.

The Var

Festival International des Arts de la Mode et de Photographie à Hyères

Villa Noailles, Hyères (information 04.98.08.01.98/www.villanoailles-hyeres.com). **Tickets** free (advance bookings only). **Date** end Apr.

Ten young fashion designers present their catwalk collections, and ten young photographers show their portfolios. There are also temporary exhibitions of fashion, photography and art.

La Bravade

St-Tropez (information Office de Tourisme, 04.94.97.45.21/www.st-tropez.st). **Date** mid May.

To honour the arrival of the headless martyr Torpes (alias St Tropez) in AD 68, locals dress as sailors, musketeers and traditional Provençaux for three days of processions.

The Riviera & southern Alps

Le Printemps des Arts

various venues in Monte-Carlo (information 00.377-93.25.54.05). **Tickets** €15. **Date** 1st 3wks Apr.

Cancelled after just six days in 2005, following the death of Prince Rainier, Monte-Carlo's festival of the musical arts usually features around 30 local and international acts, including the Ballet de Monte-Carlo. Call the information line for up-to-date billings nearer the time.

Tennis Master Series Monte-Carlo

Monte-Carlo Country Club (information 04.93.41.72.00/www.mccc.mc). **Tickets** €10-€135. **Date** 1wk mid Apr.

International men's hard-court tournament.

Cannes Film Festival

Cannes (information 04.92.99.84.22). **Date** 2wks mid May.

The celebrity film extravaganza transforms Cannes for the annual fortnight of movie business and frantic paparazzi activity around the red carpets. *See also p238* **Too hot to handle?**

Grand Prix de Monaco

Monaco (information 00.377-93.15.26.00/www.acm.mc). **Tickets** €15-€900. **Date** 1wk mid Apr.

Formula One cars zoom round Monaco's elegant streets. Book well in advance to watch them.

Summer

Fête de la Musique

Throughout France (information www.fetedela musique.culture.fr). **Date** 21 June.
Free concerts fill streets throughout the nation on the longest day of the year. Expect everything from rock, hip hop and jazz to pumping electro.

Bastille Day (le Quatorze Juillet)

Throughout France. **Date** 14 July.
Firework displays and *bals des pompiers* (open-air parties at firestations) commemorate the French Revolution, which started with the storming of the Bastille prison in Paris in 1789.

The Rhône Delta

Festival de la Nouvelle Danse

Uzès (information 04.66.22.51.51/www.uzesdanse.fr). **Tickets** €3-€25. **Date** 1wk late June.
A week of contemporary dance events, spotlighting unknown European choreographers and dance acts. Tickets are available from mid May from the Uzès Office de Tourisme (04.66.22.68.88).

Garlic Fair

Uzès (information Office de Tourisme, 04.66.22.68.88). **Date** 24 June.
This annual fair harks back to 1524 and, although interest in the event is diminishing, several producers still gather to sell cloves in the town centre.

Fête de la Tarasque

Tarascon (information Office de Tourisme, 04.90.91.03.52/www.tarascon.org). **Date** 1wk end June.
St Marthe's miraculous victory over an amphibious Rhône-dwelling beast is celebrated with music, bull-running and feasting. Founded by Good King René in 1474, the festival involves parading a model of the monster through town, as well as tributes to Alphonse Daudet's fictional hero Tartarin de Tarascon.

Rencontres d'Arles

place du Forum, place Van Gogh & other venues, Arles (information 04.90.96.76.06/www.rencontres-arles.com). **Tickets** *Exhibitions* €3-€5. *Soirées* €8-€12. *Day pass* €20-€28. **Date** 1wk early July.
With 55 exhibitions, including competitive and themed shows alongside curated collections, the Rencontres d'Arles is a major festival of contemporary art photography. Although the festival proper lasts just a week, exhibitions can be viewed until mid Sept. There's also a fringe festival, *Voies Off.*

Suds à Arles

Théâtre Antique & other venues, Arles (information 04.90.96.06.27/www.suds-arles.com). **Tickets** €10-€25. **Date** 1wk mid July.
World music festival, attracting groups from across the globe. Check out free concerts, plus dance (flamenco, tango) and music classes, and film screenings.

Nuits Musicales d'Uzès

Uzès (information Office de Tourisme, 04.66.22.68.88). **Tickets** €8-€45. **Date** 2wks end July.
Baroque, classical, jazz and Russian music concerts, staged in historic buildings.

La Feria Provençale

St-Rémy-de-Provence (information Office de Tourisme, 04.90.92.74.92). **Date** 3 days mid Aug.
Three tense days of *abrivado* (herding bulls into the ring), *bandido* (taking them out again) and *encierro* (releasing them briefly) lead up to a single *corrida portugais* (Portuguese-style bullfight).

Avignon & the Vaucluse

Festival d'Avignon

Avignon (information Bureau du Festival d'Avignon, 20 rue Portail Bocquier/04.90.27.66.50/reservations 04.90.14.14.14/www.festival-avignon.com). **Tickets** €10-€35. **Date** July.
The prestigious festival's 60th anniversary falls in 2006, so expect an especially full-bore extravaganza of performing arts, providing the usual mixture of international theatre, dance and music. The focal point for activities is the Palais des Papes.

Avignon Public Off

Avignon (information Maison d'Off Bureau d'Accueil, Conservatoire de Musique, pl du Palais, www.avignon-off.org). **Tickets** €9-€13. **Date** July.
Avignon's fringe is far more open than its parent festival: rather than cherry-picking from hundreds of applications, Public Off allows anyone to perform – so long as they are able to negotiate local-authority red tape and find a venue. The presence of fire-eaters, jugglers, sundry vaudevillians and a good many alt-musos can be assumed.

Festival Provençal

Palais du Roure & other venues, Avignon & around (information 04.90.86.27.76/www.nouvello.com). **Tickets** around €8. **Date** July.
Expect plays, singers, dance groups and debates promoting Provençal, both language and culture.

Festival de la Correspondance

Grignan (information 04.75.46.55.83/www.festivalcorrespondance-grignan.com). **Date** 5 days early July.
Nearly 100 writers and actors, mostly French, celebrate the art of the letter through readings and other events, such as calligraphy and writing workshops. The 2005 festival featured readings of Colette, Carson McCullers and Proust.

Festival de la Sorgue

L'Isle-sur-la-Sorgue (information Office de Tourisme, 04.90.38.04.78/04.90.38.67.81). **Date** July.
Singing competitions and *course de nego-chine* – a race between flower-decorated punts along the island's canals – are contested by inhabitants from five neighbouring areas (L'Isle-sur-la-Sorgue, Le Thor, Fontaine-

de-Vaucluse, Saumane and Châteauneuf de Gadagne), while non-combatants are free to enjoy the floating markets and the high-quality street theatre.

L'Eté de Vaison

Théâtre Antique, Vaison-la-Romaine (information 04.90.28.84.49/www.vaison-festival.com). Tickets €12-€40. Date 3wks from mid July.
This dance festival hosts ballet, Latino, tango and flamenco acts. Highlights of 2005 included Maurice Béjart's Ballet de Lausanne.

Les Estivales de Carpentras

Théâtre de Plein Air, Carpentras (information 04.90.60.46.00). Tickets €25-€30. Date 2wks from mid July.
A multidisciplinary line-up of music, dance and plays, staged in an open-air theatre.

Les Chorégies d'Orange

Théâtre Antique, Orange (information Bureau des Chorégies d'Orange, 18 pl Sylvain, 04.90.34.24.24/ www.choregies.asso.fr). Tickets €3.80-€200. Date early July-early Aug.
Orange's Roman amphitheatre provides a gorgeous setting for this festival of opera and recitals. The 2006 programme includes performances of Mozart's *Requiem*, Verdi's *Aïda* and Gaetano Donizetti's *Lucia di Lammermoor*.

Festival de Melon

Cavaillon (04.90.71.73.02). Date early July.
Cavaillon gets lively for a summer weekend of street performances, a procession with floats and horses, and, of course, a melon market, in honour of the ancient and mysterious 'Brotherhood of the Knights of the Order of the Melons of Cavaillon', established way back in 1988.

Festival International de Quatuors à Cordes

Luberon (information 04.90.75.89.60). Tickets €18-€25 (only available on the door). Date July-Aug.
Some of Europe's finest string quartets perform in the Abbaye de Silvacane and churches in Cabrières d'Avignon, Fontaine-de-Vaucluse, Goult, L'Isle-sur-la-Sorgue and Roussillon.

Marseille & Aix

Fête de la St-Pierre

Martigues (information Office de Tourisme, 04.42.42.31.10). Date end June.
The statue of St-Pierre, patron saint of fishermen, is carried to the port, where fishermen and their boats are blessed. The feast day is also marked in La Ciotat, Cassis and Marseille.

Argilla, Fêtes de la Céramique Aubagne

Aubagne (information Office de Tourisme, 04.42.03.49.98). Date mid Aug.
This biennial pottery fair (the next is in 2007) is France's biggest, a gathering of some 150 potters.

Festival de Marseille

Marseille (information Bureau d'Accueil, 6 pl Sadi Carnot, 04.91.99.00.20/box office 04.91.99.02.50/ www.festivaldemarseille.com). Tickets €4-€32. Date 3wks July.
Marseille's annual festival hosts international contemporary dance, theatre and music performances.

Festival International d'Art Lyrique

Aix-en-Provence (information Boutique du Festival, 11 rue Gaston de Saporta, 04.42.17.34.34/www. festival-aix.com). Tickets €25-€185.
World-renowned directors and singers feature in this prestigious international opera festival, ranging from the likes of Mozart to contemporary opera.

Festival Danse à Aix

Aix-en-Provence (information Danse à Aix, 1 pl Joan Rewald, Espace Forbin, 04.42.96.05.01/box office from June 04.42.23.41.24/www.danse-a-aix.com). Tickets €10-€30. Date 3wks mid July-early Aug.
International groups perform contemporary dance.

Festival International de Piano

La Roque d'Antheron (information 04.42.50.51.15/ www.festival-piano.com). Tickets €14-€49. Date mid July-mid Aug.
Eminent concert pianists perform in the park of the Château de Florans and other seven other venues (including the Abbaye de Silvacane). Some jazz is usually included in the month-long programme.

Musique à l'Empéri

Château de l'Empéri, Salon-de-Provence (information 04.90.56.00.82/www.musique-emperi.com). Tickets €10-€25. Date early Aug.
Chamber music, from Mozart to Strauss, is played in the chateau's courtyard.

The Var

Draguifolies

Draguignan (information Théâtres en Dracenie, bd Georges Clemenceau, 04.94.50.59.50). Date 2wks early July.
Circus, dance, theatre, concerts, juggling and fire-eating all play a role in this ten-day street festival in Draguignan and neighbouring Dracenie villages.

Festival de Théâtre de Ramatuelle

Ramatuelle (information Bureau d'Accueil, 04.94.79.25.63/www.festivalderamatuelle.com). Tickets €37. Date early Aug.
In the hill village of Ramatuelle, near St-Tropez, this festival – launched by French thesp Jean-Claude Brialy in 1985 – promotes *bonne humeur* through comedies and variety shows.

Jazz Festival de Ramatuelle

Ramatuelle (information Bureau d'Accueil, 04.98.12.64.00/www.jazzfestivalramatuelle.com). Tickets €22-€30. Date mid Aug.
Various jazz bands give concerts in Ramatuelle's outdoor amphitheatre.

The Riviera & southern Alps

Voiles d'Antibes

Port Vauban, Antibes (04.92.91.60.00).
Date early June.
Classy sailing boats race round the Cap d'Antibes
in this classic regatta. A 'village' next to the port
hosts parties during the four-day event.

Les Baroquiales

Roya & Bévéra valleys (04.93.04.22.20). **Tickets**
€8-€20. **Date** end June-early July.
After a two-year break, this festival of baroque
music – during which Alpine valley churches host
organ recitals and plays – hopes to relaunch in 2006.

Biennale de Céramique Contemporaine

Musée de la Céramique, Vallauris (04.93.64.16.05).
Tickets €3.20. **Date** early July-mid Sept.
This biennial showcase of contemporary European
ceramics, selected by a panel, will be held in 2006.

Jazz à Juan

Juan-les-Pins (information 04.92.90.53.00/
www.antibesjuanlespins.com). **Tickets** €20-€65.
Date mid July.
Enjoy jazz on the beach at this hip festival. Having
boasted impressive line-ups ever since its 1960s
inception with Count Basie, Miles Davis and Ella
Fitzgerald, it still attracts the likes of (for 2006) Keith
Jarrett and Marcus Miller, alongside pop and Latin
acts. The Jazz Off fringe has cheaper alternative gigs.

Nice Jazz Festival

Jardins de Cimiez, Nice (information Office
de Tourisme, 08.92.70.74.07/box office
04.92.09.75.56/www.nicejazzfest.com).
Tickets €29. **Date** mid-late July.
Jazz concerts are staged in the stylish Roman arena
at this poppier alternative to Jazz à Juan. Kool and
the Gang have played, as has Gil Scott-Heron.

Festival International d'Art Pyrotechnique de Cannes

La Croisette, Cannes (information 04.92.99.84.22).
Tickets free. **Date** July-Aug.
International pyrotechnicians, all of them winners
of the Vestals d'Argent prize for the best displays,
compete for the ultimate Vestals d'Or award.

Musiques au Coeur

Villa Eilenroc, Cap d'Antibes (information
04.92.90.53.00/www.antibesjuanlespins.com).
Tickets €50-€75. **Date** early July.
Choral and orchestral performances at a chic and
intimate open-air music festival.

Les Nuits du Sud

pl du Grand Jardin, Vence (information
04.93.58.06.38). **Tickets** €15. **Date**
4wks mid July-mid Aug.
Laid-back Vence speeds up for this series of outdoor
concerts of Latin American and other world music.

Festival de Musique

parvis St-Michel, Menton (information
04.92.41.76.95/www.villedementon.com).
Tickets €22-€48. **Date** end July-mid Aug.
Founded in 1950, this chamber and classical music
festival features concerts by trios and orchestras,
performed on the cobbles outside the Basilique St-
Michel in Menton's old town.

Autumn

Journées du Patrimoine

Throughout France (www.culture.gouv.fr).
Date 3rd wknd in Sept.
Historic and government buildings all over France
open up to the public for this annual architectural
heritage weekend.

The Rhône Delta

Fêtes des Prémices du Riz

Arles (04.90.93.19.55). **Date** 3rd
weekend in Sept.
Camargue's rice harvest festival kicks off on Friday
evening when the *ambassadrice du riz* – Marion
Crozat for 2005 and 2006 – arrives on the Rhône in
a boat to be blessed in the St-Pierre church by a
priest. A procession, led by the *ambassadrice* on a
Camargue pony and some decorated floats, follows
on Saturday and Sunday morning.

Avignon & the Vaucluse

Fête de la Veraison

Châteauneuf-du-Pape (04.90.83.71.08).
Date 1st wknd in Aug.
Harking back to medieval times, this wine festival
has stalls representing local vintners and artisans,
dressed in traditional costumes, selling regional
products ranging from olive oil and fine foods to
antique jewellery and medieval clothes. Spending €3
on a *verre de Veraison* will get you unlimited refills.

Marseille &Aix

Fête du Livre

Cité du Livre, Aix-en-Provence (information
04.42.26.16.85). **Date** early Oct.
The literary festival invites heavyweight guests
(Nobel winners Pinter, Grass and Naipaul have all
featured) for debates and also hosts a variety of
book-related film, art and music events.

Fiesta des Suds

Docks des Suds, Marseille (information
04.91.99.00.00/reservations 08.25.83.38.33/
www.dock-des-suds.org). **Tickets** €10-€25.
Date Oct.
Eclectic world music festival with a programme that
runs from reggae and salsa to rock and electro,
reflecting Marseille's multiracial population.

Voiles d'Antibes. *See p46.*

The Var

La Fête des Châtaignes

Collobrières (information Office de Tourisme, 04.94.48.08.00/www.collotour.com). **Date** Oct.
Chestnuts galore in France's capital of marrons glacés, with producers of chestnuts gathering to celebrate their fruits.

Rencontres Internationales du cinéma des Antipodes

St-Tropez (01.47.97.45.98/www.festivaldesantipodes. org). **Tickets** free. **Date** 3rd wk in Oct.
A chance for cinephiles to see films, documentaries and shorts from Australia and New Zealand.

The Riviera & southern Alps

Festival Mondial de l'Image Sous-Marine

Palais des Congrès, Antibes-Juan-Les-Pins (04.93.61.45.45/www.underwater-festival.com). **Tickets** €10-€12. **Date** end Oct.
Photographers, artists, filmmakers and divers all converge to discuss their underwater inspirations. Expect competitions and exhibitions.

Monaco Fête Nationale

Monaco (00.377-93.15.28.63). **Date** 18-19 Nov.
The Rocher's national day is celebrated with fireworks over the harbour, a funfair and comic *spectacles*.

Winter

Avignon & the Vaucluse

Messe des truffes

Chapel-le Notre-Dame, Richerenches (information Office de Tourisme, 04.90.28.02.00/04.90.28.05.34/ www.richerenches.fr). **Date** 15 Jan.
Truffle worship at a mass for St Antoine, patron saint of *trufficulteurs*, with the Chevaliers du Diamont Noir. The choicest truffles are later auctioned to raise funds for repairs to the church roof.

Les Hivernales

Avignon & Vaucluse (04.90.82.33.12/www. hivernales-avignon.com). **Tickets** €6.50-€26.
Date Feb.
Some 18 dance companies – from ballet through to contemporary – perform in several venues. Highlights for 2006 include Raymond Oller and the Ballet de Lorraine at the Opéra d'Avignon.

Marseille & Aix

La Chandeleur

Basilique St-Victor, Marseille (04.96.11.22.60).
Date 2 Feb.
A candlelit procession that weaves along behind the Black Virgin of the Basilique St-Victor.

The Var

Fêtes de la Lumière à St-Raphaël

St-Raphaël (information Office de Tourisme, 04.94.19.52.52/www.saint-raphael.com).
Date mid Dec-early Jan.
Throughout the Christmas period, St-Raphaël is aglow with lights, plus there's a Christmas market, street theatre groups, kids' shows and musicians.

Le Corso Fleuri

Bormes-les-Mimosas (information Office de Tourisme, 04.94.01.38.38). **Date** 19 Feb.
A colourful parade of floats covered in flowers celebrates spring, with locals dressed in flamboyant costumes. Folk and brass bands fill the streets.

The Riviera & southern Alps

Festival de Danse

Palais des Festivals & other venues, Cannes (information 04.92.99.33.83/www.festivaldedanse- cannes.com). **Tickets** €10-€28. **Date** Nov.
This contemporary dance festival is held every two years (it next happens in 2007).

Rallye Automobile Monte-Carlo

Monaco (information Office de Tourisme, 00.377- 92.16.61.16). **Date** 1wk mid Jan.
Now in its 70s, this annual event sees rally drivers careering from Monaco, up into the snow-capped mountains and back down again.

Festival International du Cirque de Monte-Carlo

Espace Fontvieille, Monaco (information 00.377- 92.05.23.45). **Tickets** €25-€90. **Date** 1wk late Jan.
For its 30th edition in 2006, the festival plays host to all its previous international winners – from Europe, China, South Korea and Russia – for a popular acrobatic extravaganza. Book in advance.

Carnaval de Nice

Nice (information 08.92.70.74.07/www.nicecarnaval. com). **Tickets** €10-€20. **Date** 2wks mid Feb.
Carnival processions saunter down the promenade des Anglais, their satiric intent inspired by *Le Roi des Dupes* – the Lord of Misrule.

Fête du Citron

Menton (information Office de Tourisme, 04.92.41.76.76). **Date** 2wks mid Feb.
This festival sees locals displaying sculptures of lemons in citrus floats. The theme for 2006 is 'Brazil'.

Napoléon à Golfe-Juan

Vallauris-Golfe-Juan (information Office de Tourisme, 04.93.63.82.58). **Date** 1st wknd in Mar.
A 400-strong Napoleonic army, reconstructs the ambitious Corsican's landing from Elba – complete with a battle fought by armed and mounted soldiers. Locals, wearing period dress, head to the beach on Sunday afternoon to sight Napoleon's ship.

The Rhône Delta

Features

Maps

Introduction

Fed by the great artery of the Rhône, this region is lush, prosperous and, above all, beautiful.

A river runs through this enchanting landscape, bringing all kinds of ships coasting through over the centuries, and setting the early precedent for the influx of trade that has come to define many of its towns. The Rhône, too, has been dammed and channelled to irrigate the fertile flood plain and keep out the sea from the flat marshes of the Camargue, while the **Pont du Gard** aqueduct was an early feat of engineering bringing water across the dry limestone plateau to nourish Nîmes. But water also remains a perpetual battle: flash floods severely hit the area a few years ago, destroying bridges in the Gard in 2002 and flooding large areas of Arles, Beaucaire and the Camargue in 2003, when a dam was breached.

The Roman past continues to mark the area. **Arles** and **Nîmes** boast some of the best preserved Roman remains in the world, so that you can really get a feel of what life in the ancient cities must have been like (and death in the extraordinarily atmospheric Les Alyscamps). Yet these two cities, despite all their tourist attractions, remain living, workaday towns with year-round populations and busy cultural programmes. At **St-Rémy-de-Provence**, the remains of Glanum present centuries of successive occupation in a glorious rural setting, yet St-Rémy itself epitomises Provençal chic with a rich Renaissance heritage, fashionable café society and memories of two famous former residents, Nostradamus and Van Gogh. Quiet **Beaucaire** and **Tarascon** point to a wealthy Provençal past, while mysterious **Aigues-Mortes** is a unique, planned city.

If the **Camargue** and the **Grande Crau** are eerie flatlands with exceptional birdlife and gigantic skies, then the jagged **Alpilles** hills, although not high, still present dramatic mountain scenery and bizarre perspectives, especially secretive **Les Baux-de-Provence**, part-medieval stronghold and part bauxite mining village, while the surrounding hills with their olive groves and vineyards hide some of France's choicest gastronomic destinations.

Pretty much everywhere in the Rhône Delta area is united by a passion for bull-fighting and gentler *course camargaise*, but there are also more rustic festivities, such as the Transhumance moving of flocks in St-Rémy, the garlic fair of **Uzès** or the Fête de la Tarasque in Tarascon, and the gathering at **Stes-Maries-de la Mer**.

The best The Rhône Delta

Things to do

Nîmes and Arles have some of the most impressive Roman remains in France. Make time to visit the **amphitheatres** in both towns (for Nîmes, *see p53*; for Arles, *see p73*), as well as the **Théâtre Antique** in Arles (*see p74*). **St-Rémy-de-Provence** is worth a look in for its chichi boutiques, while the wineries at **Aigues-Mortes** will give you something to go home with.

Places to stay

Enjoy the lovely garden at Nîmes' **Hôtel Imperator** (*see p58*) or shut yourself away in Asian-inspired luxury at St-Rémy's **Hôtel Les Ateliers de l'Image** (*see p63*). The **Grand Hôtel Nord Pinus** in Arles (*see p77*) is a bullfighters' favourite.

Places to eat

La Chassagnette in the Camargue (*see p81*) is the hip table of the moment. Michel Kayser is cooking meals fit for kings at **Alexandre** in Nîmes (*see p55*).

Culture

Stroll in the formal 18th-century splendour of **Jardin de la Fontaine** (*see p54*) in Nîmes or get an eerie history lesson at **Les Alyscamps** in Arles (*see p73*). Relax with a glass of flinty rosé at the **Caves Listel** in the Camargue (*see p82*).

Sports & activities

Horse-riding in the Camargue is one of the quintessential provençal experiences. Take your pick from a range of ranches. *See p83*.

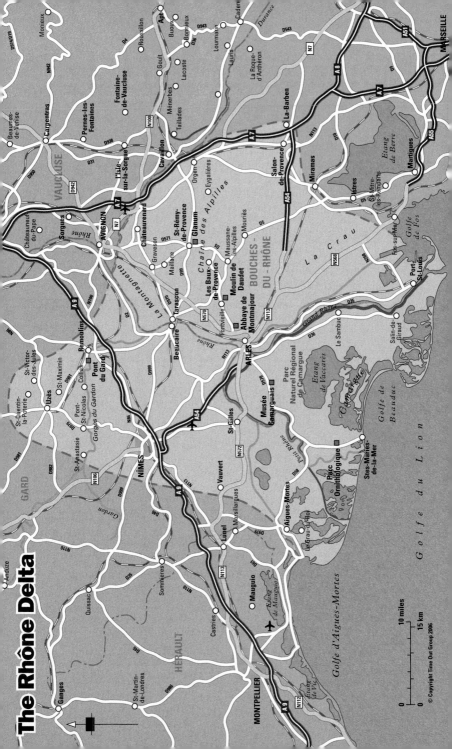

The Rhône Delta

Nîmes & Pont du Gard

Where Roman history and modernity meet.

The title 'Rome of France' is disputed with nearby Arles, but Nîmes and Arles only really have central Roman *arènes* in common. While Arles is an old-fashioned provincial town, Nîmes wears its antique treasures with nonchalance and cleverly marries a wealth of architectural heritage with daring modern interventions, as well as generating something of the buzz of a big city with its lively café society. Its two most imposing Roman remains, the Maison Carrée and the Arènes, are simply part of everyday life – even the crocodile and palm tree emblem, brought here by Roman legionnaires who had previously served in Egypt, crops up everywhere, from the nickname of the Nîmes football team (les Crocos) to traffic bollards and a bronze sculpture by Martial Raysse. Nîmes is also the most Spanish of the cities of the South, with its tapas bars, bullfights and late-night dining. At *feria* time, especially the Féria de Pentecôte in May, the party spirit takes over the whole town and cafés serving paella and sangria spill out on to the pavement.

It was a Celtic tribe that first discovered the great spring – Nemausus – that gave the city its name. Such a convenient stop on the Via Domitia between Italy and Spain was bound to attract imperial attention and by 31 BC the Romans had moved in, building roads and ramparts, a forum and a temple, the amphitheatre, baths and fountains, as well as the Pont du Gard aqueduct to supply water to a metropolis that now numbered 25,000 people.

After the collapse of the Roman Empire, Nîmes declined in importance, wracked by war and religious squabbles. It has always been non-conformist, welcoming the 12th-century Cathar heretics and becoming a major centre of Protestantism in the 16th century, which saw the town heavily embroiled in the Wars of Religion. After the revocation of the Edict of Nantes in 1685, many Protestants emigrated or converted to Catholicism, but the town prospered through the 17th and 18th centuries from dye-making and textile-production, processing the wool and silk of the region. Its tough local cotton of white warp and blue weft – already referred to as 'denim' (*de Nîmes*) in London by 1695 – became a contemporary icon after Levi Strauss used it to make trousers for Californian gold-diggers.

Perhaps as response to urban growth in neighbouring Montpellier, Nîmes's dusty image took a fashionable turn in the 1980s when flamboyant right-wing mayor Jean Bousquet, founder of the Cacharel fashion house, commissioned several ambitious projects, including a Jean Nouvel housing estate (cours Nemausus, av Général Leclerc), the Carré d'Art, a Philippe Starck bus stop and various works of art placed all over the city. This dynamism is still felt into the 21st century: the railway station was magnificently refurbished for the arrival of the TGV and has given impetus to new development south of the station.

Sightseeing

The centre of Nîmes is small enough to visit on foot, with most of the sights inside the triangle (called *l'Ecusson*, 'the shield', after its shape) formed by three 19th-century boulevards: Gambetta, Victor Hugo and Amiral Courbet.

Facing each other across the north end of boulevard Victor Hugo, the **Maison Carrée**, a superbly preserved Roman temple surrounded by a marble-paved open space on the site of the Roman forum, is daringly echoed by the glass and steel **Carré d'Art**, a modern art museum and library designed by Norman Foster.

To the east lies the heart of Nîmes, the partially pedestrianised old town, which is slowly being refurbished. Here shops and cafés are tucked within Romanesque arches, walls are half-stripped of modern accretions to reveal the ancient stonework beneath, and many 17th- and 18th-century mansions have been beautifully restored. Rue Nationale, tracing the line of the Via Domitia, leads between the covered **Halles** and the Porte Auguste, one of the original Roman gates of the city. On rue de l'Aspic, the Hôtel Fontfroide has a 17th-century double spiral staircase, while there are three early Christian sarcophagi embedded in the porch of the Hôtel Meynier de Salinelles. On rue de Fresque look out for an intact medieval stone shopfront. The place du Marché, where Nîmes's corn market used to be held, is adorned with a fountain by Martial Raysse, a modern take on the crocodile tied to a palm tree theme, and on the Grand' Rue the elegant Hôtel Rivet, now the art school, has a floor by artist Bernard Pags. On place des Herbes stands the much-altered

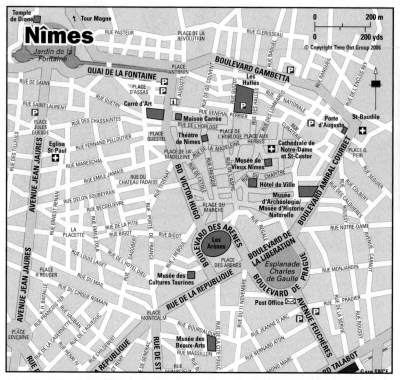

Cathédrale de Notre-Dame et St-Castor.
Next door, the elegant former bishop's palace
contains the **Musée de Vieux Nîmes**, a
collection of local curiosities and decorative
arts. On boulevard Amiral Courbet, the **Musée
d'Archéologie** and **Muséum d'Histoire
Naturelle** are both housed in an old Jesuit
college; the adjoining chapel is used for
temporary exhibitions. Near the Office du
Tourisme to the west of Les Halles, you'll
find the Ilot Littré. Once the dyers' and
spinners' district, this part of the city has
been well restored: cleaned 17th- and 18th-
century façades conceal lovely courtyards.

At the southern tip of the shield stand the
monumental **Arènes**, a beautifully preserved
Roman amphitheatre that could accommodate
20,000 visitors. Today it's perfectly suited to
bullfights and concerts. If you don't approve of
the full-blown Spanish-style *feria*, then try the
gentler Course Camarguaise (*see p60* **Feeling
bullish**). Nearby, the **Musée des Cultures
Taurines** gives further insights into the art
of bullfighting. The elegantly restored **Musée
des Beaux-Arts**, which has a good collection

of French, Dutch and Italian paintings, lies a
few streets south of the rue de la République.

West of the city centre from place Antonin,
elegant 17th- and 18th-century patricians'
houses line the canal along quai de la Fontaine,
which leads to the **Jardin de la Fontaine**,
a beautiful 18th-century formal garden. This
favourite local promenade also contains its fair
share of ancient remains, of course: on one side,
the ruined Temple de Diane; at the top of the
hill, the **Tour Magne**, a vital component of
the original pre-Roman ramparts.

Also to the north of the central triangle, in
rue de la Lampèze, is the Castellum, remnants of
a Roman water tower. Water arrived here from
the Pont du Gard, and was then distributed
across the city through thick lead pipes from
the ten holes still visible in the basin wall.

Les Arènes

*bd des Arènes (04.66.76.72.95/www.nimes.fr).
Féria box office: 4 rue de la Violette (04.66.02.80.80/
www.arenesdenimes.com).* **Open** *Mid Mar-mid Oct*
9am-7pm daily. *Mid Oct-mid Mar* 10am-5pm daily.
Closed for *feria* & concerts. **Admission** €4.45; €3.20
10-16s; free under-10s. **No credit cards.**

Les Arènes. *See p53.*

Encircled by two tiers of 60 stone arcades, this is a standard-issue Roman amphitheatre of perfect classical proportions – smaller than that at Arles, but better preserved. The arcades surround the corridors and vomitoria (exits) and the great oval 'arena' (from the *arènes*, or sands, that were spread to soak up the blood). On the exterior look out for the small carvings of Romulus and Remus, the wrestling gladiators and the two bulls' heads that support a pediment over the main entrance on the north side. The amphitheatre is an amazing piece of engineering, constructed out of vast blocks of stone by teams of slaves. You can still sit on the original stone benches and see the podium for the president of the games and sockets for the poles that held a huge awning to shelter the crowd. For the best view, climb to the top tier of seats, traditionally reserved for slaves and women. The original games included gladiator fights, as well as the spectacle of slaves and criminals being thrown to animals; dogs were set on porcupines to get the blood flowing and the crowd excited. There were also chariot races and even mock sea battles, for which the arena was flooded. After the departure of the Romans, the amphitheatre was made into a fortress, but by the Middle Ages it had become a huge tenement block. When it was finally cleared in the early 19th century, centuries of rubbish had added over 6m (20ft) to the ground level. The first corrida took place in 1853 and the *feria* is today a key event in the social calendar. Covered in winter by a high-tech glass and steel structure, the arena can now be used all year round.

Carré d'Art

pl de la Maison Carrée (04.66.76.35.80/library 04.66.76.35.50/http://musees.nimes.fr). **Open** 10am-6pm Tue-Sun. **Admission** €4.80; €3.50 10-16s; free under-10s. **No credit cards**.

Opened in 1993, the Foster-designed Carré d'Art is a masterful play of transparency and space, giving a fascinating perspective of the Maison Carrée. It houses the Musée d'Art Contemporain and the Bibliothèque Carré d'Art, a vast library and media centre. The art gallery is constructed around a light-filled atrium strung with glass staircases and provides an excellent overview of French art since 1960, including works by Raysse, Boltanski, Klein, Frize and Lavier, as well as arte povera and German and British currents, plus a strong line-up of temporary exhibitions, among them a recent survey of contemporary German art. The public library contains an important collection of early manuscripts. The chic café on the top floor offers great views.

Cathédrale de Notre-Dame et St-Castor

pl aux Herbes (04.66.67.27.72). **Open** 8.30am-6pm Mon-Sat. **Admission** free.
Nîmes's cathedral is not what it was. Although founded in 1096, it was – like much of the town – wrecked during the 16th-century Wars of Religion, and the current building is mainly a 19th-century reconstruction. The remains of a Romanesque frieze, sculpted with Old Testament scenes, are visible on the façade.

Jardin de la Fontaine & Tour Magne

quai de la Fontaine (04.66.67.65.56). **Open** *Gardens* Apr-mid Sept 7.30am-10pm daily; mid Sept-Mar 7.30am-7pm daily. *Tour Magne* Sept-June 9am-7pm daily; July, Aug 9am-10pm daily. **Admission** *Gardens* free. *Tour Magne* €2.40; €1.90 10-18s; free under-10s. **No credit cards**.
The spring that bubbles up at the heart of these lovely gardens was the reason the Romans named the city Nemausus, after its Celtic tutelary god. In

the 18th century, formal gardens were laid out by Jacques Philippe Mareschal, director of fortifications for the Languedoc. They provided a complex system of reservoirs and distributed clean water, which had been sadly lacking in the city since the Pont du Gard aqueduct was abandoned. Now the canals and still green pools, with balustraded stone terraces and marble nymphs and cupids, provide a retreat from the summer heat. On one side stand the ruins of the so-called Temple of Diana, part of a Roman sanctuary whose function remains uncertain. Behind the canals, terraces and footpaths climb up the hill. High up Mont Cavalier, on the edge of the garden, the octagonal Tour Magne was part of Nîmes's pre-Roman ramparts. Its viewing platform – 140 steps up – provides a good view over the city, the *garrigue* landscape and Les Alpilles (*see p64*).

Maison Carrée

pl de la Maison Carrée (04.66.36.26.76). **Open** *Apr-Sept* 9am-7pm daily. *Oct-Mar* 10am-5pm daily. **Admission** free.

Not *carré* (square) at all, this excellently preserved rectangular Roman temple was built in the first century BC and dedicated to Augustus' deified grandsons. With a great flight of stone steps leading up to finely fluted Corinthian columns adorned with a sculpted frieze of acanthus leaves, it has always inspired hyperbole. Arthur Young, an 18th-century British traveller, called it 'the most light, elegant and pleasing building I have ever beheld' and Thomas Jefferson, after failing to import it to America, had it copied as the model for the Virginia state capitol. It has remained in almost constant use, its functions ranging from legislative seat to tomb, from church to stables to fine-art museum. Today it contains drawings and photos relating to similar temples around Roman Gaul and a splendid fresco that was only unearthed in 1992 when the Carré d'Art was being built. Against a blood-red background sits a mythical hunter, surrounded by a border of pagan frolics (most discernibly Cassandra being dragged by her hair) and two louche-looking dwarves. Lovely as it is, the temple could do with a clean-up and suffers from constant traffic pollution.

Musée d'Archéologie & Muséum d'Histoire Naturelle

13bis bd Amiral Courbet (04.66.76.74.54/ http://musees.nimes.fr). **Open** 10am-6pm Tue-Sun. **Admission** €4.45; €3.20 10-16s; free under-10s. **No credit cards**.

Housed in the old Jesuit college, the archaeology museum contains a magnificent collection of Roman statues, sarcophagi, entablatures, coins and mosaics, as well as some gorgeous Roman glass. Pottery includes a rare pre-Roman statue, the Warrior of Grezan. Upstairs is a treasure trove of everyday items, from oil lamps to kitchen equipment, tools and cosmetic jars. The natural history museum includes some important Iron Age menhirs, a good anthropological collection and plenty of stuffed bears, tigers and crocodiles.

Musée des Beaux-Arts

rue Cité Foulc (04.66.67.38.21/http://musees.nimes. fr). **Open** 10am-6pm Tue-Sun. **Admission** €4.45; €3.20 10-16s; free under-10s. **No credit cards**.

The imposing façade of this early 20th-century building leads straight into a beautiful restoration by architect Jean-Michel Wilmotte. Seven paintings illustrating the story of Antony and Cleopatra by Nîmes-born 18th-century painter Natoire hang in the skylit central atrium around Roman mosaic *The Marriage of Admetus*. Elsewhere the eclectic collection includes Jacopo Bassano's *Susanna and the Elders*, Rubens' *Portrait of a Monk* and *The Mystic Marriage of St Catherine* by Giambono.

Musée des Cultures Taurines

6 rue Alexandre Ducros (04.66.36.83.77/ http://musees.nimes.fr). **Open** 10am-6pm Tue-Sun. **Admission** €4.65; €3.40 10-16s; free under-10s. **No credit cards**.

Further your knowledge of bull-fighting culture. Not far from the Arènes, the museum has a collection that ranges from toreador costumes and posters of bullfights to eight plates designed by Picasso.

Musée de Vieux Nîmes

pl aux Herbes (04.66.73.70/http://musees. nimes.fr). **Open** 11am-6pm Tue-Sun. **Admission** free. **No credit cards**.

This museum, housed in the 17th-century bishop's palace, was established in 1920 to preserve the tools of local industries and artefacts of regional life. The collection, much of it displayed as reconstructed interiors, comprises furniture, pottery and fabrics, including some early denim, shawls and silks.

Where to eat

Alexandre

2 rue Xavier Tronc (04.66.70.08.99/ www.michelkayser.com). **Open** noon-1.45pm, 7-9.30pm. Closed Sept-June Mon, Wed & Sun lunch, July & Aug Mon & Sun. **Menus** €38-€87. **Credit** AmEx, DC, MC, V.

Michel Kayser is one of the finest chefs active in the South of France, with his personal take on local specialities inventive yet classical in technique. Local brandade de Nîmes will never be the same again.

Au Plaisir des Halles

4 rue Littré (04.66.36.01.02). **Open** noon-2pm, 7-10pm Tue-Sat. **Menus** €19-€49. **Credit** MC, V.

A modern bistro that serves light and sophisticated cooking, making the most of fresh local produce. The interior is sleek, and there's a delightful courtyard for alfresco dining.

La Bodeguita

3 bd Alphonse Daudet (04.66.58.28.27). **Open** noon-2.30pm, 5.30-11.30pm Mon-Sat. **No credit cards**.

The tapas bar of the Royal Hôtel serves tapas (€3-€15), lunchtime plats du jour, and wine, both local and Spanish, by the glass. It has a terrace and hosts themed flamenco, tango, jazz and poetry evenings.

La Casa Don Miguel

18 rue de l'Horloge (04.66.76.07.09). **Open** *May-Sept* 11am-3pm, 6pm-1am daily. *Oct-Apr* 11am-3pm, 6pm-1am Tue-Sun. **Average** €12. **Credit** AmEx, MC, V.

Lurking under low brick vaults, this buzzing tapas bar serves good food, both hot and cold (tapas around €4 each), and puts on live music (flamenco, jazz, world, folk) on Friday and Saturday evenings.

Le Chapon-Fin

3 rue du Château Fadaise (04.66.67.34.73). **Open** noon-2pm, 7.30-10pm Mon-Thur; noon-2pm, 7.30-11pm Fri, Sat. **Average** €20-€45. **Credit** AmEx, DC, MC, V.

This long-term favourite has walls cluttered with old Bardot posters and paintings by grateful clients. Food is warming and generous, ranging from local brandade to cassoulet and Alsatian choucroute.

Gilbert Courtois

8 pl du Marché (04.66.67.20.09). **Open** *July, Aug* 8am-midnight daily. *Sept-June* 8am-7.30pm daily. **Credit** AmEx, MC, V.

This belle époque café with a comfortable terrace is a Nîmes institution for tea, coffee, hot chocolate and cakes. Simple meals are also available.

La Grande Bourse

2 bd des Arènes (04.66.36.12.12). **Open** noon-midnight daily. **Menus** €10.50-€17. **Credit** MC, V.

Recently repainted in Pompeian red and gold, this celebrated café-brasserie has a terrace looking across to the amphitheatre and serves brasserie dishes including taureau steaks and squid provençale. Service can be slow. (Take a look also at the next door café, la Petite Bourse.)

Le Jardin d'Hadrien

11 rue de l'Enclos de Rey (04.66.22.07.01). **Open** *July, Aug* noon-1.45pm, 7.30-9.45pm Tue, Thur-Sat; 7.30-9.45pm Mon, Wed. *Sept-June* noon-2pm, 7.30-10pm Mon, Thur-Sat; noon-2pm Tue, Wed, Sun. Closed Feb. **Menus** €18-€28. **Credit** AmEx, MC, V.

Sitting under the plane trees behind this dignified 19th-century house is restful after battling the throngs around the amphitheatre. Chef Alain Vinouze prepares seasonal dishes with a local bent, among them brandade and roast pigeon with olives.

Lisita

2 bd des Arènes (04.66.67.29.15/www.lelisita.com). **Open** noon-2pm, 8-10pm Tue-Sat. **Menus** €26-€65. **Credit** AmEx, DC, MC, V.

Chef Olivier Douet and sommelier Stéphane Debaille are making a real success of this stylish restaurant in the town centre, providing modern, market-sourced Southern cooking. The terrace overlooking the amphitheatre is a lighter version of the serious interior courtyard restaurant.

Magister

5 rue Nationale (04.66.76.11.00). **Open** noon-2pm, 7.30-9.30pm Mon-Fri; 7.30-9.30pm Sat; noon-2pm Sun. **Menus** €23-€40. **Credit** AmEx, MC, V.

One of Nîmes's top restaurants for smooth service and perfectly judged cooking. Try the brandade, stuffed pigeon or lamb braised in red wine with mint. The wine list offers the best of local vintages.

Restaurant Nicolas

1 rue Poise (04.66.67.50.47). **Open** noon-2pm, 7-10pm Tue-Fri; 7.30-9.30pm Sat. **Menus** €13-€24.50. **Credit** DC, MC, V.

This friendly, family-run establishment next to the Musée Archéologique has exposed stone walls, sleek lighting, all the requisite bullfighting photos and generously served home cooking.

Simple Simon

pl des Esclafidous, 11 rue Xavier Sigalon (04.66.67.55.61). **Open** 11am-9.30pm Tue-Sat. **Average** €8-€26.50. **Credit** MC, V.

Finding an English tearoom in the heart of Nîmes is a real surprise, but any expats with a sweet tooth should not hesitate to call in.

Vintage Café

7 rue de Bernis (04.66.21.04.45). **Open** noon-2pm, 8-10pm Tue-Fri; 8-10pm Sat. **Menus** €13.50-€28.50. **Credit** MC, V.

This friendly bistro, adorned with colourful paintings, is tucked into a quiet corner of the old town. Try oysters in anchovy jus or Camargue bull steak.

Wine Bar chez Michel

11 sq de la Couronne (04.66.76.19.59). **Open** 7pm-midnight daily; noon-2pm, 7pm-midnight Tue-Fri. **Menus** €12-€21. **Credit** AmEx, DC, MC, V.

Local wines are the norm round here, so this wine bar is a rare chance to sample wines from elsewhere in France. Despite the 1960s steakhouse decor, the food – fish, shellfish, beef – is reliably good.

Where to drink

Le Café Olive

22 bd Victor Hugo (04.66.67.89.10). **Open** 9am-1am Mon-Sat. **Credit** MC, V.

Old stone and contemporary furniture meet in this renovated café, which offers pan-Mediterranean cuisine, Margaritas, and evening concerts and revues.

Haddock Café

13 rue de l'Agau (04.66.67.86.57). **Open** 11am-3pm, 7pm-1am Mon-Fri; 7pm-1am Sat. **Menus** €12.50-€18.50. **Credit** AmEx, MC, V.

This popular café serves until late and hosts a busy schedule of live music and debates.

O'Flaherty's

2 bd Amiral Courbet (04.66.67.22.63). **Open** 11am-2am Mon-Fri; 5pm-2am Sat, Sun. **Credit** AmEx, DC, MC, V.

This popular Irish pub draws throngs for whiskey and Guinness, plus free live music on a Thursday.

Lulu Club

10 impasse de la Curaterie (04.66.36.28.20). **Open** 11pm-late Tue-Sun. **No credit cards.**

Lulu is a long-standing gay bar and disco, but straights are made to feel welcome too.

Le Mazurier

9 bd Amiral Courbet (04.66.67.27.48). **Open** 7am-midnight daily. **Menus** €13-€18. **Credit** MC, V.
Take advantage of this good old-fashioned belle époque brasserie for leisurely morning coffee over a newspaper on the terrace, or a pastis at the zinc bar.

Shopping

The best shopping is in the old town. For food, the covered market of **Les Halles** (rue des Halles, 7am-1pm daily) can't be beat – check out Daniel for olives and Durand for brandade, but you can't go wrong either with the cheeses and dried meats. There's also a Monday flea market on boulevard Jean-Jaurès. **F Nadal** (7 rue St-Castor, 04.66.67.35.42) is a tiny shop selling olive oil from vats, handmade soaps, herbs, honey, coffee, spices and brandade. **L'Huilerie** (10 rue des Marchands, 04.66.67.37.24, closed Mon) has spices, herbs, tisanes and beautifully packaged honeys, mustards and olive oil. Long-established boulangerie-pâtisserie **Villaret** (13 rue de la Madeleine, 04.66.67.41.79, closed Sun) is the place to buy Nîmes's other speciality, jaw-breaking croquants. For regional wines, visit the **Espace Costières** (19 pl Aristide Briand, 04.66.36.96.20, closed Sat & Sun).

Founded in Nîmes by former mayor Jean Bousquet, fashion group **Cacharel** (2 pl de la Maison Carrée, 04.66.21.82.82, closed Sun) has now relocated, but it still has a smart showcase shop facing the Maison Carrée.

Streets near the amphitheatre abound in bullfighting memorabilia, ranging from pure tat to full outfits and vintage prints. **Marie Sara Création** (40bis rue de la Madeleine, 04.66.21.18.40, closed Mon & Sun) is the place to buy the complete toreador regalia; Marie Sara was a famous bullfighter in her day. **L'Oeil du Taureau** (4 rue Fresque, 04.66.21.53.28, closed Mon & Sun) is a good second-hand bookshop. If a surfeit of Southern prints is getting you down, check out the cool contemporary furniture from Cassina, Kartell et al at the Philippe Starck-designed shop **RBC Nîmes** (1 pl de la Salamandre, 04.66.67.62.22, closed Sun) or the well-chosen mix of ethnic and funky furniture, ceramics and decorative items at **Galerie Béa** (4 pl d'Assas, 04.66.21.19.34, closed Sun).

Arts & entertainment

For local entertainment listings, pick up the freebies *Nîmescope* and the regional publication *César*, or check out www.sortiranimes.com.

Le Sémaphore

25 rue Porte de France (04.66.67.83.11/www. semaphore.free.fr). **Tickets** €5.50; €4.60 12-25s; €3.50 under-12s. **Credit** MC, V.
Le Sémaf, as it is affectionately known, offers an excellent programme of original-language (VO) films and themed weeks.

Théâtre de l'Armature

12 rue de l'Ancien Vélodrome (04.66.29.98.66/ www.larmature.org). **Box office** 9am-noon, 2-6pm Mon-Fri. **Shows** 9pm Thur-Sat. **Tickets** €6-€9. **No credit cards**.

Musée d'Archéologie. *See p55.*

The Rhône Delta

Canoeing...

This alternative theatre acts as a showcase for touring companies, staging works by contemporary writers such as Philippe Minyana.

Théâtre de Nîmes
1 pl de la Calade (04.66.36.65.00/box office 04.66.36.65.10). **Box office** 10.30am-1pm, 2.30-6pm Tue-Fri; 2-6pm Sat. **Shows** 8.30pm Tue-Sat; 6pm Sun. **Tickets** €6-€30. **Credit** AmEx, DC, MC, V.
This pretty vintage theatre is now in the hands of Macha Makeieff and Jérôme Deschamps. It hosts opera, dance and short runs of plays by top visiting directors, among them Peter Brook, Julie Brochen and Stanislas Nordey.

Where to stay

Acanthe du Temple Hôtel
1 rue Charles Babut (04.66.67.54.61/www.hotel-du-temple.com). **Rates** €36-€75 double. **Credit** MC, V.
The fussy decoration isn't for all tastes (it's a shame the owners crazy-paved the stairwell), but the hotel is spotlessly clean, friendly and well located.

Hôtel Central
2 pl du Château (04.66.67.27.75/www.hotel-central.org). **Rates** €64-€72 double. **Credit** MC, V.
This good, clean, budget hotel, just opposite the Acanthe du Temple, makes a useful base right in the centre of town.

Hôtel de l'Amphithéâtre
4 rue des Arènes (04.66.67.28.51). **Rates** €34-€76 double. Closed Jan. **Credit** AmEx, MC, V.
Surprisingly smart for the price, this well-restored 18th-century building has a lovely staircase, antique furniture and large, white-tiled bathrooms.

Hôtel Imperator
quai de la Fontaine (04.66.21.90.30/www.hotel-imperator.com). **Rates** €121-€224 double. **Credit** AmEx, DC, MC, V.

The top hotel in Nîmes is smart but unstuffy, which makes it a favourite of toreadors; it has a lovely garden, a 1930s lift and luxurious, air-conditioned rooms. Its gourmet restaurant, l'Enclos de la Fontaine, serves such specialities as fish escabeche and lacquered duck with peaches.

La Maison de Sophie
31 av Carnot (04.66.70.96.10). **Rates** €105-€230 double. **Credit** MC, V.
An exclusive *hôtel particulier* on the edge of town, elegantly decorated and with a delightful garden and swimming pool.

New Hôtel la Baume
21 rue Nationale (04.66.76.28.42/www.new-hotel.com). **Rates** €95-€120 double. **Credit** AmEx, DC, MC, V.
This 17th-century mansion has a beautiful stone staircase, spacious and well-decorated rooms, and smart bathrooms. It also has a restaurant.

L'Orangerie
755 rue de la Tour Evèque (04.66.84.50.57/ www.orangerie.fr). **Rates** €68-€130 double. **Credit** AmEx, DC, MC, V.
This charming hotel just beyond the centre has a garden, small pool, gym and good restaurant (menus €13-€49). Some rooms have private terraces.

Le Royal Hôtel
3 bd Alphonse Daudet (04.66.58.28.27). **Rates** €48-€100 double. **Credit** AmEx, DC, MC, V.
This fashionable little hotel is studiously casual, with artfully distressed walls, a palm-filled lobby, leather club chairs and friendly proprietors. Rooms vary in size but all are light and tasteful.

Resources

Hospital
Hôpital Carémeau, pl Prof Robert Debré (04.66.76.60.60).

...at the
Pont du Gard

Internet

Add On System, 11 rue Nationale (04.66.76.13.93).
Open 10am-midnight Mon-Fri, Sun; 10am-2am Sat.

Police station

av Bir Hakeim (04.66.21.73.44).

Post office

2 av Feuchères (04.66.76.69.50).

Tourist information

*Office de Tourisme, 6 rue Auguste, 30000
Nîmes (04.66.58 38.00/www.ot-nimes.fr).* **Open**
July, Aug 8.30am-8pm Mon-Fri; 9am-7pm Sat;
10am-6pm Sun. *Sept-June* 8.30am-7pm Mon-Fri;
9am-7pm Sat; 10am-6pm Sun.

North of Nîmes

Pont du Gard

The Pont du Gard is an extraordinary structure.
The limestone arches of this triple-decker
aqueduct – the highest the Romans ever built –
rise to an impressive height of 49 metres (161
feet). What is more astonishing still is that they
have managed to resist both erosion over time
and human interference. The aqueduct
originally carried drinking water from the
springs at the Fontaine d'Eure in Uzès across
the Gardon river to Nîmes, along a 50-kilometre
route (30 miles), much of it passing through
underground channels dug out of solid rock.
Fragments of water channels and lost aqueduct
arches still litter the area, and a trail through
them has been clearly signposted.

The bridge itself is built from gigantic blocks
of stone, some of them weighing as much as six
tons, which were hauled into place by pulleys,
wheels… and huge numbers of slaves. The

bridge was built with a slight bow to enable
it to withstand great water pressure; indeed,
during the devastating floods of 1988 and 2002
the Pont du Gard stood firm while several other
bridges collapsed. Crossing the bridge is in
itself a magical experience, but there is also
a little beach from which you can swim. You
can also hire canoes from Kayak Vert
(04.66.22.84.83, closed Nov-Mar, €17-€36).

In an attempt to capitalise on the millions
of people who visit Pont du Gard for free each
year, the **Public Information Centre** was
opened in 2001. It provides a film (the English
version screens at 3pm daily), an exhibition
and 600 square metres (6,500 square feet) of
interactive space for children.

Public Information Centre

*Concession Pont du Gard, Vers-Pont-du-Gard
(0820 903 330/www.pontdugard.fr).* **Open**
May-Sept 9.30am-7pm daily. *Oct-Apr* 10am-
5.30pm daily. Closed Jan. *Car park* 7am-1am
daily. **Admission** €10; €8 6-21s; free under-6s.
Credit MC, V.

Uzès & the Gardon

Charming, Italianate Uzès is often dubbed 'the
Tuscany of France'. Beautifully restored since
the town was designated a *ville d'art* in 1962,
the local pale, soft limestone has already taken
on a time-worn look, making Uzès a favourite
location for historical films such as *Cyrano
de Bergerac*. The revival of Uzès's fortunes is
seen in a proliferation of antiques shops and
restaurants, and a variety of colourful festivals
ranging from a truffle day in January and the
garlic fest on 24 June, via summer wine, dance
and baroque music events, to the National Day
of the Donkeys of Provence on 13 October.

Feeling bullish

If you're not into the full blood-and-guts drama of Spanish-style *corrida* but are fascinated by the notion of *tauromachie*, the gentler Course Camarguaise may be the answer. Events usually take place in the week before *feria*, in the Roman amphitheatres of Nîmes and Arles, with tickets available on the door. Somewhere between a comedy performance and a test of agility, Course Camarguaise pits the small, black Camargue bulls against nimble, white-clad *raseteurs*. The *raseteurs* try to grab *cocardes*, rosettes and other *attributes* that are hung from the bull's lyre-shaped horns and forehead.

Course Camarguaise has a distinguished history. Early games that pitted all sorts of animals – from dogs to lions – against bulls were recorded as early as 1402 in Arles, but were not codified into the less violent entertainment enjoyed today until the 19th century. A typical *spectacle* starts with a parade of women dressed in traditional long skirts and shawls, followed by the *capelado*, the parade of *raseteurs* – inevitably to the toreadors' march from *Carmen*. When the bull is released into the ring, *tourneurs* distract the bull and get him into a good position to charge; the *raseteurs* begin to run, followed by the bull, and attempt to grab the *attributes*, leaping over the barriers in the nick of time to avoid being spiked by the sharp horns. The most dangerous Course Camarguaise usually gets is when a bull tosses away the ringside barriers and charges round the outer passageway, to the alarm of nearby spectators.

A powerful medieval bishopric and later a major centre of Protestantism, Uzès prospered from the production of linen, serge and silk in the 17th and 18th centuries. It was also an important ducal seat and lays claim to having been the first duchy in France.

Within the ring of boulevards along the former ramparts, the arcaded place aux Herbes sums up Uzès, coming alive for the market (on Wednesday morning and all day Saturday), which is a great source of olives, baskets, provençal fabric and pottery. Behind the square is a web of small streets and squares that leads you through to the Duché d'Uzès, where the duke lives on, Republicanism notwithstanding. A guided tour includes a visit to the dungeons, complete with a holographic ghost. Beyond the ramparts, on a promenade offering views of the surrounding countryside, the 17th-century Cathédrale St-Théodorit (open 9am-6pm Mon-Sat) contains a superb 18th-century organ. The earlier Tour Fenestrelle, an arcaded round bell tower reminiscent of Pisa, is the only part of the Romanesque cathedral to survive the Wars of Religion (it made a handy watchtower). Next door, the late 17th-century bishop's palace houses the **Musée Georges Borias** with its local pottery and paintings, as well as a tribute to novelist André Gide, who was born here in 1869. Take a look also at the elegant neo-classical Hôtel du Baron de Castille on place de l'Evêché, which is now an antiques shop. In impasse Port Royal, the **Jardin Medieval** contains a remarkable collection of carefully labelled local plants and medicinal and culinary herbs. The excavated Fontaine d'Eure, a spring that originally carried water to Nîmes via the Pont du Gard, is a short walk from Uzès town centre (take chemin André Gide out of town to the Vallée de l'Alzon). At Pont des Charettes, a kilometre (half a mile) south of Uzès, the **Musée du Bonbon**, belonging to sweet manufacturer Haribo, is a nostalgia trip for adults and sheer sticky heaven for kids.

Between Uzès and Nîmes, the Gorges du Gardon are the most spectacular of a series of deep river gorges; they are visible from Pont St-Nicolas on the D979, where a fine, seven-arched medieval bridge spans the chasm. To walk along them, take a detour through Poulx, taking the D135 then the D127, to pick up the GR6 footpath through the depths; at the north-east end, the village of Collias provides wonderful views. The area is famous for its fine white clay; St-Quentin-la-Poterie, north of Uzès, is a must for pottery junkies. Over the centuries it churned out amphorae, roof tiles and bricks by the ton. The last large-scale factory closed down in 1974, but craft potters have returned; their work, often in the local green or blue glazes, can be seen in the Galerie Terra Viva adjoining the **Musée de la Poterie Méditerranéenne**. The village is a delight, its crumbling ochre houses with loggias and carved columns festooned with washing. Market day in St-Quentin is Friday morning.

Duché d'Uzès

pl de Duché, Uzès (04.66.22.18.96/www.duche-uzes.fr). **Open** *July, Aug* 10am-12.30pm, 2-6pm daily. *Sept-June* 10am-noon, 2-6pm daily. **Admission** €11; €8 12-16s, students; €4 7-11s; free under-7s. **No credit cards**.

Jardin Medieval

impasse Port Royal, off rue Port Royal, Uzès (04.66.22.38.21). **Open** *Apr-June, Sept* 2-6pm Mon-Fri; 10.30am-12.30pm, 2-6pm Sat, Sun. *July, Aug* 10.30am-12.30pm, 2-6pm daily. *Oct* 2-5pm daily. Closed Nov-Mar. **Admission** €3; free under-16s. **No credit cards.**

Musée de la Poterie Méditerranéenne

6 rue de la Fontaine, St-Quentin-la-Poterie (04.66.03.65.86/www.musee-poterie-mediterranee. com). **Open** *Apr-June, Oct-Dec* 2-6pm Wed-Sun. *July-Sept* 10am-1pm, 3-7pm daily. **Admission** €3; €2.30 12-18s, students; free under-12s. **No credit cards.**

Musée du Bonbon

Pont des Charettes (04.66.22.74.39/www.haribo. com). **Open** *July-Sept* 10am-7pm daily. *Oct-June* 10am-1pm, 2-6pm Tue-Sun. Closed 3wks Jan. **Admission** €4; €3 students; €2 5-15s; free under-5s. **No credit cards.**

Musée Georges Borias

Palais de l'Evêché , pl de l'Evêché, Uzès (04.66.22.40.23). **Open** *Feb, Nov, Dec* 2-5pm Tue-Sun. *Mar-June* 5-6pm Tue-Sun. *July, Aug* 10am-noon, 3-6pm Tue-Sun. *Sept, Oct* 3-6pm Tue-Sun. Closed Jan. **Admission** €2; €1 5-15s, students; free under-5s. **No credit cards.**

Where to stay & eat

If you want to give yourself a treat after visiting the Pont du Gard, then head for the **Vieux Castillon** (Castillon-du-Gard, 04.66.37.61.61, www.vieuxcastillon.com, double €215), which is a gloriously romantic luxury hotel.

In Uzès, family-run **La Taverne** (9 rue Sigalon, 04.66.22.47.08, www.lataverne.uzes.fr, closed end Nov, menus €21-€30) does a refined, modern take on regional cuisine, and operates a simple but tasteful air-conditioned hotel across the street (No.4, 04.66.22.13.10, double €58-€77). The **Hôtel du Général d'Entraigues** (pl de l'Evêché, 04.66.22.32.68, www.lcm.fr/savry, double €60-€150) mixes antiques and modern design. The building dates to the 15th century and has a cleverly designed swimming pool. Newly renovated **Hostellerie Provençale** (04.66.22.11.06, www.hostellerieprovencale.com, double €75-€115) has stylish bedrooms and the new owner provides a warm welcome. There are also a couple of stylish restaurants in town: **Les Fontaines** (6 rue Entre les Tours, 04.66.22.41.20, menus €23-€58), with its pretty interior courtyard, and the highly fashionable **Les Trois Salons** (18 rue du Dr Blanchard, 04.66.03.10.81, menus €21-€45).

In Arpaillargues, four kilometres (2.5 miles) from Uzès, **Château d'Arpaillargues** (Hôtel Marie d'Agoult, 04.66.22.14.48, www.chateau darpaillargues.com, closed Nov-Mar, double €69-€235, menus €30-€38) has gardens, a pool, tennis courts and barbecue-style brunches in summer. In Collias, the **Hostellerie le Castellas** (Grande Rue, 04.66.22.88.88, www.lecastellas.fr, closed Jan & Feb, double €80-€150, menus €19-€100) consists of several houses converted into a hotel, with a garden of palm trees, a pool and a restaurant. The acclaimed **Table d'Horloge** (pl de l'Horloge, 04.66.22.07.01, www.table-horloge.fr, menu €45) in St-Quentin-la-Poterie has a daily changing market menu, cooked by the elaborately named (not to mention very talented) chef Thibaut Peyroche d'Arnaud.

Resources

Tourist information

St-Quentin-la-Poterie *Office Culturel, Maison de la Terre, rue de la Fontaine, 30700 St-Quentin-la-Poterie (04.66.22.74.38).* **Open** 9am-noon, 2-5pm Mon, Tue, Thur, Fri.
Uzès *Office de Tourisme, Chapelle des Capucins, pl Albert 1er, 30700 Uzès (04.66.22.68.88/www. ville-uzes.fr).* **Open** *June-Sept* 9am-6pm Mon-Fri; 10am-1pm, 2-5pm Sat, Sun. *Oct-May* 9am-noon, 1.30-6pm Mon-Fri; 10am-1pm Sat.

Getting there & around

By air

Aéroport de Nîmes-Arles-Camargue (04.66.70.49 49) is 10km (6 miles) south-east of Nîmes. A shuttle bus heads to the town centre and train station (€4.30).

By car

For Nîmes, coming south from Lyon/Orange or north-east from Montpellier, take the A9 autoroute, exit 50. West from Arles, take the A54 autoroute, exit 1. For Uzès, take the D979 from Nîmes. Pont du Gard is 14km (9 miles) south-east of Uzès on the D981, 20km (12 miles) north-east of Nîmes on the N86 (take the Remoulins exit from the A9); from Avignon take the N100 then the D19.

By train/bus

Nîmes is on the Paris–Avignon–Montpellier line, with a TGV link direct to Paris in around 3hrs. The Nîmes *gare routière* is just behind the train station. **STD Gard** (04.66.29.27.29) runs several buses (daily except Sun) between Nîmes and Avignon and Nîmes and Uzès (some Uzès buses stop at Remoulins for the Pont du Gard and a few continue to St-Quentin-la-Poterie). There are also three buses daily to Avignon via Remoulins for the Pont du Gard (none Sun) and three between Uzès and Avignon. **Cars de Camargue** (04.90.96.36.25) runs a service between Nîmes and Arles (four daily Mon-Sat, two Sun).

Though all the main sights in Nîmes are walkable, **TCN** (04.66.38.15.40) runs the useful little La Citadine bus, which runs in a big loop from the station, passing a good many of the principal sights along the way.

St-Rémy & Les Alpilles

Snaggle-toothed hills, stylish towns and a slice of history at every turn.

Bordered by the Rhône and Durance rivers, the enigmatic Alpilles hills harbour some of Provence's most fashionable destinations.

St-Rémy-de-Provence

Chichi St-Rémy-de-Provence sits in a dramatic setting at the northern foot of the jagged Alpilles hills. Birthplace of Nostradamus (1503-66) and home to Van Gogh in 1889, today St-Rémy is a bolt-hole for many of Paris' creative elite, which has earned it a reputation as the St-Germain-des-Prés of the South.

There is no train station, but buses from nearby towns Avignon, Aix and Arles take you straight to place de la République, the main square on the east of the old town. Circular boulevards Victor Hugo, Marceau, Mirabeau and Gambetta, following the old ramparts, are the liveliest part of town, shaded by plane trees and crammed with cafés, restaurants and boutiques.

Special festivals in the town include May Day, which brings with it flowers, music and donkey-drawn carts, with a children's fair in the yard of the Ecole de la République. The Fête de Transhumance on Whit Monday is a reproduction of the exodus of flocks of sheep into the Alpilles for the hot summer months. Expect to see up to 4,000 sheep paraded through town, accompanied by donkeys and goats. Tuesday evenings (7-11.30pm, mid June-mid Sept) are enlivened by the Marché des Createurs in place de la Mairie, where craftsmen display their work. For precise details on the town's festivals, contact the tourist board (*see p64*).

For an olfactory treat, head to the **Musée des Arômes et des Parfums**, which is dedicated to the fragrant herbs and plants of Provence. Here you'll find antique perfume stills and all kinds of heady potions made from essential oils.

On boulevard Marceau, the august **Collégiale St-Martin** church was rebuilt in 1820 after the original structure caved in, and has a renowned 5,000-pipe modern organ, used for summer recitals (5pm Sat July-Sept). Follow the street to the right of the church into the old town, where narrow streets, squares with burbling fountains and Renaissance *hôtels particuliers* give a sense of St-Rémy's illustrious

St-Rémy-de-Provence.

past. Physician and astrologer Nostradamus was born in 1503 on rue Hoche, though the house is not open for visits. On place Favier, the 15th-century Hôtel de Sade, built during the Renaissance on the site of Roman baths, was the family mansion of the Marquis de Sade; today it's the **Musée Archéologique**, showing fragments found at the Roman town of Glanum (*see p67* **The road to ruins**). Most impressive are the stunning temple decorations, the distinctive pre-Roman sculptures, and a stone lintel with hollows carved to hold the severed heads of enemies. Across the square, the **Musée des Alpilles Pierre-de-Brun** presents furniture, clothing, documents and objects from a long-gone Provence in a handsome, 16th-century galleried courtyard house, once the home of the Mistral de Mondragon family. However, lack of personnel has kept the museum closed, with no definite plans for reopening. Currently, only the contemporary art exhibition on the ground floor is open to visits, with free entrance. The 18th-century Hôtel Estrine is now the **Centre d'Art Présence Van Gogh** and has varying themed exhibitions dedicated to Van Gogh, with reproductions of the artist's work. It also houses changing displays of contemporary art and a permanent exhibition dedicated to the father of Cubism, Albert Gleize, who lived in St-Rémy for the last 15 years of his life.

For a year from May 1889 Van Gogh was cared for by nuns in the psychiatric asylum adjoining the pretty **Monastère St-Paul-de-Mausole**, just south of the town, which has a Romanesque chapel and a cloister, where there is a permanent exhibition of *art brut* produced by mental patients at the hospital. During his stay, Van Gogh produced more than 150 paintings, including *Olive Groves* and *Starry Night*. Just past here, you come upon St-Rémy's impressive archaeological sites Les Antiques and Glanum (*see p67* **The road to ruins**). Normally, this would be an excuse for a pleasant country stroll but, given the speed of the traffic hurtling past, prepare for a dusty 15-minute sprint.

Centre d'Art Présence Van Gogh

Hôtel Estrine, 8 rue Estrine (04.90.92.34.72). **Open** 10.30am-12.30pm, 2.30-6.30pm Tue-Sun. Closed Jan-Mar, 3wks Nov. **Admission** €3.20; €2.30 students; free under-12s. **No credit cards**.

Monastère St-Paul-de-Mausole

Centre d'Art Valetudo, Maison de Santé St-Paul (04.90.92.77.00). **Open** *Apr-Oct* 9.45am-6.15pm Sun-Fri; 10.45am-5.15pm Sat. *Nov-Mar* by appointment. **Admission** €3.80; €2.80 students; free under-12s. **No credit cards**.

Musée des Alpilles Pierre-de-Brun

Hôtel Mistral de Mondragon, 1 pl Favier (04.90.92.68.24). **Open** (ground floor only) *Apr-Sept* 10am-6pm Tue-Sat. *Oct-Mar* 10am-5pm Tue-Sat. **Admission** €3; €2 students. **No credit cards.**

Musée Archéologique

Hôtel de Sade, rue du Parage (04.90.92.64.04). Closed for restoration until 2006. Call for admission and opening times.

Musée des Arômes et des Parfums

34 bd Mirabeau (04.32.60.05.18). **Open** *Apr-mid Sept* 10am-12.30pm, 2.30-7pm Mon-Fri; 10am-noon, 3-6pm Sat, Sun. *Mid Sept-Mar* 10am-12.30pm, 2.30-7pm Mon-Fri. **Admission** free.

Where to stay & eat

The **Domaine de Valmouriane** (Petite rte des Baux, 04.90.92.44.62, www.valmouriane. com, double €125-€335, menus €25-€48) is an idyllic countryside retreat. Situated in a pine forest in the rocky Alpilles, halfway between St-Rémy and Les Baux, the converted stone farmhouse has a tennis court, swimming pool, Jacuzzi and massage corner. The gardens are filled with herbs, which often find their way into the meals prepared in the restaurant. A few minutes from the centre of town, the **Hôtel Les Ateliers de l'Image** (traverse de Borry, 5 av Pasteur, 04.90.92.51.50, www.hotelphoto.com, closed Jan, double €165-€550) is spacious and modern, with a style inspired by Asian architecture. Photography is the central theme of the hotel, and courses and exhibitions are on offer. There is a swimming pool in the landscaped gardens, and special sushi meals prepared each evening (menus €15-€69). In the heart of town, the **Hôtel Gounod Ville Verte** (place de la République, 04.90.92.06.14, www.hotel-gounod.com, double €90-€185) has an original mix of modern decor and classical furniture. Staff are friendly and the hotel offers a swimming pool and tearoom.

Le Castelet des Alpilles (6 pl Mireille, 04.90.92.07.21, closed Nov-Mar, double €66-€89), a converted early 20th-century family home, is rustic but comfortable, with rooms overlooking a garden. Another simple but welcoming option is the **Hôtel du Cheval Blanc** (6 av Fauconnet, 04.90.92.09.28, www.hotelcheval-blanc.com, closed mid Nov-Mar, double €52-€60) in the heart of town. The intimate **Mas des Carassins** (1 chemin Gaulois, 04.90.92.15.48, closed Jan, Feb, double €99-€163; restaurant closed lunch, dinner Fri, Sat, menu €27), located ten minutes' walk from the centre of town, is a beautifully converted 19th-century farmhouse, with a swimming pool and large gardens. Just outside St-Rémy on the road to Tarascon, the **Château de Roussan** (04.90.92.11.63, www.chateau-de-roussan.com, double €60-€102; restaurant closed lunch, dinner Thur, menus €20-€24), dates from the 18th century and is set in a breathtakingly romantic park. The estate belonged to Nostradamus's brother before being transformed by his grandson-in-law, a royal official. Bedrooms have antique furniture; bathrooms are a little spartan.

The straightforward decor of **Alain Assaud** (13 bd Marceau, 04.90.92.37.11, closed Wed, lunch Thur & Sat, Nov-late Dec, Jan-mid Mar, menus €25-€40) belies the renowned chef's sophisticated seasonal cuisine. Good-value **La Gousse d'Ail** (6 bd Marceau, 04.90.92.16.87, closed Thur, Nov, Feb, menus €15-€30) has jazz nights on Wednesdays during the summer; specialities include leg of lamb with garlic cream and local *taureau*.

La Maison Jaune (15 rue Carnot, 04.90.92.56.14, closed Jan-Feb, menus €30-€57) occupies a handsomely restored 18th-century townhouse and is favoured by locals for

François Perraud's modern take on provençal cooking, seen in dishes like roast pigeon with a wine and honey sauce, and a summer dish of cold raw and cooked vegetables, prepared in an olive oil and white wine sauce. **Xa** (24 bd Mirabeau, 04.90.92.41.23, closed lunch, dinner Wed, mid Oct-mid Mar, menu €25) offers a selection of carefully prepared dishes including a starter of mussels with a mint and curry sauce and grilled sardines with a vinegar, olive oil and oregano sauce. The well-known and well-loved **Café des Arts** (30 bd Victor Hugo, 04.90.92.08.50), founded in the 1950s, has recently reopened after a disastrous period under new management and a new name. It now offers traditional meals à la carte (average €8-€18) in a chic but cosy environment, with a picturesque old-style terrace.

Shopping

St-Rémy boasts plenty of sophisticated shops – so much so, in fact, that this cache of chichi boutiques in the heart of Provence has come to be associated, in many peoples' eyes, with the 'chicification' of the region. Two of the most prominent shops are stunningly inventive *chocolatier* **Joël Durand** (3 bd Victor Hugo, 04.90.92.38.25), whose lavender chocolates make brilliant gifts, and **Le Petit Duc** (7 bd Victor Hugo, 04.90.92.08.31), where talented Dutch-born pastry chef Hermann Van Beek and his French wife Anne Daguin have resurrected a variety of ancient biscuit recipes, including pine nut *pignolats*, found in the *Traité des Fardements et des Confitures*, written in 1552 by local lad Michel de Notre-Dame, aka Nostradamus. **Fabienne Villacreces** (10 rue Jaume Roux) has beautifully cut, very feminine fashions. **NM Déco** (9 rue Hoche) offers classy cashmere, silk and linen for swanning around your converted *mas*. At **Le 16**, formerly Terre d'Art (16 rue Jaume Roux), you'll find no-fuss provençal tableware. The danger at **Vent d'Autan** (49 rue Carnot) is that the modern furniture and provençal antiques will make you want to go house-hunting. Market day in St-Rémy is Wednesday.

Resources

Internet

Café des Variétés *32 bd Victor Hugo (04.90.92.42.61).* **Open** 7am-midnight daily.

Tourist information

Office de Tourisme *pl Jean Jaurès, 13210 St-Rémy-de-Provence (04.90.92.05.22/www.saintremy-de-provence.com).* **Open** *June-Sept* 9am-12.30pm, 2pm-7pm Mon-Sat; 10am-noon Sun. *Oct-May* 9am-noon, 2-6pm Mon-Sat.

Les Alpilles, Les Baux-de-Provence & La Grande Crau

The craggy bone-white limestone outcrop of the Alpilles is one of the more recent geological formations to be thrust up from the earth's crust, and it shows: there are no smooth, time-worn edges here, just dramatically barren rock stretching south from St-Rémy. On a spur dominating the range, its surreal rock forms accentuated by centuries of quarrying, is the bizarre eyrie of **Les Baux**: not, as it appears from below, a natural phenomenon but a fortified village complete with its own ruined chateau.

The medieval Lords of Baux were an independent lot, swearing allegiance to no one and only too ready to resort to bloodshed. Their court, however, was renowned for its chivalry: only ladies of the highest birth and learning were admitted, and quibbles over questions of gallantry were often referred here. In 1372 the sadistic Raymond de Turenne became guardian of Alix, the last princess of Les Baux. Dubbed 'the scourge of Provence', he terrorised the countryside for miles around, making his prisoners leap to their death from the castle walls. On Alix's death, a subdued Baux passed to Provence, then France, only to raise its head again as a Protestant stronghold in the 17th century. Cardinal Richelieu ordered the town to be dismantled and fined it into submission.

The village lay deserted for centuries, picking up again in 1822 when bauxite (named after the place and main source of aluminium) was discovered there, and subsequently when the wild and windswept became fashionable among travellers. Beneath the ruins of the castle, the winding streets, cottages and noble mansions of the old town have been restored and are visited by two million people a year. Most day-trippers make their way back by 6pm, so if you prefer relative calm in historic surroundings, evenings are best.

As well as many beautiful buildings, the village also has some impressive museums, perhaps the most notable being the **Musée Yves Brayer**, in the Hôtel des Porcelet. This contains many of the 20th-century artist's vigorous oil paintings of the region, and also hosts two temporary exhibitions a year. The house No.4 on place de l'Eglise is also decorated with frescoes by the artist. The **Fondation Louis Jou** in the 16th-century Hôtel Jean de Brion houses the presses, wood blocks and manuscripts of the master typographer. The **Musée de Santons**, in a 17th-century building, has a collection of traditional nativity figures from the region.

Daudet's beloved **Fontvieille**.

The main reason for coming to Les Baux is a visit to the ruined **Château des Baux**. Here, you can clamber over masonry and walk along the battlements, discovering remnants of towers and windows, a dovecote, Gothic chapel, a leper's hospital, spectacular views and breathtaking sheer drops to the plateau below. Allow a good hour for a thorough visit. A free audio guide is available.

From the edge of the escarpment, there are views across the savage, unearthly rocks of the Val d'Enfer (literally, 'hell valley'), said to have inspired Dante's *Inferno* and the backdrop for Cocteau's *Le Testament d'Orphée*. Walkers can follow the GR6 footpath through the valley (access from D27) and along the crest of Les Alpilles. The **Cathédrale d'Images**, a vast old bauxite quarry, makes a dramatic setting for audio-visual shows with thousands of images projected on to the floor, ceiling and 20-metre- (66-foot) high walls. The theme changes each year. Note that the quarries a re cool (16°C or 61°F) so bring a jumper.

The lower slopes of Les Alpilles are covered with vineyards producing increasingly renowned Les Baux-de-Provence reds and rosés and Coteaux d'Aix-en-Provence whites. In the heart of Les Alpilles, the tiny village of **Eygalières** is really too pretty for its own good, now filled with overpriced interior design shops and restaurants. However, its delightful 12th-century Chapelle St-Sixte, which dominates a spartan, luminous hillside speckled with olive and almond trees, lifts the spirits. Pagan rites involving spring water from Les Alpilles were performed on the hill. Indeed, one ritual still remains: on the day of a couple's engagement the future husband drinks spring water from his fiancée's hands. If they don't marry within a year, legend has it that he'll die.

The **Moulin Jean-Marie Cornille**, a traditional olive press in the pretty town of **Mausanne-les-Alpilles**, offers guided tours of its premises, with the opportunity to buy the fruity green olive oil produced there.

To the south-west, **Fontvieille** boasts a literary landmark, the **Moulin de Daudet**. Alphonse Daudet's *Letters from my Windmill* (1860) captures the essence of life in the South, though he was accused of caricaturing the locals. Daudet never actually lived in his windmill, preferring a friend's chateau nearby, but the view from the pine-scented hilltop is delightful and the display on milling informative. You might find some characters at the Friday morning market. Just outside town are the remains of a Roman aqueduct.

Further along the road towards Arles stands the important medieval sanctuary of the **Abbaye de Montmajour**, founded by the Benedictines on a great rock surrounded by marshland. The 12th-century church, crypt and cloisters have been painstakingly pieced together over the past century by the sensitive souls of Arles. The interior, renovated by Rudi Ricciotti and used for exhibitions, is plain and serene; it's at its most human in the tiny tenth-century chapel of St Peter (closed for the forseeable future for restoration), with hermits' cells and an altar gouged out of a cave. Ask for the keys to the Chapelle St-Croix, but be prepared to hand over a form of ID in return.

Extending eastwards around the market town of St-Martin-de-Crau (the stalls appear on a Friday morning) is Grande Crau, the arid, rocky limestone 'desert' of Provence. Part of the expanse is cultivated, producing, among other things, France's only hay to be awarded an *appellation contrôlée*.

French Air Force flying school jets and hard-sell Nostradamus heritage make an unlikely couple at the sprawling commercial crossroads of **Salon-de-Provence** on the eastern edge of the Crau. In the **Maison de Nostradamus**, where the astrologer and doctor wrote his *Centuries* and lived from 1547 until his death in 1566, an audio tour talks you through kitsch waxwork tableaux: little Michel being schooled in cabalism by his uncle; the Plague; and the consecratory visit from a busty, satin-clad Catherine de Médicis. The tour lasts 40 minutes and is available in five languages. More atmospheric is Nostradamus's tomb – a simple tablet set into the wall in the Gothic **Collégiale de St-Laurent** (open noon-4pm daily), beyond the city wall. The Romano-Gothic church of St-Michel in the old town is also worth a look, as are two surviving gateways: Tour de Bourg Neuf, guarded by a black Virgin, and Porte de l'Horloge, topped by a wrought-iron belfry. Looming over Salon is the **Château de l'Emperi**, built between the tenth and 13th centuries for the bishops of Arles, and today home to a 26-room military museum and Napoleonic memorabilia. Allow two hours for a complete visit. Modern town life centres around the Hôtel de Ville, the cafés of place Croustillat and the shops of cours Gimon. The morning market is held on Wednesday. Around 1900 the arrival of the railway made Salon a boomtown. Prosperous soap barons (much of what is called *savon de Marseille* is actually made here) built themselves fanciful faux-châteaux, some of which remain, especially around the station.

Abbaye de Montmajour

rte de Fontvieille, Fontvieille (04.90.54.64.17). **Open** *Apr-Sept* 10am-6.30pm daily. *Oct-Mar* 10am-5pm Tue-Sun. **Admission** €6.10; €4.10 students, under-25s. **Credit** V, MC.

Cathédrale d'Images

Val d'Enfer, Petite rte de Maillane, Les Baux-de-Provence (04.90.54.38.65/www.cathedrale-images.com). **Open** *Mar-Sept* 10am-7pm daily. *Oct-Jan, mid Feb-Mar* 10am-6pm daily. Closed Jan-mid Feb. **Admission** €7.30; €3.50 8-18s; free under-8s. **Credit** DC, MC, V.

Château des Baux

Baux-de-Provence (04.90.54.55.56/www.chateau-baux-provence.com). **Open** *Mar-May* 9am-6.30pm daily. *June-Aug* 9am-8.20pm daily. *Sept-Nov* 9am-6.30pm daily. *Dec-Feb* 9am-5pm daily. **Admission** €7.30; €5.50 students; €3.50 under-17s; free under-7s. **Credit** MC, V.

Château de l'Emperi

Montée du Puech, Salon-de-Provence (04.90.56.22.36). **Open** 10am-noon, 2-6pm Mon, Wed-Sun. **Admission** €3.05; €2.30 7-18, students; free under-7s. **No credit cards.**

Fondation Louis Jou

Hôtel Jean de Brion, grande rue, Les Baux-de-Provence (04.90.54.34.17/www.perso.wanadoo.fr/fondationlouisjou/index.html). **Open** by appointment. **Admission** €3; €1.50 7-18s; free under-7s. **No credit cards.**

Maison de Nostradamus

rue Nostradamus, Salon-de-Provence (04.90.56.64.31). **Open** 9am-noon, 2-6pm Mon-Fri; 2-6pm Sat, Sun. **Admission** €3.05; €2.30 7-18s, students; free under-7s. **No credit cards.**

Moulin de Daudet

Allée des Pins, Fontvieille (04.90.54.60.78). **Open** *June-Sept* 9am-7pm daily. *Oct-Mar* 10am-noon, 2-5pm daily. *Apr-May* 9am-6pm. Closed Jan. **Admission** €2.50; €1.50 7-12s; free under-7s. **No credit cards.**

Moulin Jean-Marie Cornille

rue Charloun Rieu (04.90.54.32.37). **Open** 9am-6pm Mon-Sat. **Admission** €1.50.

Musée des Santons des Baux

pl Louis Jou, Baux-de-Provence (04.90.54.34.39). **Open** *Apr-Sept* 9am-7pm Mon-Fri, 10am-6pm Sat, Sun. *Oct-Mar* 9am-1pm, 2-6pm Mon-Fri; 10am-1pm, 2-6pm Sat, Sun. **Admission** free.

Musée Yves Brayer

Hôtel des Porcelet, pl François de Herain, Les Baux-de-Provence (04.90.54.36.99/www.yvesbrayer.com). **Open** *Apr-Sept* 10am-12.30pm, 2-6.30pm daily. *Oct-Mar* 10am-12.30pm, 2-5.30pm daily. Closed Tue in winter, Jan. **Admission** €4; €2.50 students, 15-18s; free under-15s. **Credit** AmEx, MC, V.

Where to stay & eat

In Les Baux, the **Mas d'Aigret** (04.90.54.20.00, www.masdaigret.com, closed Jan, double €95-€140, menu €20), right below the fortress on the D27A, is a 300 year-old building, built on the rock. Its rooms have balconies and there is a swimming pool. The **Reine Jeanne** (04.90.54.32.06, www.la-reinejeanne.com, closed mid Nov-mid Dec, Jan, double €53-€63, menus €21-€30) is slightly more moderate than its competition. It has bedrooms and apartments, some with views across the valley, and serves reliable regional dishes. Tucked away amid fig trees just off the main road leading up to Les Baux, **L'Oustau de Beaumanière** (Val d'Enfer, 04.90.54.33.07, www.oustaude baumaniere.com, closed Jan, Wed Nov-Apr, double €240-€485) is perhaps the most quietly glamorous country inn in France. Chef Jean-André Charial produces luxurious classical cooking, and there's even a seven-course vegetable menu from the hotel's own gardens (menus €89-€149). The **Cabro d'Or** (Mas Carita, rte d'Arles, 04.90.54.33.21, www.lacabrodor.com, closed Nov-mid Dec, double €145-€435) has plush farmhouse chic, and exquisitely prepared food is served inside or on a serene garden terrace (restaurant closed lunch Mon, Sun, menus €40-€90). Deep in the Alpilles, the **Domaine de Valmouriane** (Petite rte des Baux, 04.90.92.44.62, www.valmouriane.com, double €125-€335) is a luxurious converted stone farmhouse, surrounded by woods. It has a pool, a tennis court and a restaurant offering stylish regional cooking (menus €27.50-€65).

L'Oustaloun (pl de l'Eglise, Mausanne-les-Alpilles, 04.90.54.32.19, www.loustaloun.com, closed 3wks Feb, 3wks Nov, double €55-€70) has eight rooms in a 16th-century abbey and a restaurant serving regional cuisine (menus €20-€25). Another good stop for regional cuisine is **La Place** (65 av de Vallée des Baux, 04.90.54.23.31, closed Tue, menus €20-€30), which uses local ingredients in a menu that changes every three days. **Le Bistrot du Paradou** (04.90.54.32.70, closed Sun, lunch Mon, 2wks Jan, Nov, menus €39-€44, including wine and coffee) is housed in an old farmhouse on the edge of town and has been around for more than 20 years. Worth a visit for its good

The road to ruins

Just a short drive from St-Rémy, sitting in a field on the southern edge of town, are some of the most impressive traces of the Roman presence in Provence. The fascinating mishmash of remains at Glanum and Les Antiques are a much-visited attraction, and with good reason. Les Antiques consists of a wonderfully preserved mausoleum, carved with lively reliefs, put up in tribute (some experts believe) to the grandsons of Augustus, and a Roman triumphal arch that once marked the entrance to Glanum – superimposed layers of Celtic, Greek and Roman city, long buried under river silt until excavations began in the 1920s.

The sheer extent of the ruins of Glanum (entrance just up the road from Les Antiques) gives a sense of the urban buzz that reigned here in ancient Gaul. Glanum began as a pilgrimage site with a sanctuary visited by the Glaniques, a Celtic-Ligurian people, in the fifth and sixth centuries BC. The ancient Greek masonry style of many of the oldest buildings – huge blocks of precisely cut stone fitted without mortar – indicates contact with the Hellenistic world during the second century BC, but Glanum really grew after the Roman legions occupied Provence in 49 BC, building forums, basilica, public baths and theatre. Models and plans help make sense

of the visit, as do the facsimile temple columns. The south end of the site is like a corner of ancient Greece, all white limestone rocks and olive trees; you can see the sacred spring and sanctuary of the original settlers, with a deep water basin from the second century BC. The central area is the most complex, dominated by Roman temples.

Glanum
rte des Baux (04.90.92.23.79).
Open *Apr-Aug* 9am-7pm daily. *Sept-Mar* 10.30am-5pm Tue-Sun. **Admission** €6.10; €4.10 18-25s, students; free under-18s.
Credit MC, V.

provençal food on a daily-changing menu, and for the attention to detail ensured by its proud owners.

To make the most of Eygalières, stay at the **Hôtel Mas du Pastre** (04.90.95.92.61, www.masdupastre.com, closed mid Nov-mid Dec, double €115-€180), a charming converted farmhouse with a pool, Jacuzzi and newly installed *hammam* (Turkish steam bath). Smart **Bistrot d'Eygalières** (rue de la République, 04.90.90.60.34, www.chezbru.com, closed Mon, lunch Tue, Jan-mid Mar, double €120-€170, menus €75-€90) has hot young Belgian chef Wout Bru, who draws a showbiz clientele. Two chic bedrooms and two suites allow gastronomes to stagger upstairs after a heavy meal. Book well ahead.

Towering above its rivals in Fontvieille is the **Auberge La Régalido** (rue Frédéric Mistral, 04.90.54.60.22, double €106-€285, closed Jan), which offers old-fashioned haute cuisine (restaurant closed Mon, Tue, lunch Sat, menus €53-€75) and accommodation in an ancient olive mill. Among many casual bistros, **Le**

Patio (117 rte du Nord, 04.90.54.73.10, closed Wed, 2wks Dec, menus €16-€27) has a loyal following for its all-inclusive menus featuring delicious, local home-style cooking, in a rustic atmosphere; it has a pleasant interior courtyard and small garden for alfresco dining. A fine choice if you're travelling with children, or don't want anything fussy and formal, is **La Peiriero** (34 av des Baux, 04.90.54.76.10, closed mid Nov-Mar, double €84-€128), a friendly hotel with a delightful pool built into a former quarry. There are plenty of activities available, including minigolf and badminton.

In Salon, the **Hôtel Vendôme** (34 rue Maréchal Joffre, 04.90.56.01.96, double €40-€51) is housed in a 19th-century home and has a small garden. The grandest place to stay is the **Abbaye de Ste-Croix** (rte du Val de Cuech [D16], 04.90.56.24.55, www.hotels-provence.com, closed Nov-end Mar, double €170-€335), five kilometres (three miles) out of town. The rooms in former monks' cells mostly have private gardens or roof terraces, there's a pool, and the restaurant draws local bigwigs (restaurant closed lunch Mon, menus €68-€105). Far better value is the **Hostellerie Domaine de La Reynaude** in Aurons (04.90.59.30.24, double €55-€114, menus €20-€36), a converted 16th-century coaching inn in a pretty valley. Bedrooms are modern and comfortable, but the chief draw in summer is the large pool. It also has tennis and volleyball courts, and a football pitch. Bikes are on hire for rides in the surrounding countryside.

Resources

Tourist information

Les Baux Office du Tourisme *Maison du Roi, 13520 Les Baux-de-Provence (04.90.54.34.39/ www.lesbauxdeprovence.com).* **Open** *Apr-Sept* 9am-7pm Mon-Fri; 10am-7pm Sat, Sun. *Oct-Mar* 9am-6pm Mon-Fri; 10am-6pm Sat, Sun.
Salon Office de Tourisme *56 cours Gimon, 13300 Salon-de-Provence (04.90.56.27.60).* **Open** *June-Aug* 9.30am-6.30pm Mon-Sat; 10am-noon Sun. *Sept-May* 9.30am-12.30pm, 1.45-6.15pm Mon-Sat.

Beaucaire, Tarascon & La Petite Crau

Midway along the Roman road that linked Italy with Spain, **Beaucaire** (known to the Romans as Ugernum) was the locale of one of the great medieval fairs of Europe, when thousands of merchants would sail their vessels up the Rhône each July to sell silks, spices, pots, skins, wines and textiles on the expanse of land between river and castle. Later the town became known for its finely made furniture and mirrors. Today, shabby streets conceal Beaucaire's former prosperity; but closer examination reveals intricate architectural details in sculpted windows and doorways. You can check out the modern version of the market on a Thursday and Sunday. Dominating the town, the Château de Beaucaire (04.66.59.26.72, admission €8.50, €5.50 under-18s) is now a picturesque ruin. It's off-limits to the public except during afternoon falconry displays. The surrounding garden contains the **Musée Auguste-Jacquet**, where odds and ends from Roman Beaucaire are beautifully displayed.

On the opposite bank of the Rhône, bordering Languedoc, **Tarascon** is dominated by its great white-walled 15th-century **Château**, the favourite castle of Good (as in good-living) King René, with its ornately carved grand courtyard. To satisfy the king's love of material comforts, the castle was richly decorated with spiral staircases, painted ceilings and tapestries. The graceful interior still gives away the castle's lavish past. Snuggled around the castle is the old town. The rue des Halles has covered medieval arcades and the 15th-century Cloître des Cordelier. There's also a weekly market on Tuesdays and Fridays. The **Musée Souleiado** offers a history of the local textile industry – Tarascon was once a major production centre for *les indiennes*, the printed cottons inspired by imported Indian designs that have become an emblem of Provence. The museum has workshops and a boutique selling the distinctive fabrics.

To the French, Tarascon is synonymous with its fictional resident Tartarin, Alphonse Daudet's character who confirmed Parisians' preconceptions about bumbling provincials. The town is also inseparable from the Tarasque, a mythical river-dwelling beast that reputedly used to devour the odd human until St Martha happened along in the ninth century. On the last weekend of June, a model of the dreaded beast is paraded through the streets amid fireworks and bullfights.

Four kilometres (2.5 miles) north-west of Beaucaire, the **Abbaye St-Roman** is an extraordinary fifth-century abbey with chapels, cells, altars and 150 tombs hewn out of sheer rock. **Mas des Tourelles**, four kilometres (two miles) south-west on the D38, is a copy of an ancient Roman winery, and makes wine the way the Romans did – not very well. The CNRS state science research institute was involved in the recreation of the recipes, adding ingredients such as fenugreek, honey and seawater, which makes ordinary Costières de Nîmes taste like nectar in comparison. South towards Arles, **Le Vieux Mas** is a faithful reconstruction of an early 1900s provençal farmhouse, with farm animals, original equipment and regional products.

North of Tarascon, La Montagnette hill is famous for its herbs, made into a medicinal-tasting liqueur by monks at the 19th-century **Abbaye St-Michel-de-Frigolet** – *férigoulo* being the provençal word for thyme. East of here, between St-Rémy and Avignon, is the fertile Petite Crau plain, important for market gardening. Stop off at sleepy **Graveson**, which has a Romanesque church and the **Musée Auguste Chabaud**, dedicated to the powerful landscape paintings and disturbing portraits of the eponymous artist (1882-1955). Pleasant **Maillane** is the birthplace of Frédéric Mistral, revered founder of the Félibrige movement (*see p18*), whose house and garden (now **Museon Mistral**) have been preserved as he left them. **Châteaurenard**, the traffic-choked main town, is best known for its vast, mostly wholesale, fruit and vegetable market on a Sunday. Two ruined towers are all that remain of the medieval castle, which came a cropper during the Revolution.

Abbaye St-Roman
D99 (04.66.59.19.72/www.abbaye-saint-roman.com).
Open *Apr-Sept* 10am-6pm daily. *Oct-Mar* 2-5pm Sat,
Sun & school holidays. **Admission** €5; €2 students;
free under-12s. **No credit cards.**

Château de Tarascon
bd du Roi René, Tarascon (04.90.91.01.93). **Open**
Apr-Aug 9am-7pm Tue-Sun. *Sept-Mar* 10.30am-5pm
Tue-Sun. **Admission** €6.10; €4.10 18-25s; free
under-18s. **No credit cards.**

Mas des Tourelles
*4294 rte de Bellegarde/St-Jilles (04.66.59.19.72/
www.tourelles.com).* **Open** *Apr-Oct* 2-6pm daily, *Nov-
Mar* 2-6pm Sat. *July-Aug* 10am-noon, 2-7pm daily.
Closed Jan. **Admission** €4.80; €1.50 6-16s; free
under-6s. **Credit** AmEx, MC, V.

Musée Auguste Chabaud
cours National, Graveson (04.90.90.53.02). **Open**
June-Sept 10am-noon, 1.30-6.30pm daily. *Oct-May*
1.30-6.30pm daily. **Admission** €4; €2 students, 12-
18s; free under-12s. **No credit cards.**

Musée Auguste-Jacquet
In the château gardens, Beaucaire (04.66.59.47.61).
Open *July-Aug* 10am-12pm, 2-7.15pm daily. *Sept-
Oct* 10am-noon, 2-6pm daily. *Nov-Mar* 10am-noon,
2-5.15pm daily. *Apr-June* 10am-noon, 2.15-6.15pm
daily. **Admission** €4.35; €1.25 under-12s; students
free. **No credit cards.**

Musée Souleiado
39 rue Proudhon, Tarascon (04.90.91.08.80). **Open**
May-Sept 10am-6pm daily. *Oct-Apr* 10am-5pm Tue-
Sat. **Admission** €6.10; €3.05 12-18s, students; free
under-12s. **No credit cards.**

Museon Mistral
11 av Lamartine, Maillane (04.95.95.84.19). **Open**
June-Aug 9.30am-noon, 3-6.30pm daily. *Sept* 9.30-
11.30am, 2.30-6.30pm Tue-Sun. *Oct-Apr* 10-11.30am,
2-4.30pm Tue-Sun. **Admission** €4; €3 students, 12-
18s; free under 12s. **No credit cards.**

Le Vieux Mas
rte de Fourques (04.66.59.60.13). **Open** *Apr-June,
Sept* 10am-6pm daily. *July-Aug* 10am-7pm daily.
Oct-Mar 1.30-6pm Wed, Sat, Sun & school holidays.
Closed Jan. **Admission** €5.50; €4 5-16s; free under-
5s. **Credit** MC, V.

Where to stay & eat

The **Hôtel des Doctrinaires** (quai du Général
de Gaulle, 04.66.59.23.70, closed mid Dec-mid
Jan, double €51-€78) in Beaucaire is probably
the best hotel of the two towns. Set in a 17th-
century doctrinal college, dowdy but spacious
guestrooms do not live up to the vaulted
reception; its traditional cuisine is popular with
locals (menus €18-€40). A cheaper option is the
Hôtel Napoléon (4 pl Frédéric Mistral,
04.66.59.05.17), in a square near the river. It is

scheduled to become a *pension familiale,* and
will offer daily meals included in the room price
– rates were not yet available at the time of
writing. Book ahead to snag a table at **L'Ail
Heure** (46 rue du Château, 04.66.59.67.75,
menus €16-€34), the most fashionable bistro in
Beaucaire where chef Luc Andreu has rapidly
won a crowd of regulars with dishes such as
peach foie gras, sea bass in a mushroom sauce
and beef with truffles.

In Tarascon, the **Hôtel Echevins** is housed
in a beautiful 18th-century building (26 bd Itam,
04.90.9101.70, double €56-€61). **Rue du
Château** (24 rue du Château, 04.90.91.09.99,
www.chambres-hotes.com, double €78-€85)
is a charming guesthouse, situated in two
renovated buildings dating back to the 17th
and 18th centuries.

Resources

Tourist information
Beaucaire Office de Tourisme *24 cour
Gambetta, 33000 Beaucaire (04.66.59.26.57/
www.ot-beaucaire.fr).* **Open** *Apr-Sept* 8.45am-
12.30pm, 2-6pm Mon-Fri; 9.30am-12.30pm, 3-6pm
Sat. *Oct-Mar* 8.45am-12.15pm, 2-6pm Mon-Fri.
Châteaurenard Office de Tourisme *11 cours
Carnot, 13160 Châteaurenard (04.90.24.25.50).*
Open *July-Sept* 9am-noon, 3-7pm Mon-Sat; 10am-
noon Sun. *Oct-June* 9am-noon, 2-6pm Mon-Sat.
Tarascon Office de Tourisme *59 rue des Halles
(04.90.91.03.52/www.tarascon.org).* **Open** *July-Aug*
9am-7pm Mon-Sat; 9.30am-12.30pm Sun. *Sept-June*
9am-noon, 2-6pm Mon-Sat; 9.30am-12.30pm Sun.

Getting there & around

By bus
Cartreize (08.00.19.94.13, www.lepilote.com) is an
umbrella organisation for buses within the Bouches
du Rhône, including services between Avignon and
Les Baux via Châteaurenard and St-Rémy, St-Rémy
and Tarascon (Mon-Sat), Arles and St-Rémy, Arles
and Marseilles via Salon-de-Provence, Avignon and
Maillane via Châteaurenard and Graveson.

By car
For St-Rémy, the A7 exit 25, then the D99 between
Tarascon and Cavaillon. Or south of Avignon on
the N570 and the D571, via Châteaurenard. Les Baux
is 8km south of St-Rémy by the D5 and the D27.
Tarascon and Beaucaire are reached by the N570
and the D970 from Avignon or the D999 from Nîmes.
Salon is at the junction of the A7 (exit 27) and the
A54 (exit 14/15) or by the N113 from Arles.

By train
Frequent TGVs serve Avignon and Nîmes. Local
trains stop at Tarascon on the Avignon Centre Arles
line. Salon-de-Provence has several trains a day from
Avignon; for Marseille or Arles, you'll need to change
trains at Miramas.

Arles

Witness the footprints of history among the town's ancient ruins,
then party all night with the locals.

The sight of the Arlésienne in her traditional costume is one of the strongest images the South of France has to offer, and it's not just put on for the benefit of tourists. This rather staid and traditional town loves to dress up for events, which range from the bullfighting or the famous photography festival to the September rice festival (*see chapter* **The Festive South**) – all set against some of the most spectacular Roman ruins in France.

Straddling the River Rhône, Arles was badly hit by floods in 2003, although it was the modern residential areas, rather than the historic centre itself, that were affected. The town wears its history with ease; its ancient monuments are not museum pieces but part of the urban fabric. The great Roman arena is encircled by the old town like a snail in its shell, while newer buildings snuggle up to the walls of the Cathédrale St-Trophime.

The medieval centre of Arles was built over the Roman ruins and frequently incorporates earlier vestiges, such as the column embedded in the Grand Hôtel Nord Pinus (*see p77*) on the site of the original forum. The dark, narrow streets provide protection from the chilly blasts of the Mistral, and the cobbled alleys and hidden courtyards conceal centuries of history.

Arles was a Greek trading port as early as the sixth century BC, but its importance grew by leaps and bounds in 104 BC when the Romans constructed a canal to facilitate river navigation between the city and the sea. In 49 BC the city backed Julius Caesar's victorious bid to break Marseille's stranglehold on not only sea trade but the Via Domitia land route from Rome to Spain. Arles's moment of glory had arrived, and it began to acquire its rich heritage of no-expense-spared monuments. The city was home to a roaring trade in everything the Orient produced, as well as its own flourishing output of textiles and silverware.

Dark Ages battles took a relatively minor toll on the town and, by the Middle Ages, Arles had regained its clout, becoming a major centre of religious and temporal power. At its height, the kingdom of Arles included Burgundy and part of Provence. The kingdom was so influential that in 1178 Holy Roman Emperor Frederick Barbarossa pitched up and was crowned King of Arles in the newly finished cathedral.

Gradually, as the sea retreated, Marseille took over as the most important port, and in the 19th century, railway traffic replaced river traffic. Though Frédéric Mistral and his Félibrige freedom fighters fought tooth and nail to restore the area's prestige, Arles has never really regained its lost glory.

This fact has failed to dent the Arlésian attachment to local traditions. Long-running festivals, especially the exciting climax of the Easter bullfight *ferias* (*see p60* **Feeling bullish**), prompt the most colourful displays of local pride, with everyone from matrons to

Théâtre Antique. *See p74.*

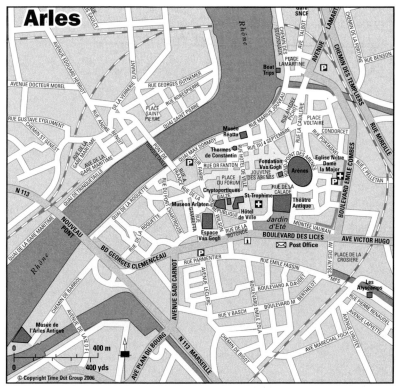

Arles

teens appears in full Arlésienne fig (lace fichus, shawls, bonnets). But just about any event will bring Arles's citizens out en masse: the Rencontres Internationales de la Photographie, which sees photo exhibitions all over town; Les Suds, Arles's world music festival; and the Fêtes des Prémices du Riz rice harvest in September (*see chapter* **The Festive South**).

Arles is irrevocably linked with Van Gogh, who arrived here in February 1888 in search of Southern light and colour, only to discover the city covered in thick snow. Undaunted, he rented the 'yellow house' and began working furiously. In the space of 15 months, punctuated by the occasional stay in the town asylum, a dispute with Gauguin and the lopping off of his own ear, he produced some 300 canvases of startling colours and contours. In truth the good citizens of Arles, like everybody else, rejected the unbalanced Dutchman, who in April 1889, terrified that he was losing his artistic grip, checked himself into the asylum at nearby St-Rémy-de-Provence. Now somewhat embarrassed by not owning a single one of the artist's works,

the city makes do with a mock-up of one of his most famous subjects, the **Café de la Nuit**, and the **Espace Van Gogh** bookshop and arts centre. The **Fondation Van Gogh**, however, pays the right sort of homage to the misunderstood genius. Its superb collection of works by contemporary masters would have pleased Van Gogh, who so much wanted to establish a community of artists here.

Sightseeing

The best view of Arles is from the top tier of the **Arènes** (Roman amphitheatre), looking across terracotta roofs and ochre walls to the River Rhône. Adjacent to the Arènes are the crumbling remains of the **Théâtre Antique** (Roman theatre), described by Henry James as 'the most touching ruins I had ever beheld'. Today they provide an atmospheric backdrop for an outdoor theatre season in June and July. Further down the hill on place de la République stands the great Romanesque **Cathédrale St-Trophime**. The magnificent 12th-century

sculpture around the doorway on the scrubbed façade is equalled only by superb cloisters next door. At the centre of the square is a fountain and an Egyptian granite obelisk, moved here from the Roman circus in the 17th century; on one side, the Hôtel de Ville with its 17th-century classical façade and celebrated vestibule vaulting. Accessible from the vestibule is the Plan de la Cour, a small medieval square with several historic municipal buildings, the 13th-century Palais des Podestats with its Romanesque doorway and windows and, next to it, a lovely 15th-century *maison commune*. Extending beneath the Hôtel de Ville are the **Cryptoportiques** (entrance on rue Baize), an underground gallery of obscure purpose dug out below the forum by the Romans.

A block away is Frédéric Mistral's pet project, the **Museon Arlaten**, which has a vast collection devoted to provençal folklore, crafts and particularly costumes, all housed in a 16th-century mansion with a courtyard built round the columns of the original Roman forum. At every turn is intriguing evidence of Arles's many layers, such as the Corinthian columns (themselves a reference to the Romans) of a 12th-century cloister door on rue du Cloître, the antique bas-reliefs on the Hôtel des Amazones in rue des Arènes, or the 18th-century bulls' heads sculpted on the façade of the Grande Boucherie in rue du 4 Septembre.

Place du Forum, next to the original forum site, is the centre of Arles life today, buzzing with cafés and restaurants, notably the Van Gogh-pastiche Café de la Nuit and hip Grand Hôtel Nord Pinus (*see p77*), where bullfighters and their acolytes congregate. All is watched over by a statue of Frédéric Mistral, leaning on his stick and looking, as he himself complained, as if he's waiting for a train. From here it is a short stroll to the banks of the Rhône, where you can walk along the quays, visit the partly excavated **Thermes de Constantin** baths complex or browse collections of Picasso and other modern masters in the **Musée Réattu**, housed in a lovely old priory with a façade that was once part of the city walls.

At the southern end of rue de l'Hôtel de Ville and the Jardin d'Eté, the shady, café-lined boulevard des Lices is great for observing *le tout Arles*, especially on Saturday mornings, when the market offers Southern colours and smells. Local cheese, olives, ham and sausages – donkey is the local speciality – are generally good buys, as are pottery and olive-wood bowls.

Further south, the necropolis of **Les Alyscamps** lies on the ancient Aurelian Way from Rome. The avenue of marble sarcophagi is a wonderfully melancholy place to stroll. The best of the tombs and sculptures, however, have been transferred to the **Musée de l'Arles Antique**, west of the old centre. Spanking new and purpose-built for the city's collection of old marbles, the museum lies on the banks of the Rhône by the site of the Roman circus, itself under excavation.

Before leaving Arles, spare a thought for another ancient monument: the Jeanne Calment retirement home is named after the woman who held the title of world's oldest person (she was able to remember Van Gogh in her mother's boulangerie) before she died aged 120 in 1997.

Les Alyscamps

av des Alyscamps. **Open** *Mar, Apr, Oct* 9-11.30am, 2-5.30pm daily. *May-Sept* 9-11.30am, 2-5.30pm daily. *Nov-Feb* 10-11.30am, 2-4.30pm daily. **Admission** €3.50; €2.60 12-18s; free under-12s. **No credit cards**.
From its beginnings as a pre-Christian necropolis until well into the Middle Ages, Les Alyscamps (the name means the Elysian Fields) was one of the most fashionable places in Europe to spend eternity. Corpses from up-country were parcelled up and floated down the Rhône with the burial fee in their mouths, to be fished out by gravediggers' assistants on the Trinquetaille bridge. By the Renaissance, many of the magnificent stone sarcophagi had been stolen or presented to distinguished visitors; in the 19th century the railway cut through one end of the cemetery. But the remaining avenue of tombs is still as wonderfully atmospheric as when Van Gogh painted it and at one end you can still visit the tiny ruined church of St-Honorat, with its Romanesque tower, and the marks where St Trophimus is said to have kneeled to bless the spot.

Les Arènes

rond-point des Arènes (04.90.49.36.86/box office 04.90.96.03.70/www.arenes-arles.com). **Open** call for times. Closed during events. **Admission** €4; €3 12-18s; free under-12s. **No credit cards**.
This amphitheatre, one of the oldest in the Roman world, was built in the first century AD to accommodate 21,000 spectators, with tunnels through which wild beasts were released into the arena. Like Nîmes, it had three storeys of 60 arcades each, but the top floor here was plundered for building stone in the Middle Ages (the rest is in remarkably good shape because it was fortified for defensive purposes). The rabble that constructed a slum within its walls a couple of centuries later was not cleared out until 1825, when restoration began.

For a true taste of Roman-style bloodlust, come for a bullfight, when the arena echoes to the sound of the spectators and the persecuted animal. It is used for both classic Spanish-style bullfighting and the more humorous, less bloodthirsty local variant, Course Camarguaise (*see p60* **Feeling bullish**). The season gets underway with the April *feria* and the *gardian* festival on 1 May, when the Queen of Arles is crowned; it culminates in early July with the award of the coveted Cocarde d'Or. Tickets are usually available on the gate, but book ahead for the *feria* and Cocarde d'Or. The arena, which also hosts concerts and films during the summer, is currently undergoing a vast restoration plan, which looks set to continue for the foreseeable future.

Cathédrale St-Trophime

pl de la République (04.90.96.07.38). **Open** *Church* 8.30am-6.30pm daily. *Cloister* 10am-5.30pm daily. **Admission** *Church* free. *Cloister* €3.50; €2.06 12-18s; free under-12s. **No credit cards.**

A church has stood here since the fifth century. The current, stunning Romanesque cathedral was built in the 12th century to house the relics of St Trophimus, a third-century bishop of Arles. Its austere nave is impressively tall, hung with Aubusson tapestries and dotted with Roman sarcophagi and 17th-century Dutch paintings. It is the portal, however, that really takes your breath away. Recently restored, its vivid carving is clearly visible: the tympanum shows Christ in glory, with life-size apostles accommodated in the columns below. The frieze – its style perhaps inspired by Roman sarcophagi – depicts the Last Judgement, with souls being dragged off to hell in chains or given to the saints in heaven. The cloister sculptures are Romanesque in the north and east arcades and 14th-century Gothic in the south and west; the two styles form a surprisingly harmonic whole. The carved columns and capitals feature a profusion of biblical characters and stories. Above the cloister, a walkway offers good views of the bell tower and the town.

Cryptoportiques

rue Baize. **Open** *Mar, Apr, Oct* 9-11.30am, 2-5.30pm daily. *May-Sept* 9-11.30am, 2-6.30pm daily. *Nov-Feb* 10-11.30am, 2-4.30pm daily. **Admission** €3.50; €2.60 12-18s; free under-12s. **No credit cards.**

These mysterious, horseshoe-shaped Roman underground galleries were constructed to support the hillside foundations of the forum and may also have been used as a religious sanctuary or to store grain. During World War II they gave refuge to members of the Resistance, and they still exude a chilly and sinister atmosphere.

Fondation Van Gogh

Palais de Luppé, 24bis rond-point des Arènes (04.90.49.94.04). **Open** *Apr-mid Oct* 10am-7pm daily. *Mid Oct-mid Mar* 9.30am-noon, 2-5.30pm Tue-Sun. Closed 1wk Mar. **Admission** €7; €5 students, 8-18s; free under-8s. **Credit** MC, V.

Work by contemporary artists in tribute to Van Gogh include a Hockney chair, a Rauschenberg sunflower in acrylic yellow and blue on steel, plus works by Bacon, Rosenquist, Lichtenstein and Viallat, and photographs by Doisneau and Cartier-Bresson. The catalogue explains how Vincent inspired each artist.

Musée de l'Arles Antique

presqu'île du Cirque Romain (04.90.18.88.88/ www.arles-antique.org). **Open** *Mar-Oct* 9am-7pm daily. *Nov-Feb* 10am-5pm daily. **Admission** €5.50; €4 students; free under-18s, all 1st Sun of mth. **Credit** MC, V.

Awkwardly placed on the fringes of the Roman circus, this modern blue triangle designed by Henri Ciriani houses the many antiquities once scattered throughout Arles's museums and archaeological sites. The well-displayed collection includes statues, capitals, pottery, jewellery, glass and villa mosaics along with maps, models and town plans. Best of all are the beautifully carved sarcophagi from Les Alyscamps, many of which date from the fourth century AD or earlier.

Musée Réattu

10 rue du Grand Prieuré (04.90.49.38.34). **Open** *Mar-Apr* 10am-12.30pm, 2-5.30pm daily. *May-Sept* 10am-12.30pm, 2-7pm daily. *Oct-Feb* 1-5.30pm daily. **Admission** €4; €3 students, 12-18s; free under-12s. **No credit cards.**

Housed in a 15th-century priory, this museum contains works by its founder, provençal artist Jacques Réattu, along with a collection of more modern work by Léger, Dufy, Gauguin and others. Most notable are the 57 drawings made by Picasso in 1971 and donated to the museum by the artist a year later to thank Arles for amusing him with its bullfights. Also by Picasso is a delicious rendering of Lee Miller as an Arlésienne painted in Mougins in 1937.

Museon Arlaten

29 rue de la République (04.90.93.58.11). **Open** *Apr, May* 9.30am-12.30pm, 2-6pm Tue-Sun. *June-Aug* 9.30am-1pm, 2-6.30pm daily. *Sept* 9.30am-1pm, 2-6pm daily. *Oct-Mar* 9.30am-12.30pm, 2-5pm Tue-Sun. Last entry 1hr before closing. **Admission** €4; €3 12-18s; free under-12s. **No credit cards.**

Frédéric Mistral used the money from his Nobel Prize for Literature in 1904 to set up this museum to preserve the traditions of Provence, thus establishing an enduring fashion for collections of regional memorabilia. Attendants wear Arlésien costume and captions come in French and Provençal only. Despite the stuffiness, this is a worthwhile and authentic collection of humble domestic and rural objects: furniture, tools, kitchen equipment, shoes and clothing. The best exhibits are a bizarre haul of traditional talismans: a fig branch burned to encourage maternal milk, a ring fashioned from the third nail of a horseshoe to ward off haemorrhoids and large quantities of equipment to prevent toothache. There are large tableaux too: a home birth; a Christmas scene with the traditional 13 desserts of Provence; and a Camargue *gardian*'s cabin.

Le Pont Van Gogh

rte de Port-St-Louis.

Van Gogh's famous Pont du Langlois has been restored (after being bombed during World War II) and moved to the southern outskirts of Arles.

Théâtre Antique

rue de la Calade (04.90.49.36.25). **Open** *Mar, Apr, Oct* 9-11.30am, 2-5.30pm daily. *May-Sept* 9-11.30am, 2-6.30pm daily. *Nov-Feb* 10-11.30am, 2-4.30pm daily. **Admission** €3; €2.20 students, 12-18s; free under-12s. **No credit cards.**

The Roman theatre, dating from the first century BC and ransacked for building stone from the fifth century on, once seated over 10,000. Today it is a mess of tumbledown columns and fragments of carved stones, its forlorn glory making it a particularly romantic setting for summer theatre and music performances. Vestiges of the original tiers of stone benches remain, along with two great Corinthian columns of the stage wall, once used as a gallows.

Thermes de Constantin

rue du Grand Prieuré. **Open** *Mar, Apr, Oct* 9-11.30am, 2-5.30pm daily. *May-Sept* 9-11.30am, 2-6.30pm daily. *Nov-Feb* 10-11.30am, 2-4.30pm daily. **Admission** €3; €2.20 students, 12-18s; free under-12s. **No credit cards.**

At the fourth-century Roman baths, once part of a larger complex of baths on the banks of the Rhône, you can still see the vaulted caldarium, warm bath, and the bricks of the underfloor heating system.

Where to eat & drink

Au Brin de Thym

22 rue du Dr Fanton (04.90.49.95.96/www.aubrinde thym.com). **Open** noon-2pm, 7-10pm Mon, Thur-Sun; 7-10pm Wed. **Menus** €17-€29. **Credit** MC, V.

Tucked behind the place du Forum, this intimate restaurant – all white beams, white tablecloths, tiled floor and bunches of lavender – serves provençal cuisine based on fresh market produce, a tasty selection of local goat's cheese, and some lip-smacking own-made puddings. The restaurant also has an adjoining provençal gift shop.

Bistrot La Mule Blanche

9 rue du Président Wilson (04.90.93.98.54). **Open** noon-2.30pm, 8-10pm Mon-Sat. **Menus** €9.15 €25. **Credit** AmEx, MC, V.

Be prepared to wait for a seat on the palm-shaded terrace of this popular address in the centre of town. The lengthy menu provides a good selection of simple grilled fish and meat, big salads and pasta, all prepared to a decent standard.

Café de la Nuit

pl du Forum (04.90.96.44.56). **Open** *Summer* 9am-2am daily. *Winter* 9am-11.30pm daily. **Average** €40. **Credit** MC, V.

This fun café has a great people-watching terrace, a lofty interior painted in vibrant Van Gogh colours and a bar decorated to look like his painting of the same name. Try the very good tagliatelle or bull daube with an inexpensive carafe of regional wine.

La Charcuterie Arlésienne

51 rue des Arènes (04.90.96.56.96). **Open** noon-1.30pm, 7.30-9.30pm Tue-Sat. Closed Aug. **Menus** €25. **Credit** MC, V.

This old charcuterie serves some of the best pork produce in Arles. The authentic Lyonnais bistro cooking comes as something of a surprise in a provençal stronghold, but in cooler months could provide a welcome change from local specialities.

Chez Ariane

2 rue du Dr Fanton (04.90.52.00.65). **Open** noon-2pm, 7-10.30pm Mon-Sat. **Average** €25. **Credit** MC, V.

New wine bar with a good choice of local wine and well-prepared plats du jour, served with a smile.

Le Cilantro

29/31 rue Porte de Laure (04.90.18.25.05). **Open** daily noon-2pm, 7.30-10pm daily. **Menus** €19-€40. **Credit** MC, V.

Chef Jêrome Laurent drags Arles's gastronomy into the 21st century with precise modern cookery of some sophistication. The perfect antidote to one too many typically provençal menus.

L'Entrevue

pl Nina Berberova (04.90.93.37.28). **Open** 9.30am-3pm, 7-11pm daily. Closed lunch Sun Oct-Apr. **Menu** €25. **Credit** V.

Part of the Actes Sud complex, this couscous restaurant has a big terrace overlooking the river, drawing in young intellectuals who enjoy the well-prepared Moroccan food and lively atmosphere.

L'Escaladou

23 rue Porte de Laure (04.90.96.70.43). **Open** noon-2pm, 6.30pm-11pm Mon, Tue, Thur-Sun. **Menus** €15-€19. **Credit** V.

An old-fashioned (and affordable) restaurant that serves simple provençal dishes (including a delicious aïoli). Popular with locals and tourists alike.

La Gueule du Loup

39 rue des Arènes (04.90.96.96.69). **Open** 7.45-9.45pm Mon; 12.30-1.30pm, 7.45-9.45pm Tue-Sat. **Menu** €25. **Credit** DC, V.

You get to this first-floor beamed restaurant through a deliciously scented kitchen where *madame* bustles around in a great white apron. Try the charlotte d'agneau with aubergines and red pepper coulis, a tarte tatin of deliciously sweet turnips with foie gras, scallop and sorrel terrine, followed by chestnut mousse with almond milk. Book ahead.

Le Jardin de Manon

14 av des Alyscamps (04.90.93.38.68). **Open** *Summer* noon-1.30pm, 7-9.30pm Mon, Tue, Thur-Sun. *Winter* 1.30pm, 7-9.30pm Mon, Tue, Thur, Sat; noon-1.30pm Fri, Sun. Closed 2wks Nov, 2wks Feb. **Menus** €14-€40. **Credit** AmEx, MC, V.

There are not a great number of restaurants down by the Alyscamps, and as its name suggests Manon has a delightful garden for alfresco dining. The interior, like the menu, features local colour combined with contemporary touches.

Lou Caleu

27 rue Porte de Laure (04.90.49.71.77). **Open** noon-2pm, 7-10pm Tue-Sat. Closed mid Jan-mid Feb. **Menus** €18-€27. **Credit** AmEx, DC, MC, V.

The best of several restaurants on a street near the Roman theatre, Lou Caleu brings a light touch to provençal cooking: witness chicken with herbs and honey, tomato stuffed with aubergine or pork daube.

The Rhône Delta

Le Malarte

2 bd des Lices (04.90.96.03.99). **Open** noon-3pm,
7-9.30pm daily. **Menus** €15-€20. **Credit** MC, V.
At some point during your visit you are sure to find
yourself on the busy boulevard des Lices, with
its slightly tacky brasseries and cafés, but you can
have an enjoyable meal at the Malarte, including
excellent petits farcis, all served with a smile.

Nightlife

Cargo de Nuit

*7 av Sadi Carnot (04.90.49.55.99/www.cargo
denuit.com).* **Open** 8pm-5am Thur-Sat. Closed
July, Aug, mid Dec-mid Jan. **Admission** varies.
Credit MC, V.
Listen to world music, rock, electronica and jazz
(both live and canned). A new team is in charge of
the restaurant, and a meal allows you entry to the
concert at a reduced rate.

El Patio de Camargue

chemin de Barriol (04.90.49.51.76/www.chico.fr).
Open 8pm-late Sat, by reservation only. **Average**
€45. **Credit** AmEx, MC, V.
This tacky Spanish complex on the banks of the
Rhône serves tapas and paella, accompanied by gui-
tars, songs and dancing from 'Chico et les Gypsies',
led by a founder member of the Gypsy Kings.

Shopping

Arles's markets take place on boulevard des
Lices on Saturdays and on boulevard Emile
Combes on Wednesdays. Both offer local fruit,
vegetables and fish, and a vast array of nuts,
spices, herbs, charcuterie and bric-a-brac. More
bric-a-brac can be found on the boulevard des
Lices on the first Wednesday of the month.

The streets of the old town, west of the arena
from rue de la République to the river, are very
pleasant for shopping (all open Mon-Sat unless
stated). Best buys are local products, such as
perfumes, incense, soaps and candles, with a
good range at upmarket chain **L'Occitane**
(58 rue de la République, 04.90.96.93.62) and
at **Fragrances** (53 rue de la République,
04.90.18.20.64). At **Santons Chave** (14 rond-
point des Arènes, 04.90.96.15.22), you can buy
provençal crèche figures and see them being
made. **L'Arlésienne** (12 rue de la République,
04.90.93.28.05) is the place to buy provençal
fabrics, waistcoats, frilly skirts, *gardian*
cowboy shirts and even a complete Arlésien
costume by the designer who dresses the
assistants in the Museon Arlaten. **Souleiado**
(4 bd des Lices, 04.90.96.37.55), the Tarascon-
based fabric producer, has a huge range of
colourful patterns for clothing and furnishing,
as well as ready-to-wear garments. **Christian
Lacroix** (52 rue de la République, 04.90.96.11.16)

Christian Lacroix.

is a native of Arles, and his exuberant style
screams South of France; gorgeous clothes
and jewellery plus children's wear, porcelain
and table linen fill this, his original shop.

Food, too, is worth seeking out. **Boitel**
(4 rue de la Liberté, 04.90.96.03.72, closed 3wks
Feb) sells regional delicacies, from handmade
chocolates to cakes, biscuits and nougat, and
also has a small tearoom. **La Charcuterie
Arlésienne** (51 rue des Arènes, 04.90.96.56.96,
closed Mon & Sun) supplies the cognoscenti
with sausages, charcuterie and a good choice of
wine. **La Maison des Gourmands** (28 rond-
point des Arènes, 04.90.93.19.38) is the place for
provençal nougat, biscuits, olive oil and honey.
Fad'Oli (46 rue des Arènes, 04.90.49.70.73) also
has a wide selections of oils and some good fast
food. For excellent wine seek out **Le Cellier
du Forum** (7 rue du Dr Fanton, 04.90.96.37.58).

The best bookshop is run by Arles-based
publisher Actes Sud (*see p77*), which has a
branch and children's bookshop in the Espace
Van Gogh. **Forum Harmonia Mundi** (3 rue
du Président Wilson, 04.90.93.38.00) is another
institution – now a France-wide chain, the
classical, jazz and world music specialist began
here in 1958. Near the Musée Réattu and the
banks of the Rhône is a small antiques enclave
with, notably, **Antiquités Maurin** (4 rue de
Grille, 04.90.96.51.57, closed Mon morning &
all Sun), a large shop crammed with provençal
furniture, paintings and objets d'art. **Livres
Anciens Gilles Barbero** (3 rue St-Julien,
04.90.93.72.04) is a bookshop stuffed full of
antiquarian books, maps, photos and postcards,
wonderful for browsing for original gifts.

Arts & entertainment

For entertainment listings, it's best to pick up
the free fortnightly listings mag *César*. You'll
find it in local shops and at the tourist office.
See also p73 **Les Arènes**.

Actes Sud

*23 quai Marx Dormoy (cinema 04.90.93.33.56/
hammam 04.90.96.10.32).* **Open** *Bookshop* 9am-
7pm Mon-Fri. *Cinema* 6.30pm, 9pm Mon-Sat;
3pm, 6pm Sun. *Hammam* men 5.30-10pm Mon,
Wed, Thur; women 9am-5pm Mon, Sat, Sun;
9am-10pm Tue-Fri.

This arts complex, beside the River Rhône, houses
its own publishing house, arts cinema, hammam and
L'Entrevue restaurant (*see p75*).

Espace Van Gogh

pl du Dr Félix Rey (04.90.49.37.53). **Open**
6am-9pm daily. **Admission** free.

A library, bookshop and exhibition space set around
a garden courtyard in the hospital where the painter
was treated, restored to look as it did in his time.

Théâtre d'Arles

bd Georges Clemenceau (04.90.52.51.51). **Open**
Box office 11am-1pm, 1-6.30pm Tue-Sat. **Tickets**
€20. **Credit** MC, V.

Restored and reopened in 2001, this splendid old
theatre offers music and lectures as well as plays.

Théâtre de la Calade

*Le Grenier à Sel, 49 quai de la Roquette
(04.90.93.05.23).* **Open** Box office 10am-12.30pm, 2-
6pm Mon-Fri. **Tickets** €6.50-€17. **No credit cards**.
Based in a former salt warehouse, this theatre company offers its own performances, opera, visiting
companies and workshops.

Where to stay

Grand Hôtel Nord Pinus

*17 pl du Forum (04.90.93.44.44/www.nord-pinus.
com).* Closed Nov-Jan. **Rates** €150-€182 double.
Credit AmEx, DC, MC, V.

This bullfighters' favourite, opened in the 19th
century, is dramatically decorated with heavy
carved furniture, Peter Beard's giant black and
white photos, *feria* posters and mounted bulls'
heads. It has an elegant bar and the Brasserie Nord
Pinus. Book well ahead at *feria* time.

Hôtel de l'Amphithéâtre

*5 rue Diderot (04.90.96.10.30/www.hotel
amphitheatre.fr).* **Rates** €49-€89 double.
Credit AmEx, DC, MC, V.

Set in a restored 17th-century building on a tiny
street, this is a gem, with warm old tiles, yellow
walls and original wrought-iron banisters. Rooms
are small but charmingly decorated, and bathrooms
well designed with big mirrors. Garage available.

Hôtel du Forum

*10 pl Forum (04.90.93.48.95/www.hoteldu
forum.com).* Closed Nov-mid Mar. **Rates**
€70-€125 double. **Credit** AmEx, DC, MC, V.

An old-fashioned hotel right in the centre of things,
the Forum has the huge advantage of having a
private garden with swimming pool to cool down in
during the torrid summers. Lots of retro charm.

Hôtel du Musée

*11 rue du Grand Prieuré (04.90.93.88.88/www.
hoteldumusee.com.fr).* Closed Jan. **Rates** €48-€78
double. **Credit** AmEx, DC, MC, V.

The rooms of this small hotel in a 16th-century mansion are elegantly decorated with provençal antiques.
Breakfast is served in a leafy inner courtyard.

Hôtel La Muette

*15 rue des Suisses (04.90.96.15.39/http://perso.
wanadoo.fr/hotel-muette).* **Rates** €51-€58 double.
Credit V.

La Muette may be a budget hotel, but it's hardly
lacking in charm, with thick stone walls and rooms
simply furnished in provençal style. The building
dates back to the 12th century.

Hôtel l'Arlatan

*26 rue du Sauvage (04.90.93.56.66/www.hotel-
arlatan.fr).* Closed Jan-early Feb. **Rates** €85-€153
double. **Credit** AmEx, DC, MC, V.

This provençal mansion is built over part of the
Roman basilica (you can see the excavations under
glass) and has a medieval Gothic tower among other
period details, carved ceilings and antiques. There
is an elegant salon with vast fireplace, an enclosed
garden courtyard and a pool.

L'Hôtel Particulier.

Hôtel Le Calendal

*5 rue Porte de Laure (04.90.96.11.89/www.le
calendal.com). Closed 3wks Jan.* **Rates** €64-€104
double. **Credit** AmEx, DC, MC, V.
This romantic hotel occupies several cleverly linked
old buildings around a large, shady garden with
tables and palm trees. Sunny rooms, each different,
look over either the Théâtre Antique or the garden.
The salon de thé serves good light meals.

Hôtel Le Cloître

*16 rue du Cloître (04.90.96.29.50/www.hotelcloitre.
com). Closed Nov-mid Mar.* **Rates** €45-€60 double.
Credit AmEx, MC, V.
A good-value hotel in a narrow street near the
Roman theatre, with a Romanesque vaulted dining
room and exposed stone walls in the bedrooms.

Hôtel Le Galoubet

*18 rue du Dr Fanton (04 90.93.18.11). Closed
Nov-Feb.* **Rates** €50 double. **Credit** AmEx, V.
Arles has many architecturally interesting hotels,
including this budget townhouse.

Hôtel St-Trophime

*16 rue de la Calade (04.90.96.88.38/www.hotel-
saint-trophime.com). Closed mid Jan-mid Feb.*
Rates €50-€70 double. **Credit** AmEx, DC, MC, V.
Housed in an atmospheric old building in the centre
of Arles, this hotel boasts a stone-arched lobby,
carved ceilings and a courtyard.

L'Hôtel Particulier

*4 rue de la Monnaie (04.90.52.51.40/www.
hotel-particulier.com).* **Rates** €159-€279 double.
Credit AmEx, DC, MC, V.
For the ultimate aristocratic high life, set up home
in the Hôtel Particulier, a majestic mansion impressively converted into an exclusive hotel, with a
Roman-style swimming pool in the walled gardens.

Resources

The 'Pass Monuments' and 'Circuit Arles
Antique' passes are available at the tourist
office, museums and sights.

Hospital

*Hôpital Général Joseph Imbert, quartier Haut
de Fourchon (04.90.49.29.29).*

Internet

Cyber.com, 87 av Dr Morel (04.90.52.02.96).
Open 1pm-12.30am daily.

Police station

1 bd des Lices (04.90.18.45.00).

Post office

5 bd des Lices (04.90.18.41.00).

Tourist information

*Office de Tourisme, esplanade Charles de Gaulle,
bd des Lices, 13200 Arles (04.90.18.41.20/www.
ville-arles.fr).* **Open** *Apr-Sept* 9am-6.45pm daily.
Oct, Nov 9am-5.45pm Mon-Sat; 10.30am-2.15pm Sun.
Dec-Mar 9am-4.45pm Mon-Sat; 10.30am-2.15pm Sun.

Getting there & around

By air

Arles is about 20km (12 miles) from Nîmes-Arles-
Camargue airport. A taxi from there takes roughly
half an hour and should cost about €30.

By bus

Cars de Camargue (04.90.96.36.25) runs
buses between Nîmes and Arles three times daily
on weekdays, and twice a day on Sat (none Sun),
and four buses Mon-Fri, between Arles and Stes-
Maries-de-la-Mer. The **SNCF** (08.92.35.35.35) runs
three or four buses daily (Mon-Sat) to Avignon.
Cartreize (08.00.19.94.13, www.lepilote.com)
runs a service between Arles and Marseille.
It's best to walk around Arles town centre.

By car

The A54 goes through Arles, with exit 5 bringing
you nearest to the centre. Otherwise take the N570
from Avignon.

By train

Arles is on the main coastal rail route, and connects
with Avignon for the TGV to Paris.

The Camargue

Wild, wild horses.

Stes-Maries-de-la-Mer.
See p81.

AUX ABORDS
DES ÉPIS

The eerily beautiful Rhône delta yields its best secrets to those willing to take to the saddle. For those reluctant to leave their car, the region can seem flat and uninteresting, with an overplayed ranch theme and the greediest mosquitoes in Europe; but take a long ride or walk and the region's charms take hold.

Nestling in the delta between the Grand and the Petit Rhône, this great flat region of marsh, pasture, salt-water *étangs* (ponds) and sand dunes is one of Europe's major wetlands, a vast protected area of 140,000 hectares (345,950 acres). The beauty of the flora and fauna cannot be overstated: pink flamingos and purple herons; black bulls and grey ponies; wild boar; beavers that thrive again here having reached the verge of extinction; wintering egrets; bulrushes and samphire; pastures and paddy fields – and dense clouds of bloodthirsty mosquitoes. It is a fragile balance; if the Rhône floods, as in 2003, the salt level in the lagoon is lowered, which disturbs the flora and fauna; the reverse happens if the sea breaks through the dykes.

It was not until the Middle Ages that the marshes were settled by Cistercians and Templars. Salt was harvested as a commodity,

as it still is in vast quantities today. With the decline of religious establishments in the 16th century, the Camargue passed into the hands of cattle-and horse-raising *gardians*, descendants of whom, dressed in black hats, high leather boots and velvet jackets, still herd small black fighting bulls on horseback. The area is dotted with white, thatched *gardian's* cabins, with one semicircular end, set against the Mistral.

In 1970 85,000 hectares (210,000 acres) of the Camargue, including **Stes-Maries-de-la-Mer** (*see p81*), became a regional nature reserve, protecting the area from rapacious developers. The reserve centres on the Etang de Vaccarès, a body of brackish water covering 6,500 hectares (16,000 acres). Numerous companies offer boat trips on the canals; try Tiki III (Le Grau-d'Orgon, 04.90.97.81.68, www.tiki3.fr, closed mid Nov-mid Mar), Aventure en Camargue (Aigues-Mortes, 06.03.91.44.63), and the Isles de Stel barges (Aigues-Mortes, 06.09.47.52.59, www.isles-de-stel.fr).

The **Musée de la Camargue**, in a converted sheep ranch between Arles and Stes-Maries-de-la-Mer, explains the region's history, produce and people, and provides information

From vine…

on nature trails. Further along, by the Etang de Ginès, the **Maison du Parc** gives information on riding and ecology and has a good view of avian antics from upstairs. For a closer brush with birdlife, visit the **Parc Ornithologique de Pont de Gau**, which replenishes stock in its aviaries and gives access to birdwatching trails along the Ginès lagoon.

The 20-kilometre (12.5-mile) walk from Stes-Maries-de-la-Mer to the salt-processing town of **Salin-de-Giraud** along the dyke, built in 1857 to protect the wetlands from the sea, allows extensive views across the reserve. The dyke is off limits to cars, though mountain bikes are tolerated. If you don't wish to part with your vehicle, various points on the D37 and C134 roads allow glimpses of herring gulls and blackheaded gulls, herons, avocets and egrets as well as the slender-billed gull and the red-crested pochard, which breed nowhere else in France. Perhaps, most impressive of all, though, are the 20,000 flamingos that roost on the Vaccarès lagoon, filtering plankton through big, hooked beaks.

East of the Etang de Vaccarès, the hamlet of **Le Sambuc** is home to the **Musée du Riz**, dedicated to the vital role played by rice in the agriculture of the Camargue: not only is it an important cash crop, but it also absorbs the salt in the soil, enabling other cereals to grow. For solitude strike out along the sea wall walk at the Pointe de Beauduc or the vast empty beach of Piémanson at the mouth of the Grand Rhône.

Across the salt lagoons, west of Arles, **St-Gilles-du-Gard** was an important medieval port forced to turn to agriculture when the sea receded. The village is dominated by its 12th-century abbey church, founded by Cistercian monks as a rest stop on the pilgrimage route to Compostela. All that remains of the original

Romanesque building after Huguenot forces wreaked havoc during the Wars of Religion is the façade and the rib vaulting of the crypt; the rebuilt 17th-century version was half the size, but the elaborate carving on the three portals rivals that of St-Trophime in Arles, and is well worth a visit. Opposite the Maison Romane is a superb 12th-century house, now home to the medieval sculpture and local memorabilia of the **Musée de St-Gilles**. St-Gilles market is held on Thursdays and Saturdays.

Maison du parc naturel & regional de la Camargue

Pont de Gau, rte d'Arles, Stes-Maries-de-la-Mer (04.90.97.86.32). **Open** *Apr-Sept* 10am-6pm daily. *Oct-Mar* 9.30am-5pm Mon-Thur, Sat, Sun. **Admission** free.

Musée de la Camargue

Mas du Pont de Rousty, D570 (04.90.97.10.82). **Open** *Apr-Sept* 9am-6pm daily (from 10am July & Aug). *Oct-Mar* 10am-5pm Mon, Wed-Sun. **Admission** €5; €2.50 10-18s; free under-10s. **Credit** AmEx, MC, V.

Musée de St-Gilles

Musée de la maison Romane, St-Gilles-du-Gard (04.66.87.40.42). **Open** 10am-5.30pm Mon-Sat. Closed Jan. **Admission** €6.50; €4 children. **No credit cards**.

Musée du Riz

Rte de Salin-de-Giraud, Le Sambuc (04.90.97.29.44). **Open** 10am-5.30pm daily. Closed Sun (Dec-Mar). **Admission** €3.50; free under-12s. **No credit cards**.

Parc Ornithologique de Pont de Gau

Rte d'Arles, 4km (2.5 miles) from Stes-Maries-de-la-Mer (04.90.97.82.62/www.parcornithologique.com). **Open** *Apr-Sept* 9am-sunset daily. *Oct-Mar* 10am-sunset daily. **Admission** €6.50; €4 4-10s; free under-4s. **No credit cards**.

...to wine: **Aigues-Mortes**. *See p82.*

Where to stay & eat

Just outside Stes-Maries-de-la-Mer begins a long succession of ranch-style hotels, all of which organise horse riding or 4WD trips. Pride of place goes to the luxurious **Mas de la Fouque** (rte du Bac du Sauvage, 04.90.97.81.02, www.masdelafouque.com, double €180-€290), whose big, stylish rooms have wooden balconies overlooking a lagoon. The boss cooks a mean leg of local lamb to enjoy after a swim in the large pool. **Mangio Fango** (rte d'Arles, 04.90.97.80.56, www.hotelmangiofango.com, closed Jan, double €75-€110) is a friendly hotel with a luxurious garden, pool, large rooms and a restaurant, which offers an outstanding half-board deal in summer (€165-€200). **Le Pont des Bannes** (rte d'Arles 04.90.97.81.09, www. pontdesbannes.com, double €163) is a converted hunting lodge with a certain rustic chic, while **Le Mas du Tadorne** (chemin Bas des Launes, 04.90.97.93.11, www.masdutadorne.camargue.fr, double €135-€180) has a pool and horse riding. The restaurant at **Hostellerie du Pont de Gau** (rte d'Arles, north-west of Stes-Maries-de-la-Mer, 04.90.97.81.53, closed Wed mid Nov-Easter, closed Jan-mid Feb, menus €19-€50) offers serious traditional cooking and good service. The **Lou Mas Dou Juge** (rte du Bac du Sauvage, Pin Fourcal, 04.66.73.51.45, double €77-€92) is a *chambres d'hôte* with seven rooms in a working farm on the Petit Rhône. East of Etang de Vaccarès, **Le Mas de Peint** (Le Sambuc, 04.90.97.20.62, closed mid Nov-mid Dec, mid Jan-mid Mar, double €205-€265, restaurant closed Wed, menus €37-€49) is the last word in Camargue style: stone floors, linen sheets, beams and log fires presided over by an owner happy to show you his bulls and let you ride his horses (€40/2hrs). Hip restaurant of the moment is **La Chassagnette** (rte de Sambuc, 04.90.97.26.96, closed Tue & Wed, menus €37-€60). Sometimes the beauty of the concept is everything: a minimalist menu, listing starters, meat or fish, cheese and pudding, may sound like any French transport café, but here food is served in a sleekly modernised barn and you can wander the organic kitchen garden as you sip aperitifs. The talented chef provides a huge country feed, at a substantial price. Dedicated cowboys can book self-catering *gardian* cabins (details from Stes-Maries-de-la-Mer tourist office, *see p82*). In St-Gilles, **Le Cours** (10 av François Griffeuille, 04.66.87.31.93, www.hotel-le-cours.com, closed mid Dec-mid Mar, double €46-€66) is a friendly and simple Logis de France; its restaurant, serving honest country food (menus €10-€28), is a local favourite.

Resources

Tourist information

St-Gilles *Office de Tourisme, 1 pl Frédéric Mistral, 1380 St-Gilles-du-Gard (04.66.87.33.75/www.ot-saint-gilles.fr).* **Open** 9am-noon, 1.30-5.30pm Mon-Fri; 9am-noon Sat.

Stes-Maries-de-la-Mer

Each May gypsies from all over Europe and the Middle East converge on Stes-Maries-de-la-Mer for an exuberant three-day pilgrimage, with flamenco, horse races and bullfights. Soon after the death of Christ, the legend goes, Mary Magdalene and assorted companions fled from Palestine by sea and washed up on the shores of Provence (*see also p14* **Crossing the holy sea**), where they were met by Black Sarah the gypsy (who may, according to another version, have travelled from the Holy Land with Mary as her maid). The local populace converted en masse and Sarah was adopted by the gypsies as their patron saint. The Church came up with some convenient relics in 1448: three sets of bones that may indeed be from first-century Middle Eastern women. The vast, fortified 12th-century church still dominates the present town, its crypt hot with hundreds of candles burning around an effigy of Black Sarah. But Stes-Maries is primarily a seaside resort, with a long sandy beach, cheap cafés and far too many shops selling provençal cowboy shirts. There's a market on Monday and Friday mornings. The low-rise hacienda-style second homes and seaside tat won't encourage you to linger, but head off down the road that follows the *plage est* (€3 in a car). The further you go the fewer tourists you see and the impressive salt marshes and vast deserted beaches provide the real Camargue. The **Musée Baroncelli** has exhibits on bullfighting and other traditions, plus the odd stuffed flamingo donated by the Marquis Folco de Baroncelli, a 19th-century aristocrat who became a Camargue cowboy.

Musée Baroncelli

rue Victor Hugo (04.90.97.87.60). **Open** varies; phone to check. Closed mid Nov-Apr. **Admission** €2; €1.30 6-12s; free under-6s. **No credit cards**.

Where to eat & stay

For a seaside-resort atmosphere but no culinary sophistication head for the **Brasserie de la Plage** (1 av de la République, 04.90.97.84.77, average €20). The **Brûleur de Loups** (67 av Gilbert Leroy, 04.90.97.83.31, closed Tue dinner, Wed & mid Nov-Dec, menus €19-€38.50) has a sea view and above-average regional specialities. Those taking the long dune walk towards Beauduc are rewarded by simple but excellent beach-hut fish restaurants. Accommodation in Stes-Maries isn't very tempting, but on the edge of town the **Hotel des Rièges** (rte de Cacharel, 04.90.97.85.07, www.hoteldesrieges.com, double €62-€75) is a typical Camargue-style ranch.

Resources

Tourist information

Office de Tourisme, 5 av Van Gogh, 13700 Stes Maries-de-la-Mer (04.90.97.82.55/www.saintes maries.com). **Open** *Apr-June, Sept* 9am-7pm daily. *July, Aug* 9am-8pm daily. *Oct* 9am-6pm daily. *Nov-Feb* 9am-5pm daily.

Aigues-Mortes

On the western edge of the Camargue, the medieval walled city of Aigues-Mortes (from the Latin 'dead waters') rises up from gloomy salt marshes and acres given over to cultivation of Listel Gris wine. This would be nobody's first choice for urban development, but Louis IX wanted to set out on a crusade from his own port rather than using the then provençal Marseille. Realising take-up for his new town would be low, he offered generous tax and trade incentives. During the Hundred Years War the Burgundians seized the town, only to have it snatched back by the Armagnacs, who, after slaughtering their enemies, stored the salted corpses in the Tour de Bourguignons. Receding sea and silting-up of the canals led to the town's decline in the 15th century. The monumental ramparts, punctuated by massive towers, make for a great walk. The most spectacular tower is the **Tour de Constance**. Built 1240-9, and containing a small chapel, it doubled as cells for political or religious prisoners. Once within the ramparts, the town has more than its share of tacky souvenir shops and despite the odd art gallery in summer the tiny centre becomes overrun with day-trippers. Eglise Notre-Dame-de-Sablons has suffered from too many refits, but its wood-framed nave has an austere charm. The Chapelle des Pénitents Blancs and Chapelle des Pénitents Gris are interesting baroque buildings that would benefit from regular openings – ask about access to the churches at the tourist office (*see p83*). Place St-Louis, the main square, is a lively hub, with exhibitions in the town hall in summer. The market takes place on Wednesday and Sunday mornings.

You can also visit the **Caves de Listel** to swig some of the flinty rosé or learn all about salt production at the **Salins du Midi**. North-east of Aigues-Mortes, the **Château de Teillan** was the former priory of the Abbaye de Psalmody, which sold the land for Aigues-Mortes to Louis IX; later additions include a Renaissance façade and 18th-century orangery.

Urban development of the contemporary kind has expanded the ports of Le Grau-du-Roi and Port Camargue into unappealing resorts; the quay of seafood restaurants at Le Grau-du-Roi does have a certain cheap and cheerful charm.

Caves de Listel

Domaine de Jarras (04.66.51.17.00/www.listel.fr). **Open** *Apr-Sept* 10am-6pm daily. *Oct-Mar* 10am-noon, 2-5pm Mon-Fri. **Admissions** €3; free under-15s. **Credit** MC, V.

Château de Teillan

Aimargues (04.66.88.02.38). **Open** *Mid June-mid Sept* 2-6pm Tue-Sun. **Admission** €4. *Park only* €3; €2.50 12-15s; free under-12s.

Salins du Midi

04.66.51.17.10/www.salins.com. **Open** 9am-6pm daily. Closed Nov-Feb. **Admission** €6.80; €5 4-12s; free under-4s.

The mane drag

What strikes you most as you enter the Camargue is the sheer number of ranches that line the sides of the roads, all of them proposing all manner of horseback outings. And there is, of course, nothing like choice to confuse the eager punter, so head to the Office de Tourisme de Stes-Maries-de-la-Mer (5 av Van Gogh, 04.90.97.82.55, www. saintesmariesdelamer.com), which can separate the trusty professionals (*see below*) from more unscrupulous operators.

If you're a beginner, head to the outstandingly helpful **Les Chevaux du Vent** (rte d'Arles, 06.09.50.42.36), a government-approved riding school, which takes its role seriously. Even an hour on a white horse in the relative cool of the evening is a more enjoyable experience when you are not being bounced along like a sack of potatoes, and the view across the Camargue is magical with pink flamingos and assorted bird life, glimpses of grazing horses and a cautious sighting of distant bulls. Part of the appeal of riding is the extra height a horse gives you, allowing panoramic views across the salt marshes, which from a car can seem bleak and uniform. The white horses seem quiet and immune to tourist chatter and incompetent riding, but look as handsome as on the postcards.

If you've got some experience, it's better to opt for one of the longer trips, especially in a slightly cooler season. Exciting possibilities include a whole-day hack, which allows you to cross the ponds and paddy fields of the Camargue, cross the Petit Rhône by ferry, and pause for a lunchtime picnic on the beach of the Grand Radeau. For the real Western fantasy you can head off across the plains for several days, staying in authentic *cabanes*, traditional small whitewashed cottages.

Based at Stes-Maries-de-la-Mer, the following centres all cater for both beginners and experienced riders: **Brenda-Centre de Tourisme Equestre** (Mas St-Georges, Astouin, 04.90.97.52.08, www.brendatourisme equestre.com); **Cabanes de Cacharel** (Hôtel Mas des Aliscornes, rte d'Arles, 04.90.97.83.41, www.camargueacheval. com); **Promenades à Cheval du Pont de Gau** (rte d'Arles (04.90.97.89.45, www.pontde gau.com). Expect to pay €28-€30 for two hours, €80-€110 for a day (includes lunch).

Tour de Constance & Ramparts

Logis du Gouverneur, pl Anatole France (04.66.53.61.55). **Open** *June-Aug* 10am-7pm daily. *Sept-Oct* 10am-6pm daily. *Nov-May* 10am-5.30pm daily. **Admission** €6.10; €4.10 18-25s; free under-18s. **Credit** MC, V.

Where to stay & eat

The restaurants on the main square are fun for an aperitif, but locals prefer the frantic bistro **Coco** (19 rue Jean Jaurès, 04.66.53.91.83, menu €12). The most entertaining restaurant within the walls is **Le Café de Bouzigues** (7 rue Pasteur, 04.66.53.93.95, menus €13-€27.50) with a delightfully grungy courtyard and modern regional cooking. **Hôtel Les Templiers** (23 rue de la République, 04.66.53.66.56, double €100-€130) has been restored with distressed elegance, but a more old-fashioned atmosphere reigns at **Hôtel-Restaurant St-Louis** (10 rue Amiral Courbet, 04.66.53.72.68, www.lesaint louis.fr, closed late Nov-mid Mar, double €62-€102). Another attractive option is **Hôtel Les Arcades** (23 bd Gambetta, 04.66.53.81.13, www.les-arcades.fr, double €92-€110). Just outside the walls, **Hôtel Tour de Constance**

(1 bd Diderot, 04.66.53.83.50, closed mid Nov-Feb, double €37-€60) is a clean and practical budget choice, while newcomer **Hôtel Canal** (440 rte de Nîmes, 04.66.80.50.04, www.hotelcanal.fr, double €44-€110) on the way into town is struggling to bring a bit of high-tech to Aigues-Mortes.

Resources

Tourist information

Office de Tourisme, pl St-Louis, 30220 Aigues-Mortes (04.66.53.73.00/www.ot-aiguesmortes.fr). **Open** *June-Sept* 9am-6pm daily. *Oct-May* 9am-noon, 1-6pm Mon-Fri; 10am-noon, 2-6pm Sat, Sun.

Getting there

By car

Leave the A54 at exit 4 and take the D570 to Stes-Maries-de-la-Mer. For Aigues-Mortes take the D570 from Arles or Stes-Maries and then the D58.

By train/bus

The nearest SNCF station is Arles from which several buses a day run to Stes-Maries-de-la-Mer. From the TGV station in Nîmes, you can get to Aigues-Mortes by train or by bus with **STDG** (04.66.29.27.29).

Avignon &
the Vaucluse

Features

Maps

Introduction

Discover Avignon, city of the arts, and the rugged beauty of the country beyond.

The land-locked Vaucluse may not be named after a river (as is the case with most French *départements*), but it does derive its name from a water source: the *val clausa* or closed valley, where water bubbles out of a deep pool at **Fontaine de Vaucluse**. Taking in Avignon and the hilly lands spreading north and east of the Rhône, the area was strongly marked both by the Avignon papacy, which injected the Papal court as a centre of scholarship and artistic production in the 14th century, and by the Wars of Religion that set village against village. Until 1793, **Avignon** remained part of a prosperous independent enclave, known as the Comtat Venaissin, also taking in Cavaillon, Carpentras, Fontaine de Vaucluse and L'Isle-sur-la-Sorgue. This period left not only the majestic Palais des Papes, worthwhile museums and cardinals' palaces of Avignon, but also a Jewish heritage unique in France, with beautiful synagogues at **Carpentras** and **Cavaillon**, and unsuspected industrial relics that include paper mills and ochre-processing.

Today, though, the **Luberon** is at the forefront of the new rural chic. Lovely scenery, attractive villages that have stayed largely within their historic limits, imposing châteaux, remote abbeys and plenty of old farmhouses ripe for conversion are combined with the worldly social gloss of villages like **Gordes** or **Lourmarin**, all within easy reach of a cultural fix in Avignon or Aix. The less-known lower-key, truffle-packed **Drôme Provençale** (the southern part of the Drôme *département*) is strongly tipped to follow. On the eastern edge of the Luberon, in the sparsely populated Alpes de Haute-Provence *département*, **Forcalquier** has more provincial feel with traces of a once-powerful past as an independent Comté while, north of Avignon, **Orange** and **Vaison-la-Romaine** offer impressive Roman remans and some of the best southern Côtes du Rhône wines, notably **Châteauneuf-du-Pape**.

The Luberon massif, the distinctively ragged **Dentelles de Montmirail**, the **Baronnies** and the astonishingly bleak **Mont Ventoux** all offer plentiful opportunities for walking, riding, cycling and rock-climbing. This range of activities gives the region a healthy and outdoorsy feel, yet it doesn't seem too wild – after all you're never far from a vineyard or a sophisticated restaurant.

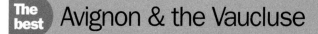

The best Avignon & the Vaucluse

Things to do

Well, there's the annual **Festival d'Avignon** (*see p44*), of course, when the city swells with an influx of performers (and spectators) from all corners of the globe. More natural delights can be found in the incredible ochre landscape of **Colorado de Rustrel** (*see p131*) or in the fascinating workings of the region's olive oil industry, at the **Musée de l'Olivier** in Nyons (*see p118*).

Places to stay

The **Hôtel de la Mirande** (*see p101*) in Avignon offers some of the area's loveliest accommodation, while **Château des Fines Roches** (*see p106*) is a 19th-century pile in a vineyard at Châteauneuf-du-Pape. But for the ultimate in provençal luxury ensconce yourself in the beautifully restored **Hostellerie de Crillon-le-Brave** in Mont Ventoux (*see p113*).

Places to eat

The region's top two restaurants are Avignon's **Christian Etienne** (*see p95*) and the **Domaine des Andéols** (*see p130*) in the Luberon. Worth a look, too, are famous **La Mirande** (*see p96*), also in Avignon, and the **Hostellerie de la Fuste** (*see p132*), just outside Manosque.

Nightlife

Avignon's clubs and music venues come alive during the summer festival but venues like **The Red Zone** (*see p97*) and **Le Bokao's** (*see p96*) are lively year-round.

Culture

The **Collection Lambert** (*see p92*), Avignon's modern art treasure trove is a must-see. Classicists may get a kick out of the **Musée Pétrarque** in the Luberon (*see p128*).

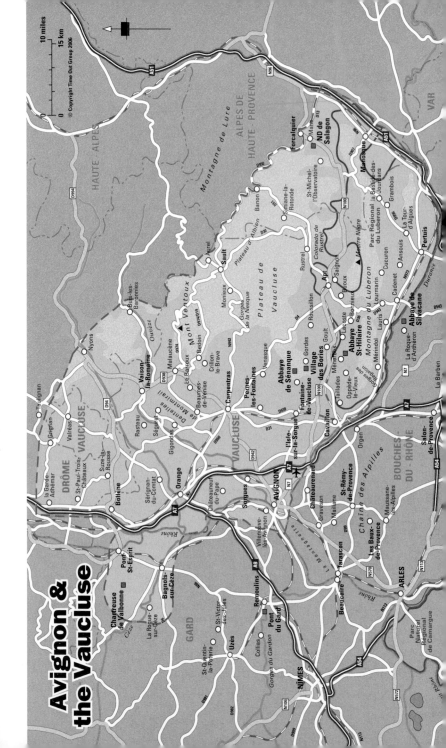

Avignon & the Vaucluse

Avignon

Holy, festive, pretty and occasionally gritty, Avignon bridges social and cultural divides.

If ever Pope Benedict XVI finds life in the Vatican too stressful, then France's own Cité des Papes awaits him. Home to the Papacy for more than a century, Avignon is crowned by the monumental Palais des Papes. His Holiness's peace and quiet may, however, be disturbed by the Festival d'Avignon, when the city becomes France's performing arts capital, attracting visitors from around the world for three weeks of theatre and music, ranging from grand classical productions to the fringe shows that seem to appear on every corner.

Approaching the city along the banks of the Rhône, the Rocher des Doms – with its gleaming virgin on top of the Cathédrale Notre-Dame-des-Doms – makes an imposing sight, along with the four kilometres (2.5 miles) of beautifully preserved ramparts, crenellated in the 19th century by ubiquitous 'improver' Viollet-le-Duc, who sadly filled in the moat. Just outside the ramparts stands the city's other top tourist attraction, the *pont* of nursery-rhyme fame – a bridge on which nobody ever dances, save perhaps a misguided tourist. Only four arches of the original 22 remain, together with a tiny Romanesque chapel, but the 12th-century Pont St-Bénezet still exerts its fascination.

Recently, the city has been restyling itself in response to the theatre crowds and the new arrivals from the TGV station, which suddenly put Avignon within easy reach of Paris. Inside the city walls, skips and scaffolding tell a story of rising house prices and restoration programmes. A surge of new bars, cafés, restaurants, hotels and shops pander to hefty wallets, with students and the thriving gay community leading the way in hip hangouts. It is a common assumption that, once the festival excitement dies down, Avignon reverts to being a cultural backwater. But compared with other places in France of a similar size the city does reasonably well: there are a few year-round theatres, a non-commercial cinema and a certain child-of-the-'60s atmosphere, with healing crystals and joss sticks still at the cutting edge.

Beyond the ramparts, Avignon tells a different story of poverty in some of the most deprived suburbs in France. Indeed it is this contrast of glamour and poverty that characterises the town, a place where designer chic rubs shoulders with urban dissatisfaction.

HISTORY

Avignon started life as a Neolithic settlement on the Rocher des Doms. Under the Romans, it flourished as a river port, but it was not until the 12th century, when Avignon's clergy became a power to be reckoned with, that the village started to think big, building towers, the Romanesque cathedral and St-Bénezet bridge.

In 1306 French pope Clément V brought his court from turbulent Rome to the safety of the independent, Vatican-owned Comtat Venaissin. After his death in 1314 six further French popes saw no reason to relocate to Rome. Their 68-year 'Babylonian captivity', as furious Italians branded it, utterly transformed the quiet provincial backwater. The population soared, and artists, scholars, architects, weavers and jewellers flocked to find patronage. The virtue industry fostered vice in equal measure: 'A sewer,' sniffed Petrarch, 'the filthiest of cities.'

Gregory XI, elected in 1370, was badgered by the persuasive St Catherine of Siena into returning to the Holy See. He took her advice, went back, and promptly died in 1378. The Italians elected a Roman pope, but the French were loath to lose their hold on the reins of power and swiftly elected Clement VII in Avignon. The rival popes excommunicated each other, sparking the Great Schism, which finally ended 40 years later when all sides agreed on the election of Martin V in 1417.

Even after the popes returned to Italy, Avignon remained papal territory. Without French censorship, and far enough from Rome to escape Vatican checks, the town flourished as an artistic, religious and publishing centre. This continued when the town was returned to France in 1791: it was to Avignon that the Félibrige (the 19th-century organisation for the promotion of Occitan culture) turned to get its Provençal-revival works into print.

Sightseeing

The terraced gardens of the Rocher des Doms, perched above the Rhône, is where Avignon started, and it's a good place to begin a visit. A miniature vineyard, sloping down the northern side, signals Avignon's role as capital of Côtes du Rhône: an example of every grape variety is represented, with the full gamut harvested during the Ban des Vendanges festival in September. From the Rocher, the view ranges over the whole city – 'its closely knitted roofs of weathered tile like a pie crust fresh from the oven', as Lawrence Durrell wrote – and takes in the Rhône and Villeneuve-lès-Avignon.

Jutting into the river below the Rocher des Doms are the four remaining arches of the **Pont St-Bénezet**. The bridge can be reached by walking along the only section of the city walls open to the public. Between the Dom and the bridge, the **Musée du Petit Palais**, a former

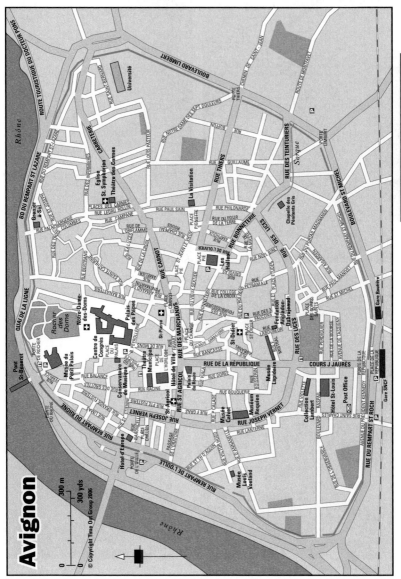

Avignon

Being streetwise in an Avignon style.

cardinal's palace, has a superb collection of early Italian and provençal paintings, and sculptures rescued from Avignon's churches.

The massive bulk of the **Palais des Papes**, more like an ogre's castle than a pontiff's palace, shares its square with **Cathédrale Notre-Dame-des-Doms** and the swagged and furbelowed former Hôtel des Monnaies (mint), now the Conservatoire de Musique. Before entering the Palais, get a sense of its solidity by walking along rue de la Peyrollerie to see its towers, embedded in sheer rock.

A little further south, place de l'Horloge is the centre of town life, with its cafés, **Théâtre Municipal** and grand 19th-century Hôtel de Ville. The square gets its name from the Gothic clock tower, Tour du Jacquemart, although the painted wooden figurines of Jacquemart and his wife have taken retirement from ringing the hour. At festival time the square is home to a whirling carousel of musicians and minstrels.

South of here, rue de la République is Avignon's main shopping thoroughfare. To the west lies the smart part of town, its streets packed with fashionable restaurants and beautifully restored mansions. On rue St-Agricol, the 15th-century carved doorway of Eglise St-Agricol (open for services only, 4-5pm Sat) has been restored, as has the church's 16th-century painting of the Assumption by Avignon artist Simon de Châlons. An alley off rue St-Agricol leads to the 15th-century **Palais du Roure**, where the aristocratic poet Folco Baroncelli was born, and where Frédéric Mistral edited *Aïoli*, his journal in Provençal.

Rue Joseph Vernet, which curves round to join busy rue de la République, is a shopaholic's dream of designer stores and handmade chocolates, set in a parade of 17th- and 18th-century *hôtels particuliers*. Off its northern end, the **Hôtel d'Europe** on rue Baroncelli has long been a favourite with visiting foreign lovers, among them the eloping Brownings and John Stuart Mill and Mrs Harriet Taylor. When Harriet died there, Mill was so distraught that he bought a house overlooking the cemetery where she was buried, furnishing it with the contents of their last hotel room.

Further south, on rue Victor Hugo, the **Musée Louis-Vouland** is a lavishly decorated private house, full of 18th-century French furniture and faïence. Back on rue Joseph Vernet, the **Musée Calvet** displays sculpture and paintings in the elegant colonnaded galleries of an 18th-century palace. In another wing is the **Muséum Requien d'Histoire Naturelle**, an old-fashioned natural history museum. Nearby, another renovated 18th-century *hôtel* contains the cutting-edge contemporary art of the

Collection Lambert. On rue Portail Boquier, check out the mixture of historic and modern at the **Hôtel Cloître St-Louis** (*see p100*), a former monastery. On one side of the cloister, the Espace St-Louis is used for art exhibitions and becomes a box office during the festival.

East of rue de la République, on a spacious paved square, the lovely **Eglise St-Didier** was built in the simple, single-aisled Provençal Gothic style. Around the corner in rue Laboureur is the **Fondation Angladon-Dubrujeaud**, a worthwhile private art museum; the **Musée Lapidaire** collection of ancient sculpture is housed nearby in a former Jesuit chapel. Across rue des Lices, not far from the tourist office, lies shady place des Corps-Saints. Stretched in front of the 14th-century Chapelle de St-Michel et Tous-les-Saints, it becomes a sea of café chairs in summer.

Heading east out of place St-Didier, rue du Roi René has several fine 17th- and 18th-century mansions; at No.22 a plaque records that this was where Italian poet Petrarch in 1327 first set eyes on Laura, the woman he was to idolise for the rest of his life. At the far end, the cobbled, boho rue des Teinturiers is one of Avignon's most atmospheric streets, winding along beside the River Sorgue, where the waterwheels of the dye works that gave the street its name are still visible. Production of the patterned calico known as *indiennes* thrived here until the end of the 19th century. Now the street is home to cafés under spreading plane trees, to second-hand bookshops and to art galleries. At No.8 the Chapelle des Pénitents Gris (open 3.30-5.30pm daily), crouched at the end of a tiny bridge, was founded in the 13th century. The chapel is believed to have witnessed its own mini version of the parting of the Red Sea: during the floods of 1433, the waters are said to have curled back either side of the aisle, allowing the consecrated host to be carried out safe and dry.

The partly pedestrianised streets north of place St-Didier are the heart of the medieval town. Most of this district was surprisingly shabby, dimly lit at night, with empty statue niches and pigeon-daubed churches, but the hand of the restorer has been busy at work. At the Hôtel de Rascas on rue des Fourbisseurs, the corbels of a projecting upper storey point to a cardinal's demands for extra airspace. Place Pie is home to Avignon's covered food market (7am-1pm Tue-Sun), while to the north, in place St-Pierre, the Gothic Eglise St-Pierre (open 2-5pm Thur, 2-6.30pm Fri, Sat) has finely carved walnut doors and a handsome belfry.

The winding streets behind the Palais des Papes lead to rue Banasterie and the Chapelle des Pénitents Noirs (open 2-5pm Sat), which has a sumptuous baroque interior painted to the last inch with gold leaf and cherubs. Round the corner on rue des Escaliers Ste-Anne, the **Utopia** arts cinema is one of Avignon's liveliest cultural centres. Opposite, the Porte de la Ligne gateway emerges beside the Rhône, close to the jetty where you can catch a new, free ferry that nips you across to the grassy Ile de la Barthelasse every 15 minutes in summer. Back inside the walls on the lively place des Carmes, the Eglise St-Symphorien (open 8am-noon daily), originally a Carmelite convent, has a 15th-century Gothic façade and some lovely polychrome wooden statues inside. Its 14th-century cloisters now rub shoulders with one of Avignon's oldest theatre companies, the **Théâtre des Carmes**. This is the university district, packed with bars, cafés and second-hand bookstores. Past the Porte St-Lazare, avenue Stuart Mill leads to **Cimetière St-Véran** (04.90.80.79.95, open 8.30am until dusk daily) where the Mills are both buried.

Cathédrale Notre-Dame-des-Doms

pl du Palais (04.90.82.12.24). **Open** 8am-6pm daily.
Despite its imposing position, this is a surprisingly unspiritual church. Apart from the Romanesque porch and a fine marble throne, most vestiges of its 12th-century origins have been obliterated by subsequent alterations: a baroque gallery, a rebuilt tower and a golden statue of the Virgin perched on its pinnacle. Even the Simone Martini frescoes have been moved to the Palais des Papes.

Collection Lambert

Hôtel de Caumont, 5 rue Violette (04.90.16.56.20). **Open** *Aug-June* 11am-6pm Tue-Sun. *July* 11am-7pm daily. **Admission** €5.50; €4 students, 12-16s; €2 6-12s; free under-6s. **Credit** MC, V.
In 2000 Parisian art dealer Yvon Lambert loaned his formidable contemporary art collection to Avignon for a period of 20 years. Housed in an 18th-century *hôtel particulier*, the 850 pieces, spanning the late 1950s to the present, are interwoven with temporary exhibitions and new commissions. Particularly strong on conceptual and minimalist art, the collection takes in painting, sculpture, installation, video and photography by names such as Nan Goldin, Douglas Gordon, Thomas Hirschhorn, Jean-Michel Basquiat, Cy Twombly and Jonathan Monk. There is a good bookshop and a courtyard café.

Eglise St-Didier

pl St-Didier (04.90.86.20.17). **Open** 8am-6.30pm daily.
This pretty example of Provençal Gothic has delicate 14th-century Italian frescoes in the north chapel. In the Chapelle St-Bénezet are relics of the bridge-building saint himself, or his skull at least.

Fondation Angladon-Dubrujeaud

5 rue Laboureur (04.90.82.29.03/www.angladon. com). **Open** 1-6pm Tue-Sun. **Admission** €6; €4 students; €1.50 7-14s; free under-7s. **No credit cards**.

Arranged like a period home, this 18th-century mansion is decorated with the collection left by 19th-century Paris couturier Jacques Doucet to local artists Jean and Paulette Angladon-Dubrujeaud. In the upper rooms, each painting, piece of furniture and objet d'art has been hung with an eye for the appropriate setting. Dutch oils are complemented by oak chests, armoires and faïence, while 18th-century French portraits occupy a lavish gilt and brocade salon. The celebrity line-up of paintings on the ground floor covers Degas, Picasso, Cézanne, Modigliani and Sisley, as well as boasting the only Van Gogh in Provence.

Musée Calvet

65 rue Joseph Vernet (04.90.86.33.84/www. fondation-calvet.org). **Open** 10am-1pm, 2-6pm Mon, Wed-Sun. **Admission** €6; €3 12-18s; free under-12s. **No credit cards**.
A beautifully restored fine art museum that displays its collection in elegant, colonnaded rooms built around a courtyard. The ground floor has Gobelins tapestries and medieval sculpture, while the 18th- and 19th-century French paintings include works by the Avignon-based Vernet family and David's *La mort de Bara*. There is a good modern section with works by Bonnard, Vuillard, Sisley, Manet and Dufy, and Camille Claudel's head of her brother Paul, who had her sent to a mental asylum near Avignon when her relationship with Rodin became too scandalous.

Musée du Petit Palais

pl du Palais (04.90.86.44.58). **Open** *June-Sept* 10am-1pm, 2-6pm Mon, Wed-Sun. *Oct-May* 9.30am-1pm, 2-5.30pm Mon, Wed-Sun. **Admission** €6; €3 12-18s; free under-12s. **No credit cards**.
First constructed in 1308 for a cardinal, the Petit Palais had its Renaissance façade and decorative tower added in the late 15th century by Cardinal Giuliano della Rovere, the future Pope Julius II. Today the series of atmospheric rooms, with original stone fireplaces and trompe-l'oeil ceilings, house magnificent medieval paintings, frescoes and sculptures, many rescued from churches destroyed in the Revolution. Note the sarcophagus of Cardinal Jean de Lagrange, with its anatomically realistic depiction of a decaying corpse, and his brutally mutilated tomb effigy. The bulk of the paintings were assembled by Gian Pietro Campana di Cavelli, a 19th-century Italian collector who went bankrupt, allowing Napoleon III to snap up his entire estate. It provides a fine introduction to the International Gothic style brought to Avignon by the mostly Sienese artists patronised by the popes, and clung to a long time after it had gone out of fashion everywhere else in Europe.

Musée Lapidaire

27 rue de la République (04.90.85.75.38/www. fondation-calvet.org). **Open** 10am-1pm, 2-6pm Mon, Wed-Sun. **Admission** €2; €1 12-18s; free under-12s. **No credit cards**.

Avignon's archaeological collection is superbly displayed in this 17th-century Jesuit chapel. As well as Greek, Gallo-Roman and Etruscan sculpture, mosaics and glass, it is rich in Egyptian sculpture, stelae and shabtis. The Gallo-Roman selection has a depiction of the Tarasque of Noves, the local man-eating monster.

Musée Louis Vouland

17 rue Victor Hugo (04.90.86.03.79/www. vouland.com). **Open** *May-Oct* 10am-noon, 2-6pm Tue-Sat; 2-6pm Sun. *Nov-Apr* 2-6pm Tue-Sun. **Admission** €4; €2.50 12-18s; free under-12s. **No credit cards**.

A 19th-century *hôtel particulier* with trompe-l'oeil ceilings houses the largely 18th-century decorative arts collection of former resident Louis Vouland. A preserved-meat salesman, Vouland spent 50 years acquiring furniture and porcelain, including faïence from Les Moustiers, Montpellier and Marseille, Ming porcelain and intricate inlaid writing desks. Among the 19th-century paintings from the Avignon School that are on display here are works by Claude Firmin and Pierre Grivolas.

Muséum Requien d'Histoire Naturelle

67 rue Joseph Vernet (04.90.82.43.51). **Open** 9am-noon, 2-6pm Tue-Sat. **Admission** free.

An old-fashioned natural history collection, the Muséum Requien is packed with rocks, minerals, stuffed animals and fossils. Buried in the archives is John Stuart Mill's collection of dried flowers and herbs, while temporary exhibitions hold the magnifying glass up to regional themes such as local insects or mushrooms.

Palais des Papes

pl du Palais (04.90.27.50.73/www.palais-des-papes. com). **Open** *Apr-Oct* 9am-7pm (9pm during festival) daily. *Nov-Mar* 9.30am-5.45pm daily. **Admission** *Apr-Oct* €9.50; €7.50 students, 8-17s; free under-8s. *Nov-Mar* €7.50; €6 students, 8-17s; free under-8s. **Credit** MC, V.

More a fortress than the palace of God's representative on earth, the Palais des Papes is a brutal power statement. The interior is strangely empty after the devastation wreaked during the Revolution, when 60 pro-papal prisoners were flung into the Tour des Latrines. During the palace's subsequent use as a prison and barracks soldiers chipped off bits of fresco to sell, but many exquisite fragments remain. The Palais is a complicated labyrinth with two interlocking parts: the forbidding Palais Vieux, built in the 1330s for the austere Cistercian monk Pope Benedict XII, and the more showy Palais Neuf, tacked on a decade later by Clement VI. You can wander at will (an audio guide is included in the entry fee) or join a guided tour (some are in English). Across the main courtyard from the ticket office is the Salle de Jésus, the antechamber of the papal council room or Consistoire, where frescoes from the cathedral are displayed. The Chapelle St-Jean next door has delightful frescoes (c1346) by Matteo Giovanetti, Clement VI's court painter. Upstairs, the ceiling of the Grand Tinel banqueting hall was once coloured blue and dotted with gold stars to resemble the sky. Next door the kitchens, with their huge pyramid-shaped chimney, could feed 3,000 guests. There are more Giovanetti frescoes, lavish with lapis lazuli and gold, in the Chapelle St-Martial. Beyond the Salle de

Eglise St-Didier. *See p92.*

The **Palais des Papes**. *See p93.*

Parement (robing room), Benedict XII's tiled study was only discovered in 1963. The papal bedchamber is followed by the Chambre du Cerf, Clement VI's study, where some delightful frescoes exude the spirit of courtly love. Vast as it is, the Chapelle Clémentine, which you come to next, was barely large enough to hold the college of cardinals when it gathered in conclave to elect a new pope. Through the Chamberlain's Room, whose raised stone slabs mark the spot where papal treasure was discovered, stairs lead up to the battlements, with a dramatic view over the city. Back on the ground floor, the Grande Audience hall has a bevy of biblical prophets frescoed by Giovanetti. The palace's empty spaces are put to good use with occasional art exhibitions, and the Cour d'Honneur is a key venue for festival productions. At weekends, a 'backstage' tour, Palais Secret (€30, including provençal brunch and wine tasting) reveals unrestored rooms, terraces and gardens usually unseen by the public, including the steam rooms, storerooms and the garden of Benoit XII. On your way out, stock up on rather expensive Côtes du Rhône at La Bouteillerie, former wine cellar to the papal banquets.

Palais du Roure

3 rue Collège du Roure (04.90.80.80.88). **Open** *Guided tour* 3pm Tue or by appointment. *Library* 9am-noon, 2-5.30pm Mon-Fri. **Admission** €4.60; €2.30 students. **No credit cards.**

The birthplace of Marquis Folco de Baroncelli-Javon, protector of the Camarguais *gardians* and promoter of the Course Camarguaise *(see p60* **Feeling bullish**)*, who devoted his life to writing poetry, breeding bulls and preserving Camarguais traditions, has a charming courtyard with fragments of frescoes and a splendid carved doorway. It is now a literary archive and library, and headquarters of the Festival Provençal (an autumn festival of theatre and music in the Provençal language; for details, contact the tourist office, *see p101*).

Pont St-Bénezet

rue Ferruce (04.90.27.51.16/www.palais-des-papes.com). **Open** *Oct-mid Mar* 9.30am-5.45pm daily. *Mid Mar-Apr* 9.30am-6.30pm daily. *Apr-July* 9am-7pm (9pm during festival) daily. *Aug-Sept* 9am-8pm daily. **Admission** *Mid Mar-Oct* €4; €3.30 students; €3 children. *Nov-mid Mar* €3.50; €3 students; €2 children. **Credit** MC, V.

The original *pont d'Avignon* was begun in 1185 by a divinely inspired shepherd boy from the Ardèche who later became St Bénezet. He lifted the first massive stone, convincing the sceptical populace that construction was possible. When completed, the bridge was 22 arches and nearly a kilometre (half a mile) long, and contributed greatly to the development of Avignon, although in 1660, after a huge flood, the avignonnais finally gave up the unequal maintenance struggle. Today, only four arches and a tiny Romanesque fisherman's chapel remain; a small museum in the reception area explains the history. Despite the song, it seems unlikely that anyone ever danced on the narrow, traffic-packed structure. It is more likely that people danced *'sous le pont'* (under the bridge): the Ile de la Barthelasse, which the bridge used to cross, was a favourite R&R spot during the Middle Ages.

Where to eat & drink

Avignon is not lacking in designer restaurants for well-heeled festival-goers, but it also has a fair number of pseudo-provençal offerings; the latter are very variable, doubtless encouraged by those who just too hungry to be discerning after a day of hitting the cultural high spots. The famous place de l'Horloge is lined with indifferent brasseries where it is best to enjoy a glass of wine and people-watch before heading off elsewhere to dine.

Le Café de la Comédie

15 pl Crillon (04.90.85.74.85). **Open** 7am-1am (7am-3am during festival) Mon-Sat. Closed Aug & 1wk Feb. **Credit** DC, MC, V.

In a calm, spacious square that's liberally dotted with restaurants, Café de la Comédie attracts a clientele of folks in their late twenties. Huddle under a plane tree and gaze upon the Renaissance façade of Avignon's first theatre.

Le Café Vert

20 rue St-Etienne (04.90.85.27.56). **Open** 12.30-2.30pm, 7-11.30pm Tue-Sat. **Menus** from €19.50. **Credit** MC, V.

This smartly turned-out little minimalist bistro offers a successful combination of North African and French cuisine. Choose an excellent tagine or a perfectly timed tuna steak, followed by superb chocolate marquise cooked in a bain-marie, presented with care and served with charm.

Le Caveau du Théâtre

16 rue des Trois Faucons (04.90.82.60.91). **Open** noon-2pm, 7-10pm Mon-Fri; 7-10.30pm Sat. **Menus** €15-€19. **Credit** MC, V.

With its background jazz, Le Caveau is a friendly bistro. It looks like a wine cellar in one room and the backstage area of a theatre in the other, plus there's a busy pavement terrace for alfresco dining. Theatre-going couples come here for good-value dishes such as pork filet mignon in garlic and honey sauce, and lemon purée with verbena coulis.

Caves Breysse

41 rue des Teinturiers (04.32.74.25.86). **Open** noon-2.30pm, 6-10.30pm Mon-Sat. Closed Aug. **Credit** MC, V.

A relaxed wine bar on the trendy rue des Teinturiers, Caves Breysse invites you to explore the wines of the region (by the glass), while sitting opposite the old watermills that line the street. As well as an excellent pit stop for a plat du jour at lunch, this is also an ideal place for an early-evening aperitif and indulging in the typically provençal pastime of people-watching.

Christian Etienne

10 rue de Mons (04.90.86.16.50/www. christian-etienne.fr). **Open** noon-2pm, 7-9.30pm Tue-Sat. **Menus** €30-€105. **Credit** AmEx, DC, MC, V.

Apart from the eateries in the city's top hotels, Christian Etienne offers Avignon's only high-flying gastronomic restaurant. The sophisticated cuisine with changing seasonal menus lives up to a fabulous setting in the shadow of the Palais des Papes. There's even an affordable lunch menu that makes the treat accessible to a wide public.

Le Cid Café

11 pl de l'Horloge (04.90.82.30.38/www.lecidcafe. com). **Open** 7am-1am daily. **Credit** MC, V.

Avignon's most popular gay bar is not hidden away down some forlorn backstreet. It is instead proudly located on the place de l'Horloge. The laid-back crowd is pleasantly mixed by day, gay by night, when there are DJs playing to different themes: disco on Monday, Latino music on Wednesday, house at weekends. All in all, Le Cid is a good place to begin checking out the city's club scene.

La Compagnie des Comptoirs

83 rue Joseph Vernet (04.90.85.99.04/www.la compagniedescomptoirs.com). **Open** noon-2pm, 7.30-11pm Tue-Sat; noon-2pm Sun. **Average** €50. **Credit** AmEx, V.

The celebrated Pourcel twins are from Montpellier, but they've done a mighty fine job of awakening Avignon to the ways of hip, urban, concept dining. The courtyard setting is spectacular in the summer, and the East-meets-West fusion cookery makes an exciting change from the provençal norm. The lounge bar has good cocktails and late-night DJs, its clientele decamping in summer to the designer 'souk' under the arches of the cloister.

L'Entrée des Artistes

1 pl des Carmes (04.90.82.46.90). **Open** noon-2pm, 7.30-10.30pm Mon-Fri. **Menus** €20-€25. **Credit** V.

On the picturesque place des Carmes in the student area of town, this great bistro offers simple but well-prepared dishes that use good, fresh ingredients, adding just the occasional modern flourish to keep the happy diners on their toes.

L'Epicerie

10 pl St-Pierre (04.90.82.74.22). **Open** 12.30-2.30pm, 7-10pm Mon-Sat. Closed Nov-Mar. **Average** €25. **Credit** MC, V.

L'Epicerie is set on one of the prettiest squares in town, in front of the magnificent 16th-century doors of the Eglise St-Pierre. It is a relaxed bistro that attracts crowds of locals and tourists with a nicely executed and typically Mediterranean menu.

La Fourchette

17 rue Racine (04.90.85.20.93). **Open** 12.15-1.45pm, 7.15-9.45pm Mon-Fri. **Menu** €29. **Credit** MC, V.

Booking well ahead is essential if you want to sample the excellent cuisine at La Fourchette, which is by far the best mid-range restaurant in town. The menu combines classic dishes with lighter, more modern combinations such as the delicious warm foie gras mould. The decor pays tribute to the utility of the fork in myriad forms.

Le Grand Café

*La Manutention, 4 rue des Escaliers Ste-Anne
(04.90.86.86.77).* **Open** noon-midnight Tue-Sat.
Menus €16.50-€30. **Credit** AmEx, DC, MC, V.
Avignon dining gets a contemporary makeover in
this converted army supplies depot next to the
Utopia cinema. The menu reads like a glossary of
modern European cooking and is as various as the
boho punters who congregate here, eager to discuss
the latest art-house movie release.

Hiely Lucullus

*5 rue de la République (04.90.86.17.07/www.hiely.
net).* **Open** noon-2pm, 7-10pm daily. **Menus** €19.50-
€45. **Credit** MC, V.
This first-floor restaurant on Avignon's main street
is where the buttoned-up bourgeoisie of the town
head for a traditional feast. Don't expect a lively
crowd or cutting-edge cuisine, but a quality feed has
been assured for generations.

La Mirande

*4 pl de la Mirande (04.90.85.93.93/www.la-mirande.
fr).* **Open** 12.30-2pm, 7.30-10pm Mon, Thur-Sun.
Closed Jan. **Menus** €35-€105. **Credit** AmEx,
DC, MC, V.
Under chef Sébastien Aminot, the restaurant of the
Hôtel de la Mirande (*see p101*) is still fit for a king,
offering foie gras, truffles and such provençal
delicacies as pigeon with black olives. There are
also sophisticated puddings from new pastry chef
Olivier Lemauviot, whose cakes enhance afternoon
tea. Eat in the rose garden or in the 15th-century
dining room. Tuesday and Wednesday nights see
an informal table d'hôte (€85) in the historic surroundings of the hotel's old kitchens, where cookery
courses are also held by guest chefs.

Numéro 75

75 rue Guillaume Puy (04.90.27.16.00). **Open**
noon-2.15pm, 8-10pm Mon-Sat. **Menus** €20-€30.
Credit MC, V.
A stylishly converted former *hôtel particulier* of the
Pernod family, Numéro 75 has a lush walled garden.
Wealthy young lovers and families crunch over the
gravel to try pork tagine, gambas a la plancha and
other Mediterranean flavours.

L'Opéra Café

24 pl de l'Horloge (04.90.86.17.43). **Open** 9am-
1am daily. **Menus** €13-€32. **Credit** DC, MC, V.
Undoubtedly the most glamorous café on the place
de l'Horloge, which isn't saying too much, this essay
in modern city chic is still devoid of local atmosphere. The food, too, is more pose than passion, yet
L'Opéra remains the place to be seen.

Simple Simon Tea Lunch

26 rue Petite Fusterie (04.90.86.62.70). **Open**
noon-7pm Mon-Sat. Closed Aug. **Average** €15.
Credit MC, V.
If any *rosbifs* have a touch of *mal du pays* this slice
of Britain, complete with beams, English china and
swirly carpets, should quickly cure the problem. The

spotlit cake table is piled with shortbread and
scones, while savoury staples like fish pie and Irish
stew are guaranteed to strike fear into the hearts of
the passing French.

Le Vernet

*58 rue Joseph Vernet (04.90.85.98.14/www.levernet.
fr).* **Open** noon-2pm, 7pm-midnight daily. **Menus**
€20-€30. **Credit** AmEx, MC, V.
Set in the lovely leafy garden of a *hôtel particulier*
on the fashionable street after which the place is
named, the Vernet is a hip spot for the yuppie crowd.
The short menu features good modern cooking; the
charming boss sources his food and wine with care.

Woolloomooloo

*16bis rue des Teinturiers (04.90.85.28.44/www.
woolloo.com).* **Open** 11.45am-2.10pm, 7.30-10.30pm
(11pm in summer) daily. **Menus** €13-€29.
Credit MC, V.
This funky HQ of Avignon's arty crowd perma-
nently buzzes with brooding students and neophyte
playwrights. They fuel their creativity with 'world
food' that sounds rather more daring on the menu
than the reasonably priced and fairly bland comfort
food that arrives.

Nightlife

Le Bokao's

9bis quai St-Lazare (04.90.82.47.95). **Open** 10pm-
5am Wed-Sat. **Admission** free Wed-Fri; €10 incl
1st drink Sat. **Credit** AmEx, DC, MC, V.
This converted barn, beside the Rhône and just
beyond the ramparts, has been elevated from mere
bar to full-blooded nightclub. Playing pumping
disco, house and techno, it's a good freebie boogie
on weekdays – if the staff like the look of you.

Delirium

1 rue Mignard (04.90.85.44.56/www.ledelirium.net).
Open 9pm-1am Thur-Sat (daily in July). **Admission**
Membership €2. **No credit cards**.
This relaxed members' club is a modern-day cultural
salon, with exhibitions and performance art. The
space unfurls like a furniture showroom, murmuring
with the beautiful and bohemian who sip inspiration
from their Melonjaia cocktails.

Pub Z

58 rue Bonneterie (04.90.85.42.84). **Open** noon-
1.30am Mon-Sat. Closed Aug. **Admission** free.
No credit cards.
A life-size zebra welcomes you into this striped bar,
which is popular with a regular crowd of rockers and
students. There's a happy hour (7.30-8.30pm), art
shows and a DJ at weekends.

The Red Lion

21-23 rue St-Jean-le-Vieux (04.90.86.40.25).
Open 10am-1.30am daily. **Admission** free.
Credit AmEx, MC, V.
This butch British pub remains popular with stu-
dents because of its extended happy hour (5-8pm).

Le Cid Café. *See p95.*

Guinness is on tap, but put aside any thoughts of real ale, even if the pub grub does include fish and chips. There's local live rock and blues (10pm-1am) on Tuesday, Wednesday and Sunday, and a free-for-all jam on Monday.

The Red Zone

25 rue Carnot (04.90.27.02.44). **Open** 9pm-3am daily. **Admission** free. **Credit** AmEx, DC, MC, V.
Very red and very popular, this bar-club near the university is where the youth of Avignon come after a night's drinking on place Pie. Varied dance nights include funk, house and salsa; on Wednesday the ladies are invited to run the bar.

Shopping

The indoor Les Halles market in place Pie is open from 7am to 1pm Tuesday to Sunday. It's a disappointing building, but a great place to stock up on fabulous olives, goat's cheese and seafood from the outstanding fishmonger. The place des Carmes holds a flower market on Saturday mornings, and a flea market on Sunday mornings. All shops are open from Monday to Saturday unless stated.

Rue de la République is the commercial centre of Avignon, with high-street names such as Zara, H&M, Monoprix and the Fnac. Peeling off down the pedestrian rue des Marchands is a maze of street-wear clothes shops and boutiques; **Les Olivades** (No.28, 04.90. 86.13.42) sells provençal fabrics by the metre and clothes, while **Mouret** (No.20, 04.90.85.39.38), Avignon's oldest shop, is an enchanting hatter frozen in the 1860s. Further east down rue Bonneterie, **Liquid** (No.37, 04.90.85.19.89) is a modern, design-led drinks shop in which to discover the region's Côtes du Rhône. **Hermès** has a grand corner premises on place de l'Horloge (No.2, 04.90.82.61.94),

heralding the transformation to Parisian designers as you head west down rue St-Agricol, finding the likes of **Christian Lacroix** (No.10, 04.90.27.13.21). **La Tropézienne** (No.22, 04.90.86.24.72, www.latropezienne.net) is a provençal food paradise, selling *calissons*, nougat and *papalines*, the local speciality (pink, spiky-coated oregano liqueur chocolates). Opposite, ice-cream shop **Deldon** (No.35, 04.90.85.59.41) is a good summer heat-buster. Rue Joseph Vernet is the city's elegance capital, with **Cacharel** (No.8, 04.90.86.19.19), **Comptoir des Cotonniers** (No.27, 04.90.14.63.84) and **Ventilo** (No.28, 04.90.85.26.51). There are more shoes than you could dream of at **Pierre Tessier** (No.85, 04.90.82.12.58), while sinful **Chocolatier Puyricard** has an outpost at No.33 (04.90.85.96.33). Running parallel, the rue Petite Fusterie is a home-decoration hotbed, with traditional antiques and garden furniture to be found at **Hervé Baume** (No.19, 04.90.86.37.66). Second-hand books in English can be found at **Shakespeare** (155 rue Carreterie, 04.90.27.38.50, closed Mon, Sun), which also doubles as a tearoom.

Arts & entertainment

AJMI

La Manutention, 4 rue des Escaliers Ste-Anne (04.90.86.08.61/www.jazzalajmi.com). **Tickets** €15; €12 students. Available through agencies or 30mins before show. **No credit cards**.
The letters belong to an association that has been promoting jazz and improvised music in Avignon since 1978. Now using the same venue as the Utopia cinema (*see p100*), it is still keenly developing dynamic and creative jazz, even going so far as to create its own recording label, AJMISeries.

Inn the family way

Avignon Festival-goers in search of high drama may feel slightly fobbed off by bedtime, retiring to their lifeless hotel after all the cloaks, daggers and controversial peeing they will have witnessed on stage. So, to keep the theatrical ferment bubbling, what could be better than shacking up with the locals for a spot of 'reality holidaying'?

France's route down this front drive of voyeurism is via its innumerable *chambres d'hôtes* (Gallic B&Bs, in other words), which began to emerge in great numbers during the 1990s and are now blazing across Provence in a trail of home-made apricot jam and lavender bags. The Vaucluse is their stronghold, where everyone seems to be throwing open their châteaux, salmon-pink bungalows and camp-beds to offer travellers the chance to cosy up to *la belle vie*. Sulky-pants France is coming over all corn-dolly, arms outstretched.

Beware, though, of the pretenders. Country-cot names like 'Mon Paradis Fleuri' can sometimes smoke-screen grim realities of the concrete block on a ring road or 'adolescent booted out of his bedroom to give you a night of dog-hair and dodgy stains' ilk.

Happily, well-housed Avignon tends to offer a high, if pricey, calibre of *chambres d'*. In fact, the farmhouse table has been well and truly turned here in recent years. These days what began as a means for lonely farmers' wives to meet people and travel the world from their *salons* has become an unrestrained exercise in bourgeois tourism. Exposed stone and rural simplicity remain the basic palette, but it's curtains to all other notions of authenticity. Enter stage right the urbanites, buying up ruins, antique pitchforks, tubs of ochre paint and copying the rest straight out of *Elle Déco*.

The backdrop, too, is shifting from the fields into town: Avignon's intra-muros addresses have shot up in the past five years.

The modern *chambres d'hôte* is something akin to a kitchen-sink drama brought up numerous pegs to portray the French middle-class, marinating in their retirement, adapting to their empty-nest syndrome, and (in some cases) revelling in their long-awaited escape to the South. Indeed, your 'hosts' may even turn out to be freelance advertising agents from Paris, sidelining in being impeccably provençal: a Madame et Monsieur 'call us Colette and Jean-Marc' charm duo, who take centre stage in your holiday, massage your curiosity for *l'art de vivre* with copious *vienoisserie*, organic peach juice and sunflowers, then pack you off home with a burgeoning inferiority complex.

Naturally, showing off is the key to their success. *Chambres d'hôtes* at their best are palaces of exhibitionism, playgrounds for the national sports of knowing better, talking about oneself and spreading the good word of being French. Madame has a lesson to teach you on everything, and a conversation addiction to boot. Bee-keeping, choosing melons, staying thin… be polite and sit it out. Hospitality here is the bosomy, intimate type. Discretion is often patchy and privacy, sleep or a quiet moment alone are usually off-limits.

The *table d'hôte* is where the spectacle reaches its climax as 'guests' are thrown together for a sitcom 'dinner party', dubbed into various languages. With lines beautifully learnt, Monsieur rolls home to appear awfully pleased to see complete strangers in his courtyard and will proceed to crack open aperitifs while Madame, your new-best-friend, emerges from the kitchen with a three-course regional feast. Play the game and sing for your supper: be engaging, breathe life into the conversational doldrums of the table. Most importantly of all, sustain a wide-eyed expression of *c'est incroyable!* as your hosts force-feed you ratatouille, accompanied by a bumper helping of reheated anecdotes from their tried-and-tested chat larder. You'll applaud their ability to goad a table of Japanese astronauts, Estonian firemen and Australian athletes into united revelry. Business contacts and corridor-creeping ensue. And so to bed, heads spinning from digestifs and comedy vignettes.

As soon as you get used to the fact that *chambres d'hôtes* are a farcical ensemble piece in social etiquette, complete with hammy stage friendliness, the experience of staying in one actually becomes quite enjoyable. As early as breakfast, everyone screws on their nicest face and greets one another with histrionically feigned interest. And what of your hosts? Can they really get anything out of it? *Mais oui.*

The fact is, you're having such faux-pally fun, with social barriers blurred in all directions, that you'll simply feel too polite to mention that your loo is blocked or the dog is in your bed. How could you possibly when Jean-Marc so kindly explained local grape varieties? Twice. Such, then, is the dramatic ambiguity. But like good guests, you keep quiet, never overstay your welcome and pay the bill.

During the Avignon Festival high-brow theatre banter is suddenly *au menu*. This city's *hôtes* are often theatre buffs, and what's more, proficient in English.

To be in the heat of the action, nab front-row beds overlooking the Palais des Papes. Exotic Sabine, a part-time doggy couturier, runs **A l'Ombre du Palais** (6 rue de la Vieille Juiverie, 04.90.85.55.17, www.alombredupalais.com, double €110-€160), offering balcony meals and lots of friends in 'dramatic' places. A few doors up, the restaurant Le Moutardier has opened the 18th-century **La Vieille Poste** (17 pl du Palais des Papes, 06.62.06.34.76, www.lavieilleposte.com, double €130), where the homely owners have been known to chauffeur guests to their dawn TGV. And for star treatment, **Bel Canto** (1 rue de la Balance, 04.90.82.02.90, double €120-€160) has a Verdi suite, kitted out by its singer hosts like a luxury yacht – think grand piano, palace panoramas and a silver-service breakfast. Be gushingly diplomatic about the paintings: they're Monsieur's handiwork.

The ex-Parisian media couple behind **La Banasterie** (11 rue de la Banasterie, 04.32.76.30.78, www.labanasterie.com, double €100-€160) speak fluent English and put on Avignon's most effortlessly elegant welcome, offering guests hot chocolate nightcaps, festival savvy and tasteful suites in their 16th-cenury home. Just inside the city walls, **Le Clos du Rempart** (34-37 rue Crémade, 04.90.86.39.14, www.closdurempart.com, double €120-€130) has an airy family apartment and, beneath the wisteria, the Lebanese hostess shares her *cuisine* and enthusiasm for dance performance.

As an escape from historic settings, **Le Limas** (51 rue du Limas, 04.90.14.67.19, www.le-limas-avignon.com, double €96-€159) hides an oasis of contemporary design and Le Corbusier furniture, favoured by architects. Wear sunglasses to face the minimalist white if you want to be able to see your fruit crumble at breakfast on the roof terrace.

For bargains, and total immersion in French-only dialogue, dine and kip chez **Madame Bally** (8 rue de la Tour, 04.90.86.00.86, double €50), who lives among her many curios; monthly apartment rentals here will suit die-hard festival addicts. Or venture ten minutes beyond the ramparts to **Chez Marie** (7 av des Chalets, 04.90.86.86.11, double €70-€95) and enjoy her garden and gold-leaf furniture-restoring skills.

Aiming further afield for a rural retreat is a lovely idea that only loses its appeal once you start hiring cars and getting lost on the schlep home. For more hassle-free natural pastures, the No.20 bus or a €10 night taxi will lead you over the river to the quasi-countryside of Ile-de-la-Barthelasse, where the comfortable **Bastide des Papes** (352 chemin des Poiriers, 04.90.86.09.42, www.bastidedespapes.com, double €115) awaits you – with its own swimming pool – among the fruit orchards. Alternatively, in villagey Villeneuve-les-Avignon, Madame Richoux operates **Les Vignes** (28 rue de la Monnaie, 04.90.89.50.31, double €93), where international guests gather around a breakfast of home-grown grapes and well-connected theatre tips.

La Galerie MMB

20 rue de la Balance (04.90.85.17.21). **Open** *Oct-June* 2-6pm Mon; 10am-noon, 2-6pm Tue-Sat. *July-Sept* 9am-7pm daily. **Admission** free.

Marie-Marguerite Buhler recently opened this contemporary art space behind the place du Palais. She shows French sculptors and painters with a taste for sombre architectural forms.

Piscine de la Barthelasse

Ile de la Barthelasse (04.90.82.54.25). **Open** 10am-7pm daily. Closed Sept-Apr. **Admission** €4.90; €3.30 after 5pm. **Credit** MC, V.

An Olympic-sized, open-air pool, which is perfect for when the city gets too hot to bear (as it frequently can in the height of the summer).

Théâtre des Carmes

6 pl des Carmes (04.90.82.20.47). **Open** *Box office* 9am-4pm Mon-Fri. **Tickets** €10-€15. **Credit** MC, V.

Avignon's oldest theatre company, Carmes, is firmly committed to radical theatre. It can also claim the title of foundationstone to the 'Off' festival.

Théâtre du Chien qui Fume

75 rue des Teinturiers (04.90.85.25.87/www.chien quifume.com). **Open** *Box office* 1hr before show. Closed Aug. **Tickets** €10-€25. **No credit cards.**

Director Gérard Vantaggioli keeps this theatre buoyant throughout the year with new productions, exhibitions and *chansons françaises* sung by a variety of his May '68 buddies. A free show on the last Friday of the month welcomes new theatre, song, dance and circus acts.

Théâtre Municipal

20 pl de l'Horloge (04.90.82.81.40). **Open** *Box office* 11am-6pm Mon-Sat; 11am-12.30pm Sun. **Tickets** €5-€60. **Credit** MC, V.

The main permanent house in Avignon, the Théâtre Municipal stages official festival productions in July and a good season of opera, ballet, comedy, and chamber and symphony music all year. Events here can be popular so be sure to book in advance.

Utopia

La Manutention, 4 rue des Escaliers Ste-Anne (04.90.82.65.36). **Open** *Box office* 11am-11pm daily. **Tickets** €5.50. **No credit cards.**

Avignon's main *version originale* (original language) cinema is a cultural hub with a packed programme and a good bar-bistro. It has a smaller offshoot at 5 rue Figuière (04.90.82.65.36). For listings and reviews, the free information sheet *La Gazette* is available city-wide.

Where to stay

For information on the wide range of *chambres d'hôtes* accommodation in Avignon, *see p98* **Inn the family way**. It is also worth remembering that many hotels increase their rates during the Festival d'Avignon (for dates, *see chapter* **The Festive South**).

La Banasterie

11 rue de la Banasterie (04.32.76.30.78/www. labanasterie.com). **Rates** €100-€150 double. **No credit cards.**

The chocoholic owners of this upmarket B&B have named a handful of luxuriously decorated bedrooms after great chocolates of the world. The 16th-century house is tucked under the Palais des Papes, in one of the most atmospheric streets in the old town. *See also p99* **Inn the family way.**

La Bastide des Papes

352 chemin des Poiriers, Ile de la Barthelasse (04.90.86.09.42). **Rates** €90-€115 double. **Credit** MC, V.

This pretty 14th-century *chambres d'hôte*, set in orchards with a pool, is a tasteful rural retreat on the Ile de la Barthelasse. Guests get free use of the spacious kitchen; take the No.20 bus to get back into town or go it alone on the Bastide's selection of mountain bikes. Minimum stay two nights. *See also p99* **Inn the family way.**

Camping du Pont d'Avignon

Ile de la Barthelasse (04.90.80.63.50/www.camping-avignon.com). Closed Nov-Mar. **Rates** €9.60-€20.50/wk 2-person tent; €250-€420/wk 4-person bungalow. **Credit** AmEx, MC, V.

A Rhône-side campsite on Ile de la Barthelasse (take Pont Edouard Daladier), with an outdoor swimming pool and mountain bikes for hire.

Hôtel Cloître St-Louis

20 rue Portail Boquier (04.90.27.55.55/www.cloitre-saint-louis.com). **Rates** €100-€250 double. **Credit** AmEx, DC, MC, V.

A contemporary steel and glass extension by Jean Nouvel has been grafted on to the 16th-century cloister, chapel wing and fountain courtyard of a former monastery. There's also a walled garden and tiny rooftop pool.

Hôtel Colbert

7 rue Agricol Perdiguier (04.90.86.20.20). Closed Nov-Feb. **Rates** €45-€77 double. **Credit** MC, V.

Part of a cluster of budget hotels on a tiny street in the middle of town, Le Colbert has clean and attractive rooms, newly redecorated and with air-conditioning. You can take your breakfast in free and easy style in the fountain courtyard.

Hôtel de Blauvac

11 rue de la Bancasse (04.90.86.34.11). **Rates** €65-€80 double. **Credit** AmEx, DC, MC, V.

A 17th-century building that overlooks a quiet, winding street leading to the place de l'Horloge, the de Blauvac has kept vestiges of its noble past. Its high-ceilinged, reasonably priced rooms are simply furnished but offer good comfort for the price.

Hôtel de Garlande

20 rue Galante (04.90.80.08.85/www.hotelde garlande.com). Closed Jan. **Rates** €69-€99 double. **Credit** AmEx, DC, MC, V.

Down a shady street conveniently close to the city centre, this cosy hotel has a certain elegance. The welcome is warm, the decoration tasteful and there are some family-sized rooms. And at these prices, the ability to walk out right into the heart of the action makes it something of a find (especially if you are able to bag a table during the festival).

Hôtel de la Mirande

4 pl de la Mirande (04.90.85.93.93/www.la-mirande.fr). **Rates** €295-€475 double. **Credit** AmEx, DC, MC, V.
This 18th-century cardinals' palace turns sleeping into a sumptuous history lesson. Aubusson tapestries, antique furniture, Pierre Frey fabrics and Venetian chandeliers transport you back in time, but the self-consciously 21st-century luxury is treated with almost papal solemnity. The hotel also has one of Avignon's best restaurants (*see p96*).

Hôtel d'Europe

12 pl Crillon (04.90.14.76.76/www.hotel-d-europe.fr). **Rates** €135-€429 double. **Credit** AmEx, DC, MC, V.
Napoleon, Victor Hugo, John Stuart Mill, Tennessee Williams and Jackie Onassis are some of the past guests at this 16th-century mansion, set around an attractive courtyard. Rooms are decorated with antiques and the good-value Sunday brunch provides an opportunity to watch the grey-haired economy in action.

Hôtel du Parc

18 rue Agricol Perdiguier (04.90.82.71.55). **Rates** €36-€47 double. **Credit** MC, V.
A few doors up from the Colbert, the Parc's balconies cascade with greenery and offer views of flower-filled place Agricol Perdiguier. The modest, rustic, beamed, stone-walled interior is cosy and clean.

Hôtel La Ferme

chemin du bois, Ile de la Barthelasse (04.90.82.57.53/www.hotel-laferme.com). Closed Nov-Mar. **Rates** €77-€88 double. **Credit** AmEx, MC, V.
It seems incredible that this attractive country dwelling on the Ile de la Barthelasse is just a ten-minute car journey from the town centre. It offers very simple accommodation, plus a beautiful tree-lined terrace for above-average alfresco dining and a swimming pool for a refreshing dip.

Hôtel Le Médiéval

16 rue Petite Saunerie (04.90.86.11.06/www.hotel medieval.com). Closed Jan. **Rates** €53-€68 double. **Credit** MC,V.
A fine 17th-century mansion has been converted into this charming small hotel, with an attractive flower-filled courtyard and impressive sweeping staircase. Some of the simply furnished rooms are studios, which include a useful kitchenette for longer stays.

Hôtel Le Splendid

17 rue Agricol Perdiguier (04.90.86.14.46/www.avignon-splendid-hotel.com). Closed mid Nov-mid Dec. **Rates** €46-€49 double. **Credit** AmEx, MC, V.

Cheerful owners the Prel-Lemoines run this simple, neat hotel just opposite the Hôtel du Parc (*see above*). Rooms are unexciting, but reliably good value, and the atmosphere is conducive to a very pleasant stay. Well worth a look.

Hôtel Mignon

12 rue Joseph Vernet (04.90.82.17.30/www.hotel-mignon.com). **Rates** €51.34-€56.34 double. **Credit** AmEx, MC, V.
A sweet little hotel on a fashionable street, the Mignon offers small but good-value rooms, comedy tiger-print wall carpeting and extremely welcoming staff. The breakfast room is so small that, to cater for the overspill, some lucky volunteers get breakfast in bed.

Le Limas

51 rue du Limas (04.90.14.67.19/www.le-limas-avignon.com). **Rates** €86-€129 double. **No credit cards.**
Starck bathroom fittings and Le Corbusier furniture contrast with the period features in this *chambres d'hôte* in an 18th-century mansion. Dynamic owner Marion Wagner serves breakfast on the roof terrace in summer and Sunday supper in winter.

Resources

The free **Avignon-Villeneuve PASSion** gives 20 to 50 per cent reductions (after the first ticket) on most museums and sights.
A decidedly tacky fleet of mini tourist trains (www.petittrainavignon.com) makes circuits of Avignon between March and October (10am-7pm daily, until 8pm July & Aug, €7) from place du Palais. Bikes can be hired from **Aymard** (80 rue Guillaume Puy, 04.90.86.32.49, closed Mon, 2wks in Aug).

Hospital

Centre Hospitalier Général, 305 rue Raoul Follereau (04.32.75.33.33).

Internet

Webzone Cybercafé, 3 rue St-Jean le Vieux (04.32.76.29.47/www.webzone.fr). **Open** Aug-June 10am-11.30pm daily. *July* 9am-3am daily.

Police station

Police municipale *10 pl Pie (04.90.86.75.43).* **Commissariat Central** *bd St-Roch (04.90.16.81.00).*

Post office

La Poste, cours Président Kennedy (04.90.27.54.00). **Open** 8am-7pm Mon-Fri; 8am-noon Sat.

Tourist information

Avignon Office de Tourisme, 41 cours Jean Jaurès, 84008 Avignon (04.32.74.32.74/www.ot-avignon.fr). **Open** *Apr-June, Aug-Oct* 9am-6pm Mon-Sat; 10am-5pm Sun. *July* 9am-7pm Mon-Sat; 10am-5pm Sun. *Nov-Mar* 9am-6pm Mon-Fri; 9am-5pm Sat; 10am-noon Sun.

Villeneuve-lès-Avignon

West of the Rhône, in the Gard *département*
over the Ile de la Barthelasse, the slightly
sprawling skyline of Villeneuve is every bit
as impressive as its big sister across the river.
To get there, take Pont Edouard Daladier, bus
No.11 or the summer Bâteau Bus from allée de
l'Oulle. This small settlement, centred on the
tenth-century Abbaye St-André, came into its
own in 1307, when King Philippe le Bel decided
it was a prime location for keeping an eye on
papal goings-on across the river. A heavily
fortified 'new town' (hence Villeneuve) sprang
up, plus a watchtower, the **Tour Philippe
le Bel**, that grew higher as Avignon became
more powerful. Its heights are now used for
exhibitions. Life is led at a more leisurely pace
in Villeneuve without any of the razzmatazz
of Avignon, and its visitors are rewarded with
some stunning architecture, a superb view and
one matchless work of art.

For the view, head to the west tower of the
Fort St-André, the fortress built around the
abbey in the 14th century, and climb along the
massive ramparts. Inside are the remains of
the **Abbaye St-André**: bewitching terraced
gardens leading to a tiny Romanesque chapel,
a ruined 13th-century church and a moving
graveyard with sarcophagi laid out like beds.

Below the fort, the **Chartreuse du Val de
Bénédiction** was once the largest Carthusian
monastery in France. The charterhouse has
been painstakingly restored, removing all
signs of the depredations suffered during the
Revolution when, to add insult to injury, the
Gothic tomb of Pope Innocent VI, who founded
the monastery in 1352, was converted into a
white marble rabbit hutch. There are monks'
cells resembling little terraced cottages, as
well as a laundry, kitchen, prisons and a herb
garden funded by beauty company Yves
Rocher. A small chapel off the cloître du
Cimetière (an enchanting open-air theatre venue
during the festival) has exquisite frescoes by
Matteo Giovanetti. 'Chocolat' guided tours on
winter Sundays culminate in a fireside tea of
hot chocolate and cake. The Chartreuse now
acts as a state-funded centre for playwrights,
whose recorded voices can be heard echoing
through the buildings, reading aloud the fruits
of their labours.

The **Musée Pierre de Luxembourg** is a
former cardinal's residence that now teems with
four floors of art, including a delicately carved
ivory Virgin and Child and 16th- and 17th-

century religious paintings by Mignard and de
Champaigne. The collection's masterpiece is the
extraordinary *Coronation of the Virgin* (1453-
54) by Enguerrand Quarton, a leading light in
the Avignon School. The entire medieval world
view is represented in the painting's detailed
landscape and depiction of human activity.

Just south of the museum, the 14th-century
Collégiale Notre-Dame has works by
Mignard and Levieux, a lavish 18th-century
altarpiece and a copy of Enguerrand Quarton's
Pietà (the original is in the Louvre).

Market day in Villeneuve is Thursday;
there's also a flea market on Saturdays.

Chartreuse du Val de Bénédiction

58 rue de la République (04.90.15.24.24). **Open**
Apr-Sept 9am-6.30pm daily. *Oct-Mar* 9.30am-5.30pm
daily. **Admission** €6.10; €4.10 18-25s; free under-
18s. **Credit** (€10 minimum) AmEx, DC, MC, V.

Collégiale Notre-Dame

pl du Chapitre. **Open** *Apr-Sept* 10am-12.30pm,
3-7pm daily. *Oct-Mar* 10am-noon, 2-5pm daily.
Admission free.

Fort St-André & Abbaye St-André

*montée du Fort (fort 04.90.25.45.35/abbey
04.90.25.55.95).* **Open** *Fort* Apr-mid May 10am-
1pm, 2-5.30pm daily; mid May-Sept 10am-1pm,
2-6pm; Oct-Mar 10am-1pm, 2-5pm daily. *Gardens*
Apr-Sept 10am-12.30pm, 2-6pm Tue-Sun; Oct-
Mar 10am-12.30pm, 2-5pm Tue-Sun. *Abbey* by
appointment. **Admission** *Fort* €4.60; €3.10 18-24s;
free under-18s. *Abbey & gardens* €4; €3 under-18s.
No credit cards.

The Red Zone. *See p97.*

Musée Pierre de Luxembourg

rue de la République (04.90.27.49.66). **Open** *Apr-Sept* 10am-12.30pm, 3-7pm daily. *Oct-Mar* 10am-noon, 2-5.30pm Tue-Sun. Closed Feb. **Admission** €3; €2 students; free under-18s. **No credit cards**.

Tour Philippe le Bel

rue Montée de la Tour (04.32.70.08.57). **Open** *Apr-mid June* 10am-12.30pm, 1.30-7pm Tue-Sat. *Mid June-Sept* 10am-12.30pm, 1.30-7pm daily. *Oct-Mar* 10am-noon, 2-5pm Tue-Sun. Closed Feb & Mon mid Sept-mid June. **Admission** €1.80; free under-18s. **No credit cards**.

Where to stay & eat

Villeneuve's hotels absorb the overflow from the Avignon festival, but are also worth considering in their own right. The luxury option is **Le Prieuré** (7 pl du Chapitre, 04.90.15.90.15, www.leprieure.fr, closed Nov-mid Mar, double €125-€225, restaurant closed Sept-June), an exquisitely restored 14th-century archbishop's palace with library, garden, pool and gourmet restaurant. A welcomingly updated option is the 17th-century **Hôtel de l'Atelier** (5 rue de la Foire, 04.90.25.01.84, www.hoteldelatelier.com, closed Nov-Dec, double €46-€91), tastefully redecorated by set designer Dominique Baroush as an airy modern-rustic guesthouse. Villeneuve also has a few upmarket B&Bs and *chambres d'hôtes*, notably the elegant **La Vigne** (28 rue de la Monnaie, 04.90.89.50.31, double €77-€93) and **Les Jardins de la Livrée** (4bis rue Camp de Bataille, 04.90.26.05.05, double €60-€90), which has a swimming pool to accompany its herbally themed rooms.

On the banks of the Rhône, **Le Vieux Moulin** (5 rue du Vieux Moulin, 04.90.25.00.26, www.avignon-vieuxmoulin.com, closed Jan, Mon & Tue except July, menus €25-€30) was an old stone-built grain depot for the trade boats; these days, it serves southern staples and is popular with large groups. **Aubertin** (1 rue de l'Hôpital, 04.90.25.94.84, closed Mon, Sun & last 2wks Aug, menus €20-€49) is the first choice for dining in Villeneuve, offering inventive regional cuisine by celebrated chef Jean-Claude Aubertin (previously of Ma Cuisine in London), which can be eaten on a pleasant terrace under the arcades.

In neighbouring village Les Angles, **C'est la Lune** (270 montée du Valadas, 04.90.25.40.55, open July-Aug daily, Sept-June Thur, Fri, lunch Wed & lunch Sat, average €30) is a North African fusion bar-restaurant, where Villeneuve's hipsters congregate to eat Moroccan-influenced provençal cuisine. By day they can then swim it off in the outdoor pool, or by night they can dance it off to the sounds of

the DJ. It's a difficult place to find, and the improvisational approach to the food won't appeal to everyone, but in the right company it's loads of fun.

Resources

A €6.86 **Passeport pour l'Art** gives entry to Villeneuve's four main attractions.

Villeneuve Office du Tourisme

1 pl Charles David, 30400 Villeneuve-lès-Avignon (04.90.25.61.33/www.villeneuvelesavignon.fr/tourisme). **Open** *Sept-June* 9am-12.30pm, 2-6pm Mon-Sat. *July* 10am-7pm Mon-Fri; 10am-1pm, 2.30-7pm Sat, Sun. *Aug* 9am-12.30pm, 2-6pm daily.

Getting there & around

By air

Caumont-Avignon (www.avignon.aeroport.fr), the local airport, is situated eight kilometres (five miles) outside the city. Flights go to London City airport via Paris Orly; there are about 20 buses a day to the city centre from the nearby Lycée Agricole.

By bus

The **main bus station** is on av Montclar (04.90.82.07.35), next to the Centre Ville train station; buses run from Avignon to Aix, Arles, Carpentras, Cavaillon, l'Isle sur la Sorgue, Nîmes and Orange, or further afield to Marseille, Nice and Cannes. Town buses and services to the TGV station are run by **TCRA** (04.32.74.18.32, www.tcra.fr).

By car

Coming south, take the A7 autoroute; from the Perpignan/Montpellier direction take the A9, exiting at Avignon nord or sud. Be careful when leaving the town to head towards the correct motorway.

By taxi

If you're in Avignon, contact **Taxis Radio Avignonnais** (Place Pie, 04.90.82.20.20). When booking taxis during the festival, allow at least an extra hour for the wait.

By train

Avignon is at the junction of the Paris–Marseille and Paris–Montpellier lines. The **Gare Centre Ville** has frequent links to Arles, Nîmes, Orange, Toulon and Carcassonne. The **Gare TGV** (08.92.35.35.35, www.tgv.com) is four kilometres (2.5 miles) south of Avignon. A bus service (*navette*) leaves from the station at the arrival of each train, taking passengers to the Gare Centre Ville, and leaves from the centre for the Gare TGV every 15mins. From July to September, a **Eurostar** (www.eurostar.com) service travels direct from London to Avignon in 6hrs 30mins; the train leaves Waterloo on Saturday mornings and returns in the afternoon. At other times of the year, you must change in Lille or Paris.

Orange & Châteauneuf-du-Pape

A Roman theatre, a mighty bridge and some celebrated papal vineyards.

Famously home to some of the most prestigious appellations of the southern Côtes du Rhône, the baking Rhône flood plain north of Avignon also beguiles visitors with the awe-inspiring Roman ruins of Orange.

Orange

Orange sits somewhat uneasily around its glorious antique theatre. Long under foreign domination, first by the Romans, later the House of Orange, it is now a fief of the Front National. The extreme right council is suspicious of the Chorégies (*see below*), Orange's venerable and prestigious opera festival, and is rumoured to routinely cancel the visits of artists coming from sexual or ethnic minorities. Don't be put off, though. Orange is a magnificent relic of the Roman city of Arausio, at its peak four times as large as today's town. Declining sharply in the Dark Ages, Orange picked up in the 12th century, as an enclave governed by troubadour-prince Raimbaut d'Orange. In 1530 the town passed to a junior branch of the German House of Nassau, and gave its name to Nassau's Dutch principality 14 years later. Thereafter Orange became a sort of Protestant buzzword (finding its way into Ulster's Orange Order and the Orange Free State) and the town itself attracted Protestant refugees from all over Provence during the Wars of Religion.

The Dutch Nassaus held on to their little piece of France against the odds, and in 1622 Maurice de Nassau built an impressive château and fortifications. Unfortunately, he used stones from the remaining Roman monuments not previously destroyed by barbarians, and only the Arc de Triomphe and the Théâtre Antique survived the pillage. In 1673, as he was embarking on another war with Protestant Holland, Louis XIV ordered the destruction of the château. Though the Treaty of Utrecht finally gave the principality to France in 1713, Queen Juliana of the Netherlands was back in 1952 to plant an oak tree on the site of the château. (It is ironic, of course, that the extreme right should peddle its ultranationalist message in a town that is historically such a newcomer to the nation.) Tourism apart, the town is home to the cavalry regiment of the French Foreign Legion, members of which you'll see strolling round town in uniform.

Geographically and emotionally, the **Théâtre Antique** dominates Orange. It is quite simply the best-preserved Roman theatre anywhere. What sets it apart is the unrivalled state of preservation of the stage wall, a massive, sculpted sandstone screen 36 metres (118 feet) high, which Louis XIV referred to as 'the finest wall in my kingdom'. The amphitheatre was a multifunctional space that hosted everything from political meetings to concerts, sporting events and plays. In the fourth century the theatre was abandoned and makeshift houses were built within the auditorium. It was not until the 19th century that restoration began and the Chorégies d'Orange was born. The Roman statue of Augustus, which presides over the stage from a niche, was placed here in 1951. A recent proposal by the local council to put a roof over the stage is a worrying development, especially when you read that it is to marry ancient and contemporary. The justification is that it should improve the already miraculous acoustic and, more importantly, allow the space to be let out more frequently for a wider range of activities.

In a 17th-century building opposite the main entrance to the theatre, the **Musée Municipal** houses an interesting collection of Roman artefacts, including a unique series of *cadastres*. These engraved marble tablets map the streets, administrative divisions and geographical features of the Orange region over the course of three successive Roman surveys (the earliest dates from AD 77). On the top floor is an unexpected curiosity: a selection of post-Impressionist paintings by Welsh artist Frank Brangwyn. The traditional printed cotton cloth known as *indiennes* is celebrated in a series of paintings by 18th-century artist GM Rossetti, while modern-day *indiennes* can be tracked down next door at La Provençale (5 pl Sylvain, 04.90.51.58.86, closed Mon, Sun & Nov-mid Feb, open afternoons Dec). There is also a Thursday morning market.

Augustus presiding over the **Théâtre Antique**.

On top of the hill of St-Eutrope, into which the curve of the theatre's seats was dug, is a pleasant park with the ruins of Maurice de Nassau's château and the Piscine des Cèdres (04.90.34.09.68, open end June-Aug), an open-air swimming pool that is a serious temptation in hot, dusty summers. It has also been the site of important recent archaeological excavations.

The old town, in front of the theatre, is a tight knot of scruffy twisting streets that liven up at festival time, but provide little architectural competition for the towering classical monuments. They do have plenty of attractive, shady squares, ideal for a pre-dinner pastis. The liveliest cafés and the majority of Orange's eating places are in front of the Roman theatre.

Out of the centre, on the northern edge of town, the Arc de Triomphe is Orange's other great Roman monument. The triumphal arch spans the former Via Agrippa, which linked Lyon to Arles. Built in 20 BC, it is the third largest of its kind in the world; the north side is a riot of well-preserved carving, with military paraphernalia arranged in abstract patterns.

Théâtre Antique/Musée Municipale

rue Madeleine Roch (04.90.51.17.60). **Open** *Mar, Oct* 9am-6pm daily. *Apr, May, June-Sept* 9am-7pm daily. *Nov-Feb* 9am-5pm daily. **Admission** €7.50; €5.50 7-17s; free under-7s. **Credit** MC, V.

Where to stay & eat

The most comfortable hotel in the centre of Orange is the renovated **Hôtel Arène** (pl de Langes, 04.90.11.40.40, www.hotel-arene.fr, closed 3wks in Nov, double €59-€104), which has 30 personalised, air-conditioned rooms, set on a paved square. Pretty in pink on the edge of the arena, the **Hôtel St-Jean** (1 cours Pourtoules, 04.90.51.15.16, closed Jan-mid Feb, double €38-€70) is an attractive budget choice,

while the unprepossessing **Glacier** (46 cours Aristide Briand, 04.90.34.02.01, www.le-glacier.com, closed mid Dec-early Jan, double €47-€70) has outstandingly helpful staff. In summer a pool is important, which condemns you to staying in one of the chain hotels just outside the town or in the **Mas des Aigras** (towards Gap, 04.90.34.81.01, closed late Dec-late Jan, Tue & Wed Oct-Mar, double €70-€106), which slightly overplays the provençal card.

The best restaurant in town is the **Parvis** (55 cours Portoules, 04.90.34.82.00, menu €22.50-€41), where Jean-Michel Berengier's imaginative cuisine takes its cue from local produce, served on a sunny terrace or in the beamed interior. A more modern approach, enjoyed on and around an attractive terrace, is found at **Le Jardin d'Adrien** (11 rue Pontillac, 04.90.51.63.04, menu €16-€28). The charming **La Table d'Angelina** (23 rue Victor Hugo, 04.90.30.28.36, average €20) is good for a light meal, while the **Café du Théâtre** (pl des Frères Mounet, 04.90.34.12.39) is the liveliest place in town for a quick drink. If you have overdosed on indigenous cuisine, **Le Saigon** (20 pl Sylvain, 04.90.34.18.19, average €25) is a decent Vietnamese restaurant beside the Théâtre Antique. For a gastronomic treat, head to the quiet village of Sérignan-du-Comtat for the **Pré du Moulin** (04.90.70.14.55, closed Feb, menus €29-€110), where the outstanding €29 lunch menu gives chef Pascal Alonso scope to show his considerable talent.

Resources

Tourist information

Office de Tourisme, 5 cours Aristide Briand, 84100 Orange (04.90.34.70.88/www.ville-orange.com). **Open** *Apr-Sept* 9.30am-7pm Mon-Sat; 10am-4pm Sun. *Oct-Mar* 10am-1pm, 2-5pm Mon-Sat.

Châteauneuf-du-Pape

The main attraction to Châteauneuf-du-Pape – just as at Sancerre or Roquefort – hardly needs to be explained. As if to reinforce the point, the road south from Orange has vines growing right to the edge of the tarmac, their grapes destined not only for the princely red that takes its name from the village but also for Côtes du Rhône and Côtes du Rhône Villages. As every second farm is a wine estate, invitations to taste and visit are thick on the ground (though it takes a certain nerve to resist buying when you have sniffed, sipped and slurped every vintage from the last ten years); the tourist office has a comprehensive list of vineyard visits. The original vineyards were planted at the initiative of the Avignon popes (commemorated in the village's name), who summered here in the castle built by wine-lover John XXII in 1316. The stringent rules regarding yield and grape varieties that were laid down in 1923 proved to be a far-sighted blueprint for France's *appellation d'origine contrôlée* regulations, sealing the reputation of the local red wine, which is a complex blend of at least eight varieties, dominated by grenache. The alluvial soil, sprinkled with heat-absorbing pebbles, the widely spaced vines and the cloud-dispersing Mistral all contribute to the muscular alcoholic content (12.5 per cent) and complex nose of the wine. More recently, white Châteauneuf-du-Pape (blending a minimum of five grapes) has made a name for itself.

All that wine money has at least been put to good use: Châteauneuf-du-Pape is an outstandingly beautiful village, tastefully restored, with a characterful town centre and a market every Friday morning. Little remains of the Château des Papes itself, destroyed in the Wars of Religion, but the views are exceptional. One winemaker, Père Anselme, has had the clever idea of opening a museum to celebrate the area's winemaking tradition: the **Musée des Outils de Vignerons**. The baskets, pruners and suchlike are interesting enough, but the shop and tasting room at the end is what this is all about. If you need a sugar rush to get out of here, there is also a good chocolate-maker, **Castelain** (rte d'Avignon, 04.90.83.54.71).

Musée des Outils de Vignerons
Le Clos (04.90.83.70.07/www.brotte.com). **Open** *July-Sept* 9am-1pm, 2-7pm daily. *Oct-June* 9am-noon, 2-6pm daily. **Admission** free.

Where to stay & eat

Châteauneuf makes the ideal base for those who are wanting to be able to spend an evening drinking some of the finest wines in the world without having to worry about driving back to the hotel. **La Garbure** (3 rue Joseph Ducos, 04.90.83.75.08, www.la-garbure.com, closed Mon & Sun Nov-Apr, 1wk in Jan, double €61-€77, menus €16-€45) is an attractive choice on the main street, as is **La Mère Germaine** (3 rue du Commandant Lemaitre, 04.90.83.54.37, www.lameregermaine.com, double €49-€68, menus €16-€85). For something more elaborate, the **Château des Fines Roches** (rte de Sorgues, 04.90.83.70.23, www.chateaufines roches.com, double €155-€200, menus €30-€75), a 19th-century pile set in a vineyard, has a good – though pricey – restaurant. For one of the best views in town, the unsophisticated **Verger des Papes** (04.90.83.50.40, menus €18-€26) has a splendid terrace up by the château. In the heart of the vineyards, **La Sommellerie** (4km or 2.5 miles down D17, 04.90.83.50.00, www.la-sommellerie, double €65-€98, menus €29-€58) has an inspired regional restaurant and some extremely comfortable rooms (where better to sleep it off than in a vineyard?).

Resources

Tourist information
Office de Tourisme, pl Portail, 84103 Châteauneuf-du-Pape (04.90.83.71.08). **Open** *July, Aug* 9.30am-7pm Mon-Sat; 10am-1pm, 2-6pm Sun. *Sept-June* 9.30am-12.30pm, 2-6pm Mon-Sat.

Musée des Outils de Vignerons.

The wine-producing monastery of **Chartreuse de Valbonne**. *See p108.*

Pont-St-Esprit & Bagnols

The 'Bridge of the Holy Spirit' spans the Rhône just where it enters Provence. Built between 1265 and 1319 by a brotherhood inspired by one Jéhan de Thianges, who was 'led by divine inspiration', the bridge was originally a more elaborate affair, boasting bastions and towers, but it remains an impressive, curved structure, with 19 of the 25 arches still in their original state. The town of **Pont-St-Esprit** was badly bombed in World War II and then, in 1951, found itself at the centre of a scandal when its bread became mysteriously poisoned. Best to put it out of your mind if you visit the Saturday morning market. It is a rather gloomy town, but rue St-Jacques (named after the pilgrims who stayed here on their way to Santiago de Compostela) is pretty. The religious paintings and artefacts in the **Musée d'Art Sacré du Gard** may not set the pulse racing, but it is beautifully located in a well-preserved medieval merchant's house that was inhabited by the same family for six centuries. Odds and ends, including some early 20th-century paintings and 220 18th-century pharmacy jars, are displayed in the **Musée Paul Raymond** in the old town hall.

Bagnols-sur-Cèze, 11 kilometres (seven miles) south, has one of the best markets in the region, as well as one of the most satisfying small museums. The old town is full of character, particularly on Wednesdays, when the market ensures that most of the centre is given over to produce of all sorts – a rare example of a thriving provençal town untouched by theme-park tourism. This is the place to stock up on local gastronomic products or good-quality provençal fabrics. Rue Crémieux, which runs up to place Mallet, is filled with fine townhouses dating from the 16th to the 18th centuries. Look up at the riotous gargoyles of No.15, and browse in the organic food shop housed in the courtyard. On the second floor of the town hall, a 17th-century mansion in place Mallet, is the town's big cultural draw: the **Musée Albert André**. In 1923 a fire destroyed the museum's patchy and parochial collection of daubs. Painter Albert André, who was standing in as curator, launched an appeal – with the help of his friend Renoir – to the artists of France to help him fill the empty walls. They responded in force, and today the museum provides an art historical snapshot of the early 20th-century figurative tradition, with works by Renoir, Signac, Bonnard, Matisse, Gauguin and others. Memories of the rich archaeological past of the town, both Celtic-Ligurian and Gallo-Roman, are housed in the **Musée d'Archéologie Léon Alègre**, while Bagnols comes right up to date with the Centre atomique de Marcoule nuclear processing plant, located outside town beside the Rhône; the plant has quadrupled the town's working population.

Perched above the River Cèze, ten kilometres (six miles) west of Bagnols, **La Roque-sur-Cèze** is a picture-postcard village with a fine Romanesque church, approached by an ancient single-track bridge. Just downstream, the Cèze cuts through limestone to form the spectacular Cascade de Sautadet, but bathers should beware: this stretch of the river sees frequent drownings. North of La Roque, in the middle of an oak forest that would not be out of place in a medieval romance, is the 13th-century **Chartreuse de Valbonne** monastery, which produces its own Côtes du Rhône wine. You can visit the richly decorated baroque church and the cloisters, and even stay in some rather basic accommodation.

Chartreuse de Valbonne

St-Paulet-de-Caisson (04.66.90.41.24/vineyard 04.66.90.41.00/www.chartreusedevalbonne.com). **Open** *May-Aug* 10am-1pm, 1.30-7pm daily. *Sept-Apr* 9am-noon, 1.30-5.30pm daily. **Admission** €4; €2.50 10-16s; free under-10s. **Credit** AmEx, DC, MC, V.

Musée Albert André

pl Mallet, Bagnols (04.66.50.50.56). **Open** *Sept-June* 10am-noon, 2-6pm Tue-Sun. *July, Aug* 10am-12.30pm, 2-6.30pm Tue-Sun. Closed Feb. **Admission** €4.20; under-16s free. **No credit cards.**

Musée d'Archéologie Léon Alègre

24 av Paul Langevin, Bagnols (04.66.89.74.00). **Open** 10am-noon, 2-6pm Tue, Thur, Fri. **Admission** €4.20. **No credit cards.**

Musée d'Art Sacré du Gard

2 rue St-Jacques, Pont-St-Esprit (04.66.39.17.61). **Open** *July, Aug* 10am-7pm Tue-Sun. *Sept-June* 10am-noon, 2-6pm Tue-Sun. **Admission** €3; €2 10-16s; free under-10s. **No credit cards.**

Musée Paul Raymond

pl de l'Hôtel de Ville, Pont-St-Esprit (04.66.39.09.98). **Open** *July, Aug* 10am-7pm Tue-Sun. *Sept-June* 10am-noon, 2-6pm Tue-Sun. **Admission** €3; €2 10-16s; free under-10s. **No credit cards.**

Where to stay & eat

In Pont-St-Esprit, the **Auberge Provençale** (rte de Nîmes, 04.66.39.08.79, closed 24 Dec-2 Jan, double €29-€32, restaurant closed dinner Sun Oct-Mar, menus €10-€20) has simple accommodation and a popular restaurant. Typical provençal fare is served at **Lou Recati** (6 rue Jean-Jacques, 04.66.90.73.01, closed Mon, Tue lunch, 2wks in Oct, menus €12-€22). One of the best places for a simple barbecue-style meal in Pont-St-Esprit is **Le Pancrace** (rte de Barjac, 04.66.39.47.81, average €30). For more lodgings in Pont-St-Esprit with more of a personal touch, there is a charming *chambres d'hôte* just out of town: **Le Mas Canet** (chemin de Gavanon, St-Paulet-de Caisson, 04.66.39.25.96, www.mascanet.com, double €47).

Near Bagnols, the luxurious **Château de Montcaud** (5km or 3 miles west of Bagnols, rte d'Alès Combe, Sabran, 04.66.89.60.60, www.chateau-de-montcaud.com, closed Nov-Mar, double €160-€350, restaurant closed lunch, menus €65-€90, bistro closed Sat & Sun, menus €30-€40) dates from the 19th-century. It has

shady wooded grounds, a nice swimming pool, a rose garden, tennis courts and a Turkish bath, and offers special half-board breaks that include tickets for Les Chorégies. The château's restaurant, **Les Jardins de Montcaud**, offers fine country cooking in a stone *mas*, with tables placed on the patio in summer. The **Château du Val de Cèze** (rte d'Avignon, 04.66.89.61.26, www.sud-provence.com, double €100-€110) has a set of comfortable bungalows in its grounds, while the best bet in the centre of Bagnols is the unexciting **Le Saint Georges** (210 av Roger Salengro, 04.66.89.53.65, www.restaurantlesaint georges.com, double €38.50-€58), which at least has a popular local restaurant. For a light meal **L'Auguste** café (8 pl Mallet, 04.66.39.18.38, menus €11-€22) is situated on a pretty square in front of the town hall. At La Roque-sur-Cèze, **Le Mas du Bélier** (04.66.82.21.39, closed Mon & Tue Oct-Mar, menus €12.50-€24.50) is a romantic waterside inn, and just outside Bagnols **Paul Itier** (04.66.82.00.24, closed Feb, menus €12.50-€26) is a charming country-style *auberge*.

Resources

Tourist information

Bagnols-sur-Cèze Office de Tourisme *Espace St-Gilles, av Léon Blum, 30200 Bagnols-sur-Cèze (04. 66.89.54.61/www.ot-bagnolssurceze.com).* **Open** *July-Aug* 9am-7pm Mon-Fri; 9am-6pm Sat; 10am-1pm Sun. *Sept-June* 9am-noon, 2-6pm Mon-Fri; 9am-noon Sat. **Pont-St-Esprit Office de Tourisme** *Résidence Welcome, 30130 Pont-St-Esprit (04.66.39.44.45/ www.ot-pont-saint-esprit.fr).* **Open** *June-Aug* 9am-12.30pm, 1.30-6.30pm Mon-Fri; 9am-12.30pm, 3-6pm Sat; 9am-noon Sun. *Sept-May* 8am-noon, 2-5.30pm Mon-Fri; 9am-noon Sat.

Getting there & around

By bus

Rapides du Sud-Est (04.90.34.15.59) runs 12 buses between Avignon and Orange every day except Sun. **Cars Auran** (04.66.39.10.40) runs buses daily between Avignon, Pont-St-Esprit and Bagnols-sur-Cèze. **Sotra Ginaux** (04.75.39.40.22) runs daily buses from Mon to Fri (less frequent in the school holidays) between Orange and Pont-St-Esprit, from Avignon to Aubernas via Pont-St-Esprit, and from Aubernas to Bagnols.

By car

Orange (A7, exit 21) is 30km (19 miles) north of Avignon. For Pont-St-Esprit and Bagnols-sur-Cèze take exit 19 off the A7 and then the N86. For Châteauneuf-du-Pape take the D68 from Orange or N7 and D17 from Avignon.

By train

Orange station (av Frédéric Mistral, 04.90.11.88.00) is on the main Paris–Avignon–Marseille line. Only a few TGVs stop here, so a change is often inevitable.

Carpentras & Mont Ventoux

Its towns cling to the rock faces, visiting cyclists fight cramp on the hill climb, but you can just enjoy a nice glass of rosé and admire the views.

Beaumes-de-Venise: home of excellent dessert wines. *See p114*.

For over half a century after it was ceded to the Holy See in 1274, Carpentras and its surrounds were part of the Comtat Venaissin, a countrified Vatican City embedded in France. Its Rhône-steeped wealth remains today, gorged puce on strawberries, cherries, wine and natural beauty.

Carpentras

Marooned and baking in the Vaucluse plain, famously hot in summer, Carpentras calmly fans itself on provençal bustle and Mistral blow-dries. Former capital of the Comtat Venaissin, the town offered a papal refuge for the Jews, albeit doused with baptismal water. Its name comes from the Gallic for a two-wheeled chariot, whose construction was the ancient speciality. The crenellated 14th-century **Porte d'Orange**, the only vestige of the ancient city walls, cowers at the steaming

ring road roaring by. Low-gear tourism is the name of the game here, with no must-see monuments bar the Friday market, so just take a stroll, soak up the atmosphere and suck on a *berlingot*, the local humbug.

The atmospheric **Musée Sobirats**, an 18th-century townhouse left to Carpentras by a pre-Revolutionary nobleman, has become a decorative arts depot for local generosity. Filled with a motley crew of Moustiers earthenware, Aubusson tapestries and Louis XV furniture donated by citizens, it is a ghostly time-warp of pan-era interior design. Up the road, the lofty 17th-century Chapelle du Collège (rue du Collège, 04.90.60.22.36, call for exhibition times and prices) puts local modern art exhibitions on the high altar. The concierge of the **Musée Comtadin-Duplessis** guards the region's customs and history behind the world's largest key, unlocking primitive local paintings and

PhD in pétanque.

the town's crest since the 13th century. Hunched behind the cathedral is a Roman triumphal arch, now less triumphantly an unofficial *pissoir*. Lacking the grandeur and preservation of its big brother in Orange, it nonetheless features an interesting carving of chained prisoners on the east side. Next door, the **Palais de Justice** boasts 17th-century Romanelli paintings (the tourist office can arrange a visit, *see p111*). This is the spiritual hub of the old town, where an open-air theatre is erected in the last fortnight of July for the patchy arts festival, Les Estivales. From here, one can explore the smart boutiques of the Passage Boyer, the result of a mid 18th-century job creation scheme and based on the Parisian glass-covered passages.

Opposite the Hôtel de Ville is the oldest **Synagogue** to have survived in France. It dates from the 14th century, though it was largely rebuilt in the 18th. You can visit the lower floor, where there are ovens for baking unleavened bread, a *piscina* for women's purification rites, and the sanctuary (men must wear a copal). Today, as the Front National approaches 40 per cent of the Carpentras vote, the Jewish community has considerably depleted, although its culture remains strong. The Jewish cemetery just outside town was desecrated in the 1990s, an event that gained widespread national attention.

South of the centre, the Hôtel-Dieu is a splendid 18th-century hospital, now housing the tourist office. Its handpainted dispensary, open in summer, is a medical sweet shop, stacking a mesmerising collection of earthenware jars, glass bottles and drawers promising rose pills, crushed poppies and dragon's blood. The baroque chapel contains the tomb of Bishop d'Inguimbert, the hospital's founder. With the medical services now trolleyed out of town, Carpentras impatiently waits for the building to be transformed into a cultural centre.

decoy bird-calls, invented by Carpentras's own Théodore Raymond. His great-grandson continues to dupe owls and cuckoos at his eco-museum five kilometres (three miles) away in St-Didier (pl Neuve, 04.90.66.13.13, www.appeaux-raymond.com, admission free).

The Cathédrale St-Siffrein (pl St-Siffrein, open 10am-noon, 2-6pm Tue-Sat) is a hotchpotch of styles and epochs, ranging from 15th-century Provençal Gothic to an early 20th-century bell tower. The 15th-century southern door is known as the Porte des Juifs. When Philippe le Bel expelled the Jews from France, many fled to the papal-controlled Comtat Venaissin, only to be bullied into Catholic baptism. The chained Jews passed through this door on their way to conversion; note the carved rats gnawing on a globe above the door. Poky chapels line the dark, baroque interior towards the resplendent Treasury, its entrance adorned by the relic of St Mors: a horse bit welded from two nails taken from the Cross, and a symbol featured in

The local black truffles, *rabasses*, rear their ugly, coveted heads from November to March, while the colour-striped *berlingots* are perennially hard to dodge. Their birthplace is now a miniature chocolate shop, eccentrically crammed with dusty marzipan cheeseboards (30 rue Porte d'Orange, 04.90.63.07.59). The Confiserie du Mont Ventoux, the last traditional *berlingot* workshop, gives sugary demonstrations in its kitchen, by appointment only (288 av Notre-Dame-de-Santé, 04.90.63.05.25, www.berlingot.net).

Musées Comtadin-Duplessis

234 bd Albin Durand (04.90.63.04.92). **Open** *Apr-Sept* 10am-noon, 2-6pm Mon, Wed-Sun. *Oct-Mar* 10am-noon, 2-4pm Mon, Wed-Sun. **Admission** €2 (with Musée Sobirats); free under-12s. **No credit cards**.

Musée Sobirats

112 rue du Collège (04.90.63.04.92). **Open** *Apr-Sept* 10am-noon, 2-6pm Mon, Wed-Sun. *Oct-Mar* 10am-noon, 2-4pm Mon, Wed-Sun. **Admission** €2 (with Musée Comtadin-Duplessis); free under-12s. **No credit cards**.

Synagogue

pl de l'Hôtel de Ville (04.90.63.39.97). **Open** 10am-noon, 3-5pm Mon-Thur; 10am-noon, 3-4pm Fri. Closed Jewish holidays. **Admission** free.

Where to stay & eat

The rustic-hip bistro **Chez Serge** (90 rue Cottier, 04.90.63.21.24, www.chez-serge.com, closed Mon & Sun, menus €14-€26.50) serves good Mediterranean staples and pizzas, with its terrace now host to a white truffle market on summer Fridays. Armenian-born Serge is a local sage on wine and bonhomie. Its modern edge has just been trumped by **Frank** (30 pl de l'Horloge, 04.90.60.75.00, closed Tue & Wed, menus €20-€33), a brassy new provençal restaurant, swathed in self-conscious ochre and purple, with a spacious courtyard lounging beneath an ancient belfry. The simpler **Les Petites Ya-Ya**, a new bric-a-brac bistro, complete with children's playroom, spills on to an airy fountain square (41 pl Galonne, 04.90.63.24.11, closed Mon, Sun & 2wks Jan, menus €15-€23). Decent hotels flank the town's western edge, notably **Hôtel du Théâtre** (7 bd Albin Durand, 04.90.63.02.90, www.hotel-dutheatre.com, double €57-€70), but for gems embedded in the centre try **Le Fiacre** (153 rue Vigne, 04.90.63.03.15, www.hotel-du-fiacre.com, double €57-€90), a characterful *hôtel particulier*, with giant rooms and frescoes. Designer tranquillity hides down a side street at **La Salamandre**, a homely guesthouse with fountain garden, lavishly decorated by its artist owner Françoise, and her dog menagerie (81 rue de la Monnaie, 04.32.85.07.53, www.salamandre-provence.com, double €75-€85, minimum stay two nights). For out-of-town treats head for the mountains. Venasque, a fortified, hilltop village, teetering 12 kilometres (7.5 miles) south-east, offers postcard views of the Mont Ventoux and vineyard plains from **La Maison aux Volets Bleus**, a florid, snug *chambres d'hôte* (pl des Boviers, 04.90.66.03.04, www.maison-volets-bleus.com, closed mid Nov-mid Mar, double €75-€90). When vertiginous on the panorama and prettiness, come down to earth with the cosy minimalism of the bistro at **L'Auberge la Fontaine** (pl de la Fontaine, 04.90.66.02.96, www.auberge-lafontaine.com, closed dinner Sun, Mon, menus €10-€18). One of Marquis de Sade's chateaux, 15 kilometres (nine miles) from Carpentras in Mazan, is now a

luxury hotel. **Château de Mazan** (pl Napoléon, 04.90.69.62.61, www.chateaudemazan.fr, closed Jan & Feb, double €90-€260, menus €30-€65) demands only slight financial sado-masochism to taste the glory of the summer terrace and underplayed sophistication of Iris Enoch's contemporary cuisine.

Resources

Internet

Wooznext, 284 av du Comtat-Venaissin, (04.90.67.13.54). **Open** 8.30am-7.30pm Mon-Fri; 10am-7.30pm Sat. Closed mid Aug-mid Sept.

Tourist information

Office de Tourisme, Hôtel Dieu, pl Aristide Briand, 84200 Carpentras (04.90.63.00.78/www.tourisme. fr/carpentras). **Open** *Sept-June* 9.30-12.30pm, 2-6pm Mon-Sat. *July-Aug* 9am-1pm, 2-7pm Mon-Sat; 9.30am-1pm Sun.

Pernes-les-Fontaines

Cherubs pout and water trickles down every winding street, refreshing your stroll through this pleasant, somnolent town. The 40 fountains that give Pernes its name and fame date from the mid 18th century. Locals goad that, if you drink from the fontaine de la Lune at the Porte St-Gilles, you'll go mad – a frenzied longing for the loo is more likely thanks to the water symphony splashing around you. The aquatic glory collects on the banks of the Nesque at the fontaine du Cormoran, crowned by an open-winged cormorant and featuring the town's emblem of a pearl and sun.

Cross the river through the Porte Notre-Dame, sole remnant of the 16th-century city walls and housing the chapel of Notre-Dame-des-Grâces. Here lies **l'Eglise Notre-Dame-de-Nazareth** (to arrange a visit, contact the tourist office, *see p112*) dating from the 11th century. Historic highpoints include the 13th-century frescoes of Charles d'Anjou's crusades, decorating upper floors of the Tour Ferrande, which overlooks the fontaine Guillaumin or 'fontaine du gigot', so-called because of its resemblance to a leg of lamb. The **Tour de l'Horloge** (rue du Donjon, open 10am-7pm daily) is all that remains of the chateau of the Counts of Toulouse, who ruled Pernes from 1125 to 1320, while it was still the capital of the Comtat Venaissin. The traditional costume is displayed in the Maison Flechier (pl Flechier, open 10am-noon, 2.30-7pm daily, closed mid Sept-mid June), a dinky museum with provençal Christmas reconstructions – freaky mannequins galore. Market day in Pernes is Saturday, but there is also a flea market on Wednesdays (held at night in July and August).

Avignon & the Vaucluse

Restaurant du Vieux Four: eating in...

Where to stay & eat

Young chef Frédéric Robert masterminds a provençal menu at **Au Fil du Temps** (73 pl Louis Giraud, 04.90.66.48.61, closed Tue, Wed, lunch Sat Oct-June, 2wks Dec & 1wk Feb, menus €30-€67), which features his wonderful beef and foie gras millefeuille. Round the corner, goose-mania hijacks the decor at the **Dame l'Oie** (56 rue Troubadour Durand, 04.90.61.62.43, closed Mon, lunch Tue & 2wks Feb, menus €16-€29), but the thematic overkill mercifully never makes it to the plate, where you'll find a subtly flavoursome regional cuisine instead. A digestive 20-minute walk south **Le Haut Traversier** (293 chemin des Traversiers, 04.90.61.55.72, www.le-haut-traversier.com, double €88-€98) is an elegant *chambres d'hôte* with swimming pool in the pine hills. One of the region's best restaurants is found clinging to a nearby rock face in the village of Le Beaucet: **Auberge du Beaucet** (04.90.66.10.82, closed Mon, Sun, Dec & Jan, menus €32-€34) makes the most of spectacular views with its new terrace. Local wines and the village's own goat's cheese are served.

Resources

Tourist information

Office de Tourisme, pl Gabriel Moutte, 84210 Pernes-les-Fontaines (04.90.61.31.04/www.ville-pernes-les-fontaines.fr). **Open** *June-Aug* 9am-12.30pm, 2.30-7pm Mon-Fri; 9am-12.30pm, 2.30-7pm Sat; 10am-12.30pm Sun. *Sept-May* 9am-noon, 2-6pm Mon-Sat.

Mont Ventoux

The hulking Géant de Provence ('giant of Provence'), Mont Ventoux, crashes in on the landscape at 1,909 metres (6,263 feet), the highest point in the Midi. Gatekeeper between the Alps and the Mediterranean, its trademark bald head of deserted white limestone looms over the skyline, sporting the incongruous toupee of a big red TV and military mast, and resisting the 250kph (155mph) winds that batter it. Petrarch was 'paralysed with amazement' when he hiked to the summit in 1336 – one of the first to get into the extreme sports lark in order to enjoy the spectacular views. On a clear day you can see from the Dentelles de Montmirail to Corsica. A UNESCO protected biosphere, Mont Ventoux has an exceptional range of vegetation, notably *épeautre* (wild barley), Greenland poppy and, of course, Côtes du Ventoux vineyards. The Ventoux is also a pilgrimage site for cyclists, who swarm here in one long, cramp-wracked phalanx from May to October. Its 20 kilometres (12.5 miles) of pure ascent are considered the most torturous stage of the Tour de France – British Olympic cyclist Tommy Simpson collapsed and died only a kilometre from the top in the 1967 race.

The main D974 summit route forks off from the Vaison–Carpentras road at Malaucène, where the tourist office (*see p113*) organises night climbs in summer. Just beyond Malaucène is the source du Groseau spring, reputedly part of an ancient Celtic cult. The unusual octagonal chapel of Notre-Dame-de-Groseau, two chapels grafted together, is all that remains of an 11th-century monastery. Just below the summit is the small ski resort of **Mont Serein** (chalet d'accueil 04.90.63.42.02), a riot of shell suits and four-wheel-drives in winter.

The big, bad climb is up the western flank from the village of Bédoin, outsized by its fine, Jesuit-style church. **Bédoin Location** hires racing bikes (chemin de la Feraille, 04.90.65.94.53, www.bedoin-location.com), and enables the pedalling public to short-cut it up in a bus and freewheel down for €46. Alternatively, it marks the start of a four-hour hike (information available at the tourist office, *see p113*). You can get provisions at the market on a Monday.

...or taking the time to look out.

For a scenic warm-up, cut in on the quieter D19, which runs past the remains of a 17th-century aqueduct to the Belvedere du Paty above the hill village of Crillon-le-Brave. The gentlest, bluest ascent is east along the D164 from Sault, one of the main centres for lavender production.

Where to stay & eat

Persuade your bank manager to let you wallow in the beautifully restored, 16th-century **Hostellerie de Crillon-le-Brave** (pl de l'Eglise, 04.90.65.61.61, www.crillonlebrave. com, closed Oct-Mar, double €155-€560, menus €74), crowning Crillon with slick sophistication and provençal warmth. Just below, **Restaurant du Vieux Four** (04.90.12.81.39, closed Mon, lunch Tue-Sat, mid Nov-Mar, menu €24) is an old bakery offering cosy suppers and plum Ventoux views. In Bédoin, the good-value **Hôtel L'Escapade** (pl Portail l'Olivier, 04.90.65.60.21, closed Nov-Apr, double €45-€50) has just spruced up its restaurant (closed Thur, menus €19-€30). For a fuelling nosh-up before the big climb, **Chez Hortense** (rte de Flassan, 04.90.65.96.06, www.chez-hortense.com, menus €24-€32) vaunts the talents of chef Diego Sanchez among antiques looted from the loft, and strung up on washing lines across the dining-room barn. Push your starting line with a cunning five-kilometre (three-mile) drive up the route du Mont Ventoux to **Le Mas des Vignes** (04.90.65.63.91, closed Mon, lunch Tue, Apr-June & Sept-Oct, lunch Mon-Sat July-Aug, menu €33) to enjoy refined food and views over the Dentelles de Montmirail. Then roll into bed just down the slope at **Le Café Guitrand** (04.90.12.82.61, closed Mon, Sun & Jan, double €50), a handy new retro hotel and café-restaurant (menus €15-€20). For the full outdoors experience, pitch up at the **Camping Municipal** above Sault (04.90.64.07.18, closed Oct-Apr, €3.30/person, tent pitch €2.85).

Resources

Tourist information

Office de Tourisme, Espace Marie-Louis Gravier, pl du Marché, 84410 Bédoin (04.90.65.63.95). **Open** *Mid June-Aug* 9am-6pm Mon-Sat; 9.30am-12.30pm Sun. *Sept-mid June* 9am-12.30pm, 2-6pm Mon-Fri; 9.30am-12.30pm Sat.

Les Dentelles de Montmirail

A show-stopping rock Mohican, the Dentelles are more magnificent than their frilly name (it means 'lace') suggests – the Jurassic limestone crest thrusts itself up into the elements, leaving an intricately jagged fang on the skyline, more like a five-year-old's chaotic grin than a dainty doily. Looped by a GR, it's riddled with stunning walks, climbs, views and amateur easels. Along its hemline, a petticoat of picturesque medieval villages churn out superior wines.

Malaucène, on the road that separates the Dentelles from Mont Ventoux, is the jumping-off point for both. It is dominated by the 14th-century fortified church of St-Michel-et-Pierre, and has a market on Wednesdays. **Le Crestet** above bags the most filmic views, spanning the full amphitheatre of Ventoux, wine valleys and Baronnies hills, meriting the hike up to its 12th-century castle (not open to the public). The village's steep alleys thread scenically around an arcaded square and its 11th-century church; inspiration indeed for the sculptor François Stahly, whose former modernist studio, no longer open to the public, can be seen poking white through the pine trees.

Southwards in **Le Barroux**, the ruined 12th-century castle (04.90.62.35.21, closed Nov-Mar) sternly surveys the Vaucluse plain. Filled with dubious art exhibitions, it stands guard over the village's rare saffron, which disappeared in the 19th century, and is now being recultivated at L'Aube Safran (*see p114*).

Cross the Col de la Chaine from Malaucène for the unmissable vine-striped descent towards terraced **Beaumes-de-Venise**, famous for its sweet dessert wine. You can taste the wine at the young *cave* **Domaine de la Pigeade** (Le Cours, 04.90.62.90.00, www.lapigeade.fr).

On the western flank, the tiny village of **Gigondas** gives its name to the famous grenache-based red wine. The Col du Cayron pass towers above, a challenge for rock-climbers. Further north, the pin-up hill village of **Séguret** plays its pretty card to a crowd of tourists, rubbernecking its tight alleys, 12th-century church and views over the plain. Waist deep in vines and trouble, the region's wine-makers are inventively trying to modernise (and avoid drowning in France's current wine crises), notably through outdoor classical concerts, and the sense-titillating wine museum in **Cairanne** (Cave de Cairanne, rte de Bollène, 04.90.30.82.05, www.cairanne.com).

Where to stay & eat

Wine is the focus in Gigondas, where **Du Verre à l'Assiette** (pl du Village, 04.90.12.36.64, closed Dec-Mar), a jovial, curio-bedecked basement cellar and terrace, serves charcuterie and salads (€8-€12) to give ballast to your voyage through local *crus*. **Restaurant-Hôtel Les Florets** (rte des Dentelles, 04.90.65.85.01, www.hotel-lesflorets.com, closed Jan-mid Mar, double €90-€125), a short drive up into the vineyards, has a florid terrace where the family's own wine accompanies outstanding local dishes (menus €24.50-€38). At the foot of the village, sporty types take a load off at the basic **Gîte d'Etape des Dentelles** (04.90.65.80.85, closed mid Jan-Mar, dormitory €15/person), where courses and information on climbing, mountain biking and hiking are on offer. Alternatively, a stately lawn and pool adorn the **Hôtel Montmirail** (04.90.65.84.01, www.hotel mirail.com, closed mid Oct-mid Mar, double €75-€103), a ten-minute drive east of Vacqueyras. For even greater elegance, live among the vines at the **Domaine de Cabasse** (between Séguret and Sablet, 04.90.46.91.12, www.domaine-de-cabasse.fr, closed Nov-Apr, double €96-€132), where pool-side comforts prevail, and sustenance comes from glossy cuisine (restaurant closed Mar-June, menus €14-€29) and the estate's own wine. Just beneath Col de la Chaine, **Ferme Le Degoutaud** (04.90.62.99.29, www.degoutaud. fr.st, double €58-€63) is a secluded, farmhouse *chambres d'hote*, with nothing but country cooking (menu €21) and unrivalled Dentelles views for company. If you're cycling up Mont Ventoux, **Les Ecuries du Ventoux** (quartier des Grottes, Malaucène, 04.90.65.29.20, closed Dec-Feb, dormitory €14/person) is a stable converted into a clean, efficient *gîte d'étape*, though the beds are wafer thin. Athletic, early-bird starts are wasted on **L'Aube Safran** (chemin du Patifiage, 04.90.62.66.91, www. aube-safran.com, double €90-€115), an airy, polished *chambres d'hôte* with pool, a strong commitment to the Barroux saffron tradition and cuisine (menu €35, restaurant closed Jan).

Resources

Tourist information

Gigondas *Office de Tourisme, pl du Portail, 84190 Gigondas (04.90.65.85.46).* **Open** *Apr-Oct* 10am-12.30pm, 2.30-6.30pm daily. *Nov-Mar* 10am-noon, 2-5pm Mon-Sat.
Malaucène *Syndicat d'Initiative, pl de la Mairie, 88340 Malaucène (04.90.65.22.59).* **Open** *June-Sept* 9am-noon, 2-5pm Mon-Sat. *Oct-May* 9am-noon, 2-5pm Mon-Fri.

Vaison-la-Romaine

Feistily independent and deeply cultured, Vaison was a town that seemed to have it all: Roman remains, vibrant music and contemporary dance scenes, and one of Provence's liveliest markets, all prettily twisted around the Ouvèze river into a knuckle of hills below the Mont Ventoux. Then on 22 September 1992, swollen by heavy rains, the Ouvèze turned into a raging torrent, sweeping away houses, a campsite and an entire industrial estate, killing 37 people. Incredibly, of the town's two bridges, it was the modern road bridge that was destroyed; the 2,000-year-old **Pont Romain** lost its parapet, now rebuilt, but otherwise held up.

Vaison has since returned to winning form; a proud, neat, Parisian holiday bolt-hole. The old town, perched on a cliff, helter-skelters up cobbled medieval streets, past fountains, towards the 12th-century château of the Comtes de Toulouse. The modern town across the river, a sea of ochre roofs, was built up from the 18th century over the original Roman nucleus of Vaison, France's largest public archaeological dig, ongoing since 1907. Bristling with ruins, modern life potters through the two whopping main excavation sites (the single ticket gives admission to both *quartiers*, the museum and the cathedral cloister, *see p115*) with the forum still lurking beneath. If you're looking for the market, Tuesday is the day – plus Thursdays and Saturdays between June and September.

Start at the museum in the **Quartier de Puymin**. Admirably organised, the collection features statues, mosaics and domestic objects. Especially striking is a marble family group, dating from 121 AD, showing a stark-naked

Emperor Hadrian standing proudly next to his elaborately dressed wife Sabina, who is clearly trying to humour her husband. Pride of place goes to a third-century AD silver bust, and writhing floor mosaics from the Peacock villa. Behind the museum is the Roman amphitheatre, pure Ridley Scott, which hosts a summer arts festival, L'Eté de Vaison, with bands like Radiohead booming off its ancient stones.

Head out past the tourist office to the **Quartier de la Villasse**. The colonnaded main street, with its huge paving stones and monumental scale, evokes the prosperity of Roman Vaison better than any other single sight. On either side are remains of shops, baths and villas, including the one where the silver bust was found. Whoever owned this property was in the money; the 5,000 square metres (53,820 square feet) *domus* had its own baths and an extensive hanging garden.

Cathédrale Notre-Dame-de-Nazareth, a ten-minute walk away on avenue Jules Ferry, is an unusual example of Provençal Romanesque, with fine carving and pure lines. Built with its cloister on the ruins of what is thought to be a Roman basilica, it has a notable 11th-century high altar on four delicate marble columns. Up the hill north of the cathedral, the Romanesque Chapelle de St-Quenin (closed to the public) has a unique triangular apse, based on an earlier Roman temple – for centuries the good citizens of Vaison thought it was Roman.

Quartiers de Puymin & de la Villasse

Open *Oct-Dec, Feb* 10am-noon, 2-5pm daily. *Mar* 10am-12.30pm, 2-6pm daily. *Apr-May* (Puymin) 9.30am-6.30pm daily; (La Villasse) 10am-noon, 2.30-6pm daily; (Museum) 10.30am-6pm daily; (Cloister) 10.30am-12.30pm, 2-6pm daily. *June-Sept* (Puymin) 9.30am-6.30pm daily; (La Villasse) 10am-noon, 2.30-6.30pm daily; (Museum) 10.30am-6.30pm daily; (Cloister) 10.30am-12.30pm, 2-6.30pm daily. *All* Closed Jan. **Admission** €7; €3.50 12-18s. **No credit cards**.

Where to stay & eat

Hostellerie le Beffroi (rue de l'Evêché, 04.90.36.04.71, www.le-beffroi.com, closed mid Dec-mid Mar, double €68-€130) offers good views and even better value from its gentrified 16th- and 17th-century buildings (with swimming pool) in the old town; the restaurant (closed Tue, lunch Mon-Fri, dinner Sat, Sun, mid Oct-Mar, menus €26-€41) adds a terrace during the summer holidays. Climb further to **La Fête en Provence** (pl du Vieux Marché, 04.90.36.36.43, www.la-fete-en-provence.com, closed Wed, Nov-Mar, double €65-€95 all year), a distinctly feminine hotel-restaurant with a dreamy, green courtyard and a cuisine of pungent, natural flavours (menu €26). Robert Bardot is Vaison's master-chef, serving heavenly garden feasts by the Pont Romain at **Le Moulin à Huile** (quai Maréchal Foch, 04.90.36.20.67, www.moulin-huile.com, closed Mon & dinner Sun, menus €40-€75), ogled from the opposite bank by the inventive kitchen at **Le Bateleur** (1 pl Théodore Aubanel, 04.90.36.28.04, closed Mon, lunch Sat, menus €18-€40), where dishes like olive oil ice-cream are par for the course. For modern reprieve, **Chez Jérémy** (47 Grande Rue, 04.90.36.20.32, closed Mon & Oct-Dec, average €20) runs a perky, young café-restaurant, pulsing on woks of meat and bean sprouts, and at the nearby **Hôtel Burrhus** (1 pl de Montfort, 04.90.36.00.11, www.burrhus.com, closed mid Dec-mid Jan, double €44-€69) on the town's buzzing bar square, you can sleep with wonderful retro furniture. Don't miss the enchanting hilltop village of Faucon, perched seven kilometres (four miles) north-east facing the Mont Ventoux, where the dynamic, new **Boulangerie des Tilleuls** has opened an alfresco tarte paradise under the lime trees (pl des Tilleuls, 04.90.36.12.91, closed Tue & lunch Sun, average €20). The stylishly minimalist **Le Laurier** (pl de la Mairie, 04.90.46.55.54, closed Mon, lunch Tue June-Sept, mid Nov-mid Dec, Jan & Feb, menus €15-€25) offers regional cuisine and organic wine from the young *vignerons* behind La Roche Buissière.

Resources

Tourist information

Office de Tourisme, pl Chanoine Sautel, 84110 Vaison-la-Romaine (04.90.36.02.11/www.vaison-la-romaine.com). **Open** *Apr-Sept* 9am-noon, 2-5.45pm Mon-Sat; 9am-noon Sun. *Oct-Mar* 9am-noon, 2-5.45pm Mon-Sat.

Getting there & around

By car

Take the A7 (exit 21) and the D950 to Carpentras. The D938 goes south to Pernes, north to Mont Ventoux and Vaison; the D7 heads to Beaumes-de-Venise and Gigondas.

By train/bus

The TGV runs to Avignon, with some services stopping at Orange. **Arnaud** (04.90.63.01.82) runs three buses a day from Marseille to Carpentras, via Pernes-les-Fontaines, three daily from Orange to Carpentras and an hourly service from Avignon. **Cars Comtadins** (04.90.67.20.25) runs four buses a day between Carpentras and Vaison-la-Romaine (also serving Malaucène) and two a day between Carpentras and Bédoin. **Cars Lieutaud** (04.90.36.05.22) runs Orange to Vaison via Sablet, north of Gigondas.

The Drôme Provençale

Scoff truffles, olives and nougat among the beautiful chateaux.

Where the sun shines the crops will grow.

The verdant Drôme Provençale isn't dragging its espadrilles. It is only a few years since the world (itself included) clicked that it had all the natural and historic assets to outshine the over-sold Luberon to the south: Roman bridges, Romanesque churches and medieval to Renaissance chateaux, all wading in vineyards, olive groves, apricot orchards, truffles and lavender. It's now doing a marvellous job of becoming the touristy 'fake-odrome' everyone dreaded. Yet, despite the odd nuclear power station and a *chambres d'hôtes* epidemic, it is still the unspoilt front garden of Provence.

The Tricastin & Grignan

The Tricastin is a Rhône-side plain, venerated for its AOC Coteaux du Tricastin wines and said to be France's leading truffle producer. Unearthed by the Gaul tribe of the Tricastanii, its ancient capital, **St-Paul-Trois-Châteaux**, has zero châteaux, but is home to the textbook 12th-century Romanesque Ancienne Cathédrale. Next door, the **Maison de la Truffe et du Tricastin** has a permanent truffle exhibition and tastings. Upriver, **Montélimar** churns France's nougat (*see p119* **Get stuck into nougat**), with the **Palais des Bonbons & du Nougat** the major formal attraction.

Head east and you'll reach **Grignan**. This graceful, perched village has just cracked the mystery behind the skull of the Marquise de Sévigné, who immortalised the **Château de Grignan** through gushy letters to her daughter. Folk myth has long maintained that, during the Revolution, her tomb in the 16th-century Collégiale St-Sauveur was opened and the crown of her head swiped so the size of her pretty little brain could be ascertained; the mayor took a peek during recent restoration work and confirmed she is indeed topless. Her memory is dug up at every opportunity, notably for the Festival de la Corréspondence in July, at the **Musée de la Typographie** (04.75.46.57.16) and for the 'Women in Literature' festival each September.

The village also boasts a stark, towering, new tourist office and exhibition gallery, courtesy of French architect *du jour* Jean-Michel Wilmotte; it makes a clean contrast with the pretty-pretty cockade of this ancient rose capital. Reclining ladylike on a hillock, the village's 12th-century feudal fort was retouched to become one of the finest examples of Renaissance architecture in south-east France. It's an elegant venue for exhibitions, theatre and concerts, with views out towards Mont Ventoux. There's also a 19th-century, columned *lavoir* in place du Mail, which dominates the marketplace, busy with stalls each Tuesday. For a shady stroll, head to the Grotte de Rochecourbière, a kilometre (half a mile) south of the public swimming pool. The Grotte cocoons a round stone table where the Marquise is said to have penned many of her letters.

South of Grignan, past the lollipop-stick-thin medieval tower at Chamaret, is the medieval hill-village of **Suze-la-Rousse**. Hovering on the west bank of the River Lez, Suze's name is derived from the Celtic 'uz' (meaning high place) and, allegedly, the auburn mane of one of the ladies of **Château de Suze**. The fortified château began life as a 12th-century hunting lodge for the Princes of Orange, before acquiring an Italianate grand courtyard that resonates to the sound of chamber music in July. The château houses the Université du Vin, created in 1978, which has its own vineyard, with 70 different grape varieties. In September the local harvest begins with wine tastings and dancing at the Ban des Vendanges; the Caves Coopératives (04.75.04.48.38) is a good year-round filling station for Coteaux du Tricastin, and there's a village market each Friday.

Château de Grignan

Grignan (04.75.91.83.55). **Open** *Apr-June, Sept-Oct* 9.30-11.30am, 2-5.30pm daily. *Nov-Mar* 9.30-11.30am, 2-6pm Mon, Wed-Sun. *July, Aug* 9.30-11.30am, 2-6pm daily. **Admission** €5.20; €3.20 11-18s; free under-11s. *Gardens* €1. **Credit** V.

Château de Suze-la-Rousse

Suze-la-Rousse (04.75.04.81.44). **Open** *Apr-June, Sept-Oct* 9.30-11.30am, 2-5.30pm daily. *Nov-Mar* 9.30-11.30am, 2-6pm Mon, Wed-Sun. *July, Aug* 9.30-11.30am, 2-6pm daily. **Admission** €3.20; €1.20 11-18s; free under-11s. **Credit** AmEx, MC, V.

Maison de la Truffe et du Tricastin

rue de la République, St-Paul-Trois-Châteaux (04.75.96.61.29/www.maisondelatruffe.com). **Open** *Summer* 3-7pm Mon; 9am-noon, 3-7pm Tue-Sat; 10am-noon, 3-7pm Sun. *Winter* 9am-noon, 2-6pm Tue-Sat; 10am-noon, 2-6pm Sun. **Admission** €3.50; €1.80 7-11s; free under-7s. **No credit cards.**

Palais des Bonbons & du Nougat

100 rte de Valence (04.75.50.62.66/www.palais-bonbons.com). **Open** *June-Sept* 10am-7pm Tue-Sun. *Oct-Dec, Feb-May* 10am-12.30pm, 2-6pm Tue-Sun. Closed Jan. **Admission** €5; €3 5-12s; free under-5s. **No credit cards.**

Where to stay & eat

In season, truffles permeate the menus of local restaurants, notably in St-Paul-Trois-Châteaux, **L'Esplan** (15 pl de l'Esplan, 04.75.96.64.64, closed lunch, late Dec-mid Jan, menus €20-€45, all-truffle menu €70) and, on the outskirts, the flamboyant new **Villa Augusta** (14 rue du Serre Blanc, 04.75.97.29.29, www.villaaugusta-hotel.com, double €145-€400, menus €42-€85, restaurant closed Mon, dinner Sun). Attempting to plug the luxury hotel gap between Lyon and Avignon, Villa Augusta is a heavy-handed restoration of a manor house built on Roman remains, with original frescoes among the piped music and parks, plus the Pourcel twins in the restaurant. For even more excess, **Le Tissonier** (04.75.04.44.03, closed dinner Sun, Mon, menus €19-€30), in an alley in Garde Adhémar, has a wonderful jumble of puppets and fishing nets on its walls.

In Grignan, the **Café de Sévigné** (pl Sévigné, 04.75.46.51.82) is good for a scenic beer, while friendly **Hôtel Sévigné** (15 pl Castellane, 04.75.46.50.97, www.hotel-sevigne-grignan.com, double €34-€118), at the foot of the château, is still undergoing a designer make-over; the restaurant (closed dinner Sun, all Mon, menus €12-€28) produces innovative food. Frou-frou 19th-century **Manoir de la Roseraie** (rte de Valréas, 04.75.46.58.15, www.manoirdelaroseraie.com, closed Jan-mid Feb & early Dec, double €162-€340, menus €34-€63) perhaps overdoes the rose motif, but is redeemed by its lawns, pool, tennis court and chef Freddy Trichet. **Le Clair de la Plume** (pl du Mail, 04.75.91.81.30, double €90-€165) is a tasteful rural-chic hotel, with trellised garden and English tearoom. Welcome newcomer **Coté Patio** (rue du Grand Faubourg, 04.75.46.59.20, closed 2wks Nov, menu €25) fills its fountain courtyard with the scent of truffle raviole, while 18th-century **Rosa Alba** (04.75.51.18.52, www.larosaalba.com, double €78-€90) is a modern-rustic guesthouse, full of books, whose hostess Frédérique is a young winegrower. **La Maison du Moulin** (quartier petit Cordy, 04.75.46.56.94, www.maisondumoulin.com, double €75-€120) is an old watermill with a pool, library and rooms decorated in glossy magazine style; it hosts lavender and truffle cookery weekends. Towards Suze, **Campsite Les Truffières** (lieu-dit Nachony, 04.75.46.93.62, www.lestruffieres.com, closed Oct-mid Apr, plot for two €13.50, electricity €4.20) has an outdoor pool.

In Suze-la-Rousse, the vine-clad terrace of **Pizzeria de la Fontaine** (pl du Champ de Mars, 04.75.98.28.67, average €9) offers down-to-earth replenishment, while elegant rest, homely suppers and a pool can be found at **Les Aiguières** guesthouse (rue de la Fontaine d'Argent, 04.75.98.40.80, www.les-aiguieres.com, double €89). For highbrow wine action, visit the 18th-century **Château La Borie** (04.75.04.81.03), a revered producer of Côtes du Rhône to the north of the village.

Further south, the luxury option is the **Château de Rochegude** (Rochegude, 04.75.97.21.10, www.chateauderochegude.com, double €170-€355, closed early Nov), a grandiose castle with restaurant (closed Nov, dinner Sun-lunch Tue Dec-Apr, menus €31-€85), park, pool and tennis court.

Resources

Tourist information

Grignan *Office de Tourisme, pl du Jeu de Ballon, 26230 Grignan (04.75.46.56.75/www.tourisme-paydegrignan.com).* **Open** *June, Sept* 9.30am-12.30pm, 2-6pm Mon-Sat. *July, Aug* 9.30am-12.30pm, 2-7pm daily. *Oct-May* 9.30am-12.30pm, 2-5.30pm Mon-Sat.

Suze-la-Rousse *Office de Tourisme, av des Côtes-du-Rhône, 26790 Suze-la-Rousse (04.75.04.81.41).* **Open** *Sept-June* 9am-noon, 2.30-6pm Tue-Fri; 9am-noon Sat. *July, Aug* 9am-noon, 2.30-6.30pm Mon-Fri; 9am-noon, 2.30-4.30pm Sat.

Nyons

Giono called Nyons 'paradise on earth': with its very own regenerative wind (the Pontias), perennial sun and a halo of olive groves, this ante-chamber to heaven is fast filling with old-people's homes and taramasalata-pink villas. Dubbed 'Petit Nice', Nyons crouches in a bowl of mountains at the opening of the Eygues Valley, pulling in the visitors with its medieval place des Arcades, the vaulted rue des Grands Forts and the remains of a feudal château. The 13th-century Tour Randonné – once a prison, but rebuilt as a chapel in the 19th century – dominates the town, looming over the bustling Thursday morning market.

The most northerly olive-growing area in Europe, Nyon produces the mild and fruity black *tanche*, the first variety in France to be awarded an *appellation d'origine contrôlée*. The olive harvest festival is in early February, and July's Les Olivades sees tastings, night markets and even a beauty contest. Olive-pressing history tours are given at the **Musée de l'Olivier** and the family-run **Les Vieux Moulins** on the banks of the Eygues. Olives are pressed next door at the new Moulin Autrand-Dozol (04.75.26.02.52, shop closed Sun) and olive-related products, local wines and tours are available at the **Vignolis Coopérative du Nyonsais** (pl Olivier de Serres, 04.75.26.95.00). **La Scourtinerie** (36 rue de la Maladrerie, 04.75.26.33.52, closed Sun) is France's last workshop (open on weekdays only) to make natural-fibre olive-pressing mats by hand. Next to Les Vieux Moulins, the 'Roman' donkey bridge, an elegant single arch actually built in the 13th and 14th centuries, is enveloped in

summer by the scent of lavender from the **Distillerie Bleu Provence**, where you can make your own eau de toilette.

For a novel dip, the Nyonsoldeïado outdoor waterworld (promenade de la Digue, 04.75.26.06.92, closed Sun) is refreshingly tame. For scenic walks, the Sentier des Oliviers takes you up through the olive groves, while the more challenging forest path along the Garde-Grosse mountain to the south provides soaring views. If you're driving in from Grignan, hug the foot of the mountain through the pretty village of Rousset-les-Vignes and take the lime-tree avenue towards **Venterol**, a radiant, picture-postcard village tumbling down the hillside, with a fine 17th-century bell tower.

Distillerie Bleu Provence

58 promenade de la Digue (04.75.26.10.42/ www.distillerie-bleu-provence.com). **Open** *May-Oct* 9.30am-12.30pm, 2.30-7.30pm daily. *Nov-Apr* 10am-12.30pm, 2.30-6.30pm daily. **Admission** €3; free under-12s. **Credit** AmEx, MC, V.

Musée de l'Olivier

allée des Tilleuls (04.75.26.12.12). **Open** 10-11.30am, 2.30-5.30pm daily. **Admission** €2; €1 students, 10-18s; free under-10s. **No credit cards**.

Les Vieux Moulins

4 promenade de la Digue (04.75.26.11.00/ http://vieuxmoulins.free.fr). **Open** 10am-noon, 2.30-6pm Tue-Sat. Closed Jan-Mar, Nov. **Admission** €4; free under-12s. **Credit** AmEx, DC, MC, V.

Where to eat, drink & stay

If your palate needs some aromatherapy, lime-blossom and fig spike the beer at the friendly provençal microbrewery **Brasserie Artisanale du Sud** (69 av Frédéric Mistral, 04.75.26.95.75, www.la-grihete.com, closed Sun). **Café de la Bourse** (04.75.26.29.75, menus €17.50-€33.50) pours crowds out on to the central place des Arcades, before they head across the square to the vapour sprays and modern-brasserie comforts of the new **Café Restaurant Les Arcades** (04.75.26.29.75, closed Tue, Nov-Feb, menus €17.50-€2.50). **Le 29** (29 rue des Déportés, 04.75.26.38.73, closed Mon & Tue Sept-June, Mon July & Aug, menus €19.90-€29.90) is a cocksure new restaurant that brings you the affordable talents of a young chef hailing from the three Michelin-starred Pic in Valence. Three sisters mother the cheap and cheerful **Hôtel au Petit Nice** (4 av Paul Laurens, 04.75.26.09.46, closed 3wks Nov, double €32.50-€45), helped by its decent €13 weekday menu (restaurant closed dinner Mon & Sun). **Une Autre Maison** (pl de la République, 04.75.26.43.09, www.uneautremaison.com, closed Nov-Jan, double €80-€135, restaurant

Get stuck into nougat

Nougat has been the emblematic bonbon of Provence since the 17th century and **Montélimar** (see p116) is its capital. Here agronomist Olivier de Serre planted the first almond trees brought to Provence from Asia, set among lavender hazy with honeybees. The Greeks are believed to have come up with the idea of mixing nuts and honey into a patty, but it was Montélimar that hit on using almonds – a nut that was not only posh but also long-lasting.

Nougat's meteoric rise up the sweet hierarchy began with the Dukes of Burgundy and Berry, who took a fancy to it on their return from Spain, but it was the car that cemented nougat's celebrity. The 30km (20-mile) summer-holiday tailbacks through Montélimar along Route National 7 filled the town with bored motorists, all itching to find something to jam shut the mouths of their yapping kids.

To merit the '...de Montélimar' appellation, nougat must contain 30 per cent almonds (slipping in a few Sicilian pistachios is allowed) and 32 per cent honey, of which 7 per cent has to be lavender honey. The derivatives are many (chocolate-coated, rose-flavoured, with salt, coconut and the sublime fig, as well as as a nougat spread) but quality and price remain high: these unassuming, unsparkling little sweets weigh in at a pricey €25/kg (about €11/lb), and that's just the pedestrian grade.

North of Montélimar's centre, the new museum **Palais des Bonbons et du Nougat** (see p117) is engagingly informative and appropriately saccharine, Wonka-worthy gimmicks abound – free sweets, Van Gogh's Sunflowers 'painted' in Carambars, a music dome spinning syrupy tunes like 'A Spoonful of Sugar', the World's Biggest Chuppa Chup (strawberry flavour, if you're wondering), all climaxing with the World's Biggest Slab of Nougat. This 1,300kg (2,870lb) cliff is the work of a young sweet-maker who has just opened workshop-boutique **Le Maître Gourmet** (12 rue St-Gaucher, 04.75.51. 30.47, www.le-maitre-gourmet.com) near the tourist office.

Most of Montélimar's nougat factories are now in the unappetising industrial outskirts to the south. You can visit their products in any shop in the town centre, but the tourist office provides a full list of weekday guided visits (Allées Provençales, 04.75.01.00.20,

www.montelimar-tourisme.com). Arrive early in the morning to watch the cuisson (cooking), which can start at 5am in the heat of summer. In warm, sugary air, copper bain-maries of scalding caramel and moussey coiffs of whipped egg white are mixed before your eyes. Even the Mistral counts as an ingredient: a blustery day means a fine, drier batch, with cooking methods adapted accordingly. The mix, knobbly with blanched almonds, is spread into moulds with gargantuan wooden spatulas, then patted down – traditionally by the hand of the maître, but nowadays with metal clubs.

You could visit an industrial giant like **Gerbe d'Or** (140 av Jean-Jaurès, 01.75. 00.63.77) to see dominos of nougat spat off the production lines at impressive speed, but there's a highly staged museum tour at **Arnaud Soubéyran** (quartier des Blaches, RN7, 04.75.51.01.35, www.nougat soubeyran.com), who've been hand-making nougat since 1837. Expect period reconstructions, a human-sized beehive and a tasting session that prepares you for the boutique and salon de thé. For more atmosphere, enter the gentle chaos of **Le Chaudron d'Or** (17 av du 52ième RI, 04.75.01.03.95, www.chaudron-dor.com) in the town centre. Here the informal tour weaves in and out of clunking 1950s machines, while women in white bonnets push and wrap. Manager Hervé Contaux banters away in English while gracefully sawing nougat into tasters. **Diane de Poytiers** (99 av Jean-Jaurès, 04.75.01. 647.02, www.diane-de-poytiers.fr), one of Henry II's mistresses, is an appropriately classy figurehead for the elegant factory and boutique that bears her name, while the delicious, retro-pink façade of **Les Trois Abeilles** (85/87 av Jean-Jaurès, 04.75.01.64.11, www.nougats-les-trois-abeilles.com) is tribute to nougat's glorious past.

Sadly, nougat's future is not so sunny. Drought, diseased bees, disastrous almond crops (the nuts are now mostly imported from California) and a price war with Chinese lavender-honey producers are pushing nougat off the menu. Try to forget about it by tucking into a nougat glacé, the ice-queen of puddings, best enjoyed at the restaurant **Aux Gourmands** (8 pl du Marché, 04.75.01.16.21).

closed lunch, menu €42) is the design choice, with a walled garden, a pool and lithe guests in hotel dressing gowns limbering up for a massage in the new hammam or a truffle cookery weekend. In Venterol, **Café de la Poste** (1 pl Sabarot, 04.75.27.33.62, closed Mon-Thur Sept-May, dinner Mon & Sun June-Aug, menus €12-€18) has been rejuvenated into a comely bistro by a young postwoman; dishes include own-made daube provençale and wild barley gratin. At the village entrance **La Ferme des Auches** (04.75.27.92.85, www.fermedesauches.com, closed Jan & Feb, double €48) is a farmhouse *chambres d'hôte*, set among vines.

Resources

Tourist information

Office de Tourisme, pl de la Libération, 26110 Nyons (04.75.26.10.35/www.paysdenyons.com). **Open** *June, Sept* 9.30am-noon, 2.30-6pm Mon-Sat; 10am-1pm Sun. *July, Aug* 9am-12.30pm, 2.30-7pm Mon-Sat; 10am-1pm, 3-5pm Sun. *Oct-May* 9.30am-noon, 2.30-5.45pm Mon-Sat.

Buis-les-Baronnies

Set in a heady landscape of apricot orchards and aromatic plants, the precipitous limestone Baronnies mountains south-east of Nyons are popular for rock-climbing, hiking and riding. Sheltered beside the River Ouvèze under the jagged Rocher St-Julien, sleepy **Buis-les-Baronnies** was the medieval capital of the Barons of Mévouillon. With the Renaissance façade of the Couvent des Ursulines (now used for art exhibitions) as its backdrop, the village enjoys a tranquillity interrupted only by the thud of pétanque and, during the July arts festival, drifting jazz and classical tunes. Since the 19th century Buis has produced almost all of France's world-class lime-blossom, hand-harvested for Europe's largest *tilleul* fair each July. Aromatic and medicinal herbs are available at the Wednesday market in place des Arcades, at *herborist* Bernard Laget (pl des Herbes, 04.75.28.16.42) or at the **Maison des Plantes Aromatiques et Médicinales**. Built into the medieval ramparts, with its own herb garden, the latter presents a small, fragrant display on lime-blossom and lavender, as well as an amusing 'smell organ'.

An hour-long walk through terraced olive groves among screaming crickets takes you to the hillside village of **La Roche-sur-le-Buis**, where the Chapelle des Pénitents is now a micro-museum of traditional farm instruments, with its tiny graveyard cultivated into an enchanting 'symbolic plant garden'.

Maison des Plantes Aromatiques et Médicinales

14 bd Eysseric (04.75.28.04.59/www.maisondes plantes.com). **Open** *July, Aug* 9am-12.30pm, 3-7pm Mon-Sat; 10am-noon, 3-7pm Sun. *Sept-June* 9.15am-noon, 2-6pm Mon-Sat; 10am-12.30pm, 2.30-5.30pm Sun. **Admission** €3.50; €1.50 12-18s; free under-12s. **No credit cards.**

Where to stay & eat

At the western end of Buis-les-Baronnies **Le Grill du Four à Pain** (24 av Boissy d'Anglas, 04.75.28.10.34, closed lunch Mon & Tue, menus €20-€30) blends sweet flavours on its garden terrace, while central **La Fourchette** (pl des Arcades, 04.75.28.03.31, closed lunch Mon July & Aug, lunch Mon & dinner Sun Sept & Dec-June, menus €15-€36) serves refined regional cuisine under the arcades. The rambling **Hôtel les Arcades** (pl des Arcades, 04.75.28.11.31, www.hotelarcades.fr, closed Dec-Feb, double €42-€57) boasts a garden, swimming pool and gentle wake-up calls from the fountain in the square. For ecclesiastical pomp **l'Ancienne Cure** (2 rue du Paroir, 04.75.28.22.08, closed mid Nov-Mar, double €60-€100), holiday home of the bishop of Valence in the 15th century, is now a gracious *chambres d'hôte*, lavishly decorated with oriental antiques.

Resources

Tourist information

Office de Tourisme, 14 bd Eysseric, 26170 Buis-les-Baronnies (04.75.28.04.59). **Open** *July-Aug* 9am-12.30pm, 3-7pm Mon-Sat; 10am-noon, 3-7pm Sun. *Sept-June* 9am-noon, 2-6pm daily.

Getting there & around

By car

Leave the A7 autoroute at exit 18 and take the D133 and D541 for Grignan, or take exit 19 and the D994 for Suze-la-Rousse. Nyons is 20km (12 miles) from Grignan by the D941 and D538, and 30km (19 miles) from Buis by the D5, D46 and D538.

By bus/train

The nearest train stations are Avignon, Orange and Montélimar. **Cars Lieutaud** (04.90.36.05.22) runs two buses every day except Sunday between Nyons and Avignon via Vaison-la-Romaine, and between Avignon and Buis-les-Baronnies. **Cars Dunevon** (04.75.28.41.54) runs two buses a day, except weekends, between Nyons and Buis. **Cars Teste** (04.75.00.27.90) runs five buses a day between Montélimar and Nyons via Grignan, plus buses between Grignan and Nyons via Valréas. **Autocars Petit Nice** (04.75.26.35.58) runs five buses each day except Sunday, from Nyons to Vaison, with 3 return journeys. Buses are less frequent in school holidays.

The Luberon

It's home, second home, to many Parisians but the charm that ensorcelled Peter Mayle is still here in abundance.

One year – 1989 – is pre-eminent in the recent history of the Luberon. It wasn't due to a particularly fine vintage of Côtes de Luberon, Côtes de Ventoux or Coteaux de Pierrevert, nor an unusually bounteous crop of lavender or olives. No – this was the year ad-man Peter Mayle published his book *A Year in Provence* and brought champagne socialists flocking in. It isn't just the Brits: worldly Parisians are just as likely to be hiding out in those designer *mas* and exchanging *bisous* at cafés. Surprisingly, the Luberon has remained largely unspoilt by the incomers, though four-fold property price increases as the newbies renovate decrepit *bastides* (there is a limit on new construction) have done nothing to ease the lot of the locals. But you'll still find local farmers sipping a *pastis* down age-old, stone backstreets.

Hill villages, fortresses and Renaissance châteaux testify to a proudly unconventional land that was heavily embroiled in the Wars of Religion. More tranquil these days, the area was in 1977 declared a Parc Régional. Its heart is the rocky limestone massif of the Montagne du Luberon, cut in two by the Aiguebrun Valley, which divides the Petit Luberon to the west from the Grand Luberon (rising to 1,125 metres or 3,690 feet at Mourre Nègre) to the east.

Still a major producer of fruit and veg, the Luberon remains pleasantly green even in high summer, and offers plenty of opportunities for walking, riding and cycling. Footpaths include the *grandes randonnées* GR6, 9, 92 and 97. 'Le Luberon en vélo' is a 100-kilometre (62-mile) bike route running partially along disused railway tracks; green and white arrows point in the direction Cavaillon–Apt–Forcalquier, green and orange arrows indicate the opposite direction, and a southern route completes the loop via Manosque, Lourmarin and Lauris.

North Luberon: from Taillades to Saignon

Once important for stone quarrying, the rugged northern flank of the Montagne du Luberon is punctuated by picturesque hill villages. At the western edge of the ridge, tranquil **Taillades** is the village that best recalls the stone-quarrying past. Houses seem to sit on blocks of cut rock

and the remains of two châteaux – one fortified, one dating from the Renaissance – face each other across a ravine. A path climbs to a chapel perched over one former quarry, now an atmospheric outdoor theatre.

Hugging the N100, the main attraction in inconspicuous **Coustellet** is its summer farmers' market (Wed evening, Sun morning, Apr-Nov), but you might also want to visit the **Musée de la Lavande**, where a film explains how the tiny purple flowers are distilled and a smelling machine demonstrates the difference between true lavender and the hybrid *lavindin*. It is run by a family that still cultivates lavender high up on Mont Ventoux.

Oppède-le-Vieux, reached through narrow country lanes to the south, perfectly symbolises the rebirth of the Luberon. The old village was abandoned during the 19th century but has been resettled since the 1960s by artists, potters and writers; it is still romantically overgrown.

Bonnieux. *See p122.*

At the top are the restored Romanesque **Collégiale Notre-Dame-d'Alidon**, with its gargoyle-adorned belltower, and the ruined castle of notorious baron Jean de Meynier. He was behind the brutal 1545 massacre of the Vaudois (or Waldensian) heretics, a proto-Protestant sect who populated many of the Luberon villages. Below the village, the *Sentier vigneron* follows quiet lanes amid vineyards, with discreet panels identifying grape varieties.

On the crest of a hill just to the east, **Ménerbes** remains a clock-stopped stone village with fine doorways that point to a prosperous past. Artists Pablo Picasso, Nicolas de Stael and Dora Maar all spent some time living here. At the top of the village, the turreted former château (not open to the public) was once a Vaudois stronghold. On the plain below, you can visit the state-of-the-art cellars of the **Domaine de la Citadelle**, where Yves Rousset-Rouard, producer of the *Emmanuelle* films, has established himself as one of the area's most respected wine makers. The visit also takes in the corkscrews of the **Musée du Tire-Bouchon**. You'll also find the Maison de la Truffe et Vin (04.90.72.52.10) has an excellent display in its cellars about the wines of the area. Between Ménerbes and Lacoste on the scenic D109, a bumpy track leads to the isolated **Abbaye St-Hilaire**, the remains of a 13th-century Carmelite priory whose cloister, chapel and garden have been lovingly restored over many years by the Bride family.

With its fortified medieval gateways and cobbled streets, the tiny, semi-deserted village of **Lacoste** should not be missed. The ruined castle at the top was the home of the scandalous Marquis de Sade on and off for 30 years until his imprisonment in 1786. Having been acquired by global fashion magnate Pierre Cardin, it now hosts an opera festival each summer. From here the road zigzags up the ramparts of **Bonnieux**. Inhabited since Neolithic times, Bonnieux became a Templar *commanderie* and later a papal outpost, although it was reunited with France back in 1793. Also of interest are a 12th-century, hilltop church, reached up cobbled steps from rue de la République; a newer parish church in the lower village, which contains four 15th-century panel paintings; the tiny **Musée de la Boulangerie**; and the remains of the towers and gates that once surrounded the village. North of Bonnieux on the way to the Roman **Pont Julien**, the **Château de Mille** (D3, rte de Bonnieux, 04.90.74.11.94) is the oldest wine château in the Luberon and a former summer residence of the Avignon Papacy. You can't visit the château itself, but you can appreciate the exterior while buying a few bottles of wine.

Out of the past

On a Sunday morning, at the height of the season, L'Isle-sur-la-Sorgue gets busier than just about anywhere else in France. And with good reason: this mini Venice is an antiques mecca. Dealers began settling here in the early 1960s, which is when the first *foires à la brocante* were held; these days, there are an estimated 300 dealers concentrated along avenue de la Libération, avenue des Quatre Otages and around the station, many of them setting up stall in picturesque canalside locations. Each Sunday, the antiques shops and arcades (open 10am-7pm Mon, Sat, Sun) are joined by squadrons of junkier *brocanteurs* who line avenue des Quatre Otages, while at Easter and on 15 August major antiques fairs flow over into nearby fields. Merchandise ranges from high-quality antiques and garden statuary to pedal cars and quirky collectibles, including many provençal items, such as gilt mirrors, armoires, carved buffets and openwork bread cabinets, printed fabrics, and Apt, Moustiers and Marseille faïence. There are also architectural salvage specialists offering old zinc bars, bistro fittings and hotel reception booths.

The different arcades have different characters: two-storey **Quai de la Gare** (4 av Julien Guigue) is the most upmarket, with plenty of fine 18th-century furniture, paintings and porcelain; **Village des Antiquaires de la Gare** (2bis av de l'Egalité), in a former carpet factory, is more ramshackle and boho; **Hôtel Dongier** (9 esplanade Robert Vasse) is set up as a series of smart interiors; **Isle-aux-Brocantes** (7 av des Quatre Otages) is accessed via a canal and abounds in vintage garden furniture and 20th-century items.

Even if there are few true bargains (some shops seem to ship entire crates of furniture direct to stores in the USA, and it's common to hear sums being discussed in dollars), prices are noticeably lower than in Paris, where a fair number of the goods end up. Needless to say, the usual bargaining rules apply. Should you succumb, transport firms can ship your purchases around the world.

In the less-known eastern half of the Luberon above Apt, the remarkably unspoiled village of **Saignon** stretches along a craggy escarpment between a square-towered Romanesque church and cemetery and a rocky belvedere. Its remote location and mountain site made the nearby hamlet of **Buoux** an important refuge during the Wars of Religion: high on the hillside (take a good pair of shoes) are ruins of the **Fort de Buoux**, demolished by Louis XIV to deter Huguenots from taking refuge here. A little further, at the end of the secluded Aiguebrun Valley, rock climbers pepper the overhanging crags, and assorted footpaths lead to Sivergues and the Mourre Nègre.

Abbaye St-Hilaire

Ménerbes (04.90.75.88.83). **Open** *Summer* 9am-7pm daily. *Winter* 10am-6pm daily. **Admission** free (donations welcome).

Collégiale Notre-Dame-d'Alidon

Oppède-le-Vieux. **Open** *July, Aug* 10am-7pm daily. *Apr-June, Sept-Nov* 10am-7pm Sat, Sun, or by appointment in the *mairie* (04.90.76.90.06). Closed Dec-Mar. **Admission** free.

Fort de Buoux

Buoux (04.90.74.25.75). **Open** dawn-dusk daily. Closed in bad weather. **Admission** €3; €2 7-16s, students; free under-12s. **No credit cards**.

Musée de la Boulangerie

12 rue de la République, Bonnieux (04.90.75.88.34). **Open** *Apr-June, Sept, Oct* 10am-12.30pm, 2.30-6pm Mon, Wed-Sun. *July, Aug* 10am-1pm, 3-6.30pm Mon, Wed-Sun. Closed Nov-Mar. **Admission** €3.50; €1.50 12-16s, students; free under-12s. **No credit cards**.

Musée de la Lavande

rte de Gordes, Coustellet (04.90.76.91.23/www.musee delalavande.com). **Open** *Early-mid Feb, mid Sept-Dec* 10am-noon, 2-6pm daily. *Mid Feb-June, early-mid Sept* 10am-noon, 2-7pm daily. *July, Aug* 9am-7pm daily. Closed Jan. **Admission** €4; free under-15s. **Credit** (shop only) AmEx, DC, MC, V.

Musée du Tire-Bouchon

Domaine de la Citadelle, Le Chataignier, chemin de Cavaillon, Ménerbes (04.90.72.41.58/www.musee dutirebouchon.com). **Open** *Apr-Sept* 9am-noon, 2-7pm daily. *Oct-Mar* 9am-noon, 2-6pm Mon-Sat. **Admission** €4; €2 students; free under-15s. **Credit** MC, V.

Where to stay & eat

At Robion, on the road between Taillades and Coustellet, **Lou Luberon** (av Aristide Briand, 04.90.76.65.04, menus €11.50-€26) looks like a simple roadside bar but serves delicious salads and carefully prepared regional dishes (except on Sundays, when it's pizza and salad only). At Coustellet itself, Olivier Gouin took over the old

family butcher **Maison Gouin** (pl du Marché Paysan, 04.90.76.90.18, closed Wed, mid Nov-early Dec, Feb-early Mar, menus €13-€33) and turned it into an haute cuisine restaurant, combined with butcher and upmarket deli. There's an informal, inexpensive menu at lunch and a more dressed-up affair in the evening.

Sadist connections abound in Lacoste: for a start, try simple *café-tabac* **Café de Sade** (rue Basse, 04.90.75.82.29, café closed mid Jan-Feb, restaurant closed mid Nov-mid Mar, menus €15-€21) for a drink, nosh and some gossip.

In Bonnieux there are several options. In an old bakery the semi-troglodyte **Le Fournil** (5 pl Carnot, 04.90.75.83.62, closed Mon, Tue & Sat lunch, Dec-Jan, menus €25-€35) is the definition of low-key provençal style, with great service and an inventive menu that uses local produce. The 18th-century **Hostellerie de la Prieuré** (rue Jean-Baptiste Auvard, 04.90.75.80.78, closed Nov-Mar, double €53-€98; restaurant closed Tue, lunch Wed, Nov-Mar, menus €19-€33.50), on the descent to Lacoste, has a chapel and vast fireplaces as reminders of its priory past; bedrooms overlook a walled garden or ramparts. On the *garrigue*-covered plateau above the village, **Le Bastide de Capelongue** (04.90.75.89.78, www.capelongue.com, double €160-€320, menus €91-€152) has 17 airy, white and cream bedrooms, and the Michelin-starred chef Edouard Loubet. Off the D194 **Les Trois Sources** (chemin de la Chaîne, 04.90.75.95.58, www.lestroissources.com, double €60-€130) is a lovely *chambres d'hôte* in an ancient building surrounded by mulberry trees. **Café de la Gare** (rte gare, 04.90.75.82.00, menus €8) is a popular and friendly restaurant in an old railway station (the last train came through here some time around the late 1980s), with terrific views and an outside terrace.

The remote **Auberge des Seguins** (Buoux, 04.90.74.16.37, double €50-€85, half-board), under the crags at the end of a valley, is a popular choice with walkers and rock climbers, and has a small *buvette* where you can stop for a drink. In Saignon, the **Auberge du Presbytère** (pl de la Fontaine, 04.90.74.11.50, www.auberge-presbytere.com, closed mid Nov-mid Feb except Christmas, double €55-€125; restaurant closed Wed, menus €26-€34) overlooks the village square, with tables set out by the fountain in summer. **Chambre de Séjour avec Vue** (04.90.04.85.01, www. chambreavecvue.com, double €75) is an old house that has been transformed with a remarkable eye for colour and design by Kamila Regent; she invites artists in residence to work and exhibit in the house, while letting out three bedrooms and an apartment. Evening meals (€25) are available on request.

Resources

Tourist information

Bonnieux *Office de Tourisme, 7 pl Carnot, 04480 Bonnieux (04.90.75.91.90).* **Open** 2-6pm Mon; 9.30am-12.30pm, 2-6pm Tue-Sat.

Lourmarin & the south Luberon chateaux

The southern edge of the range is known for its trio of Renaissance châteaux. One of the largest and liveliest Luberon villages, **Lourmarin**, with its cluster of grey-shuttered stone houses, belfry and medieval church, is the de facto gastronomic capital of the area. Despite all the antiques and gift shops, estate agents and a fabulous kitchen shop, tourism here remains civilised, with action centred on the main street where Café Gaby and Café de l'Ormeau enjoy a friendly rivalry. Lourmarin was settled by Vaudois peasants and suffered in the merciless massacre of April 1545, when much of the village was temporarily abandoned. Rebuilt, it thrived in the 17th and 18th centuries as a centre of silk production. The Protestant temple now stands at the exterior of the village. From here rue du Temple leads to the 15th- to 16th-century **Château de Lourmarin**, which presents a fortified medieval aspect from one side and the large windows of the Renaissance from the other. The château narrowly escaped destruction in the Revolution; it was restored in the early 1900s and since 1925 has hosted artists- and writers-in-residence and chamber music concerts (summer only). Don't miss the cantilever staircase and an extraordinary Renaissance fireplace, which combines classical Corinthian capitals with Native American figures from the newly discovered Americas. Albert Camus lived on the edge of the village and is buried in the cemetery alongside his wife. Lourmarin's market is on a Friday morning.

West of Lourmarin, **Mérindol** is worth a visit not so much for its second homes of today as for the moving evocation of what used to be. Climb the waymarked route des Vaudois to a ruined village that is witness to the massacre of 1545, when Jean de Meynier, president of the Parlement d'Aix, sent in his troops to implement the Decree of Mérindol, which condemned the Vaudois as heretics. Within six days 22 villages had been pillaged and burned, and an estimated 2,500 were dead. Mérindol was razed to the ground and its ruined citadel (now bearing the plaque of the Mémorial des Vaudois) remains a potent symbol. Only one large villa spoils the sense of abandon and there are hilltop views as far as the Alpilles,

Montagne Ste-Victoire and the Ste-Baume massif. Arrive on Wednesday morning if you want to visit the market.

West of Mérindol, the **Gorges de Regalon** (parking €2.30), where the river has carved out a narrow gorge, provide a welcome breath of cool air. They are as pleasant for a stroll amid wild rosemary and shrubs as for making a start on the more ambitious walk to Oppède across the range. Although dry in summer, the gorge is apt to flood after heavy rain.

More workaday than chic Lourmarin, **Cadenet** has some charming stepped streets and ancient houses, as well as the small **Musée de la Vannerie**, devoted to basketmaking, once one of the town's principal activities; the market takes place on Monday mornings. There's a statue of the drummer boy of Arcole in the main square: born in the village, he saved French troops in the war against Austria in 1796. Only foundations remain of the château that once towered above the village.

East of Lourmarin on the D27, lovely, still partly walled **Cucuron** is a tangle of narrow streets. On place de l'Horloge, a fortified bell-tower gateway leads to a ruined keep. The surprisingly large Eglise Notre-Dame-de-Beaulieu contains a fine baroque altarpiece and Gothic side chapels. Below, sunk into a rock, the Moulin à Huile Dauphin olive press (04.90.77.26.17, closed Jan-Oct, shop open all year) makes deliciously fruity olive oil and is a favourite with some of the super-chefs. On the square where the market is held on Tuesday mornings, the plane-tree-shaded Bassin de l'Etang is a large, stone water tank built in the 15th century to supply local flour mills and one of the most beautiful water features in Provence. From here footpaths lead up the Mourre Nègre, the Luberon's highest point. Further east, the Luberon is quieter and less populated. There the tiny, authentic villages **Cabrières d'Aigues** and **La Motte d'Aigues** slumber in the sunshine.

Ansouis is dominated by its Renaissance château, whose ramparts wind up around the mound. It is still inhabited by the Sabran-Pontevès family, who sometimes conduct tours themselves. The visit takes in baronial halls and massive kitchens, but the highlight is the terraced gardens. The Romanesque church is built into the edge of the ramparts. There are often concerts in the grounds over the summer. In the town, the morning market on Thursday and Saturday is the only real attraction.

Towards **Pertuis** – today dull and traffic-clogged, but useful if you need a supermarket or a train – the **Château Val Joanis** combines wine-growing with beautifully planted terraced gardens. Further east at **La Tour d'Aigues**,

Auberge La Fenière.

amid rolling vineyards, are the remains of what was once the finest of all the Renaissance châteaux. Sadly, it was destroyed by fire way back in 1792; across ample defensive ditches, only the pedimented entrance and part of the wings survive, although in its magnificent heyday the château had a park, orangerie and exotic menagerie. Two museums, the **Musée des Faïences** and **Musée de l'Histoire du Pays d'Aigues**, are housed in the cellars. La Tour d'Aigues has a Tuesday morning market.

In an area of vineyards, oak and pine forests lie **La Bastide de Jourdans**, founded in the 13th century but now much smaller than when it was a centre of silk production, and the fortified village of **Grambois** (where part of the Marcel Pagnol film biography *La Gloire de mon père* was filmed).

Château d'Ansouis
rue Cartel, Ansouis (04.90.09.82.70/www.chateau-ansouis.com). **Open** (guided tours only) *Apr-June, Sept-mid Oct* 2.30-6pm Mon, Wed-Sun. *July-Aug* 11.30am, 2.30-6pm daily. *Mid Oct-Mar* 11.30am-6pm Sun. Group visits by appointment year-round. **Admission** €6; €4.50 students; €3 6-18s; free under-6s. **No credit cards.**

Château de Lourmarin
Lourmarin (04.90.68.15.23/www.chateau-de-lourmarin.com). **Open** *Jan* 2.30-4pm Sat, Sun. *Feb-Apr, Nov, Dec* 10.30-11.30am, 2.30-4pm daily. *May, June* 10-11.30am, 2.30-5.30pm daily. *July, Aug* 10-11.30am, 3-6pm daily. *Sept* 10-11.30am, 2.30-5.30pm daily. *Oct* 11-11.30am, 2.30-4.30pm daily. Phone for details of group entry & guided tours. **Admission** €5; €2 10-16s; free under-10s. **No credit cards.**

Château Val Joanis
rte de Cavaillon (D973), Pertuis (04.90.79.88.40/ www.val-joanis.com). **Open** *Apr-Oct* 10am-7pm daily. *Nov-Mar* 2-6pm Mon-Sat. **Admission** free.

Musée des Faïences/Musée de l'Histoire du Pays d'Aigues
Château de la Tour-d'Aigues (04.90.07.50.33/ www.chateau-latourdaigues.com). **Open** *Apr-Oct* 10am-1pm, 2.30-6pm daily. *Nov-Mar* 2-5pm Mon, Sun; 10am-noon Tue; 10am-noon, 2-5pm Wed-Sat. **Admission** €4.50; €2 8-16s, students; free under-8s. **No credit cards.**

Musée de la Vannerie
La Glaneuse, av Philippe de Girard, Cadenet (04.90.68.24.44). **Open** *Apr-Oct* 10am-noon, 2.30-6.30pm Mon, Thur-Sat; 2.30-6.30pm Wed, Sun. Closed Nov-Mar. **Admission** €3.50; €1.50 students; free under-16s. **No credit cards.**

Where to stay & eat

Lourmarin has become the gourmet capital of the Luberon thanks in part to Reine Sammut at **Auberge La Fenière** (D945 rte de Cadenet, 04.90.68.11.79, www.reinesammut.com, closed mid Nov-Jan, double €140-€210, restaurant closed Mon & lunch Tue, menus €46-€110). Working against the backdrop of a stylish modern *mas*, she's particularly good at starters, often using produce from her vegetable garden. There are some attractive rooms upstairs. **Le Moulin de Lourmarin** (rue du Temple, 04.90.68.06.69, www.moulindelourmarin.com, closed mid Jan-mid Feb, double €190-€310) is a controversially converted but very comfortable watermill with an excellent bistro (menus €30-€70) run by talented chef Eric Sapet. When not in the mood for haute cuisine, locals enjoy laid-back **L'Antiquaire** (9 rue du Grand Pré, 04.90.68.17.29, closed Mon & Tue lunch in summer, Mon all day, Tue lunch, dinner Sun in winter, 3wks Nov-Dec & 3wks Jan-Feb, menus €18-€28) or the pan-Mediterranean flavours at **Maison Ollier Michel-Ange** (pl de la Fontaine, 04.90.68.02.03, closed Tue-Wed

Oct-Easter, all mid Nov-mid Dec, menus €21-€58). Well-hidden in the heart of the village **Chambres d'Hôtes de la Cordière** (impasse de la Cordière, rue Albert Camus, 04.90.68.03.32, double €60-€65) has four characterful rooms (tiled floors, roll-top baths) in an ancient house with courtyard and vaulted kitchen. Amid vineyards two kilometres (1.2 miles) east of Lourmarin, **Le Mas de Guilles** (rte de Vaugines, 04.90.68.30.55, www.guilles.com, closed Nov-Mar, double €80-€150) is a cleverly converted *mas* with swimming pool and tennis courts. Under the combe de Lourmarin, a short walk from the village, friendly **Hostellerie du Paradou** (rte d'Apt, 04.90.68.04.05, www.le paradou-lacascade.com, closed mid Nov-Jan, double €60-€65; restaurant closed Thur & lunch Fri, menus €22-€35) is a stone *mas* with spacious lawns and nine simple rooms; the restaurant serves regional food and wines.

At the top of Cadenet, **La Tuilière** (chemin de la Tuilière, 04.90.68.24.45, www.latuiliere. com, double €65-€81) offers five rooms in a big old house, with a ramshackle terraced garden, small pool and billiard table. The **Camping Val de Durance** (Les Routes, Cadenet, 04.90.68.37.75, www.homair-vacances.com, closed Oct-Mar, pitch €26 with electricity for two people) has well-spaced pitches, screened by trees. It overlooks a small public lake, which has been arranged for swimming with a small sandy beach (May-Sept 9am-8pm daily).

In scenic Cucuron, good-value **L'Horloge** (55 rue Léonce Brieugne, 04.90.77.12.74, closed Wed and 2wks Feb, €14.50-€21), housed in vaulted cellars, is a cool retreat for some quietly creative provençal cooking. **La Petite Maison** (pl de l'Etang, 04.90.77.18.60, www.la-petite-maison.com, closed mid Dec-mid Jan, menus €24.50-€84) is a favourite eaterie among local fashionistas, with chef Michel Mehdi serving imaginative versions of local staples.

There are fewer options on the Luberon's eastern slopes, but the **Restaurant de la Fontaine** (pl de la Fontaine, 04.90.07.72.16, closed lunch Tue, Wed, dinner Sun in winter, and 10 Dec-10 Jan, 2wks Feb, menu €30) at St-Martin-de-la-Brasque is justifiably popular. Grambois' welcoming **Auberge des Tilleuls** (moulin de Pas, 04.90.09.86.98/www.tilleuls. com, double €59-€64) provides five simple rooms and a good restaurant (menus €17-€37).

Resources

Tourist information

Ansouis *Office de Tourisme, pl du Château, 84240 Ansouis (04.90.09.86.98/www.ansouis.fr).* **Open** *Apr-Sept* 10am-noon, 2-6pm daily. *Oct-Mar* 10am-noon, 2-5pm daily. Closed Jan.

Cucuron *Office de Tourisme, rue Léonce Brieugne, 84160 Cucuron (04.90.77.28.37).* **Open** *July, Aug* 9am-noon, 2.30-6.30pm Mon-Sat. *Sept-June* 9am-noon, 2-4pm Tue-Sat.

Lourmarin *Office de Tourisme, 17 av Philippe de Girard, 84160 Lourmarin (04.90.68.10.77/www. lourmarin.com).* **Open** *Apr-Oct* 9.30am-1pm, 3.30-7pm Mon-Sat; 9.30am-noon Sun. *Nov-Mar* 9.30am-12.30pm, 2.30-4pm Mon-Sat.

Mérindol *Office de Tourisme, rue du Four, 84360 Mérindol (04.90.72.88.50).* **Open** 9am-12.30pm, 2-5.30pm Tue-Sat.

Cavaillon

Cavaillon is most famous for being the melon capital of France: the juicy globes are celebrated in a festival in July (*see chapter* **The Festive South**), and crop up in everything from jam to chocolates. The town injects a dose of 'real life' into the Luberon – think housing estates, lounging youths and an absurd number of roundabouts – but compensates with a thriving year-round arts scene thanks to a Scène Nationale theatre (B.P. 205 rue du Languedoc, 04.90.78.64.64, www.theatredecavaillon.com) and the **Grenier à Sons** (157 av du Général de Gaulle, 04.90.06.44.20) weekly music venue. In recent years, though, Cavaillon has been more commonly associated with militant farmers than with sightseeing, but past the anonymous periphery is an old town with relics from what was once an important medieval diocese. The big market is wholesale only, except on Mondays when there is a lively food and general goods market.

The earliest visible reminder of Cavaillon's past is the spindly first-century **Arc Romain** (pl du Clos), bearing traces of sculpted flowers and winged victories. Behind it, a footpath zigzags up the cliff to the medieval **Chapelle St-Jacques** offering panoramic views and a lovely spot of green in the middle of town. At the foot of the Arc, peer into the time-capsule **Fin de Siècle** café. The raggedy old town is presided over by the Romanesque **Cathédrale Notre-Dame et St-Véran**, with its damaged cloister, octagonal tower and sundial. A relief on one altar refers to local melon cultivation, introduced by the Avignon popes. Outside, tree-shaded place Philippe de Cabassole has some fine 18th-century houses. The baroque façade of the Grand Couvent reflects church power during the Comtat Venaissin; in the **Musée de l'Hôtel Dieu**, archaeological finds from a Neolithic settlement on St-Jacques hill are displayed in the former hospital and chapel.

Like nearby Carpentras (*see p109*), Cavaillon had a sizeable Jewish community, and its beautiful, light-filled **Synagogue** (built 1772-4) is one of the finest in France. The baby pink and blue upper level has bronze chandeliers, a rococo tabernacle and delicate ironwork. The lower level doubled as a bakery. It was a bit of a last gasp: in 1791 the Comtat Venaissin was integrated into France and French Jews were given their liberty, marking the end of Cavaillon's ghetto. The town's Jewish population today is mainly of North African origin. The synagogue now contains the **Musée Juif Comtadin**, housing tabernacle doors from the earlier synagogue, and possessions of the community.

Musée de l'Hôtel Dieu

Grand-Rue (04.90.76.00.34). Open June-Sept 9.30am-12.30pm, 2.30-6.30pm Mon, Wed-Sun. **Admission** (incl Synagogue) €3; €1.50 12-18s; free under-12s. **No credit cards.**

Synagogue/Musée Juif Comtadin

rue Hébraïque (04.90.76.00.34). Open Apr-Sept 9am-12.30pm, 2.30-6.30pm Mon, Wed-Sun. *Oct-Mar* 9am-noon, 2-5pm Mon, Wed-Fri. **Admission** (incl Musée de l'Hôtel Dieu) €3; €1.50 12-18s; free under-12s. **No credit cards.**

Where to stay & eat

Cavaillon's hotels leave quite a lot to be desired, though old-fashioned **Hôtel du Parc** (183 pl François Tourel, 04.90.71.57.78, double €56-€66) near the tourist office offers traditional style and a garden. There's no restaurant, but right next door the belle époque café **Le Fin de Siècle** (46 pl du Clos, 04.90.71.12.27, closed Tue & Wed, menus €13-€28.50) has kept its mosaic frontage and large mirrors; upstairs is a restaurant that has a loose half-board arrangement with the Hôtel du Parc (call 04.90.71.57.78 for details). There are a few other tempting tables. Upmarket, old-fashioned **Prévot** (353 av de Verdun, 04.90.71.32.43, closed Sun and 2wks Aug, menus €25-€70) is famed for its inventive summer melon menu. **Fleur de Thym** (91 rue JJ Rousseau, 04.90.71.14.64, closed Wed, menus €23-€29) offers deliciously fresh dishes that change daily. **Côté Jardin** (49 rue Lamartine, 04.90.71.33.58, closed all Sun & dinner Mon, dinner Tue in winter, 3wks Jan, menus €13-€23) has tables around a courtyard fountain and offers good-value provençal cooking, specialising in fish dishes. Outside town, the **Mas du Souléou** (5 chemin St-Pierre des Essieux, 04.90.71.43.22, www.souleou.com, double €84) is a lovely B&B set in a tastefully restored 19th-century *mas*, where M Lepaul concocts dinner (€24).

Resources

Internet is available at the tourist office.

Tourist information

Office de Tourisme, pl François Tourel, 84300 Cavaillon (04.90.71.32.01/www.cavaillon-luberon. com). **Open** *July, Aug* 9am-12.30pm, 2-6.30pm Mon-Sat; 10am-noon Sun. *Sept-June* 9am-12.30pm, 2-6.30pm Mon-Sat.

L'Isle-sur-la-Sorgue & Fontaine-de-Vaucluse

L'Isle-sur-la-Sorgue is known as the 'Venise Comtadin' for its double (in places triple) ring of canals. Dripping wheels recall a past when water powered the silk industry and, later on, the paper mills. What makes the town tick today is France's largest concentration of antiques dealers outside Paris, strung out along the canals (*see p122* **Out of the past**). In the old town, the star sight is the **Collégiale Notre-Dame-des-Anges**, whose baroque interior is a heaven full of cherubim. Outside, place de la Liberté contains the pretty belle époque **Café de France**, some galleried houses and the town's tourist office, located in the old public granary. The former Musée Donadeï de Campredon, an elegant 18th-century *hôtel particulier*, is now the **Maison René Char**. As well as recreating the study of the Surrealist poet, who was born here in 1907, the museum hosts temporary exhibitions of modern art. There's a market in town on Thursdays and Sundays.

Seven kilometres (4.5 miles) upstream (by D25), **Fontaine-de-Vaucluse** clusters around the source of the Sorgue river. Water mysteriously gushes out of a sheer cliff face into a jade-green pool, giving the ancient name Vallis Clausa ('closed valley') or Vaucluse to the whole *département*. Numerous divers, including the late Jacques Cousteau, have attempted without success to find the source; their exploits, and the geological wonders of the area, are explained in the underground museum **Le Monde souterrain de Norbert Casteret**. Above the village is a ruined castle, originally built by monks to protect pilgrims visiting the tomb of dragon-slayer St Véran. Abandoned factories hint at Fontaine's more industrial past, notably paper-making for the Comtat Venaissin. The pretty Romanesque church has a painting of St Véran and an 11th-century open altar table. Outside, a column commemorates Petrarch. Across the river, the **Musée Pétrarque** stands on the site where Italian Renaissance scholar Petrarch (1304-74) wrote his famous *Canzoniere*. Further up, past the mill, the **Musée d'Histoire 1939-1945 'L'Appel de la Liberté'** contains exhibitions on daily life during the occupation.

Le **Beaucet** is a pretty hillside village eight kilometres (five miles) north of Fontaine-de-Vaucluse (just off the D57), which offers great views of the Vaucluse mountains, a fortified château, a number of restaurants and some very interesting artisans' workshops, including **Le Jardin de Robert** (in the village centre, by the *mairie*) where two artists use the natural landscape to create living art works.

Between April and December, the Sorgue can be navigated by canoe between Fontaine-de-Vaucluse and Partage-des-Eaux. Canoes can be hired at **Canoë Evasion** (on D24 at Pont de Galas, 04.90.38.26.22, canoe hire €17 adults, €11 under-17s, free under-7s).

Collégiale Notre-Dame-des-Anges

pl de la Liberté, L'Isle-sur-la-Sorgue (no phone). **Open** 10am-noon, 3-5pm Tue-Sat. **Admission** free.

Maison René Char

20 rue du Dr Tallet, L'Isle-sur-la-Sorgue (04.90.38.17.41/www.campredon-expos.com). **Open** 10.30am-1pm, 3.30-7pm Tue-Sun. **Admission** €6; €5 students; free under-14s. **No credit cards.**

Le Monde souterrain de Norbert Casteret

chemin de la Fontaine, Fontaine-de-Vaucluse (04.90.20.34.13). **Open** *Feb-May, Sept-Nov* 10am-noon, 2-5.15pm Tue-Sun. *June* 10am-noon, 2-5pm daily. *July, Aug* 9.30am-6.45pm Tue-Sun. Closed Dec-Jan. **Admission** €5.50; €4 under-18s. **No credit cards.**

Musée d'Histoire 1939-1945 'L'Appel de la Liberté'

chemin du Gouffre, Fontaine-de-Vaucluse (04.90.20.24.00). **Open** *Mar, Nov-Dec* 10am-noon, 2-5pm (till 6pm in Mar) Sat, Sun. *Apr, May, Oct* 10am-noon, 2-6pm Mon, Wed-Sun (till 5pm last 2wks Oct). *June-Sept* 10am-6pm Mon, Wed-Sun. Closed Jan, Feb. **Admission** €3.50; €1.50 12-18s; €4.60, €2.80 with Musée Pétrarque; free under-12s. **No credit cards.**

Musée Pétrarque

quai du Château Vieux, Fontaine-de-Vaucluse (04.90.20.37.20). **Open** *Apr-May, Sept-Oct* 10am-noon, 2-6pm Mon, Wed-Sun. *June-Aug* 10am-12.30pm, 1.30-6pm. Closed Nov-Mar. **Admission** €3.50; €1.50 12-18s; €4.60, €2.80 with Musée d'Histoire; free under-12s. **No credit cards.**

Where to stay & eat

Hungry antiques browsers are served by a veritable roadshow of restaurants along the canals of L'Isle-sur-la-Sorgue. One of the best is stylish bistro **Le Carré des Herbes** (13 av des Quatres Otages, 04.90.38.62.95, closed Tue, Wed, Jan or Feb, menus €12-€28), now under the wing of Parisian chef Bernard Pacaud. The stylish **Café du Village**, within the Village des Antiquaires de la Gare (04.90.20.72.31, closed

Tue-Fri, dinner Mon, Sat, Sun, menus €18.80-€22), serves imaginatively modern market-inspired cooking (if, that is, you manage to arrive within its limited opening times). The **Rendezvous des Marchands** (91 av de la Libération, 04.90.20.84.60, open 10am-7pm Mon, Sat, Sun) is part-*brocante*, part-waterside café, offering grilled kebabs and salads. If you want to maximise every minute of antiques hunting, the **Hôtel le Domaine de la Petite Ville** (rte d'Apt, 04.90.38.40.00, double €51-€158, menus €23-€33) is a reasonably priced and central option. For calm and characterful comfort, try the **Mas de Cure Bourse** (carrefour de Velorgues, 04.90.38.16.58, double €75-€115; restaurant closed lunch Mon, Tue, mid Dec-mid Jan, menus €26-€49), an 18th-century coaching inn, with vaulted hallway, rooms *à la provençale*, large garden and pool, set in orchards three kilometres (two miles) from town. In a pretty hamlet six kilometres (four miles) south-east on the D3, **Bernard Auzet** (Petit Palais, 04.90.38.09.74) is tiny – accommodating just 15 people at a time – but serves wonderful food in a family atmosphere.

Fontaine-de-Vaucluse is strong on snacks and ice-cream, as well as river trout. The **Hostellerie Le Château** (quartier du Château Vieux, 04.90.20.31.54, closed lunch in winter, menus €22-€38) has a veranda restaurant in a waterside setting. The **Hôtel du Poète** (04.90.20.34.05, www.hoteldupoete.com, closed late Dec-mid Feb, double €70-€240) has 24 neo-provençal rooms set around imaginatively landscaped gardens (with a pool) beside the river.

In Le Beaucet, **L'Auberge du Beaucet** (04.99.66.10.82, closed Mon, Sun, Dec, Jan, menus €30-€36) offers an excellent selection of local Luberon and Ventoux wines.

Resources

Tourist information

Fontaine-de-Vaucluse *Office de Tourisme, chemin de la Fontaine, 84800 Fontaine-de-Vaucluse (04.90.20.32.22).* **Open** 10am-6pm Mon-Sat. **L'Isle-sur-la-Sorgue** *Office de Tourisme, pl de l'Eglise, 84800 L'Isle-sur-la-Sorgue (04.90.38.04.78/ www.ot-islesurlasorgue.fr).* **Open** 9am-12.30pm, 2.30-6pm Mon-Sat; 9am-12.30pm Sun.

Apt

At first glance, there doesn't seem to be much going on in Apt, with its industrial outskirts, plane trees and sleepy squares along the Calavon river. But on Saturday mornings the town comes alive, thanks to the largest market for miles around.

The Saturday market at **Apt**.

Place de la Bouquerie is the main access point for the old town, via the narrow main street, rue des Marchands. The **Ancienne Cathédrale Ste-Anne** throws an arch across the street. Now demoted to the status of parish church, it is a curious mix of Gothic and baroque with crypts dating from the fourth and 11th centuries. In 1660 Anne of Austria visited on pilgrimage to St Anne in thanks for the birth of Louis XIV and gave money to complete the Chapelle Royale. A Roman sarcophagus harks back to the town's foundation as a staging post on Via Domitia.

Nearby, the **Maison du Parc** informs visitors about the flora, fauna and geology of the Parc Régional du Luberon, and contains the child-oriented **Musée de la Paléontologie**. Next door, the **Musée de l'Aventure Industrielle**, which opened in July 2003 in an old candied fruits confectionary, traces the three industries that brought prosperity to Apt in the 18th and 19th centuries: candied fruits, cream-glazed and marbled earthenware, and the extraction of ochre. Today, although plenty of pottery can be picked up at the market, only **Faïence d'Apt** (286 av de la Libération, 04.90.74.15.31, closed Mon morning & Sun) continues to make the town's traditional marbleware. If all this mind-candy whets your appetite for the real thing, head for **Aptunion**, which is the town's biggest manufacturer of candied fruits.

Ancienne Cathédrale Ste-Anne

rue de la Cathédrale (04.90.04.85.44/www.apt-cathedrale.com). **Open** *July-Sept* 8.30am-noon, 3-7pm Tue-Fri; 10am-noon Sat, Sun. *Oct-June* 8.30am-noon, 2-4pm Tue-Fri; 10am-noon Sat, Sun. *Treasury* July-Sept (guided tours only) 11am, 5pm Mon-Sat; 11am Sun. **Admission** free.

Aptunion

on N100, quartier Salignan (04.90.76.31.43). **Open** *Factory* by appointment. *Shop* 9am-noon, 2-6pm Mon-Sat.

Maison du Parc & Musée de la Paléontologie

60 pl Jean-Jaurès (04.90.04.42.00). **Open** 8.30am-noon, 1.30-6pm Mon-Sat. **Admission** €1.50; free under-18s. **No credit cards.**

Musée de l'Aventure Industrielle

14 pl du Pastal (04.90.74.95.30). **Open** 10am-noon, 2-5.30pm Wed-Sat; 2-5.30pm Sun (July-Sept). **Admission** €4; €2 students, over-60s; free under-12s. **No credit cards.**

Where to stay & eat

At the **Auberge du Luberon** (8 pl du Fbg Ballet, 04.90.74.12.50, double €58-€82; restaurant closed dinner Sun, all Mon, lunch Tue Nov-Apr, menus €29) chef Serge Peuzin offers a special *menu aux fruits confits* in which Apt's speciality features in every course; there are also 14 bedrooms. The **Bistrot de France** (67 pl de la Bouquerie, 04.90.74.22.01, menus vary, closed Mon, Thur & Sun) features in *A Year in Provence*, but despite this starry celebrity endorsement still manages to offer good regional fare. **Picardon et Pelardon** (23 rue de Préfecture, 04.90.04.01.78) is a must for cheese lovers. It offers a huge range of *fromages* to take away, and lunch plates with cheese (naturally), salads, bread and wine. With the **Domaine des Andéols** (Les Andéols, St-Saturnin-les-Apt, 04.90.75.50.63, www.domainedesandeols.com, double €260-€650) just north of Apt, the Luberon has gained a stunning boutique hotel. Olivier Massart created nine 'maisons' from the buildings of the family farm, where encaustic, tile and oak finishes become high-voltage with the addition of classic modern furniture, contemporary art and comforts like plasma screen TVs. The grounds are a tour de force, complete with a fibre-optically lit staircase that leads to the restaurant where chef Daniel Hebert (formerly cooking at La Mirande in Avignon) produces a different menu nightly (from €55), using market produce. There's also a low-key spa has a sauna, a hammam and an indoor pool, while an infinity pool overlooks the olive groves.

Resources

Tourist information

Office de Tourisme, 20 av Philippe de Girard, 84400 Apt (04.90.74.03.18/www.ot-apt.fr). **Open** *Mid June-mid Sept* 9am-7.30pm Mon-Sat; 9am-12.30pm Sun. *Mid Sept-mid June* 9am-noon, 2-6pm Mon-Sat.

Gordes & the Plateau de Vaucluse

A principal stamping ground for the *gauche caviar*, France's champagne socialists (or the *gauche tapénade*, as they are known further south), **Gordes** is almost too pretty for its own good. Its spectacular hillside setting is dominated by the turrets of its château, drystone walls and steep, stepped alleys. The tasteful shops sell the usual range of provençal crafts and produce (there's also a market on Tuesday mornings), while the **Château de Gordes** has a semi-permanent exhibition by the Belgian painter Pol Mara (don't believe the old posters you still see mentioning Vasarely).

To the west of Gordes, the **Village des Bories** is a group of restored drystone, beehive-shaped huts. Inhabited between the 16th and 19th centuries, probably much earlier, the village attempts to reconstruct their rural lifestyle. You'll find *borie* houses, stables and sheepfolds dotted all over the hillside, as well as a photo exhibition that shows similar drystone structures in other countries.

North of Gordes, at the bottom of a wooded valley, is the **Abbaye Notre-Dame-de-Sénanque**. Founded in 1148, this is one of the great triumvirate (along with Silvacane and Thoronet) of provençal Cistercian monasteries. Set in lavender fields, the beautifully preserved Romanesque ensemble still houses a monastic community.

Surrounded by strangely eroded outcrops of ochre-red rocks, **Roussillon** is among the most picturesque of all the Luberon villages, although it can get suffocated by tourists. The houses are painted in an orange wash, which makes the entire village glow. Walk past the belfry-sundial of the Eglise St-Michel to an orientation table, and note the 18th-century façades on place de la Mairie. The town's market is held on a Thursday morning. To the left of the village cemetery, above 'car park 2', the Sentier des Ocres (closed Nov-Mar, admission €2, free under-10s), a footpath with information panels, offers spectacular views amid peculiar rock formations, the result of ochre quarrying. On the D104 towards Apt, the former ochre works have reopened as the

Conservatoire des Ocres et Pigments Appliqués. Guided tours show how the rock was made into pigment.

Reached by small lanes south of the D22 towards Rustrel from Apt, undulating green countryside suddenly gives way to the vibrantly coloured Colorado de Rustrel, a valley littered with rocks long exploited for ochre pigment in colours that vary from pale cream via yellows and orange to deep, russet red. Near the car park, a path descends to a picnic site and *buvette* and relics of disused ochre works. Wear decent shoes and do stick to the *sentiers* (colour-coded, waymarked paths) which lead you round some of the most spectacular turrets, chimneys and banks.

Abbaye Notre-Dame-de-Sénanque

3km (2 miles) N of Gordes on D177 (04.90.72.05.72/ www.senanque.fr). **Open** *Guided tours* 10.10am, 2.30pm, 3.30pm, 4.45pm Mon-Sat. Closed 2wks Jan, mornings Oct-Apr. **Admission** €6; €5 students; €2.50 6-18s; free under-6s. **No credit cards**.

Château de Gordes

Gordes (04.90.72.02.89). **Open** 10am-noon, 2-6pm daily. **Admission** €4; €3 10-17s; free under-10s. **No credit cards**.

Conservatoire des Ocres et Pigments Appliqués

Usine Mathieu, D104, Roussillon (04.90.05.66.69/www.okhra.com). **Open** *Sept-June* 9am-6pm Tue-Sun. *July, Aug* 9am-7pm daily. Closed 2wks Jan. **Tours** *July, Aug* Every 30min 10am-noon, 2-6pm daily. *Sept-June* 11am, 3pm, 4pm daily. **Admission** €5; free under-10s. **Credit** MC, V.

Village des Bories

Les Savournins, Gordes (04.90.72.04.39). **Open** 9am-sunset daily. **Admission** €5.50; €3 10-17s; free under-10s. **No credit cards**.

Where to stay & eat

In Gordes, **La Bastide de Gordes** (rte de Combe, 04.90.72.12.12, www.bastide-de-gordes. com, closed Nov-mid Dec & Jan-mid Feb, double €140-€323) is an upmarket hotel built into the ramparts, with spectacular views and both an indoor and outdoor pool. The **Domaine de l'Enclos** (rte de Sénanque, 04.90.72.71.00, closed mid Nov-mid Mar, double €100-€200) is beautifully decorated and has a nice restaurant (menu €45), and all ground-floor rooms have private gardens. Adjoining the château, **Café-Restaurant La Renaissance** (pl du Château, 04.90.72.02.02, menus €11.50-€30) has tables out on the square and very hip waitresses.

David (pl de la Poste, 04.90.05.60.13, closed Wed, dinner Sun except mid June-mid Sept, all Jan-mid Feb, menus €31.50) is the most reliable of the several bistros and snack bars dotted

about Roussillon, while the **Mas de Garrigon** (rte de St-Saturnin-d'Apt, 04.90.05.63.22, double €100-€155) is a traditional provençal farmhouse that provides nine very comfy rooms and a friendly welcome.

In Goult, just north of the N100 Avignon–Apt road, the **Café de la Poste** (pl de la Libération, 04.90.72.23.23, lunch only, closed Mon and Nov-Feb, menu €10) is another provençal restaurant to gain fame in Mayle's *A Year in Provence* – although this one also featured in Jean Becker's film *L'Eté Meurtrier*. Join locals and chic second-homers for gossip and home-cooking. British couple Nick and Maggie Denny treat their guests like old friends at **La Fontaine de Faucon** (chemin de la Fontaine de Faucon, Quartier Ste-Anne, 04.90.09.90.16, www.fontainedefaucon.com, double €100-€120), a *chambres d'hôte* in a gorgeous old farmhouse just outside the village; dinner can be served on request (menu €28).

Resources

Tourist information

Gordes *Office de Tourisme, Le Château, 84220 Gordes (04.90.72.02.75/www.gordes-village.com).* **Open** *July, Aug* 9am-12.30pm, 2-6.30pm Mon-Sat. *Sept-June* 9am-noon, 2-6pm Mon-Sat.
Roussillon *Office de Tourisme, pl de la Poste, 84220 Roussillon (04.90.05.60.25/www.roussillon-provence.com).* **Open** *July, Aug* 10am-noon, 2-6pm Mon-Sat. *Sept-June* 1.30-5.30pm Mon-Fri.

Manosque

Though it nestles at the eastern edge of the Luberon range, Manosque is very much a Durance Valley town – the largest in the sparsely populated *département* of Alpes de Haute-Provence. Housing and industrial parks now sprawl over the hillside, but for a long time the town remained within the city walls, where the not-yet-tarted-up network of narrow streets, squares and covered passageways gives an interesting perspective on what the Luberon must have been like before it became so hip. Manosque is positively moribund on a Sunday out of season and liveliest on a Saturday, when a market takes over the centre.

Porte Saunerie leads into **rue Grande**, Manosque's main shopping street. At No.14, a plaque marks the house where novelist Jean Giono (1895-1970), son of a shoemaker, was born. At No.21 is a branch of **Occitane**, the phenomenally successful Manosque-based cosmetics and skincare company that is now the town's main employer. Note also the fine 18th-century balcony at No.23. There are two historic churches, **St-Sauveur**, which features

Ancienne Cathédrale Ste-Anne. *See p129.*

in Giono's swashbuckler *Le Hussard sur le toit*, and **Notre-Dame-de-Romigier** on place de l'Hôtel de Ville, which has a fine Renaissance doorway and a black Virgin inside.

The Giono link is exploited to the full with literary competitions, bookshops and walks on the theme of 'Jean Giono, poet of the olive tree' (Haute-Provence olive oil gained an *appellation contrôlée* in 1999). The **Centre Jean Giono**, in an 18th-century *hôtel particulier*, has exhibitions and a permanent display about the writer's life and work. His own house, **Lou Paraïs** (montée des Vraies Richesses, 04.92.87.73.03), north of the old town, is open for guided visits on Friday afternoons (ring ahead).

Centre Jean Giono

3 bd Elémir Bourges (04.92.70.54.54). **Open** *Apr-June* 9.30am-12.30pm, 2-6pm Tue-Sat. *July-Sept* 9.30am-12.30pm, 2-6pm daily. *Oct-Mar* 2-6pm Tue-Sat. **Admission** €4; €2 12-18s; free under-12s. **No credit cards**.

Where to stay & eat

The best-placed hotel is the **Grand Hôtel de Versailles** (17 av Jean Giono, 08.00.10.05.38, double €26-€61), a simply furnished former coaching inn. The **Pré Saint Michel** (rte de Dauphin Manosque, 04.92.72.14.27, www. presaintmichel.com, double €58-€95)

is a beautifully decorated hotel with a very good restaurant (menus €24-€39). Manosque's top chef is **Dominique Bucaille** (43 bd des Tilleuls, 04.92.72.32.28, closed dinner Wed, all Sun & mid July-mid Aug, menus €15-€61), who offers refined seasonal cooking and an excellent wine list. **Hostellerie de la Fuste** (rte d'Oraison, 04.92.72.05.95, closed dinner Sun, Mon Oct-June, 1wk Jan, 2wks Nov, menus €17-€55) is just outside Manosque, but well worth the trip. Chef Daniel Jourdan has been there for 40 years (Dominique Bucaille started his career here), cooking wonderful dishes such as the local Sisteron lamb or trout from the nearby Durance river. It's very popular, so book ahead.

Resources

Tourist information

Office du Tourisme, pl du Dr Joubert, 04100 Manosque (04.92.72.16.00/www.ville-manosque.fr). **Open** *July, Aug* 9am-7pm Mon-Sat; 10am-noon Sun. *Sept-June* 9am-12.15pm, 1.30-6pm Mon-Sat.

Pays de Forcalquier

In the early Middle Ages, the Counts of Forcalquier rivalled those of Provence. The two were united in 1195 when Gersande, Comtesse de Forcalquier, married Alphonse, Count of Provence; their son Raymond Bérenger V craftily succeeded in marrying all four daughters to future kings. Today **Forcalquier** is light years from its illustrious past but still a lively local centre, with a big market on Monday mornings.

The sober Romano-Gothic Cathédrale Notre-Dame-du-Bourguet is almost as wide as it is long, with a triple nave and an impressive organ loft. The former Couvent des Visitandines now contains the Cinématographe cinema, the *mairie* and the **Musée Municipal**, where archaeological finds include a fine Roman head from nearby Lurs. Narrow streets next to the cathedral lead into the old town, where there are attractive houses on rue Béranger and a fancy Gothic fountain on place St-Michel. Climb past the *carrillon* up the wooded mound where the citadel was replaced in 1875 by the octagonal Chapel Notre-Dame-de-Provence, with its neo-Gothic musician angels. Forcalquier's other main sight is its cemetery, north-east of the centre, with striking landscaped walls of yew.

At **Mane**, once a market halt on the Via Domitia, houses climb up in concentric curtain walls around the feudal castle (closed to the public). On the edge of the village, the former monastery **Notre-Dame-de-Salagon** combines fascinating botanical gardens with an ethnographical museum. The 12th-century Romanesque chapel has traces of medieval frescoes, as well as modern red stained glass by abstract painter Aurélie Nemours, while assorted priory buildings contain exhibits on sage growing and bee-keeping. There's also a reconstructed forge, but the highlight is the medieval garden, which reveals that turnips, parsnips and pulses were then staples rather than what we now think of as provençal cuisine. Other gardens are planted with herbs, aromatic plants and flowers used in popular remedies. Just outside Mane, the Château de Sauvan (04.92.75.05.64) is a beautifully restored 18th-century building with extensive gardens.

The colony of white domes blistering out of the hillside above St-Michel-l'Observatoire belong to the **Observatoire de Haute-Provence** – the site was chosen for this national astronomical research laboratory because of the pure air and consequent clear skies (the position on a promontory means the views are pretty amazing too, even if you're not looking up). The **Centre d'Astronomie** tries to make astronomy accessible to the public and runs observation evenings in July and August. It often holds cinema and concert evenings also.

Centre d'Astronomie

plateau du Moulin à Vent, St-Michel-l'Observatoire (04.92.76.69.69/www.centre-astro.fr). **Open** *July, Aug* observation nights 9.30pm-12.30am Tue-Fri. *Sept-June* ring for details. **Admission** €8.70; €7 6-16s; free under-6s. **No credit cards.**

Château de Sauvan

Mane (04.92.75.05.64). **Open** *Tours* June-Sept 3.30pm Mon-Fri, Sun; Oct-May 3.30pm Sun. **Admission** €6. **No credit cards.**

Musée Municipal

pl du Bourguet, Forcalquier (04.92.75.00.14). **Open** *Apr-Sept* 3-6pm Wed-Sat. Closed Oct-Mar. **Admission** €2; free under-18s. **No credit cards.**

Observatoire de Haute Provence

St-Michel-l'Observatoire (04.92.70.64.00/www.obs-hp.fr). **Open** *Tours* Apr-Sept 2-4pm Wed; Oct-Mar 3pm Wed. **Admission** €4; €2.50 5-16; free under-5s. **No credit cards.**

Prieuré Notre-Dame-de-Salagon

Musée-Conservatoire ethnologique de Haute-Provence, Mane (04.92.75.70.50). **Open** *May-Sept* 10am-12.30pm, 2-7pm daily. *Oct-Dec, Feb-May* 2-6pm daily. Closed Jan. **Admission** €5; €2.60 12-18s; free under-12s. **No credit cards.**

Where to stay & eat

The last few years have seen something of a renaissance in Forcalquier. While the basic but clean **Grand Hôtel** (10 bd Latourette,

04.92.75.00.35, double €38-€45) still offers a good downtown location, there are several newer hotels that might take your fancy. The best is **Hôtel la Bastide St Georges** (rte de Banon, 04.92.72.14.27, www.bastidesaint georges.com, double €60-€94), newly built, with 17 well-decorated rooms and a good pool. You'll also find several café-brasseries on place du Bourguet and around place St-Michel in the old town. Olive oil emporium **Oliviers & Co** (3 rue des Cordeliers, 04.92.75.00.75, closed Tue Nov-Mar) now has outlets in New York and London, but started life in this small corner of Provence; the shop here has an excellent café.

Resources

Tourist information

Office de Tourisme, 13 pl du Bourguet, 04300 Forcalquier (04.92.75.10.02/www.forcalquier.com). **Open** *June-Sept* 9am-noon, 2-7pm Mon-Sat; 10am-1pm Sun. *Oct-May* 9am-noon, 2-6pm Mon-Sat.

Getting there & around

By bus

Cars Sumian (04.91.49.44.25) runs two buses daily between Marseille and Apt, via Cadenet, Lourmarin and Bonnieux, and two buses daily between Aix and Apt, via Cadenet and Lourmarin. **Cars Arnaud** (04.90.38.15.58, www.voyages-arnaud.fr) runs buses between L'Isle-sur-la-Sorgue and Fontaine-de-Vaucluse or Avignon, none on Sun. **Barlatier** (04.32.76.00.40) runs five buses a day between Avignon and Apt, three a day between Cavaillon and Avignon and once daily between Cavaillon and Apt and Cavaillon and Forcalquier, all Mon-Sat, none on Sun. **Express de la Durance** (04.90.71.03.00) runs two buses a day between Cavaillon and Gordes. There are no bus services to Roussillon.

By car

From A7, exit 25 for Cavaillon. D2 runs from Cavaillon to Taillades and joins the N100, the Avignon–Apt–Forcalquier road, which rings the Montagne de Luberon. L'Isle-sur-la-Sorgue is on the N100 or by the D938 from Cavaillon. To the south, the D973 runs along the Durance from Cavaillon via Mérindol and Lauris to Cadenet and Pertuis. The only road across the range is the D943 from Cadenet via Lourmarin, which then forks to Apt (D943) and Bonnieux (D36). Manosque can be reached by the D973 and N96 or the A51 from Aix. For Cadenet from Aix, take the N7 and D543/D943 via Rognes.

By train

TGV to Avignon with shuttle buses to L'Isle-sur-la-Sorgue and Cavaillon or TGV Aix-en-Provence with three shuttles a day to Manosque. Several local trains a day run from Avignon Centre Ville to Cavaillon and L'Isle-sur-la-Sorgue. Pertuis and Manosque are on the branch line from Marseille to Gap via Aix – Manosque-Gréoux-les-Bains station is 1.5 kilometres (a mile) south of the centre.

Avignon & the Vaucluse

London's weekly listings bible

Marseille & Aix

Introduction

An ancient port, fishing villages and a bastion of high culture: now that's variety.

They may seem poles apart but rough-and-ready Marseille and starchy Aix-en-Provence have far more in common than first impressions might suggest. For a start, they both have a staunchly independent spirit (which, in both cases, helped to fuel the progress of the French Revolution). Both cities have historic, well-respected universities, and they both have thriving year-round cultural scenes. In addition to Aix's prestigious Festival International d'Art Lyrique and Marseille's burgeoning Festival de Marseille, the region also benefits from dozens of smaller, equally worthwhile events and festivals. Marseille, too, boasts dynamic theatres and the most adventurous contemporary art scene in the South.

As France's oldest city, with a history stretching back 2,600 years, **Marseille** has plenty to offer tourists but can also do very well without them, thanks very much. In fact, this 'love us or leave us' attitude is really quite refreshing, given the hard-sell tourism that afflicts much of the rest of the coast. Marseille belongs to the Marseillais, and like any self-respecting *citadins*, they go on holiday in the summer. But it's a great city to visit at any time of year, and is currently in the middle of a vast urban renewal programme.

Just as life in Marseille focuses on its Vieux Port, the epicentre of the rather more chichi existence enjoyed by the residents of Aix-en-Provence is the famous cours Mirabeau and its stretch of pavement cafés. With its beautifully preserved *hôtels particuliers* and countless fountains and secluded little squares, Aix, former capital of Provence, is a shopping magnet. Paul Cézanne, who was born in the city (and whose centenary is being widely celebrated both there and throughout Provence in 2006), has left a fascinating trail of former homes, studios, favourite cafés and painterly haunts. Follow that trail from the *atelier* in Aix-en-Provence to **Montagne-Ste-Victoire** and the port at **L'Estaque**.

Despite Marseille's gritty edge, it has on its doorstep some stretches of the southern French coastline that are postcard perfect, with their pristine beaches, stunning cliffs and tranquil fishing ports. Even in the city itself, boats bob in the Vieux Port, and every other street corner offers up a glittering vista of the Med. To the east, the town gradually fizzles out into the scrub-covered limestone **Calanques**. Less well-known are the **Côte Bleue**, the pretty stretch of coast west of Marseille, and the old fishing town of **Martigue**.

The best Marseille & Aix

Things to do

The **Site Mémorial des Milles** (*see p168*) chronicles internment and deportation. See the unlovely **Docks de la Joliette** (*see p144*) being transformed. Or, just for fun, pop into the **Zoo de la Barben** (*see p176*).

Places to stay

Book a night in architectural history at **Hôtel Le Corbusier** (*see p155*) or at the charming little **Hôtel Cardinal** (*see p173*).

Places to eat

Get authentic bouillabaisse at **Le Miramar** (*see p150*) or the freshest fish at **Baie des Singes** (*see p149*). For Southern café culture, try the **Deux Garçons** (*see p168*) or quayside **Bar de la Marine** (*see p151*).

Nightlife

Get with the 'cours Ju' action at **Espace Julien** (*see p152*), plug into club culture at **Le Trolleybus** (*see p153*) or see posh students stay out late at **Le Mistral** (*see p171*).

Culture

Brush up on your modern art with Cézanne's centenary (*see p175* **Portrait of an artist**), or get the full flavour of modern Marseille by dropping some **LSD** (*see p156* **Rap and rai**).

Sports & activities

Go diving with a genuine master at **Cassis Services Plongée** (*see p161*) or catch the next Zidane playing football for Olympique de Marseille at their huge temple, the **Stade Vélodrome** (*see p148*).

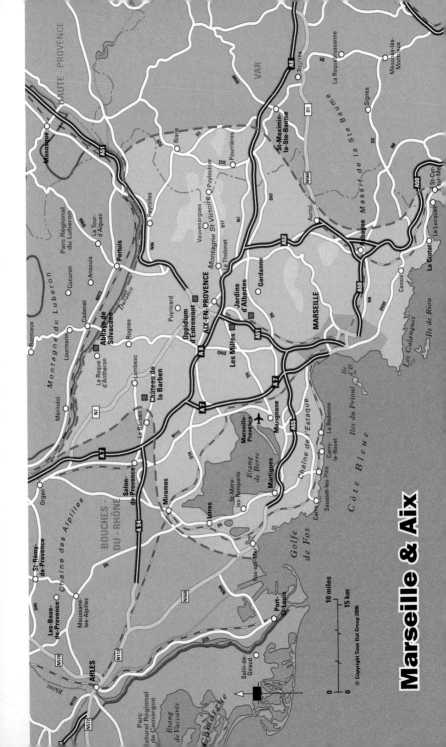

Marseille & Aix

Marseille

France's most ancient port harbours beautiful architecture,
sea-fresh cuisine and a remarkable bouillabaisse of cultures.

Like a gatecrasher at the cocktail party of
the southern French coast, Marseille has a
rugged, unpredictable charm. With the
tanned plutocrats of Monaco and the blazered
aristocrats of St-Tropez to the east, and sniffy
Aix to the north, France's second city seems
somehow larger than life, its colours even
brighter, the louche, sun-soaked terraces of its
cafés even sexier. Its famous Canebière bulges
with upfront attitude, the *quais* of its Vieux
Port teem with life and commerce, as they
have done for centuries, and yet despite all
the commotion, this is a surprisingly leisurely
town. Sit for long enough in one of its tree-
shaded squares, and the city will begin to
reveal itself to you: the metallic reports of an
unseen *pétanque* game; piano scales from an
open window; a sudden blast of rap from a
passing car; a smile from a stranger. And all
the while, the magnificent Notre-Dame-de-la-
Garde cathedral keeps watch from its hilltop,
peering down at the fuss and glory of life.

These days, Marseille enjoys a lot more
tourism thanks to the TGV phenomenon
– the extension of the high-speed train line
in 2001 that brought Marseille to three hours
from Paris. Some are quietly delighted by an
increasing flow of visitors from the capital
and boost to the economy; others seem more
reticent. For the downside of this new influx
of interest and money has been a noticeable
rise in property and restaurant prices.

Popular myths and the fishy reputation
surrounding Marseille are as widespread in
France as abroad. If the *French Connection*
movies and, more recently, Robert Guédiguian's
La ville est tranquille haven't exactly painted a
pretty bouillabaisse-suffused picture of the city;
then other images suggest a lively and upbeat
side: the omnipresent blue and white of football
team OM, Luc Besson's *Taxi* films packed with
local humour and colour, and the bold
Euroméditerranée redevelopment project.

As is so often the case here, there is no
simple truth: the oldest city in France is one
of fascinating contradictions. The sun almost
always shines but the ferocious Mistral chills
the bones in winter. The rocky coastline is
breathtaking but sought-after beaches call for a
map and hiking boots. The architecture can be
stunning but, despite much restoration in hand,
many buildings are crumbling and Marseille
has its share of modern eyesores. Some of the
neighbourhoods behind the Vieux Port remain
relatively poor while the Corniche, the coastal
road to the south, is peppered with grand stucco
villas. A dangerous reputation lingers but the
crime rate is no higher than in other major
French cities and continues to drop.

Bouillabaisse, *méchoui*, pizza and nems
may illustrate the ethnic mix here, but France's
second-largest city offers so much more. The
Marseillais will vigorously defend their city
and will tell you, in their endearingly loud
way, that it doesn't give itself over easily.

HISTORY

Life in Marseille has revolved around the
Vieux Port ever since a band of Phoenician
Greeks sailed into this strategically located
natural harbour in 600 BC. On that very day a
local chieftain's daughter, Gyptus, was to choose
a husband and the Greeks' dashing commander
Protis clearly fitted the bill. The bride came with
a donation of land and a hill near the mouth of
the Rhône, where the Greeks founded a trading

post named Massalia, a name that still crops up in modern Marseille – one of the city's best known bands is called Massilia Sound System.

Legend aside, the history of Marseille is irrevocably linked to its development as a port. By 500 BC, Massalia's Greeks were trading throughout Mediterranean Europe and from Cornwall to the Baltic. Caesar besieged the city in 49 BC, seizing almost all its colonies, and Massalia's Greeks were left with little more than their famous university and much-vaunted independence, which they were to lose and regain several times over the years.

Louis XIV ushered in the first great transformation since the arrival of the Greeks: he pulled down the city walls in 1666 and expanded the port to the Rive Neuve. The city was devastated by plague in 1720, losing more than half its population of 90,000. By the Revolution, however, its industries of soap manufacturing, oil processing and faïence were flourishing. The demand for labour sparked a wave of immigration from Provence and Italy.

Marseille enthusiastically supported the Revolution, only to turn monarchist under the First Empire and republican under the Second. By the time of Napoléon III, Algeria had become a French *département*, leading to an enormous increase in trans-Mediterranean shipping. The emperor initiated the construction of an entirely new port, La Joliette, which was completed in 1853. In 1869, when the Suez Canal opened, Marseille became the greatest boomtown in Europe. Between 1851 and 1911 the population rose by 360,000. As immigrants arrived from all over southern Europe, it acquired the astonishingly cosmopolitan population that it maintains to this day.

Marseille's heyday was soon to come to an abrupt halt. In 1934 King Alexander of Yugoslavia and Louis Barthou, the French foreign minister, were assassinated on La Canebière. In 1939 the city was placed under national guardianship when widespread corruption in local government was revealed.

Following the independence of Tunisia in 1956 and Algeria in 1962, Marseille received a mass exodus of French colonials, North African Jews and North Africans who had been involved in colonial administration. At the same time, the loss of these colonies hit Marseille's shipping trade. From 1954 to 1964 the population grew by 50 per cent, creating a severe housing shortage. New neighbourhoods were rapidly constructed to cope with the influx; areas of high unemployment throughout the 1970s and '80s, these neighbourhoods were infamous for drug dealing and crime.

Significantly, however, while Jean-Marie Le Pen and his 'France for the French' extreme-right politics have gained ground elsewhere in the region, Marseille is one place where the melting pot seems to work. The city elected a socialist council continuously from 1953 to 1995, but Jean-Claude Gaudin, the conservative mayor of Marseille since 1995, easily won the

Sitting on the dock of the bay at the **Vieux Port**. *See p142.*

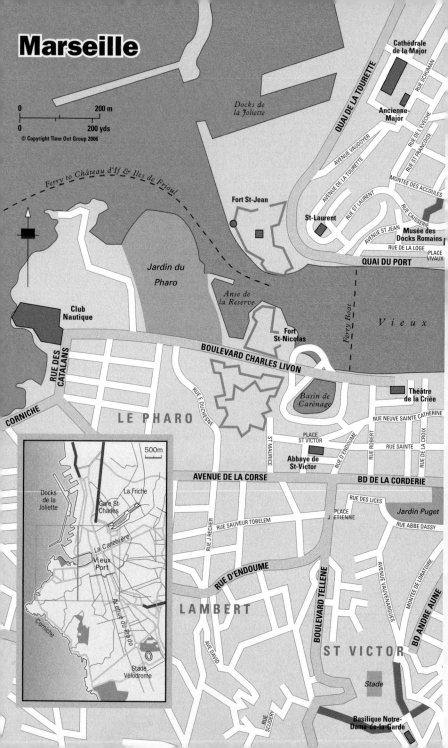

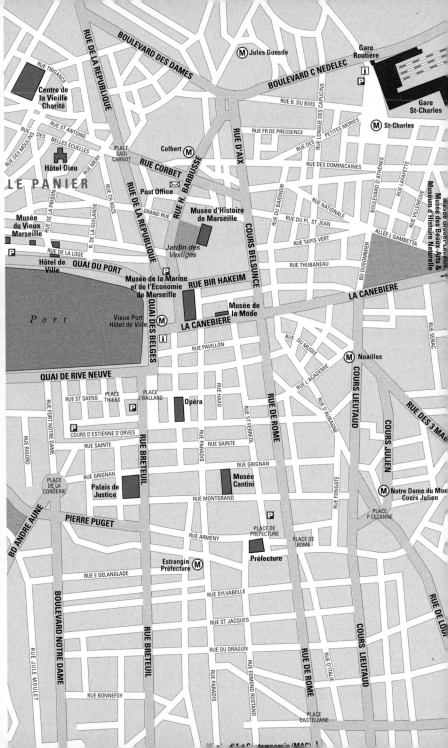

2001 municipal elections. Gaudin wisely put an optimistic spin on the city's unemployment rate, which did actually drop from 17 per cent to 14.7 per cent in June 2003.

Marseille is repositioning itself as a service and research centre, and is fast learning to capitalise on its spectacular setting and cultural facilities. If they are really serious about tourism – and indeed enhancing the feel-good factor for its 800,000 inhabitants – the authorities need to get more serious about cleaning, and not just around the Vieux Port. Suffice it to say the good citizens appear fonder of their ubiquitous dogs – and haphazardly parked cars – than the people who walk the pavements.

Sightseeing

Marseille takes in 57 kilometres (36 miles) of seafront, from L'Estaque in the north to the Calanques in the south and is laid out in 16 *arrondissements* moving clockwise from the Vieux Port, then anticlockwise in an outer semi-circle.

Vieux Port & La Canebière

If you think of Marseille as a gritty city, you'll be surprised by the beauty of the Vieux Port. Fashionable bars and avant-garde theatres rub shoulders with boat merchants; luxury yachts bob alongside fishing trawlers, which deliver the day's catch at quai des Belges (officially renamed quai de la Fraternité) to one of France's most photogenic markets. Here, you don't need to ask if the fish is fresh: the octopuses are still slithering and sea bream try valiantly to hop out of the tub. This eastern quay is the departure point for ferries to Château d'If, the Iles de Frioul (*see p148*) and the Côte Bleue (*see p158*).

From this vantage point the two forts guarding the entrance to the port come into view: **Fort St-Jean** (which will form part of the future Musée des Civilisations de l'Europe et de la Méditerranée) on the north bank and Fort St-Nicolas (closed to the public) on the south. The former, which provides a popular suntrap, was built in the 12th century and the latter under Louis XIV. Tellingly, their guns used to face towards, rather than away from, the city: the Marseillais are still proud of this display of the king's doubts about their allegiance.

The quai du Port, to the north, is the quieter side and offers pleasant strolling towards the sea. The Nazis – aided by the Vichy regime – were responsible for brutally reshaping this corner of the city, the historic St-Jean district, which was dynamited in February 1943, razing 1,500 old apartment buildings to the ground.

The ancient church of St-Laurent, reached by a flight of steps, is all that remains today. The 25,000 inhabitants of the north bank were cleared out of their homes in under 48 hours, events commemorated by an annual ceremony, when wreaths are laid in nearby place du 23 Janvier 1943, and in the **Mémorial des Camps de la Mort** around the corner. The 1950s apartment blocks that now line the *quai*, designed by architect Fernand Pouillon, look proud and elegant in their way.

They are offset by the fine 17th-century Hôtel de Ville, now surrounded by a grand new public space. Remains of much earlier shipping activity can be seen just near here in the **Musée des Docks Romains**, while the Maison Diamantée evokes the prosperous merchants' houses that stood here in the 16th century. Behind this, steps lead up to the ancient, and gradually gentrifying, Le Panier district.

The quai de Rive Neuve on the opposite bank houses some of the city's hippest bars and clubs, including the Bar de la Marine and Trolleybus, and the Théâtre de la Criée, created from the city's old fish market in the 1970s. Further along where it turns into boulevard Charles Livon, the busy road leading past Palais du Pharo towards the Corniche, is faster-paced and less pedestrian-friendly. Behind quai de Rive Neuve, a thriving restaurant and café district has sprung up on place Thiars, cours d'Estienne d'Orves and place aux Huiles. A small ferry runs from the Hôtel de Ville on the north side of the port to place aux Huiles on the south (8am-6.30pm, 50¢), but it's just as quick to walk.

Climb up behind and follow rue Sainte all the way to the ancient **Abbaye de St-Victor**, a fascinating double-decker church and once one of the most powerful abbeys in the South. On foot from here, there is a steep yet rewarding route up to Notre-Dame-de-la-Garde (*see p147*).

Running east from the Vieux Port, **La Canebière** (from canèbe: hemp in Provençal, after a rope factory once located here), the city centre's formerly glorious main drag, long served as the dividing line between the 'poor' north and the 'rich' south of Marseille. It's now rather shabby in parts and dominated by chain stores. However, the Canebière still makes for an interesting walk with its faded 19th-century wedding-cake façades, lively multicultural atmosphere and plenty of cheap places to eat. At the Vieux Port end, near the Office du Tourisme, a landscaped square leads to the colonnaded façade of the Opéra de Marseille. Across the street, the Bourse et Chambre de Commerce, decorated with ship carvings alluding to the importance of the port, now contains the **Musée de la Marine et de l'Economie de Marseille**. Nearby a modern cubic building houses the dynamic **Musée de la Mode** and a fashion-industry trade centre. At the top end of La Canebière, you can't miss the tall, imposing **Eglise des Réformés**.

To the north of La Canebière stretches the North African neighbourhood of **Belsunce**, known for its handsome 18th-century residences and as the most likely place to be mugged. This may be unfair, but best be wary of loitering lads in quiet backstreets. It's also home to the tremendous new municipal library designed by Adrien Fainsilber. At the end of the cours Belsunce in place Jules Guesde stands the imperial Porte d'Aix, a triumphal arch built 1825-33. The surrounding streets offer a vibrant experience of Marseille today: corner-shop mosques, boutiques selling cheap fabrics and gadgets, and sweetmeats of every kind. It's just minutes from the Vieux Port, but so different in mood you might have spent 24 hours on a ferry.

Abbaye de St-Victor

3 rue de l'Abbaye, 7th (04.96.11.22.60). M° Vieux-Port/bus 55, 61, 54, 81. **Open** 9am-7pm daily. **Admission** free. *Crypt* €2; free under-12s. **No credit cards.**

This spectacular, fortified medieval church was built on the remains of an ancient necropolis. The earlier church, founded in the fifth century by St Jean Cassian, was the city's first basilica and heart of a powerful abbey complex. Destroyed by Saracens in the 11th century, it was rebuilt and fortified in the 14th century. Chunks of the earlier church remain in its convoluted crypt, where sarcophagi include the tomb of St Victor, ground to death between two millstones by the Romans.

Eglise des Réformés

1 rue Barbaroux, 1st (04 91 48 57 45). M° Réformés-Canebière. **Open** 4-6pm daily. **Admission** free.

This handsome neo-Gothic church got its 'nickname' from an order of reformed Augustine monks, whose chapel stood on this site; its actual name is St-Vincent-de-Paul. Founded in 1852, it was consecrated only in 1888 due to lack of funds. The two spires, one of which houses four bells, are 69m (226ft) high.

Fort St-Jean/Musée National des Civilisations de l'Europe et de la Méditerranée

quai du Port, 2nd (04.96.13.80.90/www.musee-europemediterranee.org). M° Vieux-Port. **Open** (during exhibitions) 10am-noon, 2-7pm Mon, Wed-Sun. **Admission** €2; €1.50 students; free under-18s. **No credit cards.**

The imposing walled fortress is currently used for temporary exhibitions, which prefigure the Musée National des Civilisations de l'Europe et de la Méditerranée (due to open 2008), based around the folk art collection of the former Musée National des Arts et Traditions Populaires in Paris.

Jardins des Vestiges/ Musée d'Histoire de Marseille

Centre Bourse, 1 sq Belsunce, 1st (04.91.90.42.22). M° Vieux-Port. **Open** noon-7pm Mon-Sat. **Admission** €2.50; €1 10-16s; free under-10s. **No credit cards.**

While the foundations for the Centre Bourse shopping centre were being dug in the 1970s, remains of Marseille's original Greek walls and a corner of the Roman port were unearthed, preserved here in a sheltered enclave. The adjoining Musée d'Histoire de Marseille has a truly splendid collection, which ranges from vintage promotional posters to historical models of the city.

Mémorial des Camps de la Mort

esplanade de la Tourette, 2nd (04.91.90.73.15). M° Vieux-Port or Joliette/bus 83. **Open** June-Sept 11am-6pm Tue-Sun. *Oct-May* 10am-5pm Tue-Sun. **Admission** free.

In January 1943, following orders from Hitler, Karl Oberg, head of the Gestapo in France, declared: 'Marseille is the cancer of Europe. And Europe can't be alive as long as Marseille isn't purified… That is why the German authorities want to cleanse the old districts and destroy them with mines and fire.' These chilling words resonate in a series of haunting and fascinating pictures that capture subsequent vile events, on display in a former bunker.

Musée Cantini

19 rue Grignan, 6th (04.91.54.77.75). M° Estrangin-Préfecture. **Open** June-Sept 11am-6pm Tue-Sun. *Oct-May* 10am-5pm Tue-Sun. **Admission** €3; €1.50 10-18s, students; free under-10s. **No credit cards.**

This 17th-century mansion houses one of France's foremost Fauve and Surrealist art collections together with some fine post-war works. Highlights include a Signac of the port, Dufy from his early Cézannesque neo-Cubist phase and paintings by Camoin, Kupka, Kandinsky, Léger and Ernst. Upstairs focuses on Surrealism and abstraction, including Arp, Brauner and Picabia, plus works by Dubuffet, Balthus and Bacon.

Musée des Docks Romains

pl Vivaux, 2nd (04.91.91.24.62). M° Vieux-Port/bus 83. **Open** June-Sept 11am-6pm Tue-Sun. *Oct-May* 10am-5pm Tue-Sun. **Admission** €2; €1 10-16s, students; free under-10s. **No credit cards.**

During post-war reconstruction in 1947, the remains of a first-century Roman shipping warehouse were uncovered. This museum preserves the site intact, and documents maritime trade through terracotta jars, amphorae and coins.

Musée de la Marine et de l'Economie de Marseille

9 La Canebière, 1st (04.91.39.33.33/www.marseille-provence.cci.fr/patrimoine). M° Vieux-Port. **Open** 10am-6pm daily. **Admission** €3; €1.50 12-18s; free under-12s. **Credit** MC, V.

This grandiose building housing the city's Chamber of Commerce was inaugurated by Napoléon III in 1860. The museum charts the maritime history of Marseille from the 17th century with paintings, models, old maps and engravings, and celebrates ports of the world from Liverpool to Montevideo.

Musée de la Mode de Marseille

11 La Canebière, 1st (04.96.17.06.00/ www.espacemodemediterranee.com). M° Vieux-Port. **Open** *June-Sept* 11am-6pm Tue-Sun. *Oct-May* 10am-5pm Tue-Sun. **Admission** €3; €1.50 10-16s; free under-10s. **No credit cards.**

The fashion museum adjoining the Espace Mode Méditerranée has more than 3,000 accessories and outfits, from the 1920s to the present, displayed in changing exhibitions, ranging from thematic shows (the fashion of the Côte d'Azur during 2005) to young southern designers, such as Fred Sathal.

Musée du Vieux Marseille (Maison Diamantée)

2 rue de la Prison, 2nd (04.91.55.28.68). M° Vieux-Port/bus 83, 49B. **Open** *June-Sept* 10am-7pm Tue-Sun. *Oct-May* 10am-5pm Tue-Sun. **Admission** €3; €1.50 10-16s; free under-10s. **No credit cards.**

Reopened for temporary exhibitions only following painstaking renovation, the Maison Diamantée, so named because of its diamond-faceted Renaissance façade, was built in 1570 by wealthy merchant Pierre Gardiolle. Exhibitions give an impression of daily life in Marseille since the 18th century including furniture, photographs and provençal costume.

Le Panier, La Joliette & Les Carmes

Le Panier, rising between quai du Port and grimy (but improving) rue de la République, has been the traditional first stop for successive waves of immigrants and today is at the top of the tourist itinerary. It's hard to resist the charm of its narrow, hilly streets, steep stairways and semi-crumbling pastel-coloured houses – think Italy-meets-Tunisia. Certain Marseillais (the ones who don't live here) still think of Le Panier as a dodgy area to be avoided at night, but nowadays there is little evidence to support such fears. Its population is changing as teachers, students and arty professionals renovate flats, and chic boutiques selling pottery and soap attest to its aspirations; it remains to be seen whether Le Panier will become the Marais of Marseille.

Whether you take one of the stairways up from the Vieux Port or any of the roads leading to rue Caisserie, the striking Hôtel Dieu above catches your eye. Designed in 1753 by the nephew of Jules Hardouin-Mansart (of place Vendôme in Paris fame), its arcaded facade is typical of hospital architecture of the time,

though it was modified during the Second Empire. At the foot of the punishing Montée des Accoules, the Eglise Notre-Dame-des-Accoules has a remarkable spire and bell tower.

After it has peaked, the Montée des Accoules runs down to gently animated place de Lenche (also reached from avenue St-Jean), which is edged by a few bars, restaurants and shops. Peaceful place des Moulins is located roughly in the middle of the sector. On the north side is the stunning **Centre de la Vieille Charité**, built as a poorhouse but now home to two museums and a pleasant café. West of the Vieille Charité, with an unimpeded line to God and sea (despite the motorway roaring by alongside), is the huge, kitsch 19th-century **Cathédrale de la Major** and its predecessor l'Ancienne Major.

Behind Le Panier, the up-and-coming La Joliette area, centred around the 1860s **Docks de la Joliette**, is not so much a tourist destination as the focus of the Euroméditerranée project, anticipated as playing a key role in stimulating the city's economy. Cargo ships and a frenetic motorway make it a distinctly unpleasant place to visit, but this should change in 2006, when a tunnel replaces the flyover with an impressive esplanade. By 2008 the whole 2.7-kilometre (1.7-mile) expanse from Fort St-Jean to Arenc should be transformed into the Cité de la Méditerranée. The bold plans, overseen by architects Yves Lion and François Kern, embrace public housing, a museum and aquarium, restaurants, theatre, offices and two hotels.

Stretching from place de la Joliette to the Vieux Port runs traffic-laden rue de la République, the main Haussmann-style artery of the second *arrondissement*, and a good place to find good-value ethnic restaurants, snack joints and bakeries. This area is undergoing a make-over too, as evidenced by glossy done-up apartments and offices dotted among the rather grimier whole. This refit, another phase of the EM redevelopment, is set to continue.

Heading left down rue Jean Trinquet, some unobtrusive, smelly steps just past rue Cathala lead up to place des Grandes Carmes and an undiscovered gem Eglise Notre-Dame-du-Mont-Carmel, currently undergoing restoration to preserve its 300-plus statues, baroque interior and many paintings. This spot offers a respite and urban views across to Le Panier and the imposing residential block on place Sadi Carnot, once infamous as Nazi headquarters.

Cathédrale de la Major

pl de la Major, 2nd (04.91.90.53.57). M° Joliette. **Open** 10am-noon, 2-5.30pm Tue-Sun. **Admission** free.

The largest cathedral built in France since the Middle Ages, the neo-Byzantine Nouvelle Major was started in 1852 and completed in 1893 with oriental-style cupolas and a lustrous mosaic. The remains of the 11th-century Ancienne Major, parts of which go back to Roman times, lie in a state of disrepair.

Centre de la Vieille Charité
2 rue de la Charité, 2nd (04.91.14.58.80). M° Joliette or Vieux-Port. **Open** *June-Sept* 11am-6pm Tue-Sun. *Oct-May* 10am-5pm Tue-Sun. **Admission** *Each museum* €2; €1 10-16s; free under-10s, all Sun morning. *Exhibitions* €3; free under-10s, all Sun morning. **No credit cards.**

Constructed from 1671 to 1749 as a poorhouse, this ensemble designed by Pierre and Jean Puget has beautiful open loggias on three storeys around a courtyard, which is dominated by a magnificent chapel with an oval-shaped dome. It was renovated and reopened as a cultural complex in 1986. The former chapel now houses temporary exhibitions; around the sides are the Musée d'Archéologie Méditerranéenne and the Musée des Arts Africains, Océaniens and Amerindiens (MAAOA). The former has a superb collection of archaeological finds from Provence and the Mediterranean and the most important Egyptian collection in France outside Paris. MAAOA displays tribal art and artefacts from Africa, the Pacific and the Americas.

Docks de la Joliette
10 pl de la Joliette, 2nd (04.91.14.45.00/www.euro mediterranee.fr). M° Joliette. **Open** 9am-6pm Mon-Sat. **Admission** free.

The handsome stone warehouses of this 19th-century industrial port run along the waterfront for almost a mile and were modelled on St Katharine Docks in London. They were state of the art when opened in 1866, but as traffic declined and cargo shifted to containers, the buildings fell into disuse and there were plans to demolish them. However, they have been brilliantly renovated into office space by architect Eric Castaldi as the centrepiece of the Euroméditerranée redevelopment. The Docks are now occupied by a diverse mix of companies, bars and restaurants. An information centre in atrium 10.2 displays designs and models of the entire scheme.

St-Charles, Longchamp & the north-east

North-east of Belsunce is the main station, the Gare St-Charles, with its majestic staircase guarded by two sombre lions.

In the working-class neighbourhood of Belle de Mai behind the station, a former squat in a disused tobacco factory has become the thriving cultural centre La Friche la Belle de Mai. The surrounding area is hardly appealing on foot, although the south-east corner of Belle de Mai has also been targeted as the focus of an innovative media complex.

At the far end of boulevard Longchamp stands the grandiose Palais Longchamp, which holds the **Musée des Beaux-Arts**

La Canebière. *See p142.*

and **Muséum d'Histoire Naturelle**. Behind the palace are attractive landscaped gardens, which stay open later than the museums.

Much further out in the 13th *arrondissement*, heading past the bright blue landmark of the Hôtel du Département (which is the seat of the Bouches-du-Rhône Conseil Général) designed by British architect Will Alsop, is the Château-Gombert district. Home to a *technopôle* (technological research and business centre) as well as the delightful **Musée du Terroir Marseillais**, this is a charming little suburban village of winding roads where property is now highly sought-after. Take the time to hop on a bus and spend an afternoon wandering around here, and you'll see why.

Musée des Beaux-Arts & Muséum d'Histoire Naturelle

Palais Longchamp, bd de Longchamp, 4th. M° Longchamp-Cinq-Avenues. **Open** *Musée des Beaux-Arts* closed for renovation until 2007. *Muséum d'Historie Naturelle* (04.91.14.59.50) 10am-5pm Tue-Sun. **Admission** *Muséum d'Histoire Naturelle* €3; €1.50 10-16s; free under-10s. **No credit cards.**
No other monument expresses the ebullience of 19th-century Marseille better than the Palais Longchamp. This ostentatious complex, inaugurated in 1869, was built to celebrate the completion of an 84km (52-mile) aqueduct bringing the waters of the Durance to the drought-prone port. A massive horseshoe-shaped classical colonnade, with a triumphal arch at its centre and museums in either wing, crowns a hill landscaped around fountains. On the ground floor of the fine art museum are works by Marseille sculptor and architect Pierre Puget (1620-94); on the first floor is a superior collection of 16th- and 17th-century French, Italian and Flemish paintings. The second floor is devoted to French 18th- and 19th-century works and old master drawings. The natural history museum has zoological and prehistoric artefacts.

Musée du Terroir Marseillais

5 pl des Héros, 13th (04.91.68.14.38). M° La Rose then bus 5. **Open** 9am-noon, 2-6.30pm Tue-Fri; 2.30-6.30pm Sat, Sun. **Admission** €4; €1.60 6-14s; free under-6s. **No credit cards.**
Founded in 1928, the museum offers a charming insight into provençal culture: hand-painted 18th-century dressers, faïence, dolls and ancient kitchen gadgets such as a fig-drier.

Musée Grobet-Labadié

140 bd de Longchamp, 1st (04.91.62.21.82). M° Longchamp-Cinq-Avenues. **Open** *June-Sept* 11am-6pm Tue-Sun. *Oct-May* 10am-5pm Tue-Sun. **Admission** €2; €1 10-16s; free under-10s. **No credit cards.**
The intimate Musée Grobet-Labadié houses the private art collection of a wealthy 19th-century couple. Their 1873 mansion, scrupulously renovated, offers an intriguing glimpse into cultivated tastes of the time, ranging from 15th- and 16th-century Italian and Flemish paintings to Fragonard and Millet, medieval tapestries and 17th- and 18th-century provençal furniture and faïence.

Notre-Dame, cours Julien & Castellane

Stretching south and south-east of the Vieux Port, the densely populated sixth *arrondissement* is interestingly varied in terms of architecture and people. Its southern and western parts, along with the neighbouring seventh and eighth *arrondissements*, are considered the chic districts of Marseille. The city's most famous – and audaciously stand-out – landmark, the stripey neo-Byzantine basilica of **Notre-Dame-de-la-Garde**, rises on a peak to the south of the Vieux Port (a pleasant sign-posted climb). It can also be reached from the other side, via twisting streets and steps from the quiet Vauban district or the serene Jardin Puget.

Perched on another hill south of Noailles leading to Notre-Dame-du-Mont, is the bohemian – if that means tastefully graffitied – cours Julien, site of the former central food market (it still has a flower market Wednesday and Saturday mornings and organic food on Friday mornings). An eclectic collection of fashion boutiques, bookshops, French and

Notre-Dame-de-la-Garde. *See p147.*

ethnic restaurants, cafés with sun-soaked terraces, theatres and music venues make for a slightly uncomfortable contrast with less well-off locals, who also like to chill out here. Much of the city's youth music scene is centred around this area, bringing with it a vibrant streetlife.

It's very different in mood to the fine 19th-century apartment blocks, strung with wrought-iron balconies, that line rue de Rome in the area around the Préfecture. The regal police headquarters is fronted by cascading fountains, wide pavements much loved by skateboarders, and an attractive square, which borders the top of trendy rue St-Ferréol. South of here, place Castellane with its elegant Cantini fountain (1911-13) marks the beginning of the broad avenue du Prado, which has the grace of the Champs-Elysées without the megastores or overpriced cafés. It's also worth visiting **Parc du XXVI Centenaire** a little to the east.

Notre-Dame-de-la-Garde

rue Fort du Sanctuaire, 6th (04.91.13.40.80). *Bus 60 from Vieux Port or Petit Train de la Bonne Mère.* **Open** 7am-7pm daily. **Admission** free. Balancing on a 162m-high (531ft) peak, 'La Bonne Mère', topped by a massive gilded statue of the Virgin Mary and Child, is the emblem of Marseille and the most visited tourist site in Provence. Building began in 1853 and the interior decoration was completed in 1899. Deeply loved by Marseillais (and rightly so), its Byzantine-style interior is filled with remarkable ex-votos, including one for Olympique de Marseille. The mosaic floors were made in Venice, and alternating red and white marble pillars add to the richness of the surprisingly intimate chapel. Outside, the esplanade offers wonderful vistas in all directions.

Parc du XXVI Centenaire

sq Zino Francescatti, 8th. Mº Castellane/Périer/bus 42, 50. **Open** *Mar-Apr, Sept-Oct* 8am-7pm daily. *May-Aug* 8am-9pm daily. *Nov-Feb* 8am-5.30pm daily. **Admission** free. This agreeable 10ha (25-acre) park is a recent and as yet unfinished addition in honour of Marseille's 26 centuries of history. Stemming from the site of the former Gare du Prado, it combines paved walkways, lawns and a stream between the old platforms, and is mercifully dog-free. At the main entrance a growing list of patrons' names is engraved in stone.

La Corniche, Prado & the south-west

The Corniche Président Kennedy – known simply as La Corniche – carves along the coast from just beyond the Vieux Port to where the 8th begins near the Centre de Voile. Vantage

points, craggy coves and little beaches along the way offer stunning views of the rocky coastline, offshore islands and spooky Château d'If. The sheltered and sandy **Plage des Catalans**, encircled by cafés and restaurants, looks tempting but costs €5 per two hours. Further along, the chic little **Vallon des Auffes** inlet has a bijou harbour and a couple of upmarket restaurants. Equally sought-after, sticking out on the exposed westerly tip, is the pretty Malmousque district. It has several rocky bays and a quay, which offer refreshing although unsupervised bathing points (the most popular are in front of the Foreign Legion base down from rue de la Douane, and Anse de Maldormé and Anse Fausse Monnaie just around the corner).

Following the road south, the ominously named Plage du Prophète is a quite attractive, larger beach. All of these sunspots can be reached by strolling down through the smart residential areas of Bompard and (hilly) Roucas Blanc, occasionally a challenging up-and-down walk. The No.73 bus also offers a fun rollercoaster ride from Castellane via Périer down to Vallon de l'Oriol on the seafront. In addition the less reliable 83 runs (or rather crawls) along the Corniche between the Vieux Port and Prado.

In the eighth *arrondissement*, past the Rond-Point du Prado, stands the **Stade Vélodrome**, proud home to the city's worshipped football team Olympique de Marseille. Further along boulevard Michelet you can also stop in for a drink at Le Corbusier's landmark **Cité Radieuse**. Heading south-west between Ste-Anne and Mazargues on avenue d'Haïfa – just before César's gigantic bronze sculpture of a thumb – the **Musée d'Art Contemporain** contains an adventurous collection of contemporary art. The avenue du Prado ends at the Plage du Prado in front of a bold marble copy of Michelangelo's *David*. Along this broad recreational stretch of beach (Parc Balnéaire), you'll see *David*-like windsurfers being tossed about on the waves, as they brave Marseille's fearsome Mistral. Facing another elongated beach, the 17-hectare (42-acre) **Parc Borély**, with its horseracing track, botanical gardens, lake and château, is a haven for families, joggers and pétanque players.

Continuing on through Bonneveine and Vieille Chapelle, this stretch of coast, with its series of sand and shingle beaches, shows Marseille at its most sporty and Californian; but the picturesque ports of Pointe Rouge and Madrague de Montredon remain typically Marseillais. La Madrague also has an unofficial gay 'beach', or rather an isolated patch of rocks accessed from boulevard Mont-Rose. **Les Goudes** is located just a 20-minute walk beyond here, a seemingly remote village surrounded by barren outcrops yet still within the city limits. With its small stone houses blending into the orangey rock, it attracts fishing enthusiasts, divers and hikers; it's a great place to feast on fresh fish or wood-fired pizza. Even further along at the end of the road is the timeless village of Callelongue, which is dominated by the forbidding Massif de Marseilleveyre and too many cars at weekends.

La Cité Radieuse
280 bd Michelet, 8th (hotel 04.91.16.78.00).
M° Rond-Point du Prado then bus 21 or 22.
Guided tours ask at hotel reception or at Office de Tourisme.
Not to make the trip out here would be a terrible waste of a visit to Marseille. *La maison de fada* (the 'madman's house'), as locals once scornfully but now affectionately call Le Corbusier's 1952 reinforced-concrete apartment block (or just 'Le Corbu'), is where the architect tried out his prototype for mass housing. The vertical garden city became the model for countless urban developments. Perched on stilts, the complex contains 340 balconied flats plus a shopping floor that serves as a 'village street'. On the roof are an open-air theatre, a gym and a nursery school, offering panoramic views. The flats are mostly duplexes, in which the architect designed every detail. The Cité also contains a superb, and surprisingly affordable, hotel (*see p155*).

Musée d'Art Contemporain (MAC)
69 av d'Haïfa, 8th (04.91.25.01.07). Bus 23,
45. **Open** *June-Sept* 11am-6pm Tue-Sun. *Oct-May* 10am-5pm Tue-Sun. **Admission** €3; €1.50 10-16s; free under-10s. **No credit cards.**
Marseille's dedicated contemporary art museum is located in a hangar-like space. Its contents, which change regularly, range from perplexing to hilarious, such as Parant's *La Voiture Rouge*. In the garden are sculptures by artists including César, Absalon and Dietman.

Musée de la Faïence
157 av de Montredon, 8th (04.91.72.43.47).
M° Castellane or Prado then bus 19. **Open** *June-Sept* 11am-6pm Tue-Sun. *Oct-May* 10am-5pm Tue-Sun. **Admission** €2; €1 10-16s; free under-10s. **No credit cards.**
Surrounded by a magnificent park at the foot of the Marseilleveyre, Château Pastré was constructed in 1862 by a rich trading family. Today it houses the Musée de la Faïence, recalling the pottery industry that thrived in Marseille in the late 17th and 18th centuries, as well as other provençal production.

Stade Vélodrome (Olympique de Marseille)
3 bd Michelet, 8th. M° Rond-Point du Prado.
Club office: 25 rue Negresco, 8th (04.91.76.56.09/
www.olympiquedemarseille.com). **Open** *Shop & museum* (www.madeinsport.com) 10am-1pm, 2-6pm Mon-Sat.

This isn't a football stadium, it's a place of worship. L'Olympique de Marseille commands the sort of fervour that separatist movements might elsewhere. OM needed plenty of fighting spirit in 1993, when saviour-president Bernard Tapie, a former socialist minister, set up their victory over Valenciennes. The club clawed its way back from disgrace thanks to a crop of international talent, even though Zidane has since departed for Madrid. And in 2004 they came close (but no cigar) to bagging the UEFA Cup, having beaten Inter Milan and Liverpool on the way to the final. The Stade Vélodrome is the largest stadium in the country after Paris' Stade de France, with 60,000 seats. The best (€70) are in the Jean-Bouin stand, but the Ganay (max €60) also offers a relatively quiet viewpoint. Tickets can be bought from the stadium on match day, in advance from L'OM Café (3 quai des Belges, Vieux Port) or ring 32 29 Allo OM.

L'Estaque

The faded industrial district of L'Estaque, hugging the coast on the north-west of the city, looks like an unlikely place to have swayed the history of modern art, but it did. When Paul Cézanne first visited it in 1870, the little fishing village was already evolving into a working-class suburb living off its tile factories and cement works. The transition clearly intrigued him, because his most famous painting of the town, *Le Golfe de Marseille vu de L'Estaque* (now in the Art Institute of Chicago), has a factory chimney smoking in one corner.

The main attraction for Cézanne (and Derain, Braque, Dufy and the other artists who came here in their wake) – the remarkable light and diverse shapes of the landscape – survives today. It's not easy to pick out the locations the painters immortalised, but you can stroll around the village and up to Cézanne's favourite viaduct or take the Circuit des Peintres walking tour organised by the Marseille tourist office.

The seafront road along the so-called Plage de l'Estaque (for the most part a fenced-off private harbour) has been improved to provide better pedestrian access, although the proper beach, Plage de Corbières, is a couple of kilometres out the other side.

Ile d'If & Iles de Frioul

The Ile d'If, a tiny islet of sun-bleached white stone 20 minutes from the Vieux Port, is today inhabited by salamanders and seagulls. Its two most famous residents – Edmond Dantès and Abbé Faria, the main characters of Alexandre Dumas' *The Count of Monte Cristo* – never existed. To keep Marseille under control, François I had a fortress built here in 1524 so formidable that it never saw combat and was eventually converted into a prison. Thousands of Protestants met grisly ends here after the Edict of Nantes was revoked in 1685. But it was Dumas who put If on the map by making it the prison from which Dantès escaped: wily administrators soon caught on and kept tourists happy by hacking out the very hole through which Edmond slid to freedom in the story. The chateau is quickly visited, so bring a picnic and enjoy the clean seawater. Off-season the one café is likely to be closed.

It's easy to combine a visit to the Château d'If with the Iles de Frioul, a collection of small islands, two of which – Ile Ratonneau and Ile Pomègues – were joined by the digue de Berry in the 18th century. Aside from a few holiday flats by the marina, they consist largely of windswept rock, wonderfully isolated beaches and fragrant clumps of thyme and rosemary. Ratonneau is also the home of the impressive Hôpital Caroline, constructed 1824-28 as a quarantine hospital to protect Marseille from epidemics. Today it is a curious historic site with terrific views well worth a visit (and the slog up the hill). In June and July, it hosts the Nuits Caroline – a series of night-time events ranging from live jazz to open-air theatre (04.96.11.04.61, €23, including boat).

Château d'If

Ile d'If, 1st (04.91.59.02.30). **Open** *May-Sept* 9.30am-6.30pm daily. *Oct-Apr* 9.30am-5.30pm Tue-Sun. **Admission** €4.60; €3.10 18-25s; free under-18s.

Ferries

GACM (04.91.55.50.09, www.answeb.net/gacm) runs regular crossings (Tue-Sun, less frequent Oct-May), many of which stop at If and Iles de Frioul. Return ticket one island €10; €5 3-6s; free under-3s; both islands €15; €6.50 3-6s; free under-3s. No credit cards.

Where to eat

Bouillabaisse – which Marseillais say can only be authentically made here – is a must for any visitor: seek out a well-reputed restaurant such as Le Miramar (rather than allowing yourself to be enticed by those waiters who dart out like hungry moray eels from the seafood joints on rue Saint-Saens). Be prepared to pay at least €40 per person. Pizza is another speciality, thanks to a history of immigration from Italy.

Les Arcenaulx

25 cours d'Estienne d'Orves, 1st (04.91.59.80.30/ www.les-arcenaulx.com). M° Vieux-Port. **Open** noon-2pm, 8-11pm Mon-Sat. Closed 1wk Aug. **Menus** €28.50-€49.50. **Credit** AmEx, DC, MC, V.
In a strikingly converted former arsenal building, this restaurant amid an antiquarian bookshop, publisher and kitchen shop-cum-*épicerie* has become the

dinner rendezvous of Marseille's chattering classes. Typical of the modern southern cooking are stuffed provençal vegetables with tapenade or sardines with ginger and coriander and tempura vegetables.

Baie des Singes

Cap Croisette, Les Goudes, 8th (04.91.73.68.87). **Open** Mon-Sat (ring for further details). Closed Oct-Mar. **Average** €40. **Credit** MC, V.
Even though getting here involves arriving by boat or scrabbling over a rocky promontory, you won't be the first: President Chirac and a host of TV personalities have already done it. And you can see why – the bare white rock and blue seas could be a Greek island. The speciality is dead simple, fresh fish, presented in a basket for you to choose from before being grilled (priced by the 100g). There's a sun-bathing terrace and you can swim from the rocks.

Le Café des Epices

4 rue du Lacydon, 2nd (04.91.91.22.69). M° Vieux-Port. **Open** noon-3pm, 8-11pm Tue-Fri; 8-11pm Sat. **Average** €25. **Credit** MC, V.
For affordably ambitious cuisine with deft spicing and inventive takes on traditional favourites, Café des Epices takes some beating. Young chef Arnaud de Grammont presides over the slick interior and handful of tables out on the terrace. Delicious oysters.

Chez Michel

6 rue des Catalans, 7th (04.91.52.30.63). Bus 54, 83. **Open** noon-2pm, 7.30-9.30pm daily. **Average** €55. **Credit** AmEx, MC, V.
This Marseille institution, looking across the Anse des Catalans, is a failsafe choice for bouillabaisse or bourride; the fish are expertly de-boned by sea-weathered waiters and served with a garlicky rouille.

Le Clou

24 cours Julien, 6th (04.91.48.08.63/ 04.91.92.46.22). M° Notre-Dame-du-Mont or Noailles. **Open** noon-2.30pm, 7-11pm Mon-Thur; noon-2.30pm, 7-11.30pm Fri, Sat; 7-11pm Sun. Closed 2wks Dec. **Menu** €18. **Credit** MC, V.
At the quieter end of 'cours Ju' but compensated by a splendid garden terrace, Le Clou serves generous portions of authentic Alsatian fare. Highlights include salade paysanne with lardons and croutons, coq au Riesling with creamy spätzle noodles and pork-laden choucroute garnie.

L'Epuisette

Anse du Vallon des Auffes, 7th (04.91.52.17.82). Bus 83. **Open** 12.15-2pm, 7.45-10pm Tue-Sat. **Menus** €45-€90. **Credit** AmEx, DC, MC, V.
Young wonder-chef Guillaume Sourrieu continues to astonish, offering up mouthwatering delights at this seafood restaurant, dramatically located on a craggy stone finger surrounded by the Med. Try the shellfish risotto with violet and coriander fritter, or the caramelised scallops with bacon and lime confit. Among the desserts, the chocolate brownie with marinated bananas and Indian pepper ice-cream is a little piece of heaven.

Marseille & Aix

L'Escale

*2 bd Alexandre Delabre, rte des Goudes, 8th
(04.91.73.16.78). Bus 19, 20.* **Open** *Summer*
7.30-10.30pm Mon, Tue; noon-2pm, 7.30-10.30pm
Wed-Sun. *Winter* noon-2pm, 7.30-10.30pm Tue-Sat;
noon-2pm Sun. Closed Jan. **Average** €50. **Credit**
AmEx, MC, V.

The sleepy fishing village of Les Goudes is only 30
minutes (if you're lucky with traffic) from the centre of Marseille. Former fishmonger Serge Zaroukian
does a delicious sauté of baby squid and perfectly
cooked monkfish served with ratatouille and onion
gratin. Ideal for Sunday lunch – but it's very popular, so book ahead.

La Fabrique

*3 pl Jules Verne, 2nd (04.91.91.10.40). M° Vieux-
Port.* **Open** 7.30pm-2am Wed-Fri; noon-2am Sat,
Sun. **Average** €30. **No credit cards**.

Across the square from Café des Epices (*see p149*),
this hip restaurant has a louche, loungey feel. Low
seating, even lower lighting, chilled-out tunes – you
get the picture. But that's not to say food takes a
back seat – great main dishes could be anything
from a simple risotto to papillote de rouget aux
agrumes. Nice staff too.

Le Jardin d'à Côté

*65 cours Julien, 6th (04.91.94.15.51). M° Notre-
Dame-du-Mont or Noailles.* **Open** noon-2.30pm
Mon-Sat. **Average** €20. **No credit cards**.

The nicest restaurant on 'cours Ju', this trad bistro
offers a warm welcome and tasty, well-priced food.
It makes the corner with graffiti-strewn rue Pastoret
and its terrace is a great people-watching spot in
summer. A typical dish would be rich, hearty daube
with a creamy polenta to soak up the juices.
Quaffable house wine is also served in handy,
lunchtime-sized carafes.

La Kahena

*2 rue de la République, 1st (04.91.90.61.93).
M° Vieux-Port.* **Open** noon-2.30pm, 7-10.30pm
daily. **Average** €15. **Credit** MC, V.

This is one of the best North African restaurants in
the centre, as evidenced by its popularity (book at
the weekend), and you'll struggle to eat three courses. To start, try the chorba (spicy chickpea broth),
calamari or a substantial salad. The merguez are
good, as is the fish couscous.

Lemon Grass Restaurant

*8 rue Fort Notre-Dame, 7th (04.91.33.97.65/
www.lemon-grass-marseille.com). M° Vieux-Port.*
Open 8-10.30pm Mon-Sat. Closed 2wks Jan, 1wk
Aug. **Menus** €28-€35. **Credit** MC, V.

Contemporary interior and ambient soundtrack provide a relaxed setting for Florent Saugeron's modern fusion cooking at this restaurant hidden away
on a side street just off the Vieux Port. Dishes such
as foie gras ravioli and confit tomatoes, lamb with
spices and couscous, rice stewed in a banana leaf,
plus a vegetarian option, borrow from Europe, Asia
and the Mediterranean.

Des Mets de Provence
Chez Maurice Brun

*18 quai de Rive Neuve, 7th (04.91.33.35.38).
M° Vieux-Port.* **Open** 8-10pm Mon; noon-2pm,
8-10.30pm Tue-Fri; 8-10.30pm Sat. Closed 1-15
Aug. **Menus** €40-€58. **Credit** MC, V.

Founded in 1936, this place proudly perpetuates traditional provençal cuisine. Having ascended the
wonky old steps, you'll discover a big rotisserie in
the fireplace. The proprietor recites the daily offerings on the substantial, delicious prix-fixe.

Le Miramar

*12 quai du Port, 2nd (04.91.91.10.40/
www.bouillabaisse.com). M° Vieux-Port.* **Open**
noon-2pm, 7-10pm Tue-Sat. Closed 2wks Jan, 3wks
Aug. **Average** €60. **Credit** AmEx, DC, MC, V.

If you only have time to visit one restaurant in
Marseille, make it this one. The 1950s-vintage port-
side dining room and busy terrace are the best places
to sample the city's fabled bouillabaisse. Young star
chef Christian Buffa took over in 2003 and he is
doing fabulous things in the kitchen. One word of
advice: since bouillabaisse is always a two-course
meal (the soup, then the fish) don't order a starter.

L'Orient Exploré

*9 rue Dejean, 6th (04.91.33.54.15). M° Estrangin-
Préfecture.* **Open** 11.30am-2pm, 7-11pm Mon-Fri;
7-11pm Sat. Closed Aug. **Menu** €14.50. **No
credit cards**.

The loud rug on the ceiling doesn't distract you from
the well-rendered versions of familiar Egyptian and
Middle Eastern dishes, including felafel, kefta and
chicken kebab. The oriental cakes are tasty.

La Part des Anges

33 rue Sainte, 1st (04.91.33.55.70). M° Vieux-Port.
Open 9am-2am Mon-Sat; 9am-1pm, 6pm-2am Sun.
Credit MC, V.

Very popular with the city's thirtysomething professionals, this smart wine bar and restaurant hunts
down wines from all over France, including undiscovered off-the-wall growers, and sells many by the
glass. But the simply prepared, casually presented
food is what really sustains the crowds – gorgeous-
ly sticky gigot was a highlight of our last visit.
Cheese and charcuterie boards are also available for
grazers.

Le Peron

*56 Corniche JF Kennedy, 7th (04.91.52.15.22).
Bus 83.* **Open** noon-2.15pm, 8-10.15pm daily.
Menus €49-€63. **Credit** AmEx, MC, V.

One of Marseille's most fashionable addresses, so
you'll need to book. The dark-wood decor is sleek
and modern, the sea view one of the very best in
town and the cooking inventive (such as crisp-
skinned hake served with mustard-dressed lentils).

Pizzaria Etienne

43 rue Lorette, 2nd (no phone). M° Vieux-Port.
Open 7.30-11pm Mon-Sat. **Average** €22.
No credit cards.

Owner Stéphane Cassaro is a legendary Panier personality. Pizza is considered a starter here and main courses are enormous. Pasta can be disappointingly mushy, so go for meat, or fried squid with garlic.

P P Maulio

24 rue Sainte, 1st (04.91.33.46.13). M° Préfecture. **Open** noon-2pm, 8-11pm Mon-Fri; 8pm-midnight Sat. **Average** €25. **Credit** MC, V.

Corsican specialities (including incredible wood-fired pizzas – try the 'figatelli') are the name of the game at this cosy, popular bistro just behind the Vieux Port. The delicious wines also hail from the *île de beauté*. Service comes with a smile, and even the occasional joke.

Une Table au Sud

2 quai du Port, 2nd (04.91.90.63.53). M° Vieux-Port. **Open** noon-2pm, 7.30-10.30pm Tue-Thur; noon-2pm, 7.30pm-midnight Fri, Sat. **Menus** €43-€58. **Credit** AmEx, MC, V.

After working for Alain Ducasse, chef Lionel Lévy opened this relaxed gourmet restaurant (rather incongruously located above a Häagen-Dazs café) and has quickly won a reputation for his modern French cooking. He also holds wine and food evenings featuring top-flight producers.

Zé

19-20 quai de Rive Neuve, 7th (04.91.55.08.15). M° Vieux-Port. **Open** noon-2pm, 8-11pm daily. **Menu** €28. **Credit** MC, V.

The fusion cooking is respectable at this *Barbarella*-esque, rather self-consciously hip restaurant located on a buzzing stretch of the *quai*. Expect to see plenty of metal and black-and-white minimalism with square lines and cube stools. Expect to eat magret de canard in Coca-Cola.

Where to drink

Le Bar de la Marine

15 quai de Rive Neuve, 7th (04.91.54.95.42). M° Vieux-Port. **Open** 7am-2am daily. **Credit** AmEx, V.

This very popular quayside bar has a fading, slightly raffish air and attracts a diverse crowd. Tables on the terrace are keenly contested during the summertime *apéro* hour.

La Boutique du Glacier

1 pl Général de Gaulle, 1st (04.91.33.76.93). M° Vieux-Port. **Open** 7.45am-7.15pm Mon-Sat; 7.45am-1pm, 3.30-7.15pm Sun. **Credit** MC, V.

Despite its snappy wood-and-marble make-over, this tearoom thankfully continues to attract nice old dears, who come for the decadent cakes and ice-creams.

Café Parisien

1 pl Sadi Carnot, 2nd (04.91.90.05.77). M° Colbert or Vieux-Port. **Open** 8am-4pm Mon-Sat. **Credit** V.

Drinks are quite pricey at this handsome 1901 belle époque café but the atmosphere is stylish. Tapas are served in the evening (average €15) and Le Papou's Italian cuisine (average €20) Thur-Sat from 7.30pm.

La Caravelle

34 quai du Port, 2nd (04.91.90.36.64). M° Vieux-Port. **Open** 7am-2am daily. **Credit** AmEx, MC, V.

Hidden up a flight of stars inside the Hôtel Belle-Vue (*see p155*), la Caravelle serves breakfast and lunch but is above all a (pricey) boho cocktail bar. A handful of coveted tables on the narrow balcony offer an idyllic view of the Vieux Port.

Cup of Tea

1 rue Caisserie, 2nd (04.91.90.84.02). M° Vieux-Port. **Open** 8.30am-7pm Mon-Fri; 9.30am-7pm Sat. **Credit** AmEx, MC, V

One part tearoom, one part bookshop, this fabulous little place is one of the best pit stops in town. All manner of teas and coffees are available, plus various pastries (€3), quiche and salad (€5) or the huge, garden-fresh salade composée (€6.50).

Le Crystal

148 quai du Port, 2nd (04.91.91.57.96). M° Vieux-Port/bus 83. **Open** *May-Sept* 9am-2am daily. *Oct-Apr* 9am-6pm Mon, Sun; 9am-2am Tue-Sat. **Credit** MC, V.

This groovy café has bags of 1950s-diner appeal with red leatherette banquettes and Formica tables, but in sunny weather the foliaged terrace will be sure to lure you outside.

Les Danaïdes

6 sq Stalingrad, 1st (04.91.62.28.51). M° Réformés-Canebière. **Open** 7am-9pm Mon-Sat. **Credit** MC, V.

Le Marseillais. *See p154.*

Marseille & Aix

The blue-and-white obsession at **Stade Vélodrome**. *See p148.*

Marseille & Aix

In a tranquil square enclosed by hectic roads, this 'gay friendly' café has a large terrace out front. Busy at lunch, it offers stress-free drinking in the evening.

O'Cours Jus

67 cours Julien, 6th (04.91.48.48.58). M° Notre-Dame-du-Mont-Cours-Julien. **Open** 6.30am-7pm Mon-Sat. Closed Aug. **No credit cards.**
This is one of the more bohemian cafés along cours Julien, and its small terrace attracts a big crowd for coffee, beer and snacks.

Plauchut

168 La Canebière, 1st (04.91.48.06.67). M° Réformés-Canebière. **Open** 7am-8pm Tue-Sun. Closed July or Aug. **Credit** MC, V.
This celebrated yet down-to-earth pâtisserie and tea-room has an art nouveau interior by Rafaël Ponson, whose swirls and flourishes rival those of the towering cakes, ice-cream and chocolates.

Nightlife

Most venues don't have box offices; tickets are available from Fnac and ticket agencies. For Le Son d'Orient, *see p156* **Rap and *rai.***

L'Affranchi

212 bd St-Marcel, 11th (04.91.35.09.19/www.l-affranchi.com). Bus 40, 15. **Open** (concert nights) 9pm-3am. **Admission** €8. **No credit cards.**
L'Affranchi is a showcase for Marseille rap and reggae. It also occasionally hosts special events such as a celebration of Algerian music and cinema.

Dock des Suds

12 rue Urbain V, 2nd (04.91.99.00.00/ 08.25.83.38.33/www.dock-des-suds.org). M° National. Opening times and admission vary.
The 5,000sq m (54,000sq ft) dock hosting the Fiesta des Suds each autumn is now programming music with a world and salsa bias all year round.

Dôme-Zénith

48 av St-Just, 4th (04.91.12.21.21/www.le-dome.com). M° St-Just-Hôtel du Département/ buses 41, 53, 81, Fluobus at night. Opening times and admission vary.
A big modern venue for international rock acts and stars of French *variété*. Consult the website to find out about dates and tickets.

Espace Julien

39 cours Julien, 6th (04.91.24.34.10/infoline 04.91.24.34.19/www.espace-julien.com). M° Notre-Dame-du-Mont-Cours-Julien. Opening times and admission vary.
This long-standing, very active venue on the boho 'cours Ju' hosts music ranging from international pop and blues to local electro; small bands and DJs play in the Café Julien.

L'Intermédiaire

63 pl Jean Jaurès, 6th (04.91.47.01.25). M° Notre-Dame-du-Mont-Cours-Julien. **Open** 6.30pm-2am Mon, Tue; 5.30pm-2am Wed-Sat; 6.30pm-2am 1st Sun of mth. **Admission** free. **No credit cards.**
The hippest venue for jazz, blues and rock is crowded but friendly. Concerts at 10.30pm Wed-Sat, jam session Tue and live jazz first Sun of the month.

Le Moulin

47 bd Perrin, 13th (04.91.06.33.94/
www.concertandco.com/lemoulin). M° St-Juste.
Box office 7.30pm on day or through agencies.
Admission €10-€22. **No credit cards**.
This converted cinema has become one of Marseille's
main venues for visiting French and international
rock, reggae and world music bands.

New Cancan

3 rue Sénac-de-Meilhan, 1st (04.91.48.59.76/
www.newcancan.com). M° Réformés-Canebière.
Open 6pm-6am daily. **Admission** free-€11.
Credit AmEx, MC, V.
Marseille's largest gay club has changed little since
the 1970s. Stage shows enliven the atmosphere as
does the backroom. Mixed, uninhibited crowd.

Le Trolleybus

24 quai Rive Neuve, 7th (04.91.54.30.45/
www.letrolley.com). M° Vieux-Port. **Open**
11pm-dawn Wed-Sat. **Admission** free Wed-Fri;
€10 Sat. **Credit** MC, V.
This sprawling club is the ground zero of Marseille
nightlife and was given a facelift in 2003. Different
zones offer techno, salsa, funk… and *pétanque*. An
equally heterogeneous crowd goes from young
bankers to rappers in tracksuits.

Le Vinyl

40 rue Plan Fourmiguier, 7th (04.91.33.04.34).
M° Vieux-Port. **Open** 11pm-dawn Thur-Sun.
Admission free; €13 after midnight Sat
(plus men on Fri). **Credit** AmEx, DC, MC, V.
This club has an underground air and leans towards
Afro-Caribbean music.

Le Warm'Up

8 bd Mireille Jourdan Barry (04.96.14.06.30/
www.warmup-marseille.fr). Buses 40, 15. **Open**
8pm-2am Tue-Sat. **Admission** free Tue, Fri; €8-€12
Wed, Thur, Sat. **Credit** MC, V.
Marseille's answer to the super-club, Warm'Up has
everything from a state-of-the-art sound system and
heaving dance-floor to an oriental chill-out room and
terrace bar with a swimming pool and views of the
distant hills. DJs spin diverse sets from straight-
ahead house through electro bleeps to crisp salsa.

Shopping

Rue St-Ferréol is lined with shops including
Galeries Lafayette department store
(No.40, 04.96.11.35.00) and fashion chains.
Several chic designer places, interspersed with
tempting food stores, have also sprung up on
rues Francis Davso, Grignan and Paradis. For
a quirkier selection, head to cours Julien or
rue Thubaneau. The **Centre Bourse** (04.91.
14.00.50) near the Vieux Port is the main
shopping centre, with a Fnac store on the
second floor. Marseille has some 30 markets,
the most famous of which are fresh fish daily

on quai des Belges (quai de la Fraternité),
cours Julien (flowers Saturday and Wednesday
mornings, organic food Friday morning) and
avenue du Prado (every morning, flowers
Friday). The flea market (av du Cap-Pinède,
15th, bus 35 & 70) is worth a visit, with
antiques sold Friday to Sunday.

Ad Hoc Books

8 rue Pisançon, 1st (04.91.33.51.92/www.ad
hocbooks.fr). M° Vieux-Port. **Open** 10am-7pm
Mon-Sat. **Credit** MC, V.
English-language bookshop opened in 2001 by a former employee of Foyles in London.

Arterra

3 rue du Petit Puit, 2nd (04.91.91.03.31).
M° Colbert or Joliette. **Open** 9am-1pm, 2-6pm
Mon-Sat. **Credit** MC, V.
This workshop in Le Panier shows that *santons*
(Christmas crib figures) can be artful, not cloying.

G Bataille

25 pl Notre-Dame-du-Mont, 6th (04.91.47.06.23).
M° Notre-Dame-du-Mont-Cours-Julien. **Open**
8am-12.30pm, 3.30-8pm Mon-Sat. **Credit** MC, V.
This magnificent *traiteur* (deli) is the perfect place
to shop for a picnic of delicious cheeses, prepared
salads, cold meats, pastries, wines and olive oil.

La Compagnie de Provence

1 rue Caisserie, 2nd (04.91.56.20.94). M° Vieux-Port.
Open 10am-1pm, 2-7pm Mon-Sat. **Credit** MC, V.
This is the place to come for cubes of Marseille soap.
The classic is non-perfumed olive-oil green, but vanil-
la, jasmine and honey are also on offer.

Four des Navettes

136 rue Sainte, 7th (04.91.33.32.12). M° Vieux-
Port/bus 55, 61. **Open** 7am-8pm Mon-Sat; 9am-1pm,
4-7.30pm Sun. **Credit** MC, V.
Founded in 1781, this bakery is famous for its boat-
shaped *navettes*, orange-scented biscuits. The origins of the *navette*'s trademark shape go back to
biblical times (*see p14* **Crossing the holy sea**).

Librairie Internationale Maurel

95 rue de Lodi, 6th (04.91.42.63.44). M° Baille or
Castellane/bus 54, 74. **Open** 9am-12.15pm, 2-6.45pm
Mon-Fri; 9am-noon, 3-6pm Sat. **Credit** MC, V.
A specialist in English- and Italian-language books,
with some Russian, German and Spanish material.

Madame Zaza de Marseille

74 cours Julien, 6th (04.91.48.05.57). M° Notre-
Dame-du-Mont-Cours-Julien. **Open** 10am-1pm, 2-
7pm Mon-Fri; 10am-7pm Sat. **Credit** AmEx, MC, V.
Fashion and costume jewellery with a baroque yet
alternative edge.

La Maison du Pastis

108 quai du Port, 2nd (04.91.90.86.77./www.la
maisondupastis.com). M° Vieux-Port/bus 83. **Open**
(school holidays) 10am-7.30pm daily; (term time)
10am-2pm, 4-7.30pm Tue-Sat. **Credit** MC, V.

Marseille & Aix

A dizzying range of *pastis*, anisette and absinthe is crammed into this smart little shop. And in just five minutes of conversation, the friendly owner can take you from the very origins of the South's most celebrated drink to the intricacies of modern production and distillation. Boutique producers (including the owner himself) are the name of the game.

Manon Martin
10 rue de la Tour, 1st (04.91.55.60.95). M°
Vieux-Port. **Open** 10am-7pm Mon-Sat. **Credit** AmEx, MC, V.
This short, pedestrianised street behind the Vieux Port has become a focus for local designers, led by flamboyant hat stylist Manon Martin.

Le Marseillais
12 rue de Glandeves, 1st (04.91.33.20.45).
M° Vieux-Port. **Open** 10am-1pm, 2-7pm Mon; 10am-7pm Tue-Sat. **Credit** MC, V.
Everything from clothes and household accessories to cologne and rucksacks are branded with this slick new shop's logo (a willowy Frenchman in a stripy jumper). Inspired by the seafaring heritage of its city, Le Marseillais puts a trendy new spin on traditional styles.

Pâtisserie d'Aix
2 rue d'Aix/1 rue Nationale, 1st (04.91.90.12.50).
M° Colbert or Vieux-Port. **Open** 6am-8pm Tue-Sun.
No credit cards.
This famous Tunisian pastry shop is stacked high with pyramids of honey-drenched delights.

Rive Neuve
30 cours d'Estienne d'Orves, 1st (04.96.11.01.01).
M° Vieux-Port. **Open** 10.30am-7.30pm Mon-Sat.
Credit MC, V.
Indicative of the designer boutiques now colonising Marseille (a huge agnès b is opposite), Rive Neuve has a cutting-edge selection of men's and women's wear that includes Alberta Ferretti, Paul Smith, Coast, Camarlinghi and shoes by Alain Tondowski.

Arts & entertainment

For information, pick up weekly *L'Hebdo* from kiosks or freebies *Métro* and *Marseille Plus*.

Frac Provence-Alpes-Côtes d'Azur
1 pl Francis Chirat, 2nd (04.91.91.27.55). M°
Joliette. **Open** 10am-12.30pm, 2-6pm Mon-Sat.
Admission free.
The Fonds régional d'art contemporain has a wide-ranging collection of contemporary art, from international names to young artists, exhibited, along with special commissions, at its own gallery in Le Panier and in schools, museums and cultural centres across the PACA region.

La Friche la Belle de Mai
41 rue Jobin, 3rd (04.95.04.95.04/www.lafriche.org).
M° Gare St-Charles/bus 49a, 49b. **Open** 3-6pm
Mon-Sat. **Admission** free.

A disused tobacco factory in the scruffy (but increasingly trendy) Belle de Mai quarter, La Friche started life as an artists' squat but is now home to numerous artistic, musical, theatrical and media outfits, as well as putting on regular art exhibitions. These include Aide aux Musiques Innovatrices, Théâtre Massalia, Radio Grenouille and Georges Appaix's La Liseuse dance company.

Galérie Roger Pailhas
20 quai Rive Neuve, 7th (04.91.54.02.22/
www.rogerpailhas.com). M° Vieux-Port. **Open** 11am-1pm, 2-6pm Tue-Sat. Closed Aug. **Admission** free.
In a massive first-floor space by the Vieux Port, Roger Pailhas is one of France's rare contemporary art galleries outside Paris that counts. Over the years Pailhas has collaborated with major international artists including Dan Graham and Daniel Buren, but he also picks out young local talents, such as Corinne Marchetti who addresses contemporary culture and sexuality in witty embroidered scenes.

Gyptis Théâtre
136 rue Loubon, 3rd (04.91.11.00.91/www.
theatre online.com). Bus 31, 32, 33, 34. **Open**
Box office 1-6.30pm Mon-Fri. **Tickets** €8-€19.
Credit MC, V.
Run by director-actors Chatôt and Vouyoucas, the Gyptis' varied programme is dedicated to giving young directors, writers and artists their first break.

Opéra Municipal
2 rue Molière, 1st (04.91.55.11.10/www.mairie-marseille.fr). M° Vieux-Port. **Open** *Box office* 10am-5.30pm Tue-Sat. **Tickets** €8-€60. **No credit cards.**
The original opera was one of the city's great 18th-century buildings. Partially burnt down in 1919, it was rebuilt in art deco style preserving the original façade. Today it holds performances of opera and the Ballet National de Marseille, directed by Marie-Claude Pietragalla.

Théâtre National de la Criée
30 quai Rive Neuve, 7th (04.91.54.70.54/
www.theatre-lacriee.com). M° Vieux-Port.
Open *Box office* 10am-7pm (in person noon-6pm)
Tue-Sat; limited summer opening. **Tickets** €10-€20.
Credit MC, V.
This celebrated theatre was created from the former fish market in 1981. Director Jean-Louis Benoit, in partnership with producer and artistic consultant Frédéric Bélier-Garcia, are bringing an international slant to the operation.

Théâtre du Gymnase
4 rue du Théâtre Français, 1st (04.91.24.35.24/box office 08.20.00.04.22). M° Noailles. **Open** *Box office* 11am-6pm (in person noon-6pm). **Tickets** €20-€30.
Credit MC, V.
This candy-box of a theatre dating from 1834 was restored in 1986. Directed by Dominique Bluzet, it's one of the best-attended, most innovative theatres in France, staging its own take on everything from classics to contemporary drama.

Cup of Tea.
See p151.

Where to stay

Auberge de Jeunesse de Marseille Bonneveine

Impasse du Dr Bonfils, 8th (04.91.17.63.30/ www.fuaj.net/homepage/marseille). Mᵒ Rond-Pont du Prado then bus 44. **Closed** mid Dec-Feb. **Rates** 1st night €13.35; further nights €11.45/ person. **Credit** DC, MC, V.

Just a stone's throw from the sea and very near the Calanques, this comfortable youth hostel is a good bet if you're looking for a holiday in nature.

La Cigale et la Fourmi

19-21 rue Théophile Boudier, Mazargues, 9th (04.91.40.05.12/www.cigale-fourmi.com). Mᵒ Rond-Point du Prado then bus 22. **Rates** €15-€35/person. **No credit cards.**

These boho budget studios are particularly popular with students and backpackers and feel a little different to standard city lodgings. Each studio will sleep two to four.

Etap Hôtel Vieux Port

46 rue Sainte, 1st (08.92.68.05.82). Mᵒ Vieux-Port. **Rates** €46 double. **Credit** AmEx, MC, V.

The cours d'Estienne d'Orves façade of this former arsenal building is gorgeous, even if the rooms of this budget chain hotel feel a bit like prison cells. Still, you can't beat the location or the price.

Hôtel Alizé

35 quai des Belges, 1st (04.91.33.66.97/www.alize-hotel.com). Mᵒ Vieux-Port. **Rates** €68-€85 double. **Credit** AmEx, DC, MC, V.

Admire the panorama from one of 16 rooms (of 39) that face the Vieux Port. The other rooms don't have much of a view. All have recently been redecorated in Impressionist-inspired autumnal colours.

Hôtel Belle-Vue

34 quai du Port, 2nd (04.96.17.05.40). Mᵒ Vieux-Port. **Rates** €68-€122 double. **Credit** AmEx, MC, V.

This historic hotel above La Caravelle bar (*see p151*) has 18 tastefully renovated rooms with immaculate bathrooms. Try to get one facing the port. Pictures by local artists adorn the stairs.

Hôtel Edmond Rostand

31 rue Dragon, 6th (04.91.37.74.95/ www.hoteledmondrostand.com). Mᵒ Estrangin-Préfecture. **Rates** €49-€56 double. **Credit** AmEx, DC, MC, V.

This clean, friendly place is reasonable value and has adequate (though not spacious) air-conditioned bedrooms and an airy breakfast room.

Hôtel Hermès

2 rue Bonneterie, 2nd (04.96.11.63.63/ www.hotelmarseille.com). Mᵒ Vieux-Port. **Rates** €47-€78 double. **Credit** AmEx, DC, MC, V.

Though its rooms are small, this simple hotel just steps from the Vieux Port is good value. Three rooms on the top floor have small terraces with superb views of the harbour and Notre-Dame-de-la-Garde. There's a rooftop sundeck too.

Hôtel Le Corbusier

280 bd Michelet, 8th (04.91.16.78.00/www.hotel lecorbusier.com). Mᵒ Rond-Point du Prado/bus 21, 22. **Rates** €50-€90 double. **Credit** MC, V.

Rap and *raï*

With IAM proving that the vanguard of French rap could be made in Marseille, and the infectious Occitan energy of Massilia Sound System – where the language of the South meets Bob Marley – still an eclectic crowd-puller, a driving force in Marseille's fusion music scene is the growing number of musicians trying to escape the aftermath of civil war in Algeria. With 65 per cent of Algeria's population under the age of 25, rap on the other side of the Med has emerged as a vital means of youthful expression (in 2005 there are estimated to be in excess of 1,200 rap groups) – reacting against the electric pop of Oran's *raï* whose masters, from Khaled to Cheb Mami, have been rather homogenised by the 'globalisation' of world music. This new import that no longer feels obliged to slam in French or American English, reflecting instead the dialect of the streets of Algiers in its manipulation of '*le swiching*' (flipping between Arabic, Berber dialects and French), is known as '*le bled-rap*', or rap from the home country. (The word 'bled' in itself offers a fascinating paradox, meaning both 'back home' to Algerians and 'a small place in the middle of nowhere' to the French.)

Throw Spanish and Sephardic traditions into that same mix, and you'll find the spirit of *swiching* goes back to the grandfathers of the Jewish-Algerian tradition, Lili Boniche and Maurice el Medioni: the one an octogenarian *oud* player turned guitarist from Algiers, the other a septuagenarian pianist from Oran. Fleeing Algeria in the 1960s, they have since brushed with *Buena Vista Social Club*-type revivals: el Medioni has been sampled by Marseille DJ Aleph Beat, while 'Boniche Dub' was released by Parisian fashion label APC (in 'Boniche Dub II', the guitarist collaborates with up-and-coming French-Tunisian *oudist* and electronic sampler Smadj). Back in Algeria, these masters had already moved away from the classical Arabic-Andalucían school towards a music-hall sound, embracing influences as diverse as be-bop, flamenco and tango, as well as French *varieté*, mambo and rumba. Incorporating these styles within the poetry of *chaâbi* (the popular Kasbah singing tradition), Boniche called his blend '*Francarbe*' (French-Arab).

In 2003, the Year of Algeria in France, the group Les Orientales was created in homage to Algerian music hall. Reviving the tradition

of their 'artistic godfathers', Boniche and el Medioni, a trio of Marseille-based female vocalists (Mona Boutchebak, Saleha Moudjari and Sylvie Aniorte-Paz) sing to the strings of the Algerian Radio Orchestra and the beats of the musicians from Barrio Chino. If Mona is tipped as the next Souad Massi (Massi herself has been dubbed Algeria's answer to Tracy Chapman) then Barrio Chino, a bohemian recording studio-cum-event space in the Joliette district west of the Vieux Port, is the place to catch this new style of '*metissage*' or mixing. This might be Algerian rap blending with Cuban hip-hop, interspliced with some finger-defying gypsy flamenco and Aniorte-Paz's effortless MCing as she weaves in Spanish classics like *Besame Mucho*.

One of the rap collectives to frequent Barrio Chino is Hamma, named after the popular quarter of Algiers, from which the members of the group were driven when their homes were destroyed to make way for a luxury hotel. These young men have little patience with ersatz gangsta rap, US style. They call their festive pessimism '*le rapattitude*', their hip hop blend '*le rap ragga*', their populist expression of disgruntlement '*le rap houma*' ('street'). They experiment too with acoustic and traditional sounds, care of instrumentalists from the Paris-based Orchestre Nationale de Barbès (Barbès is the North African quarter of Paris). A percussionist associated with Hamma is Hassan Boukerrou, who also plays with Rassegna, a revelatory collective uniting traditional musicians and songs from around the Med, from Greece to Corsica, and North Africa to Italy.

These and other musical styles meld at **Le Son d'Orient** (acronym LSD, as Badis Toulabi, its charismatic founder reminds customers, while serving up a mean brew of mint tea on the teetotal premises). It's an unassuming traditional instrument shop just off the cours Julien (04.91.47.66.36, www.lesondorient. com). And Toulabi – a music journalist with a special interest in 'orientalising' western music to promote understanding of the Maghreb – has created a rug-lined haven where the roof lifts off on Friday and Saturday nights as musicians assemble for a *boeuf* or jamming session, and the desert sounds of *gnaâwi* rhythms send dancers into an ecstatic spin.

Fans of modern architecture, or those looking for something unusual, won't want to miss the opportunity to stay in the famous Cité Radieuse. Rooms are basic but imbued with lovingly preserved Le Corbusier spirit. Pricier rooms are large and there are two studios with terrace, sea view and original Le Corbusier kitchens (not for use). You may want to consider dining out, though, as cooking is not the forte here.

Hôtel du Palais
26 rue Breteuil, 6th (04.91.37.78.86). M° Estrangin-Préfecture. **Rates** €80-€100 double. **Credit** AmEx, MC, V.
In a location that is both handy for strolling around the Vieux Port but far enough removed to be peaceful at night, the Palais is a smart, efficiently run and friendly place to lay your head.

Mercure Beauvau Vieux Port
4 rue Beauvau, 1st (04.91.54.91.00/www.mercure. com). M° Vieux-Port. **Rates** €165-€236 double. **Credit** AmEx, DC, MC, V.
This historic hotel, where Chopin and George Sand once stayed, overlooks the Vieux Port. It reopened following extensive renovation a few years ago.

Mercure Prado
11 av de Mazargues, 8th (04.96.20.37.37/www. mercure.com). M° Rond-Point du Prado. **Rates** €65-€115 double. **Credit** AmEx, DC, MC, V.
This new-ish Mercure has postmodern design with furniture by Marc Newson, Ingo Maurer and Philippe Starck. Internet access in rooms on request. A good choice for business travel, yet within walking distance of the beach and Parc Borély.

New Hôtel Bompard
2 rue des Flots-Bleus, 7th (04.91.99.22.22/ www.new-hotel.com). Bus 61. **Rates** €125-€140 double. **Credit** AmEx, MC, V.
This neat, walled hotel in a quiet residential area near the Corniche has 46 air-conditioned rooms in the old wing and extension, family apartments with kitchen, and four sumptuous provençal-style *mas* (€170-€200), plus swimming pool and gardens.

Hôtel Peron
119 Corniche JF Kennedy, 7th (04.91.31.01.41/ www.hotel-peron.com). Bus 83. **Rates** €69.50-€97 double. **Credit** AmEx, MC, V.
This eccentric, family-run hotel is a study in kitsch – Moroccan, oriental, Dutch and Breton rooms were decorated in the 1960s (it's beginning to show) when it was the first hotel in Marseille to install such yet charming baths. Most have stunning sea views.

Le Petit Nice – Passédat
Anse de Maldormé, Corniche JF Kennedy, 7th (04.91. 59.25.92/www.petitnice-passedat.com). Bus 83. **Rates** €275-€410 double. **Credit** AmEx, DC, MC, V.
Sitting on its own little promontory off the Corniche, this luxurious villa has 13 sumptuous air-conditioned rooms, a swimming pool and a restaurant.

Hôtel Résidence du Vieux Port
18 quai du Port, 2nd (04.91.91.91.22/ www.hotelmarseille.com). M° Vieux-Port. **Rates** €89.50-€159.50 double. **Credit** AmEx, DC, MC, V.
This 1950s building features antique furniture, balconies (except on the second floor) and unbeatable views from every room across the Vieux Port to Notre-Dame-de-la-Garde. Book well in advance.

Hôtel Le Rhul
269 Corniche JF Kennedy, 7th (04.91.52.01.77/ www.bouillabaissemarseille.com). Bus 83. **Rates** €90 double. **Credit** AmEx, MC, V.
Though it doesn't have the character of Le Peron, the slightly pricier Rhul has the advantage of a few spacious terraces with jaw-dropping sea views and a restaurant renowned for its bouillabaisse.

Sofitel Palm Beach
200 Corniche JF Kennedy, 7th (04.91.16.19.00/ www.sofitel.com). Bus 83. **Rates** €265-€315 double. **Credit** AmEx, DC, MC, V.
This sleek hotel has stunning views of the bay and islands. Open spaces, huge windows and giant plants join with cutting-edge designs by Starck, Zanotta, Emu and Gervasoni to create a surprisingly warm feel. The salt-water pool is fed by a natural spring.

Getting there

From the airport
Aéroport Marseille-Provence (04.42.14.14.14) is 25km (15.5 miles) north-west of Marseille near Marignane. 'La Navette' coaches (04.42.14.31.27/04.91.50.59.34) run every 20mins 6.10am-10.50pm to Gare St-Charles; and from the station to the airport 5.30am-9.50pm. The trip takes about 25mins and costs €8.50. A taxi to the Vieux Port costs around €40.

By car
Marseille is served by three motorways. The A7-A51 heads north to the airport, Aix and Lyon; the A55 runs west to Martigues; and the A50 runs east to Toulon. The Prado-Carénage toll tunnel links the A55 to the A50.

By train
The main station is the Gare St-Charles on the TGV line, with frequent trains from Paris, the main coast route east to Nice and Italy, and west via Miramas and Arles. Branch lines run to Miramas via Martigues and the Côte Bleu, and to Aix and Gap. In the station SOS Voyageurs (04.91.62.12.80, open 9am-7pm Mon-Sat) helps with children, the elderly and lost luggage.

By bus
The *gare routière* is by the station on pl Victor Hugo, 3rd (04.91.08.16.40, M° St-Charles). Cartreize (08.00.19.94.13, www.lepilote.com) is the umbrella organisation for all coach services in the Bouches-du-Rhône. Eurolines (04.91.50.57.55, www.eurolines.fr) operates coaches between Marseille and Avignon, Nice via Aix-en-Provence and daily coaches to Venice, Milan and Rome, Barcelona and Valencia.

By boat

SNCM (61 bd des Dames, 2nd, M° Joliette) is the primary passenger line from the Gare Maritime de la Joliette; call 08.91.70.18.01 for Sardinia, Corsica or Italy; 08.91.70.28.02 for Algeria, Tunisia or Morocco.

Getting around

By bus & Métro

RTM (Espace Infos, 6 rue des Fabres, 1st, 04.91.91.92.10, www.rtm.fr, open 7am-6pm Mon-Fri, 9am-5.30pm Sat) runs a comprehensive network of over 80 bus routes, two Métro lines (5am-9pm Mon-Thur; 5am-12.30am Fri-Sun & OM match nights) and a tram. The same tickets are used on all three and can be bought in Métro stations, on the bus (singles only) and at *tabacs* and newsagents displaying the RTM sign. A single ticket costs €1.60 and entitles the user to one hour's travel. The Carte Libertés (€7.10 or €13) offers five or 11 journeys depending on the price you pay, each also lasting up to an hour. For unlimited travel, a one-day ticket is €4.50, weekly pass €10.30 and monthly €40. At night, a network of Fluobuses runs between the Canebière (Bourse) and outer districts.

By taxi

There are cab ranks on most main squares, or call **Marseille Taxi** (04.91.02.20.20), **Taxi Blanc Bleu** (04.91.51.50.00), **Taxi Plus** (04.91.03.60.03), **Taxi Radio Tupp** (04.91.05.80.80). Pick-up fare is €1.70, then €1.24/km in the day, €1.64/km at night.

Resources

Hospital

Hôpital de la Conception *147 bd Baille, 5th (04.91.38.30.00). M° Baille.*
Hôpital Militaire Lavéran *34 bd Lavéran, 13th (04.91.61.70.00/www.hia-laveran.fr). M° Malpassé then bus 38.*

Internet

Escaliq Cyber Café *3 rue Coutellerie, 2nd (04.91.91.65.10/www.escaliq.net). M° Vieux-Port.*
Open 11am-8.30pm Mon-Fri; 4-8.30pm Sat, Sun.
Info-Café *1 quai Rive Neuve, 1st (04.91.33.74.98/ www.info-cafe.com). M° Vieux-Port.* **Open** 9am-10pm, 2.30-7.30pm Sun.

Police

28 rue Nationale, 1th (04.91.14.29.50). M° St-Charles.

Post office

Hôtel des Postes, rue Henri Barbusse, 1st (04.91.15.47.00). M° Colbert or Vieux-Port.

Tourist information

Office du Tourisme *4 La Canebière, 1st (04.91.13.89.00/www.marseille-tourisme.com). M° Vieux-Port.* **Open** 9am-7pm Mon-Sat; 10am-5pm Sun. Other location: *Gare St-Charles, 1st (04.91.50.59.18).* **Open** *June-Aug* 11am-6pm Mon-Sat. *Sept-May* 10am-1pm, 1.30-5pm Mon-Fri.

Around Marseille

Martigues & the Côte Bleue

Beyond L'Estaque towards Carro is the relatively neglected Côte Bleue, much loved by Marseillais at weekends with its sheer cliffs, small fishing ports and rocky beaches. For once this is an area as easy to reach by train as by car – while the D5 meanders between inlets and over the red hills of the Chaîne de l'Estaque, a landscape prone to fires in summer, the railway chugs scenically over a series of viaducts along the coast (the découverte day ticket allows as many stops as you like). Tiny coves like Niolon and La Madrague-de-Gignac give stunning views of the Marseille cityscape across the bay. The main resorts are **Sausset-les-Pins**, very popular with families, and **Carry-le-Rouet**, with its crowded beach. At **Carro** there is a picturesque fishing port and is a favourite with windsurfers. It's worth making a stop too at **La Redonne**'s peaceful little harbour.

Inland, **Martigues** is a pretty, though traffic-cluttered, old town of pastel houses built alongside canals, on the edge of the heavily industrialised (and polluted) Etang de Berre, a lagoon that is surrounded by one of the largest petrochemical and oil refining complexes in Europe. The railway station is some way out towards Lavera, which means a rather long walk along main roads or waiting for an infrequent bus. An alternative is to take the coach from Marseille or Aix to the bus station (pl des Aires) in the centre. The town is the result of a merging of three villages in 1581: Jonquières, Ferrières and L'Ile Brescon, linked by a series of bridges reminiscent of Amsterdam or Venice. In Jonquières, the main sight is the bijou and wildly colourful baroque Chapelle de l'Annonciade, built 1664-71, which adjoins the church of St-Geniès. From here follow the road down to place Gérard Tenque and stroll around the many relaxed shops and cafés. On the Ile, the Eglise de la Madeleine is another fine baroque edifice with an ornately carved façade. Over in Ferrières, the modern Théâtre des Salins contrasts starkly with colour-washed fishermen's cottages. The **Musée Ziem** is a pleasant surprise containing works by Félix Ziem, Manguin, Loubon and Dufy, as well as the statue of St-Pierre, patron saint of fishermen, which is paraded from here to the port for the Fête de St-Pierre every June. The historic Eglise St-Louis-d'Anjou on nearby rue Colonel Denfert was the site of the signing of the 1581 act of union between Provence and France.

Musée Ziem
bd du 14 Juillet (04.42.41.39.60). **Open** *July-Aug*
10am-noon, 2.30-6.30pm Mon, Wed-Sun. *Sept-June*
2.30-6.30pm Wed-Sun. **Admission** free.

Where to eat & stay

In Sausset-les-Pins locals delight in the
imaginative cooking at **Les Girelles** (rue
Frédéric Mistral, 04.42.45.26.16, closed Mon,
lunch Tue in July & Aug, Wed, dinner Sun
Sept-June, Jan, menus €28-€38), which stages
jazz concerts during summer evenings. The
harbour is lined with diverse restaurants and
cafés – and boat hire shops – all in hot
competition. In Carro friendly, family-oriented
Le Chalut (port de Carro, 04.42.80.70.61,
closed dinner Mon, all Tue, menus €17-€28)
specialises in fish and shellfish. The **Auberge
de la Calanque** (port de la Redonne,
04.42.45.95.01) does appetising pizzas (€9-
€12.50). In Martigues, try the flavoursome
roast guinea fowl or delicate fish kebabs at

La Maison du Pastis. *See p153.*

Le Miroir (4 rue Marcel Galdy, 04.42.80.50.45,
closed Mon, lunch Sat, dinner Sun & all Sun
July-Aug, 1wk Nov, 2wks Dec, 2wks Easter,
menus €14.50-€30). The **Hôtel Cigalon** (37
bd du 14 Juillet, 04.42.80.49.16, double €42-€75)
is a simple, cheerfully furnished hotel.

Resources

Tourist information

Martigues Maison du Tourisme *Rond-point de
l'Hôtel de Ville, 13500 Martigues (04.42.42.31.10,
www.ville-martigues.fr).* **Open** 9am-7pm Mon-Sat;
10am-1pm, 3-6pm Sun.

Aubagne

Aubagne, 17 kilometres (ten miles) east of
Marseille, is an active commercial centre. Its
vieille ville is pleasant, dotted with tree-lined
squares and a market on Tuesday and Sunday.
Writer and filmmaker Marcel Pagnol was born
here, and the shop façades and houses have
retained (or have rather brazenly recreated)
a nostalgic feel. You can visit the **Maison
Natale de Marcel Pagnol** where he was
born in 1895 and spent his first 18 months.
The tourist office also runs a nine-kilometre
(5.5-mile) hiking tour in French (from €30.50),
or can provide directions for the Circuit Pagnol.
    Aubagne is known for its ceramics industry,
with a dozen *santon* workshops and the biennial
Argilla fair and pottery market (next in August
2007). Aubagne's other claim to fame is as the
home of the French Foreign Legion.

Maison Natale de Marcel Pagnol
16 cours Barthélémy (04.42.03.49.98). **Open** 9am-
12.30pm, 2.30-6pm daily. **Admission** €3; €1.50
5-12s; free under 5s. **No credit cards.**

Musée de la Légion Etrangère
*rte de la Thuilière, west of Aubagne on D44
(04.42.18.82.41).* **Open** *June-Sept* 10am-noon, 3-7pm
Tue-Thur, Sat, Sun. *Oct-May* 10am-noon, 2-6pm Wed,
Sat, Sun. **Admission** free.

Where to eat

La Farandole (6 rue Martinot, 04.42.03.26.36,
closed dinner Mon, 2wks Feb, menus €12.50-
€22.50) serves typical provençal cooking and
is well located for quiet dining outdoors.

Resources

Tourist information

Office de Tourisme du Pays d'Aubagne *av
Antide Boyer, 13400 Aubagne (04.42.03.49.98/
www.aubagne.com).* **Open** 9am-noon, 2-6pm
Mon-Sat.

Cassis, the Calanques & La Ciotat

Discover the delights of off-season Cassis and the geological wonder that is the Calanques.

Marseille & Aix

Cassis

Come here in the autumn or spring and what you'll find is a quiet fishing village, where the main excitement comes from Sunday morning pétanque matches by the harbour. In summer, though, it's a different story, when muscle boys and sun-worshippers abound in all their semi-clad, oiled glory, and souvenir sellers whip themselves into a *Glengarry Glen Ross* fervour.

Cassis (pronounce the last 's') is best known for its delicate white wines and dazzling Calanques. The colourful, café-lined port attracted early 20th-century artists including Dufy, Matisse and Vlaminck, though sadly none of their works have made it into the **Musée Municipal**, a meagre display of town history and bad Southern art. Cassis offers two beaches – the Plage de la Grande Mer on the sea side of the breakwater and Plage du Bestouan in a sheltered bay west of the port.

Cassis wines can best be tasted at **La Ferme Blanche** (rte de Marseille, 04.42.01.00.74), the oldest AOC Cru Classé, or **Le Clos Ste-Magdeleine** (av du Revestel, 04.42.01.70.28, closed Sat & Sun), whose vines thrive on the sunny slopes of Cap Canaille, the highest coastal cliff (416 metres or 1,365 feet) in Europe. The route des Crêtes (D141) climbs with often nail-biting views across Cap Canaille to La Ciotat.

Musée Municipal Méditerranéen d'Arts et Traditions de Cassis

rue Xavier d'Authier (04.42.01.88.66). **Open** *Apr-Oct* 10.30am-12.30pm, 3.30-6.30pm Wed-Sat. *Nov-Mar* 10.30am-12.30pm, 2.30-5.30pm Wed-Sat. **Admission** free.

Where to stay & eat

The **Hôtel-Restaurant Le Jardin d'Emile** (23 av Amiral Ganteaume, 04.42.01.80.55, www.lejardindemile.fr, closed mid Nov-mid Dec, double €80-€130) stands in a tropical garden against the old city walls and serves the best provençal cuisine in town (menu €39-€50). Winston Churchill learned to paint while staying at **Les Roches Blanches** (rte des Calanques, 04.42.01.09.30, www.roches-blanches-cassis.com, closed Nov-Mar except Christmas, double €125-€225, restaurant dinner only except July & Aug, menu €36), with its view of the port and Cap Canaille. On the port, pleasant **Hôtel du Golfe** (3 pl Grand Carnot, 04.42.01.00.21, closed Nov-Mar, double €58-€89) has a brasserie serving lunch, aperitifs and ice-creams day and night. **Hôtel Cassitel** (pl Clemenceau, 04.42.01.83.44, www.hotel-cassis.com, double €58-€90) has pleasant rooms and views over the harbour. Fish shop **La Poissonnerie Laurent** (6 quai Barthélémy, 04.42.01.71.56, closed Mon, lunch Thur & Jan, winter lunch daily, menu €20) was opened 65 years ago by Laurent Cinque and his wife Marie, now 85. She joins her grandson Laurent at their restaurant, where the morning's catch lies on icy counters. A few doors down, slick **Chez Nino** (2 quai Barthélémy, 04.42.01.74.32, average €30) also serves wonderful seafood.

Resources

Market is on Wednesday and Friday mornings.

Tourist information

Office du Tourisme, quai des Moulins, 13260 Cassis (04.42.01.71.17/www.cassis.fr). **Open** *Mar-May, Oct* 9.30am-12.30pm, 2-6pm Mon-Fri; 10am-noon, 2-6pm Sat; 10am-noon Sun. *June-Sept* 9am-12.30pm, 2-7pm Mon-Fri; 9am-12.30pm, 3-6pm Sat, Sun. *Nov-Feb* 9.30am-12.30pm, 2-5pm Mon-Fri; 10am-noon, 2-5pm Sat; 10am-noon Sun.

The Calanques

These spectacular gashes in the limestone cliffs between Marseille and Cassis were formed in the Ice Age when sea levels rose and flooded the deep valleys, leaving cavernous inlets and odd rock formations. The Calanques now form a rugged 5,000-hectare (12,355-acre) national reserve, where bushes, flowers, ferns and occasional trees cling to dry rocks, lined with trails to explore up cliffs, across mountain passes and even underwater. Eagles and falcons share the skies with seagulls, puffins and stormy petrels.

The Calanques closest to Marseille are flatter and wider than those towards Cassis. The most well known (and most visited in summer) are **Sormiou** and **Morgiou**, which are dotted with *cabanons*: run-down, century-old holiday huts, built from recycled driftwood and scrap and so cherished by Marseille families that they are passed from generation to generation, and are now listed buildings. There is no electricity on either Calanque and only one telephone booth on Sormiou for emergencies. The setting is, however, perfect for lazy swims, diving or climbing. From the Cassis side, only the first Calanque, **Port-Miou**, is fully accessible by car. Boats sail to the other inlets. The best rock-climbing is up the 'finger of God' rock spur in **En-Vau**, which has a secluded beach, or, for hardened professionals, the cliffs of **Devenson**.

Human presence in the Calanques goes back into prehistory. In 1991 Henri Cosquer, a diver from Cassis, swam into a narrow tunnel between Sormiou and Morgiou, at a depth of 37 metres (121 feet) below sea level, emerging into a huge grotto. On the walls, he found the oldest-known cave paintings – bison, horses, handprints and penguins over 27,000 years old. The cave was sealed up, but Cosquer still accompanies divers into less artistic grottos on his boat *Cro-Magnon* (*see below*).

Activities

Diving & watersports

The Calanques offer some of the best diving in France. Maestro Henri Cosquer at **Cassis Services Plongée** (3 rue Michel Arnaud, Cassis, 04.42.01.89.16, www.centrecassidaindeplongee.fr, closed mid Nov-mid Mar) organises daily dives, weather permitting.

Walking & rock-climbing

For ecologically minded, guided nature walks, rock-climbing lessons, diving and kayaking, contact **Naturoscope** (3 impasse du Meunier, Marseille, 9th arrondissement, 04.91.40.20.11) or climb, cave or scramble over and under the cliffs with **Massilia Sport Adventure** (06.12.39.59.59, www.massiliaaventure.com).

La Poissonnerie Laurent. *See p160.*

Where to stay & eat

A meal at the spectacularly located **Le Lunch** in Sormiou (04.91.25.05.37, closed mid Oct-mid Mar, average €50) is as close as you're likely to get to the local lifestyle. Bouillabaisse has to be ordered in advance; otherwise, opt for excellent grilled fish and a bottle of Cassis white. **Le Nautic** (04.91.40.06.37, closed Mon, dinner Sun, & Jan-Feb, average €30) is a decent bar-restaurant on the port at Morgiou. In Callelongue, **La Grotte** (1 av des Pebrons, 04.91.73.17.79, average €35) serves pizzas and grilled fish, but service is slow at weekends. The only place to stay in the Calanques is **La Fontasse** hostel (04.42.01.02.72, closed Jan-mid Mar, dormitory €10 for YHA members), an hour's walk from Cassis; bring food and drinking water.

Getting there

By boat

From Marseille, boats leave from quai des Belges on the Vieux Port (GACM 04.91.55.50.09, www.answeb.net/gacm) at 2pm daily July & Aug and Wed, Sat & Sun the rest of the year. A round trip to Cassis, taking in the Marseilleveyre, Calanques and islands with commentary, costs €25 and lasts about four hours (a stop-off is possible at the Iles du Frioul). From Cassis, regular boats (04.42.01.90.83, €11; €6.50 2-10s) leave 9.30am-5.30pm (10.30am in winter) from the eastern end of the port for the Circuit des trois Calanques and at set times for further afield. You can be dropped off or picked up at En-Vau or Morgiou. In July and August, there is a Spectacle Son et Lumière boat trip that leaves nightly at 10.30pm (€10).

By bus

Marseille bus 19 from Prado or Castellane runs to La Madrague de Montredon to reach the Calanques by footpath GR98. Buses 21 and 21s go to the Université de Luminy. Buses 22 and 23 from Prado to Beauvallon or Les Beaumettes lead to Sormiou and Morgiou.

By car

The single-track fire-roads to Sormiou and Morgiou are closed Easter-mid Sept, 7am-8pm, but cars are let in for those with lunch reservations.

La Ciotat & St-Cyr-sur-Mer

When the Krupp dockyard closed in 1989, 10,000 people in a town of 30,000 lost their jobs. Some 15 years later, mourning is decreed over, and the town is coming alive thanks to a new generation of industrious citizens. The graffitied dockyard factories are growing chic: 18 yacht maintenance companies have moved in and the Yacht Club (*see below*) has opened as a giant entertainment complex. From the port, ferries peddle trips to the Calanques and the **Musée Ciotaden** presents the town's maritime history.

Since the mid 19th century, La Ciotat has doubled as a genteel summer residence. Among its illustrious visitors were Auguste and Louis Lumière who made the world's first film. It showed the Toulon–Marseille train pulling into La Ciotat station and thrilled the Parisians invited to the first champagne projection in September 1895 at the Eden Théâtre, which still stands on the seafront boulevard Anatole France. The **Espace Lumière** continues the theme with photos, posters and a film archive.

Sandy white beaches curve around the Baie de la Ciotat to **St-Cyr-sur-Mer**, which boasts café life and a market on Sunday under a gilded replica of the *Statue of Liberty*, donated by sculptor Bartholdi. Its seaward extension **Les Lecques** is a wild clutter of shops and eateries and the promenade is family-friendly. Les Lecques claims to have been the Greek trading post of Taureontum, and the **Musée de Taureontum** displays the artefacts to prove it. Past the museum, a nine-kilometre (5.5-mile) footpath (waymarked in yellow) clings to the coast through old pines and oaks to La Madrague (2hrs to Port d'Alon) and Bandol (3hrs 30mins).

Espace Lumière

20 rue Maréchal Foch, La Ciotat (04.42.08.94.56). **Open** *July-Sept* 10am-noon, 4-7pm Tue-Sat. *Oct-June* 3-6pm Tue-Sat. **Admission** free.

Musée Ciotadan

Ancien Hôtel de Ville, 1 quai Ganteaume, La Ciotat (04.42.71.40.99). **Open** *June-Sept* 3-7pm Mon, Wed-Sun. *Oct-May* 3-6pm Mon, Wed-Sun. **Admission** €3.20; €1.60 12-18s, students; free under-12s. **No credit cards**.

Musée de Taureontum

131 rte de La Madrague, St-Cyr-sur-Mer (04.94.26.30.46). **Open** *June-Sept* 3-7pm Mon, Wed-Sun. *Oct-May* 2-5pm Sat, Sun. **Admission** €3; €1 12-18s, students; free under-7s. **No credit cards**.

Where to stay, eat & drink

Las Vegas in La Ciotat? Why not ? **Yacht Club La Ciotat** (quai Port Vieux, 04.42.08.14.14, www.yacht-club-la-ciotat.abcsalles.com, menu €22), a giant entertainment complex with panoramic port views, boasts a restaurant serving fusion food, concerts at weekends, dancing, movies, comedy reviews and speed-dating soirées. For a more traditional lasagne, ravioli and the freshest seafood, head to **La Mamma** (Vieux Port, 04.42.08.30.08, closed Oct-mid Nov & 2wks Feb, average €35). For wild beauty, the rustic bungalows and restaurant of **Chez Tania** (04.42.08.41.71, www.figuerolles.com, double €37-€128, menus €25-€53) lie in the nature reserve of the Calanque de Figuerolles.

The Calanque at **Port-Miou**. *See p161.*

Grand Hôtel des Lecques (24 av du Port, 04.94.26.23.01, www.grandhotelsaintcyr.com, closed Nov-mid Mar, double €63-€177, menus €26-€60) has old-world charm, an exotic garden, plus a pool and a slightly boring restaurant. **Hôtel Petit Nice** (11 allée du Dr Seillon, 04.94.32.00.64, www.hotelpetitnice.com, closed mid Nov-mid Mar, double €53-€72) has a shady pool near the beach. For sporty folks, **Hôtel-Golf Dolce Frégate** (04.94.29.39.39, www.fregate.dolce.com, rte de Bandol, St-Cyr-sur-Mer, double €134-€252) has an 18-hole course within the Domaine de Frégate vineyards (golf fees €48-€60) and two restaurants, **Mas des Vignes** (04.94.29.39.47, menus €29-€55) and **La Restanque** (menu €26.50). On the coast path past La Madrague to Bandol (or by car D559, C6), beach brasserie **Calanque Port d'Alon** (04.94.26.20.08, lunch only Mon, Wed-Sun, menu €10) grills fish on an open fire. **Riviera del Fiori** on the new port of Les Lecques (04.94.32.18.20, closed dinner Tue, all Wed & Feb, menus €19.50-€25) grills fish hand-caught by divers and simmers the local catch of rock fish in its bouillabaisse (it's best to make a reservation in advance).

Resources

La Ciotat has markets on Tuesday on place du Marché, Sunday on the port, and a farmers' market on Friday afternoon. Les Lecques's farmers' market is Wednesday and Saturday mornings in summer, with a market at St-Cyr on Sunday morning.

Tourist information

La Ciotat *Office de Tourisme, bd Anatole France, 13600 La Ciotat (04.42.08.61.32/www.laciotatourisme. com).* **Open** *June-Sept* 9am-8pm Mon-Sat; 10am-1pm Sun. *Oct-May* 9am-noon, 2-6pm Mon-Sat.
Les Lecques *Office de Tourisme, pl de l'Appel du 18 Juin, 83270 Les Lecques (04.94.26.73.73/www. saintcyrsurmer.com).* **Open** *July, Aug, Dec* 9am-7pm Mon-Sat; 10am-1pm, 4-7pm Sun. *Sept-Nov, Jan-June* 9am-6pm Mon-Fri; 9am-noon, 2-6pm Sat.

Getting there & around

By bus

Cartreize (04.42.08.41.05) runs buses between Aix-en-Provence, Marseille, Cassis and La Ciotat stations and La Ciotat to Les Lecques. **Transport St-Cyr Tourisme** (04.94.26.23.71) runs from St-Cyr station to Les Lecques and La Madrague.

By car

Leave the A50 from Marseille at exits 8 for Cassis, 9 and 10 for La Ciotat and St-Cyr. The D559 Marseille to Cassis is dramatically scenic, continuing along the coast via Les Lecques to Toulon. The D141 route des Crêtes climbs from Cassis to La Ciotat.

By train

Hourly trains between Marseille and Toulon stop at Cassis, La Ciotat and St-Cyr but stations are each about 3km (2 miles) from the centre.

Aix-en-Provence

Come for the cafés, culture and some top-quality shopping.

There's something almost cinematic about Aix. Its stately mansions, leafy streets and bubbling fountains are unreal in their prettiness, the elegant cafés of cours Mirabeau have all the manicured appeal of a film set. The people, too, look as if they might have spent an hour or two in wardrobe before stepping out of their houses. In short, this is a graceful, cultured city, more urbane than urban; it is a nursery for new artistic talent but also a refuge for wealthy, healthy retirees who enjoy the fine things in life. It is a stark contrast, in other words, to its rougher southern rival Marseille.

Aix's origins go back to Roman times. Aquae Sextiae was founded in 122 BC by Roman consul Sextius after he had defeated the Celto-Ligurian Oppidium at Entremont, the remains of which lie outside the city (see p167). Aix declined with the Roman Empire but remained important enough to have a cathedral in the fifth century.

In the 12th and 13th centuries the independent Counts of Provence held court in Aix, but it was in the 15th century that the city saw a true resurgence. In 1409 the university was founded by Louis II of Anjou, and under Good King René (1409-80), poet and patron of the arts, the city flourished and the court drew artists such as Nicolas Froment and Barthélemy Van Eyck. After its absorption into France in 1486, Aix became the capital of the Parlement de Provence – the southern arm of a centralised administration. The city boomed again in the 1600s, when the newly prosperous political and merchant class began building stylish townhouses in a new district, the Quartier Mazarin, south of the *vielle ville*. This virtually doubled the city's size. A ring of boulevards, the *cours*, replaced the ramparts. Aix elected the radical, and hypnotically ugly, Comte de Mirabeau as *député* to the *états généraux* in 1789. A brilliant orator, he played an important role in the early days of the Revolution.

In the 19th century Aix was bypassed by the main railway line and lost out to Marseille, but remained an important university and legal city with the creation of arts and law faculties and the new Palais de Justice.

Aix has expanded rapidly in the past 20 years, as new housing, business and university districts swallowed up rural villages and the grandiose agricultural bastides built by the nobility outside the city. Aix is home to a high-tech industry pole that rivals Sophia-Antipolis, numerous research institutes and France's biggest appeals court outside Paris.

Despite a reputation as the haughty bastion of the bourgeoisie, and its highbrow Festival International d'Art Lyrique every summer, Aix is a surprisingly young city, with some 40,000 students and a thriving café society.

Sightseeing

Vieil Aix

At the heart of the city – both physical and psychological – is the **cours Mirabeau**, a broad avenue lined with plane trees and handsome stone houses. Although several of these are now banks or chain restaurants, the cours Mirabeau remains every bit as important for its place in café society as the boulevard St-Germain does in Paris. At one end is place Charles de Gaulle, better known as La Rotonde, marked by an elaborate 19th-century fountain in black and white marble, with lions at the base and figures of Justice, Agriculture and Fine Art on the top.

North of cours Mirabeau lies Vieil Aix, the oldest part of the city, a remarkably well-preserved maze where graceful squares and smart mansions alternate with more secretive, winding *ruelles*. Fountains splash in almost every square, statues peer out of niches on street corners and the whole place is buzzing with small bistros, cafés and shops.

Parallel to cours Mirabeau runs rue Espariat, where the early 18th-century baroque church of **St-Esprit** and the belfry of a former Augustinian monastery nestle amid cafés and shops. Continue along rue Espariat into rue Fabrot, home to smart designer boutiques, via the glorious, cobbled place d'Albertas, a U-shape of classical façades with Corinthian pilasters, built in 1745 as a speculative venture by the powerful Albertas family. Almost opposite is the elegant 1672 Hôtel Boyer d'Eguilles, now part pharmacy, part school and part **Muséum d'Histoire Naturelle**.

Busy shopping streets rue Aude and rue Maréchal Foch lead to place Richelme, which comes alive every morning with a fruit and vegetable market under the plane trees. The door of the late 17th-century Hôtel Arbaud

(7 rue Maréchal Foch) is framed by two muscular male slaves. In beautiful place de l'Hôtel de Ville, the Gothic belfry with astrological clock and rotating figures of the seasons was a former town gateway. The grandiose **Hôtel de Ville** was the historic provençal assembly. Even the post office next door occupies a magnificent 18th-century former grain market, whose pediment, an allegory of the Durance and Rhône rivers by Chastel, is given a wonderful spark of life by a leg dangling lasciviously out of the frame.

Running north from Hôtel de Ville, rue Gaston de Saporta contains some of Aix's finest *hôtels particuliers*: Hôtel Etienne de St-Jean (No.17) contains the **Musée du Vieil Aix**; Hôtel de Châteaurenard (No.19), where Louis XIV stayed in 1660, has a staircase painted with trompe l'oeil by Daret (it now houses the city's social services, but you can visit the entrance hall); Hôtel Maynier d'Oppedé (No.23), with a fine 1757 façade, belongs to the university. The street leads into the historic core of the university with the former law faculty, now the Institut des Etudes Politiques. Opposite is the composite structure of the **Cathédrale St-Sauveur**, with its sculpted portals and fortified towers. Next door, the baroque Palais de l'Archevêché contains the **Musée des Tapisseries** (tapestries) and hosts courtyard productions during the Festival International d'Art Lyrique.

West of the town hall, place des Cardeurs is lined with ethnic restaurants. Underground car park aside, it looks as ancient as any of the other squares but, in fact, was created only in the 1960s, when an area of slums, historically the Jewish quarter, was demolished. From here, narrow streets lead to the **Thermes Sextius** (thermal baths), some fragments of medieval city wall on rue des Etuves, as well as the last surviving tower on boulevard Jean Jaurès. Just west of the baths, the **Pavillon Vendôme** still stands in its formal gardens.

South-east of the town hall, the colonnaded mass of the Palais de Justice was built in the 1820s on the site of the former Comtal palace. In front, place de Verdun (also reached from cours Mirabeau by the covered passage Agard) fills with bric-a-brac and book stalls on Tuesday, Thursday and Saturday mornings. It continues as place des Prêcheurs and place de la Madeleine, which resound to the city's main food market on the same days, in the shadow of the neo-classical-fronted **Eglise de la Madeleine**. Further east from the Palais de Justice lies the Villeneuve *quartier*, which replaced the royal gardens in the late 16th century. Several ornate *hôtels particuliers* remain on rue Emeric David

and rue de l'Opéra: Cézanne was born at No.25; at No.17 is the Jeu du Paume, a real tennis court built in 1660 and transformed into the **Théâtre du Jeu de Paume** a century later.

Cathédrale St-Sauveur

pl de l'Université (04.42.23.45.65). **Open** 8am-noon, 2-6pm Mon-Sat; 9am-noon, 2-6pm Sun (closed during services). *Cloister* 9.30am-noon, 2-6pm Mon-Sat. **Admission** free.

Aix cathedral is a hotchpotch of Romanesque, Gothic, Renaissance and baroque, reflecting its long on-off construction from the fifth to 18th centuries, with a semi-fortified exterior and rather damaged Gothic central door. At first sight the interior looks unremarkable, with three curiously linked naves, Gothic vaults and classical domes. But it has two jewels. The first is off the right-hand nave: a polygonal, fifth-century Merovingian baptistery, with crisply carved capitals and traces of frescoes (the hole in the ground is a throwback to the days of total immersion baptism). Further along to the right is a cloister, with paired capitals carved with mysterious beasts and foliage. In the central nave is the second treasure: Nicolas Froment's symbolically loaded 15th-century triptych of *Mary in the Burning Bush*, with King René and Queen Jeanne praying in the wings. At the end of the left nave, the 17th-century Corpus Domini chapel has a fine wrought-iron grille and a painting by Jean Daret.

Cours Mirabeau

Dubbed the 'Champs-Elysées of the South', stately, tree-lined cours Mirabeau was laid out in 1649 as a broad carriageway on the trace of the old ramparts, becoming the frontier between the old town of the Counts of Provence and the brand new Quartier Mazarin. Soon it became the favoured spot for local nobility to construct their mansions, notably Nos.20 and 38 on the southern side, where there was space to have a showoff façade on the street side and extensive gardens on the other. Cours Mirabeau is still the place to see and be seen today, whether you opt to promenade or simply sit and observe from a café table. In warmer months, street musicians stroll up and down, serenading diners and passers-by. The wide avenue contains mostly cafés down the sunny side (odd numbers), and banks and businesses in the shade (even). At No.53, the legendary Deux Garçons (*see p168*) still plays out its role as artistic and intellectual meeting place. There are three fountains on the cours: the Fontaine des neuf canons, the Fontaine d'eau chaude, a mossy lump bubbling out water at 34°C, and the Fontaine du Roi René, with a statue by David d'Angers of the wine-loving king holding a bunch of grapes.

Eglise de la Madeleine

pl des Prêcheurs. **Open** 8-11.30am, 3-5.30pm daily. **Admission** free.

This former Dominican convent was rebuilt in the 1690s in the baroque style. A neo-classical façade, busy with swags and garlands, was added in the

19th century. Inside there are several baroque altarpieces by Carlos Van Loo and an *Annunciation* (1444) with plunging Gothic architectural perspective, attributed to Flemish painter Barthélemy Van Eyck. The church is used for classical concerts.

Hôtel de Ville

pl de l'Hôtel de Ville (04.42.91.90.00). **Open** *Salle des Etats de Provence* 10am-noon, 3-4.30pm Mon-Fri. **Admission** free.

The town hall was built in 1655-78 by Pierre Pavillon. A wrought-iron gateway leads into a cobbled courtyard. At the back, a double stairway leads up to the Salle des Etats de Provence, the regional assembly room where taxes were voted. It is hung with portraits and mythological subjects.

Muséum d'Histoire Naturelle

6 rue Espariat (04.42.27.91.27/www.museum-paca. org). **Open** 10am-noon, 1-5pm daily. **Admission** €2.50; free students, under-25s. **No credit cards.**

Mineralogy and palaeontology collections, including hundreds of dinosaur eggs discovered on the Montagne Ste-Victoire, in a fine 17th-century *hôtel*.

Musée des Tapisseries

pl des Martyrs de la Résistance (04.42.23.09.91). **Open** 10am-12.30pm, 1.30-5pm Mon, Wed-Sun. **Admission** €2.50; free students, under-25s. **No credit cards.**

On the first floor of the former bishop's palace, the tapestry museum houses 17th- and 18th-century tapestries discovered in situ in the 19th century. There's a particularly lively series of scenes from *Don Quixote*, made at Beauvais between 1735 and 1744 after cartoons by Natier, along with costumes and model sets from opera productions from the Aix festival. Also hosts temporary exhibitions.

Musée du Vieil Aix

17 rue Gaston de Saporta (04.42.21.43.55). **Open** *Apr-Sept* 10am-noon, 2.30-6pm Tue-Sun. *Oct-Mar* 10am-noon, 2.30-5pm Tue-Sun. **Admission** €4; €2.50 students; free under-14s. **No credit cards.**

This small but worthwhile collection focuses on folk art, with *santons* (Christmas crib figures) and puppets from a mechanical crèche, plus some fine lacquered furniture and faïence. Two folding wood screens and a fragile line of mechanical puppets depict the Fête-Dieu (Corpus Christi) procession that was a feature of Aix life every June until the beginning of the 20th century. The house, with its fine entrance hall, frescoes and a tiny painted *cabinet* with ornately carved and gilded domed ceiling, gives a glimpse of 17th-century aristocratic life.

Pavillon Vendôme

32 rue Célony or 13 rue de la Molle (04.42.21.05.78). **Open** 10am-12.30pm, 1.30-5.30pm Mon, Wed-Sun. **Admission** €2.50; free students, under-25s. **No credit cards.**

This perfect pleasure dome was built by the aptly named Pierre Pavillon for the Duc de Vendôme in 1665. Set in formal gardens, the pavilion was later

extended to three storeys following the classical hierarchy of Doric, Ionic and Corinthian orders. Giant Atlantes hold up the balcony and the interior is adorned with 17th- and 18th-century furniture.

Thermes Sextius

55 cours Sextius (08.00.63.96.99/www.thermes-sextius.com). **Open** 8.30am-7.30pm Mon-Fri; 8.30am-1.30pm, 2.30-6.30pm Sat. **Treatments** from €22.70. **Credit** MC, V.

Behind a wrought-iron grille and classical façade, the Thermes now house the glass and marble pyramids of an ultramodern health spa. You can wander in and look at the small fountain, which still marks the original warm spring of the fashionable 18th-century establishment. To the right of the entrance are the remains of first-century BC Roman baths fed by the Source Imperiatrice.

Quartier Mazarin

Laid out on a strict grid plan in 1646, the Quartier Mazarin was conceived as a speculative venture and sold off in lots masterminded by Mazarin, Archbishop of Aix and brother of Louis XIV's powerful minister Cardinal Mazarin. It gradually became the aristocratic quarter and still feels very refined today. There are few shops or restaurants, other than classy *antiquaires* and select designer fashion names, but plenty of fine doorways, balustrades and wrought-iron balconies. The **Musée Paul Arbaud** occupies a townhouse on rue du 4 Septembre, the quarter's main thoroughfare, which leads into place des Quatre Dauphins, with a baroque fountain depicting four dolphins splashing in the water. On the square, at the rear of an arcaded courtyard, is the beautiful 1650 Hôtel de Boisgelin, while nearby, on rue Cardinale, is the Collège Mignet (formerly Bourbon), where Cézanne and Zola went to school. Look also at the grandiose Hôtel Bonnet de la Baume on 2 rue Goyrand.

At the far end of rue Cardinale stands the **Eglise St-Jean-de-Malte**, built by the Knights of Malta (note the Maltese cross on the fountain in front) outside the city walls at the end of the 13th century. One of the earliest Gothic structures in Provence, it has a wide nave and side chapels but no transept. The church once served as the burial place of the Counts of Provence. Beside it, the Commanderie of the Knights of Malta now houses the **Musée Granet**, the city's fine art and archaeology collection, currently closed for renovation.

Musée Granet

pl St-Jean-de-Malte. **Open** Closed until Mar 2006; ring tourist office for details.

Aix's fine art museum is at the centre of an ambitious expansion project that should eventually quadruple the available exhibition space. As well as

Wherever he laid his hat: **Atelier Cézanne**.

an important collection of 17th-century provençal painters and Flemish masters, there are several small Cézannes, a huge Ingres and works by the museum's founder, François Granet. The archaeological collection includes statues and other finds from Entremont and Roman Aix. For details on the 'Cézanne in Provence' exhibition, scheduled to start in June 2006, *see p175* **Portrait of the artist**.

Musée Paul Arbaud

2a rue du 4 Septembre (04.42.38.38.95). **Open** 2-5pm Mon-Sat. **Admission** €3; free under-10s. **No credit cards**.

Old masters from the Mirabeau family hang amid provençal faïence and manuscripts collected by scholar Paul Arbaud. Fine pieces of Marseille and Moustiers faïence, from early monochrome grotesque style based on the designs of Berain to later polychrome examples, are light years from most of the tourist production made today.

Further out

Circling the old town, the busy peripheral boulevards follow the former ramparts. Beyond here lies 'new Aix', a post-war sprawl that includes an entire new district, Quartier Sextius Mirabeau. This is home to the dynamic **Cité du Livre**, a former match factory that is fast becoming the focus of a new cultural pole. The **Centre National Chorégrapique** is expected to open in 2005 next door and the Salle de Spectacles du Pays d'Aix will be built alongside.

The Aix suburbs are still dotted with former country villas and bastides. These include the Pavillon Lenfant (now part of the University of Aix); Jas de Bouffon, a country residence bought by Cézanne's father in 1859, and now at the centre of a redevelopment zone near the **Fondation Vasarely** (2km/1.25 miles west of centre by the A8/A51); and **Château de la**

Pioline, now a hotel (*see p173*). Nearby, at Les Milles, is a brick factory turned prison camp where numerous German and Austrian intellectuals, among them Surrealists Max Ernst and Hans Bellmer, were interned during World War II, and from which nearly 2,000 Jews were deported, many to Auschwitz. The refectory is now the **Mémorial National des Milles**, which is painted with murals by prisoners. Further south, beneath the perched village of Bouc-Bel-Air, the **Jardins d'Albertas**, terraced, 18th-century formal gardens with extravagant fountains, are a testimony to the power of the Albertas family.

North of Vieil Aix, past the pyramidal **Mausoleum of Joseph Sec** – a rare example of Revolutionary architecture dating from 1792, a period when there were more pressing things to do than build – a steep hill climbs to the Lauves, where Cézanne built his last studio, the **Atelier Cézanne**. If you continue climbing, you will come to a roundabout with the remains of an ancient city gate. Continue climbing up avenue Paul Cézanne (follow signs) to the spot where Cézanne painted many of his famous scenes of Montagne Ste-Victoire: a bit of a hike, but the view is definitely worth it. The remains of the Celto-Ligurian **Oppidium d'Entremont**, site of Sextius' victory in the second century AD, lie just outside the city to the north-west.

Atelier Cézanne

9 av Paul Cézanne (04.42.21.06.53/*www.atelier-cezanne.com*). **Open** *Apr-June, Sept* 10am-noon, 2-6pm daily. *July-Aug* 10am-6pm daily. *Oct-Mar* 10am-noon, 2-5pm daily. **Admission** €5.50; €2 students; free under-16s. **Credit** AmEx, MC, V. Cézanne built this studio in 1902, and worked here until his death in 1906. Then outside the town, with views of the rocky ravines of the Montagne Ste-

Victoire, it now overlooks post-war housing developments. The first-floor studio is a masterpiece of artistic clutter, with Cézanne's easels and palettes and many of the props – fruit, vases, a broken cherub statue – that are familiar from his still lifes. A good number of events are planned to commemorate the centenary of Cézanne's death (see p175 **Portrait of the artist**), but be sure not to miss, in particular, the after-dark *Nuits des Toiles* shows that take place regularly in July and August, and the literary and gastronomic evenings that are also held in July. For both events, call or check the website for precise dates.

Fondation Vasarely

1 av Marcel Pagnol, Jas de Bouffan (04.42.20.01.09). **Open** 10am-6pm Mon-Sat. **Admission** €7; €4 7-18s, students; free under-7s. **Credit** AmEx, MC, V.
At the 'centre architectonique', Hungarian-born abstract artist Victor Vasarely (1906-97) put his theories of geometrical abstraction and kinetic art into practice on a truly architectural scale. The building itself is composed of hexagonal structures of black and white squares and circles that reflect off water. Within, the hexagonal volumes are hung with large-scale paintings, tapestries and reliefs reflecting different periods of his work. Even if Vasarely's brand of kinetic art today seems out of sync with contemporary art concerns, it remains an interesting 1970s time-warp. The Fondation also owns thousands of drawings explaining his theories.

Jardins d'Albertas

N8, Bouc-Bel-Air (04.42.22.29.77). **Open** *May, Sept, Oct* 2-6pm Sat, Sun, public holidays. *June-Aug* 3-7pm daily. Closed Nov-Apr. **Admission** 3.50; €2.50 7-16s; free under-7s. **No credit cards.**
Jean-Baptiste Albertas, president of the Cour des Comptes, dreamed of constructing a lavish rural retreat, but he was assassinated on 14 July 1790, the chateau was never built and only the gardens, laid out with terraces and pools containing sea beasts gushing water, were ever completed. During the last weekend in May, an annual sale of Mediterranean plants (along with attendant talks and events) transforms the gardens into a burst of colour.

Oppidium d'Entremont

3km (2 miles) north-west of Vieux Aix via av Solari (D14), direction Puyricard (04.42.21.97.33/www. entremont.culture.gouv.fr). **Open** 9am-noon, 2-5.30pm Mon, Wed-Sun. **Admission** free.
This Celto-Ligurian hilltop settlement developed sometime around the second century BC on the site of an earlier sanctuary and was destroyed by Romans in the second century AD at the request of the land-hungry Marseillais. Excavated sections reveal a grid plan with residential zone, plus traces of shops, warehouses and workshops.

Site Mémorial des Milles

Les Milles (04.42.24.34.68). **Open** 9am-12.15pm, 1-5pm Mon-Thur; 9am-12.15pm, 1-4pm Fri. **Admission** free.

Between 1939 and 1943, this brick factory had a quite different role that for a long time lay, if not actively concealed, quite simply ignored. Les Milles was the sole French camp that served for internment, transit and deportation. Requisitioned as early as 1939 (before the German occupation), in a period of growing xenophobia and nationalism, it was used to round up 'enemy subjects' in France, both refugees from the Spanish Civil War and German and Austrian intellectuals, many of them Jewish, who had fled the Nazi regime. Among them were two Nobel prizewinners and the Surrealist painters Max Ernst and Hans Bellmer. After June 1940, although Provence at this time was part of Free France administered by Vichy, Les Milles became a transit camp; nearly 2,000 Jews were deported from here to Auschwitz via Drancy, a transit camp near Paris. Since 1997 the former warders' refectory has become the Mémorial. In the entrance, documents and archive photos relate the history of Les Milles and other internment camps, but it is the refectory that is the most telling witness, decorated with murals by prisoners that take a subtly satiric slant in the row of caricatured warders painted in a parody of Leonardo's *Last Supper.* Across the road, at the former Gare des Milles, a railway wagon recalls those transported to Auschwitz via Drancy.

Where to eat

Antoine Côté Cour

19 cours Mirabeau (04.42.93.12.51). **Open** 7.30pm-midnight Mon; 12.30-2.30pm, 7.30pm-midnight Tue-Sat. **Average** €25. **Credit** DC, MC, V.
The fashionable folk of Aix come to this stylish and lively Italianate restaurant, which serves veal dishes, gnocchi and pasta. An ornate entrance off the cours Mirabeau leads to a beautiful courtyard perfect for summer alfresco dining.

Bistro Latin

18 rue de la Couronne (04.42.38.22.88). **Open** noon-2.30pm, 7.30-10.30pm Tue-Sat. **Menu** €21. **Credit** MC, V
This lovely restaurant boasts an intimate setting and nouvelle cuisine served at remarkably low prices. The prix fixe includes such delights as mussels and spinach in saffron sauce, roasted pork loin with honey and garlic, lamb stew, and fresh cod with fennel sauce.

Brasserie des Deux Garçons

53 cours Mirabeau (04.42.26.00.51/www.les2 garcons.com). **Open** 7am-2am daily (meals noon-3pm, 7-11.30pm daily). **Menus** €20-€30. **Credit** AmEx, MC, V.
Alias 'les 2 G', the legendary Deux Garçons café, founded in 1792 and named after the two waiters who bought it in 1840, still has its original canopied entrance and consulaire period interior with tall mirrors, chandeliers, old-fashioned cashier's desk and a salon off the side where you can read the papers or write your novel. It was the hangout of Cézanne,

Zola and a long list of famous names from Piaf and Picasso to Churchill. The food is proficient brasserie fare, but it's the elegant café buzz that counts.

Café Bastide du Cours

43-47 cours Mirabeau (04.42.26.55.41/www. cafebastideducours.com). **Open** noon-1am daily. **Average** €50. **Credit** AmEx, MC, V.

One of the most charming restaurants in Aix, the Bastide has a fabulous terrace (a smart awning and heaters make it a comfortable dining spot even out of season; tables are arranged around the bole of an enormous plane tree). Inside, a sumptuous dining room and luxurious guestrooms complete the picture. The sophisticated cooking is rooted in provençal tradition (the lamb à farigoulette is out of this world).

Café La Chimère

15 rue Brueys (04.42.38.30.00). **Open** 6.30pm-midnight Mon-Sat. **Menus** €21.50. **Credit** V.

If food is considered an art form, then La Chimère takes its art seriously. Whimsical concoctions of local, fresh ingredients are vertically arranged on platters with drizzles of sauce and garnishes such as shaved fennel or spun sugar. The decor is a rococo mix of gilt and crimson, with angels throughout. The prices are fantastic and cuisine excellent, making this an altogether fun place to spend an evening with friends.

Clos de la Violette

10 av de la Violette (04.42.23.30.71/www.clos delaviolette.fr). **Open** 7-9.30pm Mon; noon-2pm, 7-9.30pm Tue-Sat (7-9.30pm in summer). Closed 2wks Feb & 2wks Aug. **Menus** €54-€117. **Credit** AmEx, MC, V.

In a spacious garden under ancient chestnut trees, chef Jean-Marc Banzo displays a knack for producing food that is at once light, healthy and unmistakably provençal. Dishes like grilled red mullet with cabbage stuffed with squid, or a sublime croustillant of raspberries, spotlight his style. The service can be erratic, and the welcome cool.

Le Grillon

49 cours Mirabeau (04.42.27.58.81). **Open** 6am-3am daily (meals noon-3pm, 7pm-1am daily). **Menus** €12.80-€33. **Credit** MC, V.

Sit on the terrace or in the deliciously pretty, pastiche 18th-century upstairs dining room. Plenty of Aixois eat here, as do tourists. Roast lamb with herbs and daily fish dishes are simple but proficient (the pasta is best forgotten), service affable and wines by the carafe affordable.

Le Passage

10 rue Villars (04.42.37.09.00/www.le-passage.fr). **Open** 10am-midnight daily. **Menus** €15-€28. **Credit** AmEx, MC, V.

Reine Sammut, one of France's celebrity chefs, is the éminence grise behind this, the hottest table in town. Well, several tables, actually: there's a choice between the restaurant, the *salon de thé*, the *vinothèque* and the cooking school. But it's the funky

Café Bastide du Cours.

modern restaurant that we favour. Ensuring that Sammut's culinary vision is successfully transposed to the plate, chef Franck Dumont creates dishes like epaules de lapin aux graines de moutarde, pommes de terre écrasées et aïoli. Bring an appetite – and don't forget the credit card.

Le Petit Verdot

7 rue d'Entrecasteaux (04.42.27.30.12/www.lepetit verdot.com). **Open** 7-11pm Mon-Sat. **Menus** €13.50, €17. **No credit cards.**

Filled with wine barrels and a broad assortment of bottles, this charming wine bar and restaurant near to place des Tanneurs is the perfect setting for an intimate *diner à deux*. The jovial German owner and her dog make delightful hosts and the traditional regional cooking and wine are excellent. The prix-fixe menus are a steal.

La Pizza

3 rue Aude (04.42.26.22.17). **Open** noon-2pm, 7.30-11.30pm daily. **Average** €13. **Credit** AmEx, DC, MC, V.

Probably the most romantic pizzeria you'll ever have seen, La Pizza comes alive every night with tables spilling on to the cobblestones overlooking the gorgeous place d'Albertas. A wide variety of wood-fired pizzas are available, as well as pastas and risottos. Try the salmon risotto or gorgonzola gnocchi.

La Vieille Auberge

63 rue Espariat (04.42.27.17.41). **Open** 7.15-10pm Mon; noon-2pm, 7.15-10pm Tue-Sun. Closed Jan. **Menus** €15-€38. **Credit** MC, V.

A beamed, pink-washed dining room with a giant fireplace is the setting for chef Jean-Marie Merly's sophisticated cooking, seen in dishes such as pepper stuffed with brandade and red mullet stuffed with aubergine and parmesan on a red-pepper pain perdu.

Yamato (Koji & Yuriko)

4 rue Lieutaud (04.42.38.00.20). **Open** noon-2pm, 7-10pm Mon-Thur, Sun; 7-10.30pm Fri, Sat. **Menus** €27-€43. **Credit** MC, V.

Staff glide around in kimonos at this Japanese restaurant adorned with Noh masks. As well as excellent sushi and sashimi and crisp, light tempura you'll find good grilled fish and rarer specialities like *uoroke* and *sukiyaki* (strips of beef simmered at table over a flame with vegetables and noodles).

Yôji

7 av Victor Hugo (04.42.38.48.76). **Open** 7-11pm Mon; noon-2pm, 7-11pm Tue-Sat. **Menus** €20-€32.50. **Credit** AmEx, MC, V.
This Korean-Japanese restaurant has a touch of cosmopolitan glamour. The long basement is a clever mixture of alfresco dining in a courtyard, plus an lovely room with water features. Refined Japanese cuisine is paired with the chance to indulge in a sumptuous Korean barbeque thanks to cunningly designed tables.

Where to drink

For an aperitif to accompany your people-watching, cours Mirabeau and rue Espariat are the obvious choices, beginning with the **Deux Garçons** (*see p168*) and **Le Festival** (*see below*). If the market has given you an appetite for a light lunch, try **Le Pain Quotidien** on place Richelme.

Bar Brigand

17 pl Richelme (04.42.26.11.57). **Open** 9am-2am Mon-Sat; 2pm-2am Sun. **Credit** MC, V.
This is where the hip young things of Aix come to have a few drinks, swap mobile numbers and maybe, on a lucky night, slope off home with someone. But for those who just want a beer, there are 40 varieties to choose from.

Le Bistrot Aixois

37 cours Sextius (04.42.27.50.10). **Open** 6.30pm-2am Tue-Sat. **Credit** AmEx, MC, V.
Renovated after a fire, the Bistrot has the *BCBG* (French Sloanes) students queuing to get in. Inside there are drinks, billiards and a small dancefloor.

Book in Bar

1bis rue Joseph Cabassol (04.42.26.60.07/www.book inbar.com). **Open** 9am-7pm Mon-Sat. **Credit** MC, V.
Book in Bar is a cosy anglophone bookshop and café, right near the cours Mirabeau. It's a great spot not only to buy and read books, but also to meet other English speakers and search for jobs and housing on the bulletin board.

Le Festival

67bis rue Espariat (04.42.27.21.96). **Open** 7.30am-2am daily. **Credit** MC, V.
Facing the fountain at La Rotonde, this café provides an ideal spot in which to grab an outdoor table for a drink on a sunny afternoon. Sit back here and watch the world go by.

Mediterranean Boy

6 rue de la Paix (04.42.27.21.47). **Open** 8.30pm-2am daily. **Credit** AmEx, DC, MC, V.
Upstairs is a classic gay bar, tended by the venue's avuncular middle-aged patron. Downstairs is a cellar with tables, groups of people chatting away and the opportunity for heavy petting. More twilight zone than dark room.

L'Orienthé

5 rue du Félibre Gaut (06.62.16.48.25). **Open** 3pm-1am Mon-Thur; 4pm-2am Fri, Sat; 3pm-2am Sun. Closed Sun in July, 1st 2wks Jan. **No credit cards**.
Leave your shoes at the door and relax over one of 50 varieties of tea and a delectable pastry at this exotic tea salon/lounge. You sit on pillows around low tables amid candles and incense.

The Red Clover

30 rue la Verrerie (04.42.23.44.61). **Open** 8am-2am Mon-Sat. **Credit** MC, V.
The friendly, boisterous Red Clover pub is *the* spot to meet international students in Aix and serves a wide variety of beers and Irish whiskies. Don't expect to speak much French here.

Nightlife

Le Divino

Mas des Auberes, rte de Venelles (5km/3 miles from town) (04.42.99.37.08/www.divino.fr). **Open** *Club* 11pm-5am Thur-Sat. *Restaurant* 8pm-2am Tue-Sat. **Admission** *Club* €16. **Credit** MC, V.
More like a hip metropolitan club – think New York or Paris – Le Divino attracts Aix's fashion victims with its trendy decor and thumping music. Lounge at the bar or dance the night away to house hits amid a beautiful crowd.

Hot Brass Jazz Club

rte d'Eguilles (04.42.21.05.57). **Open** 10.30pm-dawn Fri, Sat. **Admission** €16-€19. **Credit** MC, V.
A short drive (or long walk) out of town, the Hot Brass offers live funk, soul, rock, blues and Latin bands, mainly local outfits. Reserve on the answerphone.

IPN

23 cours Sextius (04.42.26.25.17). **Open** 11.30pm-4am Thur-Sat. **Admission** €4 (members); €6 (non-members). **Credit** MC, V.
Always packed with students, this very popular dance spot is conveniently located in an ancient cellar in the centre of town. Great ambience and music, reasonable drink prices.

Le Mistral

3 rue Frédéric Mistral (04.42.38.16.49/www. mistralclub.com). **Open** 11.30pm-5am Tue-Sat. **Admission** €11-€15. **Credit** MC, V.
Behind a discreet entrance is this long-established haunt of *BCBG* students. This chic club is popular with international students, as it's one of the few places open for dancing past 2am. The music is a mix of pop, house and techno.

Le Sextius Mirabeau

2 cours Sextius (04.42.26.78.20). **Open** 5-11pm daily. **No credit cards**.
Le Sextius Mirabeau is a casual bar with an affordable range of drinks, a good wine selection and a small dancefloor. It's popular with students, who gather to hear live music or simply hang out with their friends. Every Tuesday is reggae night.

Marseille & Aix

Handsome, dignified **Vieil Aix**. See p164.

Shopping

Aix offers some of the most sophisticated shopping territory in the whole of Provence (all shops are open Mon-Sat unless otherwise stated). Undoubted leader of the fashion brigade is **Gago** (18, 20, 21 rue Fabrot, 04.42.27.60.19) with up-to-the-minute men's and women's designer wear and accessories, including such labels as Prada, Helmut Lang, YSL and Gucci. But you'll also find **Yohji Yamamoto** (No.3, 04.42.27.79.15) and **Max Mara** (No.12, 04.42.26.80.85, closed Mon morning) on the same street. For simpler, more casual wear **Sugar** (4 rue Maréchal Foch, 04.42.27.48.33, closed Mon morning) is worth a look. **agnès b** (2 rue Fernand Dol, 04.42.38.44.87, closed Mon morning) is just across the cours Mirabeau. There is a clutch of good children's wear shops too. These include **Catimini** (9 pl des Chapeliers, 04.42.27.51.14, closed Mon morning), colourful **Marèse** (4 rue Aude, 04.42.26.67.00) and the excellent-value **Du Pareil au Même** (14 rue Maréchal Foch, 04.42.26.48.49, closed Mon morning). Toddlers will love the traditional wooden toys sold at **Le Nain Rouge** (47 rue Espariat, 04.42.93.50.05, closed Mon morning).

Aix's culinary speciality is the *calisson d'Aix*, diamond-shaped sweets made out of almonds, sugar and preserved melon; some of the best come from **Leonard Parli** (35 av Victor Hugo, 04.42.26.05.71), who has been producing them at the rear of a pretty old shop since 1874, along with little chocolate-covered nut biscuits.

There are numerous antique and interior design shops on place des Trois Ormeaux and neighbouring rue Jaubert. **La Maison Montigny** (5 rue Lucas de Montigny, 04.42.27.74.56, closed Mon morning) has two floors of high-tech kitchen equipment and stained, restored furniture, tasteful grey linen and burnished stainless steel. **Scènes de Vie** (3 rue Jaubert, 3 rue Granet, 04.42.21.13.90, closed Mon morning) stocks sophisticated provençal pottery. Upmarket antique and fabric shops also congregate in the Quartier Mazarin, especially along rues Cardinale and Granet. For details of regular *brocantes* and antiques fairs call 04.42.52.97.10.

Perhaps the best of Aix's bookshops are the **Librairie de Provence** (31 cours Mirabeau, 04.42.26.07.23, closed Sun), which has a good fine art section, and **Librairie Paradox** (15 rue du 4 Septembre, 04.42.26.47.99, closed Sun), stocking books, videos and CD-Roms in English.

Arts & entertainment

Pick up *Le Mois à Aix*, a monthly listings magazine published by the tourist office (also available online at www.aix-en-provence.com), or the regional freebie weekly *César*, distributed in hotels and bars, for up-to-date details of events in Aix.

Centre National Chorégraphique

8-10 rue des Allumettes; (from spring 2006) 530 av Mozart (04.42.93.48.00/www.preljocaj.org). **Tickets** €8-€20.
The long-standing construction project to build the Ballet Preljocaj a home of its own looked set, at the time of writing, to be completed in spring 2006. The new building (situated just around the corner from the Cité du Livre, which currently houses the Ballet) will comprise a large concert space, as well as a number of smaller, multipurpose areas. Choreographer Angelin Preljocaj, who brings classical ballet into the 21st century, moved to Aix as a refugee from Châteauvallon when Toulon went Front National in the 1990s.

Cité du Livre

8-10 rue des Allumettes (04.42.91.98.65/www.citedu livre-aix.com). **Open** noon-6pm Tue, Thur, Fri; 10am-6pm Wed, Sat. **Admission** free.
Despite the name and the gigantic book that marks the entrance, this converted match factory covers not just literature but is a multi-disciplinary arts

centre. As well as hosting the town's annual literary festival each October and housing the historic Bibliothèque Méjanes library, it is also the home of the Institut de l'Image (art cinema, video screenings and December short film festival), the Fondation St-John Perse (04.42.91.98.85), which is an exhibition space with a collection of manuscripts by the poet, as well as the temporary home of the Ballet Preljocaj (*see p172*), plus a library of opera on video.

Espace Musical Chapelle Ste-Catherine

20 rue Mignet (04.42.99.37.11). **Concerts** 7pm Tue. **Tickets** from €3, free under-12s.
A former church, converted to be used for classical concerts – essentially chamber music events, plus a festival in Holy Week.

Galerie d'Art du Conseil Général

21bis cours Mirabeau (04.42.93.03.67). **Open** *July-Sept* 10.30am-12.45pm, 2-6.30pm daily. *Oct-June* 9.30am-1pm, 2-6pm daily. **Admission** free.
The exhibition space of the Conseil Général des Bouches du Rhône shows modern and contemporary art and photography.

Théâtre des Ateliers

29 pl Miollis (04.42.38.10.45). **Box office** 10am-noon, 2-8pm Mon-Sat. Closed Aug. **Shows** 9pm. **Tickets** €11.50; €5.50 children. **No credit cards**.
A smallish theatre, Théâtre des Ateliers works on co-productions of new work with other subsidised theatre venues.

Théâtre du Jeu de Paume

17-21 rue de l'Opéra (04.42.99.12.00/box office 04.42.99.12.12/www.lestheatres.net). **Box office** 11am-6pm (in person noon-6pm) Tue-Sat. **Tickets** €20-€35. **Credit** MC, V.
This beautiful vintage theatre was founded in 1756 on the site of the city's old real tennis court. It reopened in 2000 after major renovation works. Director Dominique Bluzet (of the Théâtre du Gymnase in Marseille) brings in successful Paris plays, as well as visiting companies from Marseille and elsewhere. It is also one of the venues for the Festival d'Art Lyrique.

3BisF

Hôpital Montperrin, 109 av du Petit Barthélémy (04.42.16.17.75/www.3bisf.com). **Open** 9am-6pm Mon-Fri. **Admission** €9; €4.50 under-15s. **No credit cards**.
3BisF provides artists' studios and an exhibition space in a hospital complex not far from the Cité du Livre. It puts on contemporary dance and theatre productions and workshops.

Where to stay

Château de la Pioline

260 rue Guillaume du Vair, La Pioline (04.42.52.27.27/www.chateaudelapioline.fr). **Rates** €155-€290 double. **Credit** AmEx, DC, MC, V.

About 5km (3 miles) out of the centre, this 16th-century chateau (downstairs is listed) has a graceful stairhall, elegant dining room and formal garden, plus a pool. Too bad the motorway's in earshot.

Grand Hôtel Nègre Coste

33 cours Mirabeau (04.42.27.74.22/www.hotelnegre coste.com). **Rates** €70-€140 double. **Credit** AmEx, MC, V.
The hospitable Hôtel Nègre Coste has a prime location and plenty of old-fashioned style, with period furniture and chandeliers downstairs and colourful bedrooms upstairs featuring antique wardrobes. Bedrooms at the front look over cours Mirabeau; quieter ones at the back have a view across rooftops to the cathedral.

Hôtel Aquabella

2 rue des Etuves (04.42.99.15.00/www.aquabella.fr). **Rates** €135-€195 double. **Credit** AmEx, DC, MC, V.
This modern 110-room hotel adjoining the revamped Thermes Sextius may lack the character of Aix's older hotels but compensates with spacious, comfortable rooms, helpful staff and a good location for exploring Vieil Aix. There's an airy reception area and a glass-walled restaurant, L'Orangerie. Special spa treatment packages are available.

Hôtel Artea

4 bd de la République (04.42.27.36.00/ www.arteahotel.com). **Rates** €63-€87 double. **Credit** AmEx, MC, V.
Hôtel Artea is a perfect spot for budget travellers who are looking for a central location. Rooms are simple and comfortable, with the larger ones easily able to accommodate groups. All rooms are equipped with en suite bathrooms.

Hôtel des Augustins

3 rue de la Masse (04.42.27.28.59/www.hotel-augustins.com). **Rates** €95-€230 double. **Credit** DC, MC, V.
Situated on a side street off the cours Mirabeau, this very appealing hotel was part of an Augustine convent until the Revolution, and only became a hotel in the 1890s. The reception has been inserted into a spectacular vaulted space and the rooms are comfortable, although the provençal-style furnishings don't quite live up to the promise of the lobby. Many famous guests are supposed to have stayed here, among them Martin Luther.

Hôtel Cardinal

24 rue Cardinale (04.42.38.32.30). **Rates** €68-€100 double. **Credit** MC, V.
Much loved by writers, artists and musicians who have come to Aix for the festival, this little hotel in the Quartier Mazarin has bags of charm. Several rooms have stucco mouldings, a couple have the original 18th-century painted overdoor panels, and all of them have been recently redecorated with high-quality fabrics, old furniture, oil paintings and new bathrooms. Suites in the annexe by Musée Granet have a kitchenette.

Marseille & Aix

Hôtel de France

63 rue Espariat (04.42.27.90.15). **Rates** €57-€70 double. **Credit** AmEx, MC, V.

An inexpensive option in a town that has fewer central hotels than you might expect. Most of its rooms are of good size, and those at the front overlook the cafés of a busy shopping street in Vieil Aix.

Hôtel Paul Cézanne

40 av Victor Hugo (04.42.91.11.11). **Rates** €118-€160 double. **Credit** AmEx, DC, MC, V.

Just a stone's throw from the train station and a short walk from cours Mirabeau, it's hard to find a more conveniently located hotel in the whole of Aix. The rooms are air-conditioned and decorated simply *à la provençale*.

Hôtel Paul

10 av Pasteur (04.42.23.23.89). **Rates** €35-€45 double. **Credit** V.

A rather dated lobby and drab rooms nonetheless provide a fantastic bargain for travellers on a budget at this hotel just north of the old town and down the hill from Cézanne's atelier. A shaded garden offers respite on hot afternoons.

Hôtel Le Pigonnet

5 av du Pigonnet (04.42.59.02.90/www. hotelpigonnet.com). **Rates** €160-€340 double. **Credit** AmEx, MC, DC, V.

Only a kilometre (about half a mile) from the town centre, this beautiful 19th-century mansion is a secluded, relaxed haven surrounded by flowers, cypress trees and bubbling fountains. It's a joy to relax by the swimming pool and soak up the sunshine. The hotel's restaurant, La Riviera (menus €38-€46), serves excellent provençal cuisine.

Hôtel des Quatre Dauphins

54 rue Roux Alphéran (04.42.38.16.39). **Rates** €65-€85 double. **Credit** MC, V.

The 'four dolphins' has 12 simple but tastefully decorated – and newly air-conditioned – rooms. The hotel is a 17th-century building, situated on a corner of one of the most pleasant streets of the Quartier Mazarin. Most guests are returnees, so be certain to book well in advance.

Hôtel St-Christophe

2 av Victor Hugo (04.42.26.01.24/www.hotel-saintchristophe.com). **Rates** €87-€97.50 double. **Credit** AmEx, DC, MC, V.

Located just off La Rotonde, the St-Christophe has comfortable modern rooms behind a 19th-century façade, done up either art deco or *à la provençale*; suites have views of the Montagne Ste-Victoire. Downstairs is the big Brasserie Léopold.

Villa Gallici

10 av de la Violette (04.42.23.29.23/www.villa gallici.com). **Rates** €250-€590 double. **Credit** AmEx, DC, MC, V.

Slightly out of the centre in an elegantly renovated bastide, luxurious Villa Gallici offers plush comfort,

with Italianate trimmings. Some rooms have private gardens, and there's a swimming pool. It also has an excellent restaurant (average €76, closed Mon, lunch Tue, Wed in winter), where chef Christophe Gavot specialises in fish.

Resources

Hospital

Centre Hospitalier du Pays d'Aix Urgences, av Tamaris (04.42.33.50.00).

Internet

Virtualis, pl de l'Hôtel de Ville (04.42.26.02.30/ www.virtualis.fr). **Open** 9am-midnight Mon-Fri; noon-midnight Sun. Closed Sat.

Police

av de l'Europe (04.42.93.97.00).

Post office

pl de l'Hôtel de Ville (04.42.17.10.40).

Tourist information

Office de Tourisme, 2 pl du Général de Gaulle (04.42.16.11.61/hotel reservations 04.42.16.11.84/ www.aixenprovencetourism.com). **Open** *June, Sept* 8.30am-7pm Mon-Sat; 10am-1pm, 2-6pm Sun. *July, Aug* 8.30am-9pm Mon-Sat; 10am-1pm, 2-6pm Sun. *Oct-Mar* 8.30am-7pm Mon-Sat; 10am-1pm, 2-6pm Sun. *Ticket office (04.42.16.11.70)* 9am-noon, 2-6pm Mon-Sat.

Getting there & around

By bike

Bikes can be hired from Cycles Zammit (27 rue Mignet, 04.42.23.19.53, closed Mon).

By bus

Aix is served by six to ten buses daily to Avignon and an hourly shuttle to Marseille airport (*gare routière* 04.42.91.26.80). Aix is also a stop on the Marseille to Nice airport service (three daily) operated by **Phocéen Cars** (04.93.85.66.61).

Although the centre of Aix is best explored by foot, there is also an extensive network of local buses serving outlying areas. Most leave from La Rotonde in front of the Office du Tourisme, where there is an information/ticket desk (04.42.26.37.28). Take No.1 to Atelier Cézanne, No.20 for the Oppidium d'Entremont, No.16 for La Pioline and Les Milles, No.4 from the old casino to the Fondation Vasarely.

By car

Leave the autoroute A8 at exits 29-31. Take the N7 from Avignon or St-Maximin-la-Ste-Baume. From Marseille, take the A51, which continues north towards Gap.

By train

Aix TGV station is 10km (6 miles) west of the city, served by regular shuttle buses. The old Aix station is on the slow Marseille–Sisteron line, with trains roughly every hour from Marseille-St-Charles.

Portrait of the artist

The 22 October 2006 marks the centenary of the death of Paul Cézanne. To celebrate his life and art, his hometown – Aix-en-Provence – is proudly hosting a season of events under the rubric 'La Mission Cézanne 2006'.

The highlight is the large-scale exhibition, entitled 'Cézanne in Provence', being held at the **Musée Granet** (*see p166*) from 9 June to 17 September. With 80 oils and 30 watercolours, it will feature the many paintings that the artist produced of provençal landscapes, as well as a number of still lifes and portraits.

In addition to this, three guided tours are being organised to the places Cézanne depicted on his canvases. Hike to the Bibémus quarries where he painted the ochre rocks, or to the Ste-Victoire mountain in Gardanne, where he developed his structural concept of painting. A trip to l'Estaque, where he stayed several times between 1869 and 1890, is another option.

The **Atelier Cézanne** (*see p167*), complete with his tools, the objects that he used as still-life models, and souvenirs, will be putting on special displays. And not to be missed is a visit to Cézanne's house in Jas de Bouffan, where he lived for nearly 40 years and painted such masterpieces as *The Card Players* and *Avenue of Chestnut Trees*.

Festivities also include music, dance and drama events, forums, seminars and contemporary art exhibitions. The aim of 'Cézanne Year' is not just about celebrating Cézanne, but affirming Provence's 'vocation' as 'a land of artists'. Visit www.cezanne-2006.com for the latest schedule.

Widely regarded as the father of modern painting, Cézanne was born on 19 January 1839, in Aix-en-Provence. One of his close school friends was the novelist Emile Zola, with whom he hooked up in Paris in 1861 after quitting his law studies. After eventually winning the support of his banker father, plus an inheritance, he was able to live comfortably in Paris, where he befriended Camille Pissarro. Several years his senior, Pissarro took Cézanne under his wing and introduced him to fellow Impressionists Claude Monet and Auguste Renoir.

After having his early works from his sober 'romantic' period rejected by the official Salon, Cézanne changed tack under Pissarro's tutelage and adopted lighter tones

and Impressionist techniques. Accepted by the group, he exhibited with them in 1874 and 1877. The critics slated his work, and Cézanne fell out with Zola after interpreting references to his lack of success in one of Zola's novels. Gradually, he drifted back to his hometown, where he concentrated on painting landscapes, bowls of fruit, and nude strangers sunbathing.

A loner by nature, Cézanne was a solitary painter who went off on his own tangent to seek 'something more solid and durable, like the art of the museums'. This meant forsaking the principles of Impressionism to concentrate on personal expression through natural representation and pictorial abstraction. Applying this rigorous system was problematic, however, and Cézanne was so dissatisfied with some of the distorted forms in his *Bathers* series that he abandoned several of the paintings. Discredited during much of his career, it wasn't until 1895, when the Paris art dealer Ambroise Vollard presented some of his works, that Cézanne became critically acclaimed. His unconventional method of painting in blocks of colour preceded Cubism, and had the largest single influence on Matisse and Picasso.

Around Aix

Montagne Ste-Victoire

The Montagne Ste-Victoire is inextricably linked with Paul Cézanne and if you are at all interested in art, you will want to see this mountain range, which at once appears both familiar and much more massive than in his paintings. The Montagne also offers rugged villages, wild landscapes for walking and the changing colours that so obsessed Cézanne, who painted it in over 60 canvases and countless watercolours as he sought out the underlying geometrical structure in the landscape.

Cézanne was born into a wealthy Aixois family in 1839 (his father had a hat business on the cours Mirabeau before founding the Banque Cézanne et Cabassol) and even while at school would go for long walks on the mountain with his friend Emile Zola (curiously, Cézanne is said to have excelled at literature and Zola at drawing). Their friendship came to an end in 1886 when Cézanne was bitterly wounded by the description of struggling painter Claude Lantier in Zola's *L'Oeuvre*, which he perceived as a portrait of himself (although it also contains elements of Manet).

The best way to approach the Montagne Ste-Victoire is in a loop, taking a detour on the way out of Aix to the Pont des Trois Sautets, now a rather urban traffic junction, also painted by the artist. Cézanne rented a room to paint in at the Château Noir, just before Le Tholonet, from 1887 and later a hut at Carrière de Bibemus quarry – before building his own atelier on the Lauves hill, with a view of the mountain (*see p176*).

At Le Tholonet, the **Moulin Cézanne** has an exhibition on local history, the *barrage Zola* (built by Emile's dad) and the friendship between Cézanne and Zola. Upstairs are temporary exhibitions of painting and sculpture. The D17 follows the southern edge of the mountain, from where a footpath leads to the hermit's chapel of St-Ser, and through the village of Puyloubier, although the easiest access for walkers is from the north off the D10.

Another artist, Picasso, is buried in the grounds of the Château de Vauvenarges (private), which he bought in 1958. Note that it's easiest to travel by car, but, in season, the tourist office at Aix-en-Provence organises weekly bus tours to the main Cézanne sites (Apr-Nov 2-7pm Thur, €26).

Moulin Cézanne
rte Cézanne, Le Tholonet (Mairie 04.42.66.90.41). **Open** (during exhibitions) *May-Oct* 3-6pm daily. **Admission** free.

West & North of Aix

Overlooking the lush plain west of Aix, sleepy **Lambesc** boasts a neo-classical church, an old *lavoir* and some fine houses, which hint at the village's 14 decades of fame (1646-1786), when it was the seat of the regional assembly. West of Lambesc, **Château de la Barben** belonged to the Abbaye de St-Victor in Marseille, before becoming a residence of King René. Later it was home to the powerful Forbin family, who brought in André Le Nôtre to redesign the gardens. The adjoining **Zoo de la Barben** is a popular family attraction, where beasts including Siberian tigers roam in the beautiful grounds.

Across the Chaîne de la Trévaresse, through rolling oak woods and Coteaux d'Aix vineyards, the D15 (or N7 and D543 from Aix) leads to the **Abbaye de Silvacane**. The third of Provence's great Cistercian Romanesque abbeys (with Sénanque and Thoronet), it was begun in 1144 on swampy lands near the Durance. It has a sober church, impressive vaulted chapter house and a refectory with contemporary stained glass by artist Sarkis. Just to the west, the small town of La Roque-d'Anthéron has a famous summer piano festival, with concerts at Silvacane and in the grounds of the Château de Florans.

North of Aix by N96, the fortified **Château de Meyrargues** (04.42.63.49.90) on a strategic hilltop is now an upmarket hotel and restaurant, with views over fragments of a Roman aqueduct. Six kilometres (four miles) further on is sleepy **Peyrolles-en-Provence**. This area lacks the cachet of the Luberon on the other side of the Durance, which means fewer tourists but you might arrive to find the cafés shut and streets deserted. This was yet another residence of Good King René. A rather grand gateway leads into what looks like a farmyard but is, in fact, the courtyard of the former royal chateau, now the *mairie* (town hall). On the other side of the village, on a rocky hillock amid some gloomy public housing and derelict industrial buildings, is the beautifully austere Chapelle de la St-Sépulcre, built on a Greek-cross plan (call the Mairie 04.42.57.80.05, to visit Mon-Fri).

Abbaye de Silvacane
La Roque d'Antheron (04.42.50.41.69). **Open** *Apr-Sept* 10am-6pm daily. *Oct-Mar* 10am-1pm, 2-5pm Mon, Wed-Sun. **Admission** €6.10; free under-17s. **Credit** V, MC.

Château & Zoo de la Barben
D572/D22 La Barben (chateau 04.90.55.25.41/ zoo 04.90.55.19.12). **Open** *Chateau* 10am-noon, 2-5.30pm daily. *Zoo* 10am-6pm daily. Closed Jan. **Admission** *Chateau* €7; €4 3-13s; free under-3s. *Zoo* €12; €6 3-13s; free under-3s. **Credit** MC, V.

The Var

Introduction

Head beyond the city limits and take the path less trodden.

There's so much more here than just the bling and glamour of St-Tropez or, indeed, the less talked-about, rather troubled Toulon. With large areas devoted to the vineyards of Bandol and the Côtes de Provence or to military training grounds, the Var has suffered less from the over-development of the coast. If there are still undiscovered stretches of coast, many of them are to be found here, down steep *caps* accessible only by foot or boat.

Over the centuries, **St-Tropez** has been raided by Saracens, Signac, Brigitte Bardot and Johnny Hallyday, but you shouldn't let its showbiz reputation and appalling traffic jams scare you off. It masters its celebrities with a certain irony and still retains an undeniable fishing village charm. There are plenty of pleasant, quieter family resorts, too, like **Sanary-sur-Mer**, **Bormes-les-Mimosas** and **Le Lavandou**, while **Fréjus** boasts an impressive Roman heritage, often unjustly neglected against neighbour **St-Raphaël**. Just inland, you soon find yourself in the wooded and remote-feeling Maures or the brick-red Estérel massifs; even Toulon sits at the foot of an impressive mountain terrain.

The Green Var around Brignoles is renowned for canoeing, walking and organic produce, but also leads to the mysterious cave in the Ste-Baume massif where the Magdalene is said to have lived out 30 years in solitude, and the pilgrimage site of **St-Maximin-la-Ste-Baume.**

In the mountainous interior, perched villages, like **Tourtour**, **Aups**, **Salernes**, **Cotignac** and **Bargemon**, with steep, narrow streets and wrought-iron belfries, have barely changed for centuries. Here, ever-so-Provençal tiles and pottery meet a cosmopolitan sheen, while the dramatic **Gorges du Verdon** provide breathtaking landscape vistas and challenging walking and rafting.

The best The Var

Things to do

Domaine du Rayol (*see p191*) is a fabulous series of exotic gardens, while the imposing **Abbaye de Thoronet** (*see p217*) and the **Basilique Ste-Marie-Madeleine** (*see p209*), last resting place of Mary Magdalene, attract religious sensibilities. In Toulon get involved with the **cours Lafayette** street market (*see p181*) or take a detached view from the **Télépherique de Mont Faron** (*see p182*). See what the peasants dug with at **Musée des Traditions Provençales** (*see p211*) or dig the cliff-face dwellings of the **Grottes Troglodytes** (*see p214*).

Places to stay

Stretch out on the private beaches at the **Golf Hôtel** (*see p184*) in Bandol or **Résidence de la Pinède** (*see p198*) in St-Tropez. Live life like a medieval lord in the grandeur of **Château de Trigance** (*see p224*) or a Renaissance monk at the **Hôtellerie du Couvent Royal** (*see p210*). Relax into your holiday with a hot spa at **Thermes de Gréoux-les-Bains** (*see p225*).

Places to eat

Get classic Med fare at **Restaurant Le Mayol** (*see p183*), a modern twist on trad cooking at **La Salle à Manger** (*see p212*) or eat on the beach at **Plage de l'Estagnol** (*see p190*).

Nightlife

For some St-Tropez glamour take a leisurely drink at **Café Le Senequier** or get a bit more upbeat at **Le Papagayo** (for both, *see p197*).

Culture

When you've had enough beach culture, enjoy the **Roman ruins** (*see p203*) in Fréjus, Cocteau's **Chapelle Notre-Dame-de-Jérusalem** (*see p204*) in the nearby forest, or the geometric modernist splendour of **Villa Noailles** (*see p187*) in Hyères.

Sports & activities

Just walking in the **Grand Canyon du Verdon** (*see p221*) is amazing, but for extra thrills try climbing (*see p222*), canyoning or cliff paragliding (for both, *see p223*). If you need to unwind after all the excitement, St-Tropez is great for messing about in **boats** (*see p196*).

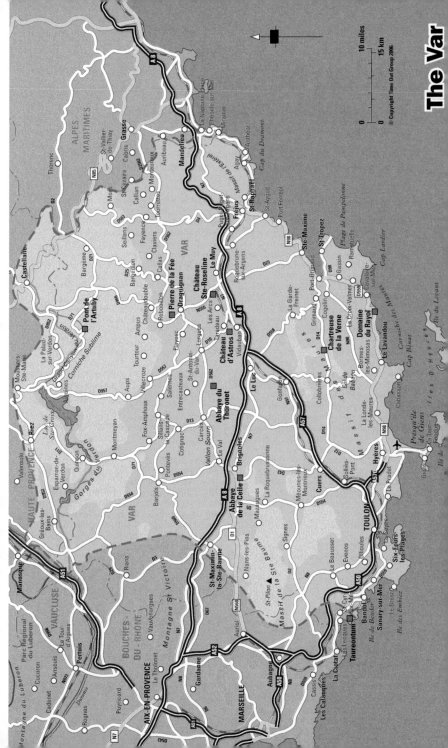

The Var

© Copyright Time Out Group 2006

0   10 miles
0   15 km

Toulon & the Western Côte

If you tire of Disney-like provençal villages, workaday Toulon – with its military port, feisty market and beautiful coastline – is a breath of fresh air.

Unless joining the French navy is your idea of a good time, Toulon won't leap to the top of your list of preferred destinations in the South. Deprivations wrought on the country's major Mediterranean naval base by bombing in World War II and some insensitive reconstruction haven't helped the city rise above its tough reputation, but the busy port, fabulous market and atmospheric old town will seem pretty appealing after an overdose of rural Provence.

The Greeks and Romans knew about the impressive natural harbour here, and exploited local deposits of murex shells to make purple dye. But only after 1481, when Toulon became part of France, did the port become strategically important. Louis XIV's military architect Vauban expanded the docks, fortified the town with star-shaped bastions and built the Fort St-Louis in Mourillon, which saw off Anglo-Spanish battleships during the War of the Spanish Succession in 1707.

In 1789, as the Revolution spread, Toulon chose to join the royal camp. In the subsequent uprising, it fell to an unknown young officer called Napoleon Bonaparte in 1793 and narrowly escaped being razed to the ground. The Royalists scuppered their own ships and blew up the shipyards so the Revolutionaries couldn't get their hands on them. In a strange re-run of history, the French scuttled their Mediterranean fleet to blockade the harbour in 1942 as the Nazis advanced. Much of the old town was destroyed in 1944 by a combination of Allied bombs and retreating Germans.

Despite the city's substantial immigrant population, it has in the past been a breeding ground for extreme-right politics: in 1995 Front National candidate Jean-Marie Le Chevallier was elected mayor. But Toulon soon came to its senses and moderate right-wing mayor Hubert Falco was duly elected in 2001.

Sightseeing

One of the most curious aspects of post-war reconstruction was the massive avenue de la République housing project that slices through the city between the port and the old town. Walk through the ghastly housing bar, however, and you discover a lively, café-lined yachting marina, from where you can take boat trips to the Iles de Hyères (*see p189*) or around the port (the only way to see the otherwise strictly off-limits military port). At the town hall annexe on quai Cronstadt, two 1657 atlantes by Pierre Puget around the door embody the agonising labour of early dock workers. The **Musée de la Marine** juts out into the westerly Darse Neuve, the 'new dock' built in 1680, and houses figureheads, ship models and marine paintings. Its ornate doorway, with figures of Mars and Minerva, is the former dockyard entrance. Nearby are the heavily guarded gates of the military port. Inside, an ancient wall is all that remains of the gruesome Le Bagne penal colony, described by Victor Hugo in *Les Misérables*, where prisoners living in hulks in the bay worked as galley slaves. Jutting out into the Rade, the Tour Royale, a fortress built for Louis XII in 1514, is today an annexe of the naval museum.

Back from the port, a couple of sex shops and 'American bars' (read fleshpots) are the last vestiges of Toulon's infamous red-light district. Known locally as 'Le Petit Chicago', the neighbourhood has undergone considerable renovation; its narrow streets and shady squares, several of which have small restaurants with terraces, are well worth a stroll. To get a better idea of the fiendishness of bygone Toulon, try the walking tours organised by the Office du Tourisme (every Tue at 10am).

In the heart of the *vieille ville*, café-filled place Puget was the site of a daily grain market in the 17th century (now a small Friday morning book and antique market); Victor Hugo lived at No.5. The Fontaine des Trois Dauphins, installed in 1780, has been growing ever since due to calcium deposits and a tiny jungle of sprouting trees. Amid tenements to the south, contemporary and historic photography exhibitions are hosted in the **Maison de la Photographie**. With a baroque façade and Gothic interior, the Cathédrale Ste-Marie on

The vineyards at **Le Castellet**. *See p184.*

place de la Cathédrale (open 9am-noon, 2.30-5.30pm daily) was built between the 11th and 17th centuries and used as an arms depot during the Revolution. A block east, cours Lafayette becomes a vast and colourful market every morning except Monday. Amid stalls overflowing with fruit and veg, you can try local snacks: perhaps la cade (a chickpea crêpe) or sweet chichi freigi (doughnuts). Halfway along the street, you'll find the historical collection of the **Musée du Vieux Toulon**.

To the east of the old town, remnants of Vauban's ramparts and the fortified Porte d'Italie can be seen, squashed behind the modern Centre Mayol shopping centre and the Stade Mayol, home of Toulon's much-loved rugby team. Near the station, the sleek mirror-and-steel **Zénith Oméga** (bd du Commandant Nicolas, 04.94.22.66.77) puts on all kinds of rock concerts.

West of the *vieille ville* lies what's left of the 18th- and 19th-century new town. On place Victor Hugo, the **Opéra de Toulon** has an opulent red and gilt Third Empire auditorium. At 6 rue Anatole France, a plaque marks where the actor Raimu, star of Marcel Pagnol's 1930s film trilogy (*Marius, Fanny, César*), was born. The Toulonnais make the most of their local celebrity: you'll find his bust on place des Trois Dauphins, a full-size statue on place du Théâtre and, on place Raimu near the port, life-size bronze figures from the famous card game scene in *Marius*. The empty chair beside César and Panisse shows serious wear – tourists like to sit on it and have their picture taken.

Further west, the lovely 19th-century former Var assembly building is now the **Hôtel des Arts**, which puts on exhibitions of contemporary art. Across the boulevard, the **Musée des Beaux-Arts** has a hotchpotch of

The view of Toulon from **Mont Faron**.

work running from Fragonard and marine paintings by Vernet up to post-war abstraction and the cartoon-influenced *figuration libre* of Combas and the Di Rosa brothers.

The best way to take in Toulon's exceptional geographic setting is to get some distance from the city proper. For the price of a return bus ticket, hop on a boat crossing to one of the four small towns around the bay. The shuttles sail along the military port, zigzag between mussel farms and, as they move outwards, offer a wonderful view of the city and the hill behind. Along the western shore in industrial **La Seyne-sur-Mer**, Fort Balaguier is where Napoleon completed the capture of Toulon in 1793, a feat honoured in the fort's **Musée Naval**. In **Les Tamaris**, there's contemporary art in the 1890s neo-Moorish **Villa Tamaris Pacha**. **Les Sablettes**, a 1950s resort designed by architect François Pouillon, opens on to a broad sandy beach, perfect for a late afternoon swim. Or follow the coastal path south towards the beach of Mar Vivo and the sweet Fabrégas cove. On a wooded peninsula, the tiny fishing port of **St-Mandrier-sur-Mer** is lined with lively restaurants.

Rising above the town – and lit up like a beacon each night – Mont Faron provides a wonderful escape from the summer heat. It can be reached by car, a nine-kilometre drive (5.5 miles) up the winding Corniche du Mont Faron, or more directly by **Téléferique** cable car from boulevard Amiral Vence (04.94.92.68.25, about every 20mins, open daily July & Aug, closed noon-2pm & Mon Sept-Nov & Feb-June, all Dec & Jan, return €6.20, €4.40 4-10s, free under-4s), which offers spectacular views over the Rade and naval docks. At the summit is the **Zoo du Mont Faron**, with big cats and monkeys, and a 19th-century fortress in which

the **Musée-Mémorial du Débarquement** commemorates the 1944 liberation of Provence (*see p19* **The other D-Day**). Billed as the 'green lung' of Toulon, the pine woods and limestone outcrops of Mont Faron are criss-crossed with footpaths and dotted with picnic tables; there are also two open-air restaurants.

East of the port, Le Mourillon is Toulon's upmarket beach suburb, with colourful old houses and tiny streets packed with shops, restaurants and bars. There's also a morning market on place Emile Claude. Beyond Fort St-Louis, built in the 1690s, the long sandy beaches of Le Mourillon have lawns, play areas and a car park, and are defiantly urban and multicultural. The recently renovated *sentier du Littoral*, once patrolled by Napoleon's customs agents, offers access to the most secret, charming parts of the coast: small sandy beaches and abrupt cliffs topped with 19th-century villas. Two tiny coves, Magaux and Méjean, hide pristine fishing villages, wonderful views and waterside restaurants; Méjean is accessible by car.

From the open greenery of Le Pradet, a footpath leads to more sandy beaches, these ones accessible only to hikers and boaters. The path continues into the woods of Le Bauo Rouge and to the **Musée de la Mine du Cap Garonne**, where you can descend a shaft to experience conditions in a mine from which copper was extracted between 1862 and 1917.

Hôtel des Arts
236 bd du Maréchal Leclerc (04.94.91.69.18/ www.cg83.fr). **Open** (during exhibitions) 11am-6pm Tue-Sun. **Admission** free.

Maison de la Photographie
pl du Globe (04.94.93.07.59). **Open** noon-6pm Tue-Sun. **Admission** free.

The Var

Musée de la Marine

pl Monsenergue (04.94.02.02.01/www.musee-marine.fr). **Open** *Feb, Mar, mid Sept-mid Dec* 10am-noon, 2-6pm Mon, Wed-Sun. *Apr-mid Sept* 10am-6pm daily. Closed mid Dec-Jan. **Admission** €5; €3.50 students under 25; free under-18s. **Credit** MC, V.

Musée de la Mine du Cap Garonne

chemin du Bauo Rouge, Le Pradet (04.94.08.32.46/www.mine-capgaronne.fr). **Open** *July, Aug* 2.30-6pm daily. *Sept-June* 2.30-6pm Wed, Sat, Sun. **Admission** €6.20; €3.80 6-18s, students under 25; free under-5s. **No credit cards.**

Musée des Beaux-Arts

113 bd du Maréchal Leclerc (04.94.36.81.01). **Open** noon-6pm Tue-Sun. **Admission** free.

Musée du Vieux Toulon

69 cours Lafayette (04.94.62.11.07). **Open** 2-5.45pm Mon-Sat. **Admission** free.

Musée-Mémorial du Débarquement

sommet du Mont Faron (04.94.88.08.09). **Open** *July-Sept* 9.45-11.45am, 1.45-5.30pm daily. *Oct-June* 9.45-11.45am, 1.45-4.30pm Tue-Sun. **Admission** €3.80; €1.55 8-16s, students under 25; free under-8s. **No credit cards.**

Musée Naval du Fort Balaguier

924 corniche Bonaparte, La Seyne-sur-Mer (04.94.94.84.72). **Open** *Mid June-mid Sept* 10am-noon, 3-7pm Tue-Sun. *Mid Sept-mid June* 10am-noon, 2-6pm Tue-Sun. **Admission** €3; €2 5-18s, students under 25; free under-5s. **No credit cards.**

Opéra de Toulon

pl Victor Hugo (04.94.92.70.78). **Open** *Box office* 10am-12.30pm, 2.30-5pm Tue-Sat. Closed July, Aug. **Tickets** €16-€59. **Credit** V.

Villa Tamaris Pacha

av de la Grande Maison, La Seyne-sur-Mer (04.94.06.84.00). **Open** (during exhibitions) 2-6.30pm Tue-Sun. **Admission** free.

Zoo du Mont Faron

Mont Faron (04.94.88.07.89). **Open** 10am-7pm daily. Closed on rainy days. **Admission** €8; €5 4-10s; free under-4s. **No credit cards.**

Where to eat & drink

Restaurants along the port specialise in seafood, including mussels raised in the bay. **Restaurant Le Mayol** (462 av de la République, 04.94.41.39.36, closed dinner Sun Sept-June, menus €25.50-€39) is a classic Mediterranean choice, named after opera singer Félix Mayol, who donated the land used for Stade Mayol and was one of Toulon's first out gays. Local dignitaries crowd to **Au Sourd** (10 rue Molière, 04.94.92.28.52, closed Mon & Sun, menu €26), by the opera, for friture with aïoli and fresh fish from Hyères and La Ciotat. Le

Cellier (52 rue Jean-Jaurès, 04.94.92.64.35, closed Sun, menus €25-€32) is perfect for season-fresh Toulon specialities, while the couscous is pure joy at **Sidi Bou Saïd** (43bis rue Jean-Jaurès, 04.94.91.21.23, closed Mon lunch & Sun, average €25), a slightly wild hangout for Toulon's North Africans.

For drinks and billiards, the **113 Café** (113 av Infanterie de Marine, 04.94.03.42.41, restaurant closed Sun, menu €25) is a bar-restaurant in a warehouse near the ferry port, with billiards, live jazz and salsa, and DJs on Friday and Saturday nights. In Le Mourillon, studeny **Bar à Thym** (32 bd Dr Cuneo, 04.94.41.90.10) is a great spot for after-beach beers. It serves tapas and has live music. **Le Navigateur** (128 av de la République, 04.94.92.34.65) is a glitzy bar where DJ Manix heats up the pre-club set.

The most pleasant dining opportunities are found outside the city. In Le Pradet, gourmet provençal cuisine is served in the gardens of **La Chanterelle** (port des Oursinières, 04.94.08.52.60, www.hotel-escapade.com, closed Jan, Feb & Mon Sept-Apr, menus €35-€45). Tucked away in the Magaud cove of Cap Brun, **Restaurant Bernard** (Anse de Magaud, 04.94.27.20.62, closed Sun night & Mon, all Oct-Mar, average €30, reservations necessary) serves very fresh fish in a quasi-luxurious beach shack. Anticipate a steep 15-minute descent from the car park on avenue de la Résistance. **Chez Daniel** (04.94.94.85.13, closed Sun night, Mon & Nov, menus €38-€75), on plage de Fabrégas, is easier to reach but just as peaceful. Locals enjoy bouillabaisse and scrambled eggs with Aups truffles on the huge terrace that overlooks the sea.

Where to stay

Toulon's long-shabby town-centre hotels show signs of improvement. The upgraded **Hôtel Little Palace** (6 rue Berthelot, 04.94.92.26.62, www.hotel-littlepalace.com, double €45-€60) has sparkling rooms, air-conditioning and a great old-town location; it belongs to the same people as the **Hôtel des Trois Dauphins** (9 pl des Trois Dauphins, 04.94.92.65.79, double €30-€40) – ask for a room with WC. Facing the gardens of the Hôtel des Arts, **New Hôtel Amirauté** (4 rue Adolphe Guiol, 04.94.22.19.67, www.new-hotel.com, double €83) is a surprisingly plush, air-conditioned hotel in a 1930s building. The new owners of classic 1960s-style **New Hôtel La Tour Blanche** (bd Amiral Vence, 04.94.24.41.57), built on stilts on the hill next to the Mont Faron cable car, were discussing major renovations as we went to press; phone for up-to-date details and prices.

The Var

Resources

Hospital
Hôpital Font Pré, 1208 av Colonel Picot (04.94.61.61.61).

Internet
Cybercafé Puget, pl Puget (04.94.93.05.54). **Open** 8am-8pm daily.

Police
1 rue Commissaire Morandin (04.98.03.53.00).

Post office
rue Prosper Ferrero (04.94.18.51.00).

Tourist information
Office de Tourisme, 334 av de la République, 83000 Toulon (04.94.18.53.00/www.toulontourisme.com). **Open** *June-Sept* 9am-6pm Mon, Wed-Sat; 10am-6pm Tue; 10am-noon Sun. *Oct-May* 9.30am-5.30pm Mon, Wed-Sat; 10.30am-5.30pm Tue; 10am-noon Sun.

The Western Côte

West of Toulon lie a string of family beach resorts, secluded hill villages and the terraced vineyards of the Bandol appellation, which produce some of the South's finest wines.

Bandol & La Cadière-d'Azur

Today the old port of **Bandol** is a massive grey parking lot, but the old town that fronts the quays is lined with palm trees, cafés and designer swimming gear, while the *ruelles* around 18th-century Eglise St-François-de-Sales buzz with shops and restaurants. The town's main market is held beside the port on Tuesday mornings, and there's a small art market in the same place every night in summer. Westward towards the bay of Renecros are elegant belle-époque homes and terraced vineyards. On the first Sunday in December, vintners bring kegs of their three-month-old baby wines to the port for a public tasting, before putting them to bed in wooden casks for 18 months.

Offshore, tiny **Ile de Bendor**, bought by pastis magnate Paul Ricard in the 1950s, has been heavily cemented with apartments. Its main attraction is the Exposition Universelle des Vins et Spiritueux (04.94.29.44.34, open 10.30am-12.30pm, 3-7pm daily July & Aug; museum closed Wed & Sat morning; gallery closed Tue & Sat morning), comprising 8,000 bottles of alcoholic spirits but, sadly, no tastings. Paul Ricard ferries (06.11.05.91.52) sail hourly from the Embarcadéro in Bandol port.

Inland from Bandol lie the pretty medieval hilltop villages of **La Cadière-d'Azur** and **Le Castellet**, a fortified village once owned by

King René of Provence – ramparts, a stern 15th-century château and a sprinkling of artsy shops remain. Outside the village, Formula One drivers test racing cars at the Circuit Paul Ricard.

The N8 continues east via the grey-stone village of **Ste-Anne-d'Evenos** and winds gently south along the River Reppe through the Gorges d'Ollioules, where steep cliffs are riddled with caves that once hid Gaspard de Besse, bandit-hero of local folklore. **Ollioules** is set amid terraced hills where locals tend olives, vines, citrus fruits and, most importantly, the flowers that end up in the town's wholesale cut-flower market. Ollioules has a normal market on Thursday morning, as well as a farmers' market on Saturdays. Medieval streets climb from the massive 11th-century Romanesque church (open 9am-noon daily) on the main square up to a ruined 13th-century château. In the eastern pine forests, **CNCDC Châteauvallon** was known for its summer dance festival until a mid 1990s run-in with Toulon's right-wing politicos. It now presents a multicultural programme of theatre, dance and music in a stunning open-air amphitheatre (June-Aug) or on an indoor stage.

CNCDC Châteauvallon
794 chemin du Châteauvallon, Ollioules (04.94.22.74.00). **Open** *Box office* 2-7pm Mon; 10am-7pm Tue-Sat. **Tickets** €20; €12 students under 25. **Credit** MC, V.

Where to stay, eat & drink

In Bandol, escape the holiday crowds on the private beach of the **Golf Hôtel** (plage Renécros, bd Lumière, 04.94.29.45.83, www.golfhotel.fr, closed Jan, Feb & 1st 3wks Dec, double €49-€120), once the casino. The low-key restaurant (average €20), also on the beach, is a good place to stroll into for lunch. A few streets back from the port, calm **Hôtel L'Oasis** (15 rue des Ecoles, 04.94.29.41.69, www.oasisbandol.com, closed Dec, double €53-€72) is a former parsonage. White linen tablecloths flap in the sea breeze at **Auberge du Port** (9 allée Jean Moulin, 04.94.29.42.63, menus €38-€48), a chic and lively brasserie.

In La Cadière, **Hostellerie Bérard** (av Gabriel Péri, 04.94.90.11.43, www.hotel-berard.com, closed Jan, double €83-€256) groups several ancient houses and an 11th-century convent together, overlooking the vineyards. In keeping with the quietly beautiful hotel, chef René Bérard serves simple but superlative provençal fare in the restaurant (closed lunch Mon & Sat, menus €45-€130). Tearoom **Le Petit Jardin** (also part of the hotel: walk down the stairs at 17 av Gabriel Péri; closed lunch Tue & Wed, average €30)

La Table du Vigneron.

serves light provençal dishes on a veranda with a panoramic view. In Ste-Anne-d'Evenos, Mme Dutheil de La Rochère offers *chambres d'hôte* at the **Château-Ste-Anne** vineyard (04.94.90.35.40, closed Oct, double €96); there's a pool under the olive trees. **Hôtel du Castellet** (3001 rte des Hauts du Camp, Le Beausset, 04.94.98.38.88, www.hotelducastellet. com, double €260-€500; restaurant closed lunch Mon, menus €65-€90) at the Circuit Paul Ricard is a luxury pit stop for racing teams and their fans – you can park your private jet at the adjoining aerodrome. Lost in the rolling hills surrounding Ollioules, **La Table du Vigneron** (724 chemin de la Tourelle, 04.94.88.36.19, www.latableduvigneron.com, closed Mon, dinner Sun & Feb, menu €45) does good seasonal cooking and offers tastings of its Domaine de Terrebrune wines.

Resources

Internet

Boss Cyber Café, 9 rue des Ecoles, Bandol (04.94.29.03.03). **Open** *July-mid Sept* 9am-1pm, 3-9.30pm Mon-Sat. *Mid Sept-June* 9am-1pm, 3-8pm Mon-Sat.

Tourist information

Bandol *Maison du Tourisme, allée Vivien, 83150 Bandol (04.94.29.41.35/www.bandol.fr).* **Open** *July, Aug* 9am-7pm daily. *Sept-June* 9am-noon, 2-6pm Mon-Fri; 9am-noon Sat.

Ollioules *Office du Tourisme, 116 av Philippe de Hautecloque, 83190 Ollioules (04.94.63.11.74/ www.ollioules.com).* **Open** *July, Aug* 9am-1pm, 4-7pm Mon-Sat. *Sept-June* 9am-noon, 2-6pm Mon-Sat.

Sanary-sur-Mer to Six-Fours

Colourful boats bob beside the quay and fishermen still sew sardine nets along the palm-lined port of **Sanary-sur-Mer**. Surely little has changed since the 1930s when Sanary was the refuge of Thomas Mann, Lion Feuchtwanger, Stefan Zweig and other German intellectuals escaping the Nazi regime. Aldous Huxley also lived here, and a young Sybille Bedford records the period in *Jigsaw*. At the western end of the port, in a 13th-century tower, the **Musée Frédéric Dumas** houses ancient diving equipment and wine amphorae – Frédéric was one of Cousteau's original 'Mousque-mers'. On hot mornings in Sanary, market vendors hawk their wares in a frenzy that competes with the seagulls; there's a daily produce market, and a flea market on the last Saturday of each month.

On the wind-battered Sicie peninsula, **Six-Fours-les-Plages** is a string of modern beach bars and restaurants, with a Saturday morning market. When the Mistral blows, angry waves make the so-called 'Brutal Beach' a surfers' paradise. On a hill to the north, the **Collégiale St-Pierre**, spanning the Romanesque and Gothic periods, is all that remains of the original village. About three kilometres (two

The Var

miles) further north, the sixth-century Chapelle Notre-Dame-de-Pepiole (open 3-6pm daily) is one of France's oldest Christian churches.

The modern beach resort of **Le Brusc** is on the site of the port of Tauroentium, founded by Phocean Greeks from Marseille; today most visitors stay only long enough to get a ferry (04.94.10.65.21) to the **Iles des Embiez**, former salt-panning islands bought by Paul Ricard in 1958. The main island houses the Institut Océanographique Paul Ricard, a research centre into Mediterranean pollution, and offers miles of footpaths and cycle tracks; bikes can be hired on the quay. If you do linger in Le Brusc, there's a market on Thursday mornings.

Collégiale St-Pierre

montée du Fort Militaire, Six-Fours-les-Plages (04.94.34.24.75). **Open** *June-Sept* 10am-noon, 3-7pm Mon, Wed-Sun. *Oct-May* 10am-noon, 2-6pm Mon, Wed-Sun. **Admission** free.

Musée Frédéric Dumas

pl de la Tour, Sanary-sur-Mer (04.94.74.80.23). **Open** *July-Aug* 10am-12.30pm, 4-7.30pm daily. *Sept-June* 10am-12.30pm, 3-6.30pm Sat, Sun. **Admission** free.

Where to eat, drink & stay

The **Hôtel-Restaurant de la Tour** (24 quai Général de Gaulle, 04.94.74.10.10, double €72-€94), on the port in Sanary, has pleasantly ageing rooms and a restaurant (closed Tue, Wed & Dec, lunch menus €20-€30, dinner menus €30-€44) serving gourmet seafood. **Restaurant L'enK** (13 rue Louis Blanc, 04.94.74.66.57, closed dinner Mon Nov-June, menu €27) produces regional dishes with exotic flair. Sanary also has a thriving bar scene: start at tiny **Café Mac'Sym's** (10 quai de Gaulle, 04.94.74.45.34) before going clubbing at **Mai-Tai** (1370 rte de Bandol, 04.94.74.23.92, open Fri & Sat only).

In Six-Fours-les-Plages, the Blussets have converted their restaurant into the breezier **Bistro du Dauphin** (36 pl des Bains, plage de Bonnegrace, 04.94.07.61.58, www.restaurant-ledauphin.com, closed Feb, Mon, dinner Thur & Sun, menus €17-€27), offering inspired cooking at moderate prices. After shopping at the local market, the chef chalks up daily specials on blackboards: lots of fish, regional meat dishes (such as tripe or calf's head), and a few adventurous sweet-savoury combinations.

In Le Brusc, family institution **St-Pierre** (47 rue de la Citadelle, 04.94.34.02.52, closed lunch Mon July & Aug, dinner Sun & all Mon Sept-June, all Jan, menus €18-€33.50, reservations necessary) serves grilled fish and an excellent bouillabaisse.

Resources

Internet

Cyber Espace @ Fenyx, 8 rue Lauzet Aîné, Sanary-sur-Mer (04.94.88.10.78). **Open** *Jan-June, Sept-Dec* 10.30am-1pm, 3-7pm Wed, Fri, Sat; 3-7pm Sun. *July, Aug* 10.30am-1pm, 3-11pm daily.

Tourist information

Sanary *Maison du Tourisme, Les Jardins de la Ville, 83110 Sanary-sur-Mer (04.94.74.01.04/ www.sanarysurmer.com).* **Open** *Jan-Apr, Nov, Dec* 9am-noon, 2-5.30pm Mon-Fri; 9am-noon, 2-5pm Sat. *May-June, Sept-Oct* 9am-noon, 2-6pm Mon-Fri; 9am-noon, 2-5pm Sat. *July, Aug* 9am-7pm Mon-Sat; 9am-noon Sun.

Six-Fours *Office du Tourisme, promenade Charles de Gaulle, 83140 Six-Fours-les-Plages (04.94.07.02.21/ www.six-fours-les-plages.com).* **Open** *Apr-June, Sept* 9am-noon, 2-6.30pm Mon-Sat. *July, Aug* 9am-1pm, 2-7pm Mon-Sat; 10am-1pm Sun. *Oct-Mar* 8.45am-noon, 2-5.30pm Mon-Fri; 9am-noon, 2-5.30pm Sat.

Getting there & around

By air

Toulon-Hyères airport is 35km (22 miles) from the city centre.

By boat

Boat services (www.reseaumistral.com) run from Toulon port to La Seyne, Les Sablettes, Tamaris and St-Mandrier. Toulon is also a ferry port to Corsica (www.corsicaferries.com).

By bus

Société des Cars et Autobus de Cassis (04.42.73.29.29) runs six buses a day between Marseille and Bandol. **Littoral Cars** (04.94.74.01.35) runs buses between Bandol and Sanary, Le Brusc, Six-Fours, La Seyne and Toulon. **RMTT** (04.94.03.87.03, www.reseaumistral.com) runs buses from Toulon to Ollioules, La Seyne and Sanary, and runs an extensive network of buses within Toulon (Nos.3, 13 and 23 go to the beaches at Mourillon; No.40 to the cable car). **Sodétrav** (08.25.000.650) runs a bus service between Toulon and Hyères.

By car

The A50 from Marseille in the west and the A57 from the east pour traffic directly into the centre of Toulon. After decades of work, a cross-city tunnel linking the two opened in 2003 – but only in one direction. Leave the A50 at exit 12 for Bandol, exit 13 for Six-Fours-les-Plages, Sanary-sur-Mer and Ollioules and exit 14 for Châteauvallon. The coastal D559 goes between Cannes and Toulon via Bandol and Sanary.

By train

Toulon is on the main TGV line from Paris and is also served by commuter trains from Marseille and Nice. Local trains between Marseille and Toulon stop at Bandol and Sanary-Ollioules.

Hyères to Les Maures

Take a breath of fresh air down on the perfect beaches, then another high in the rugged hills.

If it's unspoilt sandy beaches you want, you've come to the right place: the pristine strands along the coast from Hyères to Cavalaire are among France's finest. Inland, the wild Maures mountains offer respite from the summer crowds and heat. Ravaged by the 2003 forest fires, they are now (more or less) green again.

Hyères & Giens

Palmy Hyères led the seaside brigade in the 19th century, when its mild climate was recommended for the consumptive. It was particularly favoured by the British: Queen Victoria paid a visit in 1892. But when the fashionable season changed from winter to summer, Hyères, perched up on a hill five kilometres (three miles) from the sea, was left high and dry. Today the grand hotels have all gone, holidaymakers remain firmly on the seaside strip and the busy, multiracial town lives by salt, cut flowers and date-palm rearing as much as tourism.

Hyères's medieval *vieille ville* is reached at the end of avenue Gambetta, the main drag leading up from the coast, or through the fortified Porte Massillon. Stop at the **Biscuiterie Ré** at 8 rue Liman to stock up on traditional provençal biscuits and own-made fig ice-cream. The rue Massillon, busy with food shops, leads to café-filled place Massillon, where the much-restored, barrel-vaulted **Tour St-Blaise**, now used for exhibitions, is all that remains of a Templar monastery. Climb the steps from the square and take steep rue Ste-Catherine to the **Collégiale St-Paul**, with its medieval bell tower and Renaissance doorway; the front room is crowded with naïve ex-voto paintings. On place de la République, the 13th-century **Eglise St-Louis** (open 8am-7pm daily) was once a Franciscan monastery where Louis IX prayed in 1254 on his return from the Crusades.

Climb up above the church for Hyères's most compelling sight, the **Villa Noailles**, a masterpiece of Modernist architecture, all horizontal lines and Cubist stained glass, designed in 1924 by Robert Mallet-Stevens for avant-garde aristos Charles and Marie-Laure de Noailles. In its day, it was the scene of trysts and parties frequented by A-list bohemians including Picasso, Stravinsky, Buñuel and

Man Ray, who shot part of his film *Les Mystères du Château de Dé* here. The house was restored by the municipality in the 1990s and is now used for contemporary art and design exhibitions. Continue up the montée de Noailles to the ruins of the 11th- to 13th-century castle of the Lords of Fos, surrounded by the **Parc St-Bernard** and the equally lush **Parc Ste-Claire** (both open 8am-7pm daily summer, 8am-5pm daily winter), around the 19th-century castle once lived in by Edith Wharton.

The charms of the modern town are distinctly faded and marred by an appalling one-way system, but, near the town hall on avenue Joseph Clotis, fine belle-époque houses have become arty restaurants and tearooms, and the **Casino des Palmiers** still supplies a touch of glamour. The **Musée Municipal** on place Lefebvre contains furniture, archaeological finds and local paintings. On avenue Ambroise Thomas, the **Jardins Olbius Riquier** (open 7.30am-dusk daily) has subtropical gardens, a hothouse and a mini zoo around a pseudo-Moorish villa. Sticking up on the Costebelle hill is the pierced concrete tower of **Eglise Notre-Dame-de-la-Consolation**, which replaced an ancient church bombed in World War II.

Beach territory below the town runs either side of a long, narrow isthmus. To the east, the Plage d'Hyères is a long, over-charged stretch of sand running from the busy marina along the Rade d'Hyères bay. In the Almanarre district to the west, the **Site Archéologique d'Olbia** bears fragmentary traces of the Greek trading post of Olbia, along with Roman homes and baths and part of a medieval abbey. Jutting out between the two, the pretty though built-up **Giens** peninsula is the southernmost tip of the French Riviera. On its west side, the four-kilometre (2.5-mile) **Almanarre beach** hosts heats of the world windsurfing championships. Between here and **La Capte** beach (a long, narrow stretch of sand, perfect for children) lies the disused Etang des Pesquiers salt pans, liable to flooding in winter. On summer afternoons after 5pm, the two narrow *départementale* roads accessing the beaches have some of the worst car jams around.

At the end of the isthmus is the hilltop village of **Giens** proper. Place Belvédère hosts a market on Tuesday morning and affords fantastic views. Escape the gaping throngs by hiking down the *sentier des douaniers*, which winds through the backyards of Giens's hotels to rocky little **Port de Niel**. Locals come here to picnic or to dine on ultra-fresh fish at the excellent Poisson Rouge (*see below*).

Boats leave for the islands from **La Tour Fondue**, a squat 17th-century fortress built by Cardinal Richelieu.

Casino des Palmiers

1 av Ambroise Thomas, Hyères (04.94.12.80.80). **Open** (slot machines) 10am-4am daily; (gaming rooms) 8.30pm-4am daily. **Admission** (over-18s only, bring ID) €10 gaming rooms; free for slot machines. **Credit** AmEx, DC, MC, V.

Collégiale St-Paul

pl St-Paul, Hyères (04.94.65.83.30). **Open** *May-Sept* 10am-noon, 4-7pm Mon, Wed-Sun. *Oct-Apr* 10am-noon, 2-5.30pm Wed-Sun. **Admission** free.

Musée Municipal

Rotonde du Parc Hôtel, entrance on av Foch, Hyères (04.94.00.78.42). **Open** *May-Sept* 10am-noon, 4-7pm Mon, Wed-Sun. *Oct-Apr* 10am-noon, 2-5.30pm Mon. **Admission** free.

Site Archéologique d'Olbia

quartier de l'Almanarre, Hyères (04.94.57.98.28/www.monum.fr). **Open** *Apr-Sept* 9.30am-12.30pm, 3-6.30pm daily. Closed Oct-Mar. **Admission** €4.60; €3.10 students; free under-18s. **No credit cards**.

Villa Noailles. See p187.

Villa Noailles

montée de Noailles, Hyères (04.98.08.01.98). **Open** *Mid July-mid Sept* 10am-noon, 4-8pm Mon, Wed-Sun. *Oct-mid July* 10am-noon, 2-5.30pm Wed-Sun. **Admission** free.

Where to stay & eat

Hyères lacks the stylish accommodation of its elegant past. **Hôtel de Portalet** (4 rue de Limans, www.hotel-portalet.com, 04.94.65.39.40, double €39-€56), in the old town, is simple but clean. Overlooking La Gavine port, friendly **La Potinière** (27 av de la Méditerranée, 04.94.00.51.60, www.hotel-lapotiniere.com, closed mid Jan-mid Feb, double €55-€98) has large rooms and a private beach. La Capte is dotted with campsites and mostly downmarket hotels. The best choice is the **Hôtel Ibis Thalassa** (allée de la Mer, 04.94.58.00.94, www.thalassa.com, closed 3wks Jan, double €60-€125), a modern building with gardens, a restaurant, direct access to the spa and a private beach.

Deep in the *vieille ville*, **Bistrot de Marius** (1 pl Massillon, 04.94.35.88.38, closed Mon, Tue, mid Nov-mid Dec & mid Jan-mid Feb, menus €17-€30) serves authentic provençal cuisine on tables spilling out on to the square. Reserve for bouillabaisse. For a lighter meal or a choice of exotic teas, try **L'Eau à la Bouche** (2 pl Massillon, 04.94.35.33.85), on the opposite side of the square. In the modern town, **Le Jardin de Sadaram** (35 av de Belgique, 04.94.65.97.53, closed Mon & dinner Sun, menus €15-€18.50) serves couscous and tagines in a garden chock-full of plants, birds, bric-a-brac and unmatching chairs. Reserve for fish couscous or pigeon pastilla. Much more formal **Les Jardins de Bacchus** (32 av Gambetta, 04.94.65.77.63, www.les-jardins-de-bacchus.com, closed lunch Sat, dinner Sun, all Mon, 2wks Jan, June, menus €31-€51) does good contemporary provençal fare. On La Capte beach, **Le Paddock** (no phone, open till dusk daily), a café that boaters and jetskiers like to sail in to, is good for a drink in the tangy sea air.

In Giens, the **Provençal** (pl St-Pierre, 04.98.04.54.54, www.provencalhotel.com, closed Nov-Mar, double €80-€125) has (totally renovated) 1950s charm, a pool and terraced gardens that descend right to the sea. The **Tire Bouchon** (1 pl St-Pierre, 04.94.58.24.61, closed Wed, 2wks Oct & mid Dec-mid Jan, menus €25-€32) offers traditional provençal cooking in dowdy surroundings with breathtaking views. In the tiny cove of Port de Niel, **Le Poisson Rouge** (04.94.58.92.33, closed dinner Sun & Jan, menus €15-€45) serves fish (and clients) straight off the boat.

Resources

Internet

Maison de l'Internet, rue Soldat Bellon (04.94.65.92.82). **Open** 9am-12.30pm, 2-5pm Mon-Fri.

Tourist information

Office de Tourisme, 3 av Ambroise Thomas, 83412 Hyères (04.94.01.84.50/www.ot-hyeres.fr). **Open** *July, Aug* 8.30am-7.30pm daily. *Sept-June* 9am-6pm Mon-Fri; 10am-4pm Sat.

Iles de Hyères: Porquerolles, Port-Cros, Ile de Levant

Robert Louis Stevenson supposedly found inspiration for *Treasure Island* on the **Ile de Porquerolles**, the largest of the three islands strung across the entrance to Hyères bay. Colonised in the fifth century by the monks of Lérins (*see p239*), the islands were seized by the Saracens in 1160. The latter were turfed out by Francis I, who fortified Porquerolles with the Fort du Petit-Langoustier and the Fort Ste-Agathe, which looms over the yacht marina. Up the hill from the port, Porquerolles village was built as a retirement colony for Napoleonic officers and still resembles a colonial outpost, centred on place d'Armes, with its pungent eucalyptus trees. Here you'll find plenty of cafés, as well as stalls where you can get in supplies for a picnic. For 60 years from 1911, the village was the private property of Belgian engineer Joseph Fournier, who introduced the exotic flora. Full of well-dressed *BCBGs* (French Sloanes) cycling *en famille*, Porquerolles still feels privileged today. There are numerous bike hire outlets in both port and village. But you don't need two wheels to get to the white sand and lush backdrop of the Plage d'Argent (west) or Plage de la Courtade (east), each an easy ten- to 15-minute walk from the village through pine woods. Forest tracks lead to the more mountainous southern half of the island and the lighthouse of the Cap d'Arme; note that these may be closed during high winds in summer due to fire risk.

The lush and hilly **Ile de Port-Cros** is a nature reserve. No cars are permitted on the island, and no smoking is allowed. There are nature paths here that extend under the sea, enabling swimmers and divers to look at the lovely marine flora.

Eighty per cent of the **Ile du Levant** is still military property, though no longer a shooting range. The remaining area, Héliopolis, is a nudist colony where participating visitors, as opposed to voyeurs, are welcome.

Where to stay & eat

On Porquerolles, **Le Mas du Langoustier** (04.94.58.30.09, closed Nov-Apr, double €173-€2,997 per person, including dinner & breakfast), a short drive west of the port, has luxurious rooms, beautiful gardens, fabulous fish and a snooty reputation. Guests are met at the ferries by a minibus. Most charming of the hotels in the village is **Les Glycines** (22 pl d'Armes, 04.94.58.30.36, double €109-€269, menu €21.90), with lovely rooms in provençal hues. Bar-restaurant **L'Oustaou** (pl d'Armes, 04.94.58.30.13, www.oustaou.com, double €95-€160, menu €14.50-€22) serves pasta or plats du jour like squid cooked in its ink, and also has six rooms, some with sea views. On Port-Cros, **Le Manoir d'Hélène** (04.94.05.90.52, closed Oct-Mar, double €135-€195 per person, including dinner & breakfast) has white turrets and calm, beautiful rooms. The restaurant serves provençal classics (menus €40-€45). On the port, the family-run **Hostellerie Provençale** (04.94.05.90.43, www.hostellerie-provencale.com, closed mid Nov-Feb, double €89-€99, including dinner & breakfast) has five comfortable rooms and a cheerful restaurant.

Ferry services

There are frequent ferries in July and August; more limited services the rest of the year. **TLV** (04.94.58.21.81, www.tlv-tvm.com) runs ferries from La Tour Fondue in Giens to Porquerolles (takes 20mins, €15 return, €13.50 4-10s, free under-4s) and from Hyères to Port-Cros and Levant (takes 60-90mins, €22 return, €19.30 4-10s, free under-4s). **Vedettes Iles d'Or** (04.94.71.01.02, www.vedettesilesdor.fr) runs boats from Le Lavandou to Port-Cros and Levant (takes 35-60mins, €22 return, €18.20 4-12s, free under-4s). There are also daily services to Porquerolles and Port-Cros from Cavalaire and to Porquerolles from Toulon in summer.

Bormes-les-Mimosas

Set above the coast in the hills, the old village of **Bormes-les-Mimosas** is a picturesque clutter of colour-washed houses where sun terraces point to contemporary preoccupations but covered passages (*cuberts*) and vaulted interiors betray medieval origins. The floral handle was added to the name in 1968, to emphasise the point that Bormes had the highest density of these scented, yellow, puffball-bearing trees on the Riviera. Mimosa blooms January to March; the rest of the year, beautifully planted terraces drip with creepers and bougainvillea. On the edge of the old village, next to the Wednesday marketplace, the **Chapelle St-François** was built in 1560 in thanks to St François de Paule, who delivered the village from the plague in 1481. Place Gambetta, with its cafés and restaurants, leads into the main street, rue Carnot, from where you can wander down streets like ruelle du Moulin, venelle des Amoureux and the 83 steps of rue Rompi Cuou, or up to the remains of the medieval castle of the Lords of Fos (closed to the public). The 18th-century **Eglise St-Trophime** contains some curious polychrome wood saints' reliquaries as well as trompe-l'oeil frescoes round the choir. Further down the hill, the **Musée d'Art et d'Histoire** has some Rodin sketches plus local paintings and history. Bormes's beach suburb of **La Favière** is a modern but inoffensive low-rise development with marina, diving club, plenty of shops for swimgear and picnic fare, and a long, family-oriented sandy public beach.

The *sentier du littoral* coast path (waymarked in yellow) winds round the peninsula. Apart from the small hamlet of Cabasson and the heavily guarded 16th-century Fort de Brégançon (the French president's official summer retreat), **Cap Bénat**, which juts out south-west of Bormes, is one of the least built-up stretches of coast in the Midi. Here there's no urban sprawl, nor even any luxury villas, just the **Château de Brégançon**, source of a robust Côtes de Provence wine (*see p36*), woods, vineyards and a number of unspoiled beaches (you pay for the car park, but entrance is free). West of Brégançon, the **Plage de l'Estagnol** (parking €7-€8 Apr-Oct) is a lovely sandy strip shaded by pine woods, with shallow water, a café and a good fish restaurant (*see below*).

Musée d'Art et d'Histoire de Bormes

103 rue Carnot (04.94.71.56.60). **Open** 10am-noon, 2.30-5pm Tue-Sat; 10am-noon Sun. **Admission** free.

Where to stay & eat

Bormes Village offers the best gastronomic choices in the area; indeed, on summer evenings the village becomes one large dining room. Stylish **Restaurant La Tonnelle** (23 pl Gambetta, 04.94.71.34.84, closed Wed, lunch July-Aug, mid Nov-end Dec, menus €27-€42) is a true discovery thanks to the inventive cooking of chef Gilles Renard. At bustling **Hôtel-Restaurant La Bellevue** (14 pl Gambetta, 04.94.71.15.15, closed mid Nov-mid Jan, double €39-€50, menus €14-€21), families devour polenta, mussels, roast rabbit and ice-cream; the view *is* beautiful. Across the street, friendly **Café Le Progrès** (04.94.71.15.36) is a

good place for a drink or a dish of moules-frites. Atmospheric **Lou Portaou** (rue Cubert des Poètes, 04.94.64.86.37, closed Tue & mid Nov-mid Dec, menu €39), in a medieval tower, changes its market menu daily and is always full, so be sure to book ahead. Two of the best restaurants in Bormes face each other on the same tiny street: **La Cassole** (1 ruelle du Moulin, 04.94.71.14.86, closed lunch June-Aug, dinner Sun & Mon Sept-May, Nov-mid Dec, menus €26-€50) serves serious provençal classics in a cosy dining room and tiny courtyard with a view. **L'Escoundudo** (2 ruelle du Moulin, 04.94.71.15.53, closed Tue, 2wks Dec, Feb, menus €58-€78) has more modern decor; chefs Mathias and Fabien Dandine use fresh local produce to create lovely, authentic dishes. Near the sea, **Hôtel de la Plage** (rond-point de la Bienvenue, La Favière, 04.94.71.02.74, closed Oct-Mar, double €46-€70) has been run by the same matronly management since the 1960s (average age of staff about 70). Rooms are spotless with balconies or terraces. In Cabasson **Les Palmiers** (240 chemin du Petit Fort, 04.94.64.81.94, www.hotel-palmiers.com, closed mid Nov-mid Feb, double €80-€250, half-board obligatory July-Sept, menus €28-€45) is resolutely provincial but reliable; it has steps to the beach. At **Plage de l'Estagnol**, the animated restaurant (04.94.64.71.11, closed Oct-Mar, average €40) serves superb fish and langoustines grilled on a wood fire and big vats of bouillabaisse. Reserve for dinner, when you'll have the beach to yourself.

Resources

Bormes market is Wednesday morning. La Favière has a market on Saturday morning and Monday evening in July and August.

Tourist information

Office de Tourisme, 1 pl Gambetta, 83230 Bormes-les-Mimosas (04.94.01.38.38/www.bormeslesmimosas.com). **Open** *Apr-Sept* 9am-12.30pm, 2.30-6.30pm daily. *May-Oct* 9am-12.30pm, 1.30-5.30pm Mon-Sat. **Other locations**: La Favière, bd du Front de Mer (04.94.64.82.57); Maison de Bormes, 2273 av Lou Mistraou, Pin de Bormes (04.94.00.43.43).

Le Lavandou to Cavalaire

Le Lavandou hugs the coast east of Bormes. A concreted promenade and a couple of tower blocks hide a pretty old town, behind what was once a major fishing port, now a pleasure marina. Its glitzy seafront is animated at night. By day, the main beach gets very crowded, though the quieter, more steeply shelving Plage St-Clair further east in a bay surrounded by mountains is more attractive for bathing.

From here to Cavalaire-sur-Mer, the **Corniche des Maures** follows some of the coast's most unspoiled scenery, the view uphill from silver-sand beaches unimpeded by development. Cap Nègre and the Plage de Pramousquier were key points of the 1944 Allied landings (*see p19* **The other D-Day**).

The village of Le Rayol-Canadel is home to the fabulous **Domaine du Rayol** gardens, created in 1910 by Paris banker Alfred Courmes, who packed the grounds with exotic plants before losing all his money in the crash of 1929. Since 1989, gardening wizard Gilles Clément has added New Zealand and Asiatic gardens and a 'Garden in Motion'. Gullies, bowers and secret paths are dotted about this jungle of green and dramatic vistas and seaside drops. Buy the guided-walk leaflet, which leads you on a treasure hunt for bottlebrushes, blackboys and other unusual species. Outdoor concerts are held in July and August. Above Le Rayol-Canadel, spectacular sea views can be had from the Col du Canadel pass, which crosses over into the heart of the Maures. The idyll comes to a halt at **Cavalaire-sur-Mer**, a built-up sprawl with a long unglamorous beach.

Domaine du Rayol

av des Belges, Le Rayol-Canadel (04.98.04.44.00/ www.domainedurayol.org). **Open** *July, Aug* 9.30am-8pm daily. *Sept-June* 9.30am-12.30pm, 2.30-6.30pm daily. Closed Jan. **Admission** €7; €3.50 6-18s; €4 students; free under-6s. **Credit** MC, V.

Where to stay & eat

In Le Lavandou, the pseudo-Moorish façade of the **Auberge de la Calanque** (62 av du Général de Gaulle, 04.94.71.05.96, closed Oct-Easter, double €140-€255, restaurant closed Wed lunch, Thur, menu €32) hides a handsome

modern interior done in shades of white and blue. The restaurant, the garden and all the rooms overlook the sea; the most expensive rooms have large private terraces. By the Vieux Port, simpler **Hôtel Le Rabelais** (2 rue Rabelais, 04.94.71.00.56, www.le-rabelais. fr, closed mid Nov-mid Jan, double €60-€85) has recently redecorated rooms, some with a balcony. Pick of the fish restaurants overlooking the port is **Restaurant du Vieux-Port** (quai Gabriel Péri, 04.94.71.00.21, closed Tue, Wed & mid Nov-Feb, menus €23). Seafront eateries in St-Clair tend more towards pizza, mussels and atmosphere than great cuisine. An upmarket exception is **Les Tamaris** (chez Raymond, Plage de St-Clair, 04.94.71.07.22, closed Nov-mid Feb except 1wk at Christmas, average €40), which offers excellent fish dishes, including bourride. Luxurious **Hôtel Les Roches** (1 av des Trois Dauphins, plage d'Aiguebelle, 04.94.71.05.07, www.hotellesroches.com, closed Jan-Mar, double €240-€1,380, menus €71-€92) plunges down the cliff to the sea, and has a chic bar, antiques-furnished rooms and half-seawater pool. A short walk away, at **Le Sud** (av des Trois Dauphins, 04.94.05.76.98, closed Jan, lunch Mon-Sat in July & Aug, menu €59), brilliant chef Christophe Petra, a Bocuse disciple, changes his six-course menu every two weeks. At the time of writing, he was serving pumpkin and truffle lasagna, lobster risotto, and pigeon in a foie gras, cabbage and truffle crust. Expect lunch to last about three and a half hours.

In Le Rayol-Canadel, **Le Maurin des Maures** (bd de Touring Club, 04.94.05.60.11, closed dinner mid Nov-mid Dec, menus €13-€26.50) is always packed, as much for the fantastic atmosphere as local youngsters pile in for *babyfoot*, as for the fresh fish and provençal faves. Be sure to reserve. Overlooking the beach below the Domaine de Rayol, lovely **Hôtel**

Auberge de la Calanque.

Le Bailli de Suffren (av des Américains, 04.98.04.47.00, www.lebaillidesuffren.com, closed mid Oct-Easter, double €160-€392, menus €35-€70) is a curved 1960s building, renovated in calm, modern provençal-chic style. It has a bar, restaurant, private beach and boats available for hire.

Resources

Le Lavandou has a huge market on Thursday morning; Cavalaire's is Wednesday morning.

Internet

BPC Informatique, Résidence la Santa Cruz, av Ilaires (04.94.05.65.21). **Open** 9am-12.30pm, 2.30-7pm Tue-Sat.

Tourist information

Cavalaire *Office de Tourisme, Maison de la Mer, 83240 Cavalaire-sur-Mer (04.94.01.92.10/www. golfe-info.com/cavalaire).* **Open** *Mid June-mid Sept* 9am-7pm daily. *Mid Sept-mid June* 9am-12.30pm, 2-6pm Mon-Fri; 9am-12.30pm Sat.

Le Lavandou *Office de Tourisme, quai Gabriel Péri, 83980 Le Lavandou (04.94.00.40.50/www. lelavandou.com).* **Open** *May-Sept* 9am-12.30pm, 3-7pm daily. *Oct-Apr* 9am-noon, 3-6.30pm Mon-Sat.

The Massif des Maures

Taking the D41 out of Bormes to Collobrières, you are at once in a surprisingly feral mountain area with a hair-raisingly tortuous road that zigzags up to the Col du Babaou. The heart of the Massif, dotted with remote chapels and Neolithic menhirs, can only be reached on foot. It is crossed east–west by the GR9 and GR51 footpaths and north–south by the GR90. For the less ambitious, two short waymarked discovery footpaths leave from near the Office de Tourisme in Collobrières (*see p193*), which also organises four themed guided walks.

Surrounded by massive chestnut trees and the cork oak trees from which cork is hewn, **Collobrières** is Provence's chestnut capital. The **Confiserie Azuréenne** (bd Général Koenig, 04.94.48.07.20) sells marrons glacés and everything imaginable made with chestnuts, including soup, tea and ice-cream. Around 1850 Collobrières was an important logging centre, and 19th-century wood barons' houses contrast with higgledy-piggledy medieval streets. A ten-minute drive east, off the D14 to Cogolin, the isolated **Chartreuse de La Verne** looms like a fortress halfway up a remote hillside. Founded by a group of Carthusian monks in 1170, it was burned on several occasions in the Wars of Religion and rebuilt each time in a mix of brown-grey schist and local dark-green serpentine facing around doorways and vaults. After the Revolution the monks fled to Nice

from the Plage St-Clair. Restoration began in the 1970s and since 1983 the monastery has been occupied by a community of nuns.

Further east, picture-perfect *village perché* **Grimaud** was a Saracen stronghold before falling to the Templars. From the ruins of the 11th-century chateau at the top, there's a panoramic view of a starkly contrasting landscape – here the somber Maures mountains meet St-Tropez, with its brightly coloured villas, flashing lights and yacht-filled bay.

Reached through the cork woods north of here, **La Garde-Freinet** is a lively stopping-off point where the main street, rue St-Jacques, and place Vieille abound with bistros, *brocantes* and designer gifts, and a superb old-fashioned *quincaillerie* (hardware store). Beyond the solid 15th- to 18th-century church, rue de la Planète is the start of an energetic climb to the ruins of the abandoned original village, inhabited until the 15th century, allegedly built on the foundations of a Saracen stronghold. The **Conservatoire du Patrimoine** in the same building as the tourist office has a display about the fortress and exhibitions on local heritage and pastimes. Further west on the northern side of the Massif, near Gonfaron, the **Village des Tortues** is a conservation centre for Hermann's tortoise, found only in the Maures and in Corsica.

A busy crossroads between the Maures and St-Tropez, **Cogolin** wins no prizes for beauty, but it does qualify as a real town with an economy based around the manufacture of corks, briar pipes, bamboo furniture and carpet-making (the latter introduced by Armenian immigrants in the 1920s). Its claim to fame is the invention of the *tarte tropézienne*, a sweet brioche filled with cream, now popular throughout the region. The **Tarte Tropézienne**

World windsurfing championship. *See p187.*

pastry shop (510 av des Narcisses, 04.94.43.41.20) still prepares it according to the original recipe patented in the 1950s by Polish baker Alexandre Micka. The 11th-century church of St-Sauveur (open 8am-7pm daily) has a lovely 16th-century altarpiece by Hurlupin.

Chartreuse de La Verne

off D214 (04.94.43.45.41). Open Apr-Sept 11am-6pm Mon, Wed-Sun. *Oct-Mar* 11am-5pm Mon, Wed-Sun. Closed Jan. **Admission** €5; €3 10-16s; free under-10s. **No credit cards**.

Conservatoire du Patrimoine et des Traditions du Freinet

Chapelle St-Jean, 1 pl Neuve, La Garde-Freinet (04.94.43.08.57). **Open** 10am-12.30pm, 3-6pm Tue-Sat. **Admission** €2; free under-12s. **No credit cards**.

Village des Tortues

rte des Mayons, Gonfaron (04.94.78.26.41/www.tortues.com). **Open** *Mar-Nov* 9am-7pm daily. **Admission** €9; €6 3-16s; free under-3s. **Credit** V.

Where to stay & eat

In Collobrières, **Hôtel-Restaurant Notre-Dame** (15 av de la Libération, 04.94.48.07.13, closed Dec-mid Feb, double €33, restaurant closed Tue, menus €16-€25) is a simple Logis de France overhanging a stream. **Camping Municipal St-Roch** (closed Sept-June, €2.60 caravan/tent, €2.20 adult, €1.70 under-7s) is set on leafy terraces high above the village. For a truly rustic experience, sample the **Ferme de Peigros** (Col de Babaou, 04.94.48.03.83, lunch only, menu €22) down a track by the Col du Babaou pass, which produces its own goat's cheese. In La Garde-Freinet, **La Claire Fontaine** (pl Vieille, 04.94.43.63.76, double €40-€50, restaurant closed Sept-Mar, menus €16-€22) is a busy café and ice-cream shop in a lofty building on the main square. Bedrooms are simple but clean, none have en suite facilities, but some have a shower. The restaurant serves hearty family-style cooking. Nearby **La Colombe Joyeuse** (12 pl Vieille, 04.94.43.65.24, closed Tue, mid Nov-mid Dec & Jan, menus €16-€26), despite its name ('merry dove'), specialises in pigeon dishes.

On the D558 out of Grimaud, **Les Santons** (D558, 04.94.43.21.02, closed Nov-Mar, menus €34-€68) is a little starchy, but serves excellent pigeon, lobster and lamb in delicately flavoured sauces. For a more relaxed meal, try the **Café de France** (pl Neuve, 04.94.43.20.05, closed Oct-Feb, menu €22), a grand old café that has been pleasantly redecorated. Simple Med fare is served on the terrace. In Cogolin, **La Maison du Monde** (63 rue Carnot, 04.94.54.77.54, closed

late Jan-mid Feb, double €70-€165) has 12 stylish rooms, a pool and garden; rooms near the road can be noisy. **La Petite Maison** (34 bd Delattre de Tassigny, 04.94.54.58.49, closed Sun, €16.50-€28) is a pretty restaurant with a garden, serving warming soups and excellent fish.

Resources

Morning markets are Sunday at Collobrières, Wednesday and Saturday at Cogolin (plus Monday and Friday in summer), Wednesday and Sunday in La Garde-Freinet, Thursday at Grimaud.

Tourist information

Cogolin *Office de Tourisme, pl de la République, 83310 Cogolin (04.94.55.01.10/www.cogolin-provence.com).* **Open** *July, Aug* 9am-1pm, 2-6.30pm Mon-Sat. *Sept-June* 9am-12.30pm, 2-6.30pm Mon-Fri; 9.30am-12.30pm Sat.
Collobrières *Office de Tourisme, bd Caminat, 83610 Collobrières (04.94.48.08.00/www.collotour. com).* **Open** *July, Aug* 10am-12.30pm, 3-7pm daily. *Sept-June* 2-6pm Mon; 10am-noon, 2-6pm Tue-Sat.
La Garde-Freinet *Office de Tourisme, Chapelle St-Jean, 83680 La Garde-Freinet (04.94.43.67.41/ www.lagardefreinet.com).* **Open** *July, Aug* 9.30am-1pm, 4-6.30pm Mon-Sat. *Apr-June, Sept* 9.30am-12.30pm, 3.30-5.30pm Mon-Sat. *Oct-Mar* 9.30am-12.30pm, 2-5pm Tue-Sat.
Grimaud *Office de Tourisme, 1 bd des Aliziers, 83310 Grimaud (04.94.55.43.83/www.grimaud-provence.com).* **Open** *July, Aug* 9am-12.30pm, 3-7pm Mon-Sat; 10am-1pm Sun. *Apr-June, Sept* 9am-12.30pm, 2.30-6.15pm Mon-Sat. *Oct-Mar* 9am-12.30pm, 2.15-5.30pm Mon-Sat.

Getting there & around

By air

Toulon/Hyères airport (04.94.00.83.83) is near to Hyères port.

By bus

Sodétrav (08.25.00.06.50) operates bus services between Toulon and Hyères and from Hyères to St-Tropez, stopping at Bormes, Le Lavandou, Le Rayol-Canadol and Cavalaire-sur-Mer; there are few buses on Sun. From June to Aug, a bus connects Bormes Village and beaches at La Favière and Le Lavandou. **Phocéens Cars** (04.93.85.66.61) runs two buses a day (Mon-Sat) between Nice airport and Hyères.

By car

The A570 runs into Hyères before merging with the N98 coast road, which continues to Bormes and then cuts along the south of the Massif des Maures. The D559 at Bormes follows the coast to Le Lavandou and Cavalaire-sur-Mer.

By train

Nearest mainline stations are Toulon, Draguignan-Les Arcs and St-Raphaël. Hyères is on a branch line served by several trains a day from Toulon.

The Var

St-Tropez

Where to preen and be seen in this poseur's paradise.

A sleepy fishing village of just over 6,000 locals in winter, St-Tropez overflows with 100,000 visitors per day during the sweltering summer months. Whether you're part of the chic yachting set or just waiting for a glimpse of the rich and famous, the town lives up to its reputation as the ultimate lap of luxury. That is, of course, if you can afford it.

St-Tropez

Given the hedonistic reputation of St-Tropez, it's fitting that the arch-hedonist Nero should have put the place on the map. In the first century AD the emperor had a Christian centurion by the name of Torpes beheaded in Pisa. Torpes' headless trunk was loaded aboard a boat and set adrift with a rooster and a dog. When the boat washed up on the beach that is now named after the hapless centurion, the starving dog hadn't taken so much as a nibble of the corpse, a sure sign of sainthood.

In the Middle Ages, the small fishing community at St-Tropez was harried by Saracens until the 15th century, when 21 Genoese families were imported to show the pirates who was who. The place was still a tiny backwater in 1880 when Guy de Maupassant sailed his boat in to give the locals their first taste of bohemian eccentricity. A decade later, post-Impressionist painter Paul Signac, driven into port by a storm, fell in love with St-Tropez and bought a house, La Hune (on what is now avenue Paul Signac). He opened the internationally famed gallery, Salon des Independants, and invited his friends (then unknowns, including Matisse, Derain, Vlaminck, Marquet and Dufy) to exhibit. The time they spent in the South of France soon converted their palettes from dark northern tones to brilliant St-Tropez hues. Rich holidaying Parisians stopped in to purchase works by the up-and-coming artists, and soon began purchasing homes of their own. Colette lived here too: her only complaint about the place was that in order to concentrate on writing, she had to turn her back on the attention-monopolising view.

Another wave of personalities washed up in 1956 after Roger Vadim, his young protégée Brigitte Bardot and a film crew descended on the town to make *Et Dieu créa la femme* (*And God Created Woman*). It was no time before St-Tropez became the world's most famous playboy haunt. The millionaires and superstars are still there, but not all come out to play in the high season madness, remaining bolt-holed in their luxury sea-view abodes. And when they do venture out, they are often whisked to an ultra-discreet HIP (Highly Important Person) room. Bardot herself, who alternates between her house up in the hills and her seafront home-cum-animal-rights-HQ at La Madrague, is unlikely to be spotted swinging a baguette at the market these days. An ever-loyal flock of fans make do instead with a boat tour of the headland's A-List abodes (MMG leaves from Vieux Port, Apr-Sept daily, 04.94.96.51.00).

St-Tropez is at its most bacchanalian from May to August. Just after 'le jet set' has moved on to its next season fixture, the village is quietly bustling and more family-oriented – in winter it is pretty much deserted. Partying is not St-Tropez's only draw: Les Voiles de St-Tropez (late Sept-early Oct; for details, see www.ot-saint-tropez.com) is a yacht fest that attracts large crowds, as does Les Bravades, a huge procession paying homage to the town's patron saint, Torpes, and its most important historical and religious events, for which villagers wear traditional costumes.

Sightseeing

St-Tropez is built on a slope, with all the action sliding inexorably towards the Vieux Port. Here the richer-than-thou crowd wine and dine smugly on their gin palaces, in full view of the café terraces, where even the most sanguine holidaymaker is trapped as a gawping spectator. The port was badly bombed in World War II and reconstructed pretty much as it was, with multicoloured houses that line the quays, and later extended.

East of the Vieux Port, the **Château de Suffren** (closed to the public, although the occasional art show allows access inside) dates back to 972, and is the oldest building in town. Back from the quai Jean Jaurès, heading towards the Port des Pêcheurs, a myriad of little galleries line the side streets, and the place aux Herbes is home to a small and lively daily fish market. Stands sell fish and local produce – get there around midday to lunch on fresh oysters,

The village where God created woman: **St-Tropez**.

sea urchins and white wine. The steep rue de la Citadelle leads to a swarm of tourist-trap restaurants and the impressively walled 17th-century citadel perched at the top of the village. It contains the fairly bland **Musée Naval**, which opened in 1958 and details the citadel's extensive military history. Its highlight is the spectacular views from the ramparts. The seaside Cimetière Marin, just below the citadel on chemin des Graniers, is where film director Roger Vadim is buried.

West of the Vieux Port, those lucky enough to arrive by boat can often dock in the large Nouveau Port, in close proximity to the municipal car park and the noisy hordes piling in and out of the clubs. Situated between the old and new port areas is the **Musée de l'Annonciade**, a superb and under-visited collection of early 20th-century art housed in a 16th-century chapel. Pointillists, Fauves, Nabis, Expressionists and Cubists are all represented, and the permanent collection includes art works by Vuillard, Bonnard, Matisse, Derain, Braque and Vlaminck. The museum also stages special temporary exhibitions every summer.

Butterfly enthusiasts would also do well to make a quick stop at the **Maison de Papillons**, comprising over 4,500 carefully catalogued species, which are often displayed on painted backgrounds.

Behind the Vieux Port, St-Tropez's *pétanque*-playing fraternity hangs out on plane-tree-lined place des Lices. It's also home to a market on Tuesday and Saturday. Fruit, vegetables, charcuterie, honey and wine fill the stalls but traders are really there to catch up on the local gossip and see friends. On the hill, a kilometre south of town, the pretty Chapelle Ste-Anne (open to the public only on St Anne's day, 26 July) commands spectacular views over the bay and southern Alps.

Musée de l'Annonciade

pl Georges Gramont (04.94.17.84.10).
Open *June-mid Oct* 10am-1pm, 3-10pm Mon, Wed-Sun. *Mid Oct-May* 10am-noon, 2-6pm Mon, Wed-Sun. Closed Nov. **Admission** €5.50; €4 12-25s, students; free under-12s.
Credit AmEx, MC, V.

Musée Naval

Mont de la Citadelle (04.94.97.59.43). **Open** *Dec-March* 10am-12.30pm, 1.30-5.30pm Mon, Wed-Sun. *Apr-Oct* 10am-12.30pm, 1.30-6.30pm Mon, Wed-Sun. *July-Aug* English tours at 4.30pm Mon, Fri. Closed Nov. **Admission** €5.50; €4 8-25s, students; free under-8s. **No credit cards.**

Maison des Papillons

9 rue Etienne Berny (04.94.97.63.45).
Open 10am-noon, 2.30-7pm Mon-Sat. Closed Oct-Mar. **Admission** €4; free under-8s.

Watch life go by at **Café Le Senequier**. *See p197.*

Activities

Boat hire

Boats ranging from a little six-metre (19-foot) Semi-Rigide (€450/day) to an impressive 49-metre (160-foot) Sy Bartabas (€10,000/day) are for hire from **L'Echo Nautique** (6 rue de Clocher, 04.94.97.73.66, www.echonautique.com). **Marine Air Sport** (Pearl Beach, Ex Place des Catamarans, 06.07.22.43.97, www.marine-air-sport.com) also offers a similar range of boats for hire, many inclusive of skipper and crew, as well as jetski rental and waterskiing lessons.

Motorcyle, scooter & bicycle hire

Explore St-Tropez and the surrounding hill towns in your own time by renting two wheels from **Holiday Bikes** (14 av du General Leclerc, 04.94.97.09.39, www.holiday-bikes.com). Prices range from €10-€15 for a bicycle to €100 for a motorcycle (all prices for 24hr rental), and friendly staff will help you plan the most scenic routes around the peninsula.

Where to eat & drink

Bar du Port

7 quai Suffren (04.94.97.00.54). **Open** *July, Aug* 7am-3am daily. *Sept-June* 7am-1am daily. Closed Jan. **No credit cards**.
An ideal spot to watch celebrities and the mega-rich pull up in their yachts, the Bar du Port is a sleek combination of glass and chrome. Try the 'Ice Tropez'.

Les Boite de Sardines

3 rue St-Jean (04.94.56.48.08). **Open** 8pm-midnight Mon, Tue, Thur-Sun. Closed Nov-Mar. **Menus** from €35. **Credit** MC, V
This little Marseille-style restaurant seats about 25, and, during the summer months, its tables spill on to the tiny street outside. Try the truly phenomenal selection of sardine-based starters – the ingredients are clearly fresh off the trawlers and the cooking is unpretentious yet more than competent.

Le Café

5 pl des Lices (04.94.97.44.69). **Open** 8am-midnight daily. **Menus** €30-€39. **Credit** AmEx, MC, V.
The terrace outside Le Café doubles as a stadium for watching the endless *boules* matches that are played by locals on place des Lices. If you reckon you're good enough, ask at the bar to borrow a set of *boules* and see if you can join in.

Café de Paris

15 quai Suffren (04.94.97.00.56). **Open** 7am-3am daily. **Average** €40. **Credit** V.
The terrace of the Café de Paris looks relatively average and gives little indication of the plush, romantic interior designed by Philippe Starck. Inside, however, this sushi bar exudes mysterious chic with backlit white drapes, chandeliers and red velvet banquettes. It also offers an extensive wine list, as well as Chinese and French menu options, for those who are wary of raw fish.

Café Le Senequier

quai Jean Jaurès (04.94.97.00.90). **Open**
8am-midnight daily. **No credit cards**.
Row after row of bright red director's chairs line the
terrace outside Café Le Senequier, making it an ideal
place to yacht-watch. Try the Cocktail Senequier, a
combination of gin, strawberries and champagne,
along with any one of their spectacular desserts, all
made fresh at the pâtisserie on the premises.

Le Frégate

52 rue Allard (04.94.97.07.08). **Open** noon-2pm,
7-11pm daily. Closed mid Jan-Feb. **Menus** €23-€31.
Credit MC, V.
This little restaurant, nestled on a side street and
seating just 25, serves unpretentious provençal cuisine, including fish soups and grills.

Le Gorille

1 quai Suffren (04.94.97.03.93). **Open** *July, Aug*
24hrs daily. *Sept-Dec, Feb-June* open daily, hours
vary. Closed Jan. **Average** €20. **No credit cards**.
Located on the corner of the quai, Le Gorille is frequented primarily by locals. The friendly staff keep
the place open 24 hours a day in summer, and manage close to those hours during the rest of the year.
The menu is simple and well priced, consisting primarily of steak, seafood salads, burgers and *frites*.

Leï Mouscardïns

Tour du Portalet (04.94.97.29.00). **Open** noon-
3.30pm, 7.30pm-late daily. Closed mid Nov-mid Dec,
2wks Feb. **Menus** €67-€109. **Credit** AmEx, MC, V.
Offering its clientele a near-360º view of the sea,
Laurent Tarridec's quayside restaurant is one of the
most respected in town. The menu is seasonal and
combines local cuisine, such as *sardines argentées*,
with exclusive and exclusive delicacies, like *soup d'o-
lives vert au lait d'amandes*.

Spoon Byblos

av Maréchal Foch (04.94.56.68.20/www.spoon.fr).
Open *Mid Apr-mid Oct* 8pm-11pm daily. *July-Aug*
8pm-12.30am daily. **Average** €80. **Credit** AmEx,
DC, MC, V.
Diners at Alain Ducasse's Spoon Byblos can sit
either in the spruce dining room or outside on the
designer terrace, which is decorated with hanging
lanterns in summer. The menu has a 'concept':
choose a main ingredient, such as grilled and glazed
kebab scallops, match it up with one of three different dressings (satay sauce or citrus vinaigrette, say)
and one of three vegetable choices, like vegetarian
spring rolls. And very nice it is too.

La Table du Marché

*38 rue Georges Clemenceau (04.94.97.85.20/www.
christophe-leroy.com).* **Open** 7.30am-midnight daily.
Menus €18-€26. **Credit** AmEx, MC, V.
Celebrity chef Christophe Leroy's bistro-cum-deli
and tearoom is a rather casual reflection of his talent, but nevertheless offers good wines and fresh
seafood treats (as long as you avoid the daily *for-
mules* and go à la carte).

Nightlife

Les Caves du Roi

Hôtel Byblos, av Paul Signac (04.94.97.16.02).
Open *Easter-May, Sept-mid Oct* 11pm-5am Fri, Sat.
June-Sept 11pm-5am daily. Closed mid Oct-Easter.
Admission free. **Credit** AmEx, DC, MC, V.
The paparazzi-free basement club at Hôtel Byblos
is one of the Cote d'Azur's most exclusive and
extravagant clubs. Virtually impossible to get into
unless you arrive early or reserve a table in advance,
Les Caves has hosted private evenings for the likes
of Elton John, and internationally famous celebrities
abound. In-house DJ, Jack E, makes every night
memorable with his pounding house tunes.

Octave Café

pl de la Garonne (04.94.97.22.56). **Open** *Mar-Oct*
11pm-5am daily. *Nov-Dec* 11pm-5am Fri, Sat. Closed
mid Jan-Feb. **Admission** free (drinks obligatory).
Credit AmEx, MC, V.
A stylish piano bar with soft, loungey music,
squishy cushioned chairs, low black tables and a
chic clientèle. Liza Minnelli and the inimitable
Johnny Hallyday have been known to croon a few
tunes just for fun.

Le Papagayo

*résidences du Nouveau Port (04.94.79.29.50/www.
lepapagayo.com).* **Open** *Feb-June, Sept-mid Oct*
11.30pm-5am Fri, Sat. *July, Aug* 11.30pm-5am
daily. Closed mid Oct-Jan. **Admission** free.
Credit AmEx, MC, V.
With its port-side location and large terrace, Le
Papagayo is the perfect spot for people-watching
(celebrities like P Diddy and Bono have been known
to stop by for a drink). The club also stages fashion
shows, international nights and all manner of late-
night dance beats.

Le VIP Room

*résidences du Nouveau Port (04.94.97.14.70/www.
viproom.fr).* **Open** 7pm-5am daily. *Oct-May* 7pm-
5am Fri, Sat. **Admission** free. **Credit** AmEx, MC, V.
This southern outpost of Jean Roch's Champs-
Elysées club is where the gilded youths who slip
between Paris and St-Tropez spend their pocket
money. (You may, however, form your own views
as to whether they fully justify the 'VIP' of the club's
name.) Music is boppy and feel-good. The mezzanine houses a suitably fashionable restaurant called
Madrague (menu €29).

Shopping

Designer boutiques are popping up wherever
there is space in St-Tropez, but rues Allard and
Gambetta are the main fashion runways. The
trademark at family-run **Atelier Rondini**
(16 rue Georges Clemenceau, 04.94.97.19.55,
www.rondini.fr, closed Mon, Sun in winter,
and mid Oct-mid Nov) is 'sandales tropéziennes'
– strappy handmade Spartacus sandals also

available in funky updates; Charlotte Gainsbourg is a fan. **La Tarte Tropézienne** (pl des Lices, 04.94.97.04.69, www.tarte-tropezienne-traiteur.com) is the place to discover *la tropézienne*, a light sponge cake filled with custard cream. Relax on the mezzanine level or at outside tables while enjoying their fresh salads, delectable breads and scrumptious pastries.

Where to stay

A word of warning: if you're planning to stay in St-Tropez during high season, be sure to book months in advance.

Château de la Messardière

rte de Tahiti (04.94.56.76.00/www.messardiere.com). Closed Oct-Mar. **Rates** €200-€620 double. **Credit** AmEx, DC, MC, V.
Perched on a hilltop of parasol pines, this 19th-century castle, complete with turrets and canopy beds, once belonged to an aristocratic family whose spirit lives on in the tarot-inspired art around the lobby.

Hôtel Le Baron

23 rue de l'Aïoli (04.94.97.06.57/www.hotel-le-baron.com). **Rates** €46-€100 double. **Credit** MC, V.
Located at the foot of the citadel, this peaceful hotel is made up of ten provençal-style bedrooms, some of which come with a sea view.

Hôtel Byblos

av Paul Signac (04.94.56.68.00/www.byblos.com). Closed mid Oct-mid Apr. **Rates** €370-€690 double. **Credit** AmEx, DC, MC, V.
Opened by Brigitte Bardot in 1967 and the site of Mick Jagger's wedding over 30 years ago, the perennially trendy Byblos has 51 rooms and 44 suites that emulate a Mediterranean village of their own. With its swimming pool, fountain-filled gardens and restaurants – poolside Bayader and Alain Ducasse's Spoon Byblos (*see p197*) – guests looking for luxury won't be disappointed.

Hôtel Lou Cagnard

18 av Paul Roussel (04.94.97.04.24/www.hotel-lou-cagnard.com). Closed Nov, Dec. **Rates** €46-€110 double. **Credit** MC, V.
Not far from the glamour, but totally unaffected by it is this decent budget option, which has a leafy garden for alfresco breakfasting. All rooms are clean and comfy although the first floor can get extremely hot in summer.

Hôtel La Maison Blanche

pl des Lices (04.94.97.52.66/www.hotellamaison blanche.com). Closed 2wks Feb. **Rates** €168-€748 double. **Credit** AmEx, DC, MC, V.
The stylish facelift by minimalist designer Fabienne Villacrèces is ageing well at this exclusive yet villagey hotel. In the evening, change into something chic and laze on wicker loungers on the terrace (in arm's reach of the champagne bar, naturally).

Les Palmiers

24-26 bd Vasserot (04.94.97.01.61/www. hotel-les-palmiers.com). **Rates** €63-€195 double. **Credit** MC, V.
Just off the place des Lices, a verdant path leads to Les Palmiers' reception, and in season the branches are loaded with limes, mandarins and grapefruits. Most rooms are basic but pleasant, and those facing the courtyard have individual patios.

Le Pré de la Mer

rte des Salins (04.94.97.12.23). Closed Oct-Easter. **Rates** €130-€300 double. **Credit** AmEx, V.
This hotel is composed of three conventional bedrooms and eight self-contained studio apartments in a pretty, provençal setting slightly outside town.

Résidence de la Pinède

Plage de la Bouillabaisse (04.94.55.91.00/www. residencepinede.com). Closed Oct-Easter. **Rates** €380-€910 double. **Credit** AmEx, DC, MC, V.
Only a stone's throw from the mad summer hordes, this tranquil oasis of luxury has its own beach, a spill-over pool, an unbeatable view of the bay and fine cooking (menus €75-€104).

Le Sube

15 quai Suffren (04.94.97.30.04/www.hotel-sube.com). Closed 3wks Jan. **Rates** €150-€290. **Credit** AmEx, DC, MC, V.
Claiming status as the oldest hotel in St-Tropez, and located smack in the centre of the old port, the woody Sube is a favourite with yachting enthusiasts. A fire burns in winter in the Chesterfield-filled bar and regulars vie for seats on its minuscule balcony.

Resources

Tourist information

Office de Tourisme, quai Jean Jaurès, 83990 St-Tropez (04.94.97.45.21/www.ot-saint-tropez.com). **Open** *Apr-June, Sept, Oct* 9am-12.30pm, 2-7pm daily. *July, Aug* 9.30am-8pm daily. *Nov* 9.30am-noon, 2-6pm Mon-Sat; 2-6pm Sun. *Dec-Mar* 9.30am-noon, 2-6pm daily.

St-Tropez peninsula

When the truly chic or truly rich talk about summering in St-Trop, often as not they actually mean hiding out in Garbo-esque seclusion in the hills above the town, well away from the wannabes who frequent the old port. Here, amid parasol pines and Côtes de Provence vineyards with views down to pristine blue coves, the hill villages of Ramatuelle and Gassin retain a sense of exclusivity.

Ramatuelle began as a Saracen stronghold; it was razed in 1592 during the Wars of Religion, then rebuilt in 1620, as many inscriptions above doors testify. It still has

Mick and Bianca honeymooned at **Gassin**. *See p200.*

a fortified feel as tightly knit houses climb snail-like up around the hill; a gateway next to the church leads through to the partly pedestrianised old town. Popular for an evening meal away from the St-Trop hoi polloi, it is packed in July and August, during its jazz and theatre festivals. Ramatuelle is also just a short distance away from the Plage de Pampelonne – five kilometres (three miles) of sandy beach popular with the glitterati and hippies alike. The ever-famous Club 55 (04.94.55.55.55, www.leclub55.com) was Brigitte Bardot's choice locale to celebrate her retirement from films in 1974, and the beach was also one of the main Allied landing sites in August 1944 (*see p19* **The other D-Day**).

Smaller **Gassin**, where Mick and Bianca Jagger honeymooned in the 1970s, offers an incredible 360-degree view of the entire peninsula. Squeezing through ancient streets to its medieval fortress and church, it's easy to understand why Gassin has been named one of France's most beautiful villages. It's also utterly immersed in vineyards – take your pick of any of the AOC tasting tours.

Slightly back from the coast, **La Croix-Valmer** is a residential town with fine views across cliffs dotted with the holiday villas of discreetly well-heeled French families. Though the *croix* ('cross') in its name refers to an airborne one allegedly seen around here by the co-Emperor Constantine, the town was only built in 1934. From here, there is easy access to the stunning coastal conservation area on the Cap Lardier and the lovely Plage de Gigaro.

Where to stay & eat

Just below Ramatuelle, 500 metres from the fabulous Pampelonne beach, Christophe Leroy's **Les Moulins** (rte des Plages, 04.94.97.17.22, www.christophe-leroy.com, closed mid Nov-Feb, double €195-€289, menus €39-€70) is a combination country inn, with its five cottage-type rooms, and provençal restaurant. Vegetables come from the kitchen garden, and the dessert and cheese courses are not to be missed. Christophe Leroy has also introduced a food workshop – for €100 per person, you can participate in a four-course provençal cooking class (classes five to 15 people, book in advance). Set in cypress-dotted gardens, **La Villa Marie** (rte des Plages, Chemin Val Rian, Ramatuelle, 04.94.97.40.22, www.villamarie.fr, closed mid Dec-Jan, double €190-€610) is the latest creation from the couple behind the super-chic Fermes de Marie in the ski resort of Megève. It has 42 rooms with a 'provençal Renaissance' look, an open-air bar, a landscaped pool and a spa. Suites have distant sea views,

and you can have a massage while stretched out in the pine forest. In Ramatuelle, café-tabac and newsagent **Café de l'Ormeau** (pl de l'Ormeau, 04.94.79.20.20, open daily) is without a doubt the best place to sit and observe local life – its plant-covered terrace is an ideal vantage point. At **La Forge** (rue Victor Léon, 04.94.79.25.56, closed Nov-mid Mar, menu €35), chef Pierre Fazio and his wife serve up good provençal cuisine to a dressy crowd in a cleverly converted smithy. Check out the antiques for sale on the first floor. For excellent pizza, head over the road to **L'Estable** (rue Victor Léon, 04.94.79.10.76, average €20). Heading out of town, friendly **La Farigoulette** (rue Victor Léon, 04.94.79.20.49, closed Oct-Apr, average €30, no credit cards) offers a richly bayleaf-infused daube, anchoïade and their own freshly made pasta on the garden terrace or in the beamed stone interior. The restaurant also hosts exhibitions of local artists, and is the perfect place to start (or finish) a hike along the Sentier de la Font d'Avau. Perched just beneath the town, **Terrasse-Hostellerie Le Baou** (av Gustave Etienne, 04.98.12.94.20, closed mid Oct-Apr, double €190-€390) has spectacular views across the peninsula, pleasant rooms, a pool and a serious restaurant (menus €60-€90). Don't miss out on the local produce – both the **Temple de la Savonnerie**, with its soaps and perfumes (2 rue des Amoureux, 04.94.79.10.34, www.temple-de-la-savonnerie.com, closed Nov-Mar, except 2wks Christmas) and **Le Bar à Huile** (28bis rue St Esprit), which specialises in AOC olive oil, tapenade and home-made jams, are perfect for picking up souvenirs. In Gassin, **Le Micocoulier** (pl dei Barri, 04.94.56.14.01, closed Mon & mid Oct-Apr, menus €27-€40) serves provençal food with an Italian twist. South-east of La Croix-Valmer, the 19th-century **Château de Valmer** (rte de Gigaro, 04.94.55.15.15, www.chateau-valmer.com, closed mid Oct-mid Apr, double €153-€382) has a pool amid vines, palms and fruit trees, soothing salons and Laura Ashley or Pierre Frey fabrics. Under the same ownership, comfortable **La Pinède Plage** (Plage de Gigaro, 04.94.55.16.16, www.pinede-plage.com, closed Oct-Apr, double €153-€376, menu €48) has a restaurant and pool overlooking *la grande bleue*. The two share La Pinède's beach, which has windsurfing, kayaks and pedalos.

Resources

Tourist information

La Croix-Valmer *Office de Tourisme, esplanade de la Gare, 83400 La Croix-Valmer (04.94.55.12.12).* **Open** *Mid June-Sept* 9.30am-12.30pm, 2.30-7pm

Mon-Sat; 9.15am-1.30pm Sun. *Oct-mid June*
9am-noon, 2-6pm Mon-Fri; 9.15am-noon Sat;
2.30-6.30pm Sun.
Ramatuelle *Office de Tourisme, pl de l'Ormeau,
83350 Ramatuelle (04.98.12.64.00/www.ramatuelle-
tourisme.com).* **Open** *Apr-mid Oct* 8.30am-12.30pm,
2.30-6.30pm Mon-Sat. *Mid Oct-Mar* 8.30am-12.30pm,
3-6pm Mon-Fri.

Port Grimaud & Ste-Maxime

Hugging the curve in the bay west of St-Tropez,
Port Grimaud was designed in the late 1960s
by architect François Spoerry to look like a
miniature slice of the Venice lagoon. Kitschily
pretty, this is real estate for the seriously rich.
Visitors must park their cars in order to explore
the village by foot or boat, best in any case for
checking out the faux-Venetian bridges that
connect the islands. **Ste-Maxime** has lost the
allure it exuded in 1930s posters, and these
days it's a relatively inexpensive family-
oriented place to stay next to St-Tropez –
though the bad news is that traffic jams can
make the latter nigh impossible to reach (a
smarter move is to take Bateaux Verts' boat
service, *see below*). Sandy beaches surround the
town, and the promenade is crammed with
restaurants and live music. Ste-Maxime's only
sight as such is the stone **Tour Carrée**. Built
around 1560 by local monks, with the goal of
increasing the town's population, it has served
as a defence against pirates, a barn, a prison
and a town hall before finally being turned
into a folklore museum.

Tour Carrée
pl de l'Eglise, Ste-Maxime (04.94.96.70.30). **Open**
Sept-June 10am-noon, 3-6pm Wed-Sun. *July, Aug*
10am-noon, 3-7pm Wed-Sun. **Admission** €2.30;
60¢ 5-15s. **No credit cards.**

Where to stay, eat & drink

In Port Grimaud, the luxurious **Giraglia** (pl du
14 Juin, 04.94.56.31.33, www.hotelgiraglia.com,
closed Oct-mid May, double €245-€435) has a
pool and a garden that is perfect for boat-
watching and enjoying the sunset over St-
Tropez. Next to the Golf Club de Beauvallon
(special green rates available), **Hôtel le
Beauvallon** (bd des Collines, Baie de St-
Tropez, 04.94.55.78.88, www.lebeauvallon.com,
closed mid Oct-Apr, double €275-€540,
restaurant closed lunch, average €70, beach
restaurant €35) offers a postcard-perfect view
of St-Tropez and its *golfe*. Recently updated by
its Chinese owner, the hotel's decor now has a
palpably eastern flair, as does its exquisite
menu. Top of the line in every aspect, the hotel
is a charming place to relax, whether in their

king-size beds, private spas, or private beach.
The infinity pool, beach club restaurant and
speedboats to St-Tropez complete the luxury
package. The seafront at Ste-Maxime is lined
with restaurants, brasseries and ice-cream
parlours. **La Marine** (6 rue Fernard Bessy,
04.94.96.53.93, closed Mon & Jan, menus €21-
€35) serves seafood and other Mediterranean
fare, and **La Réserve** (8 pl Victor Hugo,
04.94.96.18.32, menus €18-€27.50) offers
inexpensive bistro classics in a huge terraced
area. The **Mas des Oliviers** (quartier de la
Croisette, 04.94.96.13.31, closed Nov-Feb, double
€49-€138), just west of the centre, has 20 rooms,
studio apartments to let on a weekly basis, as
well as a pool, tennis courts and enormous,
well-tended grounds.

Resources

Tourist information
Port Grimaud *Office de Tourisme, 1 bd
Aliziers, 83310 Port Grimaud (04.94.55.
43.83/www.grimaud-provence.com).* **Open**
June-Sept 9am-12.30pm, 2.30-5.30pm Mon-Sat
(3-7pm July, Aug). Closed Oct-May.
Ste-Maxime *Office de Tourisme, pl Simon
Lorière, 83120 Ste-Maxime (04.94.55.75.55/
www.ste-maxime.com).* **Open** *June, Sept* 9am-
12.30pm, 2-7pm Mon-Sat. *July-Aug* 9am-8pm Mon-
Sat. *Oct-May* 9am-noon, 2-6pm Mon-Sat.

Getting there & around

By air
Private jets land on the Le Môle airstrip, 35km
(21 miles) from the Massif des Maures. There is
no train station.

By bus
Sodetrav (0825 000 650, 04.94.13.33.44,
www.sodetrav.fr) runs daily buses between
St-Tropez and Toulon via Hyères. There is one
morning service a day between St-Tropez,
Ramatuelle and Gassin in July and Aug and on
Tue and Sat in Sept and June, and daily services
between St-Tropez and St-Raphaël, via Grimaud,
Cogolin and Ste-Maxime.

By boat
Les Bateaux Verts (04.94.49.29.39,
www.bateauverts.com) runs hourly boat services
from Ste-Maxime to St-Tropez from Apr to Oct.
Trans Cote d'Azur (04.92.00.42.30, www.trans-
cote-azur.com) has daily summer departures
to Nice and Cannes. For **easyCruise** sailings,
see p249 **Plane sailing**.

By car
Sweat it out on the N98 coast road. Ramatuelle is on
the D61 south of St-Tropez; for Gassin take one of the
signposted roads off the D61 or D559. Ste-Maxime is
on the D98 coast road or by A8 exit 36 and D25.

The Var

St-Raphaël & the Estérel

A Roman port, some 1920s glamour and a big hunk of red rock.

Getting a dose of vitamin sea in **St-Raphaël**.

Back in the 1880s St-Raphaël was the stomping ground of the fashionable set, as its grand hotels attest. Although a friendly enough place, it is now just an affordable resort that pulls in families with its sheltered beach and double marina. The small town of Fréjus to the north has more to interest grown-ups, boasting some of the most stunning Roman remains in the area, while to the east the Massif de l'Estérel's red volcanic rock looms over deep blue sea, providing wonderful colour contrasts.

St-Raphaël

The well-heeled pleasure-seekers who tottered down from Fréjus to found St-Raphaël would be delighted: the site of the Gallo-Roman resort is now occupied by the Casino. Thereafter the town's history was less than smooth. A bedraggled Napoleon landed here in 1799 after defeat in Egypt at the hand of the British, his arrival commemorated by a pyramid on avenue Commandant Guilbaud. But it fell to journalist Alphonse Karr (1808-90), exiled to Nice for his opposition to Napoleon III, to sort out the resort's PR: 'Leave Paris and plant your stick in my garden,' he wrote to a friend in 1864, 'next morning, when you wake, you will see it has grown roses.' Writers, artists and composers

heeded the invitation, with Dumas, Maupassant and Berlioz among those who came here.

Following their lead, Félix Martin, local mayor and civil engineer, transformed the village into a smart getaway. Further illustrious guests began to mark their stay with works of art: Gounod composed *Romeo and Juliet* here in 1869, Scott Fitzgerald wrote *Tender is the Night*, Félix Ziem painted. Following the 1920s craze for diving (Zelda used to do it drunk, from the cliffs of the Fitzgeralds' nearby hideaway) and the example shown by hosts of submerged antiquities all along the Estérel, St-Raphaël gave birth to France's first dedicated sub-aqua club. There is a plethora of diving clubs in the town to this day; among the several diving schools on the Estérel, try **Aventure sous-marine** (56 rue de la Garonne, 04.94.19.33.70, www.aventuresousmarine.fr, €46/half-day).

All that said and done, you may feel that today's St-Raph lacks atmosphere – the jungle of neon around its outskirts certainly doesn't help. The medieval and belle époque centre was largely destroyed by wartime bombing, leaving just a few wiggly old streets around the covered market on place de la République and the church of St-Pierre-des-Templiers. Built in the 12th century, this ancient church doubled as a fortress against attacks by pirates. It is home to a gilded wooden bust of St Peter that is still carried by fishermen in a torch-lit procession to the Vieux Port on the first Sunday in August.

Next door, beside the remains of the Roman aqueduct, the **Musée Archéologique** contains artefacts from the harbour, plus a display on underwater archaeology. If you are willing to dodge the in-line skaters, promenade René Coty offers a worthwhile view of the sea and the twin rocks known as the Land Lion and the Sea Lion. The promenade, opened by Félix Martin in 1882, marked the beginning of St-Raphaël's tourist heyday. Other remnants of the era are seen in the Casino, the neo-Byzantine church of Notre-Dame-de-la-Victoire-de-Lépante, the Hôtel Excelsior (built by the same architect. Pierre Aublé) and the 1914 Résidence Le Méditerranée. Modern-day St-Raphaëlites can be found at the daily food market; there's also an arts and crafts market each afternoon during the summer.

Musée Archéologique

pl de la Vieille Eglise (04.94.19.25.75). **Open** *June-Sept* 10am-12.30pm, 2.30-7pm Tue, Wed, Fri-Sun; 10am-12.30pm, 2.30-9pm Thur. *Oct-May* 10am-12.30pm, 2.30-5.30pm Tue-Sat. **Admission** (incl St-Pierre-des-Templiers) free. **No credit cards.**

Where to stay & eat

The family-run **Excelsior** (193 bd Félix Martin, 04.94.95.02.42, www.excelsior-hotel.com, double €135-€170) is a belle époque hotel on the seafront, with 34 rooms and an English pub. The owners have recently renovated the outside and smartened up the bedrooms, although they remain a touch impersonal. **Le Méditerranée** (1 av Paul Doumer, 04.94.82.10.99, www.lemediterranee.fr, double €315-€658/wk) is a large Victorian building that has been divided up into airy apartments with their own kitchenettes (useful for longer stays). **La Thimothée** (375 bd Christian Lafon, 04.94.40.49.49, double €55-€75), in a residential area to the east of town, provides good-value accommodation. It has a pool and 12 rooms, two with a view of the sea. In the centre of town, **Le Jardin des Arènes** (31 av du Général Leclerc, 04.94.95.06.34, double €33-€51) is a charming place with stained-glass windows in the stairwell, a garden and extremely helpful staff. **Les Amandiers** (874 bd Alphonse Juin, 04.94.19.85.30, www.les-amandiers.com, double €35-€76) is an elegant building close to the marina. Gastronomes make a beeline for **L'Arbousier** (6 av de Valescure, 04.94.95.25.00, closed Mon, Tue, late Dec-mid Jan, menus €27-€58), where Philippe Troncy advances his reputation as one of St-Raphaël's

most innovative chefs, sending out delicious seasonal dishes to two sunny dining rooms and a shady terrace. If you feel like a change from French food, just north of St Raphaël, by the Maeva golf course in Valescure, **La Tosca** (85 rue de Bruant, 04.94.44.63.44, menu €36, dinner only, closed Mon & Sun June-Sept, Mon, Tue & Sun Oct-May) serves excellent Italian dishes in a summery setting, with good Italian wines.

Resources

Tourist information

Office de Tourisme *210 rue Waldeck Rousseau, 83702 St-Raphaël (04.94.19.52.52/www.saint-raphael.com).* **Open** *July-Aug* 9am-7pm daily. *Sept-June* 9am-12.30pm, 2-6.30pm Mon-Sat.

Fréjus & Roquebrune-sur-Argens

Having battled through the infernal traffic system and finally arrived at **Fréjus Plage**, you may end up wondering whether you ever actually left St-Raphaël. Don't despair: the Roman town up above is worth the effort. Alongside Ostia in Italy, Fréjus was the most extensive naval base of the Roman world. It was founded as Forum Julii by Julius Caesar in 49 BC and became a naval post for Augustus' swift-sailing galleys, which defeated Antony and Cleopatra at Actium in 31 BC. The harbour was guarded by two large towers; one, the Lanterne d'Auguste, still rises high on the site of the old port. But the town is not just a living museum: with its ochre- and apricot-painted houses and squares dripping with hanging baskets, it's also a pleasant place to while away an afternoon on a café terrace. Families with children might want to visit the 20-hectare (50-acre) safari-park-style Parc Zoölogique (zone du Capitou, just off the A8, 04.98.11.37.37, www.zoo-frejus.com) or burn off some energy at the Aquatica water park (RN98, 04.94.51.82.51, www.parc-aquatica.com), which apparently contains the biggest wave pool in Europe.

It takes the best part of a day to see the scattered Roman remains of Fréjus. Most impressive is the **Amphithéâtre Romain**, which still seats up to 10,000 for bullfights and plays. Near the railway station, the half-moon-shaped Porte des Gaules was part of the Roman ramparts. On the other side of the station, around the port, the Butte St-Antoine mound formed a western citadel; it has a tower that was probably a lighthouse. The Platforme, its counterpart on the east, served as military headquarters. Further north, the **Théâtre Romain** has new seats for summer concerts.

The Var

Facing on to place Formigé, the Cathédrale St-Léonce is at the heart of the unusual fortified **Cité Episcopale** (cathedral close), which contains a fascinating 15th-century bestiary painted on the ceiling of its two-tier, 13th-century cloisters. The carved cathedral doors show Mary and Saints Peter and Paul amid scenes of Saracen butchery. Opposite is the fifth-century octagonal baptistry where excavations have uncovered the original white marble pavement and pool. Upstairs, the **Musée Archéologique** has some outstanding Gallo-Roman antiquities recovered from digs at Fréjus. Emphasising that Fréjus is also a provençal town, the **Musée d'Histoire Locale et des Traditions** concentrates on artisanal traditions and events such as the *bravade* bull run and grape harvest. Bringing things more up to date, the Port Fréjus yachting harbour opened in 1989 and is home to numerous restaurants and bars. Fréjus market takes place on Wednesday, Saturday and Sunday.

A kilometre (half a mile) north-east of Fréjus, the Villa Aurélienne (rte de Cannes, 04.94.53.11.30), a Palladian house in 22 hectares (54 acres) of gardens, hosts occasional photographic exhibitions. Further north, two surprising constructions evoke France's colonial past. On the N7 the **Pagode bouddhique Hông Hiên** (Buddhist pagoda) was built by Vietnamese soldiers who fought in France in 1917, and has an exotic garden with a collection of sacred animals and guardian spirits. Nearby, a war memorial rises above the graves of over 24,000 soldiers and civilians who died in Indochina. Jutting out amid pine woods stands the Mosquée de Missiri; built for Malian troops in the 1920s, it is a replica of their home country's celebrated Missiri de Djenné mosque.

At **La Tour de Mare**, five kilometres (three miles) north of Fréjus on the interior road to Cannes (RN7), is another curiosity, this time of more interest to art fans. Deep in a forest that enhances its mystical appeal, uniting nature and arcane symbolism, the **Chapelle Notre-Dame-de-Jérusalem** was designed by Jean Cocteau in 1961 as part of a proposed artist's colony that never took off. The octagonal chapel, built around an atrium (now glassed-in), incorporates the mythology of the First Crusade in its stained glass, floor tiles and frescoes. In the painting of the apostles above the main door can be recognised Cocteau's lover actor Jean Marais, Coco Chanel and poet Max Jacob.

North-west of Fréjus, **Roquebrune-sur-Argens** is perched on a rocky peak at the foot of the Rocher de Roquebrune. Originally a stronghold, the *castrum*, located near the

church, was once surrounded by a curtain wall destroyed in the Wars of Religion in 1592. Traces of the wall are visible in boulevard de la Liberté. Tuesday and Friday are the regular market days here.

The first left fork on the D7 north of town leads to the red sandstone Rocher de Roquebrune. At the summit stand three crosses that were made by the sculptor Bernar Veanet. Using the summit to symbolise Golgotha, Veanet has created works recalling crucifixions painted by Giotto, Grünewald and El Greco. Take the trail marked with yellow paint and expect breathtaking views.

Amphithéâtre Romain

rue Henri Vadon (04.94.51.34.31). **Open** *Apr-Oct* 9.30am-12.30pm, 2-5.45pm Tue-Sun. *Nov-Mar* 9.30am-12.30pm, 2-4.45pm Tue-Sun. **Admission** €2. **No credit cards**.

Chapelle Notre-Dame-de-Jérusalem

av Nicolaï, La Tour de Mare (04.94.53.27.06). **Open** *Apr-Oct* 9.30am-12.30pm, 2-6pm Tue-Sun. *Nov-Mar* 9.30am-12.30pm, 2-5pm Tue-Sun. **Admission** €2. **No credit cards**.

Cité Episcopale

58 rue de Fleury (04.94.51.26.30). **Open** *June-Sept* 9am-6.30pm daily. *Oct-May* 9am-noon, 2-5pm Tue-Sun. **Admission** €4.60; €4.10 groups; €3.10 18-25s; free under-18s. **No credit cards**.

Musée Archéologique

pl Calvini (04.94.52.15.78). **Open** *Apr-Oct* 9.30am-12.30pm, 2-6pm Tue-Sun. *Nov-Mar* 9.30am-12.30pm, 2-5pm Tue-Sun. **Admission** €2. **No credit cards**.

Musée d'Histoire Locale et des Traditions

153 rue Jean Jaurès (04.94.51.64.01). **Open** *Apr-Oct* 9.30am-12.30pm, 2-6pm Tue-Sun. *Nov-Mar* 9.30am-12.30pm, 2-5pm Tue-Sun. **Admission** €2. **No credit cards**.

Pagode bouddhique Hông Hiên

13 rue Henri Giraud (04.94.53.25.29). **Open** 9am-7pm daily. **Admission** €2 adults; €1.50 groups; free under-7s. **No credit cards**.

Théâtre Romain

rue du Théâtre Romain (04.94.53.58.75). **Open** *Apr-Oct* 10am-1pm, 2.30-6.30pm Mon, Wed-Sat; 8am-7pm Sun. *Nov-Mar* 10am-noon, 1.30-5.30pm Mon-Fri; 8am-5pm Sun. **Admission** free.

Where to stay & eat

The **Aréna** (145 rue Général de Gaulle, 04.94.17.09.40, www.arena-hotel.com, closed mid Dec-mid Jan, double €80-€140) in the old town offers a warm welcome, a garden and a pool, while its restaurant (closed lunch Mon & Sat, menus €38-€58) serves the best provençal cuisine in Fréjus. The **Bellevue** (pl Paul Vernet, 04.94.17.12.20, double €55) is cheaper, with smallish rooms but good views over the square. Down on the beach, the modern **Sable et Soleil** (158 rue Paul Arène, 04.94.51.08.70, double €48-€60) is bright and friendly.

La Cave Romaine (114 rue Camelin, 04.94.51.52.03, open dinner only, closed Tue, average €30) serves Italian pasta and pizzas, and grilled meat and fish. Hidden down a backstreet, tiny **Les Potiers** (135 rue des Potiers, 04.94.51.33.74, closed Tue Sept-June, 1wk Jan or Feb, menus €22.50-€33) benefits from the personal touch, courtesy of chef Richard François and his wife. Foie gras, the most tender lamb and beef, and subtle desserts await food lovers; the set menus are superb value. The **Bar du Marché** (5 pl de la Liberté, 04.94.51.29.09) offers a filling €8 *plat du jour*.

In Roquebrune-sur-Argens have a meal at **Le Gaspacho** (21 av Général de Gaulle, 04.94.45.49.59, closed Wed Sept-June, menus €11-€19). Food is traditional French and the chocolate mousse is worth every guilty calorie.

Resources

For €4.60 you can buy a seven-day pass that grants you entry to five Fréjus attractions (excluding Cité Episcopale).

Tourist information

Fréjus Office de Tourisme *325 rue Jean Jaurès, 83600 Fréjus (04.94.51.83.83/www.ville-frejus.fr)*. **Open** *Apr-Aug* 9am-12.30pm, 2-7pm daily. *Sept-Mar* 9am-noon, 2-6pm Mon-Sat.
Roquebrune Office de Tourisme *rue Jean Aicard, 83520 Roquebrune-sur-Argens (04.94.45.72.70/www.ville-roquebrune-argens.fr)*. **Open** *Apr-Sept* 9am-noon, 2-6pm Mon-Sat; 9am-noon Sun. *Oct-Mar* 9am-noon, 2-6pm Mon-Fri.

Park life in **St-Raphaël**. *See p202*.

The Corniche de l'Estérel

There are two ways in which the Corniche de l'Estérel (or, prosaically but accurately, the RN 98) will leave you breathless: either the astonishing coastal views will do the trick – or the scary hairpin bends. It's anybody's guess how the Touring Club de France got their jalopies along it when they opened the road a century ago.

Just out of St-Raphaël at **Boulouris** there are some pleasant beaches, but drive on to the **Pointe du Dramont**, ten kilometres (six miles) east. In 1897 Auguste Lutaud bought the tiny Ile d'Or, just off the point. After building a four-storey mock-medieval tower he proclaimed himself King Auguste I of the Ile d'Or and threw some of the wildest parties on the Côte. The Plage du Dramont is famous as the bit of sand where the 36th Division of the US Army landed on 15 August 1944. For a great view, take the signposted, one-hour walk up to the Sémaphore du Dramont. Another path descends to the port of **Agay**, a family resort with a sandy beach shadowed by the slopes of the Rastel d'Agay. There's a Wednesday market. The daredevil author of *Le Petit Prince*, Antoine de St-Exupéry, crashed his plane just around the bay in World War II.

The beach of **Anthéor** is dominated by the Plateau d'Anthéor, from which a path leads up to the Rocher de St-Barthélémy. Climbing to the Cap Roux peak is about a two-hour round trip. Further along the coast road is the Pointe de l'Observatoire, offering views over the crags. Steep paved paths descend through vegetation to secluded coves. It's blissful, but swimming can be dangerous when the tide is high.

Le Trayas has a pleasant, modest beach. The bay of La Figueirette, reached from the harbour of **Miramar**, was a tuna-fishing centre in the 17th century and has the ruins of a lookout tower. As you approach Miramar be prepared for a double-take when you see, perched high on the cliffs, Pierre Cardin's Le Palais Bulles, a James Bond villain's shag-pad that is open to the public for a jazz and theatre festival in July and early August. The views from the coast road at this point are among the most stunning of the Côte d'Azur, as you wind into **La Galère** and **Théoule-sur-Mer**, a friendly seaside town with some great fish restaurants and a Friday market. From here you can follow walking and mountain-biking trails up to the church of Notre-Dame d'Afrique, a place of pilgrimage for the pieds noirs.

The chief curiosity at La Napoule is the **Fondation Henry Clews**, a pseudo-medieval folly conjured out of the ruins of a Saracen castle in 1917 by Henry Clews, a failed Wall

The Var

Street banker-turned-sculptor. Today it hosts artists' residencies and workshops. There's a market on Thursday (in Mandelieu too) and Saturday and L'Oasis restaurant (*see below*) draws gastronomes, but the town of La Napoule is a bit of a downmarket Cannes, filled with yachting boors and retirement homes. You'll wish you'd stayed on the Estérel.

Fondation Henry Clews

Château de la Napoule, av Henry Clews (04.93.49.95.05/www.chateau-lanapoule.com). **Open** *Feb-Oct* 10am-6pm daily; guided tours 11.30am, 2.30pm, 3.30pm, 5.30pm. *Nov-Jan* 2-5pm daily; guided tours 2.30pm, 3.30pm. **Admission** €4.60; €3.05 3-18s; free under-3s. **Credit** MC, V.

Where to stay & eat

Overlooking the Ile d'Or, the isolated **Sol et Mar** (rte Corniche d'Or, 04.94.95.25.60, closed mid Oct-early Feb, double €95-€149, menus €30-€37) has large rooms, a saltwater pool and a provençal restaurant. In Agay, **Hotel le Relais d'Agay** (bd de la Plage, 04.94.82.78.20, www.relaisdagay.com, double €47-€82) has 33 rooms, most with beachfront views. **Hôtel-Restaurant Le Lido** (bd de la Plage, 04.94.82.01.59, closed end Oct-Feb, double €70-€95) has a private beach, friendly service and a fish restaurant.

The enchanting **Relais des Calanques** (rte des Escales, 04.94.44.14.06, double €80-€120) near Le Trayas has clifftop gardens filled with bric-a-brac, a pool, a diving creek and a restaurant (closed Tue & Oct-Mar, *plat du jour* €15). **Le Trayas Youth Hostel** (9 av de la Véronèse, 04.93.75.40.23, www.fuaj.org, closed Jan-mid Feb, rates €11.50/person) is two kilometres (just over a mile) up the hill, with rooms for four to eight. Down in the marina at Port Miramar is **La Marine** (04.93.75.49.30, open daily Apr-Sept, menus €25-€50), a very good fish restaurant with a lively bar. More expensive, but worth it for the Asian take on Mediterranean cuisine, is the **Etoile des Mers** at the **Miramar Beach Hôtel** (47 av de Miramar, 04.93.75.05.05, www.mbhriviera.com, double €155-€265, menus €37-€82).

A little further along the coast road, **La Tour de l'Esquillon** (Miramar, Théoule, 04.93.75.41.51, closed Nov-Mar, double €120-€140, menu €34), a 1920s hotel with marvellous views, recalls the era of Scott and Zelda. Théoule has plenty of tasty eating options, including fish restaurant **Le Marco Polo** (av de Lérins, 04.93.49.96.59, menus €30, closed Mon Sept-June), which dabbles a toe in the sea.

In Mandelieu-la-Napoule, **L'Ermitage du Riou** (av Henry Clews, 04.93.49.95.56, www.ermitage-du-riou.fr, closed Jan, double €126-€192, menus €39-€85) is a smart hotel with a private beach, pool and a good, highly atmospheric restaurant. At **L'Oasis** (rue Jean-Honoré Carle, 04.93.49.95.52, www.oasis-raimbault.com, closed 2wks Feb, Mon & dinner Sun mid Oct-Jan, menus €58-€115) you can splash out on Stéphane and François Raimbault's fine classical cooking and sumptuous desserts. On a simpler scale, **Boucanier** (Port de Mandelieu, 04.93.49.80.51) is down by the port; it's very French, very relaxed and serves great food.

Resources

Tourist information

Agay Office de Tourisme *pl Giannetti, 83530 Agay (04.94.82.01.85/www.esd-fr.com/agay).* **Open** *Apr-mid June* 9am-noon, 2-6pm Mon-Sat. *Mid June-Sept* 9am-8pm Mon-Sat. *Oct-Mar* 9am-noon, 2-5pm Mon-Fri.
Mandelieu Office de Tourisme *av Henry Clews, 06210 Mandelieu-la-Napoule (04.93.49.95.31/ www.ot-mandelieu.fr).* **Open** *July, Aug* 10am-12.30pm, 2-7pm daily. *Sept-June* 10am-12.30pm, 2-6pm Mon-Fri.
Théoule Office de Tourisme *1 corniche d'Or, 06590 Théoule-sur-Mer (04.93.49.28.28/ www.theoule-sur-mer.org).* **Open** *May-Sept* 9am-7pm Mon-Sat; 10am-1pm Sun. *Oct-Mar* 9am-noon, 2-6.30pm Mon-Sat.

Getting there & around

By car

For both St-Raphaël and Fréjus come off the A8 at exit 37 or exit 38; St Raphaël is also accessible via the more scenic N98 coast road. The D2098 follows the coast. For Mandelieu-la-Napoule, leave the A8 at exit 40.

By train

St-Raphaël is on the main coastal line, with TGV links from Paris, Nice and Marseille. Frequent trains from Nice and Marseille also stop at Fréjus and Mandelieu. Local trains on the St-Raphaël–Cannes line stop at Agay and Théoule-sur-Mer.

By bus

Cars Phocéens (04.93.85.66.61) runs two services daily from Nice to St-Raphaël and from Marseille to Fréjus (12.45pm, Mon-Sat); from Hyères airport there are four buses a day to Hyères bus station, where you can catch a connection (eight daily) to St-Raphaël. **Estérel Bus** (04.94.52.00.50) runs between St-Raphaël and Draguignan, via Fréjus and Roquebrune (12 daily Mon-Sat; six Sun); there's also a service between St-Raphaël and Agay (15 daily Mon-Sat; ten Sun) and frequently from Le Trayas to Cannes, via Miramar and Théoule-sur-Mer. **Bus Azur** (04.92.99.20.05) runs nine buses daily between Mandelieu and Cannes.

Brignoles & the Sainte-Baume

Pilgrims, hikers and nature-lovers all flock to the verdant Var.

Brignoles & the Green Var

It may look very twee, set among rolling green hills, but **Brignoles** is the busy commercial centre of the western villages, spewing a steady stream of traffic along the RN7. Once famous for its 'sugar plums' (now mysteriously extinct) that were sent for 1,000 years to the royal courts of Europe, it later became prosperous through bauxite mining. The place Carami bustles with café life, while the old town around it is very quiet. The tourist office (*see p208*), itself in a handsome 17th-century building, can provide a walking-tour map (*Découvrir Brignoles*) around its fine houses, towers and thick 13th-century ramparts. Stroll up the covered stairway of rue du Grand Escalier past Eglise St-Sauveur to the Palace of the Counts of Provence, built in 1264 as a summer residence. It is now the **Musée du Pays Brignolais**, which has a collection of provençal curiosities, an ancient sarcophagus, a reconstruction of a bauxite mine and a tiny plum tree (*la prune pistoline*) planted in the courtyard in an attempt to revive the Brignoles delicacy. There's a packed flea market on the promenade along the Carami river every second Sunday of the month.

Brignoles is also a springboard to the outdoor life of La Provence Verte – or the Green Var – a name inspired by the rich underground water sources that protect the region against drought. Take the D554 north from Brignoles, then the D45 at Châteauvert for the **Vallon Sourn**, the steep upper valley of the Argens river, which is a favourite area for rock-climbing, kayaking and biking. **Correns**, capital of the Argens, is the number-one organic village of France with 95 per cent of its wines and farm produce grown organically. **Domaine des Aspras**, owned by the mayor of Correns (04.94.59.59.70, closed Mon, Sun), offers wine tasting in idyllic vineyards just south of town.

Barjols, 22 kilometres (13.5 miles) north of Brignoles, lies in a valley fed by fresh-water springs. Fifteen wash basins and 32 mossy fountains have earned it the hopeful nickname of 'the Tivoli of Provence'. In Réal, the old part of town north of the Romanesque-Gothic

Peace in the valley: **Barjols**.

Eglise Notre-Dame-des-Epines built in 1014, former tanneries along streams now house galleries and artists' studios. Pretty terraces and café tables squeeze into the crooked streets, and on place de la Mairie the largest plane tree in Provence (12-metre or 40-foot circumference) has lifted up the cobblestones. Townspeople celebrate every mid January for the decidedly pagan weekend of Fête de St-Marcel, when the saint's statue is paraded through town with a garlanded ox that is later sacrificed, roasted and eaten, after a drink of water at the Fontaine du Boeuf. Atop a hill in rolling countryside east of Barjols is the village of **Pontevès**, whose ruined chateau and scenic vista make a good picnic spot.

On the southern outskirts of Brignoles by the D405, the tiny village of **La Celle** once attracted those seeking religious solace at the 12th-century **Abbaye Royale**. Today's visitors might have more venal aims, as the abbey is now partially a luxury hotel-restaurant under the sway of super-chef Alain Ducasse (*see p208*).

Tiny **La Roquebrussanne**, 15 kilometres (nine miles) south, is reached through woods beneath the odd-shaped rock formations of La Loube. The village sits squat on a plain of Coteaux Varois vineyards and serves as the central wine pressing co-operative for the region. The D64 leads east of here past two lakes (a couple of spooky holes in the earth with no visible water source) to the British-owned **Château des Chaberts** (04.94.04.92.05) vineyard, a reliable wine producer of rosés and reds, which offers tastings. South of La Roquebrussanne, the D5 winds through vineyards (try Domaine des Laou and Domaine la Rose des Vents) to the sleepy village of **Méounes-les-Montrieux**, a refreshing stop with its streams, meandering streets and shady fountain and cafés under the plane trees of place de l'Eglise.

Abbaye Royale de la Celle

La Celle (04.94.59.19.05). Open varies, ring for details. **Admission** ring for details.

Musée du Pays Brignolais

pl des Comtes de Provence, Brignoles (04.94.69.45.18). Open Apr-Sept 9am-noon, 2.30-6pm Wed-Sun. *Oct-Mar* 10am-noon, 2.30-6pm Wed-Fri; 10am-noon, 2.30-5pm Sat; 10am-noon, 3-5pm Sun. **Admission** €4; €2 12-16s, students; free under-12s. **No credit cards.**

Activities

Canoeing & kayaking

For canoe trips on the River Argens call **Provence Canoë** (D562 east of Carcès, 04.94.29.52.48, June-Aug daily, Apr, May, Sept-Nov by appointment, €13-€28).

Where to stay & eat

In Brignoles, **Hôtel de Provence** (pl du Palais de Justice, 04.94.69.01.18, closed 2wks Nov, Dec, 2wks Feb, double €46-€50, menus €13.50-€30) is the only hotel in the old town, and convenient if you don't mind cigarette smoke and the roar of passing scooters. Nearby, **Café le Central** (pl Carami, 04.94.69.11.10, closed Mon, Sun) serves a good lunchtime *plat du jour* (€8). **Lou Cigaloun** (14 rue de la République, 04.94.59.00.76, closed dinner Tue, Wed, menus €12-€25) is favoured by locals; cooking is fresh, unpretentious and 100 per cent home-made. Should you tire of provençal food, Brignoles has one of the region's few worthwhile Asian restaurants: **Chez Lee** (18 av Dréo, 04.94.69.19.74, closed Tue, menus €11-€29). Arty *chambres d'hôte* **La Cordeline** (14 rue des Cordeliers, 04.94.59.18.66, www.lacordeline. com, double €62-€95, dinner Thur & Sat only, menu €25) offers five rooms in a 17th-century residence and serves intimate family dinners and sugary plum jam *à la brignolaise* at breakfast.

Checking into a posh room at Alain Ducasse's **Hostellerie de l'Abbaye de la Celle** (pl du Général de Gaulle, La Celle, 04.98.05.14.14, www.abbaye-celle.com, double €205-€310) is the only way to go after candlelit dinner in the adjoining Gothic convent (restaurant closed Tue, Wed, 2wks Jan-Feb, menus €40-€74). Five kilometres (three miles)

east of Brignoles, **Golf Club Barbaroux** (D79, rte de Cabasse, 04.94.69.63.63, www.barbaroux. com, double €82-€108, restaurant closed Sun, dinner Mon, menus €25-€40) is a hotel-restaurant on an 18-hole golf course (fees €59). Modern rooms open on to private terraces and the woods. In La Roquebrussanne, **Hôtel-Resto de la Loube** (04.94.86.81.36, closed 2wks Dec-Jan, double €70-€80, restaurant closed dinner Mon & Tue, menus €25-€35) is a classic provençal inn with a lively bar and restaurant with terrace. At Méounes, **La Source** (04.94.48.99.83, www.les-sourciers.com, double €50, restaurant closed Tue, Wed, menus €25-€40) has four sweet rooms and a stark white restaurant, where the chef works magic on rainbow trout and crayfish from the property's own springs.

In outdoorsy Correns, you can live in the woods, in elegant privacy at **La Terrasse** (04.94.59.57.15, www.terrasse-provence.com, double €90), which has air-conditioned duplexes and a pool. For hardier sports lovers, camp at the **Camping Municipal le Grand Jardin** (Mairie de Correns 04.94.37.21.95, tent €3, adults €2.50). Originally managed by Bruno Clément (think expensive truffle lunches), now run by his disciple Bertrand Lherbette, the **Auberge du Parc** (04.94.59.53.52, www.aubergeduparc.fr, pl Général de Gaulle, double €100-€130, restaurant closed Tue, Wed, 2wks Nov, 3wks Feb, menus €32-€45) has baby-blue cupid murals and a *fumoir*. After hiking or rock-climbing in Vallon Sourn, the shady courtyard of the picturesque **Auberge de Châteauvert** (rte de Barjols, closed Tue, 04.94.77.06.60) is a good place for a late-afternoon drink.

In Pontevès, **Domaine-de-St-Ferréol** (just west of Pontevès on D560, 04.94.77.10.42, closed Nov-Feb, double €55-€64) offers upmarket *chambres d'hôte* in an 18th-century farm that bottles its own wine and has a superb pool. For the full back-to-nature experience, you can prepare your own meals in the guests' kitchen-dining room and eat them on little tables in the lovely inner courtyard.

Resources

Market in Brignoles and Barjols is Saturday.

Internet

L'Ourson Surfeur, 9 rue du Dr Barbaroux, Brignoles (04.94.69.02.22/www.oursonsurfeur.free.fr). **Open** 10am-9pm Tue-Sat.

Tourist information

Barjols Office de Tourisme *bd Grisolle, 83670 Barjols (04.94.77.20.01, www.ville-barjols.fr).* **Open** 10am-noon, 3-6pm Tue-Sat.

Brignoles Syndicat d'Initiative *Hôtel de Clavier, rue des Palais, 83170 Brignoles (04.94.69.27.51/www.ville-brignoles.fr).* **Open** 9.30am-12.30pm, 2-5.30pm Mon-Fri.
La Provence Verte Maison du Tourisme *carrefour de l'Europe, 83170 Brignoles (04.94.72.04.21/www.la-provence-verte.org).* **Open** *Mid June-mid Sept* 9am-12.30pm, 2-7.30pm Mon-Sat; 10am-noon, 3-6.30pm Sun. *Mid Sept-mid June* 9am-12.30pm, 2-6.30pm Mon-Sat.

St-Maximin-la-Ste-Baume & the Ste-Baume Massif

In the farming country between Brignoles and Aix, the **Basilique Ste-Marie-Madeleine** at St-Maximin-la-Ste-Baume soars above miles of vineyards: once a divine beacon to caravans of pilgrims, today an excellent marker for anyone travelling the A8 motorway. The basilica is the finest Gothic edifice in Provence – and one of the few outposts of this style in the largely Romanesque South – and pilgrimage site for the tomb of Mary Magdalene, buried here by her friend Maximin with whom she is said to have landed in France from Palestine at Stes-Maries-de-la-Mer (*see p14* **Crossing the holy sea**). It was founded in 1295 by Charles II d'Anjou, King of Sicily and Count of Provence, who hoped to improve his standing by building a resplendent shrine for Mary's relics, above the fourth-century crypt where her sarcophagus had been found in 1280. The interior of the

basilica contains much fascinating decoration by Dominican monks, such as the 94 choir stalls carved in walnut by Brother Vincent Funel. The altarpiece of the Passion by Antoine Ronzen was painted in 1520. Over the altar is a gilded plaster sunburst of cherubs and saints (1678-82) by Lieutaud. The monumental 18th-century organ was saved from destruction during the Revolution by Lucien Bonaparte, Napoleon's youngest brother, who used it for performances of *La Marseillaise*.

Adjoining the basilica is the **Couvent Royal**, a royal foundation begun at the same time as the church, now a lovely hotel (*see p210*). You can visit the chapel, the refectory and the Gothic cloister. Just south of the basilica, rue Colbert runs through the 13th-century medieval quarter and along the sombre arcades of the Jewish district established in 1303 in this passionately Catholic town. Street life revolves around place Malherbe, where the Wednesday market creates a turmoil of shoppers and traffic, and **Café La Renaissance** (04.94.78.00.27) tries to keep up with the demand for *pastis* at its terrace tables.

Stretching south-west of St-Maximin are the forested limestone hills of the Massif-de-la-Ste-Baume. **Nans-les-Pins** is a hiking centre on the GR9 to Signes and the Chemin des Rois royal pilgrimage route leading from St-Maximin through sacred forests to the Grotte Ste-Marie-Madeleine. In this holy cave or *santo baumo*, legend claims Mary Magdalene lived out the

Plan d'Aups, where the living is easy. *See p210.*

last 33 years of her life in solitary penitence until, too frail to walk, she was carried by angels to her old friend Maximin from St-Maximin (then known as Villalata). Each Good Friday, a procession led by Dominican monks climbs the mountain for mass inside the cave; otherwise, contact the tourist office in Plan d'Aups for guided visits. The cave is hidden in the cliffs at 950 metres (3,100 feet), and can be reached by climbing a short footpath from the Hôtellerie de la Baume (*see below*). Across the road from the Hôtellerie, the **Ecomusée de la Ste-Baume** displays ancient crafts, especially wool dyeing and weaving. The forest was also long associated with fertility rites – the GR9 footpath follows an ancient mule track past the huge oval Cave of Eggs, where medieval mothers came to 'find' (conceive) their children. **Plan d'Aups**, a village on a barren mountain plateau, has a Friday market with good farmhouse goat's cheeses and jams. Monks from the 11th-century church shop in billowing white robes along with more mundane locals. At the eastern end of the massif, the village of **Mazaugues** for centuries sent ice (to preserve fresh fish) to Toulon and Marseille from its numerous ice factories. Ice production is explained in the **Musée de la Glace**, which has ice tools and a reconstructed *glacière*.

Basilique Ste-Marie-Madeleine

pl de Prêcheurs, St-Maximin (04.42.38.01.78). **Open** 8am-11.30am, 3-5.30pm Mon-Sat; mass 8am, 11am Sun. **Admission** free.

Ecomusée de la Ste-Baume

Plan d'Aups (04.42.62.56.46). **Open** *May-Sept* 9am-noon, 2-6pm daily. *Oct-Apr* 2-5pm daily. **Admission** €4; under-14s free. **No credit cards**.

Musée de la Glace

Hameau du Château, Mazaugues (04.94.86.39.24/www.museeglace.fr.st). **Open** *June-Sept* 9am-noon, 2-6pm Tue-Sun. *Oct-May* 9am-noon, 2-5pm Sun only (call for group visits on other days). **Admission** €2.30 (museum plus *glacière* €4); free under-6s. **No credit cards**.

Where to stay & eat

Hôtellerie du Couvent Royal (pl Jean Salusse, 04.94.86.55.66, www.hotelfp-saintmaximin.com, double €75-€100, menus €26-€35) is the only place worth staying in St-Maximin. Cells inhabited by monks from 1316 to 1957 have been converted with a sense of monastic calm. The vaulted capitular room is shared by the hotel's restaurant and the **Maison des Vins du Var** (04.94.78.09.50), which does tastings there

Beween Nans-les-Pins and Plan d'Aups, the **Hôtellerie de la Baume** (D95, 04.42.04.54.84,

dormitory €7/person in groups of ten, double €25, meals €12 by reservation), a Benedictine convent, still offers accommodation for pilgrims. At Nans-les-Pins, the **Hôtel Domaine de Châteauneuf** (rte N560, 04.94.78.90.06, www.domaine-de-chateau neuf.com, closed Nov-Mar, double €152-€626, restaurant closed lunch Mon-Fri, menus €38-€70) sits in the middle of the 18-hole Golf Club La Ste-Baume. It was once a stopping point for Crusaders heading to the Holy Land; the present building later hosted Napoleon's family. Guests get preferential green fees (€50/day) and it also has a pool and tennis courts. Across the N560, the elegant **Château de Nans** (04.94.78.92.06, www.chateau-de-nans.fr, closed 1wk Nov, mid Feb-mid Mar, double €122-€183, restaurant closed Mon, Tue, menus €43-€54) dishes up divine delicacies, such as a seasonal number of wild rabbit and venison with juniper berries.

Resources

Market day is Wednesday in St-Maximin, Sunday in Nans-les-Pins.

Internet

SMI St-Maximin Informatique, 9 rue de la République, St-Maximin (04.98.05.92.70). **Open** 9am-noon, 3-6.30pm Tue-Sat.

Tourist information

Nans-les-Pins Office de Tourisme *2 cours Général de Gaulle, 83860 Nans-les-Pins (04.94.78.95.91/www.membres.lycos.fr/nanslespins).* **Open** *July, Aug* 9am-noon, 3-6pm Mon-Sat; 9am-noon Sun. *Sept-June* 9am-noon, 2-5pm Mon-Sat; 9am-noon Sun.
Plan d'Aups Office de Tourisme *pl de la Mairie, 83640 Plan d'Aups Ste-Baume (04.42.62.57.57).* **Open** 9am-noon, 3-5pm Mon-Fri; 9am-noon Sat.
St-Maximin Office de Tourisme *Hôtel de Ville, 83470 St-Maximin-la-Ste-Baume (04.94.59.84.59).* **Open** 9am-12.30pm, 2-6pm Mon-Sat; 10am-12.30pm, 2-6pm Sun.

Getting there & around

By car

Leave the A8 at exit 34 for St-Maximin, exit 35 for Brignoles, both are also on the N7.

By bus

Autocars Blancs (04.94.69.08.28), based in Brignoles, runs six buses daily between Brignoles and St-Maximin and St-Maximin and Aix, daily services between Brignoles and Barjols; around two buses a day running towards Les Arcs stop at Correns.
Phocéen Voyages (04.93.85.66.61) runs buses twice daily from Nice, and once a day from Marseille to both Brignoles and St-Maximin.

Draguignan & the Central Var

Where pigs snuffle for truffles and the *villages perchés* make artists reach for their brushes and Parisians call their mortgage brokers.

Centred around the busy hub of Draguignan, the interior of the Var *département* is a land of Côtes de Provence vineyards, truffle woods and *villages perchés* with wrought-iron belfries. The Var has been discovered by the British but many villages remain pleasantly untrafficked.

Draguignan & the Gorges de Châteaudouble

With its military barracks (the town hosts the French army artillery school) and broad boulevards laid out in the 19th century by Baron Haussmann in a dress rehearsal for his reworking of Paris, **Draguignan** doesn't conform to all those pétanque, lavender and village-fountain clichés. But once past the shopping malls, discount stores and fast food joints on the outskirts, the town centre is a pleasant place to while away a couple of hours. During the day at least, Draguignan (whose name derived from the dragon-slaying exploits of fifth-century St Hermentine) tries to emulate its prestigious past, when from 1797 to 1974 it was capital of the Var. To appreciate the town's real charm, take the pedestrianised Montée de l'Horloge to look at the 17th-century bell tower and perhaps climb its 79 steps (open 10.30am-12.30pm, 3-7pm June & July). Carry on to place du Marché, lined with elegantly dilapidated townhouses, adorned with blue shutters and hanging plants. If you can face the crowds in the summer heat, come on market days (all day Wednesday and Saturday morning) when the square and surrounding alleys are perfumed with the scents of roasting chickens, thyme, goat's cheese and pastis. There are two worthwhile museums in the old town. First is the **Musée Municipal**, housed in the summer palace of the Bishop of Fréjus. Besides a patchy collection of antiques and archaeology it has some fine sculptures and paintings, including *Rêve au coin du feu*, a marble sculpture by Camille Claudel from 1903, and *L'Enfant au béguin* by Renoir, dating from when the artist lived in Cagnes-sur-Mer. Look out, too, for the

Flayosc: where to get fortified. *See p212.*

painting *St-Pierre de Rome* by 17th-century Italian master Panini. The second museum is the recently renovated **Musée des Traditions Provençales**, which recreates traditional life through displays of agricultural tools, glass, tiles and furnishings, plus a collection of *santons*. American visitors might be interested in the US war cemetery on the boulevard John Kennedy: 861 soldiers who participated in the 1944 landings are buried here and a wall commemorates 3,000 men who disappeared.

As for the dragon, apparently it hung out in the **Gorges de Châteaudouble** north of town, reached via the scenic D955. First stop on this road is the Pierre de la Fée (fairy stone), a giant dolmen dating from 2400 BC. Further along, a dirt road on the right takes you through the beautiful vineyard of the **Domaine du Dragon** (04.98.10.23.00), once the 12th-century fortified Castrum de Dragone of the Draguignan family, where archeologists have recently discovered a medieval chapel on first-century foundations. The D955 winds along the gorge floor passing **Rebouillon**, a hamlet built like a horseshoe around a central meadow on the banks of the Nartuby. From the gorge road, Châteaudouble (also reached direct by the D45) suddenly appears high on spectacular cliffs, as the scenery changes dramatically to a far more Alpine landscape with jagged rock formations. Châteaudouble was originally called the Devil's Gap. In winter the village is full of huntsmen, buying arms for tracking wild boar.

The Var

West of Draguignan is a flatter landscape, ripe with vineyards and fruit trees. The D557 heads into the fortified village of **Flayosc**. Life revolves around the little place de la République with its timeworn fountain; unlike the majority of other fountains in the area, though, the water is not suitable for drinking. Fruit, vegetable and wine producers set up their stalls here on Monday mornings. This is also a good time to pick up some ultra-fresh pasta and own-made pesto from **Les Pâtes Flayoscaises** at 23 boulevard Jean Moulin, a small street (despite its name) that runs into the square. Shopping done, everyone relaxes on the terrace of the **Café du Commerce**. The 12th-century church, with the wrought-iron belfry characteristic of these parts, is also worth a visit at the east end of the village. In a bucolic hamlet just north of Flayosc, the 13th-century **Moulin du Flayosquet** (04.94.70.41.45, open 9am-noon, 2-6.30pm Tue-Sat) is the oldest operating olive mill in the Var. Fifth-generation owner Max Doleatto offers guided visits and tastings of olive oil.

Musée Municipal
9 rue de la République, Draguignan (04.98.10.26.85). **Open** 9am-noon, 2-6pm Mon-Sat. **Admission** free.

Musée des Traditions Provençales
15 rue Roumanille, Draguignan (04.94.47.05.72). **Open** 9am-noon, 2-6pm Tue-Sat; 2-6pm Sun. **Admission** €3.50; €1.50 6-18s, students under 25; free under-6s. **No credit cards**.

Where to stay & eat

The surrounding countryside is so seductive it generally makes more sense to stay in a *chambres d'hôtes* with a garden than in one of Draguignan's hotels. If you must spend the night here, head for the **Hotel du Parc** (21 bd de la Liberté, 04.98.10.14.50, www.hotel-duparc.fr, double €54-€63), an old-fashioned but comfortable address just oustide the old town. Some of the rooms are air-conditioned. In the same courtyard, the **Restaurant du Parc** (not part of the hotel, 04.94.50.66.44, closed Mon & Sun, menus €13-€30) has good traditional cooking and tables scattered under a huge plane tree. **Les Milles Colonnes** (2 pl aux Herbes, 04.94.68.52.58, closed Sun & 2wks Aug, dinner served mid June-mid Aug, otherwise lunch only, menu €18.50) is a lively brasserie in the old town serving up fresh market dishes. Specialities include petits farcis niçois, rougets à la tapenade and apple crumble. A stone's throw outside Draguignan, **Les Oliviers** (rte de Flayosc, 04.94.68.25.74, closed 2wks Jan, double €52-€57) is a good place to stop for the night, with sparkling clean rooms and a swimming pool in its garden.

In Châteaudouble, the view's the thing at the **Restaurant de la Tour** (pl Beausoleil, 04.94.70.93.08, closed Wed, menus €21-€28) but the food comes a close second – try the excellent game dishes and the truffle omelette if you're around between November and February. **Le Château** (04.94.70.90.05, closed Mon, dinner Sun Oct-Mar, menus €26-€50) offers modern provençal cuisine, plus own-made foie gras and views over the Nartuby gorge. In Flayosc, **L'Oustaou** (5 pl Brémond, 04.94.70.42.69, closed Mon, Wed & dinner Sun, menus €26-€42) is a well-regarded regional restaurant with a terrace. Specialities include daube provençale and pieds et paquets marseillais. At **La Salle à Manger** (9 pl de la République, 04.94.84.66.04, closed Mon & lunch Sat, menus €29-€39) Dutch chef Elisabeth Abbink uses only the freshest produce, and favours playful takes on trad dishes, such as crème brûlée of lamb, foie gras and vegetables.

Resources

Market is Wednesday and Sunday mornings in Draguignan, Monday morning in Flayosc, Tuesday in Lorgues and Friday Châteaudouble.

Hospital
Hôpital de Draguignan, rte de Montfarrat, Draguignan (04.94.60.50.00).

Internet
L'Endroit, 212 rue Jean Aicard, Draguignan (04.94.68.90.39). **Open** 3-8pm Mon; 10am-1pm, 3-8pm Tue-Thur; 10am-1pm, 3-7pm Fri, Sat.

Police
Commissariat, 1 allée Azémar, Draguignan (04.94.60.61.60).

Post office
rue St-Jaume, Draguignan (04.94.50.57.35). **Open** 8am-noon, 2-7pm Mon-Fri; 8am-1pm Sat.

Tourist information
Châteaudouble *Office de Tourisme, Hôtel de Ville, pl de la Fontaine, 83300 Châteaudouble (04.98.10.51.35).* **Open** 8-11.30am Mon-Fri.
Draguignan *Office de Tourisme, 2 av Lazare Carnot, 83300 Draguignan (04.98.10.51.05/ www.dracenie.com).* **Open** July, Aug 9am-7pm Mon-Sat; 9am-1pm Sun. Closed Sept-June.
Flayosc *Office de Tourisme, pl Pied-Barri, 83780 Flayosc (04.94.70.41.31/www.ville-flayosc.fr).* **Open** July, Aug 9am-noon, 3-6pm Mon-Sat; 9am-noon Sun. Sept-June 9am-noon, 3-6pm Mon-Sat.

Salernes, Aups & Tourtour

Salernes was made for market days, thanks to its large central square, cours Théodore Bouge, shaded by centuries-old plane trees. This is a

Out on the tiles in **Salernes**.

far more civilised spot than it was 7,000 years ago, when its citizens were cannibals (just check the proud plaque at the entrance to the Intermarché supermarket on the eastern edge of town, but don't let this dissuade you from opting for the succulent, herb-fed Sisteron lamb available here). On Wednesday and Sunday market mornings, parking places and café seats are rare finds, especially at the bustling **Café de la Bresque**. When not crammed with stalls selling fresh produce and pottery, the town is surprisingly quiet, even at the height of summer. This is the moment to explore its pretty backstreets and squares, especially the handsome place de la Révolution, which has a superb Roman fountain dribbling spring water. Down by the River Bresque, which flows along the southern side of the town, La Muie is an exceptionally pretty bathing site, with crystal-clear water and sandy banks.

Thanks to local clay, water and abundant wood from nearby forests to fuel its kilns, Salernes has been renowned for centuries for the manufacture of the hexagonal terracotta tiles, known as *tommettes,* that cover the floor of traditional provençal homes. Today there are 16 tile workshops, mostly on the western outskirts of town. Check out **Sismondini** (rte de Sillans, 04.94.04.63.06, closed Sun) and **Jacques Brest Céramiques** (quartier des Arnauds, 04.94.70.60.65, closed Sun) for traditional tiles, **Carrelages Pierre Boutal** (rte de Draguignan, 04.94.70.62.12, closed Sun)

for painted designs, and **Alain Vagh** (rte d'Entrecasteaux, 04.94.70.61.85) for colourful glazes and wacky creations from a pink-tiled Harley Davidson to a tiled grand piano.

A short drive north on the D31 brings you to the tightly knit town of **Aups**, truffle capital of the Var. Every Thursday at 10am from late November to late February there is a high-stakes truffle auction in the main square, where the precious commodity – all the more valuable as it is exempt from taxes – is sold out of car boots. The black fungi go for €600 to €1,800 per kilo; good ones should be fragrant and rather clean (not coated with earth, which may hide gravel and other disappointing substances). If the thought of chopping and cooking one of these overpriced little things makes you nervous, an excellent restaurant just around the corner, Les Gourmets (*see p214*), serves truffles year-round.

Aups life revolves around the cafés on tiny place Girard, which leads into rue Maréchal Foch, filled with boutiques hawking provençal artefacts. A little further up on avenue Albert 1er, don't miss the **Musée Simon Segal**, housed in a former Ursuline convent, and containing the work of the Russian-born artist and other lesser-known but equally impressive artists of the Ecole de Paris. **Le Moulin à Huile** (Montée des Moulins, 04.94.70.04.66) displays ancient oil-extracting equipment and a video explaining the process, and offers tastings of its award-winning olive oil.

The Var

The seven-kilometre (four-mile) drive along the D557 from Aups to Villecroze offers breathtaking views of the Var's wooded landscape as far as the Maures mountain range. Just before the entrance to the town lies the adorable 12th-century chapel of St-Victor, muffled by ancient cypresses and olive trees. The chapel is cared for by the **Académie Musicale de Villecroze** (9 rue Roger Maurice, 04.94.85.91.00, www.academie-villecroze.com) whose pupils perform here in summer (8.30pm every other Fri, Apr-Oct). **Villecroze** (meaning hollow town) is set against a cliff face riddled with caves known as the **Grottes Troglodytes** (reserve visits in May-Sept at the tourist office), which a local lord turned into dwellings in the 16th century. Until a few years ago a waterfall cascaded year-round down the cliff into a crystal-clear stream in the picturesque garden beneath. Lately, however, drought conditions have encouraged home owners to divert the water for their gardens, and it now runs dry from June to autumn.

The perched medieval village of **Tourtour** is situated just above Villecroze, reached by a twisting switchback road that gives credence to its title 'the village in the sky'. St Trinian's illustrator Ronald Searle had the good taste to settle here in the mid 1970s and hasn't moved his drawing board since. Luckily, it is too small to house many souvenir shops, while **Florence** (pl des Ormeaux, 04.94.70.56.90), the only clothes boutique, is as sophisticated as a Paris equivalent. The boules pitch below the town hall has a panoramic view over the region and is particularly picturesque on Wednesday and Saturday market days. Further up, the 11th-century church dominates the valley. The village also has a still-operational 17th-century olive press, a *lavoir* and the medieval Tour Grimaldi watchtower.

Take the quiet D51 out of Tourtour to reach the sleepy hamlet of **Ampus**, which harbours an 11th-century Romanesque church and the pretty chapel Notre-Dame-de-Spéluque, which has a beautifully sculpted altar.

Musée Simon Segal

av Albert 1er, Aups (04.94.70.01.95). **Open** *Mid June-mid Sept* 10am-noon, 4-7pm Mon, Wed-Sun. **Admission** €2.50; €1.60 10-18s, students; free under-10s. **No credit cards.**

Where to stay & eat

Aups comes alive in winter for the Fête des Truffes, on the fourth Sunday of January. A good place to sample the fungi is **Les Gourmets** (5 rue Voltaire, 04.94.70.14.97, closed Mon, late June-mid July & 2wks Dec,

The Grottes Troglodytes at **Villecroze**.

menus €14.50-€32), a discreet gastronomical restaurant on the road to Tourtour. Truffles and foie gras are served year-round; the rest of the menu changes every three months, to include game in winter, asparagus and morels in spring. A little further west, in tiny Moissac-Bellevue, the **Bastide du Calalou** (rte d'Aups, 04.94.70.17.91, www.bastide-du-calalou.com, double €77-€191) is the most comfortable hotel around Aups. Large rooms have plush furnishings and sofa-beds for children; the piano bar and library open on to a huge garden with a pool. The ultra-renovated, supernaturally clean decor feels a bit unreal, but the atmosphere is relaxed and family-oriented.

The best of the cafés and restaurants in Tourtour's main square is **L'Amandier** (pl des Ormeaux, 04.94.70.56.64, closed Mon, Nov-early Feb, menus €25-€37), whose chef likes to perfume fish and seafood with saffron, anis and three kinds of fennel (root, leaf and seed). Game is served in winter, and there's a good wine list. Just outside Tourtour, **Le Mas l'Acacia** (rte d'Aups, 04.94.70.53.84, double €50-€60) is a *chambres d'hôte* with spectacular views and a small pool. **La Bastide de Tourtour** (04.98.10.54.20, double €130-€241, restaurant dinner only except July & Aug,

menus €27.50-€49) invariably has an array of
Bentleys and Jaguars in its car park. However,
despite its fabulous views and large park, this
chateau hotel has never managed to shake off
its charmless atmosphere. On a hill below
Tourtour, the **Mas des Collines** (camp
Fournier, 04.94.70.59.30, double €80-€100,
restaurant dinner only, menus €22-€25) has
magnificent views from the balconies of its
simple rooms, and a swimming pool. A five-
minute drive out towards Villecroze, **Les
Chênes Verts** (04.94.70.55.06, closed June,
double €100, restaurant closed Tue & Wed,
menus €50-€125) is a gourmet restaurant
whose chef, Paul Bagade, does wonderful
things with truffles; it also has three
charming bedrooms.

Hidden in the countryside a few kilometres
(a mile or so) from Villecroze, **Hôtel au Bien-
Etre** (04.94.70.67.57, www.aubienetre.com,
closed Nov & Feb, double €50-€69, restaurant
closed lunch Mon-Wed, menus €24-€48) has
motel-style rooms with little terraces (although
you may find your neighbours are a little
too close for comfort). Locals come for the
sophisticated cuisine of jovial owner-chef
Michel Audier, including brouillade aux
truffes and Grand-Marnier soufflé.

Gourmets should not miss the **Fontaine
d'Ampus** (04.94.70.98.08, closed Mon-Wed,
menu €38) in Ampus. Owner-chef Marc
Haye changes his four-course menu weekly
and claims never to repeat himself. He is
particularly clever at combining herbs
and local produce to create flavours that
your taste buds will have rarely encountered.
If only the service wasn't so bossy, the place
would be a real treat.

Resources

Weekly markets are on Wednesday and Sunday
in Salernes, Wednesday and Saturday in Aups
and Tourtour.

Tourist information

Ampus *Office de Tourisme, Hôtel de Ville, 83111
Ampus (04.94.70.97.11/www.mairie-ampus.fr).*
Open 9.30am-12.30pm Mon-Fri.

Aups *Office de Tourisme, pl Mistral, 83630 Aups
(04.94.84.00.69).* **Open** *Apr-June, Sept* 9am-noon,
2-5.30pm Mon-Sat. *July, Aug* 9am-12.30pm, 3-6.30pm
Mon-Sat. *Oct-Mar* 9am-noon, 1.30pm-5pm Mon-Fri,
9am-noon Sat.

Salernes *Office de Tourisme, pl Gabriel Péri,
83690 Salernes (04.94.70.69.02).* **Open** *July, Aug*
9am-7pm Mon-Sat; 10am-1pm, 3-6pm Sun. *Sept-June*
9.30am-12.30pm, 2-6pm Tue-Sat; 11am-12.30pm Sun.

Villecroze *Office de Tourisme, rue Ambroise
Croizat, 83690 Villecroze (04.94.67.50.00).* **Open**
June-Sept 9.30am-1pm, 4-6.30pm Mon-Sat. *Oct-May*
10am-1pm, 3-5pm Mon-Sat.

Cotignac & around

Framed by an 80-metre-high and 400-metre-
wide rock face (260 feet by 1,300 feet) pierced
with caves and topped with the ruins of a
15th-century castle, lively **Cotignac** has long
seduced the British who buzz around its estate
agents. The village takes its name from *coing*
(quince), as for centuries the community has
made jelly from the fruit. Locals and would-be
locals lounge on café terraces under the huge
old plane trees that line the cours Gambetta.
The liveliest and most picturesque time to come
is on flea market days (call 04.94.76.85.91 for
dates) when the town becomes one big bric-a-
brac emporium. To witness Provençal
Romanesque architecture in its purest form
it's worth visiting the 12th-century **Eglise
St-Pierre** in the town centre, though it is
Notre-Dame-des-Grâces at the southern
entrance that holds a special place in French
history. A Paris monk dreamed that the only
way Louis XIII could have children was for
Anne of Austria to carry out three novenas,
including one at Cotignac. Lo and behold, Louis
XIV was born after the queen left the town. To
be on the safe side, Louis XIV paid his respects
here in 1660 en route to marry the Infanta
Marie-Thérèse in St-Jean-de-Luz. The medieval
rue Clastre has the oldest houses, while the
place de la Mairie has an exquisite belfry dating
from 1496. On and around the Grande Rue there
are elegant 16th- and 17th-century townhouses;
place de la Liberté boasts the prettiest of
Cotignac's 18 fountains. The magnificent
waterfall La Trompine that cascades down
the cliff from the River Cassole provides
hydroelectric power. Just outside Cotignac, the
Théâtre de Gassière, an outdoor amphitheatre,
is used for outdoor concerts in July and August.

Perhaps three kilometres (a mile) outside
Cotignac on the D13 lies the impressive
Monastère St-Joseph-du-Bessillon,
whose cloister and dormitories have been
lovingly restored by its 16 resident Benedictine
nuns. To hear the Gregorian chants and mass
in Latin is a rare, moving experience (mass
11am, vespers 5pm daily).

Continue north on the D13 to **Fox-Amphoux**,
first a Roman encampment, later a staging post
of the Knights Templar. Locals still pronounce
it 'foks-amfooks' in true provençal style, though
there are precious few locals left in the village.
In ruins only 20 years ago, it is now full of over-
restored second homes. Still, the 12th-century
Romanesque church is intact on place de
l'Eglise. Dutch painter Bram van Velde spent
a solitary year working here in 1958; due to the
absence of cafés and shops, it's still an ideal
refuge for those who like peace and quiet.

The Var

Between Fox-Amphoux and Salernes, **Sillans-la-Cascade** is a refreshingly unrestored village with a sunny square and two restaurants facing the River Bresque. Bits of 11th-century fortifications surround the 19th-century chateau; the original Renaissance edifice was levelled in the Revolution after the owner refused to pay his taxes. In front of the old chapel, a painted wooden sign indicates a 30-minute hike to *la cascade* itself, a waterfall that crashes down into a delightful cool pool.

East of Cotignac on the D50, the village of **Entrecasteaux** is dominated by the magnificent 17th-century **Château d'Entrecasteaux**. Narrowly saved from destruction during the Revolution, it was in ruins when Scottish painter Ian McGarvie-Munn – whose chequered life included a stint as commander of the Guatemalan navy – purchased it and began repairs in the 1970s. Although very long, the structure is only one room deep but it has a surrounding formal garden designed by André Le Nôtre.

Château d'Entrecasteaux

Entrecasteaux (04.94.04.43.95). **Open** (guided tours) *Apr-July, Sept-Oct* 4pm Mon-Fri, Sun. *Aug* 11.30am, 4pm, 5pm Mon-Fri, Sun. Closed Oct-Mar except for reserved bookings of over 20 people. **Admission** €7; €4 12-16s; free under-12s. **No credit cards.**

Where to stay & eat

On a quiet street in Cotignac, **Maison Gonzagues** (9 rue Léon Gérard, 04.94.72.85.40, double €115) offers five handsome rooms in an 18th-century townhouse furnished with antiques. At 27 cours Gambetta, **La Table de la Fontaine** (04.94.04.79.13, closed Mon & dinner Sun Nov-Apr, menus €20-€26) is the best restaurant on the main drag; however, a new chef was poised to take over at the time of writing. A few streets up, **Le Temps de Pose** (11 pl de la Mairie, 04.94.77.72.07, ring for opening times, average €15) is a deliciously eccentric and disorganised tearoom serving tarts and salads made with mostly organic produce. Perched on a hill on the outskirts of the village, newly opened **L'Ensoleillado** (1298 chemin de la Colle de Pierre, 04.94.04.61.61, closed dinner Sun, Mon, 1wk Nov & 1wk Jan, menu €39) has elegant food (good foie gras) in an elegant setting, but the real luxury here is the airy terrace overlooking the village and the cliffs. A few minutes' drive out of Cotignac, surrounded by vineyards, the **Clos des Vignes** (rte de Monfort, 04.94.04.72.19, closed Mon, lunch Tue mid June-mid Oct, 2wks Jan, menus €25-€35) offers lovely, carefully prepared provençal dishes. Olives grow all around **La Radassière**, just east of Cotignac (rte d'Entrecasteaux,

Château d'Entrecasteaux.

04.94.04.63.33, closed Jan, double €70), a friendly B&B where Maryse Artaud serves huge breakfasts, including preserved figs and local quince jelly; ask for one of the rooms with a bay window. On the same road, M and Mme Delamarre, former owners (and chef) of La Table de la Fontaine, will open their *chambres d'hôte*, **La Bastide des Muriers** (04.94.04.70.92, double €70-€92, menu around €18) in October 2005; meals made with fruit and vegetables from their garden should be excellent value.

In Fox-Amphoux take a room with a view at the 11th-century **Auberge du Vieux Fox** (pl de l'Eglise, 04.94.80.71.69, closed Nov-Jan, double €66-€100, restaurant closed lunch Wed, Thur, menus €18-€32). The restaurant offers a meaty menu including pork, duck and boar. As an antidote to all the prettiness, phone ahead to book lunch at **Chez Jean** (04.94.80.70.76, closed dinner, lunch Wed, 2wks Apr, menu €11.50) at the La Bréguière roundabout north of the village. Under the gaze of a stuffed owl and boar, Jean and Chantal Serre serve abundant, wholesome fare. In Sillans-la-Cascade, **Hôtel-Restaurant Les Pins** (04.94.04.63.26, double €45, menus €16-€34) offers pleasant rooms and meals in a rustic dining room. Try the fish stew with pistou in summer, game in winter.

Resources

Market day is Tuesday in Cotignac, Friday in Entrecasteaux.

Tourist information

Cotignac *Office de Tourisme, 2 rue Bonaventure, 83570 Cotignac (04.94.04.61.87/www.cotignac. provencevert.fr)*. **Open** *Apr-Sept* 9.45am-12.45pm, 3.30-6.30pm Tue-Fri; 9.45am-12.45pm, 3.30-6pm Sat. *Oct-Mar* 9am-1pm, 3-6pm Tue-Fri; 9am-1pm Sat.

Entrecasteaux *Office de Tourisme, cours Gabriel Péri, 83570 Entrecasteaux (04.98.05.22.05/ www.si-entrecasteaux.com)*. **Open** *June-mid Sept* 10am-noon, 3-7pm Tue-Sat. *Mid Sept-May* 9am-noon, 2-5pm Tue-Sat.

Sillans *Office de Tourisme, Le Château, 83690 Sillans-la-Cascade (04.94.04.78.05)*. **Open** *Mid Mar-June, Oct-Dec* 9am-noon, 2-6pm Wed-Sun. *July-Sept* 9am-noon, 3-7pm Wed-Sun. Closed Jan-mid Mar (except for last weekend of Feb).

The Argens Valley & Abbaye du Thoronet

South of Draguignan, Côtes de Provence vineyards line the gentle slopes either side of the Argens river. The most popular sport here is the estate crawl – something best done by bicycle, with a solemn promise that you'll come back later with the car to pick up those 15 cases of rosé. Avoid, however, the dangerous and noisy N7, and stick to the small roads. Most French think of **Le Muy** as the motorway exit for St-Tropez. But this small, flat, militantly working-class town has been caught in the crossfire of history a couple of times: once when the locals failed to assassinate Holy Roman Emperor Charles V and again when Le Muy was the parachute bridgehead for Operation Dragon, the August 1944 Allied liberation of Provence. The **Musée de la Libération**, where memorabilia includes jeeps, parachutes and various documents, complements a visit to the American War Cemetery in Draguignan.

Between Le Muy and Les Arcs you'll find the vineyards and chapel of the **Château Ste-Roseline**. Saintly noble lass Roseline de Villeneuve (1263-1329) used to feed starving peasants during Saracen invasions; after her death, her corpse refused to decompose and has since reclined in a glass casket in the chapel. The mainly baroque chapel has some unexpected music stands by Diego Giacometti, brother of Alberto, and a mosaic by Chagall.

Les Arcs itself has a pretty cream-coloured medieval centre that twists up steeply to the keep of the 11th-century Villeneuve castle. The **Maison des Vins** on the N7 south of town is an excellent one-stop shop for those who don't have the time or patience to tour the vineyards; it also has maps and brochures for those who do. Just outside Taradeau, the **Château St-Martin** gives a *son et lumière* show (in French or English) in the 15th-century cellar, portraying the history of provençal wines.

The D10 north to Lorgues crosses the Argens river, passing the imposing **Château d'Astros** (04.94.99.73.00), which featured in Yves Robert's film of Pagnol's *Le Château de ma mère*. **Lorgues** has a pleasant main street lined with peeling plane trees, fountains and cafés, an old town full of medieval houses and foodie destination Chez Bruno (*see p218*). Park by the 18th-century **Collégiale St-Martin** and look in at the multicoloured marble altar.

Nestled in the Darboussière forest, the **Abbaye du Thoronet** is a silent and imposing place, whose sparse, geometric lines, pure and stripped of ornament, reflect the austere lifestyle of the back-to-basics Cistercian order. Man-made reinforcements are shunned: the blocks of warm pinkish stone are held together by sheer gravity. The first of the three great Cistercian foundations of Provence (with Silvacane and Sénanque), Thoronet stays faithful to the Romanesque, though by 1160, when work began, northern France was already under the sway of Gothic. The cloister, built on different levels to accommodate the slope of the ground, has a charming fountain house. This extraordinary haven is, however, under threat. Every day lorries loaded with bauxite from nearby mines shudder past, putting enormous pressure on the building. Sadly, experts are now advocating that concrete columns be used to reinforce the site.

Abbaye du Thoronet

Darboussière forest (04.94.60.43.90). **Open** *Apr-Sept* 10am-6.30pm daily. *Oct-Mar* 10am-1pm, 2-5pm daily. Closed Sun mass (noon-2pm). **Admission** €6.50; €4.50 students under 25; free under-18s. **Credit** MC, V.

Chapelle & Château Ste-Roseline

D91 4km E of Les Arcs (www.sainte-roseline.com/ 04.94.73.37.30). **Open** *July, Aug* 2-6pm Tue-Sun. *Sept-June* 2-5pm Tue-Sun. **Admission** free. *Wine-tasting at Château Ste-Roseline (04.94.99.50.36)*. **Open** *May-Sept* 9am-12.30pm, 2-7pm Mon-Sat; 10am-noon, 2-6pm Sun. *Oct-Apr* 9am-noon, 2-6.30pm Mon-Fri; 10am-noon, 2-6pm Sat, Sun. **Admission** free. *Guided tours of wine cellars (04.94.99.50.36)*. **Tours** 2.30pm Mon-Fri. **Admission** €4; €9-€11.50 groups. **Credit** MC, V.

Château St-Martin

rte des Arcs (04.94.99.76.76). **Open** *Apr-mid Oct* 9am-6pm daily. *Mid Oct-Mar* 9am-1pm, 3-7pm Mon-Sat. **Admission** free; *son et lumière* €3.95; tastings €3.45-€10. **Credit** AmEx, MC, V.

The Var

Maison des Vins Côtes de Provence

Les Arcs (04.94.99.50.20/www.caveaucp.fr).
Open *July, Aug* 10am-1pm, 1.30-8pm daily.
June, Sept 10am-1pm, 1.30-7pm daily. *Oct-May*
10am-1pm, 1.30-6pm Mon-Sat. **Admission** free.

Musée de la Libération

Tour Charles-Quint, Le Muy (04.94.45.12.79).
Open *Apr-June* 10am-noon Sun.*July, Aug* 9.30am-
noon, 3-6pm Tue-Sat; 10am-noon Sun. *Sept-Mar*
by appointment. **Admission** free.

Where to stay & eat

In Les Arcs, book well ahead if you want to
stay at **Le Logis du Guetteur** (04.94.99.51.10,
www.logisduguetteur.com, closed mid Jan-mid
Mar, double €108-€130), which occupies part
of the Villeneuve chateau; it has 13 charming
rooms and diners eat in vaulted rooms (menus
€34-€76). You can also just stroll in for a drink
and a look around: the (rather expensive) bar
is open to non-hotel patrons. The jovial Boeuf
brothers have the gourmet scene in Vidauban
sewn up: Alain runs hearty **La Concorde** on
the main square (pl de la Mairie, 04.94.73.01.19,
closed dinner Tue, all Wed, 2wks Nov & 2wks
Feb, menus €18.50-€55), while his brother
Christian recently opened the more designer
restaurant **Bastide des Magnans** (D48, rte
de La Garde-Freinet, 04.94.99.43.91, closed
Mon & dinner Wed, menus €17-€55); both
offer solid but elegant *cuisine de terroir*. In
Lorgues, the jet set flock to be ministered
to by truffle king Bruno Clément at **Chez
Bruno** (rue des Arcs, Campagne Mariette,
04.94.85.93.93, www.restaurantbruno.com,
closed Mon & dinner Sun, menus €58.80-
€120) where the black fungus gets into
everything from lobster to ice-cream.

Resources

The markets take place on Thursday and
Sunday mornings in Le Muy, and every
Tuesday in Lorgues.

Tourist information

Les Arcs *Office de Tourisme, pl Général de
Gaulle, 83460 Les Arcs (04.94.73.37.30/www.
dracenie.com).* **Open** *July-mid Aug* 9am-12.30pm,
1.30pm-7pm Mon-Fri; 10.30am-12.30pm, 4-7pm Sat.
Mid Aug-June 9am-noon, 1.30pm-5pm Mon-Fri.
Le Muy *Office du Tourisme, 6 rte de la Bourgade,
83490 Le Muy (04.94.45.12.79/www.lemuy-tourisme.
com).* **Open** *July, Aug* 9am-noon, 4-7pm Mon-Sat;
10am-noon Sun. *Sept-June* 9am-noon, 3-6pm Mon-
Fri; 9am-noon Sat.
Lorgues *Office de Tourisme, pl d'Entrechaux,
83510 Lorgues (04.94.73.92.37).* **Open** 9am-
noon, 3-6pm Mon-Sat; 10am-noon Sun.

Bargemon & Bargème

Highway D25 slices through the countryside
towards Alpine Bargème, impressing motorists
with its display of olive groves, vineyards
and lavender in the south – as well as forests
devastated by the 2003 summer fires – before
reaching the red-faced Gorge of Pennafort.
Just to the north, **Callas** is a tidy village,
where hand-hewn stone houses cluster around
a Romanesque church and a once-splendid
castle, and spectacular views radiate south
to the Maures and Estérel massifs.

Cross the Boussague Pass directly to
Bargemon or detour through woody ravines
past **Claviers**. On the main square, the clock
ticking in the church tower is one of the few
remaining from the Revolution. Enchantingly
leafy **Bargemon** was the last link in a chain
of six perched Roman fortified settlements
stretching east to Fayence and Montauroux,
built to ward off northern invaders. Today
northern Europeans – much cherished for the
cash-flow tourism that long ago replaced local
shoe workshops – do up the residences and
stroll along the still-impressive ramparts.
Cycling enthusiasts can visit the perched
villages by following a formidable 83-kilometre
(51-mile) tour from Bargemon to Seillan and
back; official tourist office prose suggests that
five hours and 23 minutes suffice to complete it.
The **Chapelle Notre-Dame-de-Montaigu**
(ask the priest next door for the key) in the
village centre has a giant golden altar and a
miraculous statue of the Virgin, which is
brought out once a year on Easter Monday.
In the 14th-century **Eglise St-Etienne**, built
just outside the town wall next to a so-called
'Roman' (in fact, 12th-century) gate, is a
fascinating collection of votive letters.

North of Bargemon, there's a distinct
change of climate and vegetation as the
D25 loops ever upwards in hairpin bends
to the Col de Bel Homme. The road flattens
out across the military training grounds of
Camp Canjuers, where signs tell cars (perhaps
unnecessarily) to yield to tanks and a couple
of deserted villages have been left behind for
war-games. Perched at 1,097 metres (3,600
feet) on limestone cliffs, windswept **Bargème**
is the highest village in the Var, with a
population of just 15. The Amis du Vieux
Bargème in the town hall run guided tours
(2.30-5.30pm daily July, Aug) to the fortified
gateways, the 12th-century church and the
Pontevès family chateau, which was destroyed
during the Wars of Religion. Bargème is still
unspoiled (no tourist shops, no restaurants)
with only stunning beauty and the nearby
GR49 footpath as assets.

The Var

Callas. *See p218.*

Where to stay & eat

In Callas, shady place Clemenceau offers a
cool rest in the spray of the old fountain, at
the café tables of **Le St-Eloi** (04.94.76.78.06).
With 12 rooms and four suites, the **Hostellerie
Les Gorges de Pennafort** (D25 S of Callas,
04.94.76.66.51, www.hostellerie-pennafort.com,
closed mid Jan-mid Mar, double €180-€380,
restaurant closed Mon & lunch Wed, menus
€53-€130) cultivates manicured flowerbeds
in a rocky gorge far from the madding crowd.
Host Phillippe da Silva cooks excellent regional
dishes in classic cordon bleu mode and succulent
desserts. Hikers coming through the gorges
might try **Camping Les Blimouses** (D225,
Callas, 04.94.47.83.41, two people €14 for a
tent, closed mid Nov-mid Mar). In Claviers,
Auberge le Provençal (2 pl du 8 Mai 1945,
04.94.47.80.62, closed Mon & Jan, menus €10-
€20) is good for a cheap meal, with simple
French and Italian dishes (huge, wonderful
pizzas). By the *lavoir* in Bargemon, **Auberge
L'Oustaloun** (2 av Pasteur, 04.94.76.60.36,
www.oustaloun.fr, double €60-€70, closed
Jan-Feb, restaurant closed Mon & Tue, menus
€25-€28) is a family-run provençal inn with
plush, cosy rooms. Dine on trout, crayfish and
truffles in the shady terrace with a fountain; in

winter, you can eat game by the fireplace.
A young couple serve tasty regional fare
at **Restaurant La Taverne** (pl Chauvier,
04.94.84.09.17, closed dinner Wed, menus €16-
€22), which has terrace tables by a fountain.
In tiny Bargème, Annie Noël provides five
chambres d'hôte and good regional fare (menu
€18) at **Les Roses Trémières** (04.94.84.20.86,
closed Dec-Mar, double €57) in a renovated
village house. In the summer, she also runs a
small crêperie (lunch only, average €20). Just
off the GR49, **La Ferme Rebuffel** (La Roque
Esclapon, 04.94.76.80.75, www.rebuffel.com,
double €53, menu €25, reservation necessary)
has spacious new duplex rooms on a working
farm with sheep, potato fields and ponds of
ducks and geese. Meals are served in a dining
room that until 2000 housed the milking goats.

Resources

Morning markets are on Thursday in Bargemon,
Saturday and Tuesday in Callas.

Tourist information

Bargème *Office de Tourisme, Mairie, 83840
Bargème (04.94.50.23.00).* **Open** 2-5pm Mon,
Tue, Thur, Fri.
Bargemon *Office de Tourisme, av Pasteur, 83830
Bargemon (04.94.47.81.73/www.ot-bargemon.fr).*
Open *May-Aug* 9am-noon, 12.30pm,
3.30-7pm Tue-Sat; 10am-noon Sun. *Sept-Apr*
9am-12.30pm, 2-5pm Tue-Sat.
Callas *Syndicat d'Initiative, pl du 18 Juin 1940,
83830 Callas (04.94.39.06.77).* **Open** 9am-noon,
2-6pm Mon-Fri; 10am-noon Sat.

Fayence to Montauroux

Pottery and antiques are big at **Fayence**,
and on Saturday market mornings, locals both
native and international pour into the **Bistrot
Fayençais** (04.94.76.24.38) on place de la
Mairie for a drink. The **Four du Mitan**, an
ancient bread oven, has a *tableau vivant* bread-
making display. On place St-Jean-Baptiste, with
its glorious mountain vista, the 18th-century
Eglise Notre-Dame has a marble altarpiece
by provençal mason Dominique Fossatti.

West of Fayence, the D19 passes Romanesque
Chapelle Notre-Dame-de-l'Ormeau, with
its fine 16th-century altarpiece (visits 11am
Thur by Seillans tourist office, €2). Cream-
coloured fortified **Seillans** appears to be cut
out of the forest like a Cubist sculpture. Three
Roman gates lead into town, where cobbled
streets ascend to a chateau and tower. The
name Seillans is derived from the Provençal
seilhanso – the vat of boiling oil that villagers
dumped on the heads of Saracen attackers.
Today's less martial inhabitants concentrate

The Var

their energies on honey and perfume. Max Ernst lived in the village at the end of his life and 71 of his lithographs can be seen in a room on the first floor of the Office de Tourisme (04.94.76.85.91, open 3-6pm, €2).

East of Fayence, **Tourrettes** is named after the two square towers of its chateau, another home of the powerful Villeneuve family. East of here, tiny pedestrian **Callian** spirals up to an impressive feudal chateau. In summer, cool your feet in the fountain on place Bourguignon, which is fed by the same Roman aqueduct that once supplied Fréjus. The main square in nearby **Montauroux** opens on to a spectacular panorama. Montauroux has taken to selling itself as 'the village of Christian Dior'. The Dior family once owned the 12th-century **Chapelle St-Barthélémy** (open June-Sept 10am-noon Wed, 2-5pm Sat) above the village, bequeathing it to the community when the couturier died.

For lake swimming, make like the rest of the locals and head to the beautiful **Lac de St-Cassien**, a nature reserve six kilometres (four miles) south-east of Montauroux, with its protected waterline, clean water and small beaches with kid-friendly cafés.

Where to eat & stay

The **Moulin de Camandoule** (chemin Notre-Dame-des-Cyprès, 04.94.76.00.84, www.camandoule.com, double €65-€170, restaurant closed dinner Wed Apr-Sept, Wed & Thur Oct-Mar, menus €43-€65) is one of the best addresses around Fayence. Its 11 provençal-styled rooms and the restaurant, where British hostess Shirley Rilla serves classic French cuisine with Mediterranean flavours, are a treat. You can also have a more casual lunch at the restaurant by the pool, and spend the afternoon sunbathing and swimming.

In the heart of Fayence's pedestrian old town, **Hôtel La Sousto** (4 pl du Paty, 04.94.76.02.16, closed 1wk June & end Oct-early Nov, double €44-€53) provides a cheerful taste of village life. A short drive out, **Restaurant Le Castellaras** (rte de Seillans, 04.94.76.13.80, closed Mon, Tue, 1wk June, 2wks Mar & mid Nov-mid Dec, menus €43-€58) is the area's gourmet pull. *Père et fille* Alain and Hermance Carro offer creative market dishes (rolls of foie gras and elderberry, say) in a lovely garden filled with sculpture, roses, red-pepper bushes and a swimming pool. Just east of Montauroux, chef Eric Maio serves Mediterranean fare and truffles at the **Auberge des Fontaines d'Aragon** (D37, 04.94.47.71.65, www.fontaines-daragon.com, closed Mon, Tue & Jan, menus €37-€90). The **Four Seasons Resort Provence** (Domaine

de Terre Blanche, Tourrettes, 04.94.39.90.00, www.fourseasons.com, closed Jan, double €250-€1,600) is a luxury enclave with villas, spa, gym, golf course and tennis courts.

Resources

Morning markets are Tuesday, Thursday and Saturday in Fayence, Tuesday in Montauroux.

Tourist information

Fayence *Office de Tourisme, pl Léon Roux, 83440 Fayence (04.94.76.20.08/www.paysdefayence.com).* **Open** *Mid June-mid Sept* 9am-1pm, 3-7pm Mon-Sat; 10am-noon Sun. *Mid Sept-mid June* 9am-noon, 2-5.30pm Mon-Sat.

Montauroux *Office de Tourisme, pl du Clos, 83440 Montauroux (04.94.47.75.90/http://tourisme.montauroux.com).* **Open** *Mid June-mid Sept* 9am-noon, 2-6pm Mon-Sat. *Mid Sept-mid June* 9-11.30am, 2-5.30pm Mon-Fri; 9am-noon Sat.

Seillans *Office de Tourisme, pl du Thouron, 83440 Seillans (04.94.76.85.91/www.seillans-var.com).* **Open** *July, Aug* 10am-12.30pm, 3-6pm Mon-Sat; 10am-1pm, 3-6pm Sun. *May, June, Sept* 10am-12.30pm, 3-6pm Mon-Sat. *Oct-Apr* 10am-12.30pm, 3-6pm Tue-Fri; 3-6pm Sat.

Getting there & around

By car

The A8 runs along the Argens Valley. Take exit 36 (Le Muy) and then the N555 for Draguignan; the same exit and the N7 for Les Arcs and Lorgues. Salernes is west of Draguignan on the D557 and D560. Cotignac is south-west of Salernes on the D22. Bargemon is 25km (15.5 miles) north-east of Draguignan on the D562, D225 and D25. Fayence lies off the D562 between Draguignan and Grasse.

By train/bus

The station at Les Arcs-Draguignan is on the main Paris–Nice line served by TGVs and slower trains between Nice and Marseille. **Les Rapides Varois** (04.94.50.21.50) runs hourly buses to Draguignan (fewer on Sun) from Les Arcs station timed to connect with trains, two to five buses a day (Mon-Sat) between Draguignan and Aups via Tourtour and Ampus, and buses from Les Arcs station to Lorgues and Le Thoronet (Mon-Sat, none Wed in school holidays). **Autocars Blancs** (04.94.69.08.28) runs two buses a day between Draguignan and Marseille via Brignoles and Aix-en-Provence, and buses between Brignoles and Aups, Sillans, Villecroze, Salernes, Entrecasteaux, Cotignac and Lorgues. **Estérel Cars** (04.94.52.00.50) runs buses from Draguignan to St-Raphaël via Le Muy. **Transvar** (04.94.28.93.28) runs roughly four buses a day (three on Sun) between Draguignan and Toulon via Les Arcs and Vidauban. **Gagnard** (04.94.76.02.29) runs three buses a day Mon-Sat between Draguignan and Grasse, via Callas, Claviers, Bargemon and Seillans, Fayence, Callian, and Montauroux. It also runs about four buses daily between Fayence and St-Raphaël.

Gorges du Verdon

Welcome to Grand Canyon, France.

Moustiers-Ste-Marie. *See p223.*

Until potholer Edouard Martel's comprehensive explorations of the Gorges du Verdon in 1905, few beyond the local community knew about France's Grand Canyon. The place's scale alone makes this surprising: the chasm ranges in width from 215 to 1,650 metres (705 to 5,410 feet) in the eastern Upper Gorge, though it narrows dramatically in the lower section to between six and 108 metres (20 and 350 feet), while the Grand Canyon proper runs for 21 kilometres (13 miles) from south of Rougon to the reservoir at the Lac de Ste-Croix. The Gorges are beautiful as well as impressive, carved into steep limestone cliffs over millennia by the emerald-green Verdon river, with fantastic jagged bluffs nestled in an epic forested wilderness. Even more surprising, some avid Parisian nature lover suggested the best thing to do with such a large, unproductive gash would be to wall it up and make a dam. In the event, dams were built downstream at the Lac de Ste-Croix and below the Basses Gorges, but the whole inspiring, sparsely populated but much-visited area was made into a Parc Naturel Régional in 1977.

The Grand Canyon

Perilous roads perched on either side of the canyon offer a dramatic 130-kilometre circuit (80 miles), fraught with hairpin bends requiring a fair share of white-knuckled driving courage. During peak summer months, traffic jams and tempers rise as cars inch along in a sweltering crawl. The journey normally takes three hours but takes five in July and August, thanks to frequent stops along impossibly narrow roads for picture-perfect photo opportunities. The best times to go are in April, May, September or October, but even if it is hot, congested and summer, a visit is well worth the effort.

The journey is best tackled from **Castellane** (take the Grasse exit from the A8 and follow the N85), a small town on the route Napoléon. Castellane nestles beneath a massive rocky outcrop topped by the Notre-Dame-du-Roc chapel. The ascent is a difficult 20-minute walk from the centre but, once there, you can visit an interesting 18th-century shrine boasting a large statue of the Virgin covered in ex-votos. The village itself is a tightly packed maze of streets, home to at least half a dozen companies offering canyoning and rafting trips. It is also well known as a starting point for excellent mountain bike trails into the Réserve Géologique de Haute-Provence. Napoleon stopped off for a bite in March 1815 at what is now the **Conservatoire des Arts et Traditions Populaires**, though the market (Wednesdays and Saturdays) might better fulfil those needs nowadays. The **Musée Sirènes et Fossiles** has an impressive collection detailing the history of mythological mermaids combined with fossils of sirenians, marine mammals dating from the era when the sea still covered the region four million years ago. Just ten minutes north of Castellane, the Vallée des Sirènes Fossiles is where the first of these fossils were discovered.

About 12 kilometres (7.5 miles) out of Castellane, the D952 Gorges road splits in two. Turn left along the D955 to the small town of **Trigance**. Today it is little more than a jumble of artists' studios, barely worth noting except for the beautiful château. Faithfully rebuilt and restored by the loving hands of Jean-Claude Thomas, it is now a romantic getaway hotel-restaurant (*see p224*).

Ministry of hilly walks

The main points of contact for anyone who wants to explore the Gorges on foot are the regional tourist offices (at either Castellane, see p224, or Moustiers-Ste-Marie, see p225), where all manner of guides (from the written kind to the human-in-hiking-boots type) are available. Before you set out, get climate and safety information from the Parc Naturel Régional du Verdon (04.92.74.68.00, www.parcduverdon.fr).

Walk 1: The Sentier Martel

Length 14 kilometres (8.5 miles).
Time Six to nine hours (including breaks).
Difficulty Very strenuous. Do not do it alone.
Wear stout boots and bring lots of water, a map,

sweater and torch. Bring two cars, parking one at the end to save a long walk back.

It's best to start from the Chalet de la Maline, striking out from the parking lot along the signposted GR4, first tackling the long descent and then working your way back up through the Samson Couloir to the Point Sublime car park.

Shortly after leaving the Chalet, the steep, narrow trail becomes difficult, with a rock wall on one side and sheer nothingness on the other. To complicate matters, some parts are covered in loose rubble and slippery moss-covered limestone. Take a deep breath, calm your racing heart and continue along the trail – and try not to worry: it widens up again about ten minutes later.

The path is very well marked, with two painted lines (one white and one red) splashed on the cliffside, on thick tree trunks or on rocks. After about three hours of breathtaking views and some long downhill stretches, you will come to a cliff with an iron ladder that you must clamber down to continue the hike. It's not a completely sheer drop, although difficult for the faint of heart. The ladder is broken up into five stages, with much-needed places to rest along the way: there are around 240 rungs. Once at the bottom, the trail becomes a bit slippery with loose rocks and shale, snaking down to the riverbed and the plage des Baumes Frères – which is not a beach at all but a flat area with lots of pebbles. Do not swim here. Because the Verdon is controlled by two dams, the water levels can rise unexpectedly. Throughout this part of the trail you'll be confronted by disturbing signs of a stick figure running for its life before

From here, take the narrow D90 for access to the **Corniche Sublime** (D71), an engineering feat completed only in 1947. The road comprises death-defying twists and turns along the canyon's southern flank, with plunging drops a sheer 800 metres (2,600 feet) to the bright ribbon of the river below. There are plenty of scenic shots and look-out points along the way, and – happily – drivers are mostly considerate. To reach the beginning of the Corniche Sublime you need to drive over the Pont d'Artuby (Europe's highest bridge until the opening of the Millau viaduct), suspended 650 metres (2,130 feet) above the Artuby torrent. (If a simple crossing isn't enough to set your pulse racing, local tourist offices will direct you to sports clubs that

organise bungee jumping over the edge.) The first glimpse of the canyon is from the Balcon de la Mescla lookout further along the Corniche Sublime. Twisty and gut-clenchingly narrow, it winds above the gorge towards the splendidly perched town of **Aiguines**, which has the western entrance to the canyon to one side and the Lac Ste-Croix, the largest of the four Verdon lakes, to the other. The fairytale castle – a faux-Renaissance pile with multicoloured towers – is not open to the public. Aiguines was once famed for wood-turning, especially boules made from boxwood gathered by intrepid climbers from trees at the base of the gorge, but is now better known for climbing holidays; if you're interested in courses, try climbing centre La Corditelle (06.10.49.51.92, www.lacorditelle.com).

The Var

a tidal wave: this is to warn you to keep to the path or, if you do choose to wade in at your own risk, ensure you have a well-planned escape route. Check with the EDF electricity board, which controls the gates (recorded information 04.92.83.62.68).

The trail itself stays at all times above the water danger-line. It is a flat-ish tree-covered path for about half an hour, before leading back upwards along another series of vertiginous cliffs – think 200-metre drops (660 feet). Continue to follow the red-and-white trail markers upwards until you reach an open plain filled with the wonderful scents of any and all possible wild plants: raspberry bushes, ceps and mint. Moving ever upwards, you will soon find a series of tunnels; put on that sweater and pull out your torch. The first is interesting for the iron rails left over from the era when the tunnels were being dug; the second is unremarkable; the last and longest has 'windows' that let you see out over the spectacular Verdon and cliffs reflecting sunlight. From here, keep on walking, controlling your vertigo as you tiptoe across a footbridge over the Baou. Finish the hike by scrambling up to the Point Sublime car park and sink exhausted into your car. The relatively quick drive back to the Chalet de la Maline to pick up the second car should leave you plenty of time to have a well-earned victory drink at the bar.

Walk 2: The Samson Couloir

Length *Two kilometres (just over a mile).*
Time *Two hours (including pauses).*
Difficulty *Moderate: rain makes parts slippery.*

This walk through the Samson Couloir is also lovely, but it is much shorter than the Sentier Martel. It begins from the parking lot of the Point Sublime lookout. The entrance to the trail is well marked and leads immediately to a cul-de-sac with picnic tables and public toilets. After having a quick look at the Gorges from the Cauvin viewpoint, follow the GR49 trail indicated by a sign with a large painted green lizard.

The first stretch of the walk is steep and rather rocky – wear good shoes and be prepared to slide a bit. At the bottom the trail follows the riverbed to the remarkable 17th-century Tusset bridge, which bears a resemblance to the Pont d'Avignon and is a good photo opportunity. After the bridge, follow the GR49 sign: the path twists and turns upwards in a difficult climb to a clearing. Stop, breathe the pine-scented air, and take a break. After the clearing, the path is flatter. Don't miss the Rocher de la Renardière: a mysterious rock with a hole through it.

Shortly after, a splash of red paint on a tree means that the trail splits in two: one continues up along the GR49, the other downwards to another viewpoint. Take the left (down) path, cross the stream and continue until you reach a large field. On the far side is a clifftop lookout called the Rancoumas viewpoint. Black paint on the rocks shows the best places to stand for the most beautiful views: of the cliffs of l'Escales, over the Martel trail and to the village of Rougon. You will need to backtrack to return to the parking lot, but the glorious scenery means you won't regret the extra effort.

There's a market on Fridays. The high fluorine content of the water makes it vibrant green – and undrinkable. Lac de Ste-Croix is, however, a lovely place to splash about, unless the level is low, when it becomes muddy. Head down to the lakeshore beach in **Les Salles-sur-Verdon** where Verdon Loisirs (04.92.77.70.26) rents boats (€26/hr), pedalos (€8/hr) and kayaks (€5/hr).

The northern and southern roads meet in **Moustiers-Ste-Marie**. Built around its Romanesque church on the edge of a precipice, Moustiers enjoys a Mediterranean climate despite its altitude. On a rock high above town is the medieval Notre-Dame-de-Beauvoir chapel. Suspended from a chain between two rocks above the chapel is a star said to have been hung there by a knight, relieved at having returned from the Crusades unscathed. Moustiers was renowned in the 17th and 18th centuries for its faïence. After 200 years of production it was dethroned by the fashion for porcelain and English bone china, and the last oven went cold in 1874. Attempts have recently been made to resuscitate the craft, and there are now 19 workshops in operation, the output of which is given a very hard sell in the town's all-too-numerous crafts and souvenir shops. The small but excellent **Musée de la Faïence** chronicles this struggle with delicate porcelains from the end of the 17th century. Moustiers market happens on a Friday; for something more thrilling, head to Verdon Passion (rue Frédéric Mistral, 04.92.74.69.77, www.verdon-passion. com) for cliff paragliding (€130/hr) or canyoning.

The Var

Further east along the D952, the tiny village of **La Palud-sur-Verdon** is thronged with hikers and climbers sporting baggy shorts and Birkenstock sandals. There is plenty of accommodation, and a friendly grocery store sells torches and propane for cooking; the market is on Sunday. Just before La Palud, the D23 branches off to the left, offering an airy circular route that climbs more than 500 metres (1,640 feet) before plunging halfway down the side of the canyon to the Chalet de la Maline, departure point for the Sentier Martel, a six- to nine-hour walk along the valley floor (*see p222* **Ministry of hilly walks**). Just past La Palud, direction Castellane, enjoy the views from the aptly named Point Sublime.

Conservatoire des Arts et Traditions Populaires

34 rue Nationale, Castellane (04.92.83.71.80). **Open** *July-mid Aug* 10am-noon, 3-6pm daily. *Mid Aug-Sept* 10am-noon, 3-6pm Tue-Sun. *Oct-June* 10am-noon, 3-6pm Mon-Fri; also group bookings Sat, Sun. **Admission** €2; €1.50 groups; free under-7s. **No credit cards**.

Musée de la Faïence

pl du Tricentenaire, Moustiers (04.92.74.61.64/ www.ville-moustiers-sainte-marie.fr). **Open** *Apr-Oct* 10am-12.30pm, 2-6pm Mon, Wed-Sun. *Nov-Mar* 2-5pm Sat, Sun. **Admission** €2; free under-16s. **No credit cards**.

Musée Sirènes et Fossiles

pl Marcel Sauvaire, Castellane (04.92.83.19.23/ www.resgeol04.org). **Open** *June-Sept* 10am-noon, 3-6pm Mon, Wed-Sat; 10am-noon Sun. *Oct-May* group bookings only. **Admission** €4; €3 groups; €2.50 7-15s; free under-7s. **No credit cards**.

Where to stay & eat

Castellane abounds with mid-range hotels, gîtes, campsites and B&Bs. The **Hôtel du Commerce** (pl Marcel Sauvaire, 04.92.83.61.00, www.hotel-fradet.com, closed Nov-Feb, double €65) has an excellent restaurant (closed lunch Mon-Wed, menus €23-€33) and is owned by a pupil of Alain Ducasse. **Canyons du Verdon** (bd St-Michel, rte de Digne, 04.92.83.76.47, www.studi-hotel.com, closed Nov-mid Mar, double €165-€460/wk) rents rooms and studio apartments for up to four people; it has a pool. In the pedestrianised old town, **La Main à la Pâte** (rue de la Fontaine, 04.92.83.61.16, closed Tue, Wed & mid Dec-mid Feb, average €20) is a friendly bistro serving pizzas and ace salads.

Rooms at the **Auberge du Teillon** in the nearby hamlet of Garde (rte Napoléon, 04.92.83.60.88, closed mid Nov-mid Mar, double €49) are pretty straightforward, but the restaurant (closed Mon Sept-June, dinner Sun Oct-Apr, menus €18-€40) is excellent – book well ahead. The grandest option is the medieval **Château de Trigance** (04.94.76.91.18, www.chateau-de-trigance.fr, closed Nov-Mar, double €110-€165, menus €25-€60), which dominates the hilltop village of the same name with its baronial halls, four-poster beds and a vaulted restaurant.

In Aiguines, the **Hôtel du Grand Canyon du Verdon** (04.94.76.91.31) is perched on the Corniche Sublime and has a lovely panoramic restaurant. In the town centre, **Hôtel du Vieux-Château** (pl de Fontaine, 04.94.70.22.95, www.hotelvieuxchateau.fr, closed Oct-Mar, double €55-€75) has cosy rooms and a restaurant. The **Grand-Hôtel-Bain** in Comps-sur-Artuby (rue Praguillon, 04.94.76.90.06, www.grand-hotel-bain.fr, closed mid Nov-late Dec, double €48-€68) has been run by the same family for eight generations and has plain, old-fashioned rooms and traditional fare.

In the centre of Moustiers, **La Bonne Auberge** (04.92.74.66.18, closed Nov-Mar, double €65-€95) has friendly owners and 19 cheerful rooms; **Le Relais** (pl du Couvert, 04.92.74.66.10, www.lerelais-moustiers.com, closed 1wk Oct, Dec-Feb, double €59-€78) is very comfortable. Outside town, **La Ferme Rose** (04.92.74.69.47, closed mid Nov-mid Mar, except Christmas, double €75-€150) favours soft whites and exposed beams, while **La Bastide des Oliviers** (04.92.74.61.10, www.la-bastide-des-oliviers.com, double €100-€160) makes a hospitable escape. **Les Santons** restaurant (pl de l'Eglise, 04.92.74.66.48, closed dinner Mon, all Tue & mid Nov-Jan, average €70) is pricey but well worth a visit: try the roast chicken with lavender and honey (booking advised). For a gourmet experience, head for super-chef Alain Ducasse's **La Bastide de Moustiers** (chemin de Quinson, 04.92.70.47.47, www.bastide-moustiers.com, closed Dec-Mar, double €155-€355, menu €57), which has 12 warm and inviting rooms.

At La Palud-sur-Verdon, **Le Panoramic** (rte de Moustiers, 04.92.77.35.07, double €68-€78, closed Nov-Mar, menus €13-€28) has 20 basic rooms and a good-sized pool.

Resources

Tourist information

Aiguines *Office de Tourisme, av des Tilleuls, 83630 Aiguines (04.94.70.21.64/www.aiguines.com).* **Open** *July-Aug* 9am-12.30pm, 3-6pm Mon-Sat. *Sept-June* 9am-noon, 1.30-5pm Mon-Fri.

Castellane *Office de Tourisme, rue Nationale, 04120 Castellane (04.94.83.61.14/www.castellane.org).* **Open** *July, Aug* 9am-12.30pm, 1.30-7pm Mon-Sat; 10am-1pm Sun. *Sept-June* 9am-noon, 2-6pm Mon-Fri.

Come on in, the water's lovely: **Lac de Ste-Croix**. *See p223.*

See p223.

Moustiers-Ste-Marie *Office de Tourisme, Hôtel Dieu, 04360 Moustiers-Ste-Marie (04.92.74.67.84/ www.ville-moustiers-sainte-marie.fr).* **Open** *Mar-June* 9.30am-12.30pm, 2-6pm daily. *July, Aug* 9.30am-7pm daily. *Sept-Feb* 2-6pm daily.

Riez & the Basses Gorges du Verdon

West of the Lac de Ste-Croix the cliffs are only half as sheer as in the Grand Canyon and the land accommodates agriculture. Lavender is the main crop on the plateau de Valensole between the Basses Gorges and the town of Riez; it colours and perfumes the whole area in summer, and you're bound to stumble over a few lavender festivals in July and August.

Sleepy little **Riez** is pretty and unspoiled. An impressive main street that suggests it has seen better days, and four seven-metre-high (23-foot) columns in a field on the western outskirts bear witness to the town's Roman past. Across the river stands a rare early Christian monument: a sixth-century Merovingian baptistery, with more plundered Roman columns. Inside, the **Musée Lapidaire de Riez** has an interesting collection of Gallo-Roman artefacts. Ramparts surround the old town, which is dominated by a 16th-century clock tower. The western gate, the Porte Saint-Sols, opens on to the Grande Rue where flamboyant Renaissance constructions include the Hôtel de Mazan at No.12, with its 16th-century staircase. The market (Wednesday and Saturday) is a good place for local truffles, honey, lavender and faïence. Mont St-Maxime, just behind the village, provides an easy hike up to a park with lovely views over the area.

Follow the D952 south-west along the Colostre river to reach the **Château d'Allemagne-en-Provence**, a part-13th-century, part-Renaissance splendour renowned for its fine, moulded-plaster chimneypieces; the guided visits are a delight. It also has five rooms (double €80-€140) or can be rented by the week (€800-€1,600).

The best approach to the Basses Gorges is from **Quinson**, 21 kilometres (13 miles) south-west of Riez. This tiny village is the site of the ambitious **Musée de Préhistoire**. Opened in 2001, it lies in a partially buried, elliptical building designed by Lord Norman Foster. A million years of prehistory is presented using clever reconstructions, including a mock-up cave complete with paintings, dioramas of Stone Age life and archaeological finds.

The twisty but scenic D82 winds south-west over the mountain to **Esparron de Verdon**, dominated by its fortified château (now *chambres d'hôte, see p226*) and beside a lake popular for watersports. The ancient spa town of **Gréoux-les-Bains** offers a large choice of hotels, an old town crowded around a Templar castle, and the **Thermes de Gréoux-les-Bains**, a troglodyte spa (so as not to lose the therapeutic qualities of the calcium-, sodium-, sulphate- and magnesium-rich water through exposure to daylight). After a therapeutic massage, wander to the edge of town to see the **Crèche de Haute-Provence**, a doll-scale village, constructed of natural materials and evoking the harsh beauty of windswept mountain life. Gréoux market is on Thursday.

Château d'Allemagne-en-Provence

(04.92.77.46.78/www.chateauxandcountry.com/ chateaux/allemagneenprovence). **Open** *Tours* July-mid Sept 4pm, 5pm Tue-Sun; Apr-June, mid Sept-Oct 4pm, 5pm Sat, Sun. **Admission** €6. **No credit cards**.

Crèche de Haute-Provence

36 av des Alpes (rte de Vinon), Gréoux-les-Bains (04.92.77.61.08). **Open** 9am-noon, 3-7pm Tue-Sun. Closed Jan, Feb. **Admission** €4; €2.50 7-12s; free under-7s. **No credit cards**.

Musée Lapidaire de Riez

Riez Baptistery. **Open** *Mid June-mid Sept* 6pm Tue, Fri, Sat. *Mid Sept-mid June* by appointment via tourist office (04.92.77.99.09). **Admission** €2. **No credit cards**.

Musée de Préhistoire des Gorges du Verdon

rte de Montmeyan, Quinson (04.92.74.09.59/ www.museeprehistoire.com). **Open** *Feb-June, Sept-mid Dec* 10am-6pm Mon, Wed-Sun. *July, Aug* 10am-8pm daily. **Admission** €7; €5 6-18s; free under-6s. **Credit** MC, V.

Thermes de Gréoux-les-Bains

av des Thermes, Gréoux-les-Bains (04.92.70.40.00/ www.chainethermale.fr). **Open** *Mar-mid Dec* 6am-6pm daily (for 1-day visit, you must arrive before noon). Closed mid Dec-Feb. **Admission** 1 day €40; 6 days €228. **Credit** AmEx, DC, MC, V.

Where to stay & eat

There's not very much choice of places to stay or to eat in Riez itself: the **Carina** hotel (quartier St-Jean, 04.92.77.85.43, closed Nov-Mar, double €50-€58) has basic rooms and is prettier when looking out. Just outside town, on the D6 towards Valensole, the more impressive 16th-century **Château de Pontfrac** (04.92.77.78.77, www.chateau depontfrac.com, double €50-€70) has a beautiful setting and serves simple, hearty meals (menus €26-€30). Quinson's bars are strong on hunting dogs and low on gourmet facilities, but the museum happily has a café. At Esparron get a feel for the aristocratic lifestyle at the *chambres d'hôte* in the **Château d'Esparron** (Esparron de Verdon, 04.92.77.12.05, www.esparron.com, closed mid Oct-mid Apr, double €130-€200), still in the hands of the Castellane family who built it in the 12th century. Although it has something of a geriatric feel as curists come to take the waters, Gréoux-les-Bains offers plenty of hotels and restaurants. Try **La Crémaillère** (rte de Riez, 04.92.70.40.04, double €72-€78, menus €23-€32, closed mid Dec-mid Mar) for its farmhouse feel and lovely bedrooms, or the **Villa Borghèse** (av des Thermes,

04.92.78.00.91, www.villa-borghese.com, closed mid Nov-mid Mar, double €80-€130), which has a lovely garden and a small spa.

Resources

Tourist information

Gréoux *Office de Tourisme, 5 av des Maronniers, 04800 Gréoux-les-Bains (04.92.78.01.08/www. greoux-les-bains.com).* **Open** *Apr-June, Sept, Oct* 9am-noon, 2-6pm Mon-Sat; 9am-noon Sun. *July, Aug* 9am-12.30pm, 2-6.30pm Mon-Sat; 9am-noon, 2-6pm Sun. *Nov-Mar* 9am-noon, 2-6pm Mon-Fri; 9am-noon, 2-5pm Sat.

Riez *Office de Tourisme, pl de la Mairie, 04500 Riez (04.92.77.99.09/www.ville-riez.fr).* **Open** *Mid-late June, early-mid Sept* 9am-1pm, 3-7pm Mon-Sat. *July, Aug* 9am-1pm, 3-7pm Mon-Sat; 9am-noon Sun. *Mid Sept-mid June* 8.30am-12.30pm, 1.30-5.30pm Mon-Sat.

Getting there & around

By bus

Public transport is very limited. **Sumian Cars** (04.42.67.60.34) runs a daily bus from Marseille to Castellane via Aix, La Palud and Moustiers (July, Aug: Mon-Sat; Sept-June: Mon, Wed, Sat), and from Marseille to Gréoux-les-Bains via Aix (one daily, Mon-Sat). **VFD** (04.93.85.24.56) runs a service between Nice and Grenoble via Grasse and Castellane (Mon, Tue, Fri, Sat). **Guichard** (04.92.83.64.47) runs buses around the canyon (Sept-June: Sat, Sun; July, Aug: daily), linking Castellane with Point Sublime, La Palud and La Maline; it can also organise custom-made tours or airport pick-ups. Otherwise, the best option for the carless might be a day trip: try **Santa Azur** in Nice (04.97.03.60.00), which operates day trips to the Gorges du Verdon one Sun a month (Apr-Oct).

By car

For the Grand Canyon, leave the A8 at exit 42 and take the N85 to Castellane via Grasse, or take exit 36 for Draguignan and then the D955. For Quinson, leave the A8 at exit 34 at St-Maximin and take the D560/D13. From Aix-en-Provence, take the A51 or D952 to Gréoux-les-Bains; the D952 continues to Moustiers.

Lavender on the **plateau de Lavensole**. *See p225.*

The Riviera & Southern Alps

Features

Maps

Introduction

Painters, playboys and developers have all been attracted to this magical coast.

All that is best and worst about the South of France can be found in the Alpes-Maritimes *département*: a stunning natural coastline covered in some of the most banal concrete architecture of the postwar period; the glamour circuit of **Cannes**, **Monte-Carlo** and **St-Jean-Cap-Ferrat**, watersports and yachts, and pebbly, packed public beaches. The sub-tropical climate sustains citrus fruits, fabulous gardens and **Menton**'s wintering pensioners. Memories still linger of Picasso, Matisse and Renoir, and countless drab daubers, while the money that comes pouring into expat residences and film festivals sustains the haute-cuisine extravaganzas of **Mougins**.

But to concentrate just on the Riviera coastal strip would be a mistake. Just back from the sea, you find ancient olive groves and picture-perfect villages like **Haut de Cagnes**, **Coaraze**, **Peillon** and **Castellar**. Further inland are art-packed **Vence** and **St-Paul-de-Vence**, the stalactite-hung **Grottes de St-Cézaire**, the dramatic **Gorges du Loup** and the rare Alpine wildlife and wolves of the **Parc National du Mercantour**.

The eastern half of the *département* is still marked by its Italianate past (some places changed nationalities on numerous occasions), visible in the Genoese *palazzos* of **Vieux Nice**, frescoed trompe l'oeil facades of **Villefranche-sur-Mer** and the Baroque churches of **Sospel** and the upper valleys, as well as in culinary specialities such as gnocchi and ravioli.

Today, **Nice** itself is sophisticated and cosmopolitan, a vibrant commercial and congress centre with lively bars, belle époque villas and first-rate museums devoted to Chagall and Matisse, while **Monaco** provides an autocratic, princely anomaly in the midst of fiercely Republican France, with all the requisite state trappings (and more) on a miniature scale.

The best — The Riviera & Southern Alps

Things to do

Nature lovers should visit the **Gorges du Loup** (*see p297*) or **Musée Océanographique** (*see p283*). Man-made glories run from ancient artefacts from the **Vallée des Merveilles** (*see p307*) to the frescoed **Palais Lascaris** (*see p257*) and fortified **Iles de Lérins** (*see p239*).

Places to stay

If luxury is your métier, look no further than **Château Chèvre d'Or** (*see p278*), **Hi Hôtel** (*see p268*) and **Hôtel Martinez** (*see p237*).

Places to eat

Alain Llorca at **Moulin de Mougins** (*see p240*), Franck Cerutti at **Louis XV** (*see p285*) and Jacques Chibois at **Bastide St-Antoine** (*see p295*) are among the region's finest chefs. Cheaper, but nonetheless essential, is **Le Bouchon d'Objectif** (*see p233*) in Cannes.

Nightlife

To really *feel* the rich and famous, head to Monte-Carlo's **Casino** (*see p282*). But **Le Bâoli** (*see p234*) in Cannes gives you the best chance of a night out with the stars, while **Le Farfalla** (*see p233*) or **Le 72 Croisette** (*see p234*) leave you perfectly placed on La Croisette to watch them.

Culture

Time was, artists were more numerous in this region than tourists. Check out **Musée Matisse**, the extended **Musée national Message Biblique Marc Chagall** (for both, *see p260*) or the cutting-edge art at **Villa Arson** (*see p259*) in Nice, but on no account miss Matisse's finest work: the **Chapelle du Rosaire** (*see p300*) in Vence. Monte-Carlo's **open air cinema** (*see p287*) is enticingly atmospheric.

Sports & activities

Juan-les-Pins is the place for **watersports** (*see p246*), with **Plage de la Salis** (*see p243*) the favourite beach for those seeking out more leisurely pursuits. At the opposite end of the temperature scale, there's famously good Alpine skiing at **Auron** and **Isola 2000** (for both, *see p310*).

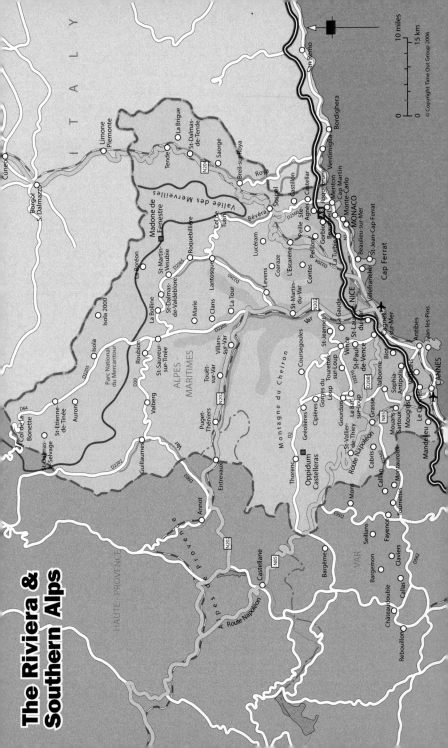

Cannes

The city's star-kissed reputation thrives – and it isn't all about the film festival.

Cannes jealously guards its status as the top international newsmaker on the festival circuit, but the fabulous two-week film extravaganza (held each year in May) is coming under local pressure to move over and share the headlines (*see also p238* **Too hot to handle**). It does so grudgingly, quick to point out that during its annual moment of glory, Cannes receives more intense global media coverage than any French city outside Paris. It's endlessly fascinating stuff too: gossipy, irreverent, full of insider info… Perfect fodder for today's celebrity-obsessed audiences, in fact. Who doesn't enjoy reading about the bizarre antics of the current crop of superstars, set against the backdrop of the red carpet, the Croisette and the Mediterranean? But enterprising visitors will soon discover there's much more to the city than its media profile.

Cannes played host to the smart set long before the festival circuit began. In 1834 the British Lord Chancellor Lord Brougham set up house here when the city was still a fishing village – an outbreak of cholera had made it impossible to continue living in Nice. He built a palatial villa, invited all his friends and for the next 34 years spent all his summers here. The British aristocracy followed en masse, transforming this once-provincial village into a glitzy watering hole for Europe's rich and famous. Art and literature flourished, nourished by the natural beauty and flair of the town.

Cannes got a fleeting taste of fame in 1939, when it was approached to host an International Festival of Cinema. Because World War II intervened, it wasn't until 1946 that the festival was finally launched, at the old Palais des Festivals (where the Noga Hilton now stands) and rather badly, if local lore has it right. Apparently, first-night guests were left to sip champagne and cool their heels while repairs were made to the projection booth, inexplicably built without its window. Things have picked up since then and the city is now justified in billing itself as a sophisticated European media festival hub. The imposing 'new' **Palais des Festivals** (opened in 1982) overlooks the bay. It is busy year-round hosting parties, festivals and conventions for international advertisers, music-makers, TV producers and a range of other conference-goers, who keep the glamour contingent high and the hotels full.

Sightseeing

The emergence of a dynamic, seasonal beach culture in Cannes is welcome news as well. Every available inch of sand is covered by sun-lotioned, often topless, bodies being bronzed in the searing summer sun. (If you prefer to leave both halves of your bikini or your trunks at the hotel, there is a straight and gay nude beach, La Batterie, by the N7 towards Antibes.) Beach volleyball fanatics and young international hipsters seem to prefer the beaches hugging the boulevard du Midi, while young families and English-speaking tourists flock to those near La Croisette. Keep in mind the fact that beach chairs, no matter which beach you choose, are off limits to anyone disinclined to pay €15-€25 per day to sit on one.

Sitting down to sip an aperitif in the late afternoon is, however, almost a rite of passage in Cannes. All those charming bistros dotting the boulevard du Midi and La Croisette fill up quickly with well-dressed people-watchers, many of whom will have toured the Croisette's famous Palais des Festivals, with its film star handprints in the pavement, viewed the celebrated trinity of **palace hotels** (the Majestic, the Martinez and the Carlton) or visited the delightful 19th-century villa called **La Malmaison**, home to art and photography exhibitions, as well as hosting the Film Festival's Quinzaine des Réalisateurs (Directors' Fortnight). After a cocktail, stroll down to the pointe de la Croisette to enjoy the vista of the sun setting over the beautiful bay of Cannes.

To the west is the port. Perched on the hill above it is the old town, which is called Le Suquet. Its pedestrianised streets are brimming with restaurants, it has one of the best food markets in the Midi and there's hurly-burly shopping around rue Meynadier. The **Musée de la Castre** occupies what's left of the 12th-century fortifications nearby and offers breathtaking views. Inside, it features a wide-ranging collection, running from a painting by Pasteur to ancient musical instruments.

Further west of the city centre is Cannes-La Bocca, a less expensive residential area with an agreeable stretch of public beach.

On the other side of Cannes is the Quartier de la Californie, which showcases the baroque architectural style of the Chapelle Bellini (in allée de la Villa-Florentina), alongside l'Eglise orthodoxe St-Michel Archange (30 bd Alexandre III), whose choral group is famous for its interpretations of Russian liturgy. The hilltop village of Le Cannet enjoys spectacular views and has been a magnet for creative types, such as artists Renoir and Bonnard and playwright Victorien Sardou. Nowadays it is filled with less famous artists and their shops, and English-speaking tourists who are snapping up and charmingly renovating pieds-à-terre, giving the village a careful facelift. Leading out from Le Cannet, the chemin des Collines is a lovely drive, winding through the hills above Cannes. And on avenue Victoria sits the elaborate, oriental-style Villa Yakimour (private, sadly), given to Yvette Labrousse by her husband, the Aga Khan. The more residential side of Le Cannet is also where you'll find La Palestre (730 av Georges Pompidou, 04.93.46.48.88, www.lapalestre.com), a large sports complex and concert venue.

Those who prefer more active nautical pursuits should contact Cannes Jeunesse Nautisme (04.92.18.88.88) and Centre Nautique Municipal (04.93.47.40.55) in Port du Mourre Rouge.

La Malmaison

47 La Croisette (04.97.06.44.90). **Open** *Apr-June* 10.30am-1pm, 2.30-6.30pm Tue-Sun. *July-mid Sept* 11am-8pm Tue-Thur, Sat, Sun; 11am-10pm Fri. *Mid Sept-Mar* 11am-8pm Tue-Sun. **Admission** €3; €2 students over 25; free students under 25, under-18s. **No credit cards**.

Musée de la Castre

Château de la Castre, pl de la Castre (04.93.38.55.26). **Open** *Apr, May, Sept* 10am-1pm, 2-6pm Tue-Sun. *June-Aug* 10am-1pm, 3-7pm Tue-Sun. *Oct-Mar* 10am-1pm, 2-5pm Tue-Sun. **Admission** €3; €2 18-25s; free under-18s. **No credit cards**.

Palais des Festivals

1 La Croisette (04.93.39.01.01/www.palaisdes festivals.com). **Admission** varies. **Credit** MC, V.

Where to eat & drink

Al Charq Spécialités Libanaises

20 rue Rouaze (04.93.94.01.76/www.alcharq.com). **Open** 11am-10pm Tue-Sun. **Average** €24. **Credit** AmEx, MC, V.

A local favourite, tucked behind the Martinez, this busy deli has absolutely the best falafel, houmous, grilled aubergine and pitta-wrapped chicken in town.

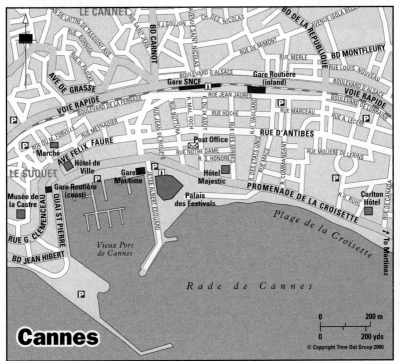

L'Annex Plage

La Croisette (in front of the Carlton) (04.93.39. 73.79). **Open** noon-3.30pm daily (evenings also for private parties). **Menu** €24. **Credit** AmEx, MC, V.

Simple and inventive cuisine makes l'Annex Plage perfect for beach-side lunches, served to you on the patio or as you lounge around in a bikini on the private beach. Try the char-grilled fish of the day or the buffalo mozzarella, fresh herb and vine-tomato salad. Swanky, modern decor and great service are an added bonus.

Astoux et Brun

27 rue Félix Faure (04.93.39.21.87). **Open** noon-3pm, 7-11.30pm daily. **Average** €35. **Credit** MC, V.

This beacon for seafood lovers is the best place in Cannes for sparkling fresh fruits de mer. Never mind the cramped tables and unimaginative decor, what you've come here for is oysters shucked to order, followed by a whole host of specials like fish casserole or the ultimate seafood platter.

Bar 4U

6 rue Frères Padignac (04.93.39.71.21). **Open** 6pm-2.30am daily. **Credit** MC, V.

Dim lighting, a large circular bar and decor of sleek geometric shapes attract the pre-club crowds to this popular bar.

Le Bouchon d'Objectif

10 rue Constantine (04.93.99.21.76). **Open** noon-2.30pm, 7-11pm Tue-Sun. Closed mid Nov-mid Dec. **Menu** €17-€27. **Credit** MC, V.

A popular spot that is a Cannes must, this tiny, unpretentious bistro serves inexpensive provençal cuisine with a sophisticated twist. Locals and tourists alike crowd the tables, making for a busy and colourful atmosphere, while a regularly changing gallery of photos adds a soft touch to the ochre and aqua room.

La Brouette de Grandmère

9bis rue d'Oran (04.93.39.12.10). **Open** 7.30-11pm Mon-Sat. **Menu** €33. **Credit** MC, V.

A tiny restaurant, 'Grandmother's Wheelbarrow' delivers value for money. The interior combines frilly curtains, a fireplace and film posters. Outside, waiters magically fit extra tables on to an already jammed pavement, while passing street performers warm up the crowd. Sit back and enjoy, but do pace yourself: the restaurant chooses the *carte* for you and it includes everything, from huge portions of good, simple food to shots of vodka and a welcome glass of champagne.

Café Roma

1 sq Mérimée (04.93.38.05.04). **Open** Sept-June 7.30am-2.30am daily. July, Aug 7.30am-4am daily. **Menus** €15-€25. **Credit** MC, V.

Put on your sunglasses and join the trendies on the terrace of this well-placed café to watch the comings and goings of the town – rich, famous and otherwise. The espressos are nice and strong and the pasta surprisingly good.

Cannelle

Gray d'Albion, 32 rue des Serbes (04.93.38.72.79). **Open** 9.30am-6.30pm Mon-Sat. **Average** €20-€25. **Credit** AmEx, MC, V.

At this café-cum-grocer you can enjoy quiches and salads, or be extravagant and savour ravioli stuffed with chicken in a mushroom and foie gras sauce. The few tables inside are nestled among irresistible displays of gastronomic delights, including a range of fine wines and caviar.

Les Coulisses

29 rue Commandant André (04.92.99.17.17). **Open** 7pm-2am daily. **Credit** AmEx, MC, V.

Fashionistas and trendsetters spill out on to the pavement terrace at Les Coulisses in the summer and crowd its small interior in the winter. It's *the* place in Cannes to see and be seen, a perfect starting point for a night out clubbing.

Le Farfalla

1 La Croisette (04.93.68.93.00). **Open** 11am-1am daily. **Menu** €15-€30. **Credit** AmEx, MC, V.

Farfalla's burnished wood, milk-bar decor acts as a magnet for bright young hipsters. The terrace provides A-grade star-ogling; alternatively, seek refuge in a booth on the mezzanine. There's a full brasserie-style menu, plus lighter salads and snacks.

Mantel

22 rue St-Antoine, Le Suquet (04.93.39.13.10). **Open** noon-2.30pm, 7-11pm Mon, Tue, Fri-Sun; 7-11pm Thur. **Menus** €32-€58. **Credit** MC, V.

Palais des Festivals. *See p231.*

Charming and discreet, this small restaurant is gathering rave reviews and faithful regulars among the rather jaded palates of Le Suquet. The fixed-price menus are excellent, the à la carte better, and the atmosphere softly elegant. Be sure to book in advance.

La Mère Besson

13 rue des Frères Pradignac (04.93.39.59.24). **Open** 7-10.30pm Mon-Sat. **Menus** €27-€32. **Credit** AmEx, DC, MC, V.
La Mère Besson is a relaxed, family-run favourite that has charmed the likes of Sophia Loren and Gina Lollobrigida. Enjoy provençal cuisine with a twist: perhaps scorpion fish baked with mussels, mushrooms and tomato, or duck breast in a creamed peppercorn sauce.

Morrison's Irish Pub

10 rue Teisseire (04.92.98.16.17/ www.morrisonspub.com). **Open** 5pm-2am Mon-Fri; 1pm-2am Sat, Sun. **Credit** AmEx, DC, MC, V.
An excellent Irish pub, with live music every Wednesday and Thursday from 10pm, and a big-screen TV tuned to English and Irish news and football. The Quays (04.93.39.27.84) is a port-side offshoot.

Le Petit Lardon

rue du Batéguier (04.93.39.06.28). **Open** 7-10.30pm Mon-Sat. **Menu** €18. **Credit** AmEx, MC, V.
Family-run and full of character, this delightful bistro offers a great mix of provençal and burgundian cuisine. Its lively atmosphere and prompt service make it ideal for a casual evening meal, and the set menu is one of the best deals in town.

La Pizza

3 quai St-Pierre (04.93.39.22.56). **Open** noon-2am daily. **Average** €20. **Credit** AmEx, MC, V.
A veritable institution in Cannes (as well as having popular outposts in Nice), this hotspot never accepts reservations. No matter: although it is constantly busy, you'll never wait more than half an hour – and the wood-fired pizza is the best in town.

Le Restaurant Arménien

82 La Croisette (04.93.94.00.58/ www.lerestaurantarmenien.com). **Open** *July, Aug* 7-10.30pm daily. *Sept-June* 7-10.30pm Tue-Sat; noon-2.30pm, 7-10.30pm Sun. Closed 1wk in Dec. **Menu** €40. **Credit** DC, MC, V.
An unusual and exotic restaurant, located at the Port Canto end of La Croisette. Expect succulent meze, including ravioli with mint, stuffed mussels and barley pasta with pistachios. Vegetarians will be in heaven here.

Le 72 Croisette

72 La Croisette (04.93.94.18.30). **Open** *May-Oct* 7am-4am daily. *Nov-Apr* 7am-9pm daily. **Credit** AmEx, MC, V.
Of all the Croisette bars, this remains the most feistily French. Battle through hordes of locals for a ringside seat to watch the rich and famous enter the Martinez (*see p237*) next door.

Villa de Lys

Majestic Barrière, 10 La Croisette (04.92.98.77.41). **Open** 7.30-10pm Tue-Sat. Closed mid Nov-late Dec. **Menus** €65-€125. **Credit** AmEx, DC, MC, V.
With theatrical decor by Jacques Garcia, a movable roof and a terrace alongside La Croisette, this swanky restaurant lives up to its reputation. Wonder-chef Bruno Oger continues to astonish with mouth-watering dishes such as lamb roast in tapenade, or caviar with green beans and a langoustine cappuccino.

Volupté

42 rue Hoche (04.93.39.60.32). **Open** 9am-7.30pm Mon-Sat. **Credit** DC, MC, V.
Volupté is a gourmet tearoom, serving teas from around the world, delicious cakes and own-made crumbles; brews have exotic names like Sailor from Hamburg and Poet's Garden. There's an associated shop at No.32 (04.93.38.20.41).

Nightlife

Le Bâoli

Port Pierre Canto (04.93.43.03.43/www.lebaoli.com). **Open** *Mid Apr-mid Nov* 8.30pm-5am daily. *Mid Nov-mid Apr* 8pm-5am Fri, Sat. **Admission** varies. **Credit** AmEx, MC, V.
Le Bâoli is the biggest player on the Cannes nightlife scene. Leonardo DiCaprio, Martin Scorsese and Tim Robbins have all stopped by this super-stylish lounge. It's usually packed, even outside festival time.

Le Lady Bird

115 av de Lérins (04.93.43.20.63). **Open** 11pm-5am Fri, Sat. **Admission** €16 (incl 1 drink), women free before midnight. **Credit** AmEx, MC, V.
The former Whisky-à-Go-Go attracts pretty young things. The main room is two storeys high and a bit of a maze, but the guests, carefully vetted at the door, don't seem to mind as they cheerfully elbow their way to the dancefloor.

Le Loft

13 rue du Dr Monod (06.21.02.37.49). **Open** *Sept-June* 10.30pm-2.30am Wed-Sat. *July, Aug* 10.30pm-2.30am daily. **Admission** free. **Credit** AmEx, MC, V.
This upmarket dance bar attracts well-dressed and beautiful youngsters. Start the night downstairs at Tantra, Le Loft's sleek bar-restaurant (open 7.30pm-2.30am), over a cocktail and Thai food (average €45).

Shopping

La Croisette, rue d'Antibes and the streets that link the two are a luxury shopper's paradise. Staff at **Chopard** (9 La Croisette, 04.92.98.07.07, closed Sun) will be happy to help you choose between platinum or solid gold for that new trinket. Then skip over to **Jacques Loup** (21 rue d'Antibes, 04.93.39.26.35, closed Mon & Sun) for the perfect shoe, making sure you stop off at the stores on **rue des Etats-Unis** (closed Sun) for avant-garde designs by

The cost of beach chair hire means most people sit on their towels. *See p230.*

the likes of Lolita Lempicka. Reasonably priced streetwear can be found at the ultra-hip **Mango** (84 rue d'Antibes, 04.97.06.63.63). In **allée de la Liberté**, a Saturday market offers regional crafts. **Forville**, behind the old port on rue du M Forville, is a magnificent covered market, selling produce every morning except Monday, when it turns into a *brocante* (flea market). **Cannolive** (16 & 20 rue Venizelos, 04.93.39. 08.19, closed Mon morning & Sun) is the place for regional goodies – olive oil, lemon and raspberry honey, rosewater – while **La Ferme Savoyard-Ceneri** (22 rue Neynadier, 04.93.39.63.68, closed Mon, Sun) has cheeses and gourmet delights. For handmade chocolates, head to **Schies** (125 rue d'Antibes, 04.93.39.01.03, closed Mon morning & Sun), while **Vilfeu Père et Fils** (19 rue des Etats Unis, 04.93.39.26.87, closed mid Oct-Mar) has the best ice-cream in Cannes. A branch of **Fnac**, selling CDs, books and electrical goods, is at 83 rue d'Antibes (04.97.06.29.29, closed Sun). **Cannes English Book Shop** is at 11 rue Bivouac-Napoléon (04.93.99.40.08, closed Sun).

Where to stay

While most mortals may never get to check into them, Cannes' famous palace hotels are still worth checking out. The exclusive trio are: **Hôtel Carlton** (*see below*), **Hôtel Martinez** and **Majestic Barrière** (for both, *see p237*)

Le Cavendish

11 bd Carnot (04.97.06.26.00/www.cavendish-cannes.com). Closed mid Dec-mid Jan. **Rates** €160-€190 double. **Credit** AmEx, DC, MC, V.
For those who have become a bit blasé about the grand hotels in Cannes, this former residence of Lord Henry Cavendish offers a true escape. Christophe Tollemar's interior conjures up a kind of 19th-century opulence with a touch of the contemporary. The soundproofed, air-conditioned rooms have elegant details like lavender-scented sheets and fresh flowers. Breakfast is a lavish affair.

Hôtel Canberra

120 rue d'Antibes (04.97.06.95.00/www.hotel-canberra-cannes.cote.azur.fr). **Rates** €90-€382 double. **Credit** AmEx, DC, MC, V.
Just by the shopping of rue d'Antibes, this neo-classical hotel has made modern use of rich reds, soft creams and black lacquer. Rooms are comfortable, and most have a terrace or balcony – breakfast outside, looking out to the garden, for a lovely moment of tranquillity. There is also a private beach.

Hôtel Carlton

58 La Croisette (04.93.06.40.06/www.ichotels group.com). **Rates** €250-€950 double. **Credit** AmEx, DC, MC, V.
Some of today's top stars have upped sticks to the super-swank Hôtel du Cap Eden-Roc (*see p246*), but this listed monument remains the first choice for festival purists. Seafront rooms are deluxe, and the new suites on the top floor provide unparalleled views of the sea and a bird's-eye view of its bathing beauties. Legend has it that architect Charles Dalmas modelled its two *coupoles* on the breasts of the famous gypsy courtesan la Belle Otéro; locals and tourists pay less ostentatious homage to contemporary celebrities by watching them arrive in their limos. Rumours persist of an ambitious programme for a new 100-room wing, spa and convention centre.

Château de la Tour

10 av Font-de-Veyre (04.93.90.52.52/www.hotelchateaudelatour.com). Closed Jan. **Rates** €155-€275. **Credit** MC, V.
Beautifully renovated in July 2005, this lovely château on the outskirts of Cannes is a refreshing change from the somewhat cynical offerings of the

Palace hotels along the Croisette. Its friendly new owners have kept and refurbished the best original features while tastefully mixing in all modern conveniences. The pool area has a great view of the sea.

Hôtel Embassy

6 rue de Bône (04.97.06.99.00/www.embassy-cannes.com). **Rates** €119-€202 double. **Credit** AmEx, MC, V.

Right in the centre of Cannes, with a garden and a rooftop swimming pool, the Embassy is a quiet, air-conditioned hotel. Rooms generally maintain a floral motif, and are clean and fresh. Good value.

Hôtel Festival

3 rue Molière (04.97.06.64.40/www.hotel-festival.com). **Rates** €95-€155 double. **Credit** AmEx, DC, MC, V.

This small, friendly hotel is well located in the middle of Cannes. Some of its recently refurbished rooms overlook the neighbouring orange trees and palms. You'll find a sauna and a whirlpool bath in the hotel spa.

Hôtel Martinez

73 La Croisette (04.92.98.73.00/www.hotel-martinez.com). **Rates** €205-€850 double. **Credit** AmEx, DC, MC, V.

While the art deco façade of the Martinez has been lovingly preserved by the bubbly Taittinger family, the sleekly renovated rooms show that this hotel is finally coming into its own. Panoramic views from the large teak terraces of the junior suites are spectacular, as is the set-up inside, inspired by the great French designers of the 1930s and '40s. Relax at the new Givenchy Spa, before spending a decadent evening at the burnished-wood and ebony Palme d'Or restaurant – and don't be surprised if you see tuxedo-clad film stars tucking into chef Christian Willer's lavish and much-praised cuisine at the table next to yours.

Hôtel Molière

5-7 rue Molière (04.93.38.16.16/www.hotel-moliere.com). **Rates** €80-€124 double. **Credit** AmEx, MC, V.

Low-key and intimate, rooms are decorated in pale provençal colours and have pretty tiled bathrooms and lush gardens. A favourite among journalists and film critics during the festival, the Molière fills up quickly – be sure to book in advance.

Hôtel Mondial

77 rue d'Antibes (04.93.68.70.00/www.hotelmondial.activehotels.com). **Rates** €110-€180 double. **Credit** AmEx, DC, MC, V.

Only a short walk from La Croisette, this 1930s art deco edifice dominates the area and looks southwards to the sea. Rooms are soundproofed and straightforward, but many have tiny balconies.

Hôtel Splendid

4-6 rue Félix Faure (04.97.06.22.22/www.splendid-hotel-cannes.fr). **Rates** €124-€264 double. **Credit** AmEx, DC, MC, V.

The original Cannes palace stands wedding-cake proud, with flags a-flutter, across from the festival HQ. Its picture-postcard charms lure a loyal clientele and its Palm Square restaurant (menus €50-€75, closed Wed) is quietly gaining quite a reputation for its mix of Thai, French and Italian cuisine.

Hôtel 3.14

5 rue François Einesy (04.92.99.72.00/www.3-14hotel.com). **Rates** €170-€500 double. **Credit** AmEx, DC, MC, V.

From a Moulin Rouge red-velvet corset/mosquito net bed to cool Japanese Zen stylings and muted browns, there is something for even the least adventurous traveller in this new addition to the city's hotels. Each floor is themed – some garishly so – but the hotel's high-end service and modern downstairs bar save it from being too Las Vegas. There's a rooftop eyrie of a pool too.

Majestic Barrière

10 La Croisette (04.92.98.77.00/www.lucienbarriere.com). Closed mid Nov-Dec. **Rates** €235-€895 double. **Credit** AmEx, DC, MC, V.

Considered the 'youngest' of the big Croisette hotels, the Majestic plays up its hip reputation as much as a palace hotel can. During the film, music or advertising festivals it positively throbs, as industry folk loudly renew acquaintances. The Villa des Lys (*see p234*) offers one of the best dining experiences in Cannes; there's also a *fumoir* (smoking room), an offshoot of the Parisian brasserie Fouquet's, and the legendary Majestic bar with its Cecil B DeMille decor.

Hôtel Carlton. *See p235.*

Too hot to handle?

The Cannes Film Festival has always been a little at odds with itself; Hollywood's finest sunning themselves on the Côte d'Azur, quaffing cocktails on yachts in between black-tie dinners and back-to-back premières, while proclaiming to be celebrating the latest subtitled musings of high-minded directors.

Give us Hot d'Or any time. The parallel awards festival for the porn industry that takes place just down the road has always seemed somehow more honest. Watching Larry Flynt surrounded by heaving beauties has none of the self-serving posturing that can accompany the earnest speeches on the *tapis rouge*. Maybe that's why the official festival organisers have done their level best to get it banned.

The black sheep of the festival circuit has been spicing things up in Cannes since 1992, holding its own parties, its own ceremonies and its own awards – just a touch sleazier, with a few more rented tuxedos – until local mayor Bernard Brochand sent his gendarmes on to the beach in 2001 and broke up the awards lunch, effectively banning the festival from the town. All he really succeeded in doing, however, was highlighting the hypocrisy of the main event (that same year, one of the top-billed films in the 'proper' festival was *Le*

Pornographe, the story of a porn director trying to bring meaning to the industry, and featuring several genuine sex scenes with a porn star called Ovidie), while Hot d'Or, undeterred, moved the celebration of its billion-dollar industry to the Lido in Paris. Observers dryly noted that maybe Cannes, which likes to portray itself as a liberal enclave in the right-wing South of France, wasn't quite so different from its neighbours after all.

Somebody in Cannes must have missed the silicon-injected glamour, though, because in 2004 Hot d'Or was once again gracing the Croisette during festival time. The most eagerly awaited parties were still being thrown on the blindingly white decks of the yacht belonging to Private (the most successful company in the business), while behind the scenes deals continued in an industry that grossed $9 billion in 2003.

With revenues going up all the time and overheads almost invariably low, these are figures the main industry players, just a few beaches down the road, must be salivating over. The rest of us are just pleased to see that Cannes has embraced what Cannes does best – packaging up glamour and success, and serving it up with the promise of instant gratification.

Villa d'Estelle

14 rue des Belges (04.92.98.44.48/ www.villadestelle.com). **Rates** €60-€1,250 double. **Credit** AmEx, DC, MC, V.

An elegant and sleekly designed manor house just off La Croisette, Villa d'Estelle is the newest hotel delight offered to visitors to Cannes. You'll find beautiful rooms, self-catering studios and apartments, furnished with every modern convenience (plasma screens, internet connections), and an intimate atmosphere. Added to the warm welcome from the hotel's proud owners, this all means they are often full – so book well in advance.

Resources

Hospital

Centre Hospitalier de Cannes (04.93.69.70.00/www.hopital-cannes.fr).

Internet

Webcenter, 26 rue Hoche (04.93.68.72.37). **Open** 10am-11pm Mon-Sat; noon-8pm Sun.

Police

Commissariat, 1 av de Grasse (04.93.06.22.22).

Post office

22 rue Bivouac Napoléon (04.93.06.26.50). **Open** 8am-7pm Mon-Fri; 8am-noon Sat.

Tourist information

Office de Tourisme, Esplanade Georges Pompidou (04.92.99.84.22/www.cannes-on-line.com). **Open** Sept-June 9am-7pm daily. *July, Aug* 9am-8pm daily. **Other locations**: Gare SNCF, rue Jean-Jaurès (04.93.99.19.77).

Getting there

By car

Leave the A8 at exit 41 or 42, or take the N7 direction Cannes.

By train

Cannes is served by the TGV from Paris (5hrs 10mins). There are regular trains along the coast to Juan-les-Pins, Antibes and Nice.

By bus

Cannes' main bus station, which is by the port, serves coastal destinations: **RCA** (04.93.39.11.39, www.rca.tm.fr) goes to Nice via the villages along the coast and to Nice airport (every 30mins, Mon-Sat). From the SNCF station RCA goes to Grasse (every 30mins Mon-Sat, hourly Sun) via Mougins. **Phocéen cars** (04.93.85.66.61) runs three services a day (Mon-Sat) to Marseille airport and one to Avignon via Aix-en-Provence.

Around Cannes

When the glamour overkill of Cannes becomes too much, and you've had enough of dyed to match poodles and wannabe starlets, don't despair. Instead, relax on a day trip to the tranquil **Iles de Lérins**, or get yourself some culture among the ceramics of **Vallauris** or in sophisticated yet charmingly rural **Mougins**.

Iles de Lérins

The Iles de Lérins are only a 15-minute boat ride from the old port of Cannes. Known to the ancients as Lero and Lerina, the islands were renamed St-Honorat and Ste-Marguerite after the siblings who founded monastic communities here in the fourth century. By the seventh century Lérins was one of Europe's key monastic institutions. Today, it's a beautiful religious backwater, where a handful of Cistercian monks make and sell a liqueur called Lérina. Visitors can wander through forests of pine and eucalyptus or swim discreetly off the rocky outcrops.

The little that remains on St-Honorat of the earlier monastery buildings was incorporated into the current Abbaye de Lérins in the 19th century. The **Monastère Fortifié** was built by the monks in 1073 to protect themselves from the Saracens.

Ste-Marguerite is more touristy. The **Musée de la Mer** in the Fort Ste-Marguerite is visited not so much for its collection of underwater archaeology as for its reputation as the prison of the Man in the Iron Mask; made famous by novelist Alexandre Dumas, the Man may have been Louis XIV's twin brother. What is certain, however, is the fact that many hapless Huguenots were confined here during Louis' religious crackdown.

Monastère Fortifié

St-Honorat (04.92.99.54.00). **Open** *July-mid Sept* (guided visits only) 10.30am-12.30pm, 2.30-5pm daily. *Mid Sept-June* 8.30am-6pm daily. **Closed** mass Sun. **Admission** free. *Guided visits* €2.50.

Musée de la Mer

Fort Ste-Marguerite (04.93.43.18.17). **Open** *Apr-Sept* 10.30am-5.45pm daily. *Oct-Mar* 10.30am-1.15pm, 2.15-4.45 pm Tue-Sun. **Admission** €3; €2 under-25s; free students, under-18s. **No credit cards**.

Getting to the islands

Planaria (04.92.98.71.38, €10 rtn to St-Honorat, €5 rtn to Ste-Marguerite) and **Horizon/Caraïbes** (04.92.98.71.36) run daily boats from Cannes old port between 9am and 5.30pm. **Compagnie Estérel Chantelclair** (04.93.39.11.82) runs daily crossings to Ste-Marguerite from promenade La Pantiero (€10 rtn, 7.30am-5pm, until 7pm July & Aug). Vintage boats, equipped with all the necessary comforts and a skipper, can be hired at **Olympique Nautique** (06.14.89.24.57) in Port Canto.

Mougins

The old village of Mougins is an extraordinary hilltop site, carpeted in flowers and bushes, with narrow lanes and restored houses built along the outlines of medieval ramparts.

In the interwar period, Mougins was discovered by the Surrealists, among them Cocteau, Picabia (who built the fanciful Château de Mai) and Picasso, who came to Mougins in the company of Dora Maar and Man Ray. Local lore has it that cash-strapped Picasso covered his room and the outside walls with art to pay for his board and lodging; the enraged owner made the still-obscure artist whitewash over them the next day. Undaunted, Picasso settled here in 1961, with his wife Jacqueline, and spent much of his time in the area until his death in 1973. Their house, l'Antre du Minotaur (the Minotaur's Lair), can be seen just opposite the strikingly beautiful chapel of Notre-Dame-de-Vie, 1.5km (a mile) south-east of Mougins (closed except for mass, 9am Sun).

Today Mougins bristles with galleries and painters, and also offers second homes for the better sort of resident – as can be discerned from all the closed-circuit cameras that peep out from behind the bougainvillea. Even the worst sort of residents are welcome, as long as they are discreet: Haitian dictator Baby Doc Duvalier used to have a pied-à-terre here.

There are a few tourist attractions in the village. The **Musée Maurice Gottlob** is upstairs in the town hall. It explores the history of Mougins using period literature. **Le Lavoir**, once the village laundry, now showcases local artists. Next to the 12th-century Porte Sarrazine, the **Musée de la Photographie** includes old cameras, a series of photos of Picasso by André Villers, and photos by Doisneau and Lartigue.

South-east of Mougins on the A8 is the **Musée de l'Automobiliste**. Adrien Maeght, son of art collectors Aimé and Marguerite Maeght, set up this ultra-modern glass and concrete tribute to racing cars and motorbikes.

Le Lavoir
av Charles Mallet (04.92.92.50.42). **Open** *Mar-Oct*
10am-7pm daily. **Admission** free.

Musée de la Photographie
Porte Sarrazine (04.93.75.85.67). **Open** *July-Aug*
10am-8pm daily. *Sept, Oct, Dec-June* 10am-6pm
daily. Closed Nov. **Admission** free.

Musée de l'Automobiliste
*772 chemin de Font-de-Currault, access Aire de
Bréguières on A8 (04.93.69.27.80/
www.musauto.fr.st).* **Open** *Apr-Sept* 10am-7pm daily.
Oct-mid Nov, mid Dec-Mar 10am-1pm, 2-6pm daily.
Closed mid Nov-mid Dec. **Admission** €7; €5 12-18s;
free under-12s. **Credit** MC, V.

Musée Maurice Gottlob
2 pl Commandant Lamy (04.92.92.50.42). **Open**
9am-5pm Mon-Fri; 11am-6pm Sat, Sun. Closed Nov.
Admission free.

Where to stay & eat

Mougins may be small, but it packs a
gastronomic punch. The **Moulin de Mougins**
(av Notre-Dame-de-Vie, 04.93.75.78.24,
www.moulin-mougins.com, closed Mon, double
€140-€190, menus €48-€150) is the most
famous of all. Brilliant young chef Alain Llorca
took it over from the legendary Roger Vergé in
2004 and faithful regulars waited with bated
breath. They were soon reassured: the decor is
sleek and modern (all cream and purple) and
the sun-drenched Mediterranean cuisine is the
freshest of the fresh. The Moulin has just three
rooms, but there are also four suites (€300-
€330). Another heavyweight on the culinary
scene here is chef Serge Gouloumes at **Le Mas
Candille** (Hôtel Le Mas Candille, bd Clement-
Rebuffel, 04.92.28.43.43, closed lunch July &
Aug, double €304-€495, menus €38-€85), who
opened here after graceful stints at Ma Maison
in Beverly Hills and the Miramar Beach in
Théoules-sur-Mer. His creations are mouth-
watering: sea bass in a rosemary clay crust or
tempura of langoustines with soya caramel and
basil. Rooms are sublimely luxurious, as are the
manicured grounds and the Shiseido spa. **Les
Muscadins** (18 bd Courteline, 04.92.28.43.43,
www.hotel-mougins-muscadins.com, closed mid
Nov-late Dec, double €139-€399), where Picasso
fell in love with Mougins in 1936, is also now
part of the Le Mas Candille empire; take
advantage of authentic, charming rooms and
indulge in the gourmet desserts downstairs in
the Café Candille. The **Manoir de l'Etang** (66
allée du Manoir, 04.92.28.36.00, www.manoir-
de-letang.com, double €125-€450) is an isolated
idyll near Picasso's final hermitage, and has
lovely views over a pond covered in lotus
flowers. At **Le Feu Follet** (pl du Commandant

Lamy, 04.93.90.15.78, www.feu-follet.fr, closed
Mon, lunch July & Aug, mid Dec-mid Jan,
menus €24-€45) Stéphane Bichon creates
spectacular dishes. Young chef Arnaud Care,
who trained with Jacques Chibois at the Bastide
St-Antoine in Grasse, has gone out on his own
at the **Brasserie de la Mediterranée** (pl du
Commandant Lamy, 04.93.90.03.47, lunch menu
€23.80, dinner menu €45). Try the tomato and
melon gazpacho or lobster with truffles. **La
Terrasse à Mougins** (31 bd Courteline,
04.92.28.36.20, www.la-terrasse-a-mougins.com,
closed Jan-mid Feb, double €107-€190, lunch
menu €25, dinner menus €45-€65) is a super-
chic hotel/restaurant with panoramic views.

Resources

Tourist information
*Office de Tourisme, 15 av Jean-Charles Mallet,
06250 Mougins (04.93.75.87.67/www.mougins-
coteazur.org).* **Open** *Mid June-mid Sept* 9am-7pm
daily. *Mid Sept-mid June* 9am-5.30am Mon-Sat.

Vallauris & Golfe-Juan

Truly, Vallauris would have had little to offer
were it not for Picasso. Georges and Suzanne
Ramié, who owned the Madoura pottery
workshop, introduced the painter to the joys of
clay in the 1940s and he single-handedly
rekindled the town's dying ceramics industry.
A mixed blessing, some might say, in view of
some of the so-called *céramique artistique* sold
along avenue Georges Clemenceau.

Vallauris seems to be split in two: there are the
busy tourist shops selling too much of the same
pottery, and then there's the deserted old town,
more famous for its Roman-style street grid than
its beauty. But don't despair, there are a few
serious workshops lurking behind the hordes of
souvenir-driven places. **Galerie Madoura** (rue
Suzanne Georges Ramié, 04.93.64.66.39, closed
Sat, Sun, Nov-mid Dec), now run by the son of
the original owners, still has the rights to
reproduce Picasso's designs in signed, limited
editions. Prices start at around €1,200.

By 1949 Picasso's passion for clay
was waning. Perhaps worried that such a
prestigious resident was about to desert them,
the good people of Vallauris gave him carte
blanche to decorate the tiny, medieval chapel
in the courtyard of the village castle – now the
Musée National Picasso. A breathtaking,
speed-painted essay on the theme of war and
peace was the result. The price of admission
also grants access to the **Musée Magnelli/
Musée de la Céramique** on the second floor
of the castle, where you'll find more Picasso
ceramics. The bronze statue of a man and sheep

The Riviera & Southern Alps

in place de la Libération is also a Picasso creation, presented to his adopted town in 1949 on condition that children be allowed to climb all over it.

Vallauris's seaward extension, Golfe-Juan, has a long series of beach-side restaurants and tourist shops and a fine, long sandy beach, sheltered from the worst of the Mistral. This is where Napoleon landed on 1 March 1815 at the beginning of the Hundred Days, his brief return to power before meeting Wellington at Waterloo. On summer weekends there's a night-time craft market (Fri-Sun June-Sept) on promenade des Ports, and Parking Aimé Berger hosts a food market on Friday mornings.

Musée National Picasso, Musée Magnelli, Musée de la Céramique

Château de Vallauris, pl de la Libération (04.93. 64.16.05). **Open** *Mid June-mid Sept* 10am-12.15pm, 2-6pm Mon, Wed-Sun. *Mid Sept-mid June* 10am-12.15pm, 2-5pm Mon, Wed-Sun. **Admission** €3.20; €1.65 students; free under-16s. **No credit cards.**

Where to stay, eat & drink

There are good eating options in Vallauris. **Le Manuscrit** (224 chemin Lintiur, 04.93.64.56.56, closed Mon, dinner Sun, dinner Tue in low season, mid Nov-mid Dec, mid Jan-mid Feb) has a beautiful terrace and nicely balanced menus (€22-€32): try the delicious snails with garlic

Vallauris. *See p240.*

cream. Old-fashioned style is the hallmark of **La Gousse d'Ail** (11 rte de Grasse, 04.93.64.10.71, closed lunch Tue, dinner Sun, Nov, 2wks in June, menus €15-€33), just behind the church. It's the bouillabaisse that's the draw at elegant **Bijou Plage** (bd du Littoral, 04.93.61.39.07, lunch menu €21, dinner menu €46). Good hotels are limited, however: try **Auberge Siou Aou Miou** (105 chemin des Fumades, 04.93.64.39.89, double €54) for its old manor-house charm.

You'll have better accommodation options if you stay down at Golfe-Juan. The selection includes the upmarket **Résidence Hotelière Open** (av Georges Pompidou, 04.93.63.33.00, www.resorts-open.com, double €75-€135) and the charming *chambres d'hôtes* of **Mas Samarcande** (138 grand bd de Super Cannes, 04.93.63.97.73, www.stpaulweb.com/samarcande, double €120), where M and Mme Diot lay on all home comforts, while basic rooms and a pool can be found at **Hôtel Beau Soleil** (impasse Beau Soleil, 04.93.63.63.63, www.hotel-beau-soleil.com, double €63-€127). Choice is good if you're peckish too. **L'Abri Côterie** (port Camille Rayon, 04.93.63.06.13, closed Dec, menus €16-€26) offers a good lunch menu (and doubles as a piano bar in summer). A must for seafood is **Nounou** (av des Frères Roustan, plages des Soleil, 04.93.63.71.73, closed Mon, Nov, dinner Sun, menus €35-€60), where steaming platters of shellfish are served amid great decor. **Restaurant Tetou** (bd des Frères Roustan, plages des Soleil, 04.93.63.71.16, closed Wed, Nov-mid Mar, lunch Mon, average €100-€125) is a beautiful New York-style restaurant.

Tourist information

Vallauris Office de Tourisme

sq du 8 Mai 1945, 06220 Vallauris (04.93.63.82.58/ www.vallauris-golfe-juan.com). **Open** *July-Aug* 9am-7pm daily. *Sept-June* 9am-noon, 2-6pm Mon-Sat.

Getting there

For the easyCruise service, *see p249* **Plane sailing**.

By bus

RCA (04.93.39.11.39, www.rca.tm.fr) buses go from the main, port-side bus station in Cannes via the villages along the coast; from the SNCF station its Grasse bus goes via Mougins (every 30mins Mon-Sat, hourly Sun). From Vallauris bus station **Envibus** (04.93.64.18.37) has frequent buses to Golfe-Juan SNCF station and to Cannes.

By car

Mougins is 3.5km (two miles) north of Cannes on N85. For Vallauris, leave the A8 at exit Antibes and follow the signs from the D435. The N7/N98 coast road runs through Golfe-Juan.

Antibes to Cagnes

One part F Scott Fitzgerald glam, one part groomed party spot and one part little Britain, this is the Riviera at its most intoxicating.

So popular now with British expats that the French often refer to it as 'Angle-tibes', Antibes and its beachside satellite Juan-les-Pins are the Riviera's current second-home honeypots, with rocketing prices to match. The seaward extensions of the next towns east, Villeneuve-Loubet and Cagnes-sur-Mer, are more downmarket, but both have magnificent medieval citadels high above the coastal strip.

Antibes & Juan-les-Pins

The Greeks set up their trading post of Antipolis in the fifth century BC. Ligurian tribes fought hard to get their hands on the town over the following centuries, forcing Antibes' residents to turn to Rome for protection in 154 BC. But the fall of Rome left Antibes prey to attacks from every passing marauder, from Barbarians to Vandals, Visigoths, Burgundians, Ostrogoths and Franks. In the tenth century, Antibes fell into the hands of the Counts of Grasse before passing to the bishops of Antibes and, at the end of the 14th century, to the Grimaldis of Monaco. It remained theirs until 1608, when Henri IV of France purchased Antibes, turning it into his front-line defence against the Savoy kingdom across the bay in Nice. This opposition partly explains the striking architectural differences between the old towns of Nice and Antibes: the latter has a certain austerity with its stone houses, rarely over three storeys, and its grey-blue shutters, while Vieux Nice, painted in shades of pink and ochre with jade-green shutters, has a more flamboyant Italian feel.

To host the initial trickle of titled and wealthy Europeans who sought winter sunshine here, a local entrepreneur opened the Grand Hôtel du Cap in 1870. But Antibes and Juan-les-Pins became a year-round playground only in 1923, when consummate hosts Gerald and Sara Murphy – friendly with the likes of Picasso, Cole Porter, Hemingway and Rudolf Valentino – persuaded the hotel to stay open all year, instead of just winter. That same summer, US tycoon Frank Jay Gould recognised the area's potential and started buying property to create hotels and a casino, while Coco Chanel launched a flowing, casual look for women that earned Juan-les-Pins the name 'Pyjamopolis'. Picasso painted masterpieces here, water-skiing

was invented, women bared skin on the beach and F Scott Fitzgerald wrote the alcohol-fuelled *Tender is the Night*, immortalising the Murphys as Nicole and Dick Diver. Antibes-Juan-les-Pins became the Riviera's first chic summer resort, to be followed by the rest of the Côte d'Azur in the summer of 1931.

These days yachties and zillionaires mix with artists and easyJetsetters (and, for that matter, easyCruisers, *see p249* **Plane sailing**) to create a genuinely cosmopolitan atmosphere. Juan-les-Pins is unashamedly touristy and near dead in the winter, but Antibes buzzes with markets, culture and café society all year. The lived-in feel of Antibes' alleys is a far cry from the brash streets of Juan-les-Pins, although both throng with crowds in the summer heat.

The conurbation of Antibes-Juan-les-Pins is a mainly unappealing mass wedged between the sea and the A8 motorway. The old districts are best approached from **Fort Carré**, which stands on the point separating the St-Roch inlet from Baie des Anges – or, even better, by sea, though it's an easy if less picturesque walk from the train station. The original fort was constructed in the 16th century to counter the Savoy threat; in the 17th century, Louis XIV's military architect Vauban gave it its eight-pointed star shape. Just to the south of the fort, Port Vauban is Europe's largest yacht marina, harbouring some of Europe's grandest pleasure craft and plenty of glitzy boutiques, where you can hire – sorry, charter – your own craft and join the yachterati. In early June the Voiles d'Antibes fills the bay with splendid sailing vessels and motor yachts for five days.

Hidden behind the sheltered ancient walls of the quay is Plage de la Gravette, a free sandy beach with gently shelving waters, in the heart of town. South of the marina, at the other end of the ramparts, is the **Musée d'Histoire et d'Archéologie**, containing reminders of the town's multi-faceted past, including Greek and Etruscan amphorae. Also squeezed within the ramparts is the **Eglise Notre-Dame-de-l'Immaculée-Conception** (04.93.34.06.29, open 8am-noon, 3-6.30pm daily), Antibes' former cathedral, built on the site of a Roman temple to Diana, a rich concoction of marble virgins, baroque stylings and deep ochres, lapis blues and blood-red walls.

Hôtel du Cap Eden-Roc. *See p246.*

The **Château Grimaldi** next door still follows the plan of the earlier Roman fort, despite rebuilding in the 16th century by the Grimaldis (*see p284* **A matter of principality**). In 1946, when Picasso (who had first painted beach life at Juan-les-Pins in 1920) rented a cold, damp room on the second floor, it belonged to a certain Romuald Dor, and already contained a small archaeological collection. Dor had ulterior motives in his offer of such prime Riviera studio space; the works Picasso left behind in lieu of rent enabled him to upgrade his lacklustre collection and re-baptise it the **Musée Picasso**. This was a fertile period for the balding Spaniard. As artists' materials were almost impossible to get hold of in 1946, Picasso used ships' paint slapped on to some odd-looking bits of wood, and discovered the joys of pottery. Picasso's treasures here are sadly limited, occupying only one floor of the collection, though the Germaine Richier sculptures and Nicolas de Staël paintings help compensate.

Just inland from the castle, the cours Masséna, the Greek town's main drag, plays host to one of the region's liveliest (and priciest) produce markets, the Marché Provençal (every morning, except Mon in winter) – market gardeners sell local produce down the centre aisle. **Balade en Provence** (25bis cours Masséna, 04.93.34.93.00, open 9am-10pm daily) stocks 50 sorts of olive oil, *pistou*, honey, hams and absinthe (with a bar where you can try out the absinthe). This area of the old town is a hive of Anglo-Frenchness and home to the long-established **Heidi's English Bookshop** (24 rue Aubernon, 04.93.34.74.11, open daily 10am-7pm) and the **Antibéa Theatre** (15 pl Clemenceau, 04.93.34.24.30), which stages plays

in English by the Red Pear Company. Just beyond the theatre, in place Nationale, comic artist Raymond Peynet's **Musée Peynet** is dedicated to cartoon art.

The old town can become frenzied in the summer months, but wander beyond the shops and restaurants into its more residential streets and you'll be amazed at how peaceful it feels. Rarely discovered by accident is the area known as the **Commune Libre du Safranier**, which has its own 'mayor', Zézé Marconi, and mission: to preserve local traditions while raising money for the poor with events such as giant street feasts. The mini village's pride shows in the flowers cascading from the bright blue shuttered windows of the stone houses along rue du Safranier, rue du Bas Castelet and rue du Haut Castelet (a decent map of Vieil Antibes will come in handy).

Heading south out of Antibes, the scenery changes dramatically from built-up citadel to leafy lap of luxury. The Cap d'Antibes peninsula is a playground for the very wealthy although most of the houses are of the classic, understated variety; definitely not the glitzy *Footballers' Wives* type. To appreciate the prosperity to the full, rent a bike from one of the many outlets along boulevard Wilson and take in the views as you wend your way up to **Parc Thuret**, a botanical testing site established in 1856 with the aim of introducing more varied flora to the Riviera – 200 new species are introduced each year and their acclimatisation carefully studied. If cycling sounds like too much exertion, take advantage of the Cap's long stretches of public beach, Plage de la Salis and Plage de la Garoupe. Both can be walked to from Antibes or Juan-les-Pins.

Water, water everywhere at **Marineland**.

Between the two, and a fair hike uphill, the **Sanctuaire de la Garoupe** has a great collection of unlikely ex-votos. At the southern tip of the peninsula, the **Musée Naval et Napoléonien** has model ships and charts and mementos of the great man, who parked his mother in Antibes on one occasion. Next to the museum is another historical landmark where most people would opt to park themselves, rather than their mothers: the Hôtel du Cap.

To the west of the peninsula, Juan-les-Pins has no pretensions to history: a sandy, forested, deserted bay until the 1920s, it was conceived for, and still attracts, the hedonists. The centre is a seething mass of boutiques and restaurants, and if it seems frantic during the day, then you should see it on a summer's night: Juan-les-Pins isn't in the habit of wasting good partying time on sleep. The beautiful beach has public and private sections; on the latter, a patch of sand with deckchair sets you back around €10 a day.

East of Antibes (a ten-minute drive by the N7) is **Marineland** marine theme park, the most visited (paid-for) attraction in the South of France. Launched in 1970, it is a must for any child visiting the Côte d'Azur and contains five parks, the best of which, Marineland itself, offers the sort of view of marine life you can only otherwise get in a cage at sea. Through the glass-surround whale tank, you can watch killer whales interact with their trainer in a relationship that strikes one as more like friends than master and subject; three out of the nine whales in the world born in captivity were born here. The dolphins occupy one of the biggest dolphin pools in Europe. There's a walk-through, underwater shark tunnel and a ray touch-pool. Then there are the other four

parks. The Little Provençal Farm, best for under-fives, has domestic animals, pony rides, an enchanted river boat ride and bouncy inflatables. Jungle of Butterflies harbours butterflies, iguanas, parrots, snakes and bats. Aqua-Splash (mid June-mid Sept, 10am-7pm daily) features seawater wave pools, a lazy river, giant toboggans and a toddlers' pool. Adventure Golf boasts three challenging minigolf courses.

Fort Carré
rte du Bord de Mer, N98 (06.14.89.17.45). **Open** *Mid June-mid Sept* 10am-6pm Tue-Sun. *Mid Sept-mid June* 10am-4pm Tue-Sun. **Admission** €3; €1.50 students; free under-18s. **No credit cards.**

Marineland
306 av Mozart (04.93.33.49.49/www.marineland.fr). **Open** *July-Aug* 10am-midnight (last entry at 10.30pm) daily. *Sept-June* 10am-5.30pm Mon, Tue, Thur; 10am-7pm Wed, Sat, Sun. Closed Jan. **Admission** €33; €24 under-12s; free under-3s. **Credit** MC, V.

Musée d'Histoire et d'Archéologie
Bastion St-André, 3 av Mezière (04.92.90.54.37). **Open** *June-Sept* 10am-noon, 2-6pm Tue-Sun. *Oct-May* 10am-noon, 2-6pm Tue-Sun. **Admission** €3; free under-18s. **Credit** MC, V.

Musée Naval et Napoléonien
bd Kennedy (04.93.61.45.32). **Open** *June-Sept* 10am-6pm Tue-Sat. *Oct-May* 10am-4.30pm Tue-Sat. **Admission** €3; free under-18s. **No credit cards.**

Musée Peynet et du Dessin Humoristique
chemin Raymond, pl Nationale (04.92.90.54.30). **Open** 10am-noon, 2-6pm Tue-Sun. **Admission** €3; €1.50 students, under-25s; free under-18s. **No credit cards.**

Musée Picasso

Château Grimaldi, pl Mariejol (04.92.90.54.20).
Open *June-Sept* 10am-6pm Tue-Sun. *Oct-May*
10am-noon, 2-6pm Tue-Sun. Closed until 2007
for renovations. **Admission** €6; free under-15s.
Credit V.

Parc Thuret

chemin Raymond (04.97.21.25.00). **Open** *May-Sept*
8am-6pm Mon-Fri. *Oct-Apr* 8.30am-5.30pm Mon-Fri.
Admission free.

Where to eat & drink

Antibes' cosmopolitan old town is lined with
cafés and bistros – the trick is finding the good
ones, which often close at lunch or, rather
oddly, during August. For an atmospheric
coffee try the age-old **Pimm's** (3 rue de la
République, 04.93.34.04.88), which still has a
few writers and lovers hiding in the woodwork,
or head to the place Nationale, cours Masséna
or boulevard d'Aguillon café strips. **L'Oursin**
(16 rue République, 04.93.34.13.46, closed dinner
Sun, Mon Nov-Apr, menus €24-€35) is
something of an oyster specialist; snails,
scallops and a daily dip of aïoli are also
available. **Le Brulot** (3 rue Frédéric Isnard,
04.93.34.17.76, www.brulot.com, closed Mon,
Tue, Sun, lunch Wed, Aug, menus €12-€38) is
famous for its socca (chickpea pancake), grilled
meats and fish, all cooked over a wood fire; it
has a pasta annexe down the street. Classy
Oscar's (8 rue du Dr Rostan, 04.93.34.90.14,
www.oscars-antibes.com, closed Mon, Sun,
mid May-mid June, menus €26-€49) has an
all-white Italian-style interior. Its most
expensive set menu is a five-course affair
featuring lobster, caviar and truffles.

Another upmarket choice is **La Jarre**
(14 rue St-Esprit, Les Remparts, 04.93.34.50.12,
closed Wed, menus €32-€40) where chef
Frédéric Ramos cooks up beautifully conceived
dishes such as grilled tuna with artichokes
and confit tomatoes with basil sauce vierge,
and yellow peach gazpacho with fresh almonds,
all served in the shade of a 100 year-old fig tree
(the garden is covered and heated in winter).
In the tiny neighbourhood known as the
Commune Libre des Safraniers, **La Taverne
du Safranier** (1 pl du Safranier, 04.93.34.80.50,
closed dinner Sun, all Mon, average €28) is a
bastion of local cuisine, serving petits farcis
(stuffed vegetables) and sardine fritters on the
lively terrace. **L'Ancre de Chine** (26 bd
d'Aguillon, 04.93.34.27.70, closed lunch Sat,
menus €14-€21) is justifiably busy, as it's
the best Chinese in town, while **L'Eléphant
Bleu** (28 bd d'Aguillon, 04.93.34.28.80, menus
€19-€40), situated right next door, serves a
wide range of excellent Thai food.

Stylish foodies make straight for Cap
d'Antibes and its luxury hotel restaurants.
Alternatively, try a knockout bouillabaisse or
platter of langoustines at the venerable **Bacon**
(bd de Bacon, 04.93.61.50.02, www.restaurantde
bacon.com, closed Mon, lunch Tue, Nov-Feb,
menus €49-€79). Overlooking the Baie des
Anges, the almost all-white dining room has a
tented ceiling that is rolled back in summer.

At Juan-les-Pins there are plenty of beach
establishments. The family-friendly **Plage
Epi Beach** (bd Guillaumont, 04.93.67.27.84,
average €24) specialises in salads and simple
grilled fish. Lively **La Bodega** (16 av du Dr
Dautheville, 04.93.67.59.02, average €24) stays
open until all hours in summer to feed revellers
from local nightlife haunts. **Bijou Plage** (bd du
Littoral, 04.93.61.39.07, menus €21-€28) serves
reliable seafood on the seafront. For a touch of
crustacean class try the **Festival de la Mer**
(146 bd Wilson, 04.93.61.04.62, average €45)
with buckets of oysters, scallops and snails.
The highly regarded **Perroquet** (3 av Georges
Gallice, 04.93.61.02.20, closed lunch July & Aug,
Nov, menus €27-€32) is possibly Juan-les-Pins'
finest with the emphasis on traditional French
cuisine. **Les Pêcheurs** (Hôtel Juana, La
Pinède, av Gallice, 04.93.61.08.70, closed Tue,
menus €65-€90) attracts a clientele more likely
to spend the day in white linen than in bathing
suits. It was here that Alain Ducasse won his
second star; chef Christian Morisset continues
the tradition of wonderful food.

Nightlife

Juan-les-Pins' annual jazz festival earns the
most international attention but, as a more
affordable club scene than St-Tropez or
Monaco, Juan attracts the young end of the
market, creating some of the liveliest nightlife
on the Côte. Without doubt, the best club is
Le Village (pl de la Nouvelle Orléans, 1 bd
de la Pinède, 04.92.93.90.00, closed Sun-Thur,
admission €16), rumoured to be the favourite
haunt of Noel Gallagher. DJs play a mix of
pop and house and the club oozes atmosphere.
The vast monastic interior is très cool, although
the hefty drinks prices could easily blow a hole
in one's pocket. Nearby, Juan icon **Whisky
à Go Go** (5 av Jacques Léonetti, La Pinède,
04.93.61.26.40, closed Nov-Mar, admission €16)
is showing its age with a kitsch 1970s disco feel.
Young upstart **Minimal** (142 bd Président
Wilson, 04.93.67.78.87, closed Sun-Thur,
admission varies) is dedicated to house music,
as is its smaller club around the corner, Le Yes
(10 av du Dr Dautheville, closed Mon-Wed).
More sedate is **Crystal** (av Georges Gallice,
04.93.61.02.51, closed mid Nov-mid Dec), a

Clubbing at **Le Village**. *See p245.*

classic early 20th-century open-air cocktail bar. The suavest hangout in town for drinks is the **Hôtel St-Charles Lounge** (4 rue St-Charles, 06.17.71.08.50, closed Jan, Feb), where DJs attempt to raise cocktail drinkers from their stylish seats. A superb club and casino on the seafront east of Antibes is **La Siesta** (rte du Bord de Mer, 04.93.33.31.31, admission €10), where in summer you can dance to pop and house in the open air and people-watch on terrace loungers – look out for its 'Deejay Superstar' nights. **Xtrême Café** (6 rue Aubernon, 04.93.34.03.90) is a fashionable bar for cocktails, apéritifs and nibbles, while **Café Cosy** (3 rue Migranier, 04.93.34.81.55, closed Mon) is a mellow place to listen to jazz. The **Hop Store** (38 bd Aguillon, 04.93.34.15.33) is a buzzing Irish bar with a domed brick roof and outside terrace. Yacht crew favourite the **Café de la Porte du Port** (32 rue Aubernon, 04.93.34.68.94), by the arches that lead to the marina, is as raucous as it gets in the classy confines of Antibes.

Activities

Watersports & yacht hire

If playing at sardines on the strand is not your thing, there are watersports galore; it was in Juan-les-Pins, they say, that water-skiing was invented in the 1930s at the beach of the glamorous Hôtel Belles-Rives, which still has its own water-skiing club. The **Ecole de Ski Nautique** (Plage Bretagne, 06.13.61.51.17) is another water-skiing specialist. For diving, **Golfe Plongée Club** (port de Golfe-Juan, 06.09.55.73.36) offers beginners' courses, while **Côté Plongée** (bd Maréchal Juin, 06.72.74.34.94, www.coteplongee.com) by the Musée Naval on Cap d'Antibes runs children's courses and exploratory and night dives. On the Antibes side of the Cap, the **Club Nautique** (Plage de la Salis, 04.93.67.22.50, www.club-nautique-antibes.com) is a professional set-up with dinghies and catamarans to hire or learn on. If a cruise is

your idea of nirvana, **Yachtbrokers International** (21 rue Aubernon, 04.93.34.04.75, www.yachtbrokers-int.com, closed Sat, Sun) can provide a six-berth, 29-knot motorboat with two crew from €1,500 a day, plus fuel, port fees, food and drink. A week on a yacht sleeping 20-22 with palatial staterooms, studies, dining rooms and a one-to-one guest to crew ratio will set you back considerably more.

Where to stay

Of all the hotels on the French Riviera, the **Hôtel du Cap Eden-Roc** (bd Kennedy, Cap d'Antibes, 04.93.61.39.01, www.edenroc-hotel.fr, closed mid Oct-mid Apr, double €360-€1,200) is probably the most exclusive, and certainly the most expensive. The gleaming white building nestles back from the coast in 25 acres (ten hectares) of woodland. It was here that the cult of the suntan was born, when American society hosts Gerald and Sara Murphy came down from Paris in the summer of 1923 and told all their friends. The hotel is pretentious enough not to accept credit cards, and can be annoyingly overrun by celebrities and their bodyguards. Smartly dressed non-residents can use the bar and swimming pool, but expect a hefty fee if you so much as glance at a towel or sun-lounger. A comparatively cheap alternative nearby is the **Hôtel Beau Site** (141 bd Kennedy, 04.93.61.53.43, www.hotelbeausite. net, closed Nov-Feb, double €68-€137), offering clean, simple accommodation and a pool. More affordable still is **Hôtel La Jabotte** (13 av Max Maurey, Cap d'Antibes, 04.93.61.45.89, www.jabotte.com, closed Nov, double €49-€84), 50 metres (160 feet) from a sandy beach but so welcoming that you might not want to leave its leafy garden. The ten rooms have been redecorated by the new owners, who run La Jabotte more like a B&B than a hotel.

In a central, peaceful location by Antibes' main square, former coaching inn **Le Relais du Postillon** (8 rue Championnet, 04.93.34. 20.77, double €45-€83) has cheery rooms overlooking the park or courtyard. Its highly regarded restaurant (closed lunch, 2wks Jan, 2wks Nov, average €30) uses fine ingredients to create melt-in-the-mouth risottos, salads and grills. Nearby, in the dead centre of town, the **Modern Hôtel** (1 rue Fourmilière, 04.92.90. 59.05, double €58-€85) has comfortable rooms with a slight 1980s feel. Somewhat cosier is the **Hôtel Le Ponteil** (11 impasse Jean Mensier, 04.93.34.67.92, closed mid Nov-Dec, double €65-€144) with its leafy exterior. For thalassotherapy spa treatments, including diet and anti-stress cures, the huge modern **Thalazur** (770 chemin des Moyennes Bréguières, Antibes, 04.92.91.82.00, www. thalazur.fr, double €110-€241) uses water pumped up from the sea. **Hôtel Juan Beach** (5 rue de l'Oratoire, Juan-les-Pins, 04.93.61.02.89, www.hoteljuanbeach.com, closed Oct-Mar, double €75-€150), a five-minute walk from the nightlife action, has acquired a lovely swimming pool and outdoor lounge area under its new owners. The **Hôtel Castel Mistral** (43 rue Bricka, Juan-les-Pins, 04.93.61.21.04, closed Oct-Mar, rates €76-€94) is a charmingly dilapidated place, handy for the beach, with a pretty terrace out front. To do Juan in style, though, stay at the **Hôtel Juana** (La Pinède, av Gallice, Juan-les-Pins, 04.93.61.08.70, www.hotel-juana.com, closed mid Jan-mid Feb, mid Nov-mid Dec, double €235-€850), a refined art deco jewel with a lovely pool and sitting area, two minutes from the sea. In a similar vein is the classic **Hôtel Belles-Rives** (33 bd Edouard Baudoin, 04.93.61.02.79, www.bellesrives.com, closed Jan, double €130-€720), which has kept its original 1920s style and furnishings. Indulge in the luxurious bars, lounges and private beach. Inexpensive charm, antiques and a sunny terrace make **La Marjolaine** (15 av du Dr Fabre, 04.93.61.06.60, closed Nov-mid Dec, double €48-€75), a few steps from Juan-les-Pins station, a truly delightful find.

Resources

Internet

Art-116, 116 bd Wilson, Juan-les-Pins (04.92. 93.14.13/www.art-116.com). **Open** 9am-11pm daily.

Tourist Information

Accueil Touristique du Vieil Antibes *32 bd d'Aguillon (04.93.34.65.65).* **Open** *July, Aug* 9am-9pm daily. *Sept-June* 9am-noon, 1.30-6pm Mon-Fri; 9am-noon Sat.
Antibes Office de Tourisme *11 pl de Gaulle, 06160 Antibes (04.92.90.53.00/www.antibes-juanlespins.com).* **Open** *July, Aug* 9am-7pm daily. *Sept-June* 9am-12.30pm, 1.30-6pm Mon-Fri; 9am-noon, 2-6pm Sat.
Juan-les-Pins Office de Tourisme *51 bd Guillaumont, 06160 Juan-les-Pins (04.92.90.53.05/ www.antibes-juanlespins.com).* **Open** *July, Aug* 9am-7pm daily. *Sept-June* 9am-noon, 2-6pm Mon-Fri; 9am-noon Sat.

Biot

Once, long ago, a clever PR company was sent into the hinterland of the Côte d'Azur to give its villages instant brand recognition. That, at least, is how it sometimes appears. Grasse is perfume, St-Paul-de-Vence is art, Vallauris is pottery and Picasso, and Biot (pronounced Bee-ot) is glass and Fernand Léger. But it was not always so. In fact, until as late as the 1950s, the name of this picturesque village was more linked to pottery. One of Léger's protégés set up a ceramic workshop in Biot dedicated to reproducing the master's designs, and Léger spent his last few years here.

A fortnight before he died in 1956, the artist acquired some land in Biot, intending to build a house. His widow, Nadia, used the site to build a fitting tribute to her husband, the **Musée National Fernand Léger**. The low-slung building is set back from the road in undulating sculpture gardens. It traces the work of this restless, politically committed artist from his first Impressionist stirrings in 1905, through boldly coloured 'machine art' of the 1920s and '30s to the later murals, stained glass, ceramics and tapestries. The museum reopened in autumn 2005 after months of renovations.

Glass came to Biot only at the end of the 1950s, when the **Verrerie de Biot** fired up its furnaces. Half working factory and half gallery, the Verrerie is just off the main D4 road, below the town walls. One can watch the unique Biot 'bubble glassware' (*verre bullé*) being blown, and there are plenty of chances to buy both here and in the village, where rue St-Sébastien is lined with shops selling the bubble glassware – one of the best is **Raphaël Farinelli** (workshop at 465 route de la Mer, 04.93.65.17.29, shop at 24 rue Sébastien, 04.93.65.01.89). The **Galerie Internationale du Verre** (04.93.65.03.00) is also worth a visit, with its collection of highly sculptural glass by US and European artists. At No.9 the **Musée d'Histoire et de la Céramique Biotoises** has a patchy but charming collection of local costumes and artefacts. Past the boutiques and bars along the main pedestrian street is the pretty place des Arcades, surrounded by Italianate loggias – a home-from-home touch brought by Genoese settlers who moved in to repopulate Biot after the Black Death. The pretty village church has two good altarpieces by Louis Bréa and Giovanni Canavesio. Classical concerts are held in the square on summer evenings. Today's Biot is a vivid mix of galleries, cafés and a tangle of beautiful little lanes; Tuesday mornings see a market held on rue St-Sébastien and the place aux Arcades. The tourist office has a walking tour leaflet.

On the way out of Biot, you can pick up tips and buy plants at the **Bonsai Arboretum**, a collection of over 1,000 bonsai in a 2,000 square-metre (21,500 square-foot) Japanese garden, tended by two generations of the Okonek family.

Bonsai Arboretum

299 chemin du Val de Pôme (04.93.65.63.99). **Open** 10am-noon, 2-6pm Mon, Wed-Sun. **Admission** €4; €2 students, 6-18s; free under-6s. **No credit cards.**

Musée d'Histoire et de la Céramique Biotoises

9 rue St-Sébastien (04.93.65.54.54). **Open** *June-Sept* 10am-6pm Wed-Sun. *Oct-June* 2-6pm Wed-Sun. **Admission** €2; €1 students; free under-16s. **No credit cards.**

Musée National Fernand Léger

chemin du Val de Pôme (04.92.91.50.30). Closed for renovations until late 2006.

La Verrerie de Biot

chemin des Combes (04.93.65.03.00/www. verreriebiot.com). **Open** *July, Aug* 9.30am-8pm Mon-Sat; 10am-1pm, 3-7.30pm Sun. *Sept-June* 9.30am-6.30pm Mon-Sat; 10am-1pm, 2.30-6.30pm Sun. **Admission** free.

Where to stay & eat

The charming **Hôtel des Arcades** (16 pl des Arcades, 04.93.65.01.04, double €52-€90, restaurant closed Mon, dinner Sun, menus €28-€32) is a 15th-century mansion that mixes ancient (huge fireplaces, four-poster beds) and modern. The owner is a collector, and the gallery-cum-restaurant displays works by artists including Vasarely, Léger and Folon. Provençal classics (hearty daube de boeuf, aïoli on Fridays) are lovingly made here with local ingredients, and staff greet you like family, particularly if you come with children. Benoît Paudrat is chef at **Le Jarrier** (30 passage Bourgade, 04.93.65.11.68, closed Mon, Tue, lunch Sat, menus €29-€45), a relaxed restaurant in a converted jar factory at the end of a laundry-festooned passageway, serving Mediterranean dishes laced with truffles, nuts and fruit. Midway down the central thoroughfare, rue St-Sébastien, **Le Piccolo** (04.93.65.16.91, menus €19-€25) dishes up grand plates of seafood and local meat on solid wooden tables. More down to earth is the traditional, lively hangout **Le Bar du Coin** (29 rue St-Sébastien, 04.93.65.10.72, menu €25) on the same street, where huge salads and grilled meats are eaten with local wine and a healthy selection of beers. The **Crêperie du Vieux Village** (2 rue St-Sébastien, 04.93.65.72.73, menu €13.50), open since 1969, serves a huge selection of crêpes, including the 'deadly sin' – a concoction involving apple, Calvados, hazelnuts, caramel and crème Chantilly – in a stone-walled, non-smoking setting. More modern is **Le Mas des Orangers** (3 rue des Roses, 04.93.65.18.10, www.lemasdesorangers.com, menu €10), with its vivid orange terrace and bright upstairs room on the main square, well-stocked *épicerie* and broad selection of teas. Tucked away in what was a 16th-century potter's workshop

near the foot of the old town, stylish **Les Terraillers** (11 route du Chemin Neuf, 04.93.65.01.59, closed Wed, Thur, late Oct-Nov, menus €35-€70) has a delightful atmosphere and a host of provençal dishes. Out-of-town elegance can be found at the **Domaine du Jas** (625 rte de la Mer, 04.93.65.50.50, www.domainedujas.com, double €120-€235), a ten-minute drive towards the sea. It has a mosaic-bottomed swimming pool set in palm trees and several homely reception rooms.

Resources

Tourist information

Office du Tourisme *46 rue St-Sébastien, 06410 Biot (04.93.65.78.00/www.biot.fr)*. **Open** *July, Aug* 10am-7pm Mon-Fri; 2.30-7pm Sat, Sun. *Sept-June* 9am-noon, 2-6pm Mon-Fri; 2-6pm Sat, Sun.

Villeneuve-Loubet & Cagnes

Zip through the beachside resorts between Antibes and Nice and you will be missing out. The interest lies just a few kilometres inland, in the medieval centres of Villeneuve-Loubet and Haut-de-Cagnes, where vine-covered houses and traditional restaurants meet fine views and a noticeable lack of tourists.

The graceful lanes of **Villeneuve-Loubet** hide more than their fair share of galleries, cafés and attractive squares. So peaceful is it that several holidaying rock and film stars have taken to hiding here from the silly-season paparazzi on the coast. The **Musée de l'Art Culinaire** celebrates one of Villeneuve's most famous sons, Auguste Escoffier, who was taken under the wing of Britain's King Edward VII after transforming cooking from a trade to an art. Escoffier later became head chef of the Savoy in London. A photograph of opera star Nellie Melba – after whom the peachy sundae was named – just about sums up the modest charms of this collection, whose highlights are the menus and cuttings elaborating tales of Escoffier's life as chef to political leaders and kings. Just above the tourist office at the foot of the old town is the **Musée d'Histoire et d'Art**. Military objects gleaned from the 20th-century French Army share the small display space with a handful of portraits and an exhibition space devoted to regional artists. Villeneuve-Loubet also has a market on Tuesday and Friday mornings.

Three kilometres (two miles) away is **Villeneuve-Loubet Plage**. This purpose-built resort stretches around the **Marina Baie des Anges**, a huge (and some might say hideous) apartment complex built 1969-70, shaped like a giant wave, which can be seen

Plane sailing

It's hard, at first, to believe that a floating orange bordello (according to some headlines) could create so many column inches. And yet, when you see said bordello moored up against the time-worn glamour of St-Tropez, Cannes and Monaco, suddenly it all makes sense. Brash, fun and frenetic, easyCruising through the playground of playboys offers an undeniable satisfaction, as you sweep past the exclusive lairs of Roger Vadim and co, all for £20 a night. Are you a crass orange invader, you begin to wonder, or do you have just as much right as the other, groomed and manicured, visitors to be sipping cocktails while staring out at the shimmering Riviera? Even if your poison is £2.75 Caipirinhas rather than their Kir Royals?

Love it or hate it, easyCruise is here to stay. Sit in the Jacuzzi for 30 minutes with a brace of cowboy-hatted babes, a chippie from Glasgow and a gaggle of American co-eds and you'll soon realise that they all love it, even if they hadn't thought they would. It's a convenient, cheap and utterly cheerful way to see one of Europe's high-end hotspots. Everyone on board sings its praises faster than you can say 'Portofino for under 30 quid' – and it's little wonder why.

From her teak decks to her shiny orange foyer, the good ship *easyCruiseOne* is top of the line in every way. With only 170 passengers and four sunny wooden decks to choose from, getting your own view of the passing coastline is a cinch. But remain on board at night and it's a different story, certainly not to everyone's taste. From the shoddy pub-style quiz (the winner gets free shots – gee, thanks) to the evening bop and the Blue Hawi (*sic*) cocktails, the snob in all of us may begin to raise his frowning, monocled head (while the hedonist deep down is giggling with every list to port). It's no surprise, then, that the decks are empty at 10am, when most easyCruisers are still in the pitch black of their cabins, swaying their way to St-Tropez.

There's a good reason why they may wait a while before turning the lights on: flick the switch on your windowless playpen to reveal a tableau of retina-searing orange, your hungover partner and the easyCruise logo emblazoned across the bedstead. It's no sight for sore eyes. Still, cabins are slickly furnished (funky ensuite bathrooms meld with comfy beds and plenty of storage for your Côte d'Azur glad rags) and, most important of all, they are soundproofed.

The 'cruise' part of the trip starts each morning at 8am, leaving plenty of time for a belt-busting easyBreakfast on board. A winch of the anchors further disorient those cocooned below deck. Above, however, it's a delight, as the orange king of the seas plies past the Cap d'Antibes, the Estoril and the Ligurian foothills on the way to its seven glamour-pot destinations: Cannes, St-Tropez, Monaco, Portofino, Genoa, San Remo and Nice. The 'easy' bit starts when the ship pulls up in the dead centre of every town, a floating hotel with seven-storey views. From here it's straight down the gangplank to a nice moules frites or a frutti di mare, and a good gape around God's own country for the Riviera first-timers on board.

As passengers swap numbers on their final morning (having, in many cases, exchanged a good deal more than that the night before), it's apparent that the wily Stelios has done it again. With rumours abroad of easyCruiseTwo, -Three and -Four in the Caribbean, Greek Islands and Bay of Naples, the big orange fortress of fun looks ready to steam on into the sunset.

for miles around and from the plane as you enter Nice; weekly visits are organised by the tourist office (10am Thur, book one day ahead). The seafront is home to an assortment of seafood and pizza restaurants, watersports activities and a long pebbly beach packed out with happy families.

Cagnes, a few kilometres down the coast towards Nice, is, in fact, three separate entities: mostly unalluring Cros-de-Cagnes on the seafront, misleadingly named Cagnes-sur-Mer, which is actually inland, and medieval Haut-de-Cagnes, perched on high and home to the UNESCO-sponsored Festival International de la Peinture each summer (contact the tourist office for details, *see p251*).

Cros-de-Cagnes was once a fishing village but today offers little more than a crowded pebbly beach, watersports hire and a string of restaurants and hotels along the beachfront, though the village centre retains some ancient charm. On the other side of the busy A8 lies **Cagnes-sur-Mer**, best known for Auguste Renoir's estate, **Les Collettes**. The artist

Musée de l'Art Culinaire.

had the house built in 1908 after his doctor prescribed a drier, warmer seaside climate for his rheumatoid arthritis. Although Renoir painted his late, almost garish *Grandes Baigneuses* here, he complained that the sun was too dazzling and concentrated in his last years on sculpture, working right up until his death in 1919, and battling against the growing paralysis in his hands. The house is preserved pretty much as he left it, and its olive-tree-filled garden is worth visiting, particularly on the evening in summer when professional storytellers visit. There's also a collection of paintings of the artist by his friends, as well as a few of the works he created here. The town also has a wonderful food and clothes market on rue du Marché that leads to the Cité Marchande, a covered market (every morning except Monday). On the slip road between the A8 and Cagnes-sur-Mer lies the **Atelier des Parfums** perfume factory. Guides take you through a history of perfume, give you a free guided tour of the factory, and let you sample one of scores of different scents. More exhilarating is the **Hippodrome Côte d'Azur** on the coast. In summer, racing is of a chariot style known as 'le Trot'. Facilities are top class with grandstands, bars and betting booths. The Cannes to Nice coastal train stops here most evenings during the summer racing season.

High on the hill within walking distance of Cagnes-sur-Mer is **Haut-de-Cagnes**, a hidden gem, as large as nearby Biot and St-Paul-de-

Vence, yet wonderfully unspoilt and calm. It's a favourite spot for contemporary artists of all persuasions, drawn by an annual arts festival but also by the Musée Mediterranéen d'Art Moderne and the Donation Suzy Solidor (a collection of 40 portraits by Cocteau, Dufy and Lempicka), both of which are housed in the dramatic **Château-Musée Grimaldi**, part Renaissance residence, part 14th-century fortress. In the centre of town the Eglise St-Pierre has fine stained glass and a marble font. To the east is the stunning Chapelle Notre-Dame-de-Protection where statues and a host of wonderful arches are backdropped by a batch of warm-coloured frescoes. Further down the coast just before Nice airport, the faceless suburb of St-Laurent-du-Var has one saving grace: discount shopping. Follow the signs for the Cap3000 shopping complex for acres of sports, shoe and clothes superstores.

Atelier des Parfums

43 chemin des Presses, Cagnes-sur-Mer (04.93.22.69.01/www.atelier-des-parfums.com). **Open** 9.30am-noon, 2-6.30pm Mon-Sat. **Admission** free.

Château-Musée Grimaldi

pl Grimaldi, Haut-de-Cagnes (04.92.02.47.30). **Open** *May-Sept* 10am-noon, 2-6pm Mon, Wed-Sun. *Oct-Apr* 10am-noon, 2-5pm Mon, Wed-Sun. Closed 3wks Nov. **Admission** €3 (€4.50 with Musée Renoir); €1.50 students under 26; free under-18s. **No credit cards.**

Hippodrome Côte d'Azur

Cagnes-sur-Mer (04.93.22.51.00). **Open** *Mid Dec-mid Mar* steeplechasing daily. *July, Aug* trotting nocturnes Mon, Wed, Fri. Closed mid Mar-June, Sept-mid Dec. **Admission** €4.50; free under-16s. Free guided visits in the morning.

Musée de l'Art Culinaire

3 rue Auguste Escoffier, Villeneuve-Loubet Village (04.93.20.80.51/www.fondation-escoffier.org). **Open** 2-6pm Mon-Fri, Sun. Closed Nov. **Admission** €5; €2.50 11-16s; free under-11s. **No credit cards.**

Musée d'Histoire et d'Art

pl de l'Hôtel de Ville, Villeneuve-Loubet Village (04.92.02.47.30). **Open** *May-Oct* 10am-noon, 2-6pm Mon, Wed-Sun. *Oct-Apr* 10am-noon, 2-5pm Mon, Wed-Sun; 9am-12.30pm Sat. Closed 2wks Nov. **Admission** €3; €1.50 students under 25; free under-18s. **No credit cards.**

Musée Renoir, Les Collettes

chemin des Collettes, Cagnes-sur-Mer (04.93.20.61.07). **Open** *May-Sept* 10am-noon, 2-6pm Mon, Wed-Sun. *Oct-Apr* 10am-noon, 2-5pm Mon, Wed-Sun. Closed 2wks Nov. **Admission** €3 (€4.50 with Château-Musée Grimaldi); €1.50 students under 25; free under-18s. **No credit cards.**

Where to stay, eat & drink

The area's most luxurious accommodation
option is **Le Cagnard** (rue Sous-Barri,
04.93.20.73.22, www.le-cagnard.com, double
€135-€285) in Haut-de-Cagnes. Its many
modern comforts have failed to disturb the
12th-century magic of the building, which offers
spectacular views. Try roast pigeon, duck or
lamb under the coat-of-arms-studded ceiling
of the restaurant (closed lunch Mon, Tue, Thur,
mid Nov-mid Dec, menus €60-€81), which
opens dramatically to reveal the sky. The **Villa
Estelle** at the foot of the old town (5 montée de
la Bourgade, Haut-de-Cagnes, 04.92.02.89.83,
www.villa-estelle.com, double €145-€185) is
a medieval coaching inn with a sumptuous
terrace. The modern, almost cool, **Grimaldi** (6
pl du Château, Haut-de-Cagnes, 04.93.20.60.24,
www.hotelgrimaldi.com, closed Feb, double
€115-€125) overlooks the delightful main
square and offers the finest meats, cheeses and
fish (restaurant closed Tue, menus €28-€40).

For those who want to sample the effects of
the local waters at Cros-de-Cagnes, **Biovimer
Spa** (Marina Baie des Anges, 04.93.22.71.71,
www.biovimer.fr), tucked into the Marina
Baie des Anges in Villeneuve-Loubet Plage,
is a modern spa with rooms and apartments.
Weekend thalassotherapy packages start at
€324; one-day use of heated outdoor seawater
pool, indoor pool, sauna, Jacuzzi, hammam and
gym starts at €53. Haut-de-Cagnes' fine range
of restaurants is centred on the montée de la
Bourgade leading uphill and the place du
Château at the top. **Fleur de Sel** near the
summit (85 montée de la Bourgade,
04.93.20.33.33, closed Wed, lunch Thur, Jan,
menus €23-€52) serves classic soupe au pistou
and imaginative seafood. **Entre Cour et
Jardin**, with its cosy vaulted cellar (102
montée de la Bourgade, 04.93.20.72.27, closed
Tue, 3wks Jan, 2wks Nov, menus €25-€35)
is innovative, too, with its gazpachos, fish
carpaccios and traditional farcis niçois. Nearby
rue Hippolyte Guis, yet another street saturated
with hanging baskets, features **Meno Grano**
(04.93.73.92.80, closed lunch, Sun, end Oct-mid
Nov, menus €20-€23), an Italian restaurant
serving such dishes as roasted veal in fig sauce
or rabbit in white wine sauce.

Good seafood can be found at the port in
Cros-de-Cagnes at **La Réserve aka Lou Lou**
(91 bd de la Plage, 04.93.31.00.17, closed lunch,
Sun, menu €38), a chic, snooty but justifiably
acclaimed restaurant. Crustaceans stud the
menu, from prawns in ginger to lobster à
l'armoricaine. At the pleasantly bourgeois
La Bourride (Port de Cros de Cagnes,
04.93.31.07.75, menu €34), chef Hervé Khobzi
serves the classic bourride (monkfish stew
flavoured with aïoli) and more creative dishes
on the glassed-in terrace or tree-shaded patio.
La Caravelle (42 bd de la Plage, 04.93.
20.10.09, menus €13-€25), near the Hôtel
Beaurivage, is more of a down-to-earth moules-
frites specialist. In Cagnes-sur-Mer, **Brasserie
des Halles** (8 rue Raimond Giacosa, 04.92.02.
77.29, closed Mon, dinner Sun, menus €12-€20)
next to the market does hearty food such as
faux-filet with sautéed potatoes.

In Villeneuve-Loubet **L'Auberge Fleurie**
(13 rue des Mesures, 04.93.73.90.92, closed Wed,
Thur, 2wks Nov, menus €19.50-€29.50) serves
hearty dishes in traditional surroundings.

Resources

Tourist information

Cagnes-sur-Mer Office de Tourisme *6 bd
Maréchal Juin, 06800 Cagnes-sur-Mer (04.93.
20.61.64/www.cagnes-tourisme.com).* **Open** *July,
Aug* 9am-7pm Mon-Sat; 9am-noon, 3-7pm Sun.
Sept-June 9am-noon, 2-6pm Mon-Sat.
**Villeneuve-Loubet Village Office de
Tourisme** *rue de l'Hôtel de Ville, 06270 Villeneuve-
Loubet (04.93.20.16.49).* **Open** *July, Aug* 9am-1pm,
3-7pm Mon-Sat; 9am-1pm Sun. *Sept-June* 9am-noon,
2-6pm Mon-Fri, 9.30-12.30pm Sat.
Villeneuve-Loubet Plage Office de Tourisme
*16 av de la Mer, (04.92.02.70.16/www.ot-villeneuve
loubet.org).* **Open** *July, Aug* 9am-1pm, 2-7pm Mon-Fri;
9.30am-12.30pm, 3-7pm Sat; 10am-1pm Sun. *Sept-June*
9am-noon, 2-6pm Mon-Fri; 9.30am-12.30pm Sat.

Getting there & around

By bus

RCA (Rapides Côte d'Azur 04.93.39.11.39) bus No.200
between Cannes and Nice runs every 20mins Mon-Sat,
30mins Sun, stopping at Antibes, Juan-les-Pins, Biot,
Villeneuve and Cagnes. Shuttle bus 10A runs hourly
between Antibes station and Biot. More information
at Antibes bus station (04.93.34.37.60). **TAM** (04.93.
85.61.81) buses run between Cagnes and Nice, serving
Biot, Antibes, Cannes, Vence and St-Paul.

By car

For Antibes-Juan-les-Pins, leave the A8 at exit 44, or
drive along the prettier N98 coast road. Juan-les-Pins
is west of Cap d'Antibes; Villeneuve-Loubet and
Cagnes are east of Antibes. In summer, avoid the N7
Antibes to Nice at the Biot junction, which becomes
one long car park, especially when Marineland is
emptying out. For Biot, take the N7 and then D4
Biot–Valbonne road, 3km (2 miles) after Antibes.

By train

Antibes is served by high-speed TGVs from Paris
and more frequent local trains, which also stop at
Juan-les-Pins, Biot, Cagnes-sur-Mer, Cros-de-Cagnes
and Villeneuve-Loubet Plage. Shuttle buses connect
Cagnes-sur-Mer and Haut-de-Cagnes and Villeneuve-
Loubet Plage and the old town.

The Riviera & Southern Alps

Nice

The hub of the Côte d'Azur, Nice is a fun, energetic town:
sometimes classy, sometimes saucy, but never boring.

Carnaval de Nice.

Thanks to its international airport, France's
fifth-largest city often serves as a jumping-off
point for the rest of the Côte d'Azur and
Provence. Increasingly, though, visitors
are rediscovering the charms of this rather
sprawling city. Just a few minutes from the
airport, the promenade des Anglais, crowned by
the flamboyant Hôtel Negresco, provides a year-
round feast for the eyes with sun-drenched palm
trees, turquoise water and bronzed in-line skaters.
The *rues piétonnes* (pedestrian streets), lined
with luxury boutiques, cater to those who come
for the glamour, but no neighbourhood is more
saucily niçois than the old town, with slanted
buildings in shades of ochre, boho boutiques,
time-warp restaurants and throbbing bars.

But how did such a sunny city come to have
a shady image? Nice was (and still is) infamous
for the financial shenanigans of its late, long-
time mayor, Jacques Médecin. This corrupt
reputation has lasted into the 21st century

with an ongoing investigation of legal favours
granted by the city and a vice scene fuelled by
Eastern European prostitution rings. The latest
scandal involves the tramway, whose planned
35 kilometres (22 miles) of lines (due for
completion by 2015) have turned much of
central Nice into a building site: it seems, not to
anyone's surprise, that transfers to the foreign
bank accounts of a city administrator may have
influenced the awarding of a major contract.

Though Nice is also said to have a high crime
rate, recent figures show it is only slightly more
dangerous than Paris and less crime-ridden
than Cannes or Antibes. In the past few years
Nice's old town has become, if not gentrified,
certainly a lot cleaner and safer than it once
was – although night-time festivities, especially
on weekends, do lead to a lot of slurred 3am
shouting matches (most of them in English).

On a higher cultural plane there is plenty
happening in the city, from the successful
summer jazz festival to the impressive
programme of the Opéra de Nice. For a city
with so many retired people, the vibe is
surprisingly youthful – the further east you
go, away from modern buildings with lifts,
the younger the population seems to get.

HISTORY

Prehistoric man set up camp some 400,000
years ago at the site known as Terra Amata at
the foot of Mont Boron, not far from where Sir
Elton John's hilltop mansion now sprawls. In
the fourth century BC Phocaean Greeks from
Marseille sailed into the harbour and founded
a trading post around another prominent hill
(now the Colline du Château), naming it Nikaïa.
The Romans arrived in 100 BC and built an
entire, no-expense-spared city on a third hill
that they called Cemenelum (today's Cimiez).
Cimiez's prime location made it an obvious
target in the Dark Ages for invading Saracens
and Barbarians, who left it in ruins, but by the
14th century the once-Greek part of the city,
including the port, was thriving again.

In 1382 Jeanne, Queen of Sicily and Countess
of Provence, was smothered to death on the
order of her cousin Charles of Durazzo, Prince
of Naples. He and another cousin, Louis of
Anjou, then staked their claims on the rich area.
After sizing up the local balance of power, the

wily Niçois decided to shun them both, opting instead to ally themselves with the Counts of Savoy. Apart from a brief period of control by Revolutionary forces between 1792 and 1814, Nice belonged to Savoy until 1860. Italian art, food and culture became intrinsic to the region.

An envious France tried several times to get Nice back. Napoleon III finally succeeded by signing the Treaty of Turin in 1860 with the King of Sardinia; the treaty was ratified later in a plebiscite (the result – some 25,700 pro-French to 260 anti-French votes – had a strong smell of election-rigging about it).

Over a century before that, however, Nice was discovered by British travellers seeking winter warmth. They raised a subscription in 1822 for the building of the seafront esplanade

still called the promenade des Anglais. By the time Queen Victoria visited in the 1890s, the Cimiez district was the place to stay. The queen pitched camp at the Régina Palace hotel, as did Henri Matisse in the 1940s.

In the early 1960s Nice became a cutting-edge artistic centre, thanks to the impetus of New Realists Yves Klein and Arman. Other artists flourished under the aegis of this movement; work by Venet, César and Ben can be seen at the Musée d'Art Moderne et d'Art Contemporain and in various public places around the city.

Today Nice takes pride in its tumultuous history, celebrating it with festivals year-round, including the Carnaval in the run-up to Lent, the Fête des Mais in May and a number of religious processions through Vieux Nice

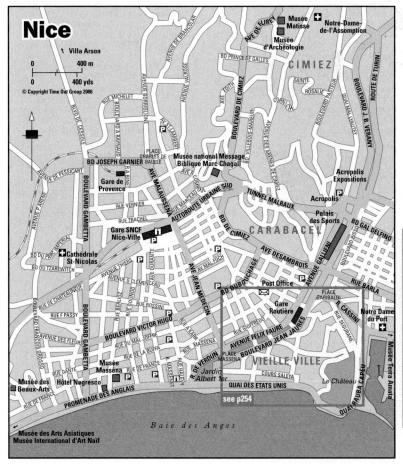

(the old town). Jean Médecin has left his mark too: the city's main shopping street is named after him and you'll still see his book on niçois cuisine in local bookshops.

Sightseeing

Vieux Nice & Colline du Château

With its ancient, pastel-coloured buildings and narrow alleys filled with countless shops, galleries and bistros, **Vieux Nice** (the old town) is certainly the most colourful quarter of the city. Though it was once shunned as crime-plagued and poverty-stricken, urban renewal encouraged young trendies to move in. They live alongside lifelong residents who still take religious festivals, such as the procession on Palm Sunday, very seriously indeed. The heart of the *vieille ville* lies just back from the seafront, along cours Saleya, where cut flowers perfume the air and stalls piled high with lush fruit and vegetables operate from dawn to lunch, Tuesday to Sunday. Niçois institution Chez Thérèse cheerfully touts chickpea socca from a stand every morning, though Thérèse herself was about to retire at the time of writing. On Monday there are antiques, junk and second-hand clothes. Shoppers and onlookers crowd bars and eateries, or seek the tranquillity and shade of the Chapelle de la Miséricorde, a superb baroque structure decorated with frescoes, gilt and a Louis Bréa altarpiece. Also of note is the tall, washed-out yellow building at the end of cours Saleya where Henri Matisse lived from 1921 to 1938. On neighbouring place du Palais de Justice there's a book and print market on Saturday. Towards the seafront, the **Opéra de Nice** is grandly belle époque. Nearby, on the quai des Etats-Unis, the **Galerie de la Marine** and **Galerie des Ponchettes** exhibit contemporary art in an old fish market.

The main square, place Rossetti, is home to two places of pilgrimage: the **Cathédrale de Ste-Réparate**, a loving tribute to Nice's patron saint that is remarkable for its glazed-tile roof, and the celebrated **Fenocchio** ice-cream parlour. The nearby baroque **Chapelle de l'Annonciation** is known locally as the Chapelle Ste-Rita, out of respect for an Italian saint still venerated in Nice as a miracle healer of terminal diseases. A few blocks north-east, through bustling streets of little shops, is the stunning **Palais Lascaris**, a treasure-trove of Flemish tapestries and 17th-century furniture. Further up, rue Droite feeds into rue St-François, busy with food shops, tourist trinkets, second-rate art and curious ecological clothing. Place St-François is the site of a disappointing little fish market (daily, except Tue), plus the city's

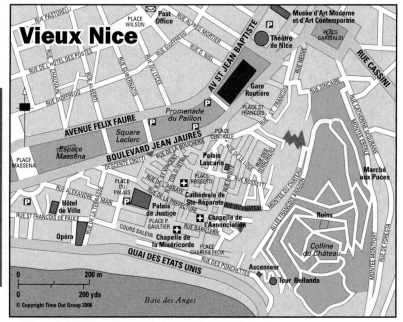

Vieux Nice. *See p254.*

17th-century former town hall and the campanile of a former Franciscan monastery (its entrance is on rue de la Tour). Bordering the old town to the north is the elegantly arcaded, though traffic-infested, place Garibaldi. Laid out between 1750 and 1780, it was later named after the hero of Italian unification, who was born in the Vieux Port in 1807.

Rising up to the east is Colline du Château, a grassy park with an impressive waterfall but no château: the castle was destroyed in the 18th century. Steps rise from rue du Château or rue Ste-Claire, but if you don't fancy the 90-metre slog up (nearly 300 feet), there's a lift (open 8am-6pm daily, 70¢ one way, €1 return) next to the 19th-century Tour Bellanda. The views over the harbour and the Baie des Anges are terrific.

Continuing round the quai or via place Garibaldi, you arrive at the attractive Vieux Port, which is lined with tall, multicoloured houses, the neo-classical church of Notre-Dame-du-Port and plenty of simple cafés where you can snack on a pan bagnat and watch ferries to Corsica. The port's possible extension has been the subject of heated debate for a few years. Though the project has now been postponed indefinitely, that doesn't stop feisty local discussions over an afternoon glass of pastis.

East of the Colline du Château, the Parc Forestier le Mont Boron is an idyllic spot for a picnic, with winding paths through acres of pines and breathtaking views down to the coast. Between the two hills, in an area dotted with 19th-century villas, the **Musée Terra**

Amata documents the area's earliest settlement. Next to this, the Castel des Deux Rois is a perfect park for children, with a small petting zoo, jets of water in summer, minigolf, plenty of grass and sophisticated playgrounds for different ages.

Cathédrale de Ste-Réparate

pl Rossetti (04.93.62.34.40). **Open** 8.30am-noon, 2-6pm daily. **Admission** free.

Located on Vieux Nice's most charming square, this 17th-century church is replete with stucco, marble and a colourfully tiled dome. It was named after a 15-year-old virgin, martyred in the Holy Land in AD 250. Her body was towed to Nice in a flowery boat by angels (landing, naturally, in what is now the Baie des Anges), but she subsequently appeared to embattled Niçois in the early fifth century. The church is an atmospheric venue for baroque music concerts and other musical events.

Chapelle de l'Annonciation

1 rue de la Poissonnerie (04.93.62.13.62). **Open** 7.30am-noon, 2.30-6.30pm daily. **Admission** free.

Join a steady trickle of locals into this lovely little gilded baroque gem and light a candle for St Rita – the patron saint of the terminally ill – to whom the chapel is dedicated.

Galerie de la Marine & Galerie des Ponchettes

59 & 77 quai des Etats-Unis (04.93.91.92.90). **Open** 10am-6pm Tue-Sat. **Admission** free.

The ancient fish market was transformed into two municipal art galleries in 1967. Temporary exhibitions often feature up-and-coming local artists.

The Riviera & Southern Alps

Angleterre-sur-mer

Britain's love affair with the French Riviera started long before Mayor Jean Médecin dubbed the Nice seafront 'la promenade des Anglais' (*pictured*) in 1931. You need look no further than a dull residential street near the Carrefour supermarket in Nice to find a tribute to English writer Tobias Smollett, whose 1763 description of almond trees flowering in January captured the British imagination.

Though sunbathing didn't catch on until the early 1920s, the British upper crust, including Queen Victoria, became such a familiar sight in Nice during the 19th-century winters that Alexandre Dumas wrote, 'Nice is an English city where you might even come across a Niçois.' Joined by Russian tsars, princes and artists flaunting their fur coats, convalescent Brits remained an important presence on the Côte d'Azur until the 1950s.

Today promenade des Anglais is again living up to its name. Peter Mayle's Luberon is yesterday's news and Nice is the new thing, thanks to low-cost flights carrying sun-starved passengers from Dublin or Durham straight to its turquoise waters and charming old town. The airport's proximity to the centre, and the city's location 40 minutes (by train or car) from Italy, make it all the more desirable.

Sue Phillips, who works for Aljazeera International, recently bought a flat in Vieux Nice, having owned properties in Brittany and Perpignan. 'I wanted sun, noise, action and colour, I wanted to be near the beach, and being close to Italy was a big plus... There is a sense of liberation here which there isn't in Perpignan and definitely not in Brittany.'

Phillips is one of hundreds of Brits who are currently colonising the Old Town, fixing up everything from medieval studios to multi-bedroom apartments with ceiling frescoes, often then letting them by the week to other refugees from the gloomy British climate.

Tristan Rutherford, a partner in the successful property agency Totally Nice, anticipated the trend two years ago. 'Seventy per cent of our clients are in their late fifties, have kids in university and haven't spent any money on themselves in the last 25 years,' says Rutherford. 'They might be from Newcastle, Liverpool, Glasgow or Luton, and they've just realised that with the low-cost airlines they can be in Nice within three to five hours. For the £30 it costs to fly to Nice they can't even get to London, and there is guaranteed sunshine here. A lot of them cry when they find their dream apartment. It's usually not the biggest house they've ever bought, but they never believed it would be possible to own property in France.'

Irish pubs and web cafés have largely replaced the Anglican church as informal meeting places for the British community, whose nocturnal festivities are making Vieux Nice all the more colourful. On the seafront, the current generation of moneyed Russians (who have spent €520 million on property between Cannes and Menton since 2000) mingles with Liverpool supporters and border-hopping Italians, who remain loyal to the French Riviera. It's no longer the belle époque, but those who are part of the Nice renaissance would agree it's still *la belle vie*.

Musée d'Histoire Naturelle

60 bd Risso (04.97.13.46.80/www.mhnnice.org).
Open 10am-6pm Tue-Sun. **Admission** free.
If you like London's Horniman Museum, you'll love this place. Lurking in its wonderful wooden display cases are the dried remains of all kinds of slippery, slithery monsters (cephalopods are something of a feature – including squids of all shapes and sizes), guaranteed to induce shivers of delighted horror in junior visitors. Temporary exhibitions, such as the recent 'Bleu Outremer' exhibition (of Australasian marine life), are of a high standard.

Musée Terra Amata

25 bd Carnot (04.93.55.59.93). **Open** 10am-6pm Tue-Sun. **Admission** €4; €2.50 students; free under-18s. **No credit cards.**
Find out what life was like on the Riviera 400,000 years ago. The highlights of this museum, built on an excavation site, include a reconstituted prehistoric cave, a human footprint in limestone, traces of fire and records of ancient elephant hunters.

Palais Lascaris

15 rue Droite (04.93.62.72.40). **Open** 10am-6pm Mon, Wed-Sun. **Admission** free.
Ornate baroque furniture, 17th-century paintings and Flemish tapestries are displayed in a wonderful miniature Genoese-style palace with frescoed ceilings depicting mythological scenes. Displays of 17th-century faïence from the Musée Masséna (*see below*) will remain on the first floor until it reopens.

The New Town

Westward, the new town of Nice takes on a completely different look. Laid out in the 18th and 19th centuries with inviting private gardens, broad city blocks and stuccoed apartments, it is divided from the old town by the River Paillon – though you'd never know it, as the river is covered over for most of its length by the pink façades of place Masséna and the Jardins Albert 1er. Smart shops congregate near here on rues de Paradis, de Suède and Alphonse Karr, while the pedestrianised eastern end of rue de France is lively with boutiques, restaurants and pizzerias.

Among the 20th-century buildings north of place Masséna is the **Musée d'Art Moderne et d'Art Contemporain (MAMAC)** with art from 1960 onward, including works from the Ecole de Nice (Arman, César, Klein). Also here is the **Théâtre de Nice**, which is breathing new life into the niçois performing arts scene.

On the seafront west of the river mouth, the promenade des Anglais is Nice's 19th-century most famous landmark, a daily parade of in-line skaters, joggers and strolling sun-worshippers. Getting safely across what is nowadays the last gasp of the N98, through manic traffic, can be a challenge, but look back once you reach the curb: the grandiose belle époque and art deco palaces that line the promenade – including the **Hôtel Negresco** and **Musée Masséna** – are a joy. Shortly before the museum, you'll come across the **Palais de la Méditerranée**, an art deco jewel built by American millionaire Frank Jay Gould in 1929. Shamefully gutted in the 1990s, preserving only the façade, it has been reborn as a luxury hotel and casino (*see p271*).

A few blocks back from the promenade des Anglais, broad boulevard Victor Hugo is lined with belle époque villas. Further west, the **Musée des Beaux-Arts** has a small but notable collection, including the plaster study for Rodin's *Le Baiser*. A kilometre (half a mile) further on is the **Musée International d'Art Naïf Anatole Jakovsky**, while just before the airport, the **Musée des Arts Asiatiques** nestles among the botanical species and giant hothouse of the Parc Floral Phoenix.

The beach itself, though long, is not particularly spectacular, being pebbly and rather steep in spots. While some stretches are open to anyone and have attractions ranging from parascending to sandpits, other parts are carved up into private beach concessions. One of the nicest is Castel Plage, down below the *vieille ville*; it has its own restaurant.

Slicing north-west through the new town from place Masséna, avenue Jean Médecin – currently in shreds due to work on the tramway – is Nice's prime shopping street. At its northern end is the main train station, to the west of which, across boulevard Gambetta, stands the Russian Orthodox **Cathédrale St-Nicolas**, Nice's most-visited attraction. Further north, **Villa Arson** puts on adventurous contemporary art in a lovely garden setting. Also worth seeing is the **Musée Masséna** (65 rue de France), a collection of Empire salons containing the work of primitive painters, pieces of armour and Napoleon's coronation robe and death mask. The museum will, however, be closed for renovation until at least 2006 – call for details (04.93.88.11.34).

Cathédrale St-Nicolas (Eglise Russe)

av Nicolas II (04.93.96.88.02). **Open** *June-Sept* 9am-noon, 2.30-6pm daily. *Oct-May* 9.30am-noon, 2.30-5pm daily. **Admission** €2.50; free under-12s. **No credit cards**.
If you visit only one church, go and see this beautiful pink and grey marble, brick and tile oddity, with its five brilliantly coloured onion-domed cupolas. Built between 1903 and 1912, it is filled with intricate carvings, icons and frescoes, and a marvellous iconostasis. In the garden behind the cathedral, a small chapel remembers Grand Duc Nicolas Alexandrovitch, son of Tsar Alexander II, who died here in 1865 at the age of 21.

Musée d'Art Moderne et d'Art Contemporain (MAMAC)

promenade des Arts (04.93.62.61.62/www.mamac-nice.org). **Open** 10am-6pm Tue-Sun. **Admission** €4; €2.50 students; free under-18s. Free to all 1st & 3rd Sun of mth. **No credit cards.**

This sprawling, multi-level marble building provides a home for European and American art from the 1960s onwards, staging first-rate shows. There's a room dedicated to the Nice School (Arman, César, Klein and Sosno) and permanent displays of work by such artists as Keith Haring and Jean Tinguely.

Musée des Arts Asiatiques

405 promenade des Anglais (04.92.29.37.00/ www.arts-asiatiques.com). **Open** *May-mid Oct* 10am-6pm Mon, Wed-Sun. *Mid Oct-Apr* 10am-5pm Mon, Wed-Sun. **Admission** €6; €4 concessions. **Credit** V.

Designed by Japanese architect Kenzo Tange, this impressive, minimalist, glass and metal structure boasts a small but stunning collection of rare pieces that range from a 12th-century Japanese Buddha to the latest in Asian high-tech design. Don't miss the tea pavilion under the gingko trees (€10; you can make reservations on 04.92.29.37.02).

Musée des Beaux-Arts

33 av des Baumettes (04.92.15.28.28). **Open** 10am-6pm Tue-Sun. **Admission** €4; €2.50 students; free under-18s. **No credit cards.**

Built for a Ukranian prince in 1878, this Genoese-inspired villa houses a fine collection of 15th- to early 20th-century art. Highlights include works by niçois pastel artist and pioneering lithographer Jules Cheret, *Le Tango* by Van Dongen, and canvases by Bonnard, Sisley, Dufy, Signac and Kisling.

Musée International d'Art Naïf Anatole Jakovsky

Château Ste-Hélène, av Val-Marie (04.93.71.78.33). **Open** 10am-6pm Mon, Wed-Sun. **Admission** €4; €2.50 students; free under-18s. **No credit cards.**

Once the home of perfume creator René Coty, this lovely pink villa now houses a private collection that traces the history of naïve art from the 18th century to the present. Work shown here includes Bombois, Séraphine, Rimbert and Grandma Moses.

Villa Arson

20 av Stephen Liegeard (04.92.07.73.73/www.villa-arson.org). **Open** *June-Sept* 2-7pm Mon, Wed-Sun. *Oct-May* 2-6pm Mon, Wed-Sun. **Admission** free.

Villa Arson is at the sharp end of young, avant-garde art. You can listen to heated discussions in the small café (8.30am-5pm Mon-Thur; 8.30am-3pm Fri), or study at the related art school.

Cimiez

To the north of the city centre, Cimiez, once the Roman settlement of Cemenelum, is Nice's most luxurious neighbourhood: an affluent hillside swathed in large villas, Roman ruins and sweeping belle époque apartments. You can walk up to Cimiez in about 30 minutes from Vieux Nice or place Masséna, or take the bus (No.15 from place Masséna, No.17 from avenue Jean Médecin); otherwise, arm yourself with a car, plenty of patience and a map.

Just off the lower reaches of boulevard de Cimiez is the newly expanded **Musée national Message Biblique Marc Chagall**, showing large-scale biblical works. Further up, sweeping round the corner of boulevard de Cimiez and avenue Régina, you can't miss the Excelsior Régina Palace. Designed by Biasini, the hotel where Queen Victoria stayed each year from 1897 to 1899 and Matisse lived between 1938

Cours Saleya. *See p254.*

and 1943 is now a smart apartment building. At the top of the hill, the fabulous **Musée Matisse** stands in the centre of a park dotted with olive trees, behind the ruins of the Roman amphitheatre and the **Musée d'Archéologie**. **Eglise Notre-Dame-de-l'Assomption** and its 16th-century Franciscan monastery are nearby, flanked by a glorious rose-perfumed garden and the cemetery in which Matisse and Dufy are buried. Further down rue Grammont, take a look at Nice's most unusual church: designed by Jacques Droz, Eglise Ste-Jeanne d'Arc is a radical 1930s reinforced-concrete structure, nicknamed 'the egg'.

Eglise Notre-Dame-de-l'Assomption (Musée Franciscain)

pl du Monastère (04.93.81.00.04). **Open** *Church* 9am-noon, 2-6pm daily. *Museum* 10am-noon, 3-6pm Mon-Sat. **Admission** free.

At the edge of the gardens of Cimiez, this church is a heavy-handed 19th-century reworking of a 16th-century building. Inside, three Louis Bréa altarpieces survive. The adjoining 16th-century monastery includes a couple of pretty cloisters – one with some strange, perhaps alchemical murals – as well as the Musée Franciscain, where the uncomfortable ends of Franciscan martyrs are documented.

Musée d'Archéologie

160 av des Arènes (04.93.81.59.57). **Open** 10am-6pm Mon, Wed-Sun. **Admission** €4; €2.50 students; free under-18s. **No credit cards**.

This smart archaeological museum charts Nice's history from 1100 BC up to the Middle Ages through an impressive display of ceramics, sculpture, coins, jewellery and tools. Outside are first- to fourth-century ruins on the ancient site of Cemenelum, with vestiges of the Roman public baths, paved streets and a 4,000-seat stone amphitheatre – now used as a venue during the Nice Jazz Festival.

Musée Matisse

164 av des Arènes (04.93.81.08.08). **Open** 10am-6pm Mon, Wed-Sun. **Admission** €4; €2.50 students; free under-18s. **Credit** MC, V.

In the scruffy park next to the Roman amphitheatre, Matisse's 17th-century villa (with modern extension) houses a fascinating collection, tracing the artist's development from dark, brooding early works through to the colourful paper cut-outs. One room holds sketches for the Chapelle du Rosaire (*see p301*).

Musée national Message Biblique Marc Chagall

av du Dr Menard (04.93.53.87.20/www.musee-chagall.fr). **Open** *July-Sept* 10am-6pm Mon, Wed-Sun. *Oct-June* 10am-5pm Mon, Wed-Sun. **Admission** €5.50; €4 students; free under-18s. **Credit** MC, V.

Dedicated to long-time Riviera resident Chagall, this museum reopened in May 2005 after a three-month renovation and enlargement. The collection includes a stunning selection of paintings on Old Testament

themes, notably the Song of Songs. Chagall provided mosaics, sketches and stained glass for the gallery, which holds temporary shows and small-scale acoustic concerts in the lovely amphitheatre (8.30pm Thur, tickets €8 from Fnac or 1hr before show).

Where to eat

L'Allegro

6 pl Guynemar (04.93.56.62.06). **Open** noon-1.45pm, 8-10pm Mon-Fri; 8-10pm Sat. Closed Aug. **Menus** €18.30-€53.40. **Credit** MC, V.

In a Venetian setting, under the watchful eyes of characters from the commedia dell'arte, savour exquisite own-made ravioli, risotto and fresh pasta, cooked right in front of the eager customers. You'll have to book in advance.

L'Auberge de Théo

52 av Cap de Croix (04.93.81.26.19/www.auberge-de-theo.com). **Open** noon-2pm, 7-10.15pm Tue-Sat; noon-2pm Sun. Closed 25 June-15 July. **Menus** €16.50-€30.50. **Credit** V.

Near the Chagall and Matisse museums (*see above*), an area where restaurants are far from plentiful, this trattoria with an open-air patio is a perfect place for Italian specialities, including cep pasta and tagliata.

La Baie d'Amalfi

9 rue Gustave Deloye (04.93.80.01.21). **Open** noon-2pm, 7-11pm daily. Closed July. **Menus** €19-€28. **Credit** MC, V.

Pizza, pasta and fish enthusiasts are in heaven in this bustling old-style mansion. Try the risotto with courgette flowers and scampi, or the gnocchi.

Bistrot du Port

28 quai de Lunel (04.93.55.21.70). **Open** noon-2.15pm, 7-10.30pm Mon, Thur-Sun; noon-2.15pm Tue. **Menus** €13.80-€48. **Credit** DC, MC, V.

At this big yellow brasserie on the old port, excellent specialities include warm lobster salad with olive tapenade and Grand Marnier soufflé. Service is friendly; wines top-notch, but affordable.

Brasserie Flo

2-4 rue Sacha Guitry (04.93.13.38.38). **Open** noon-2.30pm, 7pm-midnight daily. **Menus** €22.40-€31.80. **Credit** AmEx, DC, MC, V.

Not to be missed. Set in an old theatre, this restaurant has its kitchen where the stage used to be and the best seats are on the upper balcony. Food is good, uncomplicated provençal – the *Faim de Nuit* menu is perfect late at night. Be sure to book ahead.

Le Chantecler

Hôtel Negresco, 37 promenade des Anglais (04.93.16.64.00). **Open** 12.30-2pm, 8-10pm daily. **Menus** €45-€130. **Credit** AmEx, DC, MC, V.

The dust has settled after the most recent change of chef (Bruno Turbot is now commanding the kitchen), with Le Chantecler again turning out the kind of food you would expect from such a prestigious address. At lunch, the €45 *Menu Plaisir* gives the illusion of a major splash-out – but beware the pricey wines, which could turn fantasy into reality. The brasserie, La Rotonde, also offers an excellent (more affordable) menu conceived by Turbot.

Chez René Socca

2 rue Miralheti (04.93.92.05.73). **Open** 9am-10pm Tue-Sun. Closed Jan. **Average** €10. **No credit cards**. Rustic wooden tables spill out into the street from this Vieux Nice landmark, the oldest and most popular address for socca. Stern waiters slam down your drinks and you have to fetch the steaming niçois specialities yourself – but you're here for the food, not for airs and graces.

La Cigale

7 av de Suède (04.93.88.60.20). **Open** 10am-midnight daily. **Menus** €28-€35. **Credit** AmEx, MC, V. This Lebanese restaurant-deli provides an international option besides pizza on designer-boutique

row. Try yummy chicken shish kebab and scrumptious honey-soaked pastries. La Cigale is liveliest on weekend nights, when a belly dancer performs.

Delhi Belhi

22 rue de la Barillerie (04.93.92.51.87). **Open** 8pm-midnight Mon-Sat. **Average** €40. **Credit** MC, V. A favourite of Nice's British expats despite the unfortunate name, Delhi Belhi dishes up some of the best Indian food on the Côte d'Azur in a softly lit, sweet-smelling dining room just behind the cours Saleya market (*see p254*). To sample several dishes, order a thali – a vegetarian version is available.

Don Camillo

5 rue des Ponchettes (04.93.85.67.95). **Open** noon-2pm, 7-11pm Mon-Fri; 7.30-10.30pm Sat. **Menus** €32-€56. **Credit** AmEx, MC, V. The Don Camillo has shed its staid decor for a swish look that matches the modern cuisine. Stéphane

Baie des Anges. *See p255.*

The Riviera & Southern Alps

Viano reinvents the niçois classics, serving dishes such as porchetta-style rabbit and loup (the local name for sea bass) cooked a la plancha.

L'Estrilha

11-13 rue de l'Abbaye (04.93.62.62.00). **Open** 7-11pm Mon-Sat. **Average** €23. **Credit** AmEx, MC, V.
The speciality of this Vieux Nice restaurant is the delicious amphore: a copious mixed fish, tomato, white wine and basil stew, baked in a clay pot and served steaming at the table.

Fleur de Jade

8 rue d'Italie (04.93.88.34.01). **Open** noon-2pm, 7-10pm daily. **Menus** €14.50-€29. **Credit** AmEx, MC, V.
The hum of a brimming fish tank accompanies clients as they make their foray into wonderfully prepared Vietnamese dishes: noodle soup, lacquered duck and fresh fruit flambéed with rice wine.

Le Frog

3 rue Milton Robbins (04.93.85.85.65). **Open** 7pm-midnight Mon-Sat. **Average** €30. **Credit** AmEx, MC, V.
With T-bone steak and cheesecake on the menu, this Tex Mex bistro is a slice of North America in the heart of Vieux Nice – even the wines are mostly from the New World. There's live music nightly after 9pm.

Le Grand Balcon

10 rue St-François-de-Paule (04.93.62.60.74). **Open** noon-2pm, 7.30-11pm Mon-Fri; 7.30-11pm Sat, Sun. **Menus** €32-€50. **Credit** AmEx, MC, V.
Here fashionable Parisian decorator Jacques Garcia has created the mood of a comfortable English library. Chef Marc Hamel, previously at La Petite Maison (*see p263*), offers a tropical menu favouring fish, but do try the excellent chicken breast with basil and coconut or the balsamic duck breast.

Le Grand Café de Turin

5 pl Garibaldi (04.93.62.29.52). **Open** 8am-10pm Mon, Tue, Thur-Sun. **Average** €25. **Credit** AmEx, DC, MC, V.
Providing some of the best shellfish in town, this classic niçois brasserie is on the perfect corner for people-watching. Since it opened in 1910 it has been jammed with locals slurping oysters. Service can be testy, but the atmosphere is the real thing.

Indochine

5 av Thiers (04.93.88.75.29). **Average** €10. **Open** 9am-11pm daily. **Credit** MC, V.
The best of the Asian fast-food restaurants around the train station, Indochine serves lacquered duck (made each day on the premises) and a respectable array of other own-made dishes, in a no-frills setting.

Indyana

11 rue Gustave Deloye (04.93.80.67.69). **Open** 7pm-midnight Mon, Sun; noon-2pm, 7pm-midnight Tue-Sat. **Average** €50. **Credit** AmEx, DC, MC, V.
This swanky dining spot serves Franco-Japanese fusion cuisine that's well matched with the ethno-

loft decor. Regulars are an intriguing mix of fashionistas, arty intellectuals and stiff business suits.

Le Karr

10 rue Alphonse Karr (04.93.82.18.31). **Open** noon-2.30pm, 7-11.30pm Mon-Sat. *Bar* 8am-12.30am Mon-Sat. **Menus** €14.50-€40. **Credit** AmEx, DC, MC, V.
Dressed up in beige and black, this is a casual restaurant that attracts a good-looking, stylish crowd, conjuring an atmosphere that is as much Paris as it is Nice. The equally good-looking food leans to dishes such as aubergine 'caviar' with tuna or chèvre salad with honey and spices. Live music (Fri, Sat) adds an intimate note.

Kei's Passion

22ter rue de France (04.93.82.26.06). **Open** 7.30-9.45pm Mon, Sat; noon-2pm, 7.30-9.45pm Tue-Fri. **Menus** €22-€80. **Credit** MC, V.
Japanese chef Keisuko Matsushima (ex-Pourcel Brothers, ex-Regis Marcon) continues to wow his local clientele with such creations as cold asparagus soup with sea urchin cream and roast lobster in a curried vinaigrette.

La Merenda

4 rue de la Terrasse (no phone). **Open** lunch & dinner Mon-Fri. Closed 3wks Aug. **Menus** €25-€30. **No credit cards**.
Tiny and always packed, La Merenda serves the ultimate version of every niçois classic. To reserve, stop by in person on the day of your meal.

La Mousson

167 promenade des Flots Bleus, St-Laurent-du-Var (04.93.31.13.30). **Open** *July, Aug* 6.30-9.30pm daily. *Sept-June* noon-1.30pm, 6.30-9.30pm Tue-Sat. **Menus** €25-€41. **Credit** MC, V.
Truly exquisite Thai cuisine, a stone's throw from the airport at the seaside port of St-Laurent-du-Var. Highlights include the spicy beef sautéed with Thai basil and caramelised mango with sticky rice.

Le Parcours

1 pl Marcel Eusebi, Falicon (04.93.84.94.57). **Open** 8-10pm Tue; 12.30-2.30pm, 8-10pm Wed-Sat; 12.30-2.30pm Sun. **Menus** €35-€50. **Credit** MC, V.
Jean-Marc Delacourt left the prestigious Château de la Chèvre d'Or (*see p278*) in Eze to open up this cosy restaurant in the hills above Nice. Plasma screens, strategically placed amid calmly minimalist decor, reveal what's happening in the kitchen. Menus, which change every three days, are gorgeous and reasonably priced. Book ahead.

La Part des Anges

17 rue Gubernatis (04.93.62.69.80). **Open** noon-8pm Mon-Thur; noon-2pm, 7-10pm Fri, Sat. **Average** €20. **Credit** AmEx, MC, V.
You'll inhale a captivating aroma as you approach this intimate wine cellar with a few tables. Within, owner and sommelier Olivier Labarde offers expert advice on his superb selection of local and rare vintages, as well as delicious French regional cooking.

La Petite Maison

11 rue St-François-de-Paule (04.93.85.71.53). **Open**
noon-2pm, 7.30-11.30pm Mon-Sat. **Average** €45.
Credit AmEx, MC, V.
This venerable restaurant draws colourful locals at
noon, top models and cinema stars by night. Start
with the niçois hors d'oeuvres (pissaladière, stuffed
vegetables and so on), then have sea bass cooked in
a salt crust and finish with fabulous house ice-cream.

La Pizza

34 rue Masséna (04.93.87.70.29). **Open** 11am-1am
daily. **Average** €20. **Credit** MC, V.
So popular is La Pizza that it has another two
branches in this shopping street alone, as well as an
enthusiastically patronised outlet in Cannes. The
place's success comes down to its straightforward
and succulent speciality, cooked in a wood-fired
oven, and its democratic pricing. A stress-free
experience, even with kids.
Other locations: Le Québec, 43 rue Masséna
(04.93.87.84.21); La Taverne, 27 rue Masséna
(04.93.87.77.57).

Restaurant du Gésu

1 pl du Gésu (04.93.62.26.46). **Open** noon-
1.45pm, 7.30-10.30pm Mon-Sat. **Average** €18.
No credit cards.
The festive terrace here is jammed year-round
with locals and tourists alike. Service is jovial and
customers are happy to bandy jokes about while
savouring simple niçois cooking in all its splendour.
Everything is prepared on the premises, including
the fresh gnocchi, and the prices make dining feel
like a gift from Gésu himself.

Terres de Truffes

11 rue St-François-de-Paule (04.93.62.07.68). **Open**
noon-2pm, 8-10pm Tue-Sat. **Menus** €30-€35. **Credit**
AmEx, MC, V.
Truffles meet fast food in this stylish wood-panelled
bistro-cum-deli, created by celebrity chef Bruno
Clément, who is based in the town of Lorgues.
Truffles come with everything, from sandwiches
and delectable truffle-studded warm brie to the
caramelised truffle ice-cream.

L'Univers de Christian Plumail

54 bd Jean Jaurès (04.93.62.32.22). **Open** noon-2pm,
7.30-10pm Mon-Fri; 7.30-10pm Sat. **Menus** €18-€65.
Credit AmEx, MC, V.
Renowned niçois chef Christian Plumail has transformed a former brasserie into an unpretentious
haven for simple yet refined Mediterranean cuisine
at surprisingly affordable prices.

Le 22 Septembre

*3 rue Centrale (04.93.80.87.90/www.le22septembre.
com)*. **Open** 7-11pm Tue-Sat. **Menus** €12-€15.
Credit MC, V.
This budget eatery in Vieux Nice is a magnet for
stylish students and savvy young couples. The food
is hearty and tasty – try the beef stroganoff, the sea
bass with basil butter or the fried camembert.

La Zucca Magica

4bis quai Papacino (04.93.56.25.27). **Open** noon-
2.45pm, 7pm-midnight Tue-Sat. **Lunch menu** €17.
Dinner menu €27. **No credit cards**.
It's looks a bit like Halloween all year round at this
bizarrely decorated restaurant, whose Italian chef
serves some of the best vegetarian food in Nice – if
not the world. Come with the heartiest possible
appetite: our winter visit revealed a five-course,
no-choice menu that included a cheesy polenta,
cheese-filled focaccia and ricotta-stuffed vegetables.
And yes, you will be expected to clear your plate.

Where to drink

Au Pain Quotidien

1 rue St-François-de-Paule (04.93.62.94.32).
Open 7am-7pm daily. **No credit cards**.
Part of a Belgian chain, this high-ceilinged café with
wooden tables on a terrace is the perfect spot for
breakfast. Dip into jars of decadent praline spreads
and jams laid out on the long *table d'hôtes*.

Le Bar des Oiseaux

5 rue St-Vincent (04.93.80.27.33). **Open**
8pm-12.30am Tue-Sun. **Credit** MC, V.
Expect plenty of local atmosphere at this popular
restaurant, bar and theatre. Live bands and live
birds (in cages, most of the time), plus uproarious
comic sketches written by proprietor Noëlle Perna.

Café Borghèse

9 rue Fodéré (04.92.04.83.83). **Open**
8am-midnight Mon-Sat. **Credit** MC, V.
Located behind the church of the old port, this is the
place for cappuccino, aperitifs, antipasti platters and
copious portions of gnocchi and ravioli.

Chez Pipo

13 rue Bavastro (04.93.55.88.82). **Open**
5.30-10pm Tue-Sun. Closed Nov, Sat in July
& Aug. **No credit cards**.
This lively port-side spot has a huge wood-burning
oven and long tables where old-timers gossip in
Niçois dialect. The perfect place for an early-evening
snack of socca and a glass of local rosé.

La Civette du Cours

1 cours Saleya (04.93.80.80.59). **Open**
7.30am-2.30am daily. **Credit** DC, MC, V.
This is the friendliest and cheapest place for an aperitif on the cours Saleya, complete with niçois nibbles.

Crêperie Granny's

5 pl de l'Ancien-Sénat (no phone). **Open**
8.30am-7pm daily. **Credit** MC, V.
The place to go with kids, this inviting crêperie-café
behind the cours Saleya market has a train set,
puzzles and guinea pigs to keep the little ones occupied, and serves food all day.

Fenocchio

2 pl Rossetti (04.93.80.72.52). **Open** 10am-midnight
daily. Closed Dec & Jan. **Credit** MC, V.

The Riviera & Southern Alps

ASIAN ARTS MUSEUM

MUSEUM OF THE GENERAL COUNCIL OF THE ALPES-MARITIMES

405, PROMENADE DES ANGLAIS
ARÉNAS - 06200 NICE, FRANCE
TEL : +33 (0)4 92 29 37 00 FAX : +33 (0)4 92 29 37 01
WWW.ARTS-ASIATIQUES.COM
OPEN EVERY DAY EXCEPT TUESDAY
MAY 2 TO OCTOBER 15 : 10 A.M. TO 6 P.M.
OCTOBER 16 TO APRIL 30 : 10 A.M. TO 5 P.M.
CLOSED MAY 1 AND ON CHRISTMAS AND NEW YEAR'S DAY

CONSEIL GENERAL
DES ALPES-MARITIMES

Settle at a table by the fountain on the cathedral square and choose from a superb range of own-made ice-cream and sorbets, some made of local citrus fruits.

La Havane
32 rue de France (04.93.16.36.16). **Open** 4pm-2.30am daily. *Restaurant* 4pm-2.30am Tue-Sun. **Credit** AmEx, MC, V.
No one can resist dancing in this restaurant-bar, where a hot Cuban group plays nightly.

Johnny's Wine Bar
1 rue Rossetti (04 93 80 65 97). **Open** 4pm-12.30am daily. **No credit cards**.
Rather inexplicably, this wine bar with wooden tables and stools outside and a Canadian flag has become the watering hole of choice for British expats. It must have something to do with the cheap Algerian wine, served here by the jug.

Nocy-Bé
4-6 rue Jules Gilly (04.93.85.52.25). **Open** 7pm-midnight daily. **No credit cards**.
At this cosy Moroccan boutique, which doubles as a tearoom, you can shop till you drop… on to a cushion for some invigorating mint tea and pastries.

Oliviera
8bis rue du Collet (04.93.13.06.45). **Open** *May-Oct* 10am-10pm Mon-Sat; 10am-6pm Sun. *Nov-Apr* 10am-10pm Tue-Sat; 10am-3pm Sun. **No credit cards**.
Nadim Beyrouti runs Nice's most fascinating olive-oil shop, which is dedicated to the finest provençal oils. His freshly made dishes, such as aubergine caviar with chèvre and vegetable lasagne, serve as the perfect vehicle for his discoveries.

O'Neill's Irish Pub
40 rue Droite (04.93.80.06.75/www.puboneills.com). **Open** 5pm-2am Mon-Fri; 1pm-2am Sat, Sun. **Credit** MC, V.
All the friendly Irish fixings: burnished wood, cheery staff, beer on tap and a busy happy hour (5-9pm).

Pâtisserie Cappa
7-9 pl Garibaldi (04.93.62.30.83). **Open** 7.30am-7.30pm Tue-Sun. Closed Sept. **Credit** MC, V.
Venture under the arches for heavenly pastries, mousse cakes and tourte de blettes to take away or consume on the terrace. In summer there is a small selection of exceptional ice-creams and sorbets, made on the premises.

Nightlife

For other concert venues, notably **Palais Nikaïa**, *see p267* **Arts & entertainment**.

Le Barrio
73 quai des Etats-Unis (04.93.92.94.04). **Open** 8pm-2.30am Tue-Sun. **Admission** free. **Credit** MC, V.
Nightly salsa lessons (€8-€12) for dance fans; newcomers crowd in to watch, sipping tropical cocktails for courage while the regulars take up the beat.

Restaurant du Gésu. *See p263.*

Blue Boy Enterprise
9 rue Jean-Baptiste Spinetta (04.93.44.68.24/ www.blueboy.fr). **Open** 11.30pm-5am daily. **Admission** free (€10 Sat). **Credit** V.
Blue Boy is the best-known gay disco in town. Young boys prance and dance, Riviera queens cosy up or bitch, and everyone else just hits the booze and shortly thereafter the dancefloor.

The Riviera & Southern Alps

Le Blue Whales

1 rue Mascoïnat (04.93.62.90.94). **Open** 5.30pm-4.30am daily. **Admission** free. **Credit** DC, MC, V.
A relaxed, thirtysomething crowd frequents this better-than-most pub, where you can shoot pool and dance to a DJ or to live music that ranges from jazz funk to salsa.

La Casa del Sol

69 quai des Etats-Unis (04.93.62.87.28). **Open** *Mid May-Sept* 6.30pm-2.30am daily. *Oct-Dec, Feb-mid May* 7pm-2.30am Tue-Sat. *Jan* 7pm-2.30am Fri, Sat. **Credit** AmEx, MC, V.
This before- and after-hours tapas bar has a lively atmosphere and a Spanish-Latino beat (DJs Thur-Sat). Dress cool, clean and casual to get past the door.

Dizzy Club

26 quai Lunel (04.93.26.54.79). **Open** 11.30pm-5am Wed-Sat. **Admission** free (€15 Fri, Sat). **Credit** MC, V.
One of the few clubs where you can actually have a conversation at the bar. Sleek decor, a piano-bar, a dancefloor with live bands (working everything from jazz to electro) and DJs draw pretty people aged between 25 and 50.

Le Ghost House

3 rue Barillerie (04.93.92.93.37). **Open** 8pm-2.30am daily. **Admission** free. **Credit** DC, MC, V.
Trip hop, drum 'n' bass and house fans flock to this tiny club in Vieux Nice, which leads the way on the Nice electronic scene. DJs play out from Wednesday to Saturday night.

Le Grand Escurial

29 rue Alphonse Karr (04.93.82.37.66). **Open** 7.30pm-5am Fri, Sat. **Admission** €16. **Credit** MC, V.
A cavernous disco (full in the summer) with a surprisingly cosy restaurant/lounge on the mezzanine.

Wayne's

15 rue de la Préfecture (04.93.13.46.99/ www.waynes.fr). **Open** noon-1am daily. **Admission** free. **Credit** AmEx, MC, V.
This live-music mecca for anglophones in Vieux Nice attracts young party-goers with live bands, theme nights and karaoke on Sundays.

Shopping

The split-level Etoile mall, department store Galeries Lafayette, book and record emporium Fnac and countless clothing chains line avenue Jean Médecin. Luxury labels congregate on rue Paradis (Chanel, Emporio Armani, Kenzo, Sonia Rykiel), avenue de Suède (Yves Saint Laurent, Rolex, Louis Vuitton) and avenue de Verdun (Cartier, Hermès). Food stores and funky speciality emporia clutter the narrow streets of Vieux Nice. Although the cours Saleya market (mornings, except Mon) is a foodie must, the Niçois prefer to buy their local produce and

fish at the more down-to-earth marché de la Libération, which ordinarily takes place just north of the train station along avenue Malaussena but has been moved to boulevard Joseph Garnier during work on the tramway.

L'Atelier des Jouets

1 pl de l'Ancien Sénat (04.93.13.09.60). **Open** 10.30am-7pm Mon, Tue, Thur-Sat; 2-7pm Wed; 10.30am-6.30pm Sun. **Credit** AmEx, DC, MC, V.
A charming, old-fashioned toy shop on a pretty square in Vieux Nice, packed with everything from soft toys, puzzles and puppets to stocking fillers.

Au Brin de Soleil

1 rue de la Boucherie (04.93.62.89.00). **Open** 9.30am-7pm daily. **Credit** AmEx, DC, MC, V.
A haven for those seeking provençal interior furnishings. You'll find handpainted faïence, bed covers, kitchenware, candles and soaps.

Boutique 3

3 rue Longchamp (04.93.88.35.00). **Open** 1-6.30pm Tue-Sat. Closed Aug. **Credit** MC, V.
Check out designer Jacqueline Morabito's creamy linen tablecloths, flowing white shirts, shawls, ceramic dishes and range of gourmet goodies.

Une Cabane sur la Plage

1 pl du Jésus (04.93.76.82.46). **Open** 4.30-7.30pm Mon; 10.30am-7.30pm Tue-Sat; 10.30am-1.30pm Sun. **Credit** MC, V.
This friendly Vieux Nice boutique stocks feminine clothing that's perfect for the city's laid-back seaside vibe. Labels include Noa-Noa and Jayko; there's also menswear by Komodo and clothes made of hemp.

La Chapellerie

36 cours Saleya (04.93.62.52.54). **Open** 9.30am-1pm, 2-6.30pm daily. **Credit** V, MC.
Check out every imaginable sort of hat, from the basic beret to frilly things with serious plumage.

Diagram

11 cours Saleya (04.93.80.33.71). **Open** 10am-1pm, 3-8pm Mon-Sat; 10am-1pm Sun. **No credit cards.**
Eschewing provençal kitsch, this shop – which faces the flower market – sells exquisite tableware and furniture from France and Asia, at reasonable prices.

Façonnable

7, 9 & 10 rue Paradis (04.93.87.88.80). **Open** 10am-7pm Mon-Sat. **Credit** AmEx, DC, MC, V.
The menswear label that began with this shop now has stores in every major city, selling elegantly preppy sportswear, suits and ties. Womenswear is sold at the premises at No.10.

Fayences de Moustiers

18 rue du Marché (04.93.13.06.03). **Open** 9.45am-7pm Mon-Sat. **Credit** AmEx, MC, V.
The only shop in Nice selling the delicately handpainted porcelain that comes from Moustiers, stocking everything from cream jugs to fruit bowls. Pricey, but the real thing.

Matarosso Bookstore/Gallery
2 rue Longchamp (04.93.87.74.55). **Open** 10am-12.30pm, 4-7.30pm Tue-Sat. **Credit** MC, V.
This pioneer niçois gallery also offers contemporary art books, original editions and engravings.

Le Shop
37 rue Droite (04.93.62.83.13). **Open** 11.30am-7pm daily. **Credit** MC, V.
Showcasing the work of young French designers, Le Shop sells light-hearted clothing for men, women and children.

Star Dog & Cat
40 rue de France (04.93.82.93.71). **Open** 9.30am-noon, 2.30-7pm Mon-Sat. **Credit** AmEx, DC, MC, V.
Buy a souvenir for your dog or cat at this temple for pampered pets. Treasures include diamanté dog collars, Burberry-check coats and bejewelled bowls.

Village Ségurane
main entrance on rue Ségurane (no phone). **Open** 10am-noon, 3-6.30pm Mon-Sat. **Credit** AmEx, MC, V.
When Elton John went on a decorating spree for his villa in Mont Boron, this is where he shopped: a two-storey village of antiques shops, stacked together.

Arts & entertainment

For music and theatre listings, buy the weekly French-language *Semaine des Spectacles* available from newsagents, or pick up *Le Pitchoun*, a free French-language guide to clubs, restaurants and leisure activities.

Acropolis
1 esplanade Kennedy (04.93.92.83.00).
Open/tickets vary by event; call for details.
A modern mega-structure that hosts special events, conventions, concerts, ballet and opera.

Fenocchio. *See p263*.

Casino Ruhl
1 promenade des Anglais (04.97.03.12.33). **Open** *Slot machines* 10am-5am daily. *Gaming rooms* from 8pm Mon-Fri; from 5pm Sat, Sun. **Admission** (over-18s only, bring ID) *Slot machines* free. *Gaming rooms* €12. **Credit** AmEx, MC, V.
A modern expanse of gaming rooms, offering French and English roulette, blackjack, punto banco, craps and clanging slot machines.

Cinémathèque de Nice
3 esplanade Kennedy (04.92.04.06.66/ www.cinematheque-nice.com). **Films** 2.30pm, 5pm, 8pm Tue-Sat; 2.30pm, 5pm, 8pm, 10pm Fri, Sat; 3pm Sun. **Tickets** €3; €6 3-film pass. **No credit cards.**
Nice's cinematheque puts on an international selection of classic films, including high-quality recent releases, screened in their original language.

Galerie Soardi
8 rue Desiré Niel (04.93.62.32.03). **Open** 9am-7pm Mon-Sat. Closed Aug. **Admission** free. **Credit** AmEx, DC, MC, V.
In the former atelier of Henri Matisse you'll now find a private gallery that presents innovative shows of young artists and representatives of the Ecole de Nice. It also sells lithographs, frames and arty gifts, and offers cultural excursions.

Opéra de Nice
4 rue St-François-de-Paule (04.92.17.40.40/ www.opera-nice.org). **Open** *Box office* 9am-6pm Mon-Sat. **Tickets** €8-€80. **Credit** MC, V.
This small 19th-century gem of an opera house on the edge of Vieux Nice is decked out in sumptuous red velvet, with crystal chandeliers and lashings of gold. It attracts top-notch visiting artists to perform not only opera, but also symphonies and ballet.

Palais des sports Jean Bouin
2 rue Jean Allègre (04.97.20.20.30). **Open** varies by event; call for details. Closed Aug. **Admission** *Pool* €4.40; €3.60 2-8s. *Ice rink* €4.30; €3.50 2-8s (skate hire €2.70). **No credit cards.**
The Palais des sports is a vast municipal complex next to the Acropolis. It has a well-kept, Olympic-sized indoor pool and a covered ice rink – a bit of a rarity on the Côte d'Azur.

Palais Nikaïa
163 rte de Grenoble (04.92.29.31.29/04.92.29.31.12/ www.nikaia.fr). **Open** *Box office* 1-6pm Mon-Fri. **Tickets** vary by event; call for details. **Credit** V.
This massive, state-of-the-art, modular concert hall-cum-stadium hosts crowd-pleasing rock and classical stars, plus sporting events.

Théâtre de la Photographie et de l'Image
27 bd de Dubouchage (04.97.13.42.21). **Open** 10am-6pm Tue-Sun. **Admission** free.
A restored vintage theatre that now provides a vast space for big-name photography exhibitions. It also hosts lectures, holds an internet archive and has a convivial coffee bar.

The grand old **Opéra de Nice**. *See p267.*

Théâtre National de Nice

promenade des Arts (04.93.13.90.90). **Open** *Box office* 2-7pm Tue-Sat. **Tickets** *Grande salle* €7.50-€30. *Petite salle* €16-€20. **Credit** AmEx, DC, MC, V.
One of the most important theatres in the South of France, the Théâtre National de Nice is now directed by Daniel Benoin, staging high-profile productions of French and foreign classics and a variety of contemporary drama.

Where to stay

Nice has plenty of hotels of all price ranges to choose from, from the budget yet boutique **Villa La Tour** to the queen of them all, **Le Negresco**. The city's cheap hotels are clustered around the train station, but some mid-range options are great value, especially in the off-season. You might also consider renting a flat in Vieux Nice for a few days: contact **Nice Time** on 06.81.67.41.22 or at landry.ph@free.fr.

Hi Hôtel

3 av des Fleurs (04.97.07.26.26). **Rates** €180-€390 double. **Credit** AmEx, DC, MC, V.
Looking less futuristic than it did when it opened, this hotel is nonetheless the funkiest place to stay in Nice, with its experimental living spaces in jellybean colours. The tiny rooftop pool has a fabulous view, interiors are by up-and-coming designer Matali Crasset and there are DJ soirées on weekends. It would be wise to eat elsewhere, however, as the hippie-style health food supplied by Hédiard wildly misses the mark.

Hôtel Albert 1er

4 av des Phocéens (04.93.85.74.01/www.hotel-albert-1er.fr). **Rates** €90-€145 double. **Credit** AmEx, MC, V.
Just steps from the flower market, this charming hotel offers a friendly welcome with oak bedsteads, sleek whites and cornflower blues, and views out to sea or over the gardens.

Hôtel Atlantic

12 bd Victor Hugo (04.97.03.89.89). **Rates** €188.85-€231.05 double. **Credit** AmEx, MC, V.
Beyond the sumptuous belle époque stained-glass lobby – used by François Truffaut as a location in his film *Day for Night* – the Atlantic's modern, renovated rooms are spacious and comfortable.

Hôtel Beau Rivage

24 rue St-François-de-Paule (04.92.47.82.82). **Rates** €150-€600 double. **Credit** AmEx, DC, MC, V.
Matisse once lived in the Hôtel Beau Rivage, but he probably wouldn't recognise it these days: it's been freshly renovated in sleek modern style, with light switches that can lead to confusion after one too many drinks from the minibar. A stay here is otherwise a seamless experience. The hotel has its own beach, but rooms don't offer sea views.

Hôtel de la Fontaine

49 rue de France (04.93.88.30.38/www.hotel-fontaine.com). **Rates** €82-€120 double. **Credit** AmEx, MC, V.
This immaculate and simply designed hotel has cheerfully tiled bathrooms and a lovely inner courtyard. The cost of a room includes a substantial breakfast buffet.

Hôtel du Petit Palais

17 av Emile Bieckiert (04.93.62.19.11/www.hotel-petit-palais.com). **Rates** €76-€144 double. **Credit** AmEx, MC, V.

On a quiet street in Cimiez, this 25-room belle époque hotel may not be the *dernier cri* in terms of its decor, but the panoramic view and lush garden make up for it. Playwright and film director Sacha Guitry lived here in the 1930s.

Hôtel Excelsior

19 av Durante (04.93.88.18.05/ www.excelsiornice.com). **Rates** €90-€120 double. **Credit** AmEx, MC, V.

Located on a quiet street, this impressive building, dating back to 1898, has clean, old-fashioned rooms and a small garden where breakfast is served.

Hôtel Gounod

3 rue Gounod (04.93.16.42.00/www.gounod-nice.com). **Rates** €100-€140 double. **Credit** AmEx, DC, MC, V.

A dusty-rose, belle époque exterior hides standard, but chic, modern rooms with balconies. Guests can use the rooftop pool next door at Hôtel Splendid (*see p271*). The Gounod closes from mid-November to mid-December each year.

Hôtel La Pérouse

11 quai Rauba-Capeau (04.93.62.34.63/www.hotel-la-perouse.com). **Rates** €150-€420 double. **Credit** AmEx, MC, V.

This secret treasure, cut into the cliff of the Colline du Château, has breathtaking views over the Baie des Anges. Just steps away from Vieux Nice, it's wonderfully tranquil – the sundeck, sauna and stunning pool with a sea view add to the sense of luxury. Some of the rooms are very small, however, and staff can be snooty.

Hôtel La Petite Sirène

8 rue Maccarani (04.97.03.03.40/www.hotel-la-petite-sirene-nice.cote.azur.fr). **Rates** €107-€143 double. **Credit** AmEx, MC, V.

Near boulevard Victor Hugo, this hotel is cute and quiet. Rooms are clean and comfortable, and attentive staff at reception provide a lovely welcome.

Hôtel Le Floride

52 bd de Cimiez (04.93.53.11.02/www.hotel-floride.fr). **Rates** €49-€66 double. **Credit** AmEx, MC, V.

Only a ten-minute walk from the centre of town and right near the Chagall museum (*see p260*), this modest hotel nonetheless boasts a fine view from the top floor. The place closes for the month of January.

Hôtel Le Grimaldi

15 rue Grimaldi (04.93.16.00.24/www.le-grimaldi.com). **Rates** €95-€175 double. **Credit** AmEx, MC, V.

This elegant, upmarket, boutique hotel offers the kind of personalised hospitality often lacking in the glitzy Riviera palaces. Each room is different, but tastefully decorated with provençal fabrics.

Hôtel Les Cigales

16 rue Dalpozzo (04.97.03.10.70/www.hotel-lescigales.com). **Rates** €80-€130 double. **Credit** AmEx, MC, V.

This family-run hotel in a renovated *hôtel particulier* has cheerful, well-soundproofed rooms, some with small balconies looking over the garden.

Hôtel Masséna

58 rue Gioffredo (04.92.47.88.88/www.hotel-massena-nice.com). **Rates** €115-€200 double. **Credit** AmEx, MC, V.

An abundance of modern comforts lurk behind the splendid belle époque façade of this recently renovated building near place Masséna. Like the recently refurbished lobby, the rooms are decorated in a bright and sunny provençal style; many of them have great people-watching balconies that look over the street. Large baths, an internet connection in most rooms, fluffy green rugs and a friendly welcome are bonuses.

Hôtel Negresco

37 promenade des Anglais (04.93.16.64.00/ www.hotel-negresco-nice.com). **Rates** €315-€525 double; €830-€1,650 suite. **Credit** AmEx, DC, MC, V.

You can't miss this pink and white wedding cake. Built by Edouard Niermans, 'the Offenbach of architecture', it was initially considered a folly. But the Negresco eventually managed to draw in everyone from crowned heads-of-state to captains of industry. The sumptuous bedrooms range from oriental to Napoleon III pomp, though the bathtubs are oddly Las Vegas. There's no pool, but there is a private beach.

Hôtel Oasis

23 rue Gounod (04.93.88.12.29). **Rate** €67-€105 double. **Credit** AmEx, MC, V.

This tranquil, centrally located hotel once lodged illustrious Russians, among them Chekhov and Lenin. The biggest rooms (Nos.110, 124 and 210) look over a splendid, shady garden.

Hôtel Palais Maeterlinck

30 bd Maurice Maeterlinck (04.92.00.72.00/www.palais-maeterlinck.com). **Rates** €250-€700 double. **Credit** AmEx, DC, MC, V.

Once a villa belonging to Belgian writer Count Maurice Maeterlinck, this sprawling neo-classical palace on the Basse Corniche is now a hotel boasting luxurious rooms, an excellent restaurant and lovely outdoor pool. There's also a small, man-made beach for guests; located at the bottom of the cliffs, you'll be glad of the cable car on the way back. The atmosphere is somewhat stiff and formal, but the views are superb.

Hôtel Solara

7 rue de France (04.93.88.09.96). **Rates** €65-€75 double. **Credit** AmEx, MC, V.

Although its front entrance looks a bit dodgy, rooms at the Solara are bright and tidy. The hotel's central location too makes it good value.

have a Nice time

Stay in the charming boutique hotel that is the Hotel Massena and enjoy a stay exceeding all your expectations. Superbly situated in the heart of Nice, you will be only minutes walk away from all the main distractions; the Old Town, the beach and some fabulous shopping. Inside the hotel you will discover an intimate atmosphere, complimented by an attentive personnel and the classic Provencal character that runs through from the delicate frescoes in the hall to the cosy and luxurious bedrooms.

SPECIAL
OFFER
Readers
10%
Discount
from 90 € to 190 €
On presentation of this guide

★ ★ ★ ★
HÔTEL MASSÉNA
58, rue Gioffredo - 06000 Nice
Tel. 0033 492 47 88 88 - fax 0033 492 47 88 89
www.hotel-massena-nice.com

Hôtel Splendid
50 bd Victor Hugo (04.93.16.41.00/www.splendid-nice.com). **Rates** €220-€245 double; €330-€350 suite. **Credit** AmEx, MC, V.

This long-established four-star hotel has plenty to recommend it, not least its conveniently central – but pleasingly tranquil – location and the views from its top floor, where you'll find a heated pool and terrace. Rooms are modern, comfortable and spacious, and some (the pricier ones) have balconies.

Hôtel Suisse
15 quai Rauba-Capeau (04.92.17.39.00). **Rates** €90-€165 double. **Credit** AmEx, MC, V.

The Hôtel Suisse could probably get away with charging double the price given its enviable location overlooking the Baie des Anges and its understated contemporary decor. Most of the smallish but comfortable rooms have balconies, and the hotel gets a fresh coat of paint every year.

Hôtel Villa La Tour
4 rue de la Tour (04.93.80.08.15/www.villa-la-tour.com). **Rates** €62-€131 double. **Credit** AmEx, MC, V.

Set in an 18th-century convent, this is the only hotel in Vieux Nice. It's stunning value too, with compact, individually decorated rooms and a roof garden.

Hôtel Windsor
11 rue Dalpozzo (04.93.88.59.35/www.hotel windsornice.com). **Rates** €80-€165 double. **Credit** AmEx, MC, V.

This cult address is an arty oasis. Avoid the cheaper 'standard' rooms and insist on one that has been decorated by a contemporary artist, such as Ben, Peter Fend or Lawrence Weiner; there's also an exotic garden, aviary, hammam and small gym.

Mercure Marché aux Fleurs
91 quai des Etats-Unis (04.93.85.74.19/www.mercure.com). **Rates** €75-€143 double. **Credit** AmEx, MC, V.

Never mind the basic decor and matching florals: the service is dynamic and attentive, the €10 breakfast buffet is all-you-can-eat, and lovely views stretch out over the Baie des Anges.

Palais de la Méditerranée
13-15 promenade des Anglais (04.92.14.77.00/www.concorde-hotels.com). **Rates** €280-€550 double. **Credit** AmEx, DC, MC, V.

This luxury hotel opened in 2004, keeping the façade of the fabulous art deco Palais de la Méd. Most rooms have fantastic sea views, but a heads-on-beds policy means the owners have squashed in too many floors, making the ceilings rather low. The hotel's many security features include having its own fireman. There's a pool and a restaurant headed by the talented chef Bruno Sohn.

Villa Victoria
33 bd Victor Hugo (04.93.88.39.60/www.villa-victoria.com). **Rates** €90-€155 double. **Credit** AmEx, DC, MC, V.

This comfortably renovated belle époque villa has a spacious bar area with wrought-iron furniture. Rooms are decently sized, if heavily floral, but the real treat is a luxuriant garden with a rose pergola.

Resources

Municipal museums are free the first and third Sunday of the month. If you plan to visit several different museums, getting a **Passe-Musées** is a good idea: for a fixed rate of €6 you get seven days of single visits to all municipal museums; for €18.30 (€9.15 concessions) you can make 15 visits over a year. **Cartes Musées Côte d'Azur** are available in €10 (one day), €17 (three consecutive days) or €27 (seven days) varieties, valid for the whole region.

Hospital
Hôpital St-Roch, 5 rue Pierre Dévoluy (04.92.03.77.77/www.chu-nice.fr).

Internet
Internet cafés abound in Nice. One of the friendliest is the **E-mail Café** (8 rue St-Vincent, 04.93.62.68.86), which has become a meeting place for British expats.

Police
1 av Maréchal Foch (04.92.17.22.22). **Open** 24hrs daily.

Post office
21-23 av Thiers (04.93.82.65.00). **Open** 8am-7pm Mon-Fri; 8am-noon Sat.

Tourist information
Office du Tourisme et des Congrès, 5 promenade des Anglais (08.92.70.74.07/www.nicetourisme. com). **Open** 8am-8pm Mon-Sat; 9am-7pm Sun. **Other locations**: Aéroport Nice Côte d'Azur, Terminal 1; Gare SNCF, av Thiers.

Getting there

From the airport
Nice airport is 8km (five miles) west of the city centre. Bus No.98 runs between the airport and the *gare routière*, No.99 runs between the airport and the main SNCF station (every 20mins Mon-Sat, every 30mins Sun, €4), No.23 from terminal 1 only to St-Maurice via the station. A taxi to the city centre will cost about €35.

By bus
The *gare routière* (5 bd Jean Jaurès, 04.93.85.61.81) is the hub for most Côte d'Azur coach services, among them the international buses that run via Nice from Rome to Barcelona and from Venice to Nice via Milan. **Cars Phocéens** (04.93.85.66.61) on place Masséna runs buses between Marseille and Nice via Aix and Cannes (four daily, Mon-Sat; two on Sun), and to Toulon, via Cannes and Hyères (two daily, Mon-Sat). **RCA** (04.93.85.64.44, www.rca.tm.fr) runs regular buses along the coast to and from Cannes and Menton.

Nice's corking neighbour

Industrial outskirts give way to wooded countryside as you drive up the steep route de Bellet on the western side of Nice. Only a small brown sign, 'Vignobles de Bellet', indicates that you are entering France's smallest AOC (Appellation d'Origine Contrôlée) region – 400 hectares (7.4 acres), 300 metres (984 feet) above sea level, but still within the city of Nice.

Fourteen vineyards share the AOC label, the best-known of which is **Château de Bellet** on chemin de Saquier (No.440, 04.93.37.81.57), a winding road that leads to several of the winemakers' properties (though the signs are not easy to spot and most of them are closed to the public at weekends). So steep are the hills that you are often looking at a sheer drop rather than soft slopes lined with vines – mechanical harvesting is simply not a possibility here. To make the winemaker's job even more difficult, the land is divided into tiny parcels, often some distance apart.

Bellet's producers are passionate about their wines – if they weren't, they would have long ago sold their property to developers rather than continue tending rare grape varieties on arid soil made up of sand and pudding stone. Some, such as Dutch billionaire Cornelis Kamerbeek of **Château de Crémat** (442 chemin de Crémat, 04.92.15.12.15), are recent (and controversial) arrivals, whereas local personality Guislain de Charnacé has been defending Bellet wines at the head of Château de Bellet for 30 years.

Off the chemin de Saquier, a series of narrow, rocky lanes lead to **Clos St-Vincent** (collet des Fourniers, 04.92.15.12.69), run since 1993 by Roland Sicardi and Joseph Sergi. The initial impression is forbidding: two Dobermanns growl menacingly behind the iron gate. 'Get back into your car while I open the gate and tie up the dogs,' warns a voice through the intercom. A few seconds later, Sergi is introducing the now-docile Margaux and Pétrus. His wines are exemplary, particularly the floral rosé made only with *braquet*, a grape variety so local that many inhabitants of Bellet bear the name. *Rolle* is another ancient grape variety typical of this region, while *la folle noire*, used in full-bodied red wines, is named for its unpredictable yield.

It's unusual to find Bellet wines outside Nice, and the prices reflect that scarcity – it rarely sells for less than €20 a bottle (€30 and upwards in restaurants), though you can pay around €13 if you buy directly from the producer. It's worth the money both to savour the quality of the wines themselves, which are best enjoyed with local *cuisine niçoise*, and to taste a piece of history – whether they are friends or foes, Bellet's producers are united in trying to prove (through DNA tests) that their wines are the oldest in France.

The easiest way to get to Bellet is by car, turning off the promenade des Anglais on to the boulevard de la Madeleine and following the signs to the route de Bellet. The No.62 bus, which leaves from the Magnan bus stop about every 30 minutes, follows the entire loop around the vineyards and takes you to the village of St-Roman-de-Bellet.

Nearly every wine shop in Nice stocks wine from Bellet producers, but long-established **Cave Bianchi** (7 rue de la Terrasse, 04.93.85.65.79), near the cours Saleya market, has a particularly good selection. To buy direct from producers, contact **Les Coteaux de Bellet** (325 rte de Saquier, 04.93.85.13.92), **Propriété Nicoletti** (95 corniche Fleurie, 04.93.83.03.76), or simply get in touch with the individual vineyards.

By car

You can leave the A8 at exit 54 or 55, but it's more scenic to take the N7 or N98 along the coast (expect traffic jams in summer and during rush hour).

By train

The main SNCF station (3 av Thiers, www.sncf.com) is served by frequent trains from Paris and Marseille. Local services to Menton also stop at Gare Riquier, near the port and in the old town. The Gare St-Augustin is near the airport. The private Gare de Provence, just north of the main station, is the departure point for the narrow-gauge Var Valley Train des Pignes.

Getting around

By bus

An extensive bus network, including four Noctambus night buses, is run by Lignes d'Azur (10 av Félix Faure, 08.10.06.10.06, open 7.15am-7pm Mon-Fri, 8am-6pm Sat; 29 av Masséna, open 8.15am-noon, 2-5pm Mon-Fri). Tickets cost €1.30. Bus-hop passes (€4, daily; €15, weekly), are available from Lignes d'Azur, *tabacs* and newsagents.

By taxi

Nice taxis are notoriously expensive. To order a taxi, call Central Taxi Riviera (04.93.13.78.78).

The Arrière-Pays

Mere minutes from Nice, the hinterlands known as the Arrière-Pays are about the furthest thing imaginable from the fast-paced energy of the Côte d'Azur's urban centres. A quietly delightful mini wilderness of olive groves, pine woods, wild flowers and precariously perched villages, the region offers cooling summer breezes, spectacular panoramas and rustic cuisine.

Just 18 kilometres (11 miles) north of Nice on the D2204/D15, **Contes** juts out from a steep slope overlooking the Paillon de Contes torrent. Once a Roman settlement, this quiet village found itself in the limelight in 1508 when the Bishop of Nice was called in to rid the place of a nasty plague of caterpillars. Legend has it that he succeeded through force of pious good will, giving the townsfolk good reason to build the Chapelle Ste-Hélène in 1525; the chapel is remarkable today for the tiny Renaissance fountain in its courtyard. This area is also famous for all things olive: olives are still pressed (between December and March) in a 17th-century water-powered mill at the Site des Moulins (04.93.91.74.20). Olive oil, salted olives and tapenade are on sale at the Gamm Vert agricultural co-operative (rte de Châteauneuf, 04.93.79.01.51, open 8.30am-noon, 2.30-6pm Tue-Sat).

In tiny **Châteauneuf-de-Contes**, 4.5 kilometres (three miles) to the west, the 11th-century Madone de la Vieille Ville church is worth a look. A well-marked 30-minute walk leads to the atmospheric ruins of Vieille Châteauneuf.

On the main square of **Coaraze**, self-styled *village du soleil* ('village of the sun'), the town hall bears dazzling modern sundials by Jean Cocteau and other artists. The village is a maze of vaulted passageways, cypress-lined gardens and fountains. Also of interest is the unusual Chapelle Notre-Dame de la Pitié, otherwise known as the 'Blue Chapel' for its monochrome scenes depicting the life of Christ. At the top of the village is the old cemetery, with cement boxes provided for burials since the rocks are too hard even for pickaxes. The name Coaraze supposedly derives from *caude rase* ('cut tail'): wily medieval inhabitants caught Old Nick napping and grabbed hold of him, obliging him to shed his lizard-like tail to escape; a modern pavement mosaic illustrates the tale.

Travel 16 kilometres (ten miles) north-east of Nice on the D2204/D21 and you'll find **Peillon**, isolated on a rocky spur above olive groves. The village has not a single quaint boutique, the wise residents having banned upmarket tourist development. Instead there are narrow cobblestoned streets, pantiled roofs and an unbeatable panorama of the valley. Not to be missed is the minuscule Chapelle des Pénitents Blancs at the entrance to the village. The chapel is kept closed to protect the 15th-century frescoes of the Passion, attributed to Giovanni Canavesio, but the works can be viewed through a grating by means of coin-operated

Coaraze.

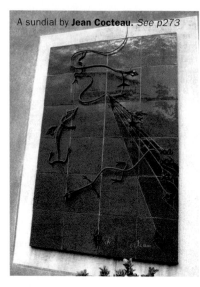

A sundial by **Jean Cocteau.** *See p273*

de lapin (rabbit stew) and heavenly nougat ice-cream. Rooms are simple but comfortable, and overlook the valley. At the edge of the village, five cosy rooms, a panoramic terrace and a pool are a nice surprise at the **Relais de Feuilleraie** (04.93.79.39.90, double €48-€60, menus €15-€32). In Peillon, the **Auberge de la Madone** (2 pl Auguste Arnulf, 04.93.79.91.17, www.chateauxhotels.com/madone, double €90-€200) is a long-standing romantic hideaway; it closes for three weeks in January, and from November to Christmas Eve. The restaurant (open 12.30-2pm, 7.30-9pm, reservations only, closed Wed, lunchtime Thur, menus €30-€70) features refined Nissart specialities, cooked by chef Milo and his son Thomas, who trained under super-chef Alain Ducasse. The view from the flower-lined terrace is one of the best in the Arrière-Pays. In Peille, stop for a pastis and pissaladière at the café **Chez Cauvin** (5 pl Carnot, 04.93.79.90.41, open lunch only Mon, Thur & Sun, lunch & dinner Fri, Sat, dinner reservations required, menus €17-€25).

lights. Further upstream – or a lovely 90-minute ridge walk from Peillon – **Peille** is a quiet village with handsome Romanesque and Gothic doorways and a ruined feudal castle at the top. Peille's feisty inhabitants, who accepted numerous excommunications in the Middle Ages rather than pay taxes to the bishop, speak their own dialect, known as Pelhasc.

At the bottom of the Peillon valley, the agricultural township of **L'Escarène** was once an important staging post on the Route du sel ('salt road') from Nice to Turin; for once, a piece of modern engineering – the viaduct of the Nice–Sospel railway – complements the view of the old town. Further up the Route du sel, the fortified medieval crossroads of **Lucéram** is worth a detour for its 15th-century Eglise Stes-Marguerite-et-Rosalie (rue de l'Eglise, closed Mon & Tue), which has a striking Italianate, onion-domed, yellow and pink belfry. Outstanding altarpieces by the Bréa school recount the story of St Marguerite, a shepherdess-martyr who was burned at the stake. She was also one of Joan of Arc's favourite voices-in-the-head.

Where to stay & eat

One of the most quietly celebrated Arrière-Pays destinations is the **Auberge du Soleil** (5 chemin Camin de la Beguda, 04.93.79.08.11, closed Nov-mid Feb, double €62-€85, menus €23-€28) in Coaraze, where the bucolic vista is a treat for city-sore eyes. Try the giboulette

Resources

Tourist information

Coaraze *Office du Tourisme, 7 pl Ste-Catherine, 06390 Coaraze (04.93.79.37.47).* **Open** *Apr-Sept* 10am-12.30pm, 3-6pm Tue-Fri. *Oct-Mar* 10am-12.30pm, 3-6pm Tue-Fri; 10am-12.30pm Sat.
Contes *Syndicat d'Initiative, pl d'Albert Olivier, 06390 Contes (04.93.79.13.99/www.ville-contes.fr).* **Open** 2-5pm Mon-Fri.
Lucéram *Maison du Pays, la Placette, 06440 Lucéram (04.93.79.46.50).* **Open** 10am-noon, 2-6pm Tue-Sat.
Peille *Syndicat d'Initiative, Mairie, pl Carnot, 06440 Peille (04.93.91.71.71).* **Open** 9am-noon Mon-Fri.
Peillon *Syndicat d'Initiative, Mairie, 672 av de l'Hôtel de Ville, 06440 Peillon (04.93.79.91.04).* **Open** 8.30am-noon Mon, Tue, Thur; 8.30am-noon, 2-5.30pm Wed, Fri.

Getting there

For the easyCruise service, *see p249* **Plane sailing**.

By car

The starting point for getting to the Arrière-Pays is the D2204 Paillon valley road, which begins at the Acropolis roundabout in Nice as bd J-B Verany.

By train/bus

The Nice–Sospel line (between four and six trains daily) stops at Peillon, Peille and L'Escarène, but only L'Escarène has a station within easy reach of the town; Peillon and Peille are a 5km (three-mile) walk from their respective stations. There are buses from Nice to Peille (three daily, Mon-Sat), to L'Escarène and Lucéram (four daily, Mon-Sat) and to Contes and Coaraze (two daily, Mon-Sat); for details call the Nice *gare routière* (04.93.85.61.81).

The Corniches

The long and winding road.

The very names Villefranche and Cap-Ferrat conjure up images of speedboats, millionaires' mansions and bronzed beauties. While all that does exist, this is perhaps the world's most democratic playboy's playground, supplying activities, sights and a patch of sun for everyone. The three Corniche roads that wind between Nice and Menton – low (Basse), middle (Moyenne) and high (Grande) – give you flashes of azure sea, green manicured gardens and oh-so-pretty villages. The Basse Corniche (N98 – also known as the Corniche Inférieure) hugs the coast, passing through all the towns and resorts. To take some of the strain, the wider Moyenne Corniche (N7) was hacked through the mountains in the 1920s. The highest route – the Grande Corniche (D2564) – follows the ancient Roman Aurelian Way, and is the most spectacular of the three.

The glamour of the Corniches has its tragic side too. On 13 September 1982 a car carrying Princess Grace of Monaco and her daughter Stéphanie swerved off the N53, a treacherous descent full of hairpin bends that leads from the Grande Corniche to the Moyenne Corniche. Stéphanie survived; her mother did not (*see p284* **A matter of principality**). There's no memorial, but a bunch or two of fresh flowers can generally be seen by the roadside.

Basse Corniche: Villefranche-sur-Mer

Used as a fine natural shelter by ancient Greeks and Romans, Villefranche proper was founded in the 14th century by Charles II of Anjou as a duty-free port. The seaside town's stacked dusty-rose, ochre and apricot houses and trompe-l'oeil frescoes redefine the term 'picturesque'. You might still see old women mending fishing nets beside the tiny cobblestoned port; in the old town rue Obscure, an eerie vaulted passageway, has changed little since the Middle Ages; and the Combat Naval Fleuri, held on the Monday before Ash Wednesday, is a surreal sight, with dozens of fishing boats bedecked with flowers invading the harbour.

The deep harbour between the headlands of Mont Boron to the west and Cap-Ferrat to the east was used as a US naval base until France withdrew from the military wing of NATO in 1966. The quayside, lined with brasseries and overlooking a long sandy public beach, is a haven of high-class entertainment compared to the days when it used to service sailors. At the western end of the port, the postage stamp-sized **Chapelle de St-Pierre-des-Pêcheurs**, once a store for fishing nets, was covered in 1957 with lively frescoes by Jean Cocteau; these depict the life of St Peter. At the top of the old town, the **Eglise St-Michel** (04.93.76.69.94, open 9.30am-7pm daily) is a handsome 18th-century, Italianate church. It boasts an impressive organ, built in 1790 by the Niçois Grinda brothers and still played during Sunday mass (celebrated each week at 10.30am). Wander through the old streets west of the church to the 16th-century Citadelle. It was built by the Dukes of Savoy and comes complete with a drawbridge. It now houses the voluptuous female figures of local sculptor Antoniucci Volti (in the **Musée Volti**) and 100 minor works by artists such as Picasso, Hartung, Picabia and Miró (in the **Musée Goetz-Boumeester**). The citadel is also used for outdoor theatre and film shows, mainly in summer. Villefranche buzzes year-round, especially during the provençal market, held in place du Marché on Saturday mornings, and the Sunday antiques market, on avenue Albert 1er.

Chapelle de St-Pierre-des-Pêcheurs

quai Courbet (04.93.76.90.70). **Open** *Mar-June* 10am-noon, 3-7pm Tue-Sun. *July-Sept* 10am-noon, 4-8pm Tue-Sun. *Oct-Feb* 9.30am-noon, 2.30-5pm Tue-Sun. Closed mid Nov-mid Dec. **Admission** €2; free under-12s. **No credit cards**.

Musée Volti, Musée Roux et Musée Goetz-Boumeester

Citadelle, av Sadi Carnot (04.93.76.33.27). **Open** *Sept-June* 9am-noon, 2.30-5.30pm Mon-Sat. *July, Aug* 10am-noon, 2.30-7pm Mon, Wed-Sat; 2.30-7pm Tue, Sun. Closed Nov. **Admission** free.

Where to stay & eat

The always refined **Hôtel Welcome** (3 quai Amiral Courbet, 04.93.76.27.62, www.welcome hotel.com, closed early Nov-late Dec, double €91-€194) is a splendid yellow and blue portside establishment, although it now bears little resemblance to the hotel of the same name in which Jean Cocteau fraternised with young sailors amid opium fumes in the 1920s. The airy rooms all have balconies, most of which overlook the port. The 21 rooms of the **Hôtel de la Darse** (32 av Général de Gaulle, 04.93.01.72.54, www.hoteldeladarse.com, doubles €42-78) are neat and tidy, and the hotel is just seconds from the port, minutes from Villefranche's heart. Back down on the quay, the **Fille du Pêcheur** (04.93.01.90.09, 11am-11pm daily, average €33) and **L'Oursin Bleu** (04.93.01.90.12, closed mid Jan-mid Feb, Tue in Nov & Dec, menu €32) sit side by side; octopus and seafood tapas is a winner at the former, grilled meats and tuna tournedos at the latter. The fisherman who supplies both restaurants moors his boat 20 metres away in the port and, if you're moored there and the need arises, he can be telephoned to provide you with a lift from your boat. In place Amélie Pollonais friendly **Le Cosmo Bar** (04.93.01.84.05, average €38) offers quality fish and some of the best salade niçoise on the Riviera. It's also great for breakfast before the antiques market on Sunday. Carrying on down towards the beach, catch Villefranche's trendy set at **Carpaccio** (promenade des Marinières, 04.93.01.72.97, average €30), with its cigar cave and summer restaurant-to-yacht shuttle service. The titular finely sliced meats and fish are the order of the day; a platter of beef, squid or swordfish comes in at around €20.

Resources

Tourist information

Office de Tourisme, Jardin François Binon, 06230 Villefranche-sur-Mer (04.93.01.73.68/ www.villefranche-sur-mer.com). **Open** *July, Aug* 9am-7pm daily. *June, Sept* 9am-noon, 2-6.30pm Mon-Sat. *Oct-May* 9am-noon, 2-6pm Mon-Sat.

Basse Corniche: Cap-Ferrat

The lush, secluded peninsula jutting out between Villefranche and Beaulieu is a millionaires' paradise of high-hedged, gilded mansions. The promontory is also a walker's dream, with a stunningly beautiful, rocky, ten-kilometre (six-mile) path that winds around the Cap en route to the Plage des Fosses, a pebbly beach ideal for small children. Swimmers can also drive or walk to tree-lined La Paloma beach, five minutes south of Port St-Jean.

The approach to the Cap is dominated by the **Villa Ephrussi-de-Rothschild**, an Italianate extravaganza built for Beatrice de Rothschild in the early 1900s. Inside, Beatrice had appropriate settings recreated for her immense art collection, which focuses on the 18th century but also includes Impressionist paintings and various oriental knick-knacks. The villa is surrounded by fountain-filled

Spanish, Japanese and Italian gardens, with arresting views. On the eastern side of the peninsula, luxury yachts have replaced many of the fishing boats at St-Jean-Cap-Ferrat. Still, it's a delightful spot for an evening drink, which simply has to be followed by a stroll along the marina and Port St-Jean. Further west, the **Zoo du Cap-Ferrat** has 300 species, from flamingos and talking cockatoos to otters and zebras – all of them more likely to impress little ones than budding botanists.

Villa Ephrussi-de-Rothschild

1 av Ephrussi-de-Rothschild (04.93.01.33.09/guided group visits 04.93.01.45.90/www.villa-ephrussi.com). **Open** *Sept-June* 10am-6pm daily. *July, Aug* 10am-7pm daily. **Admission** €9; €6.50 7-17s; free under-7s. **Credit** AmEx, MC, V.

Zoo du Cap-Ferrat

117 bd du Général de Gaulle (04.93.76.07.60/ www.zoocapferrat.com). **Open** *Apr-Oct* 9.30am-7pm daily. *Nov-Mar* 9.30am-5.30pm daily. **Admission** €13; €9 3-10s; free under-3s. **Credit** MC, V.

Where to stay & eat

The stately **Grand Hôtel du Cap-Ferrat** (71 bd Général de Gaulle, 04.93.76.50.50, www.grand-hotel-cap-ferrat.com, closed Jan & Feb, double €205-€2,525) is partially hidden in magnificent fragrant gardens near the tip of the peninsula. Non-residents can eat at the classically elegant Le Cap restaurant (average €105), dine on the terrace in summer or stop for a drink at the hotel's Somerset Maugham Bar, to which the writer occasionally wandered from his nearby home for gin tonics with friends; for a €60 entrance fee, you can take the funicular to Le Club Dauphin, a spectacular spill-over pool. **La Voile d'Or** (av Jean Mermoz,

Casino de Beaulieu-sur-Mer. *See p277.*

04.93.01.13.13, www.lavoiledor.fr, closed mid
Oct-mid Apr, double €229-€829, menus €68-
€85) by Port St-Jean might be mistaken for an
impressive family villa. Guests revel in amazing
balcony views, a sauna, the private beach and a
waterside pool. The small yet refined menu at
the restaurant is an extravaganza of sea bass,
scallops and duck. **Capitaine Cook** (11 av
Jean Mermoz, 04.93.76.02.66, closed Wed &
lunch Thur, menus €23-€28), just 50 metres
(165 feet) up the hill, cracks out fish fillets and
oysters on its charming vine-covered terrace.
 In St-Jean itself, **Le Provençal** (2 av Denis
Séméria, 04.93.76.03.97, menus €35-€160)
prides itself on its seafood mêlée, which
contains lobster galore. The **Hôtel Brise
Marine** (58 av Jean Mermoz, 04.93.76.04.36,
www.hotel-brisemarine.com, closed Nov-Jan,
double €135-€150) is an ochre- and turquoise-
trimmed villa with a tangled garden, near La
Paloma beach. **Résidence Bagatelle** (11 av
Honoré Sauvan, 04.93.01.32.86, double €85-
€125, closed Nov-Mar), on a quiet backstreet
between St-Jean and Beaulieu, has modestly
priced rooms and an overgrown citrus garden.
The simply decorated **La Frégate** (11 av
Denis Séméria, 04.93.76.04.51, double €45-€75)
is even less expensive, although full board costs
an extra €57-€72 in July and August. For great
food, join the St-Jean locals in the **Restaurant
du Port** (7 av Jean Mermoz, 04.93.76.04.46,
closed Tue) for three-course menus (€16.50-
€26.50) of flambéed prawns, grilled sea
bream and sardines.

Resources

Tourist information

*Office de Tourisme, 59 av Denis Séméria, 06230
St-Jean-Cap-Ferrat (04.93.76.08.90).* **Open** *July, Aug*
8.30am-6.30pm daily. *Sept-June* 8.30am-6pm Mon-Fri;
9am-5pm Sat.

Basse Corniche: Beaulieu-sur-Mer

A charming belle époque resort that has
long been a favourite for holidaying European
aristocrats, Beaulieu still has an old-world feel,
with genteel (but non-designer) boutiques and
ubiquitous palms. Well-heeled Sunday strollers
and their yapping dogs jostle for space on the
scenic promenade Maurice Rouvier, which links
the port of Beaulieu via the clean public beach
to St-Jean-Cap-Ferrat via the late David Niven's
pink castle. Gustave Eiffel and Gordon Bennett,
legendary director of the *New York Herald
Tribune*, lived here. So did archaeologist
Theodore Reinach, who was so enamoured

of ancient Greece that he built a fastidious
and not-to-be-missed reconstruction of a fifth-
century BC Athenian house. Situated in front
of the Baie des Fourmis – so-called because of
the ant-like black rocks dotted about – the **Villa
Kérylos** is now a museum, with sunken marble
bath, reclining sofas and antique-looking
frescoes galore (plus hidden modern amenities
such as showers). Up the road towards the
port de Plaisance marina, the **Musée du
Patrimoine Berlugan** covers local history
since Palaeolithic times. On the seafront, the
Casino, a turn-of-the-19th-century jewel
offering roulette, blackjack and baccarat for
the wealthy Cap-Ferrat crowd, is deliciously
retro. So is the **Tennis Club de Beaulieu-
sur-Mer**, a quaint club with eight clay courts
that can be rented by the day. Less rarified
pleasures can be found at the food market on
place Charles de Gaulle, which also sells clothes
and homeware (daily, except Sun out of season).
  The Basse Corniche continues eastwards
through the ribbon development of Eze-Bord-
de-Mer and on to **Cap-d'Ail**, which would
have little to recommend it were it not for the
splendid pebbly beach, Plage la Mala, equally
prized by the Monaco jetset and Italian day-
trippers. Be prepared for a wearying trek
down the steps (and up again).

Casino de Beaulieu-sur-Mer

*4 rue Fernand Dunan (04.93.76.48.00/
www.partouche.com).* **Open** *Gaming room* 9pm-4am
daily. *Slot machines* 11am-4am daily. **Admission**
(over-18s only, bring ID) *Gaming room* €11. *Slot
machines* free. **Credit** AmEx, DC, MC, V.

Musée du Patrimoine Berlugan

av des Hellènes (04.93.01.68.66). **Open** *Sept-July*
1-6pm Fri, Sat. **Admission** free.

Tennis Club de Beaulieu-sur-Mer

*4 rue Alexandre 1er de Yougoslavie
(04.93.01.05.19).* **Open** *Courts* 8am-10pm daily.
Office July, Aug 9am-noon, 4-8pm daily; Sept-June
9am-noon, 2-6pm daily. **Admission** €15/day per
person. **No credit cards**.

Villa Kérylos

*impasse Gustave Eiffel (04.93.01.01.44/www.villa-
kerylos.com).* **Open** *Feb-Nov* 10am-6pm daily. *Dec,
Jan* 2-6pm Mon-Fri; 10am-10pm Sat, Sun & school
hols. **Admission** €7.80; €5.50 7-18s, students; free
under-7s. **Credit** AmEx, MC, V.

Where to stay & eat

Relaxed yet stylish bistro **Les Agaves** (4 av
Maréchal Foch, 04.93.01.13.12, closed lunch,
mid Nov-mid Dec, menu €35), by the train
station in the Palais des Anglais, is popular
for its seasonal, creative cooking. Italianate
Le Métropole (15 bd Leclerc, 04.93.01.00.08,

www.le-metropole.com, closed late Oct-Dec, double €170-€1,270) has scented gardens running down to the sea, floral rooms, a heated pool and a restaurant (menus €55-€88) that serves inspired, seafood-heavy dishes. Celebrities and royalty once flocked to the fin-de-siècle **Florentine Hôtel La Réserve** (5 bd Leclerc, 04.93.01.00.01, closed Nov-late Dec, double €170-€2,440), with its spa and stunning pool; the hotel restaurant serves refined but pricey Mediterranean cuisine (menus €135-€170), including liberal sprinklings of caviar, foie gras and game. Blue and white **Hôtel Le Havre Bleu** (29 bd du Maréchal Joffre, 04.93.01.01.40, www.hotel-lehavrebleu.fr, double €57-€62) is an aged villa with simply decorated guestrooms. Lively retro-colonial **L'African Queen** (port de Plaisance, 04.93.01.10.85, average €40) offers carpaccios and the possibility of rubbing elbows with passing celebrities. Next door, **La Max** (04.93.01.65.75, closed Mon, average €35) is a seafood specialist with a yachty clientele.

Resources

Tourist information

Office de Tourisme, pl Georges Clemenceau, 06310 Beaulieu-sur-Mer (04.93.01.02.21/www.ot-beaulieu-sur-mer.fr). **Open** *June-Sept* 9am-12.30pm, 2-7pm Mon-Sat; 9am-12.30pm Sun. *Oct-May* 9am-12.30pm, 2-6pm Mon-Sat.

Moyenne Corniche: Eze

An eagle's nest of a place, with views to match, picturesque Eze is perched 430 metres (1,410 feet) above the shimmering Med. The village started life as a Celto-Ligurian settlement, passing over the ages from Phoenicians to Romans, Lombards to Saracens. Its glorious vistas inspired Nietzsche, who would stride up here in the 1880s from his Eze-Bord-de-Mer home, composing the third part of *Thus Spake Zarathustra* in his head. The steep mule path he took (now called sentier Frédéric Nietzsche) snakes through olive and pine groves. Allow 75 minutes and take a bottle of water for the uphill slog from the Basse Corniche.

During the Eze d'Antan Festival on the final weekend of each July, the village is swamped by sword-toting knights and colourful pageantry. In what remains of Eze's castle, at the summit of the village, the **Jardin Exotique** is a prickly blaze of flowering cacti and succulents, offering a sweeping panorama over red-tiled roofs to the coast. Aside from the metal workshops, cutesy art gallery and souvenir shops and perfectly rejuvenated provençal lanes, there is little else of substance to see in

Eze; but a place where donkeys still haul their cargoes of groceries up the steep lanes must surely be worth a visit.

Jardin Exotique

rue du Château, Eze (04.93.41.10.30). **Open** *July-Aug* 9am-8pm daily. *Sept-June* 9am-6pm daily. Closing times vary, depending on daylight. **Admission** €4; free under-12s. **No credit cards**.

Where to stay & eat

Nestling beneath the castle ruins, the **Nid d'Aigle** (rue du Château, 04.93.41.19.08, closed early Jan-early Feb, average €30) is an informal, family-run restaurant that specialises in local dishes such as artichokes with goat's cheese and Ligurian *pasta pistou*. **La Troubadour** (4 rue du Brec, 04.93.41.19.03, closed Mon, Sun, mid Nov-mid Dec, menus €32-€47) serves up classical French cuisine with a provençal twist in its olde-worlde interior. The sumptuous rooms at the **Château de la Chèvre d'Or** (rue du Barri, 04.92.10.66.66, www.chevredor.com, double €270-€680) have sweeping coast views; there's also a pool, and the restaurant (menus €60-€130) serves some innovative dishes, such as sea bass carpaccio and duck breast with peaches. The newly renovated **Château Eza** (rue de la Pise, 04.93.41.12.24, double €150-€890) is a mini castle at the top of endless crooked steps. The view from its precipitous terrace is one of the greatest views in the world.

Resources

Tourist information

Office de Tourisme, pl Général de Gaulle, 06360 Eze (04.93.41.26.00/www.eze-riviera.com). **Open** *Apr-Oct* 9am-7pm daily. *Nov-Mar* 9am-6pm Mon-Sat.

Grande Corniche: La Turbie

Built under Napoleon, the Grande Corniche winds along what was the Aurelian Way (known for this stretch as the Via Julia Augusta) for 32 kilometres (20 miles) over breathtaking drops: it's a favourite of wannabe Formula One drivers, masochistic cyclists, scenery lovers and fans of Hitchcock's *To Catch a Thief*.

Dominating the road is La Turbie (from *tropea*, Latin for trophy), a spectacularly located village that is often shrouded in mountain mist. Sleepily charming, it consists of little more than a row of ancient ochre houses, two town gates and the 18th-century church of St-Michel-Archange, with its host of 'attributed to' and 'school of' works. What puts the village on the map is the Roman **Trophée des Alpes**, a partly restored curve of white Doric columns

Get a clear water revival at **Plage des Fosses**. *See p276.*

set in a hilltop park. The Trophée was erected in 6 BC to celebrate Augustus' victory over rowdy local tribes; it bears a copy of an inscription praising Augustus, though the huge statue of the victor that once adorned the monument has long since gone. Inside the adjoining museum is a scale model of the original, and diverse artefacts that were unearthed on the site. Little pieces of history lurk everywhere in the village, from the odd carved doorway to vestiges of the ancient city wall.

If it's sport, not history, you're after, the **Monte-Carlo Golf Club** is an 18-hole course with a vertiginous view. Star-gazers should head north of La Turbie to **Eze Astrorama**, a wildly popular astronomical show (combining planetarium, telescopes and videos).

Eze Astrorama

rte de la Revere (04.93.41.23.04). **Open** *July, Aug* 6-11pm Mon-Sat. *Sept-June* 6-11pm Fri, Sat. **Admission** €7, €5 children (€10, €7 under-12s Wed, Sat & conference days); free under-6s.

Monte-Carlo Golf Club

rte du Mont Agel (04.93.41.09.11). **Open** *Oct-May* 8am-6pm daily. *June-Sept* 8am-8pm daily. **Admission** €90 Mon-Fri; €110 Sat, Sun. **Credit** MC, V.

Trophée des Alpes

18 av Albert 1er, La Turbie (04.93.41.20.84). **Open** *Mid May-mid Sept* 9.30am-6pm daily. *Mid Sept-mid May* 10am-1.30pm, 2.30-5pm Tue-Sun. **Admission** €4.60; €3.10 18-25s; free under-18s.

Where to stay & eat

Besides its rather luxurious guestrooms and central location, La Turbie's **Hôtellerie Jérôme** (20 rue de Compte de Cessole, 04.92.41.51.51, closed early-late Dec, doubles €100-€140) boasts a classy restaurant (closed Mon & Tue, menus €55-€98), where regional recipes are given a Ligurian twist. For full-on comfort, head to **Roquebrune Vista Palace** (rte de la Grande Corniche, 04.92.10.40.00, www.vistapalace.com, closed Feb, double €160-€1,200). Clinging to a precipice off the Grande Corniche, the hotel is a St-Moritz-style wedge of dated 1970s grandeur. Its restaurant, **Le Vistaero** (closed lunch mid May-Sept, menus €85-€110), produces classic French cuisine.

Getting there & around

By train

Villefranche, Beaulieu, Eze-Bord-de-Mer and Cap-d'Ail are served by regular trains from Nice. Beaulieu is also served by faster Italian trains on the Nice-Genova run, but not by the French TGVs.

By bus

RCA (04.93.85.61.81, www.rca.tm.fr) runs several useful buses: No.100 travels along the Basse Corniche between Nice and Menton; No.112 (Nice–Beausoleil) stops in Eze (and terminates there on Sun); No.116 runs daily (except Sun) between Nice and Peille via La Turbie. **Lignes d'Azur** (08.10.06.10.06) runs the No.81 bus from Nice to Cap-Ferrat, while the No.83 shuttles between Eze-Bord-de-Mer and Eze village.

Monaco & Monte-Carlo

Welcome to Trumpton-on-Sea, where the royal family makes the headlines and the residents make millions – but what lies beneath?

Port Hercule.

There's trouble brewing in paradise. With the passing of Prince Rainier III, the autocratic ruler who transformed the tiny principality of Monaco from a sedate gambling resort into a glamorous, billion-dollar tax haven, increasing its GDP 180-fold, major changes are afoot. Under Rainier, tax from offshore banks and companies accounted for 50 per cent of the state budget. No income tax was levied – hence it became home to racing drivers, tennis stars and entertainment legends.

On the eve of his accession in July 2005, Prince Rainier's son Albert II began measures to lift the veil of secrecy on Monaco's opaque but lucrative banking customs. Non-residents (in particular EU citizens) will be forced to show more transparency in their financial dealings. 'I want to create the model state,' declared Albert on Accession Day.

Amid fireworks and the free quayside banquet laid on for Monégasque citizens (some 6,000 of the 32,000 population of this 2.2 sq km/ 0.8 sq mile cliff-top playground), talk wasn't of models – but of an air hostess. Two months before Albert's accession, *Paris Match* broke

the sensational news that Albert had had a love child with Air France stewardess, Togo-born Nicole Coste. Two-year-old Alexandre is the latest in a long line of royal scandals that have affected the Grimaldi clan (*see p284* **A matter of principality**), descended from the Genoese pirate who seized the rock in 1297. Prince Rainier III's marriage to Hollywood star Grace Kelly, which brought Monaco into the post-war glamour circuit, has kept the francophone gossip press busy since 1956. Princess Grace's fatal car crash in 1982 is still shrouded in myth.

Myth and glamour bring today's tourists to Monaco. Swelled by budget-air travellers to Nice, a short, cheap and easy train ride away, they hang around Monaco's centrepiece Casino to gawp at the valet-parked Rolls-Royces, glimpse the ersatz good looks of surrounding Monte-Carlo (the regal figurehead of Monaco's six districts) and group for holiday snaps in front of the pristine yachts bobbing imperiously in nearby Port Hercule.

For those here on the cheap, Monaco needn't be that expensive – certainly no more so than Paris. The string of two- and three-star hotels near the train station, a pavement or so away in France (you can tell by the phoneboxes and postboxes), are reasonably priced. Dining and going out needn't break the bank. Most (glitzy if bland) nightspots only charge entrance at weekends – few have strict dress codes. The free public beach at Larvotto, made with imported fine sand, has a reasonably clean stretch of sea, with fish swimming almost up to the water's edge. These attractions, coupled with a handful of sights, mainly high up around the Palais Princier, are accessible by a cheap,

frequent local bus service and an essential network of public lifts. Hard to spot on the free maps distributed at key spots around the principality, these lifts make light work of the punishing inclines from seafront to clifftop.

One oft-quoted myth about Monaco is that it is only the size of Hyde Park. Try walking it. Another is that there's a policeman to guard every 55 residents. They don't have to. This Trumptonesque stick of rock, with its own red-and-white flags, stamps, international dialling code (00.377), phonecards and laws (no topless

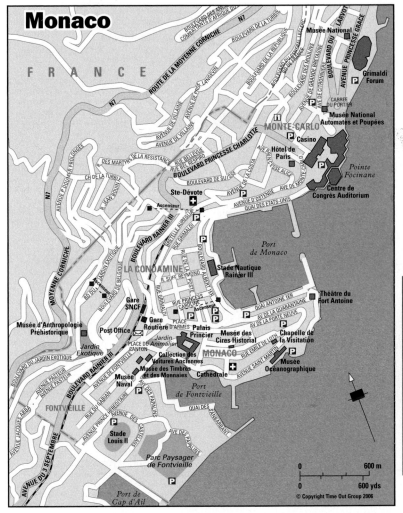

The Riviera & Southern Alps

bathing, no public singing), is festooned with CCTV cameras. Alleyways, passages and lifts you wouldn't dream of entering elsewhere (certainly not in nearby Genoa) are all under surveillance. Trust flourishes. Restaurants don't bother to tether their terrace tables when closed. Your hotel may not ask for your passport. Unlocked mopeds clutter prime pavement space. (Those sheer walls forming the hairpin bends of the famed Grand Prix city-centre circuit see action all year round.)

Everything, in fact, fights for space here. Row upon row of bland housing blocks, pitted with balconies overlooking balconies (much of Monaco is residential and plug-ugly), car parks, tiny patches of green, Ferrari paraphernalia and Rainier portraits in shop windows – everything and everybody struggles for a piece. What's going to happen if they bring in income tax? Or the Grimaldis suffer one scandal too many, and the line dies out? Legally, France would claim Monaco back, and who'd want another Nice?

Sightseeing

The first thing you will want to see is the Casino, the former Opera House, built by the man responsible for creating the similar edifice in Paris. Still under a huge renovation project, it dominates place du Casino, with its fountains and grass verges, lined with Monaco's finest lodgings (Hôtel de Paris), finest restaurant (Louis XV) and finest bar (Bar Américain). Braided flunkies abound. This is the Monaco you came for, the Monte-Carlo of legend, *The Persuaders* locations you used to watch on Sunday afternoons. It won't disappoint.

The other main draw is the harbour at La Condamine, which forms half of the Grand Prix circuit each May. Lined with the downmarket terrace bars at sea level on quai Albert Ier, and landmark destinations – Stars 'n' Bars, Quai des Artistes – on quai Antoine Ier, it's busy noon and night. From here, through the tunnel on bus routes Nos.5 and 6, the harbour at Fontvieille is a more low-key and pleasant diversion. Much here is built on land reclaimed from the sea. Nearby is Stade Louis II, home to local football club AS Monaco and host of the European Super Cup every August. Beneath the tunnel, between Fontvieille and La Condamine, high up in Monaco-Ville, is the Palais Princier and surrounding sights, the best being the Musée Océanographique. This is the oldest part of the principality – and tourist central, lamentably rustic, with souvenir shops offering Ferrari tat and stamp collections. Interestingly, street signs are given in French and a local language not dissimilar to Corsican. Monaco's pirate past is never far behind.

Cathédrale de Monaco

av St-Martin (00.377-93.30.87.70). **Open** *July-Sept* 8am-6.45pm daily. *Oct-June* 8am-6pm daily. **Admission** free (no entry during mass).

Monaco's cathedral was built in 1875 in a sort of Romanesque, kind of Byzantine style. It contains a 15th-century altarpiece by Louis Bréa, a grandiose marble altar, tombs of the princes of Monaco – and a simple slab in honour of Princess Grace.

Collection des Voitures Anciennes

terrasses de Fontvieille (00.377-92.05.28.56). **Open** 10am-6pm daily. **Admission** €6; €3 8-14s; free under-8s. **No credit cards.**

Prince Rainier's vintage car collection, from a 1903 de Dion-Bouton to a 1986 Lamborghini Countach.

Eglise Ste-Dévote

pl Ste-Dévote (00.377-93.50.52.60). **Open** 8.30am-6.30pm daily. **Admission** free.

This port-side church was built in 1870 on the site where, according to legend, Monaco's patron saint was guided ashore by a dove after surviving a shipwreck off Africa. Medieval pirates stole the saint's relics, only to be caught and their ship set on fire. A replica ship goes up in flames in front of the church every 26 January.

Jardin Animalier

terrasses de Fontvieille (00.377-93.25.18.31). **Open** *Oct-Feb* 10am-noon, 2-5pm daily. *Mar-May* 10am-noon, 2-6pm daily. *June-Sept* 9am-noon, 2-7pm daily. **Admission** €4; €2 under-14s. **No credit cards.**

After a visit to Africa in 1954, Prince Rainier procured countless varieties of monkeys and sundry other wild beasts and exotic birds for this mini zoo.

Jardin Exotique et Grotte de l'Observatoire/Musée d'Anthropologie Préhistorique

62 bd du Jardin Exotique (00.377-93.15.29.80/ www.jardin-exotique.mc). **Open** *Mid May-mid Sept* 9am-7pm daily. *Mid Sept-mid May* 9am-6pm daily. **Admission** €6.80; €3.50 6-18s; free students, under-6s. **Credit** MC, V.

Inaugurated in 1933, this succulent wonderland of nearly 7,000 bizarrely shaped tropical specimens has everything from giant Aztec agaves to ball-shaped 'mother-in-law's cushion' cacti. The grotto inside the garden contains a stalactite- and stalagmite-lined Neolithic dwelling 60m (200ft) underground. The museum traces the story of Stone Age life on the Riviera, with bones galore from extinct animal species and impressive Cro-Magnon skeletons, all found in the Grimaldi caves (which can be visited in Balzi Rossi, just over the border in Italy).

Musée de la Chapelle de la Visitation

pl de la Visitation (00.377-93.50.07.00). **Open** 10am-4pm Tue-Sun. **Admission** €3; €1.50 6-14s; free under-6s. **No credit cards.**

This 17th-century chapel houses religious paintings by Rubens, Zurbaran and Italian baroque masters.

Musée des Souvenirs Napoléoniens et Collection des Archives Historiques du Palais

pl du Palais (00.377-93.25.18.31). **Open** *June-Sept* 9.30am-6.30pm daily. *Oct, Nov* 10am-5pm daily. *Dec-May* 10.30am-noon, 2-4.30pm Tue-Sun. Closed mid Nov-mid Dec. **Admission** €4; €2 8-14s; free under-8s. **No credit cards**.

Bonaparte buffs will enjoy the vast display of objects and documents from the First Empire, while the more Monaco-smitten can peruse an exhibit of historic charters and Grimaldi medals.

Musée National Automates et Poupées

17 av Princesse Grace (00.377-93.30.91.26/www. monte-carlo.mc/musee-national). **Open** *Apr-Sept* 10am-6.30pm daily. *Oct-Mar* 10am-12.15pm, 2.30-6.30pm daily. **Admission** €6; €3.50 6-14s; free under-6s. **No credit cards**.

A variety of 18th- and 19th-century dolls and mechanical toys is set into motion several times daily at this kooky museum. It's well worth visiting if the fabulous but temporary Barbie designer collection is still on show.

Musée Océanographique

av St-Martin (00.377-93.15.36.00/www.oceano.mc). **Open** *Apr-June, Sept* 9am-7pm daily. *July, Aug* 9am-7.30pm daily. *Oct-Mar* 10am-6pm daily. **Admission** €11; €6 6-18s; free under-6s. **Credit** MC, V.

Set in a beautiful fin-de-siècle building on 85m (279ft) of sheer cliff rising from the sea in Monaco-Ville, this wonderful aquarium was founded by renowned oceanographer Albert I in 1910. The old-style museum on the first floor is dedicated to his activities, with vast whale skeletons, original equipment and meticulously surveyed maps of Arctic islands. Downstairs is the aquarium, including the shark lagoon and reconstructed tropical reefs bright with colourful movement. Lantern-eye fish, long-horned cowfish, fish shaped like rocks, razor shrimps that can also be used as knives when bone dry, medusas and moray eels give rise to shrieks of 'Rigolo!' from darkened corners of this eerie basement. Each tank features a smiley-face sticker to indicate whether or not it's ethically sound to eat its residents (sardines – thumbs up!). There's a bar on the roof terrace and a restaurant.

Palais Princier

pl du Palais (00.377-93.25.18.31). **Open** *June-Sept* 9.30am-6.20pm daily. *Oct* 10am-5pm daily. Closed Nov-May. **Admission** €8; €4 8-14s; free under-8s. **No credit cards**.

The sugary palace, built over a 13th-century Genoese fortress, is closed to the public when the prince is in residence (signalled by a red-and-white banner). The 30min tour takes in the frescoed gallery, sumptuous bedrooms, state apartments with Venetian furnishings, the throne room and the mosaic courtyard. The changing of the guard takes place at 11.55am daily in the palace square.

Trips & tours

Aquavision

quai des Etats-Unis (00.377-92.16.15.15/www.aqua vision-monaco.com). **Tours** *June, Sept* 11am, 2.30pm, 4pm Mon-Sat. *July, Aug* 11am, 2.30pm, 4pm, 5.30pm daily. **Admission** €11; €8 3-18s. **No credit cards**.

This hour-long boat trip gives visitors the chance to see how Monaco looks from the Med – as well as to plunge underwater at Cap d'Ail and see sea life through a glass-hulled catamaran.

Héli Air Monaco

Héliport, avenue des Ligures (00.377-92.050.050/ www.heliairmonaco.com). **Open** 8am-7pm Mon-Fri. **Admission** €52. **Credit** AmEx, MC, V.

Héli Air runs 10min panoramic helicopter tours of the principality. Four passengers are required for everyone to pay the minimum fare of €52 each – phone ahead to book.

Monaco-Tours

38 quai Jean-Charles Rey (00.377-92.05.64.38). **Open** *Feb-May, Sept-mid Nov* 10.30am-5pm daily. *June-Aug* 10am-5pm daily. **Admission** €7; free under-5s. **Credit** MC, V.

Karé(ment). *See p285.*

A matter of principality

As Albert II's Accession Day fireworks exploded over Port Hercule and the speakers blasted out the apocalyptic wailing from *The Dark Side of the Moon*, a drunken local in a nearby bar looked over and said: 'Atlantis'. The scene on boulevard Albert 1er (named after the new ruler's great-grandfather) did seem like the sinking of some lost kingdom.

Many in Monaco fear that with Albert's accession, the whole live-fast, tax-free ethos of Albert's father, Prince Rainier III, will be gone. In his 56-year reign, ending with his death in April 2005, the wily Rainier made two smart, long-term moves. First, he married Grace Kelly and thrust Monaco on to the international jet-set circuit. Second, he made Monaco an offshore tax haven: banks and companies paid the autocrat minimal tax, but it was enough to finance half the state budget. No longer were the Grimaldis reliant on profits from the Société des Bains de Mer (SBM), set up a century before to manage the new casino, spa baths and opulent hotels.

In 1297 the Grimaldis – then a bunch of Genoese pirates – seized the rock, a bare plateau of olive groves and lemon orchards. Then, when nearby Roquebrune and Menton opted out of Monégasque rule in 1848, it lost its main source of revenue: a tax on lemons. Charles III duly set up SBM, taking ten per cent of its profits. A judicious loan to the French government got Charles the architect Charles Garnier to design the Casino, plus a railway to ship in gamblers. And, in 1870, a flourishing Monaco was able to abolish local taxes for nationals and residents.

When Rainier took over in 1949, the principality was passé, but his marital and financial dealings soon pushed Monaco back into the big time – at a price. Under the glare of the gossip press, his marriage became shaky and daughters Caroline and Stephanie got hitched with a string of elephant trainers and trapeze artists; one husband was killed in a speedboat race. After Princess Grace's mysterious death in a car crash in 1982, Rainier retreated with his secrets for two sad decades. Questions arose concerning the principality's financial probity.

Little seemed to affect honourable, sports-mad, unattached Albert. After his father died, under pressure from the EU, Albert declared that Monaco's financial institutions should show more transparency. Europe applauded: the majority of Monaco's residents are EU citizens. With Albert's blessing, on the eve of his accession in July 2005, the National Council voted in a first law to criminalise financial misdeeds in the principality.

But the world wasn't listening. It was far more interested in the first scandal to taint honest Albert – he had had a love child with Togo-born stewardess Nicole Coste. In an open interview with French TV, Albert admitted responsibility for two-year-old Alexandre – although his son can never ascend the throne (only offspring of Catholic marriages are eligible) – and even left the door open should there be any other illegitimate offspring. He then followed in his namesake great-grandfather's footsteps, setting off on an expedition to Spitsbergen in the Arctic – and an uncertain future.

Kitsch little tourist trains in national colours run to and from the Musée Océanographique to 18 key spots around the principality. Tours last half an hour and commentary is provided in ten languages.

Where to eat & drink

Baltik

1 av des Citronniers (00.377-97.70.64.06). **Open** 9am-5am Mon-Fri; 5pm-5am Sat, Sun. **Menu** €17. **Credit** AmEx, MC, V.

The most palatable of the Monte-Carlo venues near the Casino, this low-key lounge restaurant is centred around a sturdy octagonal bar counter propped up by all kinds of nighthawks. It's a long way down-market from where it thinks it is, but therein lies the charm – and it does make an effort with a decent programme of DJs and chanteurs.

Bar Américain

Hôtel de Paris, place du Casino (00.377-92.16.28.64). **Open** 10.30am-2am daily. **Credit** AmEx, DC, MC, V.

Old-school cocktail bar and café, overlooking the Casino, with tables spilling out into the exquisite lobby of the Hôtel de Paris (*see p287*). Inside, a jazz trio plays the *Chariots of Fire* theme in the corner while immaculately attired bar staff serve suitably pricey (€22) cocktails (Race & Gamble, Grand Prix, Jackpot, Last Lap), rare armagnacs and bottles of local Monaco beer in frosted glasses (€11). Smart dress please, at any time, with jacket and tie required as the evening wears on.

Columbus Bar

23 av des Papalins (00.377-92.05.90.00). **Open** 10am-1.30am. **Credit** AmEx, DC, MC, V.

A destination bar by the lobby of the hippest hotel in town, over in Fontvieille, Columbus is brown, minimalist and ideal for an early-evening snifter. Fresh fruit Martinis (€15) include lemon, passion fruit and melon versions; Mojitos (€15) come in fiery varieties; champagne starts at €15 a glass, and there are any number of rare whiskies. Not much in the way of food, but there is a brasserie across the lobby.

L'Eden Bleu
32 port de Fontvieille (00.377-99.99.99.69/www. lamouledor.com). **Open** noon-2.30pm, 7.30-11pm Tue-Fri, Sun; 7.30-11pm Sat. **Average** €25. **Credit** DC, MC, V.
This friendly Belgian brasserie on the Fontvieille waterfront serves Monaco's freshest moules, cooked in 15 styles with frites, or pasta with seafood.

Huit et Demi
4 rue Princesse Caroline (00.377.93.50.97.02). **Open** noon-2.30pm, 7-11pm Mon-Fri; 7-11pm Sat. **Average** €38. **Credit** AmEx, DC, MC, V.
Red velvet Fellini-esque surroundings and a huge terrace harbour gaggles of gossiping Italians, English and Monégasques. Superbly fresh Mediterranean fare includes beignets de courgettes and sea bream en papillotte; the soup of fresh fruits with own-made lemon sorbet is divine.

Louis XV
Hôtel de Paris, pl du Casino (00.377-92.16.29.76/ www.alain-ducasse.com). **Open** 12.15-1.45pm, 8-9.45pm Mon, Thur-Sun; 8-9.45pm Wed (late June-late Aug). Closed mid Feb-early Mar, late Nov-late Dec. **Menus** €105-€190. **Credit** AmEx, DC, MC, V.
This jewel box of a dining room offers the ultimate Riviera gilt trip and one of the most glamorous outdoor terraces in the world. It was Alain Ducasse's first restaurant and is still his best, although now he merely flies in to supervise. The food is a contemporary update of the sturdy, peasant food native to the coast and hinterlands from Nice to Genoa, complemented by a remarkable cellar.

Quai des Artistes
4 quai Antoine 1er (00.377-97.97.97.77/www.quai desartistes.com). **Open** noon-2.30pm, 7.30-11pm daily. **Lunch menu** €21. **Dinner average** €40. **Credit** AmEx, DC, MC, V.
Situated beside the Marlborough Gallery, this spacious terrace brasserie overlooking the harbour is aiming to transform the quai Antoine 1er into an arty hangout. It's too formal for that, but the seafood is superb, the €21 lunch deal a bargain for these parts and the service first-class.

La Salière
14 quai Jean-Charles Rey (00.377-92.05.25.82). **Open** noon-2.30pm, 8-11pm daily. Closed Sat & Sun lunch in Aug. **Menu** €30. **Credit** AmEx, MC, V.
The best of the attractive options around Fontvieille harbour, Stefano Frittella's landmark Italian eaterie serves inventive versions of standard favourites,

attracting the occasional famous name to his warm-hearted establishment. There are daily specials at €20 and wood-fired pizzas.

Sport Aviron Snack Bar
3 av Président J-F Kennedy (00.377-93.50.51.30). **Open** noon-3pm Mon-Sat. **Average** €15. **No credit cards.**
Although you won't find it in many guides, this is a great place for lunch: the upstairs restaurant of the Monaco Rowing Club, which is signified by a pair of red-and-white oars and the proud foundation date of 1888. A simple dining room is filled with the local seafaring fraternity, chatting in Italian and Monégasque dialects while tucking into mountainous portions of pasta (€8) and relaxing over a few too many grappas afterwards. Non-members are welcome for a €1 surcharge on the laughably modest bill. Stockfish on Fridays. Harbour views too.

Zébra Square
Grimaldi Forum, 10 av Princesse Grace (00.377-99.99.25.50). **Open** noon-3pm, 8pm-midnight daily. **Average** €45. Closed Feb. **Credit** AmEx, DC, MC, V.
Cool sister operation of its namesake counterpart in Paris, Zébra Square is a trendy bar-restaurant atop the Grimaldi Forum (take the lift by the main entrance). The small after-hours lounge bar is a destination in itself, but most are here for modern provençal cuisine, impeccably served in the low-lit dining room and on the seaview terrace.

Nightlife

Monaco's options aren't all glitzy – in fact, its late-opening clubs and bars (*see p284*) have plenty to appeal to the average punter. None of it is particularly adventurous, but there are a handful of waterfront venues you'd be happy to find anywhere else on the Côte. Many flock to the string of piano bars on avenue des Spélugues, which leads up from the Casino, but the scene here is generally more wanky than swanky and is best avoided. A better bar crawl is to be had around the harbour, with two levels of unpretentious quayside venues and the catch-all **Stars 'n' Bars**. Pick up a copy of the monthly *By Night* freebie booklet for details of happy hours and dress codes in town.

Karé(ment)
Grimaldi Forum, 10 av Princesse Grace (00.377-99.99.20.20/www.karement.com). **Open** 9am-4.30am daily. **Credit** AmEx, DC, MC, V.
This hip new cocktail and tapas bar, with a terrace from which to view passing cruise ships, has been packed since it opened in 2004. The tapas are actually oriental dishes served on dinky square black trays by black-shirted staff; it's more a nightspot, really. Cocktails (€15), including a Karé(ment) Sling of Bombay Sapphire and cherry Marnier, are only served until 11pm, after which a DJ keeps the crowd busy on the dancefloor and the lip-shaped furniture.

McCarthy's

7 rue du Portier (00.377-93.25.87.67/www.monte-carlo.mc/mccarthys). **Open** 6pm-5am daily. **Live music** *June-Aug* daily. *Sept-May* Thur-Sat. **Credit** AmEx, DC, MC, V.

Genuine snugs form the interior of this accommodating, late-night Irish bar – the main local expat hangout. Happy hour runs from 6pm to 9pm but the bar's pretty busy until its daily dawn closure. TV sports and standard pizzas complement the Guinness and Foster's.

La Note Bleue

Plage Larvotto, av Princesse Grace (00.377-93.50.05.02/www.lanotebleue.mc). **Open** *June-mid Sept* 9am-11pm daily. *Mid Sept-May* 9am-7pm daily. **Live music** *June-mid Sept* Thur-Sun. Closed Mar, Thur in Nov. **Average** €60. **Credit** DC, MC, V.

Calling itself a 'plage restaurant jazz lounge', La Note Bleue is the perfect place to squander a balmy summer night. By day, this Larvotto seafront venue hires out loungers on its private section of beach by the jetty and lifeguard observation-post; by dusk, tea lights transform the terrace into a romantic music bar. Strong fruit Daiquiris (€12), glasses of champagne (€10) and bottles of wine (€20) come up from the busy bar counter by the stage, which sees live action every weekend in summer (no entrance fee). A kitchen serves salads and meaty mains (€15-€20) from 7.30pm.

Le Sporting Club

av Princesse Grace (00.377-92.16.22.77). **Open** *July-Aug* 8.30pm-late daily. *Sept-June* 8.30pm-late Wed-Sun. **Admission** *Concerts/shows* €60-€145 (incl 1st drink). **Credit** AmEx, DC, MC, V.

Le Méridien Beach Plaza. *See p288.*

This six-hectare (15-acre) seaside complex is frequented by royalty, models, pop stars, Middle Eastern princes and miniskirted demoiselles in Cartier. Jimmy'z (00.377-92.16.36.36, open July, Aug 11.30pm-dawn daily, Sept-June 11.30am-dawn Wed-Sun), the disco for beautiful people, requires chic dress and an ample wallet. Le Sporting d'Eté entertainment complex hosts big-name crooners.

Stars 'n' Bars

6 quai Antoine 1er (00.377-97.97.95.95/www.starsnbars.com). **Open** *July, Aug* 10am-5am daily. *Sept-June* 11am-midnight Mon-Thur; 11am-2am Fri-Sun. **Credit** AmEx, MC, V.

Everyone comes to this harbourfront sports bar, with its four-square island bar counter manned by the glass-juggling Fabio and lined with young(ish) cosmopolitans on the flirt. Inside is a two-floor operation, decked out with motor-racing paraphernalia, with drivers' overalls inlaid into the tables heaving with humongous Tex-Mex hamburgers (€15). There's an internet station by the reception area and a separate bar counter serving the busy terrace.

Shopping

Luxury knows no bounds in Monte-Carlo, from the rash of jewellery shops near the Casino to the designer boutiques along boulevard des Moulins and avenue Princesse Grace. In place du Casino, the **Galerie du Metropole** is an upscale three-storey mall and home to the realistically priced Fnac CD, book and hi-fi store. Rue Grimaldi offers the flip, hip side of fashion. True Monégasques shop in the **Centre Commerciale** in Fontvieille, a large mall with a mega-supermarket.

Arts & entertainment

Le Cabaret du Casino

pl du Casino (00.377-92.16.36.36). **Show** 10.30pm Wed-Sat. Closed mid June-mid Sept. **Admission** *Show & dinner* €67. **Credit** AmEx, DC, MC, V.

Slick cabaret shows offer an alternative to gambling. *Let's Be Wild,* with its jazzy Cotton Club and African jungle theme, incorporates live animals and film music, in a red-velvety nightclub atmosphere and among Hollywood frescoes.

Casino de Monte-Carlo

pl du Casino (00.377-92.16.20.00/www.casino-monte-carlo.com). **Open** (over-18s only, ID essential) *Salons européens* noon-late daily. *Slot machines* 2pm-late Mon-Fri; noon-late Sat, Sun. *Salons privés* 4pm-late daily. *Club Anglais* 10pm-late daily. **Admission** €10 (€20 for salons privés & Club Anglais). **No credit cards.**

The ornate gambling house was dreamed up in 1863 by Monaco's prince to generate revenue. Old-fashioned precepts still apply: no clergymen or Monégasque citizens are allowed into the gaming rooms. For men, a sports jacket and tie are de rigueur. Roulette has a €5 minimum bet, stakes are higher in the salons privés and the Club Anglais, which offer chemin de fer, trente-et-quarante, black-jack and craps.

Grimaldi Forum

10 av Princesse Grace (00.377-99.99.30.00/www. grimaldiforum.com). **Open** *July, Aug* 10am-8pm Mon-Sat. *Sept-June* noon-7pm Mon-Sat. **Admission** varies. **Credit** AmEx, DC, MC, V.

This vast, ultramodern exhibition and cultural centre is a multi-levelled modular glass and steel complex with everything from concert halls and seasonal art or trade shows to a cybercafé. The Forum now features destination restaurant Zébra Square and nightspot Karé(ment) (for both, *see p285*), each with their own lift by the main entrance.

Monte-Carlo Country Club

155 av Princesse Grace (04.93.41.30.15/ www.mccc.mc). **Open** *July, Aug* 8am-9pm daily. *Sept-June* 8am-8.30pm daily. **Admission** (1-day pass) €36; €26 under-18s. **Credit** AmEx, MC, V.

The swankiest club on the Riviera has clay tennis courts, squash, a gym and a heated open-air pool (open May-Oct) with airjets, waterfalls and a counter-current basin for aquatic workouts.

Open air cinema

terrasses du Parking des Pecheurs (00.377-93.25.86.80/www.cinemasporting.com). **Open** *Mid Aug-mid Sept* 9.30pm daily. **Admission** €10-€15. **No credit cards**.

On a warm summer evening, sit under the stars with a glass of rosé and watch the latest movie on top of the rock, at this version originale cinema with the largest open-air screen in Europe. Seating is on cushioned chairs, or slightly more expensive reclining sunloungers with tables for your drinks.

Stade Louis II

3 av des Castelans (00.377-92.05.74.73/www.asm-foot.mc). **Open** *Guided tours* 10.30am, 11.30am, 2.30pm, 4pm Mon-Fri. **Admission** €4; €2 under-12s. **No credit cards**.

This modest sports complex, plonked in a residential district of Fontvieille, houses an Olympic-sized pool, basketball court and boxing gym below the 18,500-capacity football ground where top-league club AS Monaco plays home matches. Games are poorly attended, meaning tickets are often available at the office inside the main entrance. Away fans are placed in the only uncovered section of the ground, the Populaires at the Cap d'Ail end. The 40min stadium tour is disappointing: there isn't much to see, with neither trophy room nor club museum. Access is by buses Nos.5 or 6 from town, where you'll find the equally modest club shop at 16 rue Grimaldi.

Where to stay

With the current fad for luxury spa breaks, nearly all of Monaco's high-end hotels are being given the once-over. The Société des Bains de Mer, which operates the key venues in the principality – the Casino, Les Thermes Marins and the **Hôtel de Paris** – is opening a four-star spa and leisure hotel complex in Larvotto at the end of 2005. The **Hôtel Métropole** saw a complete refurbishment in 2004, **Le Méridien Beach Plaza** now has a high-tech top floor, and the second phase of the renovation of the **Hôtel Hermitage** was completed in 2004. In 2006 a new Novotel will be opened on the site of Radio Monte-Carlo, while the five-star **Port Palace** continues to win international acclaim despite an ugly street-level exterior. For those arriving on spec, the **tourist office** (*see p288*) can reserve, free of charge, a room for you for that day only.

Those on a budget will find two-star hotels on boulevard du Général Leclerc, an easy hop from the train station by bus Nos.2 and 4.

Hôtel Columbus

23 av des Papalins (00.377-92.05.90.00). **Rates** €245-€335 double. **Credit** AmEx, DC, MC, V.

Launched by Ken McCulloch, founder of the wildly successful Malmaison chain, this hip lifestyle hotel on the Fontvieille harbour has given a contemporary spin to Monaco's stuffy, old-world image. The rooms are decked out in soft lavenders and creamy beiges, with luxurious leather upholstered beds and a cabinet equipped with a CD player and internet. The bar is a haunt of Formula One drivers, presided over by part-owner David Coulthard.

Hôtel de Paris

pl du Casino (00.377-92.16.30.00/www.sbm.mc). **Rates** €390-€790 double. **Credit** AmEx, DC, MC, V.

This grande dame of luxury hotels shares its history with Monte-Carlo itself. Inspired by the Hôtel du Boulevard des Capucines in Paris, it was opened in 1864 as Charles III began to construct an elegant resort around the adjacent Casino. Famous guests – Verdi, Alexandre Dumas, General Grant – flooded in. Extended seven times since, it now boasts four superb restaurants (including the exquisite Louis XV, *see p285*) and the equally elegant Bar Américain (*see p284*). It also provides easy access to the spa facilities at Les Thermes Marins.

Hôtel Helvetia

1bis rue Grimaldi (00.377-93.30.21.71/www.monte-carlo.mc/helvetia). **Rates** €79-€105 double. **Credit** AmEx, MC, V.

Only a stone's throw from the port, the Helvetia is a clean and affordable hotel. The decor is unremarkable, but staff are friendly.

Hôtel Hermitage

sq Beaumarchais (00.377-92.16.40.00/www.sbm.mc). **Rates** €355-€850 double. **Credit** AmEx, DC, MC, V.

The most elegant of Monaco's luxury hotels, the refurbished Hermitage saw two new floors added in 2004 to its Princes and Beaumarchais wings. The glass-roofed foyer was also restructured – but the centrepiece is still Gustav Eiffel's stained-glass dome, which covers the winter garden. Many of the already comfortable rooms were also renovated; the more expensive rooms have balconies with harbour views. Guests can enjoy exquisite seafood at the rooftop Vistamar restaurant and have direct access to Les Thermes Marins spa.

Hôtel Métropole
4 av de la Madone (00.377-93.15.15.15/www. metropole.com). **Rates** €355-€440 double, up to €2,000 suite. **Credit** AmEx, DC, MC, V.
Fully refurbished, with a new spa and seawater swimming pool having opened in the spring of 2005, this high-end establishment is looking to give the Hôtel de Paris (*see p287*), a short walk across place du Casino, a run for its money. Its luxuriously equipped rooms also come in deluxe and prestige varieties, ranging up to junior suite or suite. Joël Robuchon's terrace restaurant provides inventive French-Med cuisine.

Le Méridien Beach Plaza
22 av Princesse Grace (00.377-93.30.98.80/ www.lemeridien.com). **Rates** €240-€375 double. **Credit** AmEx, DC, MC, V.
With its high-tech rooftop tenth floor (whose sea-facing rooms command a €100-€150 surcharge), the Beach Plaza is now the second largest hotel in the principality, with a prime location right by the city beach at Larvotto. Three restaurants, two swimming pools, a beauty and fitness centre, saunas and vast conference centre equip this top-class leisure and business hotel for just about anything.

Port Palace
7 av Président J-F Kennedy (00.377-97.97.90.00/ www.portpalace.com). **Rates** €250-€325 double, €990-€1,600 suite. **Credit** AmEx, DC, MC, V.
Hermès design director Leila Menchari is responsible for the fine and sleek interior of this super-stylish five-star contemporary hotel. Right by Port Hercule harbour, it has Carrara marble and Rubelli fabrics, not to mention sharkskin on its lift walls. The sixth-floor terrace restaurant is overseen by Michelin-starred chef François Pillard and beauty treatment is provided by Clé de Peau Beauté, rarely seen outside Japan. On the downside, it has no pool. But all rooms from 'superior' to 'executive suite' have a harbour view.

Villa Boeri
29 bd du Général Leclerc (04.93.78.38.10/www.hotel boeri.com). **Rates** €55-€68 double. **Credit** AmEx, DC, MC, V.
Within a short walk of the Casino, you won't find cheaper than the small, friendly Boeri. It's the last of a line of budget lodgings a few doors over the Monégasque border in Beausoleil, and provides 30 clean, comfortable rooms, some with sea-facing balconies. Try also the nearby three-star **Olympia** at No.17bis (04.93.41.85.04), with rooms in the €100 range. Both are an easy hop from Monte-Carlo station by bus Nos.2 and 4.

Resources

Hospital
Centre Hospitalier Princesse Grace, av Pasteur (00.377-97.98.99.00).

Internet
Stars 'n' Bars, *see p286.*

Police
Police Municipale, pl Marie (00.377-93.15.28.26).

Post office
Postes et Télégraphes, 1 av Henri Dunant (00.377-97.97.25.25). **Open** 8am-7pm Mon-Fri; 8am-noon Sat.

Tourist information
Direction des Tourismes et des Congrès de la Principauté de Monaco, 2A bd des Moulins, 98000 Monaco (00.377-92.16.61.16/www. monaco-tourisme.com). **Open** 9am-7pm Mon-Sat; 10am-noon Sun.

Getting around

The six-line colour-coded **bus** network is easy, cheap and convenient. Single tickets (€1.45) and four-journey (€3.50) varieties are available on board, change given. Maps are posted at each stop. **Taxis** are parked around the Casino; otherwise, call 00.377-93.15.01.01 or 00.377-93.50.56.28.

Monaco has its own **phone cards**, **stamps** and **dialling code**, 00.377, dropped when calling internally. For France, dial 00.33. The currency is, as in France, the euro.

Getting there

For the easyCruise service, *see p249* **Plane sailing**.

By air
The nearest airport is at Nice (*see p252*), 16km (ten miles) away. There is a direct bus service to Monaco Casino from Nice airport (€12.50, 50mins). Héli Air Monaco (*see p283*) runs a helicopter service (€85, €50 under-12s, free under-2s, 7mins). Alternatively, you can take the regular bus (€4, 15mins) from Nice airport to the railway station, then the train to Monaco Monte-Carlo.

By bus
A regular bus service runs between the Nice and Menton *gares routières*, stopping at boulevard Albert Ier at Monaco harbour.

By car
Leave the A8 autoroute at exit 57 or 58 or take the N98 (Basse Corniche), the coast road from Nice to the west and Cap Martin and Menton in the east.

By train
Monaco Monte-Carlo station is served by regular trains on the Cannes–Nice–Menton–Ventimiglia line. From Nice, the journey costs €3.10 and takes under 15mins. A few TGV trains connect directly with Paris (6hrs).

Roquebrune to Menton

Land of swank and citrus fruits.

In the pink at **Menton**. *See p290.*

Roquebrune-Cap-Martin

The illustrious – Empress Eugénie, Churchill, Coco Chanel, Le Corbusier and WB Yeats – and notorious – African dictator Emperor Bokassa – have all been drawn to the beautiful **Cap-Martin** promontory. The pine, fir, olive and mimosa trees seem to have been planted by God with the express purpose of concealing the luxury hideaways, most of which are hidden from mere mortals in the Domaine privé du Cap-Martin.

The well-maintained Sentier Douanier winds around the edge of the peninsula, passing by Le Corbusier's tiny modular beach shack Le Cabanon (call the tourist office for visits, 10am Tue & Fri), set just before the pointe de Cabbé. To the west, the curved Plage du Golfe Bleu is a favourite landing spot for hang-gliders. The architect, who drowned while swimming here in 1965, had the foresight to design himself an impressive memorial in the cemetery (open 10am-7pm daily) of the handsome old village of **Roquebrune**, which rises above Cap-Martin. It started life in the tenth century as a fortified

Carolingian fiefdom, then for five centuries from 1355 belonged to the Grimaldis, before being incorporated into France in 1860. Up steep stairways at the top of the village is the **Château de Roquebrune**, which would have been Disneyfied by its English owner in the 1920s had the locals not kicked up a fuss. It has four floors of historical displays, including armour and a dungeon.

For the energetic, the Sentier Massolin is little more than a giant staircase leading from Roquebrune village down to the coast via Carnolès, a popular but much less exclusive seaside suburb that sprawls between the Cap and Menton. It has a bustling shingle beach. There are two more secluded beaches just below Cap-Martin Roquebrune rail station, as well as plenty of tiny paths to the water.

Château de Roquebrune

pl William Ingram (04.93.35.07.22). **Open** *Feb, Mar, Oct* 10am-12.30pm, 2-6pm daily. *Apr-June, Sept* 10am-12.30pm, 2-6.30pm daily. *July, Aug* 10am-12.30pm, 3-7.30pm daily. *Nov-Jan* 10am-12.30pm, 2-5pm daily. **Admission** €3.70; €1.60 7-18s, students; free under-7s. **No credit cards**.

Where to stay & eat

On the water's edge, the **Hôtel Westminster**
(14 av Louis Laurens, 04.93.35.00.68, www.
westminster06.com, closed mid Nov-mid Jan,
except Christmas & New Year, double
€75-€91) is a small, reasonably priced gem,
with glorious views. A secluded shingle cove
lies at the end of a winding path just down the
street. In the thick of the seafront action, the
freshly renovated **Hôtel Reine d'Azur** (29
promenade du Cap-Martin, 04.93.35.76.84,
double €70-€82) has modest rooms and its own
gravelly garden – ask for a room with a balcony
facing the sea. On the eastern tip of Cap-Martin
is the friendly, modern **Hôtel Alexandra** (93
av Winston Churchill, 04.93.35.65.45,
www.hotel-alexandra.net, double €60-€112),
where most rooms have Jacuzzi baths and
balconies with views towards the bay of
Menton and Italy. In Roquebrune village,
Au Grand Inquisiteur (18 rue du Château,
04.93.35.05.37, closed Mon, Tue & July, menus
€24-€37) serves up gastronomic beef and fish
dishes. For a breathtaking sea view, dine on the
terrace of the **Hôtel-Restaurant des Deux-
Frères** (pl des Deux Frères, 04.93.28.99.00,
www.lesdeuxfreres.com, closed mid Nov-mid
Dec, double €75-€110), an adorable ten-room
hotel at the foot of the *vieux village*. Its elegant
restaurant (closed Mon, lunch Tue & dinner
Sun, menus €24-€45) serves provençal cuisine
with an international twist (perhaps John Dory
with Colombo spices, coconut and wild rice) and
the small rooms, some with sea views, are
exquisitely romantic – two apartments are also
available in the village. The neighbouring
tearoom **Fraise et Chocolat** (06.67.08.32.20),
adorned with children's drawings, is a fine
choice: kids love the giant strawberry
marshmallows. Across the square, atmospheric,
troglodyte café **La Grotte** (3 pl des Deux
Frères, 04.93.35.00.04, closed Wed) offers
salads, plats du jour and pretty good pizza.

Resources

Tourist information

*Office de Tourisme, 218 av Aristide Briand,
Carnolès, 06190 Roquebrune (04.93.35.62.87/
www.roquebrune.com). Open July, Aug 9am-7.30pm
daily. Sept-June 9am-12.30pm, 2-6pm Mon-Sat.*

Menton

Menton's famously mild climate has brought
forth two crops in abundance: lemon trees and
the elderly invalids. One fortnight each
February the latter watch the former being
juiced, iced, painted on plates and amassed in
gigantic kitsch floats for the Fête du Citron
– in such quantities that the low level of prized
local production has to be enhanced by cheap
imports from Spain. The town's festive calendar
otherwise extends to a street theatre and young
musicians' fair in May, classical music evenings
in July, the prestigious Festival de Musique
every August and a Mediterranean garden
event in mid-September. The streets feel sedate
even in high season, except for the lively
pedestrian rue St-Michel, which attracts the
hordes with its sunny café terraces, ice-cream
shops and lurid soaps.

After more than six centuries of Monégasque
domination, Menton voted to become French in
1860. In the same year, British physician Henry
Bennet recommended Menton for its healthy
air. Before long, wealthy Britons and Russians
began gracing its shores, bringing tearooms
and botanical gardens, and staying in grand
belle époque hotels, now sadly demolished or
turned into flats. Writers, artists and musicians
– among them Monet, Maupassant, Flaubert
and Liszt – also sojourned here. The sea air
wasn't always restorative, however. TB
sufferers Robert Louis Stevenson (who
discovered opium in Menton) and Katherine
Mansfield, in her tiny villa Isola Bella, found
the seaside dampness worsened their condition.

The tone of present-day Menton is still set by
its dilapidated belle époque villas. But there's
modernity too: artist-aesthete-poet Jean Cocteau
left his mark, as did architect-designer Eileen
Gray, whose minuscule 1930s cube-house is
visible on the route de Castellar.

Menton has few nocturnal hotspots, and even
the gambling at the **Casino** is low-key. Year-
round, however, smartly dressed Italians stroll
the seafront promenade du Soleil, scooping up
fruit in the excellent covered market behind the
quays (you'll find the best produce outdoors,
where the market gardeners are clustered), or
sunbathe topless on the pebbly beach. Indeed,
border-hopping is a favourite pastime, with
many Italian workers commuting into France
daily and Mentonnais heading into Italy for
bargains at the Ventimiglia market each Friday
or to load up on olive oil, Italian wine and
parmesan at the supermarket.

The **Musée des Beaux-Arts** in the Palais
Carnolès, the 18th-century summer retreat for
the Princes of Monaco, has European paintings
ranging from Italian primitives and a beautiful
Virgin and Child by Louis Bréa to modern
artists including Graham Sutherland.
The palace is surrounded by the Jardin des
Agrumes, an extravaganza of 400 citrus trees.

Just north towards Gorbio, the Eglise Russe
(12 rue Paul Morillot, 04.93.35.70.57; services
5pm Sat, 10am Sun) is worth a look.

Casino de Menton

av Félix Faure (04.92.10.16.16). **Open** *Slot machines* 10am-3am daily. *Salle de jeux* 8pm-3am Mon-Fri, from 5pm Sat, Sun. **Admission** (over-18s only; bring ID) *Slot machines* free. *Salle de jeux* €10. **Credit** AmEx, MC, V.

Musée des Beaux-Arts

Palais Carnolès, 3 av de la Madone (04.93.35.49.71). **Open** 10am-noon, 2-6pm Mon, Wed-Sun. **Admission** free.

Where to stay & eat

The belle époque **Hôtel Aiglon** (7 av de la Madone, 04.93.57.55.55, www.hotelaiglon.net, closed late Nov-mid Dec, double €86-€205, menu €29.90), set back from the beach towards Carnolès, is the epitome of old Riviera charm. It has a garden with towering banana palms, rooms with frescoes and a pool. **Hôtel des Ambassadeurs** (3 rue des Partouneaux, 04.93.28.75.75, double €330-€490, lunch menu €35, dinner menu €75) is a mini palace with a central location, grand entrance and vast bedrooms. An Alain Ducasse-trained chef has recently taken over the restaurant, making it Menton's finest gastronomic address. The charming **Hôtel Paris-Rome** (79 av de la Porte de France, 04.93.35.70.35, closed Nov & Dec, double €67-€89) faces Garavan Bay, a 15-minute walk from the old town. It has been owned by the same family since 1908 and now houses the best-value restaurant in town (closed Mon): prix-fixe menus at €24 (lunch) and €34 (dinner) consist of sophisticated south-west-inspired cuisine (roast lobster with apple rémoulade, foie gras cream and rocket). Looking over the sea in Garavan, the recently renovated **Hôtel Napoléon** (29 av de la Porte de France, 04.93.35.89.50, double €84-€219) targets a clientele that hasn't yet reached retirement with modern furniture, bright colour schemes, high-speed Wi-Fi internet access in every room, an outdoor swimming pool, a fitness room and – to reward yourself after exertions – an ice-cream parlour where sundaes are sold by weight. Every room has a furnished balcony. The vintage 1950s lobby of **Hôtel Moderne** (1 cours Georges V, 04.93.57.20.02, double €55-€70), just minutes from the train station, would look at home in a gallery, but the rooms are really quite plainly furnished – they do have balconies, though.

In the heart of the old town, stone-vaulted **Braijade Meridiounale** (66 rue Longue, 04.93.35.65.65, closed lunch July & Aug, Tue Sept-June, menus €25-€42) is a favourite for local specialities, such as tripe, aïoli or brochettes grilled over an open fire; it may be closing temporarily for renovations, so be sure

to call ahead. Highly recommended **Pistou** (9 quai Gordon Bennett, 04.93.57.45.89, closed Mon, menu €14.10) sits on the Vieux Port overlooking the Plage des Sablettes. It specialises in shellfish, bouillabaisse and paella. **La Coquille d'Or** (1 quai Bonaparte, 04.93.35.80.67, closed Tue, 1st 2wks Nov, average €40) serves excellent provençal-style seafood in glitzy surroundings. Looking a bit shabby from the outside but full of food-loving seniors within is the Italian-run **Restaurant Angelo** (15 av de Verdon, 04.92.41.06.12, closed 1st wk July, menus €21-€28), near the Casino. Here grilled fish and delicious seafood pasta dishes are served on square plates; bouillabaisse is available for €27 per person (at least two people). Newcomer **Torréfaction Noailles** (15 av Félix Faure, 04.93.78.28.56) serves a selection of tasty coffees made with freshly roasted beans.

Resources

Internet access

Café des Arts, 16 rue de la République (04.93. 35.78.67). **Open** 7.30-11am, 2.30-10pm Mon-Sat.

Tourist information

Office de Tourisme *Palais de l'Europe, 8 av Boyer, 06500 Menton (04.92.41.76.76/www.ville dementon.com).* **Open** *Mid June-mid Sept* 9am-7pm daily. *Mid Sept-mid June* 8.30am-12.30pm, 2-6pm Mon-Sat; 9am-12.30pm Sun.
Service du Patrimoine *Hôtel d'Adhémar de Lantagnac, 24 rue St-Michel (04.92.10.97.10).* **Open** 10am-12.30pm, 1.30-6pm Tue-Sat.

Getting there

By bus

RCA Menton (08.20.42.33.33) runs a regular daily service from Menton's *gare routière* (next to the train station) along the Basse Corniche to Nice, stopping at Carnolès, Roquebrune and Monaco, and hourly shuttle buses from Carnolès to Roquebrune village.

By car

Leave the A8 at exit 58 and follow the Grande Corniche down to Roquebrune, exit 59 for Menton (last exit before Italy), or one of the three Corniches from Nice. Gorbio is 9km (5.5 miles) north-west of Roquebrune-Cap-Martin on the narrow D23. For Ste-Agnès, take rte des Castagnins from Menton, which becomes the D22 (13km/8 miles). Castillon is 10km (6 miles) up the D2566 Sospel road from Menton. Castellar is 6km (4 miles) up the D24.

By train

Local trains on the Nice–Ventimiglia line stop at Roquebrune-Cap-Martin (just before the headland), Carnolès (just beyond), Menton and Menton-Garavan stations. There are also daily TGV connections between Paris and Menton.

The Riviera & Southern Alps

Grasse & the Gorges du Loup

Good scents made the fortune of this town, and it's still the place for a whiff of the perfume industry before branching out into the wilds.

Grasse

Perfume may have made Grasse, but the forward-thinking town seems happy to splash around more than just eau de toilette to bring in the tourist trade. In 2004 the train linking Grasse to Cannes and the rest of the Côte d'Azur was finally put back on track, reigniting interest in a town often written off as a day trip for factory discounts. Now a mere 20 minutes from the sea, Grasse is on the up and up: savvy investors are snapping up real estate to meet an increasing demand for authentic pieds-à-terre. Coupled with recent cultural subsidies, this has created an atmosphere of optimism and excitement around town, yet – unlike picture-perfect Valbonne (*see p298*) and Mougins – Grasse's town centre seems determined to hang on to its earthy charm: children play in the streets, washing hangs from the windows and men of all ages loiter in tiny squares sipping *pastis* and playing *pétanque*.

Grasse was already of interest in the days of Catherine de Medici, who decided that its balmy microclimate and the reputation of its tanning industry made it ideal for turning out perfumed gloves – the must-have for every Renaissance it girl. When gloves went out of fashion, the Grassois continued to make perfume, perfecting the art until the cosmetic world sat up and took notice. The town still boasts easily toured factories that now extract their precious floral essences for the likes of Dior, Chanel and Yves Saint Laurent. Just a few decades ago the fields of the Plan de Grasse were filled with flowers ready for harvest, but these days the view of the valley is less romantic and fragrant, with more factories than lavender or freesias. Still, Grasse retains plenty of old-world charm: steep staircases with hidden doorways jostle for space with the tacky glitz of the boulevard du Jeu de Ballon, which climbs up past the municipal casino. Much of the old town is pedestrianised, although some roads that are apparently open to traffic are so narrow they hardly look wide enough to accommodate anything larger than a pushchair.

Musée International de la Parfumerie. *See p295.*

Cours Honoré Cresp, the main square, is home to a cluster of museums (park underneath the square and continue on foot to avoid traffic jams). The **Musée International de la Parfumerie** provides a useful, though not always easy to understand, introduction to the area's chief industry. Exhibits include perfume bottles from antiquity and Dior's 1947 New Look Bar Suit. The most interesting bit is easily missed: in a greenhouse on the roof you can smell different plants and herbs. Closed in late 2004 for an ambitious two-year renovation project, the museum now displays part of its collection across the street at the **Musée d'Art et d'Histoire de Provence**, a museum giving an insight into the lives of the 19th-century provençal bourgeoisie. Almost opposite, in the

The sunny streets of **Grasse**. See p293.

18th-century Hôtel Pontevès-Morel, is the **Musée de la Marine**, dedicated to Admiral François Joseph Paul (1722-88), Count of Grasse, whose defence of Chesapeake Bay during the siege of Yorktown helped bring the American War of Independence to an end. From here, wander down through the touristy shops of rue Jean Ossola where the collection of the **Musée Provençal du Costume et du Bijou** is housed in the magnificent 18th-century home of the Marquise de Clapiers-Cabris, sister of flamboyant Revolutionary politician Mirabeau. Then turn right down rue Gazan into place du Petit Puy. The square is dominated by the Cathédrale Notre-Dame-du-Puy, a prime piece of Lombard-influenced Romanesque, mauled in the 17th and 18th centuries. In its right aisle are several paintings by a young Rubens; it also houses *The Washing of the Disciples' Feet*, a rare religious subject by local boy Fragonard.

Head down the steps to the side of the Hôtel de Ville towards the place des Herbes, once Grasse's herb and vegetable market. Then head up rue Droite (very crooked, despite its name), passing the Maison Doria de Roberti at No.24, which has a remarkable Renaissance stairwell. At the top look out for the portal and Gothic window of the old Oratory Chapel, incorporated into the façade of Monoprix. Turn left here and

head for cobbled place aux Aires, with its lovely three-tiered fountain and street cafés. Every morning except Monday, the square hosts a flower and fresh produce market.

At the far end of the *jardin public* from the perfume museum stands the **Villa-Musée Fragonard**, an elegant 17th-century country house where artist Jean-Honoré Fragonard (1732-1806) sought refuge from the Revolutionary powers. The son of a not particularly successful glove-maker, Fragonard took himself to Paris. There, he offered to Louis XV's favourite, the Comtesse du Barry, five paintings representing the steps of amorous conquest; Fragonard's chocolate-box works were soon all the rage, but they were little liked by the children of the Revolution who, after all, decapitated most of his clients. The villa has sketches and etchings, plus trompe l'oeil murals by Fragonard's 13-year-old son.

Grasse's three big perfume houses (**Parfumeries Fragonard**, **Galimard** and **Molinard**) all offer factory tours, letting you see the distilling and blending process. Fragonard's Historic Factory, dating to 1782, is in the centre of town and has a collection of stills and perfume bottles upstairs. Its modern Fabrique des Fleurs, opened in 1986, is where perfumes are made today. At Galimard's Studio

The Var

des Fragrances, you can take an initiation course and, under the advice of Le Nez, mix up your own fabulous creation, to be funnelled into a charming glass bottle. The flowers at the heart of Grasse's perfume success are celebrated in the Expo-Rose in May and the Jasmine Festival on the first weekend of August. At other times of year head to the Jardin de la Princesse Pauline on avenue Thiers, which has spectacular views among jasmine, roses and other aromatic plants. Further out in nearby Plascassier, the plants of the **Domaine de Manon** find their way into Chanel No.5, Guerlain's Jardin de Bagatelle and Patou's Joy.

If you've had enough of perfumeries, another good buy is olive oil. After a decline following World War II, olive cultivation is on the increase and the local *olive de Nice* has been awarded an *appellation d'origine contrôlée*. On the outskirts of Grasse, try the Moulin à Huile Conti (138 rte de Draguignan, 04.93.70.21.42, closed Sun, Mon Feb-Oct). The shop is open year round, but the mill is in action only during pressing season (Nov-Jan).

If all this shopping is making you itch, head for a swim to the Olympic-sized pool at Espace Culturelle Altitude 500 (57 rte Napoléon, 04.93.36.35.64, open July & Aug), which offers breathtaking views and is less crowded than the beaches below.

Domaine de Manon

36 chemin du Servan, Plascassier (04.93.60.12.76/ www.domaine-manon.com). **Open** *May-mid June* (roses) 2-5pm daily. *Aug-Oct* (jasmine) 8-10am daily. **Admission** €6; free under-12s. **No credit cards.**

Musée d'Art et d'Histoire de Provence

2 rue Mirabeau (04.93.36.80.20/www.museesde grasse.com). **Open** *June-Sept* 10am-12.30pm, 1.30-6.30pm daily. *Oct, Dec-May* 10am-12.30pm, 2.5.30pm Mon, Wed-Sun. Closed Nov. **Admission** €3-€4; €1.50-€2 10-16s; free under-10s. **Credit** MC, V.

Musée de la Marine

2 bd du Jeu de Ballon (04.93.40.11.11). **Open** 10am-noon, 2-5pm Mon-Fri. **Admission** €3; €2.20 students; €1.50 12-18s; free under-12s. **No credit cards.**

Musée International de la Parfumerie

8 pl du cours Honoré Cresp (04.93.36.80.20/www. museesdegrasse.com). **Open** *June-Sept* 10am-7pm daily. *Oct-May* 10am-12.30pm, 2-5pm Mon, Wed-Sun. **Admission** €3-€4; €1.50-€2 10-16s; free under-10s. **No credit cards.**

Musée Provençal du Costume et du Bijou

2 rue Jean Ossola (04.93.36.44.65/www.fragonard. com). **Open** *Feb-Oct* 9am-6pm daily. *Nov-Jan* 9am-12.30pm, 2-6pm daily. **Admission** free.

Parfumerie Fragonard

Historic Factory *20 bd Fragonard (04.93.36.44.65/www.fragonard.com).* **Fabrique des Fleurs** *Les Quatre Chemins, 17 rte de Cannes (04.93.77.94.30).* **Open** *Feb-Oct* 9am-6.30pm daily. *Nov-Jan* 9am-12.30pm, 2-6pm daily. **Admission** free.

Parfumerie Galimard

Factory *73 rte de Cannes (04.93.09.20.00/ www.galimard.com).* **Open** *May-Oct* 9am-6.30pm daily. *Nov-Apr* 9am-noon, 2-6pm Mon-Sat. **Admission** free.
Studio des Fragrances *rte de Pégonas.* **Open** by appointment. **Admission** €35. **Credit** AmEx, MC, V.

Parfumerie Molinard

60 bd Victor Hugo (04.93.36.01.62/www.molinard. com). **Open** *Apr-Sept* 9am-6.30pm daily. *Oct-Mar* 9am-12.30pm, 2-6pm Mon-Sat. Visits finish 1hr before closing. **Admission** free.

Villa-Musée Fragonard

23 bd Fragonard (04.97.05.58.00/www.museesde grasse.com). **Open** *June-Sept* 10am-6.30pm daily. *Oct, Dec-May* 10am-12.30pm, 2-5.30pm Mon, Wed-Sun. Closed Nov. **Admission** €3-€4; €1.50-€2 10-16s, students; free under-10s. **Credit** MC, V.

Where to stay & eat

Without question Jacques Chibois is one of the hottest chefs on the Riviera. His **Bastide St-Antoine** (48 av Henri Dunant, www.jacques-chibois.com, 04.93.70.94.94, double €235-€650, lunch menu €53, dinner menu €130-€170) serves exquisite food (truffles are a speciality) and has near-perfect service. Set in a century-old olive grove below Grasse, it has 11 elegant rooms that look over the greens; expansion plans are in the works. Located unhappily close to the *gare routière*, **Café Arnaud** (10 pl de la Foux, 04.93.36.44.88, open Fri & Sat, lunch Mon-Thur, menus €14-€17) is one of the oldest restaurants in Grasse. Original thinking and consistently good food has made cosy **Le Gazan** (3 rue Gazan, 04.93.36.22.88, menus €16-€26) an institution. **La Voûte** (3 rue du Thouron, 04.93.36.11.43, menus €22-€25) draws lots of locals for its provençal specialities and French classics; from April to October it opens a lively outdoor annexe, Côté Place. **Le Moulin des Paroirs** (7 av Jean XXIII, 04.93.40.10.40, reservations necessary Sat & Sun, closed end Sept-mid Oct, menus €16-€58) serves a superbly tender pigeon à la royale in a candlelit, converted olive mill. Good curry – curry period – is rare on the Côte d'Azur: those with a craving should try **Le Punjab** (3 rue Fabreries, 04.93.36.16.03, menus €19-€26.50). **Le Perchoir** in the Casino de Grasse (bd Jeu de Ballon, 04.93.36.91.00, www.casino-grasse.com, dinner only, closed Mon & Tue Oct-June, menu €28) has a certain Vegas style and a huge upstairs terrace; have a drink in the kitsch **Lounge Bar**, before heading into the casino (bring your passport as ID). The **Clos des Cypres** (87 chemin de Canebiers, 04.93.40.44.23, double €99-€125) is a lovely five-room, 19th-century villa set in good acreage of pine, olive and cypress trees. South-west Grasse has the delightful **Bastide Saint-Mathieu** (35 chemin Blumental, 04.97.01.10.00, www.hotel-bastide-saint-mathieu-grasse.cote.azur.fr, double €270-€340), dating to the 18th century but with all modern comforts. Near Auribeau-sur-Siagne, a short drive out of town, **Moulin du Sault** (rte de Cannes, Moulin Vieux, 04.93.42.25.42, closed Mon, dinner Sun, menus €28-€46) is perfect for a special occasion, thanks to its stunning terrace, mill stream and wheel, and superb food. Five minutes on foot up the route Napoléon towards Digne, the **Hôtel Sainte Thérèse** (39 av Yves Emmanuel Baudoin, 04.93.36.10.29, www.hotelsainte therese.com, double €60-€68) is a former Carmelite hospice. Rooms are basic, but the terrace has sea views. There are more great views at the quiet, out-of-the-way **Auberge La Tourmaline** (381 rte de Plascassier, 04.93.60.10.08, double €68) and friendly, central **Hôtel des Parfums** (bd Eugène Charabot, 04.92.42.35.35, www.hoteldesparfums.com, double €96-€126), which has a pool and gym. **Hôtel Le Victoria** (7 av Riou Blanquet, 04.93.40.30.30, www.le-victoria-hotel.com, closed Jan, double €52-€79) is a mid-sized hotel with pool, nice gym and reasonable restaurant; plans to renovate are afoot, so call ahead.

Resources

Internet

Le Petit Caboulot, 8 pl de la Foux (04.93.40.16.01). **Open** 8am-7.15pm Mon-Sat. Closed 2wks Sept.

Tourist information

Office de Tourisme, 22 cours Honoré Cresp, 06130 Grasse (04.93.36.66.66/www.grasse-riviera.com). **Open** *July-Sept* 9am-7pm Mon-Sat; 9am-1pm, 2-6pm Sun. *Oct-June* 9am-12.30pm, 2-6pm Mon-Sat.

West of Grasse

A surprising hinterland awaits along the route Napoléon (N85, rte de Digne) north-west out of Grasse: you soon find yourself climbing through impressive, arid mountain scenery. After about 12 kilometres (7.5 miles) you'll find the medieval village of **St-Vallier-de-Thiey**, which sits on the plateau de Caussols, a good vantage point for spotting *bories*, the dry-stone

The **Gorges du Loup**. *See p297.*

igloos once occupied by shepherds. Nearby is the **Souterroscope de Baume Obscure**, where underground waterfalls crash past stalactites and stalagmites. (Bring a sweater, as it's a constant 12°C.) Further north towards Castellane and the Gorges du Verdon (*see p221*) the scenery gradually gets more Alpine, going through pine forests and crossing the 1,054-metre (3,458-foot) Col de Luens pass.

South of St-Vallier towards Cabris are the **Grottes des Audides**. This cave system, inhabited in prehistoric times, was discovered by a shepherd in 1988. In the adjoining Parc Préhistorique, dioramas illustrate the lives of the original inhabitants.

But the richest and most popular village in the area has to be **Cabris**, which boasts a large green on which the anglophone Cabris Cricket Club (www.cabriscricket.com) plays matches. There are numerous cafés and restaurants. Perched above the River Siagne is the larger, unspoiled medieval village of **St-Cézaire-sur-Siagne**, famed for its fantastically preserved architecture and magnificent views. Look out for the Gallo-Roman sarcophagus in the entrance to the 12th-century cemetery chapel. Most visitors come to see the **Grottes de St-Cézaire**. The rust-red stalagmites and stalactites are famous for the variety of their shapes – toadstools, animals, flowers – some of which emit an eerie musical sound when struck.

Grottes des Audides

1606 rte de Cabris (04.93.42.64.15). **Open** *July, Aug* 11am-6pm Tue-Sun. *Sept-June* 2-6pm Wed-Sun. Closed late Aug-early Sept. **Admission** *Caves* €5; €3 4-11s; free under-4s. *Parc Préhistorique* €3; €2.50 4-11s; free under-4s. **No credit cards**.

Grottes de St-Cézaire

9 bd du Puit d'Amon (04.93.60.22.35/www.lesgrottes desaintcezaire.com). **Open** *June, Sept* 10.30am-noon, 2-6pm daily. *July, Aug* 10.30am-6.30pm daily.

Oct 2.30-5pm daily. *Nov, Jan* 2.30-5pm Sun. *Feb, Mar* 2.30-5pm daily. *Apr, May* 2.30-5.30pm daily. Closed Dec. **Admission** €6; €4.50 13-18s; €3 6-12s; free under-6s. **Credit** AmEx, MC, V.

Souterroscope de Baume Obscure

chemin Ste-Anne, St-Vallier-de-Thiey (04.93.42.61.63). **Open** *May-June, Sept* 10am-5pm Mon-Sat; 10am-6pm Sun. *July, Aug* 10am-6pm daily. *Oct-Apr* 10am-5pm Tue-Sun. Closed mid Dec-mid Feb. **Admission** €7.65; €3.80 5-12s; free under-4s. **Credit** MC, V.

Where to stay & eat

In St-Vallier-de-Thiey **Le Relais Impérial** (85 rte Napoléon, 04.92.60.36.36, www.relaisimperial.com, double €41-€73) is cosy and clean; it has a restaurant. **Le Préjoly** (pl Cavalier Fabre, 04.93.60.03.20, closed Jan, double €38-€77) is a welcoming country inn with 17 rooms and a restaurant (04.93.42.60.86, closed Tue evening & Wed in winter, menus €16.50-€24.50) serving high-quality classical cuisine. Towards St-Cézaire **L'Hostellerie des Chênes Blancs** (2020 rte de St-Vallier, 04.93.60.20.09, www.chenes-blancs.com, closed Sept-Apr, double €67-€129) has a pool, tennis courts and restaurant (menus €21.50-€29.50).

In Cabris the charming **Mas du Naoc** (chemin du Migranié, 04.93.60.63.13, www.lemasdunaoc.com, double €100-€120) has plenty of authentic high-end provençal style and lovely hosts. **L'Horizon** (100 promenade St-Jean, 04.93.60.51.69, closed mid Oct-Mar, double €80-€130) has a pool, terrace and renovated bedrooms. **Le Vieux Château** (pl du Panorama, 04.93.60.50.12, www.aubergeduvieuxchateau.com, double €60-€100, restaurant closed Mon, Tue & Jan, lunch menu €24, dinner menu €37) is a charming hotel-restaurant carved out of the old castle, with provençal food and just four double rooms – book well ahead. **Le Petit Prince** (15 rue Frédéric Mistral, 04.93.60.63.14, closed Dec-mid Jan, menus €20-€29) serves a great rabbit with lavender and raspberry vinegar, and has a terrace. **Le Mini Grill** (5 pl du Puits, 04.93.60.55.58, closed lunch Wed, menu €19), with its off-road terrace, is handy for children.

Resources

Tourist infomation

Cabris Office de Tourisme *4 rue Porte Haute, 06530 Cabris (04.93.60.55.63).* **Open** *May-Sept* 9am-12.30pm, 2-5.30pm Mon-Sat. *Oct-Apr* 9am-12.30pm, 1.30-5pm Mon-Sat. Closed Christmas.

St-Cézaire Office de Tourisme *3 rue de la République, 06530 St-Cézaire-sur-Siagne (04.93.60.84.30/www.saintcezairesursiagne.com).* **Open** 10am-noon, 3-6.30pm Tue-Fri; 10am-noon Sat, Sun.

St-Vallier Office de Tourisme *10 pl du Tour, 06460 St-Vallier-de-Thiey (04.93.42.78.00/www.saintvallier.com).* **Open** *Mar-June, Sept, Oct* 9am-noon, 3-6pm Mon-Sat. *July, Aug* 9am-noon, 3-6pm Mon-Sat; 10am-noon Sun. *Nov-Feb* 9am-noon, 3-5pm Mon-Sat.

The Gorges du Loup

The unusual fortified village of **Tourrettes-sur-Loup**, its outer houses forming a rampart, is built on a rocky peak surrounded by precipices. Producing so many violets (celebrated in the Fête des Violettes in early March) it's known as the 'Violet Village', this lovely medieval town has been a mecca for sculptors, potters and painters. Today, there are more than 30 workshops and galleries. The Grand'Rue is lined with earnest (and expensive) shops. There are some handsome altarpieces in the 15th-century church, including scenes from the life of the Virgin, as well as a Bréa triptych. **Confiserie Florian** is a visit for a rainy day; it makes sweets and chocolates flavoured with violets, lemon verbena and citrus using traditional methods. There are tours in English.

Once part of the estate of the Counts de Grasse, **Le Bar-sur-Loup** has all the authentic charm of a well-kept medieval village. The town sits on a hillside surrounded by beds of jasmine, orange trees and violets, its narrow streets winding around a massive 16th-century castle with four corner towers and a ruined keep. The Gothic church of St-Jacques contains a 15th-century altarpiece, as well as a famous *danse macabre*, portraying tiny courtly dancers being shot by Death, judged unworthy by St Michael and hurled into hell. When he's in the area, a less saintly Michael (Schumacher) takes a spin at **Fun Kart** (plateau de la Sarée, rte de Gourdon, 04.93.42.48.08, www.fun-karting.com).

Tortuous bends and overhanging cliffs, accompanied by the sound of crashing waterfalls, lead you into the Gorges du Loup. Canyoning is dangerous, so organise a private guide: Destination Nature (69 rue Georges Clemenceau, La Colle-sur-Loup, 04.93.32.06.93, www.loisirs-explorer.com/destination-nature) is affordable and reliable. Qualified guides organise half- to two-day canyoning trips, as well as mountain hiking. If you are experienced enough to do it on your own, consult *Les Guides Randoxygène* at tourist offices. Along the D6, amid lush vegetation, a huge monolith marks

The Riviera & Southern Alps

the entrance to the spectacular Saut du Loup. The waters of the Loup swirl furiously through this enormous, eroded cauldron, gushing down through vegetation petrified by the lime carbonate of the spray.

Perched between Grasse and the Loup Valley lies **Gourdon**, a medieval citadel that kept watch against marauding Saracens. The 13th-century **Château de Gourdon** blends French and Italian Romanesque influences and has gardens laid out by André Le Nôtre in the 17th century. It houses the Musée Historique (the usual weaponry and torture implements, plus a Rembrandt and a Rubens) and the Musée de la Peinture Naïve (Douanier Rousseau-type daubs and one example of the real thing).

Château de Gourdon

Gourdon (04.93.09.68.02). **Open** *June-Sept* 11am-1pm, 2-7pm daily. *Oct-May* 2-6pm Mon, Wed-Sun. **Admission** €4; €3 12-16s, students; free under-12s. **No credit cards**.

Confiserie Florian

Pont du Loup, Tourrettes-sur-Loup (04.93.59.32.91). **Open** *July, Aug* 9am-6.30pm daily. *Sept-June* 9am-noon, 2-6.30pm daily. **Admission** free.

Where to stay & eat

In Tourrettes-sur-Loup **Chez Grande Mère** (pl Maximin Escalier, 04.93.59.33.34, closed Wed, lunch Sat, Nov-mid Dec, menus €17-€22) has a cosy fire and makes fabulous lentil soup.

Bacchanales (21 Grand'Rue, 04.93.24.19.19, closed Tue, Wed, early Dec, mid Jan-Feb, menus €35-€48) is a local favourite for traditional provençal dishes, and has a great vegetarian selection. **Le Mas des Cigales** (1673 rte des Quenières, 04.93.59.25.73, double €72-€92) is a lovely bed and breakfast with pool and tennis courts. **Relais des Coches** (28 rte de Vence, 04.93.24.30.24, closed Mon & Tue, Jan, lunch July & Aug, open dinner daily July & Aug, menu €38) offers traditional French fare, and Sunday roast cooked by a Yorkshire chef (noon-6pm, €25). The **Auberge de Tourrettes** (11 rte de Grasse, 04.93.59.30.05, www.aubergedetourrettes.fr, closed Jan & Feb, double €112-€130) has six cosy rooms, a lovely terrace and an excellent restaurant (menu €45).

Restaurants are few and far between in Le Bar: try **La Jarrerie** (av Amiral de Grasse, 04.93.42.92.92, closed Tue, lunch Wed, Jan, menus €25-€45) for hearty provençal fare. In Gourdon the **Auberge de Gourdon** (04.93.09.69.69, menus €16.50-€20.50) is a bar-tabac-restaurant with local charm, heavy provençal accents and simple, honest dishes. **Le Mas au Loup** (1389 ancienne rte Vence Grasse, 04.93.59.32.68, www.lemasauloup.com,

double €60-€75) has two cosy rooms and lovely views. If you have a tent, the **Camping Rives du Loup** (2666B rte de la Colle, pont du Loup, 04.93.24.15.65, 2-person tent €13.50-€17.50, large tent/caravan €18.50-€22.50) is a well-organised site in a lovely setting.

Resources

Tourist information

Le Bar Office de Tourisme *pl Francis Paulet, 06620 Le Bar-sur-Loup (04.93.42.72.21/www.bar-sur-loup.com).* **Open** *Apr-June, Sept* 3-6pm Mon; 10am-1pm, 3-6pm Tue-Fri; 10am-1pm Sat. *July, Aug* 10am-1pm, 3-7pm Tue-Sun. *Oct-Mar* 9.30am-noon, 3-5pm Tue-Fri; 3-6pm Mon; 10am-1pm Sat.
Gourdon Syndicat d'Initiative *pl Victoria, 06620 Gourdon (04.93.09.68.25/www.gourdon-france.com).* **Open** *July, Aug* 9.30am-1pm, 3-7pm. *Sept-June* 10.30am-1pm, 2-6pm daily.
Tourrettes-sur-Loup Office de Tourisme *2 pl de la Libération, 06140 Tourrettes-sur-Loup (04.93.24.18.93/www.tourrettessurloup.com).* **Open** *Mid Sept-mid June* 9.30am-6.30pm Mon-Sat. *Mid June-mid Sept* 9.30am-6.30pm daily.

Valbonne was planned on a chequerboard design in the 17th century by the monks of Lérins, clearly inspired by the plans of Roman towns, as part of a bid by Augustin de Grimaldi, Bishop of Grasse, to repopulate a region devastated by plague. The village is bordered by 'rampart houses' with an entrance gate on each of its four sides. Today it has several glass workshops, notably for perfume flasks. At the heart of the village is place des Arcades, where the Fête du Raisin celebrates the late-ripening servan grape at the end of January. The parish church is part of the former Chalaisian Abbey and is in the form of a Latin cross with a square chevet. The abbey, under restoration, contains the small **Musée des Arts et Traditions Populaires**.

In the shadow of Valbonne lies **Sophia-Antipolis** (www.saem-sophia-antipolis.fr), a 150 square-kilometre (58 square-mile) bid for high-tech prestige, where 20,000 people from more than 60 countries work in R&D-intensive companies, keeping the already high property prices in the area bubbling over. Work on this perfectly landscaped, perfectly soulless science park – the 'Milton Keynes of the Riviera' – began in 1969; today 1,300 companies share the site.

South-west of Valbonne, **Mouans-Sartoux** attracts contemporary art pilgrims. The Renaissance château was converted into the **Espace de l'Art Concret** in 1990 by artist Gottfried Honegger. The permanent collection

Valbonne. *See p298.*

includes works by Honegger, Albers, André, LeWitt and Morellet, exhibited along with three- or four-month themed shows dedicated to geometrical abstraction and minimalist art.

Espace de l'Art Concret

Château de Mouans-Sartoux (04.93.75.71.50). **Open** *July, Aug* 11am-7pm daily. *Sept-June* 11am-6pm Tue-Sun. **Admission** €3; €1.50 12-18s, students; free under-12s. **No credit cards**.

Musée des Arts et Traditions Populaires

rue Paroisse, Valbonne (04.93.12.96.54). **Open** *May-Sept* 3-7pm Thur-Sun. Closed Oct-Apr. **Admission** €2; €1 12-18s. **No credit cards**.

Where to stay & eat

The **Hôtel Les Armoiries** (pl des Arcades, 04.93.12.90.90, www.hotellesarmoiries.com, double €89-€159) occupies a 17th-century building and its rooms are very comfortable, although some are a little on the small side.

Just outside Valbonne **Château la Bégude** (rte de Roquefort-Les-Pins, 04.93.12.37.00, www.opengolfclub.com, closed mid Nov-mid Dec, double €80-€328) is a lovely restored manor with 34 beautifully decorated rooms and a restaurant (closed dinner Sun Nov-Mar, lunch menu €31, dinner menu €43) with a terrace overlooking the golf course. The **Bastide de Valbonne** (107 rte de Cannes, 04.93.12.33.40, www.bastide-valbonne.com, double €95-€250), with four charming rooms and a large pool, is surrounded by golf courses. The **Bistro de Valbonne** (11 rue de la Fontaine, 04.93.12.05.59, closed Mon lunch, Sun, Thur lunch mid June-mid Sept, Sat lunch mid Sept-mid June, lunch menu €16.80, dinner menus €27-€33) serves French classics and superb smoked wild Baltic salmon. If you like Moroccan food, book a table at low-lit and intimate **La Pigeot** (16 rue Alexis Julien, 04.93.12.17.53, closed lunch June-Sept & late Dec-early Jan, average €35). At **Lou Cigalon** (4-6 bd Carnot, 04.93.12.27.07, closed Mon & Sun, lunch menu €26, dinner menus €34-€65) owner-chef Alain Parodi is getting rave reviews for his modern spin on provençal cuisine.

Resources

Tourist information

Valbonne Office de Tourisme *1 pl de l'Hôtel de Ville, 06560 Valbonne (04.93.12.34.50).* **Open** *Mid June-mid Sept* 9am-12.30pm, 1.30-5.30pm Mon-Sat. *Mid Sept-mid June* 9am-12.30pm, 1.30-5.30pm Mon-Fri; 9am-12.30pm Sat.

Getting there & around

By bus

Rapides Côte d'Azur (04.93.36.08.43) runs buses daily between Grasse and Cannes, Nice airport, Vence, Grasse and St-Cézaire, some of which stop at Cabris, and between Grasse and St-Vallier-de-Thiey (Mon-Sat). For the Gorges du Loup, take No.511 from Grasse to Pont du Loup. **TACAVL** (04.93.42.40.79) operates several services (Mon-Sat) between Grasse and Le Bar-sur-Loup. **STCAR** (04.93.12.00.12) No.3VB runs from Cannes direct to Valbonne about every hour (less on Sun) and the No.5VB (four buses Mon-Fri) goes via Sophia-Antipolis. **Sillages** (04.92.28.58.68, www.sillages-stga.tm.fr) also runs buses in the area.

By car

The N85 (route Napoléon) is a dual carriageway between Cannes and Grasse, continuing towards Digne via St-Vallier-de-Thiey. From Nice take the D2085 at Cagnes towards Le Bar-sur-Loup and Grasse. For Cabris, take the D4 out of Grasse, then the D13 to St-Cézaire. The D2210 winds from Vence towards Grasse via Tourrettes-sur-Loup and Le Bar, with side roads turning off up the Gorges du Loup.

The Riviera & Southern Alps

Vence & St-Paul

Home of Matisse's masterpiece and the final resting places of Lawrence and Chagall, arty Vence and St-Paul are the cultural hotspots of the Côte d'Azur.

Vence

A Ligurian tribe was already calling this part of France home long before the Emperor Augustus and his jack-sandalled hordes marched in and decided to call it Vintium instead. Set in a strategic position ten kilometres (six miles) back from the sea, Vence was a bishopric from the fourth to 19th centuries, and boasts two patron saints. The first was fifth-century bishop Véran, who organised the town's defences against Visigoth invaders (though Saracens would later succeed where the Barbarians had failed, razing the cathedral and much of Vence to the ground). The second, 12th-century bishop Lambert, defended the town's rights against its rapacious new baron, Romée de Villeneuve, setting a trend of rivalry between nobility and clergy that was to last until the bishopric was dissolved after the Revolution. Perhaps Vence's most popular prelate – though this one was never canonised – was 17th-century bishop Antoine Godeau, a gallant dwarf, poet and renowned wit who was a founding member of the Académie Française.

In the 1920s Vence became a popular pit stop for artists and writers, including Paul Valéry, André Gide and DH Lawrence, who died here in 1930. A simple plaque in Vence cemetery marks the place where Lawrence lay for five years before he was cremated at the behest of his widow and his ashes shipped to Taos, New Mexico. However, Frieda Lawrence's lover, Ravagli, who was entrusted with the task, apparently boasted that he had dumped the ashes somewhere between Marseille and Villefranche to save himself the trouble.

Walls still encircle some of the medieval *vieille ville*, which manages to retain its old-world feel despite the modern sprawl outside. The boulevard Paul André follows the old ramparts and offers sweeping views to the Alps. Outside the western Porte Peyra, one of five original town gates, place du Frêne is named after its giant ash tree planted to commemorate Pope Paul III's visit to Vence in 1538. The gate leads into place Peyra, site of the Roman forum. Between the two squares, the 17th-century **Château de Villeneuve** was the long-time residence of the Lords of Villeneuve, Provence and Vence. The **Fondation Emile**

Hugues is now located within the château, and organises two major types of art exhibitions. The first focuses on major modern artists who visited or resided in Vence, such as Matisse and Chagall; the second is a general multimedia exploration of contemporary art. It also includes a small but well-stocked gift shop selling information and books about the exhibitions and the chateau itself.

At the centre of the *vieille ville*, the **Ancienne Cathédrale Notre-Dame-de-la-Nativité** (open 9am-6pm daily) has been constructed over a Roman temple of Mars. A column of this temple is visible from place Godeau. In the fourth century the first Christian church was built on this site – eventual destructionsled to the present construction. Recent renovations were attempted in 1988 by 477 volunteers; however, the project remains incomplete due to a typically Mediterranean bureaucratic glitch. The Cathédrale's Roman origins can be seen in inscriptions worked into the baroque façade on place Clemenceau and in the pre-Christian sarcophagus (third chapel on the right), where St Véran is said to have been buried. A Chagall mosaic of Moses in the waters, created by the artist in 1979, can be viewed on the wall of the baptistery, and some charmingly irreverent 15th-century carvings by Jacques Bellot are located on the choir stalls. The most beautiful corner of the church, to the left of the altar, is the Chapelle du Saint Sacrement. A neat alcove, the chapel features typical Romanic decoration (sculpted Carolingian slabs) and an amazing Gothic wooden door. Place Clemenceau is also the location of Vence market each morning, with stalls selling everything from second-hand clothes to an extensive range of local olives.

The **place du Grand Jardin**, an open, airy square edged with cafés, is located just outside the medieval town, and is the perfect vantage point for watching local *boules* players. Locals wander about on daily business, and it's here that you really get the feeling of being part of Vence. In July tourism seriously picks up for the **Nuits du Sud** (04.93.58.40.17, www.nuitsdu sud.com) music festival with a month of Latin, salsa, jazz and French-Arabic music.

One of the biggest tourist attractions is the **Chapelle du Rosaire**, designed by Matisse as a gift of thanks to the Dominican nuns who cared for him. It is one of the most exquisite and significant pieces of 20th-century art work on the coast. Matisse himself called it 'the culmination of a whole life dedicated to the search for truth.' A fifteen-minute walk (extremely well marked from the western Porte Peyra) or a five-minute train ride (€4.50 return per person – ask in the tourist office), the roads leading to the Chapelle, and the views from them, are breathtakingly beautiful. South-west of town, located on 3.5 hectares (nine acres) of land, **NALL (Nature, Art & Life League) Art Association** is comprised of ten studios where artists, including painters, sculptors, writers and musicians, live and work. Art students also work as assistants to Nall, the artist-founder. Within the house, which was designed and built by Nall, the mosaics and international objects collected on his journeys reflect the eccentric nature of the man.

Also of interest to art fans is the **Galerie Beaubourg**. Originally based in Paris, Marianne and Pierre Nahon moved their gallery to just west of Vence, on the road to Grasse, 20 years ago. The concept of this (by-appointment only) gallery is 'modest art'; the art works featured in the collection are defined as affordable and accessible to everyone. Incorporating indoor and outdoor exhibition spaces, the gardens surrounding the gallery are dotted with enormous bronze sculptures, with pieces by Niki de Saint Phalle, Arman and Julian Schnabel. These art works act as a preview to the extensive contemporary collection located within the chateau itself. The pièce de résistance is the Jean Tinguely chapel, featuring his weird and wonderful *Grande Odalisque*. The gallery and gift shop, with art works for sale, are no longer located on the Galerie premises, but in the centre of Vence.

To the north-east of Vence, St-Jeannet is a wine-producing village dominated by the dramatic rock outcrop known as Le Baou, which can be ascended by a waymarked path. La Gaude (15 kilometres, or nine miles, east of Vence) is comparatively dull, but is nonetheless a well-preserved and friendly little perched village dating from 189 BC. It's also a good place to start a walking tour of the surrounding countryside: there are six marked walks, the one to Vence taking an hour and ten minutes, and the one to Le Baou an hour and a half. The tourist office has maps.

Chapelle du Rosaire

466 av Henri Matisse, Vence (04.93.58.21.10). **Open** 10-11.30am, 2-5.30pm Tue, Thur; 2-5.30pm Mon, Wed, Sat (2-5.30pm Fri during school holidays); mass 10am Sun. Closed mid Nov-mid Dec. **Admission** €2.50; €1 6-16s; free under-6s. **No credit cards**.

Château de Villeneuve Fondation Emile Hugues (Art Moderne et Contemporain)

2 pl du Frêne, Vence (04.93.58.15.78). **Open** *July-Oct* 10am-6pm Tue-Sun. *Nov-June* 10am-12.30pm, 2-6pm Tue-Sun. **Admission** €5; €2.50 12-18s; free under-12s. **No credit cards**.

Galerie Beaubourg

Château Notre-Dame des Fleurs, 2618 rte de Grasse, Vence Cedex (04.93.24.52.00). **Open** by appointment only. **Admission** €5; €2.50 12-18s; free under-12s. **No credit cards**.

NALL (Nature, Art & Life League) Art Association

232 bd de Lattre, Vence (04.93.58.13.26/www.nall. org). **Open** *May-Sept* 3-6pm Mon, Sat, Sun. Closed Oct-Apr. **Admission** €3. **No credit cards**.

Where to stay & eat

Super-chef and proprietor Jacques Maximin at **Restaurant Jacques Maximin** (689 chemin de La Gaude, Vence, 04.93.58.90.75, www.restaurant-maximin.com, closed dinner Sun, all Mon, mid Nov-mid Dec, menus €40-€95) is a provençal legend, and you'll see why once you tuck into a starter like his salad of artichoke hearts, broad beans, squid, penne and parmesan. It's pricey, but well worth it, whether you eat outside in the lush garden, or inside the chic restaurant itself, which features paintings and sculptures by modern and contemporary artists, such as Arman and César. **La Closerie des Genêts** (4 imp Marcellin Maurel, 04.93.58.33.25, double €37-€58) has ten chintz-draped rooms, a shady garden and a terrace, and is located just outside the old city centre. Recently renovated **Hôtel Miramar** (167 av Bougearel, plateau St-Michel, 04.93.58.01.32, www.hotel-miramar-vence.com, double €77-€152), perched on the eastern edge of Vence, is a delightfully converted ancient manor with pool, terrace and panoramic views of St-Jeannet, the sea and the surrounding hillsides. The centrally located **Hôtel Le Provence** (9 av Marcellin Maurel, 04.93.58.04.21, closed mid Jan-mid Feb, double €39-€67) is cute and centrally located. While slightly out of the centre, the charming **Hôtel Villa Roseraie** (51 av Henri Giraud, 04.93.58.02.20, double €95-€146) has a magnificent garden with pool. An exclusive hotel since 1970, the luxurious **Château du Domaine St-Martin** (av des Templiers, BP 102, Vence, 04.93.58.02.02, www.château-st-martin.com, suites €240-€750) offers elegant accommodation, ranging from junior suites with balconies and sea views to private villas. The hotel also has stunning views and an excellent Italian-influenced restaurant headed up by chef Phillippe Guerin (menus €45-€100). Best of all, you can cut out all those winding roads by availing yourself of the hotel's private helipad. Located on a quiet wooded hill, the **Hôtel Cantemerle** (258 chemin Cantemerle, 04.93.58.08.18, www.hotelcantemerle.com, double €175-€195) offers a selection of spa options, such as shiatsu and Thai massages, as well as aromatherapy and reflexology. Each room has its own private terrace, and the grounds comprise indoor and outdoor pools, a Turkish bath (and a bar and restaurant for the evening retox). **L'Auberge des Templiers** (30 av Joffre, 04.93.58.06.05, www.restaurant-vence.com, closed lunch Mon, Tue & Wed in summer, menus €39-€59) has great mod-Med cuisine cooked up by internationally trained (but Vence-born) chef Stéphane Demichelis and served in the sun-dappled garden in summer. The 15th-century **Auberge des Seigneurs** (pl du Frêne, 04.93.58.04.24, closed mid Nov-mid Dec, double €70-€85) has been an inn since 1895, and is the perfect hotel in which to cosy up during the winter months. Its restaurant specialises in roast meats, such as rib-eye steak and lamb, cooked over a grill in the huge fireplace at one end of the dining room (closed Mon, lunch Tue-Thur, menus €20-€39). Don't miss the incredible antique sink to the right of the entrance, which has been carved from a single piece of marble. In the heart of Vence's *vieille ville*, **Le P'tit Provençal** (4 pl Clemenceau, 04.93.58.50.64, closed Mon, lunch Tue, Nov, late Feb-early Mar, menus €24-€30) offers an absolutely ideal mix of beautiful presentation and exquisite food, and is well worth dedicating a lazy afternoon to. At the nearby **La Terrasse du Clemenceau** (22 pl Clemenceau, 04.93.58.24.70, www.brasserie-clemenceau.com, closed Mon, dinner Sun, 3wks Nov, 2wks Mar, menu €24), local specialities such as *petits farcis*, rabbit and oven-roasted lamb with herbs can be enjoyed on the terrace, beneath enormous shady trees that cover half of the picturesque square. Located in the countryside, on the road to St-Paul-de-Vence, the **Hôtel du Baou** (le plan du Bois, 04.93.59.44.44, www.hotel-baou-la-gaude.cote.azur.fr, double €59-€89) in La Gaude is the perfect starting point for country ramblings – and its pool will be much appreciated when you return.

Resources

Tourist information

La Gaude Syndicat d'Initiative *20 rue Centrale, 06610 La Gaude (04.93.24.47.26/www.mairie-lagaude.fr).* **Open** 9am-12.30pm, 2.30-5.30pm Tue-Fri; 9am-4pm Sat.

St-Jeannet Syndicat d'Initiative *35 rue de la Soucare, 06640 St-Jeannet (04.93.24.73.83/ www.saintjeannet.com).* **Open** *June-Sept* 9am-6pm daily. *Oct-May* 9.30am-noon, 2.30-5pm Tue-Sat.
Vence Office de Tourisme *8 pl du Grand Jardin, 06140 Vence (04.93.58.06.38/www.ville-vence.fr).* **Open** *July-Aug* 9am-7pm Mon-Sat; 9am-1pm Sun. *Sept-June* 9am-6pm Mon-Sat.

St-Paul-de-Vence & La Colle-sur-Loup

St-Paul-de-Vence might have been just another picturesque village, rather than the mega-tourist attraction it's become, if it were not for the many artists who have chosen to reside and create here over the past century. Now a *quartier général* of modern art, it's also home to one of the most important modern art museums in France, the Fondation Maeght.

St-Paul flourished in the Middle Ages thanks to its vines, figs, olives and orange trees, as well as hemp and linen. François I put up the almost-intact ramparts in 1540 after the town helped him beat off arch-enemy, Emperor Charles V. The town went into a decline until the 20th century. Picasso, Matisse, Braque and Dufy were just some of the daubers who pitched up here after World War I, paying for their board and lodging at La Colombe d'Or (*see p304*) with paintings that still adorn the hostelry's walls. In the 1960s art collectors Aimé and Marguerite Maeght created the **Fondation Maeght** for their remarkable private collection.

St-Paul's narrow medieval lanes are filled with day-trippers in high season and lined with bougainvillea, jasmine and geraniums along with hard-sell artists' studios and shops selling antiques, crafts and souvenirs. **Rue Grande**, the main street, is well worth visiting for the fabulously smart foodie shops selling perfectly packaged olive oil and designer chocolates, in between chic boutiques and touristy tack. In the **Eglise Collégiale** on place de la Mairie (open 8am-8pm daily), only the choir remains from the original 12th-century building; later adornments include St Clément's chapel, a masterpiece of baroque stucco, and a painting of St Catherine of Alexandria, attributed to Tintoretto. Sip wine and snack on low-cost local cuisine under the huge shady plane trees at **Café de la Place** (pl de Gaulle, 04.93.28.003), all while observing France's most famous *terrain aux boules*. Celebrities line up to challenge local champions and Japanese players travel huge distances for regional tournaments, but rookies are also welcome (a set of two *boules* can be rented from the tourist office at €5/hr). Walk around the ramparts of the old city walls

Lose yourself in the winding streets of **St-Paul-de-Vence**.

to enjoy panoramic views of the mountains, the sea and the huge number of luxury villas that are sprinkled across the hills of the surrounding countryside. The **Port de Nice** leads to the beautiful **cemetery**, overlooking the Mediterranean, where Chagall is buried (open June-Sept 7.30am-8pm, Oct-May 8am-5pm). In a pinewood forest just north-west of St-Paul, the **Fondation Maeght** is one of the Côte's star attractions, with over 200,000 visitors per year. Opened in 1964, this extraordinary low-slung construction set in grounds bristling with art works was designed by Catalan architect José Luis Sert to house Aimé and Marguerite Maeght's collection of approximately 9,000 art works. The Fondation is a maze, with no fixed route and nothing resembling a hanging plan. Some works do have places of their own, by virtue of being part of the fabric of the place: Giacometti figures in the courtyard; a Miró labyrinth peopled with sculptures and ceramics, including the half-submerged *Egg*; mural mosaics by Chagall and Tal-Coat; the pool and stained-glass window by Braque; Pol Bury's fountain; Calder's bobbing mobiles. But the Fondation's more moveable Braques and Légers, Kandinskys and Mirós, Bonnards and Chagalls disappear into storage to make way for temporary exhibitions, including the annual summer show. Located near the Fondation Maeght, the more commercial **Galerie Guy Pieters** was opened by the Belgian gallery owner in 2000. The gallery exhibits and sells an alternative collection of American pop art and French *nouveau réalisme*, including

Christo, Niki de Saint Phalle, Arman and Robert Indiana. For truly modern art, head into town where the **Galerie Catherine Issert**, established in 1975, exhibits all manner of cutting-edge contemporary works within its spacious white interior.

South-west of St-Paul-de-Vence, unspoiled La Colle-sur-Loup has an attractive 17th-century church, but is best known for antiques. The main drag of antiques shops on rue Yves Klein is open daily (4-6pm), and an antiques market is held every second Sunday of the month. The **Maison des Arts** offers residential art, cooking and 'creative thinking' courses (most popular are its full- or half-day painting courses, available with full board), located within a beautiful 18th-century house. It also exhibits the work of local artists. However, what really puts La Colle on the map is L'Abbaye, a 12th-century monastery that is now a stunning hotel and restaurant (*see p304*).

Fondation Maeght
chemin des Trious (04.93.32.81.63/www. fondation-maeght.com). **Open** *Oct-June* 10am-12.30pm, 2.30-6pm daily. *July-Sept* 10am-7pm daily. **Admission** €11; €9 10-18s; free under-10s. **Credit** AmEx, MC, V.

Galerie Catherine Issert
2 rte des Serres (04.93.32.96.92/www.galerie-issert.com). **Open** 11am-1pm, 3-7pm Mon-Sat.

Galerie Guy Pieters
chemin des Trious (04.93.32.06.46/www.guypietersgallery.com). **Open** *June-Oct* 10am-7pm Mon-Sat. *Nov-May* 10am-1pm, 2-6pm Mon-Sat.

Maison des Arts

*10 rue Maréchal Foch, La Colle-sur-Loup
(04.93.32.32.50/www.maisondesarts.com).*
Art courses €450-€1,000/wk.

Where to stay & eat

Accommodation is expensive in St-Paul, but
the **Hostellerie les Remparts** (72 rue
Grande, 04.93.32.09.88, closed mid Jan-mid Feb,
double €39-€80) in the centre of the *vieille ville*
combines style and value. Six of its nine
charming rooms face the beautiful countryside
to the west, while the other three look over the
old town's winding streets. The Hostellerie
manages two restaurants, the best of which,
Les Remparts de Saint Paul (closed dinner
Sun, all Mon, mid Jan-mid Feb, menu €30), can
be entered from the town's high street and
features a selection of tasty delights such as
beignets de fleurs de courgettes, as well as local
wines, meats and fishes. During the summer,
expect to book two months in advance for a
room, or minimum ten days ahead for a table,
at **La Colombe d'Or** (pl des Ormeaux,
04.93.32.80.02, www.la-colombe-dor.com, closed
late Oct-mid Dec, 2wks Jan, double €270-€330,
half-board €360-€420 per person). The world-
renowned hotel is open only to guests, as are
the treasures left here in lieu of payment by
former clients, including then unknowns like
Picasso, Modigliani, Miró, Matisse and Chagall.
A meal on the celebrated, fig-shaded terrace is
still an occasion, with its combination of earthy
food (average €65) and jet-set clientele. You can
also pick up a copy of the only book about the
history of La Colombe d'Or, on sale in the
frescoed reception area for €53. A deluxe hotel
located in the centre of the town, **Le Saint
Paul** (86 rue Grande, 04.93.32.65.25,
www.lesaintpaul.com, double €210-€580 high
season, closed Jan-mid Feb) is a 16th-century
mansion with a superior restaurant (menu €68),
expertly managed by chef Frederic Buzet.
Comme à la Maison (montée de l'Eglise,
angle rue Grande, 04.93.32.87.81) serves large
salads, toasted sandwiches and the like, as well
as local dishes with an exotic twist, such as foie
gras with rose-petal jelly (average €15). During
the winter months, hot wine with cinnamon
is available to counter the effects of the frosty
wind. Chagall once stayed at the **Hôtel le
Hameau** (528 rte de La Colle, 04.93.32.80.24,
www.le-hameau.com, closed mid Nov-mid
Feb, double €140-€190), where beautiful white
buildings encompass 17 provençal-themed
rooms. The flower-covered terrace is perfect for
breakfast, or lounging by the swimming pool.
La Ferme de St-Paul (1334 rte de La Colle,
04.93.32.82.48, closed lunch Tue & Wed,

average €40) serves fine, classic provençal
cuisine in a converted 18th-century farmhouse.
Designed by the famous architect Fernand
Pouillon and set in an eight-hectare (19-acre)
park with views of the sea, **Le Mas d'Artigny**
(rte de la Colle, 04.93.32.84.54, www.mas-
artigny.com, double €150-€450) has rooms,
self-catering apartments and villas with private
pools and gardens, plus a heated outdoor pool
open year-round. Award-winning chef Francis
Scordel gives the restaurant and its food a
sophisticated air (menus €38-€85). Another
outstanding hotel, and one that's ideal for
celebrity-spotting, is the recently opened **Le
Mas de Pierre** (rte des Serres, 04.93.59.00.10,
www.lemasdepierre.com, double €270-€750),
a silent oasis of tranquillity located in the valley
to the west of St-Paul. The staff, meticulous and
helpful without being invasive, preside over the
spa, outside pool and Jacuzzi, as well as a small
aviary and greenhouse. The restaurant is
headed up by outstanding chef Alexis Mayroux,
and offers an excellent-value lunch menu for
€37, as well as an à la carte dinner menu based
on seasonal specialities (average €52). Weekend
packages are also available. It's the lounge,
cloisters, pool and restaurant that give such
a special atmosphere to the romantic medieval
monastery **L'Abbaye** (541 bd Honoré
Teisseire, La Colle-sur-Loup, 04.93.32.68.34,
www.abbaye-lacolle.com, double €120-€250).
Several celebrities, such as Roger Moore's
daughter, have been married in the beautiful
Protestant chapel.

Resources

Tourist information

La Colle-sur-Loup Office du Tourisme
*28 rue Maréchal Foch, 06480 La Colle-sur-Loup
(04.93.32.68.36/www.ot-lacollesurloup.com).*
Open *July, Aug* 9am-7pm daily. *Sept-June* 9am-noon,
2-6pm Mon-Sat.
St-Paul-de-Vence Office de Tourisme *2 rue
Grande, 06570 St-Paul-de-Vence (04.93.32.86.95/
www.saintpaulweb.net).* **Open** *June-Sept* 10am-7pm
daily. *Oct-May* 10am-6pm daily.

Getting there

By car

Exit the A8 at junction 48 and follow the D7 to St-
Paul. Continue north along the D7 until it becomes the
D2, when you arrive in Vence. Coming from the north,
exit the N202 at Carros and continue along the D2210
to Vence, turning south on to the D7 to St-Paul.

By bus

From Nice, Transport Alpes-Maritimes
(www.cg06.fr/tam-html) runs a regular bus
service (No.400) to Vence via St-Paul.

Into the Alps

Just half an hour uphill and Riviera decadence makes way for vertiginous roads, thick forests and white water.

Take a peak at the **Gorges de la Vésubie**. *See p308.*

When it's time to take a break from the high-fashion, high-energy coastline, head up to the Alps. Steep crags, just waiting to be scaled, walked or scrambled over, dominate the deeply scored valleys of the Roya, the Vésubie, the Tinée and the Haut Var. Isolated mountain villages scattered throughout are warmly welcoming, justifiably proud of their hospitality, their authenticity and their tiny baroque chapels with frescoes worthy of the best museums. Walking, skiing, canyoning and mountain biking bring nature-lovers in droves; but even for the less enthusiastic traveller, the sheer natural power of the region makes it easy to throw away those carefully planned holiday itineraries, and just relax and go with it.

One of the most impressive parts of this region is the huge swathe of territory near the border with Italy, the Parc National du Mercantour (*see also p311* **Shaggy dog story**). It has some 600 kilometres (373 miles) of waymarked footpaths. Here, as well as free-roaming, bell-clanking sheep and goats, you'll find chamoix and marmots, rare imperial eagles, eagle owls, snow grouse, the recently reintroduced lammergeyer (a bearded vulture that lives mainly on bones), as well as Alpine ibex or *bouquetin* that roam between the Mercantour and the adjacent Parco Naturale delle Alpi Marittime in Italy (officially twinned with its French cousin since 1987).

The Roya & Bévéra valleys & the Vallée des Merveilles

In 1860 Savoy and the rest of the County of Nice officially became a part of France under the reign of Napoléon III, but the upper valleys of the Roya and its tributary the Bévéra were granted to Vittorio Emanuele II, sovereign of the new kingdom of Italy. A nice little gesture between the rulers, since they were Vittorio's favourite hunting grounds. The inhabitants of the valleys stubbornly stayed essentially French, at least in spirit, but it was not until 1947 that they were allowed to decide which side of the border they wanted to be on.

Charming **Sospel**, a sleepy, sprawling town beside the River Bévéra, is the mountain gateway to the Roya Valley and a great place to stock up on the outstanding local olive oil; market day is Thursday. It was the second largest city in the County of Nice in the 13th century, thanks to its crucial situation along the Mediterranean salt route; the 11th-century Vieux Pont (old bridge) still spans the river in two graceful arcs, its tower (now the tourist office) was once the toll gate that gave passage, for a price, to a steady stream of mules on the salt trail from Nice to Turin. Sospel is split in two: the oldest house on the south bank (Palais Ricci) bears a plaque describing Pope Pius VII's stay here. The streets abound with charming squares and sculpted fountains, with the most imposing one found in place de la Cabraïa. It has two levels and was used as a drinking trough for the flocks of goats that used to be gathered here for auction. The main highlight is the floridly baroque Eglise St-Michel (open 3-6pm daily) on place St-Michel, with its stucco façade, trompe l'oeil murals and François Bréa's splendid early 16th-century *Immaculate Virgin* surrounded by angels.

From the church you can hike across to the north bank to visit place St-Nicholas with its old houses and pretty paving. Note the beautifully carved stone lintels and the elegant provençal fountain. From here, you can hike a kilometre south of the village (on the D2204) to the **Musée du Fort St-Roch**, a fascinating relic of the Maginot Line. Built in 1932, this underground world was a marvel of 1930s technology, and from what appears to be the entrance to a garage on the side of a cliff visitors embark on a trip through seemingly endless galleries, containing officers' quarters, munitions, a hospital, some impressive kitchens and (of course) a wine cellar.

North-west of Sospel, the narrow D2566 climbs alongside the Bévéra river through the Turini forest, rich in maple, beech, chestnut and spruce trees. Several roads meet at the 1,604-metre (5,262-foot) Col de Turini, a popular spot to start hiking or cross-country skiing at the edge of the Parc National du Mercantour (for more information, call 04.93.03.60.52). For a wonderfully scenic drive, take the D68, which runs through the Authion Massif. The Monument aux Morts, a few kilometres along, pays tribute to those who died in the Austro-Sardinian war of 1793 and against the Germans in 1945. Further along are the Cabanes Vieilles, stark ruins of an old Napoleonic military camp that was damaged in the fighting of 1945. At the Pointe des Trois-Communes at the far edge of the camp, there is a marvellous panorama of the peaks of the Mercantour and the Pré-Alpes.

North of Sospel is the D2204, which climbs over the 879-metre (2,884-foot) Col de Brouis before dropping into the Roya Valley proper at **Breil-sur-Roya**. A tranquil village of red-tiled pastel houses and picturesque streets, it has survived practically intact since the Middle Ages. Breil has several small industries (leather, olives, dairy farming, each well represented at market on a Tuesday). It has also become an internationally renowned centre for canyoning, rafting and kayaking. The main square, place Bracion, is flanked by two churches. The façade of one of the churches, the Chapelle Ste-Catherine, is very Italian Renaissance with two Corinthian columns flanking the portal. But spare time, too, for the flamboyant 18th-century church of Sancta-Maria-in-Albis (open 9am-noon, 2-5pm daily). This is but one of seven historic, finely decorated organs in the area that are put into service in Les Baroquiales baroque music festival every summer. Also of note is the unusual and colourful A Stacada: a festival that takes place every four years (next in 2006) where villagers dressed in medieval costume parade through the town, periodically stopping to perform scenes portraying the abolition of the *droit du seigneur*. For more information, contact the tourist board (*see p.308*).

Originally a Ligurian settlement and then a Roman colony, **Saorge** lies in a rugged setting, its cluster of Italianate houses and bell towers with shimmering fish-scale-tile roofs clinging to the side of a mountain at the entrance to the breathtaking Roya Gorge. It is the most spectacular Roya village: a narrow cobbled street winds up to the 15th-century Eglise St-Sauveur, which was built by hauling stones up on the back of mules and contains another of those magnificent carved organs. This one was built in 1847 by the Lingiardi of Pavia, shipped by sea from Genoa and then carried to Saorge, also on the back of a mule. Despite these achievements, there are no boutiques and only one pizzeria and one restaurant. South of the village is the not-to-be-missed **Couvent des Franciscains**, whose lovely cloister is filled with painted sundials and 18th-century frescoes depicting the life of St Francis of Assisi. Beyond the monastery's cypress-lined terrace, a mule track leads to Madone del Poggio, a ruined Romanesque abbey (closed to the public).

The last stop before the climb over into Italy, **Tende**, 20 kilometres (65 miles) from Saorge, is surrounded by peaks that become seriously Alpine. Tende is a market town (Wednesday is market day) where hikers and nature-lovers gather to gear up before heading off into the Mercantour or the Vallée des Merveilles. Anyone intending to visit the Vallée des Merveilles should not miss the modern **Musée** des **Merveilles**, which has a diorama and interactive exhibits as well as various Bronze Age artefacts. It's dry stuff, but informative.

The **Vallée des Merveilles** itself is a high and isolated valley enclosed on all sides by mountains and dominated by Mont Bégo. It can be reached from St-Dalmas-de-Tende, five kilometres (three miles) south of Tende (the Association des Taxis Accompagnateurs, 04.93.04.73.21, can provide transport), where a paved mountain road branches west to Casterino, jumping-off point for two way-marked footpaths – the direct route via the Refuge de Fontalbe, the only refuge accessible by car and then a 30-minute walk, or the longer northern route via the Refuge de Valmasque. Western access is from Madone de Fenestre in the Vésubie Valley (*see p308*), via the high-altitude Refuge de Nice. A magnificent, rock-strewn valley dominated by the 2,872-metre (9,423-foot) Mont Bégo, it contains at least 50,000 engravings, most dating from 2500 BC to 500 BC, although there are more recent interlopers. Bronze and Iron Age shepherds chipped away at the red rocks to depict apparently familiar objects – cattle, ploughs, field systems. One of the most famous – and a symbol of the Vallée des Merveilles – is the so-called Sorcerer, a bearded giant who appears to be shooting lightning bolts from his hands. For guided 4WD tours of the valley contact Franck Panza (groups €63/person/day, 04.93.04.73.21, www.ifrance.com/panzamerveilles.com). For more information, contact the Tende tourist office (*see p308*).

Heading downstream from Tende, a side road leads east to picturesque **La Brigue**. Once a powerful medieval stronghold, the village nestles under the ruin of its chateau in a pretty valley on the River Levense. It has three wonderful baroque churches, of which the 15th-century La Collégiale St-Martin (La Place, open 9am-6pm daily), with some fine primitive paintings of the Nice School, is the only one open to the public. The real treat lies further east, where the mountain chapel of Notre-Dame-des-Fontaines (to arrange a visit, contact La Brigue tourist office, *see p308*), a site of pilgrimage since antiquity, conceals a series of frescoes that has earned it the moniker the 'Sistine of the Alps'. The nave frescoes by Giovanni Canavesio push beyond the Gothic into a touching, though still primitive, foretaste of the Renaissance.

Couvent des Franciscains

Saorge (04.93.04.55.55). **Open** *Apr-Oct* 10am-6pm Mon, Wed-Sun. *Nov-Mar* 10am-noon, 2-6pm Mon, Wed, Sun. *Nov-Mar* 10am-noon, 2-5pm Mon, Wed, Sun. **Admission** €4.60; free under-18s. **No credit cards**.

Musée des Merveilles

av du 16 Septembre 1947, Tende (04.93.04.32.50/www.museedesmerveilles.com). **Open** *May-mid Oct* 10am-6.30pm Mon, Wed-Sun. *Mid Oct-Apr* 10am-5pm Mon, Wed-Sun. Closed 2wks Mar, 2wks Nov. **Admission** €4.55; €2.30 14-18s; free under-14s. **Credit** AmEx, MC, V.

Musée du Fort St-Roch

16 pl Guillaume Tell, Sospel (04.93.04.00.70). **Open** *Apr-June, Oct* 2-6pm Sat, Sun. *June-Aug* 2-6pm Tue-Sun. Closed Nov-Mar. **Admission** €5; €3 5-13s; free under-5s. **No credit cards**.

Where to stay & eat

Along the route to Sospel from Nice, perched up on the heights, is the highly recommended **Pierrot-Pierrett** (rte de Sospel, 04.93.35.79.76, closed Mon, Nov-mid Jan, double €67-€76) with scrumptious regional cuisine (menus €27-€39) and a luxurious garden. Just outside Sospel, the homely, wood-and-whitewashed interior of **L'Auberge Provençale** (rte de Col de Castillon, 04.93.04.00.31, www.auberge provencale.fr, double €65-€110, menu €21-€34) offers a cosy welcome, while in town the leisurely Bel Acqua restaurant (closed lunch Tue & Wed, menus €21-€31) of the **Hôtel des Etrangers** (7 bd de Verdun, 04.93.04.00.09, closed Nov-Feb, double €65-€80) is a local institution and the food, including a tank of justifiably worried-looking trout, is first-class. Right in the centre of Sospel is charming **Le St-Pierre** (14 rue St-Pierre, 04.93.04.00.66, www.sospello.com, double €68-€100), which has five wonderfully rustic rooms .

At the Col de Turini, modern, log-cabin-like **Les Trois Vallées** (04.93.04.23.23, double €48.80-€91.50, breakfast included) has a restaurant (menus €15.50-€39). Friendly **Les Chamois** (04.93.91.58.31, double €45) has comfortable rooms iand good food (menu €20).

Out of Breil-sur-Roya, beside the Roya on the N204, the **Hôtel Restaurant Castel du Roy** (146 rte de l'Aigora, 04.93.04.43.66, www.castelduroy.com, closed Nov-Easter, double €58-€80, restaurant closed Mon) has comfortable rooms and exquisitely served regional cuisine (try sea perch with a provençal *tian* or local trout; menus €25-€35). A youthful, sporty and friendly option is the **Gîte d'Etape** (392 chemin du Foussa, 04.93.04.47.64, double €29-€36, breakfast included).

In Saorge, restaurant **Le Bellevue** (5 rue Louis Périssol, 04.93.04.51.37, closed Tue, end Nov-mid Dec, menus €17-€26) has a panoramic view. There are no hotels in Saorge but trekkers flock to the **Gîte Bergiron** (04.93.04.55.49, €11/person in a dorm, €28 with dinner) behind the Franciscan monastery.

In Tende, **L'Auberge Tendasque** (65 av du 16 Septembre 1947, 04.93.04.62.26, menus €13-€20) serves the famous truite au bleu, where the fish hardly pauses from tank to plate. In nearby St-Dalmas-de-Tende, **Hôtel Restaurant Le Prieuré** (av Jean Médecin, 04.93.04.75.70, double €46-€64, restaurant closed Mon & dinner Sun Nov-Mar, menus €10-€22) offers pristine rooms and immaculate grounds – a comfortable stop for those allergic to mountain refuges. Cosy and familial, **Le Terminus** (across from the train station, 04.93.04.96.96, double €49.50-€61.50) is an easygoing hotel with a mountain inn feel. If you want to try one of the Vallée des Merveilles refuges, contact **Club Alpin Nice** (04.93.62. 59.99, www.cafnice.org, dorm €13.50).

At La Brigue, **La Cassoulette** (20 rue du Général de Gaulle, 04.93.04.63.82, closed Mon, dinner Sun, Mar, menus €18-€28) is a tiny, convivial bistro, chock-a-block with statuettes of barnyard birds. It offers divine foie gras, duck confit and desserts (book ahead). **Hôtel Restaurant Le Mirval** (3 rue Vincent Ferrier, 04.93.04.63.71, closed Nov-Mar, double €54-€64, restaurant closed lunch Fri, menus €16-€22) has utilitarian but quite spacious modern accommodation; it also organises 4WD excursions into the surrounding valleys.

Resources

Tourist information

Breil-sur-Roya Office de Tourisme *17 pl Bianchéri, 06540 Breil-sur-Roya (04.93.04.99.76 /www.breil-sur-roya.fr)*. **Open** *Jan-June, Sept-Dec* 8.30am-12.30pm, 1.30-5.30pm Mon-Fri; 9am-1pm Sat. *July, Aug* 9am-1pm, 3-6pm Mon-Sat; 9am-1pm Sun.
La Brigue Office de Tourisme *Mairie, pl St-Martin, 06430 La Brigue (04.93.04.60.04)*. **Open** *May-Sept* 9am-12.30pm, 1.30-5.30pm daily. *Oct-Apr* 9.30am-12.30pm, 1.30-4.30pm daily (closed Sun Dec-Feb). Closed mid Jan-mid Feb.
Sospel Office de Tourisme *19 av Jean Médecin, 06380 Sospel (04.93.04.15.80)*. **Open** *Mid May-mid Oct* 9.30am-12.30pm, 2.30-6pm daily. *Mid Oct-mid May* 9.30am-12.30pm, 2.30-5.30pm daily.
Tende Office de Tourisme *103 av du 16 septembre 1947, 06430 Tende (04.93.04.73.71/www.tendemerveilles.com)*. **Open** *May-Oct* 9am-12.30pm, 2-5.30pm Mon-Sat. *Nov-Apr* 9am-12.30pm, 2-5pm Mon-Sat.

The Vésubie Valley

Fed by the snows of the Alpine ranges, the Vésubie river flows through one of the most beautiful valleys above Nice. The best way into the upper valley is the D19 out of Nice, which rises almost imperceptibly past villas and pastures to the village of **Levens**, an atmospheric cluster of stone houses with an excess of burbling fountains. The town hall boasts some amusing frescoes on the life of Marshal Massena in the style of strip cartoons, painted in the 1950s, and there is a stunning view from near the War Memorial that extends out over the junction of the Var and the Vesubie. Beyond Levens the mountains begin with a vengeance as the road clings to the side of the **Gorges de la Vésubie** – which can also be negotiated on the lower D2565 route. Soon after the two roads meet is the turn-off for **Utelle**, a village that projects like a balcony over the Vésubie Valley below. This isolated village has managed to keep its original character: old houses with sundials and a church with a pretty Gothic porch and doors carved with scenes from the life of local boy St Véran. The nearby Chapelle des Pénitents-Blancs has a carved wooden version of Rubens' *Descent from the Cross*, while the shrine of Madone d'Utelle stands on a barren peak six kilometres (four miles) further on; try to visit in the morning, before the clouds roll in. A plain terracotta church, it owes its existence to a ninth-century shipwreck on the patch of sea that, on a clear day, can be seen far below. Believing they had been saved from drowning by the Virgin, who appeared on the mountainside bathed in light, grateful Spanish mariners climbed up here to build a shrine.

The road up to St-Martin-Vésubie continues past Lantosque to **Roquebillière**, a crumbling old village with a modern offshoot opposite, built after a landslide in 1926 that claimed 17 lives. Down by the river on the same side as the modern village is the unusual church of St-Michel-de-Gast-des-Templiers. Built by the Knights Templar and later taken over by the Knights of Malta, it is full of abstruse Templar symbolism; on one capital there is a carving of the Egyptian baboon god Thot. The altarpiece from the Nice School is dedicated to St Anthony and there is a fine collection of priestly vestments in the sacristy. The key is kept by the voluble Madame Périchon, who lives in the house opposite the church.

At **Berthemont-les-Bains** you'll find a modern spa. The sulphurous, 30ºC (86ºF) waters were used by the Romans to treat respiratory diseases and rheumatism. Today they are funnelled into various indoor pools where clients relax after a therapeutic massage at the **Station Thermale de Berthemont-les-Bains** (04.93.03.47.00, closed Oct-Apr, rates €33-€44, weekly rate €210).

St-Martin-Vésubie is a good place to refuel and pick up supplies and information. The pocket-sized place Félix Faure links the main valley road with rue Cagnoli, St-Martin's

The unspoilt village of **Utelle**. *See p308.*

pedestrian backbone. A little paved channel
of water, known as a *gargouille*, runs the
whole way down the steeply inclined street.

The road west to the church of **Madone
de Fenestre** criss-crosses a mountain stream.
Push on to the end, where a large mountain
refuge and a tin-roofed church are surrounded
by a cirque of high peaks. The church is only
two centuries old, but its miraculous icon of the
Madone de Fenestre (kept down in St-Martin in
winter) dates from the 12th century. Allow at
least an hour and a half for the rewarding walk
up past a lake to the Col de Fenestre on the
Italian border. Madone de Fenestre also gives
access to the Vallée des Merveilles.

Perched on a rocky spur that overlooks
St-Martin, **Venanson** is home to the tiny
Chapelle Ste-Claire on place St-Jean, which
has lively 15th-century frescoes of the life of
St Sebastian. If it's closed, collect the key from
the Hôtel Bellavista (04.93.03.25.11) opposite.

West of St-Martin, the D2565 continues up
to the Col St-Martin (1,500 metres or 4,921 feet),
which links the Vésubie and Tinée valleys. Just
right from the Col is a *via ferrata*, a protected
climbing route with handrail that will certainly
do its best to get your pulse racing. There are
three routes, blue, black and red depending on
their difficulty, and even the easiest takes an
hour and a half. Ask at the tourist office for
details and equipment. Just below the pass is
the aspiring resort of **La Colmiane**, where,
in June and July, you can career down the
mountain on a *trottinerbe,* a sort of kid's scooter
with huge soft tyres, from the top of the Pic de
Colmiane lift. In winter, it's a small ski resort.
The charms of **St-Dalmas-de-Valdeblore**,
the first village over the pass, are more sedate.
The Eglise de l'Invention de la Ste-Croix, a fine

Romanesque church with its very own piece
of the Holy Cross, once belonged to a powerful
Benedictine priory.

Where to stay & eat

Just above Utelle on the Madone d'Utelle road,
Le Bellevue restaurant (04.93.03.17.19, closed
Mon, menus €12.50-€28) has views that live
up to the name and serves traditional home
cooking. In nearby Lantosque, **L'Ancienne
Gendarmerie** (Le Rivet, 04.93.03. 00.65, closed
Nov-Feb, double €65-€110, restaurant closed
Mon & dinner Sun, menu €17.90) really was
a police station – hence the sentry box outside
– and offers eight rooms and a small swimming
pool perched above the river. Up in the village,
the **Bar des Tilleuls** (04.93.03.05.74) is a good
place for a *pastis* under the lime trees.

In Roquebillière, the friendly *chambres
d'hôte* **Ferme les Cartons** (Quartier Gordon,
04.93.03.47.93, double €45, including breakfast)
has lovely views and charmingly rustic rooms.
The **Hotel des Thermes** in Berthemont-les-
Bains (04.93.03.40.43, double €60) has 22 rooms
with a charming garden and terrace.

In St-Martin-Vésubie, **La Treille** (68 rue
Cagnoli, 04.93.03.30.85, closed dinner Wed &
Thur except in school holidays, Dec-mid Feb,
menus €20-€24), towards the top of the main
street, is a friendly restaurant with good wood-
fired pizzas (dinner only), classic meat and fish
dishes and a panoramic terrace at the back.
La Taverne du Pelago (Lac du Boeron,
04.93.03.22.00, lunch only, closed Nov, Dec,
menu €23) looks out over the lake and serves
lovely roast lamb and great local cheeses. **La
Bonne Auberge** (La Place, 04.93.03.20.49,
closed mid Nov-mid Feb, double €45-€52) lives

The Riviera & Southern Alps

up to its name, offering solid mountain hospitality (menus €18-€25) in a cheerful building overlooking the valley. The slightly more luxurious **Edward's Parc Hôtel La Chataigneraie** (04.93.03.21.22, closed Oct-May, double €60-€70) is a little frayed but still a good place to relax, with the aid of a heated outdoor swimming pool and minigolf.

Resources

Tourist information

St-Martin-Vésubie Office de Tourisme *pl Félix Faure, 06450 St-Martin-Vésubie (04.93.03.21.28/ www.saintmartinvesubie.fr)*. **Open** *June, Sept* 9am-noon, 2-6pm daily. *July, Aug* 9am-7pm daily. *Oct-May* 9am-noon, 2-6pm Mon-Sat; 9am-noon Sun.
Bureau des Guides du Mercantour *pl du Marché, St-Martin-Vésubie (04.93.03.31.32)*. **Open** 10.30am-12.30pm, 4-5.30pm daily. Closed Sept-June.

The Tinée Valley

Most Niçois see this road as a bit of scenery on the way to the ski resorts of Isola 2000 or Auron, but the upper reaches of the Tinée Valley are worth a visit in their own right. The Tinée flows into the Var just where the latter changes direction to head south to Nice. A few side roads wind their way up to the *villages perchés* of **La Tour** and **Clans**. The former has some vivacious 15th-century scenes of vices and virtues in the Chapelle des Pénitents-Blancs and an ancient but working oil mill. In well-preserved medieval Clans, the Chapelle de St-Antoine features frescoes of the life of the saint. On the east side of the valley, **Marie** is a pretty hamlet of only 60 inhabitants with an excellent hotel-restaurant, Le Panoramique (*see p311*).

Approaching **St-Sauveur-sur-Tinée**, the iron-rich cliffs turn a garish shade of puce – quite a sight at sunset. St-Sauveur is a one-horse town, with little to retain the visitor, but it is also the jumping-off point for a spectacular route west via the ski resort of **Valberg** into the Haut Var Valley, whose source lies just below the Col de Cayolle, one of the finest of all the gateways into the Mercantour.

Above St-Sauveur, the Tinée Valley heads north through the Gorges de Valabre before broadening out below Isola, a siesta of a village amid chestnut groves, with a solitary 15th-century bell tower and, rather incongruously given the pace of life around these parts, **Aquavallée** (04.93.02.16.49, 11am-8pm Mon-Fri, 10am-8pm Sat, Sun, admission €4-€9), a covered fun pool with sauna, gym, steam room and squash courts. Further incongruities lie in wait up the side road that ascends the Chastillon torrent to the ski resort of **Isola**

2000. The 1970s British design of this blight on the landscape has not aged well, but from here you can walk into the surrounding high peaks or continue by car over the Col de la Lombarde pass into Italy.

St-Etienne-de-Tinée, near the head of the valley, is a surprisingly lively market town of tall, pastel houses and Gothic portals, which celebrates its shepherding traditions in the Fête de la Transhumance on the last Sunday in June. It has a cluster of interesting frescoed churches, though you need to go on a tour organised by the tourist office (*see p312*) to see them. For information on tours and the Fête de la Transhumance, contact the tourist office direct.

The prize for the most unexpected sight in the Alpes-Maritimes must go to the Chapelle de St-Erige (open by appointment, collect the key from the tourist office, *see p312*) in the lively ski resort of **Auron**. This little wooden chapel – commissioned by wealthy parishioners in the 15th century, when this upland plain was covered in summer cornfields – is almost overwhelmed by the faux-Swiss-chalet hotels that surround it. Inside, it's another story – a series of stories, in fact, told in vivid frescoes dating back to 1451. Scenes of the life of Mary Magdalene alternate religious mysticism with the secular spirit of the troubadour poets.

North of St-Etienne the D2205 soon becomes the D64 to Barcelonnette, the highest paved road in Europe. When the pass is open (June-Sept) bikers, motorists and even cyclists slog up to the Col de la Bonette, where the road loops to encircle the bare peak of Cime de la Bonette. From the highest snack bar in Europe (2,802 metres or 9,193 feet), a short path takes you up to the viewing table at 2,860 metres (9,383 feet) for a spectacular panorama.

Alternatively, leave the D2205 north of St-Etienne and head left to the ravishingly pretty mountain village of **St-Dalmas-le-Selvage**, the highest in the Alpes-Maritimes. Most of the houses still have their original larchwood roofs, open under the eaves where the corn was traditionally laid out to dry. The parish church has two early 16th-century altarpieces, and inside the tiny Chapelle de Ste-Marguerite in the centre of the village are frescoes by Jean Baleison, which were discovered behind the altar in 1996.

Activities

Skiing

The two main resorts with the widest choice of options are Auron and Isola 2000. **Auron**, at 1,600 metres (5,249 feet) altitude, offers 130 kilometres (81 miles) of pistes and 25 assorted téléphériques, télésièges and téléskis to get to them, as well as Surf-

Shaggy dog story

Ignoring country borders with carefree indifference, the intrepid wolf has been slipping over the Franco-Italian frontier in increasing numbers since 1992, happily setting up camp in the wilds of the Mercantour. Since then, a bitter battle has been raging between ecologists and shepherds. The latter are terrified that their flocks will be killed, the former thrilled that the perhaps 50 wolves in the park are thriving against earlier odds predicting extinction. In the ecologists' scientific opinion, *les chiens errants* (stray dogs) are to blame for recent attacks since, contrary to dogs, wolves only kill to eat. The shepherds, on the other hand, are not nearly so philosophical – they just want the attacks on their sheep to stop.

A first investigative report was ordered by the French government, with little practical effect except to confirm that there were wolves – 27 of them – in the Mercantour. Sheep continued to die, wolves continued to roam, and the conflict continued to simmer. It reached boiling point in 2002, when the Minister for Ecology and Sustainable Development released provisional numbers relating to flock damage: 2,304 sheep killed by vicious wild dog/wolf attacks. Bad enough from a shepherd's point of view, but what triggered the explosion was an unexpectedly

gory event in the commune of Moulinet. A flock of sheep was attacked by two wolves, resulting in 407 dead animals. Only six were actually bitten, but the rest, reacting in mass terror, flung themselves off a cliff to their deaths in the ravine below.

Tensions started to run high and Parliament ordered another investigation. The resulting report gave ambiguous advice: wolf-friendly zones ought to have borders, outside of which the wolves could be shot. This proved unworkable and in July 2004, in the face of continued pressure and another grisly meeting between a flock of sheep and the bottom of a ravine, the government agreed to a limited cull. Three *départements* were permitted to kill up to four wolves, amounting to a tenth of the current known population and 50 per cent of the annual population growth. Environmentalists were, predictably, outraged. With fewer than 500 wolves in Italy and about 1,500 in Spain, wolves remain an endangered and internationally protected species. But wolves do, as is their immutable nature, attack sheep.

The answer to the question of the big, bad wolf is nowhere in sight. But if you fancy going in search of one, there's plenty of useful information about visiting Mercantour at www.parcsnationaux-fr.com.

---

land, a huge playground for snowboarders, with a half-pipe and runs for beginners. Purpose-built resort **Isola 2000** offers 48 runs, including five blacks, heli-skiing and one of the largest snowboarding and mini-skiing clubs in France. Passes cost around €20-€25. And if 1970s concrete is not your style, try the rustic chalets north of the station. **St-Dalmas-le-Selvage** mainly offers cross-country skiing, with over 35 kilometres (22 miles) of pistes, plus snowshoe and skidoo excursions, while **Valberg** is a smaller station but probably the most fiestily French.

For weather conditions call **Météo Neige** (08.92.68.10.20) or **Météo France** (3250 from France only), or visit www.auron.com.

Where to stay & eat

It's worth planning a lunch or dinner stop in Marie, where the relaxing family-run hotel-restaurant **Le Panoramique** (pl de la Mairie, 04.93.02.03.01, double €45) provides five scenic rooms and fine meals, including seasonal game (restaurant closed Tue-Thur, menus €17-€28). In Isola (the village, not the ski resort), **Au Café d'Isola** (pl Jean Gaïssa, 04.93.02.17.03,

closed Oct-Apr, average €7.50) does decent pizzas and snacks and also has a few guestrooms (double €44.30). The comfortable **Hôtel Le Régalivou** (8 bd d'Auron, 04.93.02.49.00, double €50-€65) has a summer restaurant (July, Aug only) serving solid regional dishes (menus €13-€25). The town also has a well-run municipal **campsite** on a small watersports lake, a three-minute walk from the centre (Plan d'Eau, 04.93.02.41.57, €8.50-€11 two people). The **Hôtel Chastellares** (pl Central, 04.93.23.02.58, closed Apr-June, mid Sept-Nov, double €70-€98 with half-board) in the centre of Auron has lovely balconies and a good restaurant. **L'Auberge de l'Etoile** (04.93.02.44.97, closed mid Oct-May, Mon-Thur in Sept, menu €25) in St-Dalmas-le-Selvage hides not a little sophistication beneath its rustic decor, which is enlivened by fake Van Goghs. Booking is essential. There is also a homely **Gîte d'Etape** (04.93.02.44.61, dormitory €10) in the village, designed for walkers doing the GR5 long-distance path, but open to all-comers.

Resources

Tourist information

Auron Office de Tourisme *Grange Cossa, 06660 Auron (04.93.23.02.66/www.auron.com).* **Open** *May-June, Sept-Nov* 9am-noon, 2-5.30pm Mon-Sat. *July-Aug, Dec-Apr* 9am-noon, 2-6.30pm daily.

Isola 2000 Chalet d'Acceuil *06420 Isola (04.93.23.15.15/www.isola2000.com).* **Open** *July, Aug, mid Dec-Apr* 9am-noon, 2-7pm daily. *May-June, Sept-Nov* 9am-noon, 1.30-5.30pm Mon-Fri.

St-Etienne-de-Tinée Office de Tourisme *1 rue des Communes de France, 06660 St-Etienne-de-Tinée (04.93.02.41.96).* **Open** 9am-noon, 2.30-6pm Mon-Sat; 9am-noon Sun.

The Upper Var Valley

The River Var flows into the Mediterranean just next to Nice airport at St-Laurent-du-Var, but in the upper reaches it offers Alpine scenery and perilously perched villages. Although you can follow the route by the N202 from Nice airport, this is one place where the train trip on the **Train des Pignes** (*see below*) is worth the journey in itself. Built in 1891-1900 between the Gare de Provence in Nice and Digne-les-Bains in the sparsely populated Alpes de Haute-Provence, it was part of an ambitious plan to provide a direct rail link between the Alps and the Côte d'Azur. The one-metre narrow-gauge railway runs over 31 bridges and viaducts and through 25 tunnels, climbing to an altitude of 1,000 metres (3,280 feet).

Beyond Plan du Var the mountains close in on either side at the forbidding Défilé de Chaudan, beyond which the Var abruptly changes direction, heading west. **Villars-sur-Var** is a *village perché* with some good Renaissance art in the church of St-Jean-Baptiste, but its main claim to fame is as the centre of the tiny Bellet wine appellation, which occupies a mere 31 hectares (77 acres); the white is definitely worth trying. At **Touët-sur-Var**, space is so tight that the village church straddles a mountain stream. The valley opens out a little at **Puget-Théniers**, an old Templar stronghold and birthplace of Auguste Blanqui, one of the leaders of the Paris Commune of 1870, who is commemorated by a stirring Aristide Maillol monument on the main road.

Cradled in a curve of the river, **Entrevaux** is a handsome fortified village. Perched way above on a perilous ridge is a fortress built by Louis XIV's military architect Vauban in the 1690s. Until 1860, this was a border town between France and Italy. The twin towers that guard the entrance to the village across a single-arched bridge are almost Disney-picturesque, but once inside it is a sturdily practical place, with tall houses, narrow lanes

and a 17th-century cathedral built into the defensive walls. The castle itself is a steep, appetite-building climb from the town up a zigzag ramp; it's an atmospheric old pile, with dungeons and galleries to explore.

Beyond Entrevaux, the Train des Pignes continues towards Digne-les-Bains via the old town of **Annot**, where the houses are built right up against huge sandstone boulders, and **St-André-les-Alpes** on the Lac de Castellane. The Var Valley backtracks again in a route that can be traced by the D2202 along the dramatic red-schist Gorges de Dalious to its source way north in the Parc de Mercantour.

Resources

Tourist information

Puget Office de Tourisme-Maison de Pays *2 rue Alexandre Borety, 06260 Puget-Théniers (04.93.05.05.05).* **Open** *Mar-Oct* 9am-noon, 2-6pm daily. *Nov-Feb* 9am-noon, 2-5pm daily.

Getting there & around

By bus

Bus travel is limited here. **Rapides Côte d'Azur** (04.93.35.91.17) runs services between Menton and other destinations in the Roya Valley. **TRAM** (04.93.89.47.14) buses run twice daily between Nice and St-Martin-Vésubie, Mon-Sat, and once daily Sun. In summer, one a day continues to La Colmiane, only Wed morning and evening, Fri evening, Sat morning and Sunday in winter. Infrequent buses also serve Le Boréon and Madone de Fenestre in summer. **Santa-Azur** (04.93.85.92.60) runs daily services between Nice, St-Etienne-de-Tinée and Auron, and between Nice, Isola and Isola 2000.

By car

For the Roya and Bévéra valleys take the D2566 from Menton to Sospel, then the D2204 north for Breil-sur-Roya. Alternatively, the Roya Valley can be ascended from Ventimiglia in Italy on the S20, which crosses into France at Olivetta San Michele, 10km (6 miles) before Breil. The N202 follows the Var Valley from Nice airport; the D2565 branches off here along the Vésubie Valley (also reached by D2566/D70 from Sospel via the Col de Turini); the D2205 follows the Tinée Valley.

By train

Around five trains a day travel the Nice-Cuneo line stopping at Menton, Sospel, Breil-sur-Roya and Tende.

Train des Pignes (04.97.03.80.80). Trains depart from the Gare de Provence in Nice (4bis rue Alfred Binet) and arrive at the Gare Digne-les-Bains. There are four daily departures in each direction; Nice to Digne takes just over three hours and costs €17.65 (€14.10 students, 12-18s; €8.85 4-12s) one-way; Nice to Entrevaux takes an hour and a half and costs €9. Trains are modern, with two carriages, but steam trains complete with staff in costume still ply the route on Sunday from May to October.

Directory

Features

Directory

Getting There & Around

By air

Airlines from the UK

The continuing popularity of low-cost airlines means air-travel options remain broad.

Air France *UK 0845 142 4343/ USA 1-800 237 2747/France 08.20.82.08.20/www.airfrance.com.* Paris to Avignon, Marseille, Montpellier, Nice and Nîmes.

British Airways *UK 0870 850 9850/US 1-800 247 9297/France 08.25.82.54.00/ www.britishairways.com.* London Gatwick to Marseille, Montpellier; Heathrow, Gatwick and Birmingham to Nice.

British Midland *UK 0870 607 0555/France 01.48.62.55.65/ www.flybmi.com.* Heathrow and Nottingham to Nice.

Easyjet *UK 0870 600 0000/France 08.25.08.25.08/www.easyjet.com.* Gatwick, Stansted, Aberdeen, Bristol, Liverpool and Luton to Nice; Gatwick to Marseille.

Ryanair *08.92.55.56.66/ www.ryanair.com.* Luton and Stansted to Nîmes.

Airlines from the USA

From the USA, most flights involve a Paris connection.

Delta *US 1-800 241 4141/France 08.00.35.40.80/www.delta.com.* Daily from New York JFK to Nice.

Airports

Marseille and Nice are the two main airports in this part of the South of France.

Aéroport Avignon-Caumont *04.90.81.51.51.* Served by Air France from Paris Orly.

Aéroport de Nîmes-Arles-Camargue *04.66.70.49.49.* 10km (6 miles) south-east of Nîmes; 20km (12 miles) from Arles.

Aéroport Marseille-Provence *04.42.14.14.14/www.marseille. aeroport.fr.*

Actually situated 28km (17 miles) north-west of town, in Marignane, but buses run every 20mins to Marseille rail station and every 30mins to Aix-en-Provence.

Aéroport Montpellier Méditerranée *04.67.20.85.00/ recorded times 04.67.20.85.85/ www.montpellier.aeroport.fr.*

Aéroport Nice-Côte d'Azur *08.20.42.33.33/www.nice.aeroport.fr.* France's second airport, located 7km (4 miles) west of the centre of Nice. Most airlines use Terminal 1; Air France flights use Terminal 2.

Aéroport de Toulon-Hyères *04.94.00.83.83.* Near Hyères port.

Helicopter services

Air St-Tropez *04.94.97.15.12.* Between Nice and St-Tropez; costs €784 for five people, plus tax.

Héli-Air Monaco *00.377-92.05.00.50.* Nice to Monaco, €89.08 per person.

Nice Hélicoptères *04.93.21.34.32.* Cannes–Nice return, around €135 per person, plus tax.

By train

One of the quickest and most efficient ways to travel within France is by train. French trains are run by the **SNCF** state railway (www.sncf.com).

Train lines

Mainline services

The French **TGV** (high-speed train) runs to the South from Paris Gare de Lyon and Lille, via Lyon, to Avignon. There it splits west to Nîmes and east to Aix-en-Provence, Marseille, Toulon, Draguignan-Les Arcs, St-Raphaël, Cannes, Antibes, Nice, Monte-Carlo and Menton (not all trains stop at all stations). Note that the highest-speed track currently only reaches Marseille and Nîmes. It takes around 2hrs 40mins to Avignon, 3hrs to Aix, Marseille and Nîmes, 5hrs 30mins to Nice. On slower, long-distance trains from

Menton and Nice, you can travel overnight by **couchette** (a bunk-bed sleeping car, shared with up to five others) or **voiture-lit** (a comfier sleeping compartment for up to three). Both are available in first- and second-class, and must be reserved ahead.

Eurostar

UK 01233 617575/France 08.92.35.35.39/www.eurostar.com. For the Eurostar to the South of France, change on to the TGV at Lille or Paris. From July to September a weekly Eurostar goes direct from London Waterloo to Avignon Central in just 6hrs 15mins.

Local trains

The local **SNCF** network is most extensive in the Rhône Valley and along the coast. Out-of-town stations usually have a connecting *navette* (shuttle bus) to the town centre. Sometimes SNCF runs buses (marked 'Autocar' in timetables) to stations where the train no longer stops; rail tickets and passes are valid on these. **Métrazur** runs along the coast, stopping at all stations between Marseille and Ventimiglia in Italy. There's also a Marseille–Aix–Gap line and two mountain lines from Nice: the Roya line via Sospel, and the privately run Train des Pignes (from Gare de Provence).

Fares & tickets

You can buy tickets in all **SNCF** stations from counters or by French-issued credit card at automatic ticket machines, also from some travel agents. Phone bookings can be made on 3635 or 08.92.35.35.35 (7am-10pm daily). Bookings can be made online at www.sncf.com or www.tgv.com, and paid online or at ticket machines; certain tickets can be printed out directly at home. The **TGV** can be booked up to two months ahead; you always have to reserve seats to travel on the TGV. For all train journeys you must **composter votre billet** – date-stamp your ticket in the orange *composteur* machine on the platform before you start the journey.

In the UK, tickets for through travel can be booked from any mainline station or travel centre. Otherwise try the **International Rail Centre**

(0870 751 5000, www.international-rail.com) or the **Rail Europe Travel Shop** (179 Piccadilly, London W1V OBA, 0870 584 8848, www.raileurope.co.uk).

Fares & discounts

Fares vary according to whether you travel in normal (*période normale*) or peak (*période de pointe*) hours; discounts are sometimes still available within these times, but first-class travellers pay the same rate at all times. *Découverte à deux* gives a 25% reduction for two people travelling together on a return journey, and there are discounts for up to four adults travelling with a child under 12. Every Tuesday www.sncf.com advertises special *dernière minute* offers, while a *prem* (available every day) gives low prices for selected cities if bought in advance. You can also save 25%-50% by buying special discount cards for under-12s, 12-25-year-olds and over-60s. Children under four travel free.

International passes

A Eurodomino pass allows unlimited travel on France's rail network for a 3-8 day duration within one month, but must be bought before travelling to France. There are discounted rates for children aged between four and 11, young people between 12 and 25 and for the over-60s. Passes for North Americans include Eurailpass, Flexipass and Saver Pass, which can be purchased in the USA.

Bicycles on trains

For long-distance train travel, bicycles need to be transported separately, and must be registered and insured. They can be delivered to your destination, though this may take several days. On Eurostar bikes can be transported as hand luggage in a bike bag, or checked in up to 24hrs in advance of your journey. Bikes can be transported on many local trains (indicated by a bicycle symbol in timetables). You can also consult *SNCF Guide Train + Vélo*.

By bus & coach

Travelling round France by bus takes some determination.

Eurolines

UK 01582 404511/France 08.92.69.52.52/www.eurolines.com. Regular coaches from London Victoria to Avignon, Marseille, Toulon and Nice.

Local buses

The coastal area is reasonably well served by buses, and city centres have regular services. Services are more limited in the country and run by myriad local companies. Rural buses often cater for schools and workers, meaning there may be just one bus in the morning, one in the evening and none on Sundays/school holidays. Towns of any size should have a bus station (*gare routière*), which is often near the train station.

By car & motorbike

Much of Europe heads south during July and August. Coast roads and motorways crawl at snail's pace, especially around St-Tropez or between Cannes and Menton. Roads are at their worst on Saturdays and around the 14 July and 15 August public holidays. Look for BIS (Bison Futé) signs, which attempt to reduce summer traffic by suggesting diversions on backroads.

Car ferries & Eurotunnel

Brittany Ferries *UK 0870 366 5333/France 08.25.82.88.28/ www.brittanyferries.com.* Poole to Cherbourg, Plymouth to Roscoff, Portsmouth to St-Malo or to Caen.

Eurotunnel *UK 0870 535 3535/ France 03.21.00.61.00/www.euro tunnel.com.* Takes cars from Folkestone to Calais, through the Channel Tunnel.

Hoverspeed *UK 0870 240 8070/ France 00.800-12.11.12.11/www. hoverspeed.com.* High-speed Seacats run Dover to Calais and Newhaven to Dieppe.

P&O Stena Line *UK 0870 598 0333/France 08.25.12.01.56/www. posl.com.* Dover to Calais and Portsmouth to Cherbourg or Le Havre.

SeaFrance *UK 0870 571 1711/ France 08.03.04.40.45/www.sea france.com.* Dover to Calais.

Driving in France

Roads

French roads are divided into *autoroutes* (motorways, marked A8, A51 etc), *routes nationales* (national 'N' roads, marked N222 etc), *routes départementales* ('D' roads) and tiny rural *routes communales* ('C' roads).

Autoroutes & tolls

The distance from Calais to Nice is 1,167km (725 miles); from Caen to Nice 1,161km (721 miles). Dieppe to Avignon is 854km (531 miles), Calais to Avignon 965km (600 miles). For Provence, the quickest route from Calais is via Paris (but avoid the Périphérique ring road at rush hour) and the A6 Autoroute du Soleil to Lyon and the Rhône Valley. A less-trafficked route to western Provence is the A10–A71–A75 via Bourges and Clermont-Ferrand. www.via michelin.com, www.mappy.fr and www.autoroutes.fr can help you plan your route. 08.92.68.10.77 and Radio 107.7 FM give traffic information.

French autoroutes are toll (*péage*) roads, although some sections – especially around major cities – are free. At *péage* toll-booths, payment can be made by cash or credit card. From Calais to Menton, expect to spend around €80 on tolls, Nice airport to Monaco costs €3.20, Aix-en-Provence to Nice €14.

There are *aires* approximately every 20-30km (10-20 miles); simple ones offer picnic tables and toilets; larger ones have 24hr petrol stations, cafés, shops and sometimes summer activities and tourist information.

Motorail

A comfortable though pricey option is the Motorail: put your car on the train in Calais or Paris and travel overnight down to the coast. Services do not run every day, except in high summer, and you may have to travel on a different day to your car. Couchettes are mandatory. For UK bookings, contact **Rail Europe** (0870 241 5415, www.frenchmotorail.com).

Paperwork

If you bring your car to France, you will need to bring the relevant registration and insurance documents, and, of course, your driving licence. New drivers need to have held a licence for at least a year.

Speed limits

In normal conditions, speed limits are 130kph (80mph) on autoroutes, 110kph (69mph) on dual carriageways and 90kph (56mph) on other roads. In heavy rain and fog, these limits are reduced by 20kph (12mph) on autoroutes, 10kph (6mph) on other roads; limits are also reduced on days of heavy air pollution. The limit in built-up areas is 50kph (28mph), 30kph (17mph) in some districts. Recent government policy has been to rigorously enforce speed limits; automatic radars have been installed all over France since 2003, which can automatically send off a speeding fine for breaking the speed limit by as little as 6kph.

Directory

Breakdown services

The AA or RAC do not have reciprocal arrangements with French organisations, so take out additional breakdown insurance, for example with **Europ Assistance** (UK 01444 442211, 0870 737 5720). Local 24hr breakdown services include **Dépannage Côte d'Azur** (04.93.29.87.87). Autoroutes and routes nationales have emergency telephones every 2km (1.2 miles). *See also p321* **Emergencies**.

Driving essentials

● It is now obligatory to carry a luminous (Hi-Glow or DayGlo) vest in your car; you'll have to put the vest on before even stepping out on the hard shoulder, so don't keep it in the boot or anywhere inaccessible. Fines for failure to comply can be severe.
● At intersections where no signposts indicate the right of way, the car coming from the right has priority. Roundabouts follow the same rule, though many now give priority to those on the roundabout: this will be indicated either by stop markings on the road or by the message 'Vous n'avez pas la priorité'.
● Drivers and all passengers must wear seat belts.
● Children under ten are not allowed to travel in the front, except in special baby seats facing backwards.
● You should not stop on an open road; pull off to the side.
● When drivers flash their lights at you, they are warning that they will not slow down and you should keep out of the way. Oncoming drivers may also flash their lights to warn you when there are gendarmes lurking on the other side of the hill.
● Carry change, as it's quicker to head for the exact-money queue on *péages*; but cashiers do give change and *péages* accept credit cards.
● Motorbikes must have headlights on while in motion; cars must have their headlights on in poor visibility.
● All vehicles have to carry a full spare set of light bulbs and drivers who wear spectacles or contact lenses must carry a spare pair.
● The French drink-driving limit is 0.5g alcohol per litre of blood (about a large glass of wine). Above 0.8g/l and you can have your licence confiscated on the spot.
● Key phrases for motorists include: *Cédez le passage* Give way. *Vous n'avez pas la priorité* Give way, you do not have right of way. *Passage protégé* No right of way. *Rappel* Reminder.

Fuel

Only unleaded (*sans plomb*) and diesel (*gasoil*) are available, but a special unleaded petrol is available for cars that run on leaded fuel. Petrol tends to be most expensive on autoroutes, so many drivers fill up at the supermarkets. Petrol stations can be scarce in rural areas (it's especially hard finding one that opens on a Sunday), though some supermarket stations have 24hr pumps that accept Carte Bleue.

Parking

In high season, you have to get up very early to get a parking space at the beach. Inland, some highly touristed villages now have compulsory car parks, and car parks are often the best option in the main cities. Parking meters have now largely been replaced by *horodateurs* (pay-and-display machines), which take either cards, available from *tabacs*, or coins. Parking may be free over lunch, on Sundays and on public holidays. Check exact details on the machine or display panels.

Vehicle hire

To hire a car you must normally be 25 or over and to have held a licence for at least a year. Some hire companies will accept drivers aged 21-24, but a supplement of €8-€15 per day is usual. Remember to bring your licence and passport with you.

Car hire companies

ADA *01.41.27.49.00/www.ada.fr.*
Avis *08.20.05.05.05/UK 0870 010 0287/www.avis.co.uk.*
Budget *UK 0870 153 9170/ www.budget.com.*
Europcar *08.25.35.23.52/ www.europcar.com.*
EasyCar *No phone reservations/ www.easycar.com.*
Hertz *01.39.38.38.38/UK 0870 850 2654/www.hertz.com.*
Interrent *08.99.70.02.92/ www.interrent.fr.*

Car hire rates

Hiring a car in France is expensive. Consider fly-drive packages; it can also work out cheaper if you arrange car hire before leaving home. SNCF offers a train/car rental scheme, in assocation with Avis. There are often good weekend offers (Friday evening to Monday morning). Week-long deals are better at the bigger hire companies – with Avis or Budget, for example, it costs around €250/wk to hire a small car, with insurance and 1,700km (1,000 miles) included. Most international companies will allow the return of a car in other cities or even countries. Low-cost operators, such as ADA, may have a high excess charge for dents or damage. Rates with EasyCar vary according to demand when you book.

By bicycle

Cycling is an excellent way to see Provence, but if you bring a foreign-made bike, be sure to pack some spare tyres – French sizes are different.

Bike hire

Holiday Bikes
www.holiday-bikes.com
Franchise network with 20 branches along the Côte d'Azur, between Bandol and Menton, plus Avignon and Forcalquier. Bicycles, scooters and mopeds can be hired at individual agencies or on the web. Prices start at €14/day. Note that prices vary from branch to branch.

SNCF
Bikes can be rented from some SNCF stations (around €15/day plus €150 deposit), and returned to any station in the scheme. *See also p315* **Bicycles on trains**.

On foot

Provence is crossed by several well-signposted, long-distance *sentiers de grande randonnée* (GR), as well as local footpaths, all described in Topo guides, available from bookshops and newsagents. On the coast, some of the most beautiful *caps* (headlands) have waymarked paths, while walking in the Calanques gives access to spectacular unspoilt beaches. The best periods for walking are spring and autumn; access may be limited during the height of summer in areas where there is a high risk of fire. Be sure you have plenty of water and sun protection. *See also p322* **Maps** and *p324* **Sport & activity holidays**.

Hitch-hiking

Allô-Stop
8 rue Rochambeau, Paris (01.53.20.42.42).
A safer method of hitchhiking than just taking your chances on the kerb with a waved thumb and a smiley cardboard sign, this agency puts hitchhikers in touch with drivers. You should call several days in advance. There's a fee of €4.50-€10.50, depending on distance; you then pay €0.36/10km to the driver (Paris to Nice costs around €36).

Accommodation

There is a huge variety of places to stay in the South, from the grandest seafront palace hotel to the simplest mountain refuge, via villas, gîtes, campsites, country auberges and *chambres d'hôtes*. Book ahead in summer (it's essential if you want to stay on the coast), but outside the peak period of mid July to mid August you shouldn't have too much trouble finding accommodation. Many hotels and most campsites close from November to around March; some reopen just for the Christmas break. Certain tourist offices offer a free booking service and, if you arrive in peak season with nowhere to stay, most will know which hotels have last-minute vacancies.

Camping

French campsites (*les campings*) can be surprisingly luxurious. Many are run by local councils. Prices range from €8 to around €26 per night for a family of four, with car, caravan or tent. Camping rough (*camping sauvage*) is discouraged, but you may be given permission if you ask. Be very careful when camping in areas that may be a fire risk.

Campsites are graded from one-star (minimal comfort, water points, showers and sinks) to four-star luxury sites that offer more space for each pitch and above-average facilities. To get back to nature look out for campsites designated 'Aire naturelle de camping', where facilities will be absolutely minimal, with prices to match. Some farms offer camping pitches under the auspices of the Fédération Nationale des Gîtes Ruraux; these are designated 'Camping à la ferme' and again facilities are usually limited.

Information

The French Federation of Camping and Caravanning (FFCC) *Guide Officiel* lists 11,600 sites nationwide. *Michelin Green Guide – Camping/Caravanning France* is also good.

Chambres d'hôtes

Chambres d'hôtes, in private homes with a maximum of five bedrooms, are the French equivalent of British bed and breakfasts. Sometimes dinner en famille is also available. It is often an upmarket (and pricey) option; many are beautifully decorated rural farmhouses or even châteaux.

The following guides, available from government tourist offices, provide listings. Most tourist offices have a local list, but it is worth simply looking out for roadside signs, especially in rural areas (we also list selected *chambres d'hôtes* in the **Where to stay** sections). Gîtes de France (*see below*) has some *chambres d'hôtes* on its books.

Chambres et tables d'hôtes: listings for 14,000 French B&Bs.

Chambres d'hôtes prestige: a selection of 400 luxury B&Bs, plus 100 luxury gîtes.

Châteaux accueil: a selection of B&Bs in private châteaux.

Thomas Cook Welcome Guide to Selected Bed & Breakfasts in France: 500 personally inspected B&Bs.

B&B Abroad

5 Worlds End Lane, Orpington, Kent BR6 6AA (01689 882500/0845 330 2500/www.hotelsabroad.com). A straight-forward B&B booking service; can include ferry bookings.

Gîtes & holiday rentals

If you want to live as a local, there are plenty of opportunities to rent self-catering accommodation. Properties range from simple farm cottages to grand manor houses – even the odd château.

On the coast, holiday rentals range from luxury villas near St-Tropez to purpose-built (and often cramped) flats or *résidences de Tourisme* in the newer coastal resorts. Rentals are usually by the week or month and normally run Saturday to Saturday; book well ahead for July and August. Weekend rentals may be possible in winter. Individual tourist offices usually also have lists of rental properties. Alastair Sawday's *Special Places to Stay: French Holiday Homes* (www.specialplacestostay. com) lists holiday rentals all over France.

Fédération des Gîtes Ruraux de France *Maison des Gîtes de France, 59 rue St-Lazare, 75009 Paris (01.49.70.75.85/www.gites-de-france.fr).*
France's best-known holiday cottage organisation was set up after World War II to stimulate the rural economy by offering grants to owners to restore rural properties and let them out as holiday homes. Note that some will be off the beaten track and the use of a car, or at the very least a bicycle, is usually essential. You will often be expected to supply your own bed linen, but most have owners living nearby who will tell you where to buy local produce (or provide it themselves).
Prices average €250-€460 per week in August for a two- to four-person gîte. Properties are inspected by the Relais Départemental and given an *épi* (ear of corn) classification from one to five according to level of comfort. Prices tend to be much lower than for UK-based agencies, but many properties are also correspondingly more basic; check carefully for details such as an independent entry or garden or whether the gîte is in the same building as the owner. **Brittany Ferries** (Brittany Centre, Wharf Road, Portsmouth PO2 8RU, 0870 536 0360) is the UK agent for Gîtes de France, although its brochure only lists a small selection.

Clévacances *05.61.13.55.66/ www.clevacances.com.*
This association of holiday flats, houses and *chambres d'hôtes* doesn't exist in all *départements*, but is more recently established and well reputed for its more up-to-date rating system.

Directory

UK-based agencies

Balfour France *8878 9955/
www.balfourfrance.com.*
Top-of-the-market rentals along
the Côte d'Azur and Luberon, often
grand villas with endless terraces,
swimming pools and views over
the Med. Expect to pay £2,000–
£3,500/wk for an eight-person villa.

French Affair *7381 8519/
www.frenchaffair.com.*
A long-established company that lets
privately owned villas and houses in
Provence and other parts of France
(notably the Dordogne), including
refurbished stone farmhouses and
recently built *mas* and bungalows;
most have swimming pools. Prices go
from around £500/wk to £2,800/wk,
including ferry crossing, depending
on size and location of the property.

**Riviera Retreats/Kestrel
Travel** *01672 520651/France
04.93.24.10.70/www.kestrel
travel.com.*
Well-equipped, upmarket villas
and yachts on the coast between
St-Tropez and Monaco, or in the chic
hinterland around Vence and Grasse.
Prices from around £2,000/wk to a
money's-no-object £25,000/wk.

Gîtes d'étape & refuges

Gîte d'étape accommodation –
often found in mountainous
areas, or along long-distance
footpaths – is intended for
overnight stays by hikers,
cyclists, skiers or horse-riders.
These gîtes are often village-
run and tend to be spartan,
with bunks and basic facilities.
It is always wise to book. *Gîtes
de neige*, *gîtes de pêche* and
gîtes équestre are all variations
on the *gîte d'étape*, for skiers,
anglers and horse riders
respectively.

Mountain *refuges* (shelters)
range from large and solid
stone houses to basic huts. All
have bunk beds; many offer
food – often of surprisingly
high quality. Many are only
open from June to September;
they should always be booked
in advance. Prices vary from
€6 to €14 per person. Lists are
available from local tourist
offices or from the Club Alpin
Français (*see p324*).

Hotels

French hotels are generally
reasonably priced when
compared to much of what is
available elsewhere in Western
Europe, but the South of
France is, along with Paris,
the most expensive French
region. Hotels are graded from
no stars to four-star and even
four-star luxe, according to
factors such as room size,
lifts and services, but the star
system does not necessarily
reflect quality or welcome,
nor facilities such as air-
conditioning or computer
sockets: an old building may
lack a lift but be otherwise
charming. For this reason
we do not list star-ratings.
The majority of French hotels
are small, family-run affairs;
many close in winter.

Prices & reservations

You can usually get a decent room
with an adequate bathroom from
around €45 for two, though prices
are higher on the coast. Prices are
usually given per room rather than
per person, and will be posted on the
back of the door. We quote the price
for double rooms, but many hotels
will also have triples, quadruples or
suites suitable for families, or can
provide an extra bed or cot for a
child (there may be a supplement).
Breakfast is not normally included:
expect to pay from €6 in a budget
hotel to €25 in a luxury hotel. During
peak season hotels often insist on
demi-pension (with lunch or, more
usually, dinner included). All hotels
charge an additional room tax (*taxe
de séjour*) of 15¢–€1/person per night.
When booking, you may be asked for
a deposit; most places accept a credit
card number; some are satisfied with
a confirming fax. When booking a
room, it is normal to look at it first;
if it doesn't suit, ask to be shown
another (rooms can vary enormously
within the same hotel).

Hotel groups & chains

Best Western
*08.00.90.44.90/www.bestwestern.fr/
www.bestwestern.com.*
Huge international grouping of
privately owned, mainly three-
star hotels of varying styles from
historic coaching inns to modern
constructions.

Châteaux & Hotels de France
*01.40.07.00.20/www.chateaux
hotels.com.*
A group of independent, upmarket
hotels, ranging from more moderate
to luxury, as well as a few B&Bs in
private châteaux.

Concorde Hôtels *08.00.05.00.11/
UK 0800 028 9880/www.concorde-
hotels.fr.*
This French luxury group has in
its portfolio hotels as classy as the
Martinez in Cannes, the Palais de la
Méditerranée in Nice and the Belles-
Rives in Juan-les-Pins.

Logis de France *Fédération
Nationale des Logis et Auberges
de France, 83 av d'Italie, 75013
Paris (01.45.84.70.00/www.logis-
de-france.fr).*
France's biggest hotel network acts
as a sort of quality-control stamp for
over 5,000 private, often family-run,
hotels. Located in the countryside or
small towns, all have a restaurant,
most are one- or two-star.

Groupe Accor
www.accorhotels.com.
This is the biggest hotel group in
the world, ranging from the luxury
Sofitels to budget Etap and Formule
1 chains, which may be in industrial
estates or by motorways. It also runs
the mid-range Hôtels Ibis and
Novotels, as well as upmarket
Mercures, usually in towns.

Relais & Châteaux
*01.45.72.90.00/www.
relaischateaux.com.*
A consortium of luxury hotels, with
upmarket restaurants, often located
in handsome châteaux.

Relais du Silence *01.44.49.79.00/
www.silencehotel.com.*
A grouping of peaceful independent
hotels in châteaux or grand houses.

Special offers

The **Bon Week End en Villes**
(www.bon-week-end-en-villes.com)
scheme offers two nights for the price
of one at weekends, at selected hotels.
Participating cities include Aix-en-
Provence, Avignon and Marseille,
usually from November to March.
Les Escapades Provençales pass
offers three nights for the price of
two in hotels in the Vaucluse
(excluding Avignon) in winter.

Youth hostels

To stay in most *auberges de
jeunesse* you need to be a
member of the International
YHA or the Fédération Unie
des Auberges de Jeunesse
(27 rue Pajol, 75018 Paris,
01.44.89.87.27, www.fuaj.org).

Resources A-Z

Addresses

All addresses in France have a five-figure postcode before the town's name, starting with two numbers that indicate the *département*. This may be the only address in small rural communes; bigger places have street names; major cities are divided into *arrondissements*.

Age restrictions

You must be 18 or over to drive and 16 to consume alcohol in a public place. The age of consent is 15.

Beauty spas

Thalassotherapy

The French will often devote an entire holiday to thalassotherapy – therapeutic seawater massage and seaweed treatment. Children are generally not welcome (although some spas offer babysitting services and postnatal packages). Expect to pay €46-€75/day.

Biovimer Spa Marina *Baie des Anges, Cros-de-Cagnes (04.93.22.71.71/www.biovimer.fr).*
Thalassa Hyères *allée de la Mer, La Capte, Hyères (04.94.58.00.94).*
Thalazur Antibes *770 chemin des Moyennes Bréguières, Antibes (04.92.91.82.00).*
Thermes Marins de Monte-Carlo *2 av de Monte-Carlo (00.377-92.16.40.40).*

Inland spas

The natural thermal spa at Aix concentrates on beauty and fitness; Gréoux is more focused on medical treatments. Grape cures are available in the Vaucluse (contact Avignon Office de Tourisme, 04.32.74.32.74).

Thermes de Gréoux-les-Bains *av des Thermes, Gréoux-les-Bains (08.26.46.81.85).*
Thermes Sextius *55 cours Sextius, Aix-en-Provence (04.42.23.81.81).*

Business

Business people in France will invariably prefer to meet you in person, even if it's to discuss something that could easily have been dealt with over the phone. Shake hands and remember that French is a more formal language than English: use the *vous* form, unless it's someone you know well.

Most major banks can refer you to lawyers, accountants and tax consultants; several US and British banks provide expatriate services. The standard English-language reference is *The French Company Handbook*, published by the International Herald Tribune (01.41.43.93.00).

Business media

Dailies *La Tribune* and *Les Echos*, and the weekly *Investir*, are trusted sources. *Capital*, its sister magazine *Management* and the weightier *L'Expansion* are worthwhile monthlies. *Défis* has tips for the entrepreneur; *Initiatives* is for the self-employed. BFM (96.4 FM) is an all-news business radio station. Online, you'll find stock quotes at www.boursarama.com and www.lesechos.com, and company and market profiles at www.kompass.fr.

English Yellow Pages *08.92.68.83.97/04.92.90.49.34/ www.englishyellowpages.fr.* Free A-Z of English-speaking businesses in the Alpes-Maritimes and Var, aimed at expats.

Congress centres

Acropolis *1 esplanade Kennedy, Nice (04.93.92.83.00).*
Centre des Congrès Auditorium *bd Louis II, Monte-Carlo, Monaco (00.377-93.10.84.00).*
Centre de Rencontre Internationale *13 bd Princesse Charlotte, Monte-Carlo (00.377-93.25.53.07).*
Palais des Congrès *Parc Chanot, 2 bd Rabatau, Marseille (04.91.76.16.00).*
Palais des Festivals *La Croisette, Cannes (04.93.39.01.01).*

Useful addresses

Banque Populaire de la Côte d'Azur *International Branch, 22 bd Victor Hugo, 06000 Nice (04.93.82.81.81/www.cotedazur. banquepopulaire.fr).* Banking advice in English.
British Chamber of Commerce *25bis bd Carnot, Nice (04.97.08.11.30).*
Centre de Ressources Côte d'Azur *Chambre de Commerce et d'Industrie Nice Côte d'Azur, 20 bd Carabacel, Nice (04.93.13.74.36/ www.businessriviera.com).* Information centre.

Services

Computer services

Gale Force *13 av St-Michel, Monte-Carlo (00.377-93.50.20.92/ www.galeforce.com).* In English.

Travel advice

For up-to-date information on travel to a specific country – including the latest news on safety and security, on health issues, and on local laws and customs – contact your home country government's department of foreign affairs. Most have websites packed with useful advice for would-be travellers.

Australia
www.dfat.gov.au/travel

New Zealand
www.mft.govt.nz/travel

UK
www.fco.gov.uk/travel

Canada
www.voyage.gc.ca

Republic of Ireland
www.irlgov.ie/iveagh

USA
http://travel.state.gov

Directory

Loca Centre *1330 av Guilbert de la Lauzière, Europarc de Pichaury, Batiment B5, 13865 Aix-en-Provence (04.88.71.88.35/www.locacentre.com).* Rentals of laptops, PCs, printers and scanners. A branch in Marseille too.

International couriers

DHL *0800 202 525/www.dhl.com.*
FedEx *0800 123 800/ www.fedex.com.*

Translation services

Accents *Pauline Beaumont, 120 chemin des Serres, 06510 Gattières (04.93.08.38.38/pauline.beaumont@ worldonline.fr).*

Children

Plenty of kids' activities are laid on in France, and many hotels have family rooms or can add a cot (*lit bébé*). Disposable nappies (*couches jetables*) are easy to find.

Activities & sightseeing

The beach and the sea are the easiest way to amuse children, and private beach concessions with sunloungers and parasols are the easiest of all; just book your parasol close to the shore and watch the kids make sandcastles. Main resorts and beaches are monitored by trained lifeguards in summer. But do be careful with the intense midday sun – most French families leave the beach between noon and 3pm.

In the main cities, many theatres and museums organise activities and performances for children, especially on Wednesdays and Saturdays.

Even small villages often have a playground, which can be a good place to meet other families. Museums and monuments generally have reduced rates for children: under-18s are free at state museums. Popular family attractions include zoos at Fréjus and La Barben, Marineland at Antibes and the Aquarium in Monaco (for listings, see the relevant chapters).

Eating out

Eating out with children is a normal part of French life, and children are usually welcome. It's especially easy during the day at cafés or restaurants with a terrace. Many places offer a children's menu, will split a prix fixe between two kids or will give you an extra plate so that you can share with your children.

Transport

When hiring a car, be sure to book baby and child seats in advance. For train fares, *see p314.*

Customs

There are no limits on the quantity of goods you can take into France from another EU country for personal use, provided tax has been paid in the country of origin. Beware bringing in fake designer goods from the markets at Ventimiglia and San Remo: the goods may be confiscated and you might have to pay a fine.

Personal limits are:

● up to 800 cigarettes, 400 small cigars, 200 cigars or 1kg loose tobacco.
● 10 litres of spirits (over 22% alcohol), 90 litres of wine (under 22% alcohol) or 110 litres of beer.

For goods from outside the EU:

● 200 cigarettes or 100 small cigars, 50 cigars or 250g loose tobacco.
● 1 litre of spirits (over 22% alcohol) and 2 litres of wine (under 22% alcohol) and beer.
● 50g perfume.

Visitors can carry up to €7,600 in currency.

Tax refunds (détaxe)

Non-EU residents can claim a refund on VAT (TVA) on some items if they spend over €175 in one day. Ask for a *bordereau de vente à l'exportation* form in the shop and when you leave France have it stamped by Customs; then post the form back to the shop.

Disabled travellers

Travel & transport

Location de Véhicules Equipés et Automatiques *51 rue Celony, 13100 Aix-en-Provence (04.42.93.54.59/www.lvea.fr).* Rents cars specially adapted for disabled drivers; around €100/day.
Eurotunnel *03.21.00.61.00/ UK 0870 535 3535/www.euro tunnel.com.*
The Channel Tunnel car-on-a-train is good for disabled passengers; you may stay in your vehicle and get a 10% discount.

Groupement pour Insertion des Handicapés Physiques (GIHP) *04.91.11.41.00.*
Information on disabled transport.

Taxis

Taxi drivers cannot legally refuse to take disabled people or guide dogs, and must help them get into the taxi.

Trains

SNCF runs train carriages designed to accommodate wheelchairs. For information call 08.00.15.47.53. People accompanying handicapped passengers get free travel or reductions, as do guide dogs.

Holidays & accommodation

Tourist offices should be able to provide information on sights and hotels accessible to the disabled. Disabled parking is indicated with a blue wheelchair sign; the international orange disabled parking disc is also recognised. To hire a wheelchair or other equipment, enquire at the local pharmacy. In Nice, part of the public beach has been adapted for wheelchairs with ramp access and a concrete platform.

Gîtes Accessibles à Tous (Gites de France, 59 rue St-Lazare, 75009 Paris, 01.49.70.75.85, www.gites-de-france.fr) lists holiday rentals equipped for the disabled. The *French Federation of Camping and Caravanning Guide* and the *Michelin Green Guide – Camping/Caravanning France* both list campsites with disabled facilities.

Useful addresses

Association des paralysés de France *01.40.78.69.00.*
RADAR (Royal Association for Disability & Rehabilitation) *Unit 12 City Forum, 250 City Road, London EC1V 8AF (7250 3222/ www.radar.org.uk).*

Drugs

Possession of drugs is illegal in France. Possession of even a small amount of cannabis for personal use could land you in jail and incur a large fine.

Electricity & gas

Electricity in France runs on 220V, so visitors with British 240V appliances can use a converter (*adaptateur*), available at hardware shops. For US 110V appliances, you will need a transformer (*transformateur*), available at Fnac and Darty chains.

Embassies & consulates

For general enquiries, passports or visas, you usually need the consulate rather than the embassy. A full list of embassies and consulates appears in Pages Jaunes under 'Ambassades et Consulats' (or see www.pagesjaunes.fr).

Consulates in the South

British *24 av du Prado, 13006 Marseille (04.91.15.72.10)*.
Canadian *10 rue Lamartine, 06000 Nice (04.93.92.93.22)*.
Irish *152 bd JF Kennedy, 06160 Cap d'Antibes (04.93.61.50.63)*.
US *12 bd Paul Peytral, 13286 Marseille (04.91.54.92.00); 7 av Gustave V, 06000 Nice (04.93.88.89.55)*.

Embassies in Paris

Australian *01.40.59.33.00/ www.france.embassy.gov.au*.
British *01.44.51.31.00/ www.amb-grandebretagne.fr*.
Canadian *01.44.43.29.00/ www.amb-canada.fr*.
Irish *01.44.17.67.00*.
New Zealand *01.45.01.43.43/ www.nzembassy.com/france*.
South Africa *01.53.59.23.23/ www.afriquesud.net*.
US *01.43.12.22.22/www.amb-usa.fr*.

Emergencies

Police 17
Fire (Sapeurs-Pompiers) 18
Ambulance (SAMU) 15
EDF/GDF 08.10.12.61.26
Emergencies from **mobile phone** 112
See also below **Health**.

Gay & lesbian

France is a generally gay-tolerant country and the Riviera has long been a stamping ground for pink

people. Gay bars, saunas and discos abound in Nice, Toulon, Marseille, Nimes, Aix and Avignon, there are Gay Pride marches in Marseille and Cannes, and an infrastructure of groups is slowly developing. Nice's Coco Beach is a 24hr cruising point. Other gay beaches include the ritzy Plage de St-Laurent-d'Eze and Plage St-Aygulf at Fréjus. La Batterie, just outside Cannes, is a straight and gay nude beach.

Associations & information

Centre Gai et Lesbien
11 rue Regal, 30000 Nîmes (04.66.67.10.59). **Open** 7-9pm Thur. Support and advice.
www.gay-provence.org
Lists gay-friendly hotels and B&Bs, activities and assocations.
www.france.qrd.org
France-wide directory of gay and lesbian associations and events.

Health

All EU nationals staying in France are entitled to use the French Social Security system, which refunds up to 70% of medical expenses (but sometimes much less, for example for dental treatment). From 1 January 2006 the E111 will be replaced by the European Health Insurance Card (EHIC). It is easiest to apply for one online at www.dh.gov.uk (provide your name, date of birth and NHS or NI number). The E112 form is still valid for those already receiving medical care, such as routine maternity care. Non-EU nationals should take out insurance before leaving home. Fees and prescriptions are paid in full, then reimbursed in part on receipt of a completed *fiche*.

Accident & emergency

For emergency numbers, *see above* **Emergencies**. Note that the Sapeurs-Pompiers (fire brigade), who are also trained paramedics, will usually be called to accidents rather than the SAMU.

Complementary medicine

Most pharmacies sell homeopathic medicines. For alternative medicine practitioners, ask in the pharmacy or check www.pagesjaunes.fr.

Contraception & abortion

For the pill (*la pilule*) or a coil (*stérilet*) you will need a prescription. Visit a GP (*médecin généraliste*) or gynaecologist (*gynécologue*); look in the Pages Jaunes (www.pagesjaunes. fr) or ask at a pharmacy for a recommendation. You can buy condoms (*préservatifs*) and spermicides from pharmacies. French pharmacies also dispense the morning-after pill (*pilule du lendemain*) without a prescription. Abortion (*avortement* or *interruption volontaire de la grossesse*) is legal up to 12 weeks and can be reimbursed by French Social Security; consult a gynaecologist or look for the local 'Planning Familial' centre in the telephone directory.

Doctors & dentists

A complete list of practitioners is in the Pages Jaunes under 'Médecins Qualifiés'. To get a Social Security refund, choose a doctor or dentist with 'Médecin Conventionné' after the name. Consultations cost at least €20, of which a proportion may be reimbursed if you are entitled to use the French Social Security system (*see above*). A *médecin généraliste* is a general practitioner, though you are also free to go to the specialist of your choice – whose fees may be two or three times higher.

Helplines & house calls

In cases of medical emergency, dial 15 for an ambulance or, in most large towns, ring the Service d'Aide Médicale d'Urgence (SAMU) – the numbers will be given at the front of telephone directories. The Sapeurs-Pompiers (fire brigade) also have trained paramedics.
Alcoholics Anonymous South of France *04.93.82.91.10*.
Centre Anti-Poisons *04.91.75.25.25*.
Nice Médecins *04.93.52.42.42*. Local doctor service for home visits.
SOS Help *01.46.21.46.46*.
Open 3-11pm daily.
Paris-based helpline in English.

SOS Médecins *08.10.85.01.01.*
Can send a doctor on a house call.
A home visit before 7pm starts at
€38 if you don't have French Social
Security, €23 if you do; the fee goes
up after 7pm.

Hospitals

For a complete list, consult the Pages
Blanches (www.pagesblanches.fr)
under 'Hôpital Assistance Publique'.

Opticians

Any optician can make small repairs
and, if you bring your prescription,
supply new glasses. Drivers are
required by law to carry a spare pair.

Pharmacies

Pharmacies, which sport a green
neon cross, have a monopoly on
issuing medication. Most open from
9am or 10am to 7pm or 8pm. Staff
can provide basic medical services
such as disinfecting and bandaging
wounds, attending to snake or insect
bites (for a small fee) and will
indicate the nearest doctor on
duty. French pharmacists are
highly trained; you can often
avoid visiting a doctor by describing
your symptoms and seeing what they
suggest. They are also qualified to
identify mushrooms, so you can take
in anything you aren't sure about.
Towns have a rota system of
pharmacies de garde at night and
on Sundays. Any closed pharmacy
will have a sign indicating the
nearest open pharmacy.

STDs, HIV & AIDS

SIDA Info Service *08.00.84.08.00.*
Open 24hrs daily.
Confidential AIDS information in
French; some bilingual counsellors.

ID

You are required to keep your
passport or *carte de séjour*
with you at all times.

Insurance

Insurance is often required
for sporting activities. *See
also p321* **Health**.

Internet

Big youth- and student-oriented
cities such as Aix and Marseille
abound in cybercafés, but
availability in rural areas and
villages is much more variable.
Wi-Fi is now available in some
hotels and airports, often using
prepaid cards; free wireless
access isn't common, but there
are several places in the South
of France that do offer the
service – they are listed at
http://wififreespot.com.

ISPs

America Online *08.26.02.60.00/
www.aol.fr.*
Club-Internet *08.26.02.70.28/
www.club-internet.fr.*
Free *www.free.fr.*
Wanadoo (France Télécom)
08.10.63.34.34/www.wanadoo.fr.

Language

See p328 **Essential
Vocabulary**. For courses,
see p325; for food terms, *see
p30* **Decoding the menu**.

Legal advice

Mairies (town halls) may be
able to answer legal enquiries;
phone for details of free
consultations juridiques. They
will also be able to recommend
an *avocat* (lawyer) or *notaire*
(solicitor), both are addressed
as 'Maître'. English Language
Yellow Pages can give names
of English-speaking lawyers
in the Côte d'Azur over the
phone (08.92.68.83.97).

Lost & stolen property

To report a crime or lost
belongings, visit the local
gendarmerie or *commissariat
de police* (*see p324* **Police &
crime**). If you want to make
an insurance claim, you'll need
a police report. Phone numbers
are given at the front of local
directories; in an **emergency**
dial 17. If you lose a passport,
report it first to the police,
then to the nearest consulate
(*see p321* **Embassies &
consulates**).

Maps

Tourist offices can usually
provide free town maps (*plans*).
The large-format Michelin
Atlas or 1:1,000,000 (1cm:10km)
No.989 sheet map (*carte routière
et touristique*) for the whole of
France are good for driving.
Michelin Carte Régionale
No.528 Provence, Côte d'Azur
is a good 1:200,000 (1cm:2km)
all-purpose map of the region.
For walking or cycling, the
Institut Géographique National
(IGN) maps are invaluable.
Top 100 (1:100,000, 1cm:1km)
and Top 50 (1:50,000, 2cm:1km)
maps mark all roads and most
footpaths; the IGN blue series
1:25,000 (4cm:1km) has even
greater detail.

Media

English-language press

Most of major British and US papers,
including Paris-based *International
Herald Tribune*, can be picked up
from newsagents (*maisons de la
presse*) in major towns, at train
stations and airports.

Local English press

Riviera Reporter (04.93.45.77.19) is
a glossy magazine aimed at foreign
residents, carrying local information,
news and small ads; it can be picked
up at English bookshops. The
monthly *Riviera Times* (www.riviera
times.com) has local news, events
and classifieds. *The Connexion* is
an A4-sized news and ads freebie.

French press

As well as the French national dailies
Le Monde (centre-left), *Libération*
(left), *Le Figaro* (right) and sports
daily *L'Equipe*, the French are
attached to their local papers:
Nice-Matin (www.nicematin.fr), *La
Provence* (www.laprovence-presse.fr),
Var-Matin (www.varmatin.com),
Le Dauphiné Vaucluse and *La
Marseillaise* cover most of Provence
and the Côte d'Azur. Free news
dailies are booming in Marseille, with
20 Minutes and *Metro*, plus free *La
Marseillaise* offshoot *Marseille Plus*.
A vast range of magazines includes
news weeklies *L'Express*, *Nouvel
Observateur*, *Le Point* and *Marianne*,
women's mags *Elle*, *Marie-Claire*,
Jalouse, *Vogue*, and gossip essentials
Paris Match, *Gala* and *Voici*.

Radio

FM radio

Note that many stations' wavelengths vary from area to area.

87.8 France Inter State-run, MOR music and international news.
91.7/92.1 France Musique State classical music channel with concerts and jazz, and lots of talk.
93.5/93.9 France Culture Highbrow state culture station.
105.5 France Info 24hr news, economic updates and sports. Broadcasts repeat every 15mins, so it's good for learning French.
RTL The most popular French station, mixing music and talk.
Europe 1 News, press reviews, sports, business and interviews.
NRJ Very popular pop channel.
Nostalgie Golden oldies.
Rire et chansons French comedy acts, mixed with pop.

Local FM stations

88.8 FM Radio Grenouille Marseille station, with hip coverage of culture, events and new music.
98.8 FM Radio Monte-Carlo
106.3/106.5 FM Riviera Radio Parochial English-language radio, with small ads and local gossip.

BBC World Service

6.195 to 12.095 MHz shortwave.

Television

Terrestrial channels

France has six terrestrial channels. The biggest, **TF1**, features movies, reality shows, soaps and news with star anchors Patrick Poivre d'Arvor and Claire Chazal. **France 2** is a similar state-run version, minus the reality shows. **France 3** has regional news, sports, documentaries and Sunday's *Cinéma de Minuit*, with classic films screened in their original language (VO). **Canal+** is a subscription channel, with recent movies, exclusive sport and late-night porn. **Arte** is a Franco-German hybrid specialising in intelligent arts coverage, films and themed evenings. Its wavelength is shared with educational channel **La Cinquième** (6.45am-7pm). **M6** rotates music videos, imported series and some excellent magazine programmes.

Cable TV & satellite

Cable and satellite channels include **LCI** for 24hr news and business bulletins; documentaries on **Planète**, **Histoire** and **Voyages**; **Téva** for women's programmes and good sitcoms in VO; **Mezzo** for classical

music and dance; **Eurosport** for sport; **Canal Jimmy**, **13e Rue**, **Série Club**, **RTL9** for sitcoms and police series; and **TMC** for sitcoms and classic movies. Foreign-language channels include **BBC World**, **BBC Prime** and **CNN**.

Money

The euro (€)

The euro (€) is the official currency in France and 11 other participating European Union nations. Coins exist in 1, 2, 5, 10 and 50 centime denominations and 1 and 2 euros; notes are in 5, 10, 20, 50, 100, 200 and 500 denominations. Try to avoid €200 and €500 notes as few shops are willing to accept them.

ATMs

If your cash-withdrawal card has the European Cirrus symbol, withdrawals can be made from bank and post office cash machines by using your PIN. Credit card companies charge a fee for cash advances, but rates are often better than bank rates. Cash machines are widespread in major cities and towns, but can be few and far between in rural areas.

Banks

French banks usually open from 9am to 5pm Monday to Friday (some close for lunch between 12.30pm and 2.30pm); some also open on Saturday. All close on public holidays (usually from noon on the previous day).

Bank accounts

To open an account (*ouvrir un compte*) you need proof of identity, regular income and an address in France. You'll probably have to show your passport or *carte de séjour*, a utility bill in your name and a payslip or a letter from your employer. Students need a student card and may need a letter from their parents. French banks are tough on overdrafts, so try to anticipate any cash crisis in advance and work out a deal for an authorised overdraft (*découvert autorisé*). Depositing foreign-currency cheques is slow, and incurs high charges, so use wire transfer or a bank draft in euros.

Credit cards

Major international credit cards are widely used in France, especially Visa (linked to the French Carte Bleue); American Express and Diners Club coverage is more

patchy. French-issued cards have a security microchip (*puce*) that enables them to be slotted into a card reader and transactions authorised by keying in a PIN; non-French cards generate a credit slip to sign.
In case of credit card loss or theft, call the following 24hr services, which have English-speaking staff.
American Express *01.47.77.72.00.*
Diners Club *08.20.00.07.34.*
MasterCard *01.45.67.84.84.*
Visa *08.92.70.57.05.*

Natural hazards

For details on heat and floods, *see also p326* **Climate**.

Insects

For every tourist there is at least one mosquito in the South, particularly in the Camargue. Plug-in vaporisers are a good defence and are available in most supermarkets. Campers should beware of a spider that bites exposed skin at night, producing a scratchy rash. Black scorpions are sometimes found from late spring to autumn.

Fire

Fire is a major risk during the dry summer period, and each year there are usually several serious fires, some of them caused deliberately. Always be careful when walking or cycling on open mountain or in woodland; campfires are strictly banned and certain paths are closed in high summer or on windy days.

Opening times

Shops are generally open 9.30am-7pm, earlier for food shops. The sacred lunch hour is still largely observed, which means that many shops and offices close at noon or 1pm and reopen at 2pm or later. Many shops also close for the morning or all day on Monday. Hypermarkets (*grandes surfaces*) usually stay open through lunch. Most shops close on Sundays, though *bureaux de tabac* (cigarettes, stamps) and newsagents are often open Sunday mornings, and *boulangeries* (bakers) may be open every day. Public offices and *mairies* (town halls) usually open 8.30am-noon,

Directory

then 2-6pm; for banks, *see p323* **Banks**. Except in peak season, many museums close for lunch. They also close on certain public holidays, notably 1 Jan, 1 May and 25 Dec. National museums usually close on Tuesday.

Police & crime

Police in urban and rural areas come under two different governmental organisations. The **Gendarmerie nationale** is a military force serving under the Ministère de la Défense and its network covers minor towns and rural areas. The **Police nationale** serve under the Ministère de l'Intérieur in main cities. Some cities also have **Police municipale**.

Beware of car crime. Police advise leaving nothing visible in parked cars. In Nice there has also been a spate of car jackings – car theft as people are parking; petrol theft is not unknown in rural areas.

If you are robbed, you need to make a statement at the police station or gendarmerie for your insurance claim.

Postal services

Postes (post offices) are usually open 9am-noon and 2-7pm Monday to Friday, and 9am-noon on Saturday. In main post offices, individual counters are marked according to the services they provide; if you just need stamps, go to the window marked 'Timbres'.

If you need to send an urgent letter or parcel overseas, ask for it to be sent through 'Chronopost', which is faster but more expensive. Chronopost is also fastest for parcels within France; packages up to 25kg are guaranteed to be delivered within 24hrs.

For a small fee, you can arrange for mail to be kept poste restante, addressed to Poste Restante, Poste Centrale (for main post office), then the town postcode and name. You will need to present your passport when collecting mail.

Stamps are also available at tobacconists (*bureaux de tabac*) and other shops selling postcards and greetings cards. For standard-weight letters or postcards (up to 20g within France and 10g within the EU) a 50¢ stamp is needed.

Telegrams can be sent during *poste* hours or by phone (24hr); to send a telegram abroad, dial 08.00.33.44.11.

Fax and photocopying facilities are often available at post offices and newsagents. Many supermarkets have coin-operated photocopiers.

Religion

The presence of the British in the South of France over the past two centuries means there are several Anglican churches. For more information contact:
Intercontinental Church Society *1 Athena Drive, Tachbrook Park, Warwick CV34 6NL (0192 643 0347/www.ics-uk.org).*
Holy Trinity Church *rue du Canada, Cannes (04.93.94.54.61).* **Service** 10.30am Sun.
Monaco Christian Fellowship *9 rue Louis Notari, Monaco (00.377-93.30.60.72).* **Service** 11am Sun.
St Michael's Anglican Church *11 chemin des Myrtes, Beaulieu (04.93.01.45.61).* **Service** 10am Sun.

Removals

For international removals use a company with experience in France that is a member of the International Federation of Furniture Removers (FIDI) or the Overseas Moving Network (www.omnimoving.com).
Overs International *Unit 8, Abro Development, Government Road, Aldershot GU11 2DA (01252 343646).*

Smoking

Despite health campaigns and a law that insists restaurants provide non-smoking areas (*zones non-fumeurs*), the French remain enthusiastic smokers. Cigarettes are officially only on sale in *tabacs*, which tend to close at 8pm, and 2pm on Sundays.

Sport & activity holidays

Enquire at local tourist offices about swimming and tennis facilities; there is also useful sports information on the regional tourist board website (www.crt-paca.fr).

Climbing

Les Guides randoxygène (available from main tourist offices) are excellent guides for climbers and walkers, with detailed trails in the region. Dozens of climbing clubs provide courses, plus guides and monitors for day outings.
Club Alpin Français *14 av Mirabeau, Nice (04.93.62.59.99/ www.cafnice.org); 3 rue St-Michel, Avignon (04.90.41.92.15).*

Cycling

Taking your own bike (*vélo*) to France is relatively easy (*see p315*). Some youth hostels also rent out cycles and arrange tours; for details, contact the YHA (*see p318*). Package cycling holidays are offered by various organisations; luggage is normally transported each day to your next destination. The IGN 906 Cycling France map gives details of routes, cycling clubs and places to stay. The **Cyclists Touring Club** (Cotterell House, 69 Meadrow, Godalming, Surrey GU7 3HS, 0870 873 0060, www.ctc.org.uk) can provide members with cycle and travel insurance, detailed touring itineraries and information sheets about France; its tours brochure lists trips to the region. The club's French counterpart is the **Fédération Française de Cyclotourisme** (01.56.20.88.88, www.ffct.org).

Golf

For Provence's golf courses, contact the **Fédération Française de Golfe** (01.41.49.77.00, www.ffg. org). **Cordon Rouge Villas** (01253 739749) and **French Golf Holidays** (01277 824100, www.golf-france.co.uk) offer golf holiday packages out of the UK.

Horse riding

Horse riding and pony trekking are popular, with *centres équestres* all over the region (for the Camargue, *see p83* **The mane drag**). Foxcroft Travel (01834 831841, www.foxcroft travel.co.uk) offers French equestrian holidays out of the UK. For further information, contact the **Association Drôme à Cheval** (04.75.45.78.79, www.drome-a-cheval.com) or the **Ligue Régionale de Provence des Sports Equestres** (298 av du club Hippique, 13090 Aix-en-Provence, 04.42.20.88.02, www.provence-equitation.com).

Skiing

There are several ski resorts in the Alpes-Maritimes; the three with the best facilities are Auron, Valberg and Isola 2000.
Fédération Française de Ski *04.50.51.40.34/www.ffs.fr.*

Watersports

Antibes and Cannes are major watersports centres, and there's great diving at the Iles de Lérins, the Iles de Hyères and the Calanques. Canoes and rafts are popular in the Gorges de Verdon and on the River Argens. For detailed listings pick up the *Watersports Côte d'Azur* brochure or go to www.france-nautisme.com.
Comité Régional de Voile Alpes-Provence *46 bd Kraemer, Marseille (04.91.11.61.78).*
Comité Régional de Voile Côte d'Azur *Espace Antibes, 2208 rte de Grasse, Antibes (04.93.74.77.05).*
Fédération Française de Canoë-Kayak et des Sports Associés en Eau-Vive *01.45.11.08.50/www.ffck.org.*
Fédération Française d'Etudes et de Sports Sous-Marins *24 quai Rive-Neuve, Marseille (04.91.33.99.31).*
Ligue Régionale Canoë Alpes-Provence *14 av Vincent Auriol, Bagnols-sur-Cèze (04.66.89.47.71/www.canoe-alpesprovence.com).*

Walking

Each *département* has its own ramblers' organisation that arranges guided walks. The Club Alpin Français in Nice (*see p324* **Climbing**) organises day-long hikes with coach/minibus transport. *See also p322* **Maps**.
Fédération Française de Randonnée Pédestre *01.44.89.93.93/www.ffrp.asso.fr.*

Study & students

For cookery courses, *see p26* **DIY cuisine**.

Language courses

Actilangue *2 rue Alexis Mossa, 06000 Nice (04.93.96.33.84/fax 04.93.44.37.16/www.actilangue.com).*
Alliance Française *310 rue de Paradis, 13008 Marseille (04.96.10.24.60); 2 rue de Paris, 06000 Nice (04.93.62.67.66).*
Azurlingua *25 bd Raimbaldi, 06000 Nice (04.97.03.07.00/ www.azurlingua.com).*
Centre International d'Antibes *38 bd d'Aguillon, Antibes 06600 (04.92.90.71.70/www.cia-France.com).*
ELFCA (Institut d'Enseignement de la Langue Française sur la Côte d'Azur) *66 av de Toulon, 83400 Hyères (04.94.65.03.31/www.elfca.com).*
International School of Nice *15 av Claude Debussy, 06200 Nice (04.93.21.04.00/04.93.21.84.90/ www.isn-nice.org).*

Student discounts

To claim discounts in museums, cinemas and theatres you need an **International Student Identity Card**. ISICs are only valid in France if you are under 26. Under-26s can also get discounts of up to 50% on trains with the **Carte 12/25**. The **Carte Jeune** (€18.29 from Fnac) also gives a range of discounts.

Universities

The **Université d'Aix-Marseille** has arts, humanities and law faculties located in Aix, and science and mathematics faculties in Marseille; Aix-Marseille III (04.42.21.59.87, 04.91.28.81.18) is the most international part. Contact the **Institut d'Etudes Françaises pour Etudiants Etrangers** (23 rue Gaston de Saporta, Aix-en-Provence, 04.42.21.70.90) about courses for foreign students.

Other universities include **Avignon** (04.90.16.25.00, www.univ-avignon.fr), **Toulon** (04.94.14.20.00, www.univ-tln.fr) and **Nice-Sophia Antipolis** (04.92.07.67.07, www.unice.fr).

Useful organisations

Central Bureau for Educational Visits & Exchanges *10 Spring Gardens, London SW1A 1BN (020 7389 4004).*

Centre des Échanges Internationaux *1 rue Golzen, 75006 Paris (01.40.51.11.71).*
Non-profit organisation, running sporting and cultural holidays, and educational tours for 15-30-year-olds.
Socrates-Erasmus Programme *UK Socrates-Erasmus Council, RND Building, The University, Canterbury, Kent CT2 7PD (0122 776 2712/www.erasmus.ac.uk).*
This scheme enables EU students with a reasonable standard of written and spoken French to spend a year of their degree taking appropriate courses in the French university system. The UK office publishes a brochure, but applications must be made through the Erasmus co-ordinator at your home university.
Souffle *Espace Charlotte, La Crou, 83260 (04.94.00.94.65).*
An umbrella organisation for courses in French as a foreign language.

Telephones

Telephone numbers are always ten figures, written in sets of two, e.g. 01.23.45.67.89. If you want numbers to be given singly rather than in pairs as is customary, ask for *chiffre par chiffre*. Regional telephone numbers are prefixed as follows: Paris & Ile de France 01; North-west 02; North-east 03; South-east and Corsica 04; and South-west 05. Mobile phones start 06. When calling from abroad, omit the zero. The code for dialling France is 33; for Monaco it is 377.

Public phones

Public phone boxes use phone cards (*télécartes*),which are available from post offices, stationers, stations, *tabacs* and some cafés. To make a call from a public phone box, lift the receiver, insert the card, then dial the number. To make a follow-on call, do not replace the receiver but press the green 'appel suivant' button and dial.

International calls

Dial 00 followed by the country's international code.
Australia *00 61*
Canada *00 1*
Ireland *00 353*
Monaco *00 377*
New Zealand *00 64*
South Africa *00 27*
UK *00 44*
USA *00 1*

Directory

Special rates

In France numbers that start with the following prefixes are charged at special rates:

0800 Numéro vert Freephone.

0801 Numéro azur 11¢ first 3mins, then 4¢/min.

0802 Numéro indigo I 15¢/min.

0803 Numéro indigo II 23¢/min.

0867 23¢/min.

0836/0868/0869 34¢/min.

Cheap rates

Within France cheap rates apply between 7pm and 8am both on weekdays and at weekends.

Mobile phones

France has just three mobile phone operators, offering myriad subscriptions and prepaid card systems. The operators are Bouygues, France Telecom/ Orange and SFR.

Misterrent *www.misterrent.com.* This internet-based company will work out which of its nationwide network of outlet franchises is nearest to you, then bike a phone to you from there.

Rentacell *08.10.00.00.92/ www.rentacell.com.* Rentacell offers mobile phone rental for €8/day or €30/wk; calls within France cost 76¢/min, international calls cost €1.22/min, and incoming calls are free. There's same-day delivery to your hotel or an airport if you're staying in Cannes or Nice.

Phone directories

Phone directories can be found in all post offices and in most cafés. The Pages Blanches provides a listing of people and businesses in alphabetical order. Pages Jaunes lists businesses and services by category. Both are available on www.pagesjaunes.fr.

24-hour services

French directory enquiries *(renseignements)* 12.

International directory enquiries 32 12 then country code (eg. 44 for UK, 1 for USA).

Telephone engineer 13.

International news (French recorded message, France Inter) dial 08.36.68.10.33 (34¢/min).

To send a telegram (all languages): international 08.00.33.44.11, within France 36.55.

Speaking clock 36.99.

Time

France is one hour ahead of Greenwich Mean Time (GMT) and six hours ahead of New York. The clocks change between summer and winter time on the same date as the UK. The 24hr clock is frequently used in France when giving times: 8am is *huit heures*, noon *(midi)* is *douze heures*, 8pm is *vingt heures* and midnight *(minuit)* is *zéro heure*.

Tipping

By law a service charge of 10-15% is included in the bill in all restaurants; leave a small extra tip of 50¢-€2 on the table if you are particularly pleased. In taxis, round up to the nearest 50¢ or €1; give €1-€2 to porters, doormen, hairdressers and guides. In a bar or café, just leave small change.

Toilets

Anyone may use the toilet in a bar or café, although it's polite to at least have a *café* at *le zinc*. Ask for *les toilettes* or *le WC* – pronouced 'vay say'. You may have to get a token *(jeton)* from the bar. Public toilets vary; some are still squats.

Tourist information

France has an efficient network of tourist information offices (Office de Tourisme or Syndicat d'Initiative), often present in even tiny villages, with information on accommodation, sporting facilities, cultural attractions and guided visits; some also have hotel booking and ticket reservation services.

For information before you travel, there are French government Tourist Offices in the UK (178 Piccadilly, London W1, 0906 824 4123) and USA

(444 Madison Avenue, NY 10022, 212 838 7800). Otherwise, consult the French Government Tourist Office's official internet site www.franceguide.com.

Visas

To visit France, you need a valid passport. Non-EU citizens require a visa, although USA, Canada, Australia and New Zealand citizens do not need a visa for stays of up to three months. If in any doubt, check with the French consulate in your country. If you intend to stay in France for more than 90 days, then you are supposed to apply for a *carte de séjour*.

Weights & measures

France uses the metric system. Remember that all speed limits are in kilometres per hour. One kilometre is equivalent to 0.62 mile (1 mile = 1.6km). Petrol, like other liquids, is measured in litres (1 UK gallon = 4.54 litres; 1 US gallon = 3.79 litres).

When to go

Climate

The climate is generally hot and dry, except for spring, when there may be heavy rainfall, and November, which can be blustery, cold and wet. The coast has a gentle Mediterranean climate with mild winters (minimum daytime temperatures of 10°C/50°F) and hot summers (30°C/86°F or more). Temperatures can rise into the 40s°C (100s°F) in the middle of the day. Stay in the shade, wear a sunhat and drink plenty of water.

In Provence, the Mistral, a harsh, cold wind, blows down the Rhône Valley and howls through the streets of Arles, Avignon and Marseille, bringing winter (and at times spring) temperatures down dramatically. It usually lasts three or four days, but can go on as long as ten days. The area has also seen dramatic storms in recent years, causing flash floods in autumn. The high mountains usually have snow November to March. Although summer is generally dry, there are often dramatic thunderstorms along the Riviera in late August. Average sunshine on the French Riviera is six hours in January, 12 hours in July.

Information

For local forecasts dial 08.92.68.12.34 followed by the *département* number. Otherwise, look at www.meteo.fr, www.lachainemeteo.com and www.meteoconsult.com, or dial 3201.

Public holidays

On public holidays, banks, post offices and public offices will be closed. Food shops – in particular *boulangeries* (bakeries) – will still open, even on Christmas Day. It is common practice, if a public holiday falls on a Thursday or Tuesday, for French businesses to *faire le pont* ('bridge the gap') and take Friday or Monday as a holiday too. The most fully observed holidays are 1 Jan, 1 May, 14 July, 15 Aug and 25 Dec.

1 Jan New Year's Day (Nouvel an). **Easter Monday** (Lundi de Pâques). **1 May** Labour Day (Fête du Travail). **Ascension Day** a Thur, 40 days after Easter (Ascension). **8 May** Victory Day (Fête de la Libération), marking the end of World War II. **14 July** Bastille Day (Quatorze Juillet). **15 Aug** Assumption Day (Fête de l'Assomption). **1 Nov** All Saints' Day (Toussaint). **11 Nov** Armistice Day (Fête de l'Armistice). **25 Dec** Christmas Day (Noël).

Women

Women need feel no more threatened in the South of France than in any other European country; indeed women alone will be more comfortable than in many places. The usual safety precautions should be taken in big cities at night. Be careful on trains, especially sleepers. You may receive compliments – more a cultural difference than sexual harrassment. A polite 'N'insistez pas!' ('Don't push it!') should turn off any unwanted attention. For contraception and abortion, *see p321*.

International Women's Club of the Riviera *04.92.60.47.75.* Coffee mornings for newcomers.

SOS Viol Informations *08.00.05.95.95.* Freephone service in French, dealing with rape. Alternatively, dial 04.91.33.16.60.

Working in the South of France

Anyone coming to work in France should be prepared for bureaucracy. Documents regularly required include a passport and a legally approved translation of your birth certificate (embassies have lists of translators).

Carte de séjour

Officially, EU citizens and non-Europeans alike who are in France for more than three months must apply at the local *mairie* (town hall) for a *carte de séjour*, valid for five years. Those who have had a *carte de séjour* for at least three years, have been paying French income tax, can show proof of income and/or are married to a French national can apply for a ten-year *carte de résident*.

Job-hunting

All EU nationals can work legally in France, but must apply for a *carte de séjour* (*see above*) and a French social security number from the Caisse Primaire d'Assurance Maladie. Some job ads can be found at branches of the Agence National Pour l'Emploi (ANPE, www.anpe.fr), the French national employment bureau. This is also the place to sign up as a *demandeur d'emploi* and thereby qualify for French unemployment benefit. Offices are listed under Administration du Travail et de l'Emploi in the Pages Jaunes. In the UK, International Job Advice (Whitehall 2, Whitehall Quay, Leeds, LS1 4HR, 0113 307 8090, www.europa.eu.int/eures) publishes information on working in France.

Seasonal employment

Foreign students can get *autorisation provisoire de travail* (a temporary work permit) for part-time work during the holidays. Seasonal work is available mainly in the tourist industry, for which you'll need to be able to speak decent French. Other work possibilities are gardening, house-sitting and teaching English. Grape- and fruit-picking is very difficult to set up in advance (for more details, *see p37* **A fruitful enterprise**). A good search engine for jobs is www.pacajob.com.

Weather

Average daily maximum and minimum temperatures.

	Marseille	Nice	Nîmes
Jan	10°C (50°F) / 2°C (36°F)	13°C (55°F) / 5°C (41°F)	10°C (50°F) / 2°C (36°F)
Feb	12°C (54°F) / 2°C (36°F)	13°C (55°F) / 6°C (43°F)	12°C (54°F) / 4°C (39°F)
Mar	15°C (59°F) / 5°C (41°F)	15°C (59°F) / 7°C (45°F)	15°C (59°F) / 5°C (41°F)
Apr	18°C (64°F) / 8°C (46°F)	17°C (63°F) / 10°C (50°F)	18°C (64°F) / 8°C (46°F)
May	22°C (72°F) / 11°C (52°F)	20°C (68°F) / 13°C (55°F)	22°C (72°F) / 11°C (52°F)
June	26°C (79°F) / 15°C (59°F)	23°C (73°F) / 15°C (59°F)	26°C (79°F) / 15°C (59°F)
July	29°C (84°F) / 17°C (63°F)	26°C (79°F) / 19°C (66°F)	30°C (86°F) / 18°C (64°F)
Aug	28°C (82°F) / 17°C (63°F)	27°C (81°F) / 19°C (66°F)	29°C (84°F) / 17°C (63°F)
Sept	25°C (77°F) / 15°C (59°F)	24°C (75°F) / 17°C (63°F)	25°C (77°F) / 15°C (59°F)
Oct	20°C (68°F) / 10°C (50°F)	21°C (70°F) / 13°C (55°F)	20°C (68°F) / 11°C (52°F)
Nov	15°C (59°F) / 6°C (43°F)	16°C (61°F) / 9°C (48°F)	14°C (57°F) / 6°C (43°F)
Dec	11°C (52°F) / 3°C (37°F)	14°C (57°F) / 6°C (43°F)	11°C (52°F) / 3°C (37°F)

Directory

Essential Vocabulary

In French, as in other Latin languages, the second-person singular ('you') has two forms. Phrases here are given in the more polite *vous* form. The *tu* form is used with family, friends, young children and pets; you should be careful not to use it with people you do not know sufficiently well. You will also find that courtesies such as *monsieur, madame* and *mademoiselle* are used much more than their English equivalents. *See p325* for information on language courses and *p30* **Decoding the menu** for food terms.

General expressions

yes *oui*; no *non*; OK *d'accord/ça va*
good morning/good afternoon/
hello *bonjour*
hi (familiar) *salut*
good evening *bonsoir*
goodbye *au revoir*
how are you? *comment allez vous?/ vous allez bien?*
how's it going? *comment ça va?/* (familiar) *ça va?*
Sir/Mr *monsieur* (*M, Mr*); Madam/ Mrs *madame* (*Mme*); Miss *mademoiselle* (*Mlle*)
please *s'il vous plaît*; thank you *merci*; thank you very much *merci beaucoup*
sorry *pardon*; excuse me *excusez-moi*
do you speak English? *parlez-vous anglais?*
I don't speak French *je ne parle pas français*
I don't understand *je ne comprends pas*
please speak more slowly *parlez plus lentement, s'il vous plaît*
leave me alone *laissez-moi tranquille*
how much?/how many? *combien?*
have you got change? *avez-vous de la monnaie?*
I would like... *je voudrais...*
I am going *je vais*; I am going to pay *je vais payer*
it is *c'est*; it isn't *ce n'est pas*
good *bon(ne)*; bad *mauvais(e)*
small *petit(e)*; big *grand(e)*
beautiful *beau/belle*
well *bien*; badly *mal*
expensive *cher*; cheap *pas cher*
a bit *un peu*; a lot *beaucoup*; very *très*; with *avec*; without *sans*

and *et*; or *ou*; because *parce-que*
who? *qui?*; when? *quand?*; which? *quel?*; where? *où?*; why? *pourquoi?*; how? *comment?*
at what time/when? *à quelle heure?*
forbidden *interdit/défendu*
out of order *hors service/en panne*
daily *tous les jours* (*tlj*); except Sunday *sauf le dimanche*

On the phone

hello (telephone) *allô*; who's calling? *c'est de la part de qui?/ qui est à l'appareil?*
hold the line *ne quittez pas/ patientez s'il vous plaît*

Getting around

when is the next train for...? *c'est quand le prochain train pour...?*
ticket *un billet*; station *la gare*; train station *gare SNCF*; platform *le quai*; bus/coach station *gare routière*; bus/coach *autobus/car*
entrance *entrée*; exit *sortie*
left *gauche*; right *droite*; interchange *correspondence*
straight on *tout droit*; far *loin*; near *pas loin/près d'ici*
street *la rue*; street map *le plan*; road map *la carte*
bank *la banque*; is there a bank near here? *est-ce qu'il y a une banque près d'ici?*
post office *la Poste*; a stamp *un timbre*

Sightseeing

beach *une plage*; bridge *un pont*; cave *une grotte*; wine cellar *une cave*; church *une église*; Protestant church *un temple*; market *marché, les halles*; museum *un musée*; mill *un moulin*; town hall *l'hôtel de ville/ la mairie*; exhibition *une exposition*; ticket (for museum) *un billet*; (for theatre, concert) *une place*; free *gratuit*; reduced price *un tarif réduit*; open *ouvert*; closed *fermé*

At the hotel

do you have a room (for this evening/for two people)? *avez-vous une chambre (pour ce soir/pour deux personnes)?* full *complet*; room *une chambre*; bed *un lit*; double bed *un grand lit*; (a room with) twin beds *(une chambre) à deux lits*; with bath(room)/shower *avec (salle de) bain/douche*; breakfast *le petit déjeuner*; included *compris*; lift *un ascenseur*; air-conditioned *climatisé*; swimming pool *piscine*

At the café or restaurant

I'd like to book a table (for three/at 8pm) *je voudrais réserver une table (pour trois personnes/à vingt heures)*
lunch *le déjeuner*; dinner *le dîner*
coffee (espresso) *un café*; white coffee *un café au lait/café crème*; tea *le thé*; wine *le vin*; beer *la bière*; a draught beer *une pression*
mineral water *eau minérale*; fizzy *gazeuse*; still *plate*; tap water *eau du robinet/une carafe d'eau*
the bill, please *l'addition, s'il vous plaît*

Behind the wheel

give way *céder le passage*; it's not your right of way *vous n'avez pas la priorité*; no parking *stationnement interdit/stationnement gênant*; deliveries *livraisons*; residents only *sauf riverains*
pedestrian *piéton*
toll *péage*; speed limit 40 *rappel 40kph (25mph)*
petrol *essence*; unleaded *sans plomb*; diesel *gasoil*
traffic jam *embouteillage/bouchon*; speed *vitesse*
dangerous bends *attention virages*

Numbers

0 *zéro*; 1 *un, une*; 2 *deux*; 3 *trois*; 4 *quatre*; 5 *cinq*; 6 *six*; 7 *sept*; 8 *huit*; 9 *neuf*; 10 *dix*; 11 *onze*; 12 *douze*; 13 *treize*; 14 *quatorze*; 15 *quinze*; 16 *seize*; 17 *dix-sept*; 18 *dix-huit*; 19 *dix-neuf*; 20 *vingt*; 21 *vingt-et-un*; 22 *vingt-deux*; 30 *trente*; 40 *quarante*; 50 *cinquante*; 60 *soixante*; 70 *soixante-dix*; 80 *quatre-vingts*; 90 *quatre-vingt-dix*; 100 *cent*; 1,000 *mille*; 1,000,000 *un million*

Days, months & seasons

Monday *lundi*; Tuesday *mardi*; Wednesday *mercredi*; Thursday *jeudi*; Friday *vendredi*; Saturday *samedi*; Sunday *dimanche*
January *janvier*; February *février*; March *mars*; April *avril*; May *mai*; June *juin*; July *juillet*; August *août*; September *septembre*; October *octobre*; November *novembre*; December *décembre*
spring *printemps*; summer *été*; autumn *automne*; winter *hiver*

Directory

Further Reference

Books

Non-fiction

Maurice Agulhon & Noël Coulet
Histoire de la Provence. A short
political and economic history, in
French. Que sais-je? PUF, 2001.
James Bromwich *The Roman
Remains of Southern France.*
No stone unturned. Routledge, 1996.
Ed. Ronald de Leeuw *Letters of
Van Gogh.* Vincent writes to beloved
brother Theo. Penguin, 1997.
Alain Ducasse *Flavours of France.*
By the star chef. Artisan, 1998.
**Noëlle Duck & Christian
Sarramon** *Provence Style.*
How to get the sun-bleached look in
your home. Flammarion, 2002.
Kenneth Frampton *Le Corbusier:
Architect and Visionary.* Corb's ideas
and work. Thames & Hudson, 2001.
Jamie Ivey *Extremely Pale Rosé.*
Hunt for the palest rosé in France.
Weidenfeld & Nicolson, 2006.
Andrew Jefford *New France: A
Complete Guide to Contemporary
French Wine.* Mitchell Beazley, 2002.
Ed. Hugh Johnson *Touring in
Wine Country: Provence.* Vineyard
companion. Mitchell Beazley, 1993.
Louisa Jones & Vincent Motte
*Gardens of Provence; Gardens of the
French Riviera.* Flammarion, 2002.
John Richardson *The Sorcerer's
Apprentice: Picasso, Provence and
Douglas Cooper.* Gossipy account of
Picasso and his dealer. Cape, 1999.
Gustaf Sobin *Luminous Debris.*
Speculations from Southern places
and *objets.* UC Press, 2000.
Rupert Wright *Notes from the
Languedoc.* From a mayor to a
matador. Ebury, 2005.

Fiction & literature

JG Ballard *Super-Cannes.* An expat
couple get themselves mixed up in
murder in a Riviera business park.
Flamingo, 2001.
Sybille Bedford *Jigsaw.* Wry
account of a childhood and strange
neighbours in Sanary-sur-Mer.
Penguin, 1999.
Alphonse Daudet *In the Land of
Pain.* Short memoir about failing to
recover from syphilis. Cape, 2002.
Carol Drinkwater *The Olive Farm.*
British actress and a Frenchman fall
for an olive farm. Abacus, 2001.
Alexandre Dumas *The Count of
Monte Cristo.* Ripping yarn of prison,
treasure and revenge. Various edns.
F Scott Fitzgerald *Tender is the
Night.* Wealthy American socialites
on the Riviera. Various edns.

Jean Giono *The Man who Planted
Trees.* Eco-fable for grown-ups by
gritty Southern writer. Harvill, 1992.
Jean-Claude Izzo *One Helluva
Mess.* The first in Izzo's Marseille
detective trilogy. Arcadia, 2001.
Peter Mayle *A Year in Provence.*
Former ad man copes with the
Luberon locals. Penguin, 1989.
Petrarch *Canzoniere.* Italian poet
falls in love in Avignon. Various edns.
Tobias Smollett *Travels through
France and Italy.* Cantankerous
letters of novelist and doctor on
his travels. Various edns.
Patrick Süskind *Perfume.* A
smelly thriller set in the 18th-century
Grasse perfume trade. Picador, 1989.
Emile Zola *La Fortune des Rougon.*
The first of Zola's Rougon-Macquart
saga is set in Plassans, a loosely
disguised Aix-en-Provence. Plassans
also features in *L'Oeuvre,* about a
struggling artist. Various edns.

Films

La Baie des anges (1963) Jeanne
Moreau plays a compulsive gambler
in Nice and Monte-Carlo, in Jacques
Demy's ravishing New Wave film.
Et Dieu créa la femme (1956)
Director Roger Vadim's classic
launched the teenage Brigitte Bardot,
with St-Tropez in the background.
The French Connection (1971)
Gene Hackman stars as a tough New
York cop brought to the Riviera on
the trail of a drug smuggling ring.
**Les Gendarmes et les
extraterrestres** (1978) Aliens
land in St-Tropez; a classic comedy
with Louis de Funes.
Goldeneye (1995) James Bond tears
along the Corniche, then cashes his
chips at the Monte-Carlo casino.
Herbie Goes to Monte-Carlo
(1977) Disney's VW beetle, all tuned
up for the Paris to Monte-Carlo road
race, falls for a pert little Lancia.
**Jean de Florette/Manon des
Sources** (both 1986) Depardieu
and Auteuil battle it out over water,
based on Pagnol's *L'Eau des Collines.*
Marius et Jeannette (1997) Robert
Guédiguian's portrait of a working-
class friendship in l'Estaque.
Marius/Fanny/César (1931, 1932,
1936) Sentimental trilogy, a Pagnol-
scripted homage to Marseille.
La Piscine (1968) Alain Delon and
Romy Schneider hang out around the
pool above St-Tropez.
Swimming Pool (2002) Charlotte
Rampling and Ludivine Sagnier hang
out around the pool in the Luberon.
Taxi (1998) Stunts galore in the Luc
Besson-scripted and -produced car
chase caper through Marseille.

To Catch a Thief (1955) Cary
Grant and Grace Kelly in a Hitchcock
crime riddle set on the Riviera.
Two for the Road (1967) Albert
Finney and Audrey Hepburn in
marital crisis on the Riviera.

Music

Bizet *L'Arlésienne Suite.*
The provençal signature tune.
Gounod *Mireille.* Camargue opera.
IAM *Revoir au printemps.*
Soul-infused Marseille rappers
joined by Redman and Beyoncé.
Poulenc *La Dame de Monte-Carlo.*
Soprano monologue, complete with
lyrics by Cocteau.
Rolling Stones *Exile on Main
Street.* Recorded in 1971 at Keith
Richard's Côte d'Azur villa.
Troublemakers *Doubts &
Convictions.* Marseille electro trio.

Websites

Official tourist sites

Each chapter contains full contact
details for local tourist offices,
including their websites.
www.alpes-haute-provence.com
www.crt-paca.fr Provence–Alps–
Côte d'Azur (PACA) region.
www.drome-tourisme.com
www.franceguide.com France-
wide official government tourist site.
www.guideriviera.com
The Alpes-Maritimes.
www.provenceguide.com
The Vaucluse.
www.tourismevar.com The Var.
www.visitprovence.com
The Bouches-du-Rhône.

Unofficial & media

www.cityvox.com City guides.
www.cote.azur.fr What's on and
tourist information in the Var and
Alpes-Maritimes.
www.documentsdartistes.org
Contemporary artists in the South.
www.festivals.laregie-paca.com
Summer festivals; site under
construction as we went to press.
www.luberon-news.com
Bilingual guide to villages, hotels,
rentals, restaurants, wine, markets,
events and property.
www.nicematin.fr Regional daily.
www.provenceweb.fr
Good bilingual guide, covering
hundreds of villages and towns.
www.riviera-reporter.com
Expat, English-language mag, with
community events and small ads.

Directory

Index

Advertisers' Index